# Game Coding Complete, Fourth Edition

Mike "MrMike" McShaffry and David "Rez" Graham

**Course Technology PTR**
*A part of Cengage Learning*

COURSE TECHNOLOGY
CENGAGE Learning™

Australia • Brazil • Japan • Korea • Mexico • Singapore • Spain • United Kingdom • United States

COURSE TECHNOLOGY
CENGAGE Learning™

**Game Coding Complete, Fourth Edition**
**Mike "MrMike" McShaffry and David "Rez" Graham**

**Publisher and General Manager, Course Technology PTR:** Stacy L. Hiquet

**Associate Director of Marketing:** Sarah Panella

**Manager of Editorial Services:** Heather Talbot

**Senior Marketing Manager:** Mark Hughes

**Acquisitions Editor:** Heather Hurley

**Project and Copy Editor:** Marta Justak

**Technical Reviewers:** James Leitch and Sascha Friedmann

**Interior Layout Tech:** MPS Limited, a Macmillan Company

**Cover Designer:** Tre Ziemann

**Cartoon Artist:** Steph Laberis

**Indexer:** Kelly Talbot

**Proofreader:** Gene Redding



Library of Congress Control Number: 2012930785

ISBN-13: 978-1-133-77657-4

ISBN-10: 1-133-77657-4

**Course Technology, a part of Cengage Learning**

20 Channel Center Street

Boston, MA 02210

USA

Cengage Learning is a leading provider of customized learning solutions with office locations around the globe, including Singapore, the United Kingdom, Australia, Mexico, Brazil, and Japan. Locate your local office at: **international.cengage.com/region**

Cengage Learning products are represented in Canada by Nelson Education, Ltd.

For your lifelong learning solutions, visit **courseptr.com**

Visit our corporate website at **cengage.com**

Printed in the United States of America
4 5 6 7 8 9 19 18 17 16 15

***Dedication from Mike McShaffry***

*This book and my life are dedicated to my wife and my best friend, Robin*

***Dedication from David Graham***

*This book is dedicated to my grandfather, William Chace*
*The potion was just sugar water after all*

# Foreword

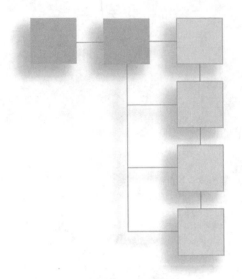

*by Warren Spector*

## For Mike McShaffry

Let me start by admitting a couple of things. First, I've never written a foreword for a book before. I've written books but never a foreword. Honestly, I usually skip right over these things when I'm reading a book, so odds are that no one is ever going to read what I'm writing here anyway. That makes it safe for me to move on to admission number two: I'm not a programmer. Never have been, and I fear, never will be, despite some valiant efforts on my part (if I do say so myself). I've done okay despite not knowing a blessed thing about programming. I'm not looking for sympathy or anything, but I am here to tell you that a day doesn't go by when I don't think, "Damn, if only I knew my z-buffers from my BSP trees!" If you're already a programmer, you've got a huge leg up on me when I tried to get into the electronic game biz! (And if you're not a programmer, do as I say and not as I do—learn to program ASAP. Mike has some advice about how to do that in the pages that follow. Pay attention.)

Okay, so with those two confessions out of the way, I figure there's a fair chance any credibility I might have had is pretty well shot. Luckily for you folks, the guy who wrote this book has credibility to burn. Mike McShaffry (or "Mr. Mike" as he's known to most everyone in the game biz) is the real deal. Mike is a genuine survivor. He is a guy who can talk the talk because, Lord knows, he's walked the walk enough times to earn some talking time.

Mike's experience of game development runs the gamut in a pretty remarkable way. He was there when teams were a dozen folks, and he's been around in the era of 20, 30, and 50-person teams. He's done the startup thing, worked for the biggest publishers in the business, worked on "traditional" games and decidedly untraditional ones—everything from *Ultima* to *Blackjack*, single player, multiplayer, online and off, and just about everything else you can imagine. When it comes to PC games, he speaks with the authority of someone who's worn just about every hat it's possible to wear—programmer, designer, project leader, director of development, studio head....

And I've had the privilege of watching him learn and grow with each new project and each new role. I was there when Mike got his first game job. I was one of the folks at Origin who interviewed him back in the Bone Ages, back in the 20th century, way back in 1990, when he applied for a programming job at Origin. (Seems like forever, doesn't it, Mike? Whew!)

He started out as "just" a programmer on *Martian Dreams,* a game I produced for Origin, but by the end of the project, he was the engine that drove that game to the finish line. The game wouldn't have happened without Mike. His drive, dedication, love of games, knack for on-the-fly design, natural leadership skills, and ability to combine right brain and left brain (to say nothing of his willingness to work crazy hours) drove all of us to work that much harder and ensured that the game ended up something special (at least to those of us who worked on it together—it sure didn't sell many copies!).

I honestly don't even remember if I ever gave Mike the title "Lead Programmer" officially on *Martian Dreams,* but he sure deserved it. The guy was a machine, working longer hours than most people I've worked with (and that's saying something in the game business). He also managed to do more and better work in those hours than any human being should be allowed to. It just ain't fair to the rest of us mere mortals. When Mike was on, there was no touching him. And he was almost always on—after *Martian Dreams,* Mike did it again and again, on *Ultima VII, VIII, IX,* and a bunch of others. Scary really.

In retrospect, all those hours and all the hard work that seemed so necessary back in the days when we were all younger and more foolish than we are now was probably an indication that Mike, like the rest of us, didn't have a clue about software development or game design or much anything else. (Okay, we had a pretty good handle on the effects of sugar and caffeine on the human body, but that's about it.) We had to work so long and so hard just to have a chance in hell of ending up with something worthwhile.

Reading this book, I couldn't help but marvel at how much Mike's learned over the years and wonder how much more Mike—and the rest of us—would have gotten done, how much better our games might have been, if we'd had the benefit of the kind of information in the pages that follow. There just wasn't anyone around back then who knew enough about games, programming practices, and software development. We were making it up as we went along.

Today, there are plenty of books out there that can teach you the typing part of programming. There are even some books that go a bit further and teach you what makes game coding different from coding a word processing program or a billing system for your local health care providers (or, as we used to call 'em, "doctors"). But even now, there just aren't many books that combine hard-core game programming advice with equally hard-core development processes, debugging, and team-building information.

Development process? Team building? Who cares about all that? You just want to write code, right? If you're like a lot of programmers I know, that's just what you're thinking. And, man, are you wrong. There might have been a time when coders could just close their doors and type, not caring about how their work fit into the bigger picture of a game's development. Maybe that was true 10 years ago or more (probably not, but maybe). Well, it sure isn't true anymore. With teams getting bigger all the time, with timelines stretching and budgets bloating, process and team issues are everyone's concern nowadays.

Mike gets that, something that becomes clear in the very first chapter, when he says, "Being the best developer you can be requires that you have intimate knowledge about the real demands of the industry." Amen, brother. That, in a nutshell, is what makes this book special. Most people think enthusiasm and talent are enough to get them into the game business and to ensure success once they land that all-important first gig. "I play games all the time," they say, "and I'm a kickass coder, so what more is there to know? Sign me up!"

Well, I'm here to tell you that there's plenty more to know, and that's probably the single most valuable lesson this book has to offer. Games are insanely complex, and their creation involves a unique combination of art and science (some call it "magic," and they're not far wrong). Game development is demanding in a way that can only be appreciated after a stint in the trenches. At least, I used to think that was the case, but that's where Mike comes in. Having been in the trenches, he can save you the trouble and pain and scars and relationship breakups and company failures that all too often go along with game development. No matter what you may think, it isn't all glory, fame, wealth, and intense personal satisfaction (though there is a better than fair share of that last item).

There's a ton of great stuff in Mike's book. And I love all the insider bits found in Mike's "Tales from the Pixel Mines."

Of course, there's plenty of nuts-and-bolts stuff for folks who are already programmers but want to know what makes game programming so special (and believe me, it is). But even programmers will benefit from the other ton of stuff that often gets short shrift in the typical programming book—all that Big Picture stuff that doesn't involve code samples.

These areas are critical for being the most effective developer you can be, whether you're a programmer or not. This is all stuff you can't get just anywhere. You have to have lived through the process (and the pain!) a bunch of times. Or you have to find a mentor and spend years sucking his or her brain dry. Or you can stop reading this foreword and start reading this book.

What are you waiting for?

*—Warren Spector,*

*Founder of Junction Point Studios*

# Foreword

*by Bo Lasater*

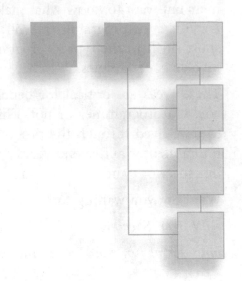

## For David "Rez" Graham

Rez has done a lot of really cool things in his career and met a lot of great people along the way. Therefore, I was very honored when he asked me to write the foreword for this book.

I think he picked me because I'm one of the keepers of his Origin story. Origin stories are fun—no matter how many bad guys Spider-Man defeats, the fans still want to hear about how he was bitten by a radioactive spider—and they are also instructive. If you are reading this, you too may be thinking about how to craft your own Origin story that culminates in an exciting career in video game programming. You can learn a lot from Rez's story.

I met Rez in 2005 when he came to interview at a little company I was running called Super-Ego Games. We were convinced back then that people needed an interactive situation comedy playable on consoles, and we were going to give it to them. (How we got there and what happened next is an interesting and cautionary tale in and of itself for another time.) At the time of Rez's interview, we had convinced a publisher of the same thing and were ramping up a team of very talented individuals.

Believe it or not, Rez came to us not as an engineering prospect but as a quality assurance lead with an interest in game design. When Rez walked into our office, the first thing we noticed wasn't his height, though he's very tall, nor his combat boots, vintage black army jacket, or faded black combat fatigues, but rather his 10-inch blue mohawk.

The next thing we noticed was the ease with which he spoke to the four or five of us in the room interviewing him. This was a bigger deal than it sounds, because all of us were more experienced, had bigger degrees from fancier colleges, and were mohawkless. And, it was an interview for heaven's sake!

The third thing we noticed was his passion and knowledge of games. More than just playing a lot of games, he was extraordinarily thoughtful and articulate about what he liked and why.

The fourth thing we noticed was *Farmer Bill's Almond Farm.* This was a demo game that Rez had built to teach himself game programming. It had simple graphics and a crude interface for sure, but it was full of original ideas well realized and lots of fun, nonetheless. We were smart enough to see that a singular talent lay behind it. (If we were really smart, we would have published the game on Facebook a couple of years before *Farmville* came out.)

As you have guessed by now since I'm writing this, we hired Rez. Before I go on about the next stage, I'd like to call out some things for those of you who are interested in breaking in to the industry.

First of all, QA is a great way to get into games. The entry hurdles are typically lower than other positions, and the skills you gain can prepare you well for many disciplines in game development—programming, design, project management, and production.

Second, being able to explain a point of view on what makes games fun is very important. Many game companies go deep here in interviews for almost any position. Not only is it to determine if you have the passion to fuel the drive and determination to make it in games, but more importantly, to see if you "get" the product. A game studio pulls off this incredible choreography of many and varied talents to create a product that is itself a choreography of sounds and pictures, whose purpose is to engage and delight its user. Decisions made by almost anyone can affect the final experience of the product. People have to work autonomously, often with limited oversight and supervision. The best insurance that mistakes don't get made is making sure that all of the employees share the same vision and alignment. We're knowledge workers, after all. Making smart decisions is what we do.

Getting a product doesn't mean preferring it or even liking it. Rez and I have made games for male and female, young and old. We don't have the luxury or curse of being all of those things at once, but we can put ourselves in the mindset of our players and learn what they want. The ability to understand and articulate why a game will delight its audience is a big part of "getting" a product.

Third, mohawks are cool in the games industry. We're creative types by and large and self-expression is welcome.

Finally, showing up with something you built is awesome. It demonstrates passion, competence, and vision much better than words alone can. Moreover, making a demo actually gives you competence and vision and confidence. (By the way, this book will help you build the demo that will give you real confidence.)

Rez started in QA with a promise from us to make him a designer when he proved himself a bit. The proving didn't take long at all. Rez was a diligent checker with lots of great input. When he took on a nasty group of bugs around our UtilEcon AI system, I quickly realized that he should be tweaking the parameters directly instead of telling us about them. Voilà, he was now a designer. Very soon, he started implementing tools to help us visualize and manage the system's data more easily. Before long, he had taken over a lot of the coding on the core system itself.

Rez then faced a decision point. He could go down the design path or the engineering path. In spite of Rez's keen fashion sense and artistic leanings, he followed his inner child and became an engineer. Looking back, I realize Rez had figured out what pros like Sid Meier of *Civilization* fame knows. Anyone in a game company can have design input if he has good ideas, but only a programmer gets to tell the machine exactly what to do without any middle men.

Rez took up coding fulltime, and a star was born! In the months that followed, Rez integrated himself into many of our key systems like graphics, animation, story events, and user interface. His hunger to learn was insatiable, he was a pleasure to work with, and he did what had to be done to get his projects done.

After Super-Ego Games, Rez spent a year at Planet Moon. He worked on a DS game called *Brain Quest*, which was a small kid's game. After that he worked on the AI, animation, and save game systems for *Drawn to Life: The Next Chapter* for the Wii. His next stop was at Slipgate where he worked on an MMO doing client programming and some UI work. Next was Play First where he worked on *Diner Dash* for the iPad before it shipped and on *Wedding Dash* for the iPhone 4. Rez's latest stop is at EA where he has worked on AI for the *Sims Medieval* and the *Pirates & Noble* expansion. He is currently the AI programmer for a new unannounced *Sims* project.

Anyone who has worked with Rez has the same impression. He has more energy than anyone has a right to have, and is upbeat and funny even in the grimmest hours of a project or a company's life cycle. His enthusiasm is infectious. Hanging out with him, you realize that game coding is the highest and best calling a human can have and is definitely the most fun. If you ask Rez to explain his latest project, make sure you had a good night's sleep the night before and drink a lot of coffee, because it will be a torrent of words and ideas.

Luckily, you can absorb his thoughts at a more leisurely pace through the pages of this book. It will give you the benefit of years of interesting and challenging work in the heart of game development, filtered and focused by a first-class intellect and guided by a personality who wants nothing more than to share the thrill of this exciting field.

Enjoy!

*—Bo Lasater,*

*Executive Producer at Kixeye*

# Acknowledgments

## Mike's Acknowledgments

**Mom and Grandma Hawker**

Thanks for never saying I'd never amount to anything playing games all the time; you believed in me, and it paid off.

**Dad and Lynn**

Thanks for showing me I should never be afraid of hard work.

**Phil Hawker**

Thanks for giving me a sense of humor—I think I put it to good use here.

**Warren Spector and Richard Garriott**

Thanks for believing a geeky college kid could help make the games I loved to play.

**Fourth Edition Beta Testers**

James Leitch and Sascha Friedmann

**Cover Artist**

The cover was created by Tre Ziemann. He is currently a 3D Artist at King's Isle in Austin, Texas.

**Fourth Edition Editors**

Thanks to Heather Hurley, acquisitions editor, for picking up the book for a fourth edition.

Thanks to my editor Marta Justak for making me look like a writer.

## Rez's Acknowledgments

**My Father, Robin Graham**

Thanks for giving me my first programming book, my very own computer, and introducing me to science fiction.

**My Mother, Susan Angelos**

Thanks for letting me walk my own path in life and for never telling me to quit ruining my life playing video games.

**Bo Lasater and Steve Matthews**

Thanks for hiring a passionate kid with no degree and no experience. I owe a lot of my success to your willingness to take a chance on me.

**Steph Laberis**

Thank you for supporting yet another project that consumed so much of my time.

**Cartoons**

The cartoon inserts were created by Steph Laberis. She is currently an illustrator and character designer living in Berkeley, California.

**Last but not least, Robin McShaffry**

Thank you for letting Mike come out to play.

# About the Authors

**Mike McShaffry**, aka "Mr. Mike," started programming games as soon as he could tap a keyboard—in fact, he somehow skipped seventh grade math entirely in favor of writing games in BASIC on an ancient Commodore Pet. In his single-minded pursuit of programming knowledge, he signed up for an extended stay at the University of Houston. To his surprise and the Dean of Mathematics, he actually graduated five and one-half years later. Shortly after graduation, he entered the boot camp of the computer game industry: Origin Systems. He worked for Warren Spector and Richard Garriott, aka "Lord British," on *Martian Dreams*, *Ultima VII: The Black Gate*, *Ultima VIII: Pagan*, *Ultima IX: Ascension*, and *Ultima Online*.

Exactly seven years from the day he was hired, Mike arranged his escape, and in 1997 formed his first company, Tornado Alley. Tornado Alley was a garage startup whose goal was to create *No Grownups Allowed*, a massively multiplayer world for children—something that was sure to land Mike and anyone else at Tornado Alley front and center of a Congressional hearing. While *No Grownups* never left the tarmac, a kid's activity program called *Magnadoodle* by Mattel Media did, and in record development time.

The entrepreneurial bug, a ravenous and insatiable beast, finally devoured enough of Mike's remaining EA stock to motivate him to take a steady gig at Glass Eye Entertainment, working for his friend Monty Kerr, where he produced *Microsoft Casino*. Ten short months later, Monty asked Mike and his newly assembled team to start their own company called Compulsive Development, which worked exclusively with Microsoft on casual casino and card games.

Mike served as the primary coffee brewmaster and head of studio, and together with the rest of the Compulsive folks, 20 great people in all, produced three more casual titles for Microsoft until August 2002. Compulsive was acquired by Glass Eye Entertainment to continue work on Glass Eye's growing online casual games business.

Mike was hungry for AAA console work, and in 2003 he got what he wanted: Ion Storm's *Thief: Deadly Shadows* team called Mike in to create their third-person camera technology and to work on fine-tuning character movement at the 11th hour. What started as a two-week contract turned into almost a year of labor working side-by-side with programmers who used to call Mike "boss."

While it was great to be "one of the boys" again, it couldn't last forever. Mike was recruited to start an Austin studio for Maryland-based BreakAway Games. BreakAway Austin's focus was AAA console development and high-end simulations for the U.S. military and DoD contractors. Mike and three of the BreakAway Austin team actually visited the USS Harry S. Truman, one of the U.S. Navy's CVN class Nuclear Aircraft Carriers. They flew out, landed on the carrier, spent four days and nights with the officers and crew, and got launched to go back home. Afterward, they created *24 Blue*, a training simulator that mimics the insane environment of the deck of the carrier, jets and everything.

After BreakAway Austin, Mike founded a consulting company called MrMike. He figured that nearly 18 years in the gaming industry was enough to firmly establish that as a good identity for the company. For nearly two years, he helped small game companies choose their game technology, firm up their production practices, and pitch game ideas to industry publishers like Microsoft, EA, THQ, and others. One of his clients, Red Fly Studio, made him an offer he couldn't refuse, and he jumped back into a full-time gig.

Mike took the position of Executive Producer and helped ship *Mushroom Men: The Spore Wars*. He still works at Red Fly Studio as their Director of Product Development and sometime coffee maker. He still makes coffee and tries to give good advice to the programmers, artists, designers, audio guys, and producers working for him.

He still writes code when he can—most recently working with the Unity game engine, playing around in C#, and writing mad improvements to the GameCode4 engine.

If Mike's fingers aren't tapping away at a keyboard, he's probably either "downhilling" on his mountain bike or enjoying good times with his friends in Austin, Texas.

**David "Rez" Graham** is a self-taught programmer and has been an avid gamer ever since he could pick up a video game controller. He's always been fascinated with games and in 1996, his father gave him his very first programming book. Rez devoured that book with passion and immediately began attempting to write his very own game. Six months and 5500 lines of code later, *Farmer Bill's Almond Farm* was born. This was a very simple adventure game with crude graphics written for DOS 6.2. Rez never stopped and kept on writing games.

In 1998, he managed to break into the video games industry as a game tester working on *Sim City 3000* before going to Microprose to work for its tech support team. After the studio shut down in late 1999, Rez worked outside of the industry at Kodak managing a team of IT professionals to keep their tech support group running.

In late 2005, the time was right to return to the video games industry, and Rez landed a job at Super-Ego Games, first working on their source control systems as a QA engineer and quickly moving into design and engineering. In less than a month, Rez was working on the AI code for *RatRace.* He spent over two years there and shipped a kid's game called *Barbie Diaries: High School Mystery*, where he worked on several minigames and expanded the AI systems. The rest of the time, Rez worked on a variety of systems for *Rat Race* for the PlayStation 3. In early 2008, Rez left Super-Ego Games and spent a year working at Planet Moon, where he worked on a small kid's game for the Gameboy DS called *Brain Quest.* After that, Rez worked on *Drawn to Life: The Next Chapter* for the Wii doing AI, animation, and game saving.

In 2009, Rez moved to a company called Slipgate, which was a part of Gazillion, where he worked on the client for an MMO. After leaving Slipgate, Rez went to work on casual iPhone and iPad games for a company called PlayFirst. He shipped *Diner Dash: Grillin' Green* for the iPad and was the lead engineer for *Wedding Dash* for the iPhone 4.

Today, Rez is working at EA as the lead AI programmer for an upcoming *Sims* game. He has been at EA since mid-2010, and the last project he shipped was *The Sims Medieval* and the *Pirates & Nobles Adventure Pack*. Rez has spoken at The Game Developer's Conference on several occasions and frequently talks to high-school and college students about how to break into the game industry.

In his spare time, Rez enjoys running table-top RPGs, playing a little music, drawing, and working on various side projects and AI experiments.

# Contents

# Introduction

*by Mike McShaffry*

## Welcome to the Fourth Edition

The first edition of this book was published in the summer of 2003, just as I was making some big transitions of my own. The first edition gave me a chance to stand back and show programmers what really goes on in the world of game development. Writing the book was a challenge, but the rewards were many. I heard from programmers all around the world who enjoyed the book and found the stories, insight, and programming tips to be helpful. The second edition was almost a complete rewrite. The book went from around 700 pages to 1,110, and it was more popular than the first edition. In 2009, the third edition added AI, multiprogramming, Lua, and C# with the help of my friends James Clarendon, Jeff Lake, Quoc Tran, and David "Rez" Graham.

Three years later, I made a call to my publisher, Cengage Learning, and asked if a fourth edition would be a good idea. They said yes, and somehow I had to figure out how to find time to write it.

One of my friends, the co-author from the AI chapter of the third edition, and the only person second to me in posting threads on the book's website, Rez, was a natural choice to help me. I called him, but I didn't get the answer I expected. He not only wanted to help, but he wanted to do half the book with me and become partners.

What you hold in your hands is the result.

## Where Is the Code? Must I Actually Type?

Shortly after the publication of the first edition of this book, I made a website to provide resources and helpful information for readers. This site also became a great place for downloading the book's source code examples and all manner of interesting stuff. The site has really grown since the first edition, and now it has become quite a resource center. So if you are looking for additional help, the source code, or you want to share your thoughts with other game programmers, point your browser to one of these two places:

www.mcshaffry.com/GameCode/

www.courseptr.com/downloads

The book has never included a CD because the source code will get fixed and tweaked even as this book goes to press and long thereafter. Good suggestions and fixes even come from readers like you. Grab the code from the GameCode website (or the publisher's), and you'll be assured of getting the latest source code and information.

## How This Book Is Organized

The book is organized into four parts:

- **Game Programming Fundamentals (Chapters 1–4)**: Exposes some stuff that you'll want in your game programming toolbox, like a good random-number generator. It also introduces the major components of games and how they interact. After you read the chapters in this part, you'll have a good working knowledge of the real architecture that game developers use.
- **Get Your Game Running (Chapters 8–9)**: It's now time to learn how to get all of the main building blocks of your game together, including the initialization and shutdown code, the main loop, game actors, user interfaces, and input device code. You'll find your first meaty game code examples. Often, many programming books just gloss over this stuff and jump right into the cool 3D code. But, in reality, this is the stuff you really need to know to create a successful game, no matter what type of game you want to build.
- **Core Game Technologies (Chapters 10–18):** The tougher code examples are in this section, such as 3D programming, scripting with Lua, game audio, physics, and AI programming.
- **Advanced Topics and Bringing It All Together (Chapters 19–24):** In this section, you'll find chapters on networking, programming with threads, creating

tools in C#, and bringing all the code in the book together to make a little game. You'll also see some great debugging tricks and an entire chapter on how it feels to be there when you release a commercial game.

Throughout the book, you'll see a few insets that are identified by the following cartoons:

A "Gotcha" is something to watch out for, most likely because either Rez or I have already made the mistake for you, and you can avoid it.

Best practices have been figured out through years of hard-won lessons. Follow these "Best Practice" lessons, and you'll be happier for it.

Both Rez and I have tons of stories won from hard work and late nights working on real games. We like to interrupt each other a lot, so you can recognize our stories by these cartoons.

## What You'll Need

If you're a programmer and you've had some game programming experience, you'll be able to follow along nicely. Take a moment to flip through the pages, and you'll see this book is written for programmers. Nonprogrammers could probably get something from the book, too, but there is more code in this book than noncode.

The code is written in C++, Lua, and C#. If you don't know these languages, you'll probably struggle a little with the code samples, but I'll bet you can get enough from the comments and the explanations to get your money's worth.

All of the code in this book works under Visual Studio 2010, or at least it did when it was copied into Microsoft Word, which is how Rez and I wrote the book. Apologies ahead of time for making no attempt whatsoever to make sure the code worked in other compilers like CodeWarrior or GNU C++. I hope you'll forgive us. We figured our time would be better spent by covering as much technical ground as possible, instead of working on multicompiler–compatible code.

The Lua code was written using the Decoda IDE. Since Lua isn't a compiled language, you don't have to use any special editor; Notepad will work just fine. However, there is a DEPROJ file included with the Lua scripts so if you happen to use Decoda, the project is all laid out for you.

The code in this book also has a heavy Windows bias. I'm a Windows programmer, and I was a DOS programmer before that. I've had some brief forays into UNIX on the *Ultima Online* server code, but I'm hardly an expert. Much of the code in this book assumes that you are using Windows, and I didn't change the code to support cross-compiling into other operating systems for much the same reason as I chose a single compiler. It was simply better for me to cover lots of technical issues than for me to check my code under LINUX.

As far as graphics APIs are concerned, I assume you'll use DirectX 11 or later. The code supports both Direct3D 9 and Direct3D 11, but only Direct3D 11 is covered in the book. I don't have anything against OpenGL, of course, but I'm just not an expert in the nuances of it. Basically, if you have a good working knowledge in C++, C#, Windows, and a passing knowledge of DirectX, you'll be fine. You don't have to be godlike in your skill, but you should be pretty comfortable coding in these areas.

If you are a complete newbie and perhaps only know a little C++, don't feel dejected and don't return this book! I have a plan for you. Throughout this book, I'll refer to other tomes of knowledge that helped me learn how to program. They can help you, too, and you can use them in conjunction with the humble collection of knowledge you hold in your hands. With a little concentration, you can bootstrap yourself into programming prowess. I learned more about programming in C++, DirectX, and Windows by looking at working code, of which there is plenty included in these pages for you to enjoy.

## Third-Party Libraries

This book uses STL for common data structures. If you don't know anything about STL, you'll see some good examples in this book, and I'm sure you'll be able to follow the code. I'm not attempting to teach you STL, which is something that is beyond the scope of this book. Instead, go read *The C++ Standard Library: A Tutorial and Reference* by Nicolai M. Josuttis. After you get your bearings, go read Scott Meyer's books on STL because both books are fantastic.

STL is a body of code that is extremely well tested, has a widely understood API, and is available on almost every development platform. If you haven't seen it yet, stop reading right now and do a little research. You'll never have to write code for common data structures like linked lists, resizable arrays, and trees ever again. I've saved hours of grief using `<list>`, `<vector>`, and `<map>`.

Whatever happens, don't get caught writing your own linked-list class or tree when STL would have worked. All implementations are extremely well tested. Every bug or implementation oddity has already been exposed and discussed on the Internet. Your own code, on the other hand, is not.

## Source Code and Coding Standards

I despise technical books that include source code that doesn't compile. I cursed the name of every author and editor who created those books, filled with errors and broken code. I'm now doomed to join their ranks.

Microsoft Word just doesn't handle C++ source code very well. Since this book is printed in black and white, the code highlighting has to be turned off. I understand now why so many programming books are crawling with errors. I apologize to every author and editor I maligned. Until I wrote this book, I had no idea how difficult it was, and now Rez feels exactly the same way. Enough groveling! Rez and I will make a valiant effort to check and recheck the source code in this book, and we'll do what we can to set anything right if anything is broken.

Now that my conscience is at ease, you should know something about how to read the source code in this book.

## Where the Code Comes From

Every line of source code has its beginning in an actual game. Of course, the code is not 100 percent verbatim. My front door would be knocked down by a wave of lawyers from Microsoft, Electronic Arts, Mattel, Eidos, and who knows what else. You should see the agreements from EA that Rez had to sign before working on this project! Instead, the code has been sufficiently tweaked to protect my intellectual property and everyone else who was crazy enough to employ Rez and me. The original code is much harder to read anyway. It usually contained optimizations and external references that I couldn't easily include in any form. Since they came from over 30 years of combined coding experience, you can imagine the wide variety of style and structure. If you want to make your own game, the source code in this book should give you a head start. You'll find some great skeletal work on which you can hang your own code. I'm even hoping that some of the code in here will save you some headaches so you can concentrate on your game.

The code in this book was written and tested on the Windows platform under Visual Studio 2010 using the DirectX 9 and 11 applications framework. Console programming is a different beast, and where it makes sense, these differences are pointed out. If you're looking to use this code on a Windows box but want to know how programming the same thing on the Xbox 360, PS3, or the Wii is different, you're holding the right book.

The source code is covered under the GNU Lesser General Public License. You can read about this license here: http://www.gnu.org/licenses/lgpl.html, but basically it means that you can do what you like with the code as long as you give Rez and me credit. If you are crazy enough, you can even use this code in a commercial game. But don't say Rez and I didn't warn you.

## Coding Standards and Style

Source code standards are important. I'm not necessarily a standards dictator. I can find room for other opinions on code style, and I'm happy to adopt reasonable standards when and where I must. I look at it like trying to learn a bit of the local language if you travel abroad. The locals will appreciate it, and you might even learn something.

Origin Systems didn't have company-wide coding standards. I was part of no less than three standards committees while I was there, to no avail. Every time we attempted to discuss C++ bracing style, the meeting simply broke down into a screaming match. There were many programmers at Origin who simply wouldn't adapt to anyone else's style. It got so bad that somebody wrote a little utility that would parse a source file and change the bracing style from one to the other. Madness!

Your coding standards and style exist solely to communicate useful information to other programmers and sometimes a future version of yourself.

Rez and I use a coding style in this book extremely similar to what we use professionally. The only departures are those that make the code simpler to read. For example, the source code in the book frequently eliminates obvious error detection and handling. If we used every line of source code exactly as it appeared in real projects, this book would have to be twice as long. It was a tough trade-off, but it's better to have more examples and leave the obvious stuff out of the book.

## Using Prefixes

Modern IDEs like Visual Studio expose the type of an identifier with a tooltip, so programmers don't have to clutter the prefix with redundant information. Instead, the prefixes show scope, primarily. Here they are:

- **g**: Use with global variables—`g_Counter`
- **m**: Use with member variables—`m_Counter`
- **p**: Use with pointer variables—`m_pActor`
- **V**: Use with virtual functions—`VDraw()`
- **I**: Use with Interface classes—class `IDrawable`

I've seen some crazy use of prefixes that attach three or more characters to the front of any identifier. It must be hard to program in Hungary. The problem with this style is that every identifier that has the same prefix looks exactly alike. That's why the prefix should be as small as possible and separated from the identifier with an underscore—it conveys useful information without overpowering the identity of the variable name. In your own code, feel free to add more prefixes to this list as you find good use for them. Just don't go overboard!

Prefixing variables for scope is an excellent use for prefixes. Programmers who change the value of something with global scope need to be slapped in the face so they can take proper precautions. Class member variables have a different scope than local variables. The "m" prefix is a clean way to differentiate locals and members when they are used in the same method, such as constructors.

Virtual functions are powerful, and therefore dangerous when used to evil ends. A prefix on virtual functions reminds programmers that they should call the parent's overloaded virtual function, and that the cost of calling the function is high.

I find it useful to apply a prefix to interface classes, ones that only define pure virtual functions and no data members, so programmers feel safe multiply inheriting from them. I avoid multiple inheritance of noninterface classes, and I advise you to do the same. The resulting code can be very confusing and hard to maintain.

## Capitalization

I use capitalization to distinguish different classes of identifiers and make identifiers easier to read.

- **Variables and Parameters:** Always start with lowercase and use a capital letter for each compound word—`g_BufferLength`, `m_BufferLength`, `returnValue`.
- **Classes, Functions, Typedefs, and Methods:** Always start with uppercase and capitalize each compound word—`SoundResource`, `MemoryFile`.
- **Macros & Constants:** Use all capitals and separate compound words with underscores—`SAFE_DELETE`, `MAX_PATH`.

The first two capitalization styles help programmers distinguish between definitions of class and instances of those classes:

```
SoundResource soundResource;
MemoryFile memoryFile;
```

Macros, a source of frequent pain and suffering, should boldly state their existence in all capitals. If you want to find the definition of a macro, it's easy to search for the `#define MACRO_NAME`. This sets them apart from functions or methods.

## Const Correct Code

I try my best to make code const correct, and the code in this book is no exception. I'm sure some of you hard-core const correct programmers will be able to throw a few thousand `const` keywords in where I've forgotten them. Const correctness is a pain, but it's important. Adding const to member variables, function returns, pointers, and references communicates important information to other programmers.

## Strings and Localization

If you make your game for English speakers only, you're slashing your sales. Europe and Asia, especially mainland China, are hungry for quality games. Most players will put up with English, but they'd rather get their hands on a good translation in their native language. Good localization technique deserves an entire book and a master's degree in foreign cultures.

I tend to use `std::string` and `std::wstring` throughout the book. It is an incredibly useful string class, and while not everyone agrees, it's the one I'm most comfortable with.

One final note about strings in real game code: Debug strings or names for objects are fine as literals. You can declare them at will:

```
if (impossibleError == true)
{
   OutputDebugString(_T("Someone enabled the impossible error flag!"));
}
```

## Commenting

Really good code comments itself, and I'm hoping the code in this book does exactly that. Good variable names and logic should obviate the need for wordy explanations. In this book, I'll sprinkle comments in the code where I think they do some good, but you'll usually find some meaty explanation immediately after the code sample.

In a real game, the meaty explanation should be inserted into the code, perhaps at the beginning of the file, so that other programmers can figure out what's going on. What seems obvious the moment you type the code degrades linearly with time to a confusing mess. For me, total confusion sets in approximately three months after I write the code. How could I possibly expect anyone else to understand it if I'm completely lost in something I wrote myself?

I always start projects with the intention of putting good comments in my code. I always end projects disappointed in other programmers and myself—we just didn't have enough time. That happens. Projects under pressure will see comments disappear because the programmers are spending 100 percent of their time coding like mad. The best policy is to start with a lean, light commenting policy and keep it up as long as you can. If there comes a point in the project where comments are dwindling, try to make a good effort to go back in the code base after the project releases to document the code. A good friend of mine at Microsoft told me that shipping the product was a good feature. I agree.

## Error Handling

There is very little error handling code in this book, so little that when I look at it, I cringe. The fact is that robust error code gets a little wordy, and I wanted to spend time on the lines of code that will teach you about making games. You can use any form of error checking you want, and I talk about some different options in the chapter on debugging.

Every hard exit in your game should have an error message that is presented to the player: "Bummer – your game is hosed because of some bug in objectdata.cpp, line 6502". Use `FILE` and `LINE` to identify the offending code. Unique error codes are a hassle to maintain. This data can be invaluable for the development team and customer service after the game ships. Many a patch or workaround traces its roots to a few hundred telephone calls and emails that finger a particular error code.

Most games create their own `assert()` macros and error logging system, and this book is no different. Throughout the code in the book, you'll see `GCC_ASSERT()`, which replaces the typical CRT `assert()` macro. It functionally behaves in the same way. You may also see `GCC_ERROR()` and `GCC_LOG()`. The first will display an error message, while the second will log the string to the debugger, assuming you have the correct tag enabled. This is described in detail in Chapter 23, "Debugging and Profiling Your Game."

## Memory Leak Detection

Most everywhere in the source code, you will see memory allocations use `GCC_NEW`:

```
m_PCMBuffer = GCC_NEW char[bytes];
```

`GCC_NEW` is defined in debug builds as:

```
#define GCC_NEW new(_NORMAL_BLOCK,__FILE__, __LINE__)
```

You'll learn more about this in Chapter 23, but suffice it to say for now that doing this helps you find memory leaks.

#### GOTO: NOT JUST A BAD IDEA—IT WAS NONEXISTENT!

At Origin Systems, a particular programmer on *Martian Dreams* used `goto` at a frequency you'd find unpleasantly surprising. The new version of the Borland compiler was on everyone's desks, fresh from the presses. He'd just finished installing it and went to lunch. I went to his machine and edited the compiler executable. I changed the keyword `goto` to `goat`. When he came back from lunch, three or four of us were poring over the Borland docs in my office. We told him that Borland's software engineers decided to eliminate `goto` from their implementation of C. He didn't believe us until he compiled a small test program in his newly installed compiler and received "unexpected identifier or keyword: goto" message for his trouble. We told him the truth before he reached someone at Borland's customer service department.

## Companion Website Downloads

Visit the companion website for this book at http://www.mcshaffry.com/GameCode/, where you can find the most up-to-date resources for this book, especially the source code.

The source code for this book is hosted by Google Code at this address:
http://code.google.com/p/gamecode4/

You may download the companion website files from www.courseptr.com/downloads. Please note that you will be redirected to the Cengage Learning site.

# Chapter 1

*by Mike McShaffry*

## What Is Game Programming Really Like?

Programming games can be very different from other kinds of programming. Some of the good aspects of game programming have to do with the bleeding edge challenges you run across and the fact that sometimes you actually see your name scroll across a credits screen. Games are cool, and everybody loves them. If you meet a fan at a computer game store, that person is usually really happy to meet you. You get to play with some great technology from manufacturers like Nintendo, Microsoft, Sony, Apple, and others. Software development kits from companies like Unity, Havok, Epic, Valve, and others are also a lot of fun to play with. They can give you a real boost in game development and can bootstrap your game from nothing to something cool in record time.

The not-so-cool side of professional game programming involves the inherent unknowns that come with your work. The sweaty underbelly of this industry can be blamed mostly on insane deadlines and work hours, project management problems, ever-changing SDKs, hardware and operating systems, the tricky problem of creating "fun," and intense competition from other game developers. Hopefully, this book can give you some perspective on the industry and at the same time show you the fun and not-so-fun aspects of game development. I'll try to point out some things that I've learned over the past few years. Read this chapter, and you might be able to dodge a few of these problems.

## The Good

Programming jobs in the games industry change fast. In fact, they've even changed with each new edition of this book. Programming used to be a really broad activity because there were so many problems to solve and there were so few good and experienced game programmers out there who could solve them. In the real early days, game programmers did everything: code, art, sound, and game design. Now you tend to see very specialized game programmers for niche areas of game technology: Character movement, network communications, database, physics, and audio are just a few. When I accepted my first job in the computer game industry, my second choice was a job with American General Life Insurance. They wore ties. Their employees took drug tests. I would have had the distinct privilege of working on a beta version of Microsoft's C++ compiler, programming little sales tools for insurance agents. Did I make the right decision or what?

Face it—most programming jobs are downright boring. If you know where to look, you can still find really interesting ones even outside the games industry. They might be jobs you can't talk about, working on ultra high budget simulations and control software, finding cures for disease through molecular protein folding analysis, and games. Everything else falls quickly into the "Did you put a cover sheet on your TPS report?" category.

**The Games Industry Is More Secretive Than the Pentagon**

In 2010 I was approached by Electronic Arts to work at their Sims studio on "a brand new Sims game." That was all they would tell me. It wasn't until I went into the on-site interview and signed a non-disclosure agreement that they told me this new game was *The Sims Medieval*. The project I'm working on as of the writing of this book is even more secretive. We don't tell potential candidates anything at all except that it's a Sims game, even after signing a non-disclosure agreement.

### The Job

Here's my bottom line: Games are great to work on because they are as much about art as they are science. When I wrote the first edition of this book, I put a lot of thought into why I found game programming immensely satisfying even with all of the pressures and challenges. I came to the following conclusion—I like blending the artsy side of my left brain and the engineering side of my right brain, especially when I'm in new territory. When I was on *Thief: Deadly Shadows*, I got to work on character movement—talk about a tweak fest. I had to look carefully at the character movement and understand why it "felt" wrong. I played tons of *Splinter Cell* to see how they solved some sticky problems. The "art" involved understanding how character movement was supposed to "feel." Once I had a clue, I had to convert that feeling to a piece of code that fixed the problem—that was science, mostly math. Two sides of your brain working together can solve some really cool problems. Even if you understand the science, sometimes it's up to you to tweak it, like an artist tweaks a smile on a portrait.

It's great to take a game design discussion with you to lunch. You can have a heated debate on whether the master zombie characters came from outer space or originated here on Earth—the result of some tragic experiment. You get the weirdest looks, as someone screams, "Damn it, everyone knows that it's better for the zombies to come from space!"

I have the most fun coding, especially when things are going well. Game code can be pretty difficult stuff, and you frequently have to break some new ground here and there. This is especially true when you are playing with new hardware like the latest console development kits. When working at Red Fly Studio on *Thor 3DS,* no one had worked on stereoscopic 3D rendering before, and it was both fun and tricky to figure out how to do it right. Sometimes you can break new ground when you figure out how to implement a customized version of a classic algorithm so that it runs fast enough to be in a game instead of a textbook.

Probably the best part of game coding is starting from scratch and allowing everything in your libraries to be refreshed and rewritten if necessary. While you are finishing, you can't make drastic changes, and you are forced to live with some annoying hacks and hastily designed objects. When the project is done and you are starting the next one, there's nothing better than throwing off those shackles. Refactoring, reorganizing, and rewriting an older system so that it really shines is extremely rewarding. Games probably offer more freedom than other types of programming projects because game code can have a very short shelf life. Of course, I say that knowing full well that some of my code might very well still be alive in *Ultima Online,* 10 years after it went live. Still, the state of the art moves pretty fast, and as a game developer you'll be pedaling as fast as you can.

## The Gamers

If you work in the games industry, people want to know about your company and your projects. They talk to you about your job because it's high profile. They want to know when they can play your game. Depending on the company you work for and what game you are working on, you may not be able to say a single word about it. (Secrecy can be very important when working with companies like Nintendo or LucasArts.) Every now and then, you'll find someone who played a game you worked on and enjoyed it. It's great when fans get a buzz going about a game that's still in the design phase, or they start talking about the next version before you're back from vacation. They set up websites devoted to your game and argue endlessly about stuff that even the development team finds minor.

Another category of people you come into contact with is the hopeful would-be game programmer. I enjoy these folks, and I do everything I can for anyone who has talent and is willing to increase his or her skills—if I didn't, you wouldn't be reading this book! With today's independent development scene and increasingly savvy hobbyists, there is also an increase in amateur developers. These developers are taking things a step beyond the more casual hobbyist level to create things that are intensely interesting. Some even graduate to cult status, or better yet, to the professional ranks. With iTunes, the Android Marketplace, Xbox Live Arcade, Steam, and Facebook, anyone can make his own game, actually sell it, and potentially make a living. The best revenge is being able to tell your parents that playing all those games actually did you some good.

**A Demo Is Better Than a Resume**

One of the best programmers I ever worked with started out as a dedicated amateur. This guy was so dedicated that he rewrote a large portion of *Ultima VII* on his own time and actually made a fantastic graphics engine that had Z-sprites before I even knew what they were. He showed us a demo that simply blew the minds of the *Ultima* programming team. We hired him.

## Your Coworkers

The best people are those closest to you—the development team. By the end of a project, they're like your family. Certainly you've seen them more than your family, and I've even seen teammates become family. Programmers, artists, animators, designers, audio engineers, composers, testers, and project managers make an odd mix of people. You wouldn't think that these people could all hang out and get along. But they do, mostly anyway.

Most of your interactions in game programming are with other programmers. One big difference between the game industry and other more traditional programming jobs is that there's a significant portion of programmers who are self-taught in games. I believe that game programmers as a whole look more to a person's skill than a university diploma. That's not to say that self-taught coders are slackers by any shake of the stick. Instead, they tend to be absolutely brilliant. One difference between the self-taught hackers and the programmer with formal training is that hackers tend to design and code things before they realize that someone has already solved the problem. Sometimes, you'll catch them describing a cool data structure they just came up with, and you'll realize they are talking about a B+ tree. Their strength comes from their amazing ability to see right to the heart of a problem and fearlessly begin to solve it. One of the most brilliant programmers I ever met never graduated high school.

The creative insight that artists conjure up makes working with them so fantastic. Probably the weirdest thing about working with artists on computer games is that you realize that artists and programmers are the same kind of people working with different sides of their brain. Artists can push you hard to achieve the look they are going for. Sometimes on a busy day, your first reaction to them asking crazy things of you is to brush them off. Instead, take a moment to visualize their goal and see if there's a way to make it happen. At Red Fly Studio, artists ruled the roost (the CEO was an artist), and our games always benefited from programmers trying hard to make the artists happy. One bit of advice, though—artists find it very difficult to remember that not every texture needs to be 2048 × 2048, and they will sometimes create assets that couldn't run on an army of computers, much less one that a normal person owns. When that happens, try to be patient and give them gentle reminders.

Animators have intense relationships with programmers, because getting a character to act in the game as the animator intends can be pretty tricky. The programmer working with a character animator has to constantly balance how good the character looks with how responsive the character feels. Take jumping, for example. When players press the jump button, they want the character to jump immediately, but in practice that looks a little goofy, since there's no time for the character to "wind up" to the jump as a real person would. Detecting the character's surroundings and animating to make him react properly to it can also be a challenge. Finally, animators love to change animations to make them better, but the problems of changing something critical, like jump distance, can have a drastic effect on level design—making easy things impossible or vice versa. Again, gentle corrections and good communication are key.

Game designers are a truly special breed of people. Almost every other discipline in game development has easy access to work in other industries—programmers, artists, composers, even producers can work using the same tools and thought processes as they do making games. Game designers, however, tend to transform into writers, playwrights, movie directors, historians, teachers, philosophers, poets, and any number of other things. Great game designers bring an amazing understanding of what drives human behavior and what fantasies humans would like to have. All this, as you might expect, can create some very interesting personalities—from the collaborative inspirer to the egomaniacal dictator. As a programmer working among designers, being able to understand their vision and help them create it is likely one of the most important skills you can have beyond the technical ones.

I've always enjoyed working with audio engineers and composers. One thing I can pass on is that the last content that gets tweaked or made in games is generally audio. Story is usually told through voice-over, sometimes with well-known actors. Final sound effects can't really be perfected until all the animations and particle effects are completely and absolutely final. What this means to you is that anytime something you are working on runs a little behind, you basically steal a little time from the guys who work last, which tends to be audio. Even so, you'll never find a more laidback and fun group of people. How they can be so pressed and keep a better attitude than almost everyone else on the whole team I'll never know.

I've tried very hard to have a great relationship with game testers. They can be everything from a high school kid working part-time to a real test engineer formally trained in software quality assurance. Either way, they are your last, best hope to release a game that will be fun to play and free of game-stopping defects. They can sometimes be frustrated game designers, but most of the time they are just game enthusiasts who really know the difference between fun and "meh." Listen to them, try to be patient when they keep telling you your code is broken, again, and they'll save you from introducing some bug that gets mentioned in a Metacritic review.

Producers, or project managers, I know the best because I've spent probably as much if not most of my career managing as I have coding. They are typically obsessive-compulsive organizers, energetic, gregarious, and team cheerleaders. They can also be like that guy in *Office Space* asking you where your weekly report is, which never goes over very well. Best advice I can give you is to put yourself in their shoes—playing a live action resource allocation game and trying to get thousands or even millions of creative works all completed in the right order and the right time, hopefully without asking everyone on the team to work every weekend for the next two years. Most producers want the best game possible without killing the team, and with any luck, they want to see that the team has some fun while doing it. Remember that, and you'll see their pesky questions in a new light.

All told, this group of people brings an incredible amount of talent and diversity to a team—and that is something you just can't get in many other jobs.

## The Tools—Software Development Kits (SDKs)

One of the most popular SDKs is DirectX from Microsoft. It provides APIs useful for creating game software, albeit only on devices that run Microsoft operating systems. There are many more: SDKs for physics, SDKs for rendering 3D graphics, SDKs for audio, networking, even AI. You probably could make a professional game without using any of them, but I wouldn't recommend it. You don't need all of them, but most certainly you'll use one or two. They boost your development schedule and give you some confidence that your graphics or audio system has been well tested and might even be well known by other programmers that will help you make your game.

When I first started writing this section, it was in "The Dark Side" section at the end of this chapter. I felt a little guilty about giving SDKs such a bad rap. After all, if they are really useless, why do I use them on every project? The truth is that SDKs give you a huge leg up. The source code that accompanies this book could never have been written or maintained without them. That said, they can also be a huge pain in the butt. SDKs are widely used, so they can't appeal to the odd needs of every project. Some of the expensive ones come with source code as you see with open source SDKs, which is critical for debugging problems. You can even make changes and recompile the SDK, but any customizations you perform might be invalidated by their next version. Most of the time, you have to be satisfied with begging and pleading the company that created it to add your wacky feature or just support the custom mod yourself. Perhaps the SDK engineers will find your idea interesting and add your idea to the mix.

The real hassle comes when you grab their latest version. You'll usually find that the new version isn't compatible with your code base, and you'll spend hours or days getting your game to compile again. In writing the fourth edition of this book, this happened to me—many SDKs needed some code changes to become functional again or to take advantage of new features and capabilities. Basically, if you don't have to upgrade for some compelling reason, don't bother. Spend the time making your game better. As they say, "If it ain't broke, don't fix it."

Do yourself a favor and try to find SDKs that that are widely used or are from companies that commit to support earlier APIs or have become stable enough that you only have to change your code to utilize new additions, rather than random changes to old APIs. Anything else is madness.

**Self-Inflicted Wounds**

Red Fly used TRI's Infernal Engine for all our games until about 2011. During that time, the programmers at Red Fly were improving the engine almost at the same speed as the TRI programmers—but not in the same way or even with the same programming philosophy. Ultimately, the two engines had to be brought back together because the Gen3 version of the engine had platform support for Sony PlayStation 3 and Nintendo 3DS. It took one programmer almost six months to reintegrate tens of thousands of individual changes so Red Fly could have the best of both worlds.

## The Hardware

Games run on cool hardware. Well, most games do. At Red Fly, the *Thor* project was one of the first games released on Nintendo's 3DS system, featuring stereoscopic 3D rendering. *Thief: Deadly Shadows* used the very latest in audio and video hardware for the PC, especially the new 5.0 EAX environmental audio system from Creative, and it also ran on the fairly new Xbox. Way back in the day, the *Ultima* games from Origin Systems pushed hardware so hard that players would usually buy a new computer every time an *Ultima* came out. At the time, this was like spending $2,500 on a new game. Many of the big-budget PC titles are created on hardware that has yet to reach any serious market penetration, which means that the hardware manufacturers are constantly sending game developers the latest greatest stuff and even a T-shirt every now and then. An established developer can still call any hardware company out there and get on their developer program. You don't exactly get free hardware anymore, but you do get access to the developer forums, news about updates, and other things you'll find useful. That can save your day if you find that your game crashes on the hottest video card or with one of the latest new controllers—you can't fix the bug just by hoping it goes away.

The developer programs offered by hardware manufacturers are a great resource. Most of them have special developer websites and prerelease hardware programs. They also have dedicated engineers who can help you with a specific problem. An engineer at ATI verified a particular bug on one of the Microsoft projects I worked on, and they had a new driver ready in a few days. Of course, I was happy to have the big gorilla named Microsoft standing behind us, but most hardware companies are really responsive when it comes to diagnosing weird driver problems.

## The Platforms

There is a wide variety of gaming platforms, and they never stop growing. For many years, we only had to deal with consoles and desktops. Since 2001, games have popped up on handheld devices like the Nintendo 3DS, Sony's Vita, the iPhone/iPad, Android devices, and many others. The biggest growth in gaming from the third edition of this book to the fourth edition by far is Web-based gaming, especially Facebook and Google+.

At the time of this writing, the big consoles on the market are the Wii from Nintendo, the Xbox 360 from Microsoft, and the PlayStation 3 from Sony. At first, the battle seemed to sway to Nintendo, which came in third place during the PS2/Gamecube/Xbox era. Late in the cycle, Microsoft and Sony seem to be winning. Since the 1950s and the very first computers, it was always software that sold the hardware, which is a fact that will never change. PlayStation 2 won the last time because it had the best games, period. The Wii came out strong because of its wide appeal to gamers of all ages. But due to the fact that Microsoft and Sony strongly support all their developers, not just their internal teams, they have gained ground, and it looks like the Wii is fading. Still, if it weren't for Nintendo taking a big risk on the Wii motion controls, we probably wouldn't have seen them from the much more conservative Microsoft or Sony. Fading or not, they are still influential, and the games industry is used to surprises from Nintendo.

**My Nephew Makes *Mushroom Men* Better**

One thing most games go through is something called *blind playtesting*. This is when you let someone who has never seen the game come in and give it a try. Usually, this happens with some developers watching and cringing, as they see a new player have trouble with something they designed. My then 10-year-old nephew, Sam, was a blind playtester for *Mushroom Men: The Spore Wars* and actually found a pretty important bug. It turned out that the special weapons Pax could build could only be used while standing in one place—and my nephew immediately noticed this. One of the programmers, Kain, was able to fix the bug and show Sam how his comments made the game better.

The best part of developing for consoles is the fact that you'll never have to worry about supporting a hellish grid of operating system and hardware configurations that are guaranteed to change at least twice during your development cycle. You do have to deal with standards compliance with the console manufacturers, which can be quite difficult if you've never had the experience.

Tables 1.1 and 1.2 list the various platforms on the market and their hardware specifications.

**Table 1.1 Capabilities of Last Generation Consoles**

| Platform | Xbox | PS2 | GameCube |
|---|---|---|---|
| CPU | 733MHz | 294.9MHz | 485MHz |
| Graphics Processor | 250MHz | 147.5MHz | 162MHz |
| Maximum Resolution | 1920 × 1080 | 1280 × 1024 | Up to HDTV |
| Memory | 64MB RAM | 40MB RAM | 43MB RAM |
| Controller Ports | 4 | 2 (4 optional) | 4 |
| Media | 4x DVD-ROM (3.2–6.4GB) | 5x DVD-ROM (3.2–6.4GB) | 3x DVD-ROM (1.5GB) |
| Digital Sound | Dolby 5.1 DTS in gameplay | Dolby Pro Logic II | Dolby 5.1 for DVDs |
| Hardware Audio Channels | 64 | 48 | 64 |
| Hard Disk | Yes—8GB | Add-on | No |
| Internet | 10/100 Ethernet port | Optional modem/ broadband | Optional modem/ broadband |
| DVD Movies | Yes | Yes | No |

There's a serious leap in capability from that first table to the second, isn't there? The change from the PS2 to the PS3 is nothing short of remarkable. But hardware capability doesn't mean you'll sell more—a great lesson that sometimes less is more.

When I wrote the second edition in 2004, I had a line about desktop hardware that said: "After all, you can't find CPUs topping 2GHz in the console world...." Funny how times change—today that statement is completely wrong. A few years after this edition is published, it will be wrong again! I also wrote that consoles were always lacking behind desktops for raw processing and graphics power. That statement isn't as true in the PS3/Xbox360 era and certainly won't remain true when their successors start to emerge.

Desktops are still ahead when it comes to memory and hard drive storage, but they are falling behind in cool controllers, like you see with the Wii. With all the consoles being Internet-capable and having space on their hard drives, consoles even get to send updates. The lines are definitely blurring. But the cool controllers aren't driving the popularity of PC games anymore; instead, it is social gaming on sites like

**Table 1.2 Capabilities of Next-Generation Consoles**

| Platform | Xbox360 | PS3 | Wii |
|---|---|---|---|
| CPU | 3.2GHz PowerPC Xenon with three cores | 3.2GHz cell—Also has seven single-threaded special purpose processors (SPEs) | 729MHz IBM Broadway |
| Graphics Processor | 500MHz ATI | 550MHz NVIDIA | 243MHz ATI |
| Maximum Resolution | Up to 1080p HDTV | Up to 1080p HDTV | Up to 480p |
| Memory | 512MB RAM @ 22.4Gbps | 256MB RAM @ 25.6Gbps | 60MB RAM @ 1.9Gbps |
| HDMI | Yes | Yes | No |
| Controller Ports | 4 (wired and wireless) | 7 (wired and wireless) | 4 |
| Media | 12x DVD-ROM (3.2–6.4GB) | Blu-ray (3.2–6.4GB) | Proprietary DVD (1.5GB) |
| Digital Sound | Dolby 5.1 DTS | Dolby 5.1 DTS | Dolby 5.1 for DVDs |
| Hardware Audio Channels | n/a | 320 hardware, no limit with software | 64 |
| Hard Disk | Yes—20–120GB | Yes—20–120GB | No |
| Internet | 100Mbs Ethernet | Gigabit Ethernet | Built-in wireless |
| DVD Movies | Yes | Yes | No |
| Blu-ray Movies | No | Yes | No |

Facebook and Google+. Those games begin as free to play, but very quickly they begin to ask you to spend small amounts of money on more energy. Even more insidious, these games ask you to use your social network to "help" you play, thus using you as a way to spread the word about their game while they take your money at the same time. Brilliant. A little disgusting maybe, but brilliant.

Still, the dizzying array of hardware and operating system combinations on desktops makes compatibility a serious problem. You'll spend a serious amount of time chasing down some crazy bug that only happens on some archaic version of Windows or on some rare video card. What a hassle!

Take a look at Table 1.3 and compare it to Table 1.2. You'll see pretty quickly that what was sitting under your TV will be in your pocket in just a few years. Not only that, but the input/output of these devices has all kinds of fun things to play with—GPS, front-and-back facing cameras, accelerometers, multi-touch screens, Bluetooth local networking, and fast Internet connections. just to name a few. Some of the best innovation in game design comes from having new ways to interact with the virtual universe, simulated by the device and other humans playing the game. One of the most innovative things I've seen recently is experiments in augmented reality, where you can use a pad or a phone as virtual goggles into the real world, with game characters seemingly moving about on your desktop, living room floor, or on top of someone's head in the subway. This kind of creativity and genuine fun in game development is one of those things that makes me want to get up every day and go to work. I never know how the day will turn out or what new things I'll see.

On desktops and even handhelds, like phones and pads, you might find it useful to find ways to support older legacy hardware while you make your game look good on the bleeding-edge gear. The CPU delta on PCs can be nearly 10:1, and the graphics delta is worse. People who play casual games hold on to their computers a long time,

**Table 1.3 Capabilities of Latest Handheld Devices**

| Platform | iPad2 | Droid Bionic | Sony Vita |
|---|---|---|---|
| CPU | 1GHz Apple A5 | 1GHz ARM9 (dual core) | 1GHz ARM9 (quad core) |
| Graphics Processor | 200MHz PowerVR SGX535 | GeForce Tregra 2 | PowerVR SGX543 |
| Maximum Resolution | 1024 × 768 HDTV | 960 × 540 | 960 × 544 |
| Memory | 16–64GB RAM | 16GB RAMSD adds 32GB RAM | 512MB RAM 128MB VRAM |
| HDMI | Yes | No | No |
| I/O | Touch screen, front and back cameras, GPS | Touch screen, front and back cameras, GPS | Touch screen, playstation controls, front and back cameras |
| Internet | 3.1Mbps 3G WiFi 802.11 a/b/g/n | 3.1Mbps 3G WiFi 802.11 b/g/n | WiFi 802.11 b/g/n |

so you'll probably still find video cards out there that don't support shaders for that type of gamer. A good game will configure itself to create the best experience it can on the hardware. If you have a hard-core audience, make sure that your options screen lets them tweak every setting possible. Let the flamethrowers turn on multi-channel MP3 decompression, full dynamic lighting and shadows, full-screen graphics effects like motion blur and bloom, ultra-high texture and model density, stereo 1600 × 1200 × 32 displays, and quasi-telepathic AI. Each of these options deserves separate testing paths on all the hardware configurations.

It makes you glad you can send patches over the Internet.

## The Show

The game industry throws awesome tradeshows and parties. Find out for yourself and register for the Electronic Entertainment Expo (E3), usually held in Los Angeles in May. E3 requires you to be part of the industry to get registered, so if you don't have a game job, then launch a game review website and call yourself "press." Everybody else does. When you get there, play every game you can and dork around with the latest console gear. The show floor is where the game companies pull out all the stops to attract attention. You've got to go see for yourself. It's unbelievable.

**Sneaking Around Is Definitely a Best Practice**

Throughout this book, I'll be including a number of "best practice" tips from my years of experience as a developer. I couldn't resist including this one for your first "best practice" dose. It can be a lot of fun to snag party invitations from the in-crowd and talk your way into the "by invitation only" areas. A friend of mine who worked for Dell was able to get into virtually every private area of the show just by showing up, flashing his Dell credentials, and talking like he was someone important. Almost everyone bought it. It's all good fun.

If you want to learn about game development, go to the Game Developer's Conference in San Francisco, which is held in March. It's brutally expensive, but you'll find the cream of the game development crop telling willing crowds some of their secrets. Before you sign up for any of the workshops, roundtables, or sessions, it's a good idea to do a Google search on the speakers and get an idea of what they've worked on recently. Choose the sessions that have speakers with the most game industry experience and subject matter you're ready to hear—some of them are fairly advanced. If you find yourself short of the cash to register, sign up to volunteer. Sure you have to work the show, but you will get some time for yourself, and even just an hour or two will be worth it.

## The Hard Work

Every job has its good parts and parts you just have to slog through. Game programming is no different. First, game programming can be extremely frustrating at times. Many before me have argued that programming games is the most challenging form of programming there is. Bad things are a matter of perspective; some people find these things challenging, while others find them burdensome. You'll have to judge for yourself.

### Game Programming Is Freaking Hard

It's not uncommon for a game programmer to do something completely new and try to hit a deadline at the same time. I'm not talking about a modification of a data structure to fit a certain problem; I'm talking about applying experimental and theoretical designs to a production system that meets deadlines. On *Ultima VII,* one programmer wrote a 32-bit memory management system that was based on a little-known Intel 486 processor flag and hand-coded assembly, since there were no 32-bit compilers or operating systems we could use. On *Ultima VIII,* one of the low-level engineers wrote a multithreaded real-time multitasker two years before Win32 went beta. On *Ultima IX,* the graphics programmer figured out how to make a software rasterizer appear to pump 32,000 textured polygons per second on a first generation Pentium. Everyone knows what *Ultima Online* did—found a way to get every *Ultima* fan playing in Britannia all at the same time. I can't even begin to talk about the innovation that had to happen there just to get this system to work.

It would be one thing if this stuff were all research, where results come when they may and the pressure is bearable as long as the funding for your project is there. A game project is different because the schedule is relentless. For all the media press about how late games are, I'm surprised that you see some of them at all, given the fact that so much technology has to be created and somehow the game has to be fun all at the same time.

**Richard Garriott Uses Jedi Mind Tricks**

Technology isn't the only thing that makes game programming hard. Game designers will push you farther than you ever thought you could go. I remember very well a conversation the senior staff at Origin had with Richard Garriott about the world design for *Ultima IX*. The team was pushing for a simple design that was reminiscent of the old *Ultima* games—the outdoor map was separate from the city maps. This was a simple design because each map could be loaded at once, and no complicated map streaming would be required. Richard didn't go for it. He wanted a seamless map like *Ultima VII*. This was a much harder problem. We knew going into the meeting that if we couldn't convince Richard to use a simpler world design we'd have a hard time making our deadlines. We steeled ourselves with resolve, and armed with our charts and graphs and grim schedule predictions, we entered the conference room. Two hours later, we all walked out of the room completely convinced that Richard was right, a seamless map was the way to go. I wish I knew how he does that!

## Bits and Pieces

Games are built from more than code. Go find any PC game you bought recently and take a look at the directory where you installed it. You'll find the expected EXE and DLL files, with a few INIs or TXT files, too. You'll also find gigabytes of other stuff with file extensions that don't necessarily map to any program you've ever seen. These other files hold art, models, levels, sounds, music, scripts, and game data. This data didn't just fall out of the ether. Every texture was once a PNG or TIF file. Every sound was once a WAV, probably converted to MP3 or OGG. Each model and game level had its own file, too, perhaps stored in a 3ds Max file. Even a small game will collect hundreds, if not thousands, of these bits and pieces, all of which need to be catalogued and organized into a manageable database of sorts.

Very few software projects share this problem. The only thing that comes close is a website, and there just aren't that many assets. After all, they have to get sent over the Internet, so there can't be that many—certainly not enough to fill up a Blu-ray disc, and a compressed one at that.

#### Losing Files Is Easier Than You Think

Logistically, these things can be a nightmare to manage. I worked on a project where an artist wiped every file he'd worked on without even knowing it. Art files would get changed on the network, but wouldn't get copied into the build, or even worse, the artist would change the name of a file, and it would get lost forever. When you have thousands of files to look though, it's sometimes easier to just repaint it. Luckily, there are tools like Perforce, Subversion, or Git to help manage this problem. The situation is certainly better than when I started, where I think our best file management scheme was a pad of paper.

## That's Not a Bug—That's a Feature

Actual bug: I was walking along and the trees turned into shovels and my character turned into a pair of boots and then the game crashed.

You certainly won't see a bug report like that working on a database application. Seriously, some of these reports convince you beyond any shadow of doubt that the testers are certifiably crazy. Or your code could be crazy. My bet is on the code being crazy.

You might wonder why I put something so amusing in the "hard" section of working on games. There are plenty of funny bugs; stuff goes wrong in a game and has a bizarre result. Luckily, Quality Assurance (QA) should find it because it will be funnier for you as a developer than it will be for players whose crashed game destroyed their save files and ruined all their progress, forcing them to start again from the beginning. Trust me, most players will "rage quit" at that moment.

Beyond the funny bugs, there's a dark side.

One bad thing is just the sheer volume of bugs. Games tend to be rushed into testing, and the QA department does what they are paid to do and writes up every problem they observe. I think they hope that eventually the producers will get the point and stop sending proto-ware into the test department. They hope in vain because the pressure to call the game "testable" is usually too much for the project management to bear. It's too bad that there tends to be no solid definition of "testable" unless you work in QA. From their point of view, it's pretty obvious.

The heavy bug volume weighs on everyone, developers and testers alike. They end up creating a logistical nightmare. The graphical reports that get spit out by the bug database are watched like the stock market; only this time, a steep upward curve tends to have a negative effect on team morale. The worst part by far is what happens when the team can't quite keep the bug count under control, which typically happens when they are still focused on finishing the game's content and features. To stay ahead, the project leadership gathers together and does "triage"—a process where they kill off bugs without the team ever really seeing it. The bug simply becomes a feature, maybe a weird screwed-up annoying feature, but a feature all the same.

**You Won't Be Able to Fix Every Bug**

There's nothing like having the rug pulled out from underneath you because a bug that you intended to fix is marked "won't fix" by the team leadership. You might even have the code fixed on your machine, ready to check in for the next build. Instead, you get to undo the change. The final straw is when some critic on the Internet bashes the programmers for writing buggy code and even points out the very bug that you intended to fix. Most programmers I know are perfectionists and take a lot of pride in their work, and because of that they lose sleep over bugs. As evil as this seems, making those decisions is as tough as knowing your code has a bug that you aren't allowed to fix. Believe me, I've done that a few thousand times.

## The Tools

Richard Garriott, aka Lord British and creator of the *Ultima* RPG series, once said that the computer game industry is a lot like the movie industry. He also said that at the beginning of every game project we start by inventing new cameras, film and processing techniques, and projectors. He said that 10 years ago, and while there is great middleware out there for sound and graphics and even complete turnkey game engines like *Unreal 3*, many game projects end up writing their own development tools from scratch.

**Before We Made the Game, We Made the Tools**

Most games have level or mission editors. When we developed the *Ultima* games, we spent the first year or so of development writing the game editor—a tool that could import graphics, sounds, and models from all the art and modeling software like Photoshop, LightWave, 3ds Max, Maya, and others. *Ultima IX*'s level editor was fully networked and used TCP/IP to communicate peer-to-peer to all the designers and programmers running it. They could even edit the same map at the same time, since smaller portions of the map could be locked out for changes. The editor could launch into game mode at the press of a button, so the designers could test their work. *Ultima Online's* editor was much more like the game than *Ultima IX*. UO already had a client/server system up and running, and it used a special god client to change the map levels and add new assets to the game.

Other games use a simpler strategy, a wise choice if you don't need 20 people building seamless maps and levels. The basic game level is assembled in a modeling tool like 3ds Max. A special editing tool usually loads that level and drops in special actions, dynamic object generators, and characters, almost as if you were playing the game. If you are developing a smaller game with a small team, there's no need to have a complicated, multiperson-aware tool. In fact, with a little work you can make 3ds Max act like your level editor—just don't try this on an AAA title.

There are a number of game engines on the market from Unity, Epic, Crytek, Valve, Trinigy, and others. The days of creating custom level and mission editors may be over, but you'll still have to write quite a bit of custom tools and code to make your game unique. So, worry not, the job of the game programmer is safe for a long time.

## The Dark Side

There are plenty of factors that make game coding a fluid and unpredictable task. The design of the game can change drastically during development, motivated by many factors inside and outside the development team. Mounting schedule slippage and production pressure leads to the legendary "crunch mode" so prevalent on many game projects. Dependant software tools like console SDKs and your licensed game engine change constantly, challenging software teams to keep up. Unlike many software projects, games frequently must support a wide variety of operating systems, graphics APIs, and platforms.

## Hitting a Moving Target

Most industry software projects are carefully designed and planned. Systems analysts study customer requirements, case studies of previous versions of the software, and prospective architectures for months before the first line of code is ever written. *Ultima VIII*'s architecture was planned by seven programmers in a single afternoon on a whiteboard.

Architecture notwithstanding, you can't design "fun." Fun is a "tweakable" thing, not something that exists in a design document. You hope like hell that the original design will result in a fun game, but the first playable version frequently leaves you with the distinct impression that the game needs some more chili powder and a little more time on the stove.

Sometimes, the entire design is reworked. *Ultima IX*'s architecture and game design changed no less than three times in development. I was there for two of them and didn't stick around for the third. When a game is in development for multiple years, it's easy for new hardware technology to blaze past you. In *Ultima IX*'s case, 3D accelerated video cards were just coming into their own as we were putting the finishing touches on what had to be the finest software rasterizer anyone ever wrote. It never saw the light of day.

**Sometimes Your Game Is Just Plain Boring**

*Ultima VIII*'s map design had a hub-and-spoke model. The hub was an underground dungeon that connected every other map. We released the game to QA, and word came back that it was completely boring. The culprit was a sparse central map that wasn't much more than an underground maze with a few bad guys hanging out here and there. It wasn't good enough. Two designers worked day and night to rework the central map. Puzzles, traps, monsters, and other trickery finally added a little spice. The central map ended up being one of the best parts of the whole game.

## Crunch Mode (and Crunch Meals)

Every now and then you end up at a technological dead-end and have to start completely over. I was brought into the late stages of a Mattel project that was supposed to be in the test phase in about two weeks. I took one look at the code and realized, to my horror, that the entire graphics engine was using Windows GDI. Unless someone out there knew something I didn't, the GDI in 1999 couldn't texture map polygons. In less than five weeks, the entire project was rebuilt from scratch, including a basic 2D vector animation tool.

Those five weeks were really more like fifteen weeks. The tiny development team worked late into each night and dragged themselves back each morning. There were no weekends. There were no days off. I'd estimate that we worked 90-hour workweeks on that project. You might think that unreasonable, and that nobody should have to work like that. That project was only five weeks. It was nothing compared to the pixel mines of Origin Systems circa 1992. Back then, Origin had something called the "100 Club." The price of entry was working 100 hours in a single workweek. The last time I counted, there were only 168 hours in seven days, so the folks in the 100 Club were either working or sleeping.

#### The Infamous Origin Hostel

To facilitate a grueling schedule, the teams built bunk beds in the kitchen. Company kitchens are no place for bedding. My office was unfortunately located right across the hall, and I observed the kitchen/bedroom getting higher occupancy than the homeless shelter in downtown Austin. After about a week, I began to detect an odor emanating from across the hall. It seemed that the brilliant organizers of Hotel Origin never hired a maid service, and that an unplanned biology experiment was reporting its initial results via colorless but odorous gasses. Origin management soon liquidated the experiment.

It's not uncommon for companies insisting on long hours from salaried employees to provide meals. These "crunch meals" are usually ordered out and delivered to the team. Origin was able to get a local deli to bill them instead of requiring a credit card, so they began to order from them almost every night. Months went by, and everyone on the development team knew every item on the menu by heart and knew exactly which bits of food were most likely to survive delivery intact. Fifteen years later, I can still tell you what's on the menu at Jason's Deli, and even though the food is good, I rarely eat there.

At the ripe old age of 38, I signed on to full-fledged crunch mode at Ion Storm to help finish *Thief: Deadly Shadows.* Let me tell you something—the older you get, the harder it is to stay awake and code. I actually cheated a little and came in early, but the long hours still were pretty tiring, especially after the fourth month.

At Red Fly, things were better, but crunch mode was still a reality. The simple fact was that publishers' budgets and deadlines never allowed a game to be developed in a manner that allowed 40-hour workweeks. For those of you who have heard of EA spouse, the scandal that supposedly changed the games industry, I'm here to tell you that the long hours were simply outsourced to third-party developers. To stay alive, Red Fly had to work harder and faster than everyone else—and even then we still had layoffs.

Good grief—when will this industry ever learn?

**The Centinal**

Sometimes there's a badge of honor attached to working late hours. My old boss at PlayFirst called it "The Centinal," which was a special club reserved for those who had worked over 100 hours in a single week. Basic math will tell you that there are only 168 hours in an Earth week. Mike and I are both long-standing members of this not-so-exclusive club. That having been said, there's an interesting camaraderie that gets forged when you spend that much time with a group of people. We all come together to make something great because we believe in the project and refuse to ship something that's not fun. When it gets to be 3 a.m. on a Tuesday night and you know that tomorrow night is going to be even longer, the walls of social etiquette come tumbling down.

## Bah Humbug

Computer games are a seasonal business. They sell like crap in the summer, and profits soar at Christmas time. Of course, they only soar for your project if you're not still working on it. This puts a significant amount of pressure on development teams. Sometimes, the pressure begins before the team starts working. If you work on downloadable titles, you can't earn money until you ship the game, so getting it done before the holiday rush is important. If you are working on a retail title, things are more difficult because of the time it takes to get your game on store shelves.

This lead time varies from publisher to publisher. A big company like Microsoft has a huge manufacturing pipeline that includes everything from the latest version of *Halo* to their latest version of *Office*. I once worked on a game that shipped the same month as Windows XP. I'll bet that if you were standing on the assembly line, you'd be hard pressed to notice the brief flash of dark green as 50,000 boxes of my game whizzed by. You shouldn't be surprised to see that a publisher like Microsoft requires you to finish your title by September or even August in order to make the shelves by the holiday season.

Other publishers are more nimble, and they might be more accommodating if you've got a AAA title coming in hot and steep as late as November. You won't get the best sales if you release after Thanksgiving, but even getting out the week before Christmas is better than missing the season altogether. It's always best to have everything in the can before October if you want to see your game under Christmas trees.

Basically, Christmas is only merry if your game is done.

## Operating System Hell

Microsoft Excel doesn't need to support full-screen modes, and it certainly doesn't need to worry about whether the installed video card has the latest shaders. That's one of the reasons that games get some special dispensations from Microsoft to qualify for logo compliance. Logo compliance means that your game exposes certain features and passes quality assurance tests from Microsoft. When your game passes muster, you are allowed to display the Windows logo on the box—something that is good for any game but especially important for mass-market games.

One Microsoft game I worked on had to pass QA testing for Windows 98, Windows ME, Windows 2000, and all versions of Windows XP. By 2002, Microsoft wasn't supporting Windows 95 anymore, which was a good thing. It was hard enough building an old box for our Windows 98 test machine. The OS that required the most tweaking was Windows XP, mostly because of the new requirement that the *Program Files* directory was essentially read only for nonadministrator accounts. Most games store their dynamic data files close to the executable, which will fail under Windows XP Home. These drastic changes to Windows XP motivated many game companies to drop support for all Windows 9x platforms by the end of 2004. For a big company, Microsoft can move pretty fast, and as a game programmer, you have to keep up.

The hell doesn't even stop there—some games choose to write graphics engines that work under DirectX and OpenGL. Some graphics middleware supports this natively, so you don't have to worry about it. Why would you bother? Performance.

Most video cards have DirectX and OpenGL drivers, but it's not guaranteed that you'll achieve equal performance or graphics quality under both. The performance differences are directly proportional to the effort put into the drivers, and there are cases where the OpenGL driver beats DirectX soundly. Of course, there are mirror cases as well, where DirectX is the way to go. Even better, the quality of the drivers changes from operating system to operating system. The result of all this is a huge increase in effort on your side. Even if you choose one particular graphics API, you still have to support a wide array of operating systems. This increase in effort simply widens the market for your game. It doesn't make your game fun or provide a deeper experience. It just keeps it from misbehaving on someone's computer.

I almost forgot—what about iOS and Android? If you are writing games for these platforms, you still have to deal with the differences between OS releases: Android 2.0 is different than 2.1 or 2.2. iOS is the same way. If you decide to support a wide variety of platforms and operating systems, I highly suggest you consider using a game engine like Unity, which hides a lot of these problems and simply lets you make your game. Doing it yourself is a big problem, and to be honest, not one that makes any financial sense.

Moving games to very dissimilar platforms can be nigh impossible, such as a direct port of a PC game to a handheld device. The lack of a keyboard or game controller, different screen resolution, radically difference graphics performance, and smaller secondary storage preclude some games from being directly portable even if the operating system is the same. That doesn't even begin to address the inherent design concerns that differ sharply from handhelds to desktops—the players on these devices simply want different things out of gaming.

## Fluid Nature of Employment

The game industry, for all its size and billions of dollars of annual revenue, is not the most stable employment opportunity out there. You can almost guarantee that if you get a job in the industry you'll be working with a completely different set of people every two years or so, and perhaps even more often than that.

Every year at the Origin Christmas party, employees were asked to stand up as a group. Everyone who had worked there less than a year was asked to sit down, followed by second and third year employees. This process was repeated until only a handful of people were left. This was usually by the fourth or fifth year. In my sixth year, I became the twelfth most senior person in the company by time of service, and Origin had hundreds of employees. This can be fairly common throughout the industry—but you can find some companies that are different by the nature of their product or culture. They are just harder to find, unfortunately.

The stresses of incredibly short schedules and cancelled projects have chased many of my friends out of the industry altogether. Whole studios, including two of my own, take root for a while and then evaporate or get bought. Your boss today will not be your boss tomorrow, especially if your boss attempts to do something crazy, like start his own game studio! Weirder yet, the boss you have today might actually be working for you tomorrow, or vice versa. I've had that happen more than once!

**I Remember You!**

The longest job I've ever had in the video games industry was just over two years. If you look at all the companies I've worked for, only about half of them still exist. It's very rare to find any kind of stability in this industry. One interesting side effect of this is how often you run into the same people. There's a UI designer at EA who I've worked with at three separate companies. Mike and I live in different states, and we still find people we've both worked with. For example, the lead gameplay programmer at Slipgate was hired into the industry several years ago by Mike. This just goes to show you that if you're difficult to work with, you won't last long. We all know each other.

## It's All Worth It, Right?

There's something odd about human psychology. After a particularly scary or painful experience, some of us will say to ourselves, "Hey, that wasn't so bad. Let's do it again!" People who make games do this all the time. The job is incredibly difficult and can drive you completely mad. Your tools and supported operating systems change more often than you'd like. Some days you delete more code than you write.

Taking three steps forward and five steps back is a good recipe for long hours, and you'll get an "all you can eat" buffet of overtime. It will get so bad that you'll feel guilty when you leave work before 7 p.m. on a Sunday night. When crunch mode is over, and you get back to a normal 60-hour workweek, you'll wonder what to do with all the extra time on your hands.

Why bother? Is it possible that that boring job at American General Life Insurance was a better option for me? Not a chance. There are plenty of good things, many of which I mentioned at the beginning of this chapter, but there's one I've held for last that beats them all: After all the work, lost weekends, and screaming matches with producers and testers, your game finally appears on the retail shelves somewhere. A few weeks after it ships, you start looking. You make excuses to go to Wal-Mart, GameStop, and Best Buy and wander the software section. Eventually, you see it. Your game. In a box. On the shelf.

There's nothing like it. As you hold it in your hands, someone walks up to you and says, "Hey, I was thinking of buying that game. Is it any good?" You smile and hand him the box saying, "Yeah, it's damn good."

# Chapter 2

*by Mike McShaffry*

## What's in a Game?

There are tons of reasons programmers get attracted to games: graphics, physics, AI, networking, and more. Looking at all of the awesome games that have been released over the past few years, such as *Halo, Grand Theft Auto, Gears of War,* and others, you might first think that all of the major technology advances have been in the area of graphics or physics programming. There is certainly more than meets the eye, and after seeing for myself how some games are architected, I often wonder how they even function.

When building a game, programmers will typically start with a DirectX sample, import some of their own miserable programmer art, put an environment map or a bump map on everything in sight, and shout "Eureka! The graphics system is finished! We'll be shipping our game by next weekend!"

By the time the next weekend rolls around, the same newbie game programmers will have a long laundry list of things that need to be done, and there are a number of subtle things that they will have completely missed—like how to manage memory and game processes properly. These hidden systems are usually the heart of every game, and you're never aware of them when you play games because you're not supposed to be aware of them.

This book is about more than just the visible parts. It is primarily about how to glue all these parts together in a way that won't drive you and your programming colleagues insane. This chapter takes the first step, and it shows you a high-level view of how commercial games are (or should be) architected.

After you finish this chapter, you'll have a good understanding of the main components of game code and how they fit together. The rest of this book digs into the details of these systems and how they work.

The important lesson to learn here is that you'll be able to build much better games if you really understand the architecture, the components, and how everything fits together. In other words, think and plan before you start coding, because a great foundation can hold a big game, where a crappy one simply can't hold up to the strain. We all hear this good advice over and over, but it's easy to neglect because it takes a lot longer to get something up and running. Think of this like you would approach building a house. Don't be like the guy down the street who just starts putting up walls without really thinking through how big his house needs to be, whether it needs a second floor, and how he wants to live in it.

## Game Architecture

There are as many ways to assemble the subsystems of a game as there are game programmers. Being a game programmer, I'll give you my opinion of what the subsystems are, what they do, and how they communicate. You may do things differently, and that's perfectly fine by me, especially since what I'm going to present is geared toward understandability, not necessarily efficiency. Once you understand something, you can find your own path to making it run pegged at 60Hz or better, but you sure can't get something to run that fast if you have no idea what's going on.

I can't say this enough—you don't have to do things my way—but since my way is the easiest for me to describe, it makes some sense that I'll preach a little of my own opinions. As you read this chapter, think first about what problems I'm solving with this system and at least grab hold of the subsystems and what they do on their own. If you come up with a better way to build this mousetrap, call me, and I'll hire you.

Let's start at the top level and work our way down. You can take every subsystem in a game and classify it as belonging to one of three primary categories: the application layer, the game logic layer, and the game view layer (see Figure 2.1). The application layer deals with the hardware and the operating system. The game logic layer manages your game state and how it changes over time. The game view layer presents the game state with graphics and sound.

If you think this architecture sounds familiar (and you're familiar with MFC's document/view architecture), you're exactly right, but don't burn this book in disgust just yet. While I loathe programming in MFC as much as the next person, there is amazing flexibility in separating a game into these three independent systems. Another popular design pattern, the Model-View-Controller, seeks to separate the logic of a

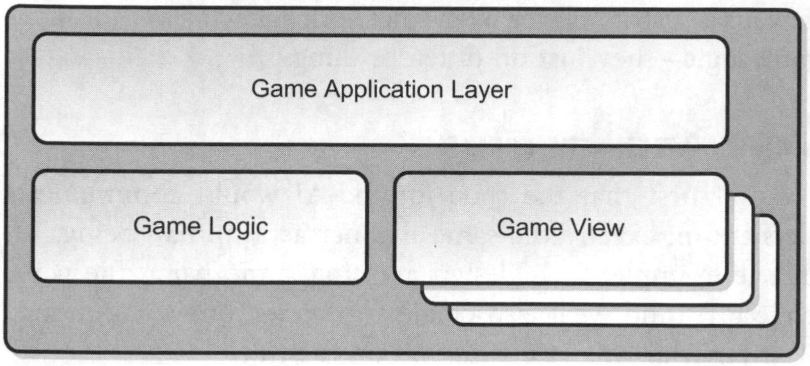


**Figure 2.1**
High-level game architecture.

system from the interface used to present or request changes to data. The architecture I propose encapsulates that and adds a layer for hardware or operating system–specific subsystems.

The application layer concerns itself with the machine your game runs on. If you were going to port your game from Windows to iOS or Android, or from the PlayStation 3 to Xbox 360, you would rewrite most of the code in the application layer, but hopefully not much else. In this area, you'll find code that deals with hardware devices like the mouse or a gamepad, operating system services such as network communications or threading, and operations such as initialization and shutdown of your game.

The game logic layer is your game, completely separated from the machine your game runs on or how it is presented to the player. In a perfect world, you could simply recompile all the source code related to your game logic, and it would run on any platform or operating system. In this area, you'll find subsystems for managing your game's world state, communicating state changes to other systems, and accepting input commands from other systems. You'll also find systems that enforce rules of your game system's universe. A good example of this is a physics system, which is the authority on how game objects move and interact.

The third and last system component is the game view. This system is responsible for presenting the game state and translating input into game commands that are then sent to the game logic. What's interesting about the game view is that it can have different implementations, and you can have as many views attached to your game as your computer can handle. One type of game view is for your players; it draws the game state on the screen, sends audio to the speakers, and accepts input through the user interface. Another type is the view for the artificial intelligence (AI) agent, and a third might be a view for a remote player over a network. They all get the same state changes from the game logic—they just do different things.

## Applying the Game Architecture

It might seem weird to you at first that the code for the AI would communicate through the same pathways and in exactly the same manner as a human being. Let me give you a more concrete example. Let's design a racing game using the game logic and game view architecture, and we'll also create two views: one for a human player and one for an AI driver who will race with you on the track.

The game logic for a racing game will have the data that describes cars and tracks and all the minute properties of each. For the car, you'll have data that describes how weight is distributed, engine performance, tire performance, fuel efficiency, and things like that. The track will have data that describes its shape and the properties of the surface all along the route. You'll also have a physics system that can calculate what happens to cars in various states of acceleration and steering, how they respond to the track, change in input controls, or even collisions with each other.

For inputs, the game logic cares about only four things for each car: steering, acceleration, braking, and perhaps the emergency brake. If your cars have guns on them, like we all wish, you would also have an input for whether the fire trigger is down. That's it; the game logic needs nothing else as input to get the cars moving around the track.

Outputs from the game logic will be state changes and events. This includes each car's position and orientation and the position and orientation of the wheels in relation to the car's body. If the game supports damage, you'll also have damage statistics as an output. If your cars have guns, a state change could also be whether the weapon is firing and how much ammo is left. Another important game state, especially the way I play racing games, is collision events. Every time a collision happens, the game logic sends an event with all the collision data. Events and state changes are sent to game views.

The game view for the human has a lot of work to do to present the view of the game state. It has to draw the scene from the player's selected point of view, send audio to the speakers, spawn particle effects—especially when bad drivers like myself are scraping down the guardrails—and rumble the force feedback controls. The view also reads the state of the game controller and translates that into game logic commands. A good example of this is to notice the right trigger pressed to full throttle, and it sends the "Accelerator at 100%" command to the game view or changes in the left thumbstick to "Steer left at 50%." These commands are sent back to the game logic. Take a look at Figure 2.2 to see what I mean:

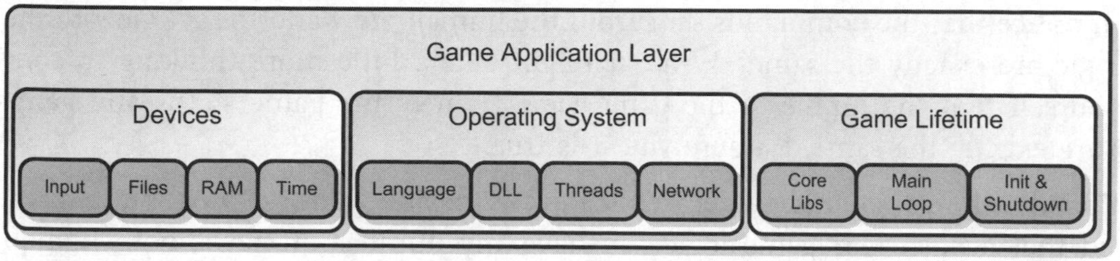


**Figure 2.2**
A closer look at the application layer.

Imagine what happens when a player mashes the A button on the controller—the normal control for the emergency brake in my favorite Xbox 360 racing game. The human view interprets this as a request to hit the emergency brake on my Ferrari and sends a message to the game logic. The game logic evaluates the request, sets `m_bIsEmergencyBrakeOn` to true, and sends a state update back to the human view. The human view responds to this message by playing a sound effect or maybe showing something on the screen. Another example is the throttle setting. The controller sends a message to the game view that the right trigger is pressed 82%. The view interprets this as a command to set the accelerator to 82% and sends a request to the game logic. The game logic determines that the rear tires have broken loose by looking at the car, its weight, the tires, the track condition, and other factors. It sends a message back to the game view that the rear tires are spinning, and the game view can then respond by playing a sound effect.

You can see that the game controller's thumbstick or button state doesn't affect the game state directly. Instead, the controller's state is interpreted by the game view and converted into commands, which are sent to the game logic by an event. The game logic receives events generated by the view and uses those commands, along with its physics simulation, to figure out what is happening in the game universe. The state changes in the game world get sent back to the view, so it can draw polygons, play sound effects, and rumble the controller.

The game view for the AI is a little different. It will receive the same game state events received by the human game view, such as which track the race is occurring on, the weather conditions, and the constantly updated positions, orientations, and velocity of cars on the track. It will take this information and recalculate what commands to send into the game logic. For example, in response to the "Go" event from the game logic, the AI might send an "Accelerator at 100%" command back to the game logic. While negotiating a turn, it might send "Steer left at 50%" to the game logic.

Did you notice that the commands sent from the human view and the AI view to the game logic are exactly the same? While it might take a little more thinking to convince yourself that the inputs to the game view, namely the game status and game events, are exactly the same, I assure you it is true.

I mentioned before that this game architecture is flexible. You've probably already surmised that a particular game logic can have any number of views, both human and AI. If the interfaces for the human and AI views are exactly the same, it is a trivial matter to swap a human player, or even all human players, with AI players. But wait, it gets better.

You could create a special DVR game view that does nothing but record game events into a buffer and play them back. In a sense, the game logic is entirely short circuited, but since the game state changes and events are exactly the same, they can be presented in the DVR view with very little recoding. Of course, if you want a "rewind" feature, you've got some extra work to do because the game events don't necessarily go equally back in time as they go forward!

You could also create a special game view that forwards game status and events to a remote player across the Internet. Think about that: The game logic doesn't have to care whether the players are local or separated by thousands of miles. The remote view should be pretty smart about collecting game states and events, compressing them into as few bytes as possible, and shipping them via TCP or UDP to the remote player. The game commands received from the remote player should go through a verification filter, of course. You can never be too sure about remote players, or remote game logics, for that matter.

One thing to note—players with different views can be advantaged or disadvantaged. For example, those who play on 4:3 screens can't see quite as much as those playing on 16:9 screens. Taken a step further, you can easily see that any differences in view definitions can give any consumer of that view a huge edge or take it away. Be cautious with your view definitions, whether it has to do with something obvious like screen size or the types of events the view receives from the game logic.

I hope I've convinced you that this architecture is a good way to go. I'll be quite honest and tell you that it isn't an easy architecture to code, especially at first. You'll go through a phase where you are sure there is an easier way, and you'll want to abandon this event-driven architecture where game logic is completely separate from the view. Please be patient and resist the urge. Given some time, you'll never go back to a simpler, but less flexible design.

**Make It So, Number 1!**

One day, while working on a Sims project as an AI programmer, the lead engineer came up to me with some AI tasks related to a new object the designers wanted to get into the game. They wanted special Sim behavior for this object. After explaining the designs, he guessed that it would take a couple of weeks to implement. I smiled and shook my head. "It'll take two or three days, tops." That's the difference between good architecture and bad architecture. Good architecture is flexible and easy to change.

## Application Layer

The contents of the application layer are divided further into different areas that deal with devices, the operating system, and your game's lifetime (refer to Figure 2.2).

### Reading Input

Games have an amazing variety of user input devices: keyboard, mouse, gamepad, joystick, dance pad, steering wheel, cameras, accelerometers, GPS, and my personal favorite, the guitar. Reading these devices is almost always completely dependent on calls to the operating system and device drivers. The state of these devices should always be translated into game commands. Some of these commands might be sent back to the game logic, such as "fire missile," while others might be handled by the game view, such as "show me my inventory." Either way, you'll likely write an entire subsystem to read these devices and interpret them as commands.

This same system should also be configurable. I play console shooters with an inverted Y-axis, but many people like it the other way around, even though I'll never understand why. If you have a system that reads devices as input and sends game commands as output, you can create the system to read a configuration file to match controls with commands. Then all you have to do is modify this data file, and you'll have completely configurable controls.

One thing is critical: You can't simply change the game state directly when you read user input. Every bit of game sample code out there does this; you can see where games make direct changes to data simply because the W key was pressed. This is a vastly inflexible system and will haunt you later, I guarantee it.

### File Systems and Resource Caching

File systems read from and write data to storage systems such as DVD-ROM, hard disk, and SD cards. Code in this subsystem will generally be responsible for managing game resource files and loading and saving the game state. Managing resource files can be pretty complicated—much more so than simply opening a JPG or an MP3 file.

A resource cache is one of those hidden systems I told you about. An open world game like *Grand Theft Auto* has gigabytes of art and sound, and the system only has a fraction of the memory needed to load everything. Let me explain why a resource cache is important with a little metaphor. Imagine the problem of getting a crowd of people out of a burning building. Left to their own devices, the crowd will panic, attempt to force themselves through every available exit, and only a small fraction of the people will escape alive.

Now imagine another scenario, where the evacuation is completely organized. The crowd would divide themselves into single file lines, each line going out the nearest exit. If the lines don't cross, people could almost run. It would be very likely that even a large building could be completely evacuated.

This analogy also works well for game resources. The burning building is your slow optical media, and the doors are the limited bandwidth you have for streaming this media. The bits in your resource file represent the crowd. Your job is to figure out a way to get as many of the bits from the optical media into memory in the shortest possible time. That's not the entire problem, though. A resource cache is exactly what the name implies—commonly used assets like the graphics for the HUD are always in memory, and rarely used assets like the cinematic endgame are only in memory while it's playing, and most likely only a piece of it at that.

The resource cache manages assets like these in a way that fools the game into thinking that they are always in memory. If everything works well, the game will never have to wait for anything, since the resource cache should be smart enough to predict which assets will be used and load them before they are needed.

Every now and then, the cache might miscalculate and suffer a cache miss. Depending on the resource, the game might be able to continue without it until it has been loaded, such as the graphics for an object in the far distance. In that case, the graphic can fade in once it is safely in memory. In other cases, the game isn't so lucky, such as a missing audio file for a character's lines. Since they are synched to the facial animations, the game has to wait until the audio is loaded before the character can begin speaking. If it does that, players will notice a slight pause or "hitch" in the game.

So it's not enough to write a little cache that knows whether resources exist in memory at the moment they are needed. It has to be clever, predicting the future to some extent and even providing the game with a backup in case the cache suffers a miss.

Luckily, I've included an entire chapter on the subject of file systems and the resource cache. This just might be one of the most under-discussed topics in game development.

## Managing Memory

Managing memory is a critical system for games, but it is largely ignored by most game developers until they run out of it. Simply put, the default memory manager that comes with the default C-runtime libraries is completely unsuitable for most game applications. Many game data structures are relatively tiny things, and they belong in different areas of memory, such as RAM or video memory. A general memory manager tries to be all things to all applications, where you will know every detail about how your game needs and uses memory. Generally, you'll write your own memory manager to handle allocations of various sizes and persistence and more importantly to track budgets.

**Virtual Memory—Can Be Good, Can Be Bad**

Windows can use virtual memory, and when a game runs out of physical memory, the OS will automatically begin to use virtual memory. Sometimes, Windows games can get away with this, but it is a little like playing Russian roulette—at some point, the game will slow to a crawl. A console game is completely different. For example, if your game allocates a single byte larger than the available memory, it will crash. Every game programmer should be as careful about memory as console programmers. Your game will run faster and will simply be more fun. Create some way to track every byte of memory, which subsystem is using it, and when any one of these areas exceeds its memory budget. Your game will be better for it.

## Initialization, the Main Loop, and Shutdown

Most software waits for the user to do something before any code is executed. If the mouse isn't moving and the keyboard isn't being hammered, an application like Microsoft Excel is completely idle. This is good because you can have a bunch of applications up and running without a large CPU overhead. Games are completely different. Games are simulations that have a life of their own. Without player input, they'll happily send some horrific creature over to start pounding on your character's skull. That will probably motivate a few button presses.

The system that controls this ongoing activity is the main loop, and it has three major components: grabbing and queuing player input, ticking the game logic, and presenting the game state to all the game views, which means rendering the screen, playing sounds, or sending game state changes over the Internet.

At the highest level, your game application layer creates and loads your game logic, creates and attaches game views to that logic, and then gives all these systems some CPU time so they can do their jobs. You'll learn more about this in Chapter 5, "Game Initialization and Shutdown," and Chapter 7, "Controlling the Main Loop."

## Other Application Layer Code

There are lots of other important subsystems in the application layer, including the following:

- The system clock
- String handling
- Dynamically loaded libraries (DLLs)
- Threads and thread synchronization
- Network communications
- Initialization
- Main loop
- Shutdown

The system clock is critical for games. Without it, you have no way to synchronize game animations and audio, move objects at a known speed, or simply be able to time your credits so that people have enough time to read them. Almost every game subsystem will care about time: physics, animations, user interface, sound, and so on. Some systems have multiple methods of getting access to the system clock, each with different levels of resolution or precision. If you choose one that has poor precision, such as the Windows `WM_TIMER` message, your game will suffer from jittery animations, bad synchronization between animations and audio, and other problems.

Game programming becomes more global year after year, and generally games that sell well in one language will also sell well if they are translated or *localized*. If you structure your game correctly and factor all language-specific files, such as strings into separate files, you'll find it a lot easier to translate your game into a similar language. Note that I said "similar language." Although it is possible to structure a game to be in completely different languages like English and Japanese, remember that you don't just have a technology barrier to multilingual gaming. You also have a cultural barrier—not every game is one that can cross cultures easily.

Most operating systems have a way to dynamically swap code in and out of memory at runtime. This is critical for conserving valuable memory space or replacing a subsystem entirely. You might use a DLL to swap a DirectX for an OpenGL renderer, for example.

Today's multicore desktops and consoles make multithreaded and multicore programming a must. I actually remember a time when games didn't use threads—instead everything ran in a single execution path. It was easier in some ways, but harder in others. Threads are used for audio streaming data, AI, and if you are clever, even physics. I've read in other places that shall remain nameless that suggest you can use threads for everything. Don't believe this for a minute; if every subsystem used separate threads, it could be extremely difficult to manage thread synchronization, and I guarantee the system would be challenging to debug.

Network communications is another service provided by the operating system. This network code will generally provide your game with a way to make a network connection with another computer and a way to read and write data from the network stream. The definition of what actually gets sent and how received data is interpreted is actually coded in the game view and game logic layer. I'll talk more about that shortly.

The last group in the application layer is responsible for your game's life cycle: initialization, the main loop, and shutdown. I've also included in this group your core libraries that standardize basic data structures and templates, as well as your script interpreter.

Initialization can be something of a nightmare. Many game subsystems have complicated interrelations, and they tend to depend on one another. We'll discuss details of the initialization sequence in Chapter 5.

Most games use scripting languages. Whether it is UnrealScript, Python, Lua, or something a game team creates from scratch, these systems and the scripts they run are critical components for today's commercial game development. You'll learn more about scripting languages, and Lua in particular, in Chapter 12, "Scripting with Lua."

## Game Logic

The game logic (see Figure 2.3) is the heart and soul of your game. It defines the game universe, what things are in the universe, and how they interact. It also defines how the game state can be changed by external stimulus, such as a human player pressing a gamepad key or an AI process taking action to kill you. Let's take a closer look at all of the components of the game logic system.

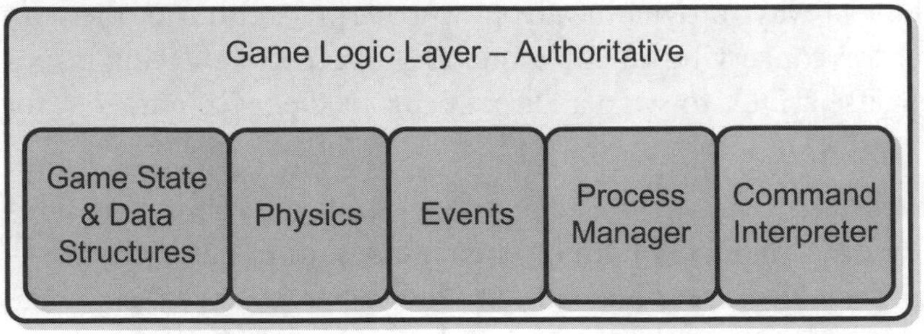


**Figure 2.3**
Game logic and its subsystems.

## Game State and Data Structures

Every game will have a container for game objects. Simple games can use a list structure, but more complicated games will need something more flexible and optimized for quick local searching or streaming. Your game engine must be able to traverse the object data structures quickly to change an object's state, and yet it must be able to hold a flexible array of properties for each object. These two requirements are frequently at odds with each other; one is quick to search, the other is easy to extend.

*Ultima* used a simple two-dimensional array of object lists. It was easy to find objects within a given range of a map location, and each grid square was small enough to have a quickly traversable list of objects. *Thief: Deadly Shadows*, on the other hand, used a simple list of objects, but it was heavily tangled by internal pointers. If two objects needed to know about each other, such as an elevator button and the elevator door, they were linked by the game editor. This solution actually worked quite well and is commonly used.

Object properties, such as hit points, engine horsepower, and wacky things like that tend to be stored in custom data structures whose efficiency can be anything from fantastic to dismal. *Ultima Online* used text strings to define properties on objects, which had the benefit of easy and flexible development at some cost in memory storage. *Thief: Deadly Shadows* had an extremely complicated property system that was actually object oriented; you could define object properties for an archetype, like a barrel, but overload existing properties or even create totally new ones for a particular barrel that was placed only once in the game universe. The system was memory efficient since it never copied property data, but it ran at some extra cost in CPU time because the property system was essentially a tree structure. There are tradeoffs no matter how you do it.

It's easy to confuse the game logic representation of an object with the visual representation of an object. The game logic holds the object state, such as the amount of damage an object has—probably stored in an integer. The visual representation, managed by the game view, holds model data and textures that convey the state visually to the player, such as a bloody arm stump. A bloody arm stump texture is completely different from `m_damage = 30`.

You might feel that it would be better to store all of these things in a single C++ object—how much damage had been done and whether the arm texture is healthy or bloody. In a way you are right—but maybe not in exactly the way you think. Most modern games create special objects that contain all of the various definitions that make that game object unique. Some of the classes in the collection belong to the game view, such as the skeletal mesh object used by the renderer to display the actor. Others might belong to the game logic, such as data that tells the physics system how heavy the actor is and how it will collide with other physical objects in the game. Other objects might describe game specific data, such as a character's hit points; this too would belong to the game logic. When any game logic data changes, the game logic broadcasts an event. In the previous example, when damage is increased on the actor, the game logic sends a special event informing all of the game subsystems. The renderer reacts to this event by changing the texture. More on this later.

I wish I had more time in this book to go exhaustively over low-level game data structures, but to be honest, they are extremely custom and are finely tuned to suit the requirements of a particular game. My suggestion to you is to make sure that you have an excellent knowledge of classic data structures such as linked lists, hash lists, trees, B-trees, and all those other things you learn in classic data structures texts. Games absolutely use these structures, or perhaps abuse them, to get the results they need.

## Physics and Collision

Physics falls under the general category of "rules of your game universe" and is solidly a member of your game logic. It defines everything from how actors move when they fall under gravity to what they do when they tumble around and come into contact with other actors.

You certainly don't need a complicated physics system to have a fun game, but you can bet your bottom dollar that a bad physics system will completely remove the fun from any game. There's a great game concept that says that when something is completely abstract, it's easy to ignore unrealistic representations of things. When you inject reality into a game, even small errors create complaints from your players. You can prove this to yourself by looking at the movements of a stick figure on one of those old Flash games on the Internet and comparing it to the best human animations in a game like *Battlefield 3*. You'll forgive the stick figure for moving in weird ways because it is so abstract, but you'll be upset with the *Battlefield* character for the smallest mistake in facial animation—(one of the hardest things to animate, by the way)—because the character looks so realistic we find it difficult to accept when it does anything unrealistic.

This concept has to do with human psychology and how we observe things. It comes into serious play when you create any game technology that approaches reality, as physics systems do. You'll spend a staggering amount of time making the tiniest tweaks to your system to remove the smallest movement problems, because that tiny mistake in reality is glaring.

## Events

When the game logic makes changes in the game state, such as creating or moving an actor, a number of game systems will respond. Here's an example. Imagine that one actor in your game is a portable radio. The graphics system will need to create polygons and textures so you can see the radio. The sound system will create a sound effect so your radio will play some great music—perhaps a little Jimi Hendrix. AI processes might respond to the presence of the actor. In this case, they might just chill out and enjoy the sublime guitar from our boy Jimi. All three of these subsystems—the graphics system, the audio system, and even the AI system—need to know that this radio exists and what it is doing. These systems are notified through events. Just like a Windows application hears about a `WM_MOUSEMOVE` event, your game systems can listen and react to a game event for practically any change in game state or input from a player. There are also global game events, such as events to inform subsystems that a new level has been loaded or the game is being saved.

Many games create an event system that defines these events and the data that accompanies them. Different subsystems register with the Event Manager to listen for events that they'll react to. A good example of this is the sound system; it might register to listen for object collision events so that it can play the appropriate sound effect when two objects are smashed together.

Event-based architectures tend to make your game system clean and efficient. Instead of making API calls to four or five subsystems when an object collision is detected, the code simply sends an event to the Event Manager, and all the subsystems that registered to receive event notifications of this type will get notified in turn.

The event code is the glue that holds this entire game architecture together. The application layer holds the event registry, subsystems register to listen to events they care about, and other subsystems send events as needed. These events get sent to only the subsystems that have subscribed to them.

Chapter 11, "Game Event Management," will dig into this system and show you how it works.

## Process Manager

Any simulation of a game world is usually composed of discrete bits of very simple code, such as a bit of code to move an actor along a linear path or parse a Lua script. Acting on a single game object has the effect of combining these simple state changes into something more complex. These bits of code are usually organized into classes, and they can be instantiated for any game object. If you were to create a "move along this path" class and a "run Lua script" class and instantiate them both on one object, you'd create an interesting and complicated interaction from two simple pieces of code.

This is the heart of another important game subsystem: the Process Manager. It keeps a list of processes and gives each one a little CPU time by calling it once every game loop. A great example of this is a pathfind process. It acts to move an actor from one place to another, and when the destination is reached, it simply terminates and ceases acting on the actor.

#### Learning Our Lessons from *Ultima VII*

After *Ultima VII*, all of the programmers met in the courtyard of Origin Systems with a plan to redesign the *Ultima* technology for *Ultima VIII*. We had a nice sunny day, a whiteboard, and real motivation to make a much better system. We realized that any code that operated on an actor or group of actors for a period of time could be encapsulated in a cooperative process, and it could even be responsible for its own lifetime. When its job was done, it would kill itself off. The best thing of all was that the entire thing could be managed from a single class that contained a list of every running process. This technology eventually evolved to become almost as useful and complex as a simple operating system, managing both cooperative and real-time processes.

On *Ultima*, we found it very useful to allow processes to have dependencies on one another, where one process would wait for another to complete before starting. A good example of this is something you might use for a Molotov cocktail: One process tracks the parabolic movement of any game object until it collides with something, and another process manages a fireball explosion. Your game can string these processes together to create some amazingly cool effects.

You'll learn more about this system in Chapter 7.

## Command Interpreter

A game logic needs to respond to external commands. For a human playing a racing game, these commands will send input to the game logic's representation of the car: acceleration, braking, and steering. An AI process will do exactly the same thing. External entities, such as a human holding a gamepad or an AI process using a command-based interface, can communicate to the game logic *with exactly the same commands.*

You might ask why this is necessary. In any racing game, there should be someplace in the code that says "If button A is down, set emergency brake" or something like that. I know it seems like a lot of extra work, but that breaks the separation between game logic and game views that I have found to be so important when creating games.

What should happen is this: The game view presents an interface to the human player that changes the "Button A is pressed" state into a game command, "Set Emergency Brake." That game command is then sent to the game logic, but here's the rub: The code that actually sets the emergency brake state on the data structure representing the car is actually in the game logic. This code only sets the emergency brake in response to a command—not through a direct tweak to the `m_bIsEmergencyBrakeOn` member of a class somewhere.

I can hear you whining about this, and I'm not even sitting near you. Let me try to show you how cool this is before you call me a complete freak.

If your game logic can accept commands through an event-based interface instead of direct API calls to game logic classes, you can create a programming language for your own game, just like you see in so many games that have heavy mod hooks like *Unreal.* The command interpreter you use for your game will probably have an ultra-efficient low level, but there's nothing keeping you from coding a higher level interface that accepts console input. Then you could actually type something that would get sent right to the scripting interpreter, such as `SetCarProperty(2, E_BRAKE_PROPERTY, true)`, and guess what will happen? Car two will lock up the tires and go spinning out of control, all at your command.

#### *Unreal's* Command Console

Ion Storm's core code base was basically *Unreal Warfare*, a modified version of *Unreal 2*, and thus had an amazing console command system that could be used to control almost anything. You could add or remove properties, move actors, make AIs blind, deaf, dumb, or even all three. The console system could even take input from a file, creating a weird meta-programming language for the game. Believe me, it was nice to have—

because even if your game doesn't have a rigorous separation between game logic and game view, you can still create a command interpreter that provides a very low-level way to tweak your game while it is running.

## Game View for the Human Player

A game view is a collection of systems that communicates with the game logic to present the game to a particular kind of observer. This observer can be a human being with a controller of some kind, like a keyboard or a plastic drum set, but it can also be an AI agent, whose view of the game state will determine the AI process's next course of action.

The game view for a human being has a lot of work to do (see Figure 2.4). It must respond to game events and figure out how to draw the scene, send output to the speakers, translate controller input into game commands, and more. Let's look at the main areas.

### Graphics Display

The display renders the objects that make up a game scene, the user interface layer on top of the scene, and perhaps even streaming video. The renderer should draw the screen as fast as it possibly can. The display can be one of the biggest suckers of CPU budget in a game and should therefore scale well with the capabilities of a wide range of CPUs and GPUs (graphic processing units). For PC or handheld games, it should also perform well under different hardware configurations and operating system releases. Generally, the game engine will disable expensive but nonessential features, such as full screen effects, in order to run at the best frame rate they can.

Video cards will draw all the polygons you stuff into the GPU, even if it takes them forever. Forever, by the way, is defined as anything more than 50ms, giving you a frame rate of 20fps, even if that's all your game does. The real problem a 3D engine has is choosing which polygons to draw to make the most compelling scene.

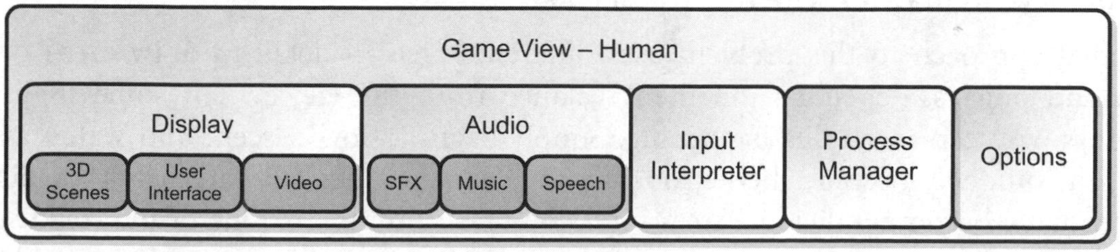


**Figure 2.4**
Subsystems that create a game view for a human player.

**Figure 2.5**
Microsoft Flight Simulator X.

Consider the problem of a flight simulator like Microsoft *Flight Simulator X*. When the plane is on the ground, the display looks a lot like every other 3D game out there. You see a few buildings, a few other planes, and a runway. You might also see some scenery in the distance, such as a mountain range or a city skyline (see Figure 2.5).

Once the plane is up in the air, you have a different story altogether. You've increased the viewable surface by a few orders of magnitude, and therefore you've increased the potential viewable set of polygons. Players who attempt a naive approach of simply drawing all the polygons will learn quickly that they can't get their plane more than 150 feet off the ground. The frame rate will fall in inverse geometric proportion to the altitude of the plane because that's how many more polygons you have to draw to achieve a realistic look.

The actual approach to this problem uses different levels of detail to draw areas of terrain and objects, depending on their distance from the viewer. On some flight simulators, you can catch this happening. Simply begin a slow descent and watch as the terrain suddenly becomes better looking; the green patches will increase in detail and eventually become individual trees until you crash into them. One of the trickier parts of most 3D engines is getting the levels of detail to transition smoothly, avoiding the "popping" effect.

Another problem is avoiding overdraw. If your game is in a complex interior environment or deep in the concrete canyons of New York City, you'll achieve the fastest frame rate if you only draw the polygons that you can see. Again the naive approach is to simply draw all of the polygons in the view frustum, omitting any that are facing away from the camera. This solution will most likely result in a disastrous frame rate in certain areas but not others, even if the camera is pointed straight at an interior wall. When the game is bogging down like this, it is drawing an enormous number of polygons behind the wall, only to be covered up by the bigger polygons close to the camera. What a waste!

You'll need some advanced tools to help you analyze your level and calculate what areas can be seen given a particular viewing location. Umbra Software (www.umbra-software.com) has developed sophisticated PVS (potentially visible set) and portal technologies to do this either offline or on the fly, but many games can use a simple portal or occlusion culling technique. Competitive games are all pushing the envelope for the illusion of extremely complicated worlds. The trick is to create these worlds so that your environments behave well with whatever culling technique is best for your renderer. Add to that mix of technology some nice levels of detail, and you can get a game that looks good when objects are close up or far away.

Since 3D engines are only capable of drawing so much scenery per frame, an amazing amount of effort must go into creating the right level of design. Any environment that is too dense must be fixed, or the frame rate will suffer along with your reviews.

**Your Artists Need to Know What Your Engine Can Do**

The most common mistake made on 3D games is not communicating with the artists about what the graphics engine can and can't do. Remember that the world environment is just a backdrop, and you'll still need to add interactive objects, characters, special effects, and a little bit of user interface before you can call it a day. All these things, especially the characters, will drag your performance into the ground if the background art is too aggressive. Try to establish CPU budgets for drawing the background, objects, characters, and special effects early on and hold your environment artists and level designers to it like glue. Measure the CPU time spent preparing and rendering these objects and display it for all to see.

## Audio

Audio is one of my favorite areas of game development, and I've been lucky enough to work with some of the best audio engineers and composers in the business. Game audio can generally be split up into three major areas: sound effects, music, and speech.

Sound effects are pretty easy things to get running in a game. You simply load a WAV file and send it into DirectX with volume and looping parameters. Almost every sound system is capable of simulating the 3D position of the object relative to the listener. You just provide the position of the object, and the 3D sound system will do the rest.

Music can be really easy or really hard. Technically, it's not really different from sound effects unless you want to get into complicated mixing of different tunes to reflect what's going on in the game. Anyone who's played *Halo* knows how effective this can be; the distinctive combat music tells you you'd better reload your shotgun.

Speech is much trickier—not just technically, but keeping track of all the bits and pieces recorded in the studio and matching them with a 3D lip-synched character. This usually involves anything from a total hack to a carefully hand-tweaked database of mouth positions for each speech file to a tool that can automatically generate this data.

You'll see a good introduction to game audio in Chapter 13, "Game Audio."

## User Interface Presentation

The user interface for a game doesn't look like something drawn by the Windows GDI. Game interfaces have a creative flair, and they should. This means that the user interface needs to be baked fresh every time, especially since every health meter and HUD are different for every game.

The irony of this is that games still need things like a button control, so players can easily click OK for whatever thing the game is asking about. These controls aren't hard to write, but if you're like me, you hate rewriting something that already exists and is well understood by both coders and players. You'll probably roll your own and hopefully keep that code around from game to game so you won't have to rewrite it ever again. Another option is licensing Iggy from RAD Game Tools or Scale-Form GFx, which lets your artists create your entire UI in Flash and import the results directly into your game.

I'll cover these topics more in Chapter 10, "User Interface Programming."

## Process Manager

Having a little déjà vu? You aren't crazy, because you saw this same heading under the game logic group just a few pages back. It turns out that game views can use their own process manager to handle everything from button animations to streaming audio and video. Keep this in the back of your mind as you read about the Process Manager in Chapter 7. You'll use it all over your game.

### Options

Most games have some user-configurable options like sound effects volume, whether your controls are Y-inverted or not, and whether you like to run your game in 4:3 or in 16:9 widescreen. These options are useful to stick in something simple like an XML file so that anyone can easily tweak them, especially during development.

### Multiplayer Games

One thing you might not have considered—this event-based, logic/view architecture makes it simple to have a multiplayer game. All you need to do is attach more human views to the same game logic. Okay, I'll come clean. It's a little more trouble than that because each view needs to share what is likely a single display from the application layer, figure out how to iterate the additional controls, and so on. That stuff is fairly easy compared to getting the overall architecture built to support multiple players, especially if it wasn't designed to do so from the very beginning.

## Game Views for AI Agents

A great argument for the harsh breakdown between game logic and game views is that humans and AI processes can interact with the game logic through exactly the same event-based interface. An AI agent's view of a game generally has the components shown in Figure 2.6.

The stimulus interpreter receives the same events that all other game views receive: object movement, collisions, and so on. It's up to the AI programmer to determine how the AI will react to each event the AI agent receives. It would be easy enough for an AI process to ignore certain events or react to events that are filtered by the human view, and this would certainly affect what the AI process would do.

For example, AI agents might react to sound effects, which are the result of game events such as objects colliding, footsteps, or noisy objects like radios being activated. If an AI is supposed to be deaf, it merely filters the sound events. If an AI is

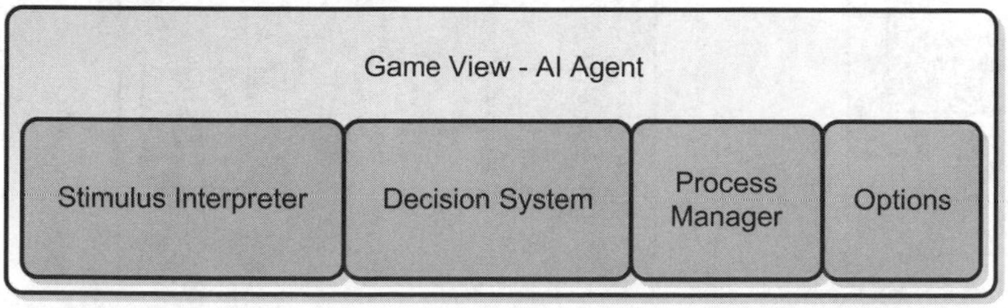


**Figure 2.6**
An AI agent's view of the game.

supposed to be blind, it filters any event about the visible state of an object. You can set the nature of an AI agent's behavior completely by controlling what stimuli the AI agent receives.

The second part of an AI view is the decision system. This is a completely custom written subsystem that translates stimuli into actions. Your AI agent might be able to send commands into the game your human can't, giving it extra abilities such as opening locked doors. The reverse is also true, and the combination of AI stimulus filters and command sets can have a great effect on how smart your AI agents are.

If your AI needs to solve difficult problems, such as how to navigate a complicated environment or make the next move in a chess match, then you might need a process manager just as in the game logic and game view. You might use this to have AI spread its evaluation of stimuli and decisions over time, amortizing the cost of these expensive calculations over many frames.

Finally, you'll certainly want a list of AI options that you can tweak through a simple text file. The stimulus filter and decision set options are certainly enough to warrant a large options file, but more importantly, your AI options can be extremely useful for AI tuning during development. Even if you eventually hard code the AI parameters, you'll certainly want an instantly "tweakable" version while your game is in development.

## Networked Game Architecture

If you implement the game architecture that I've been beating you with since the beginning of this chapter, you can write two additional classes and transform your single-player game into a networked, multiplayer game. That might seem like an insane boast, but it is completely true. Well, nearly completely true. Look at Figure 2.7 to get another look at how game views interact with the game logic.

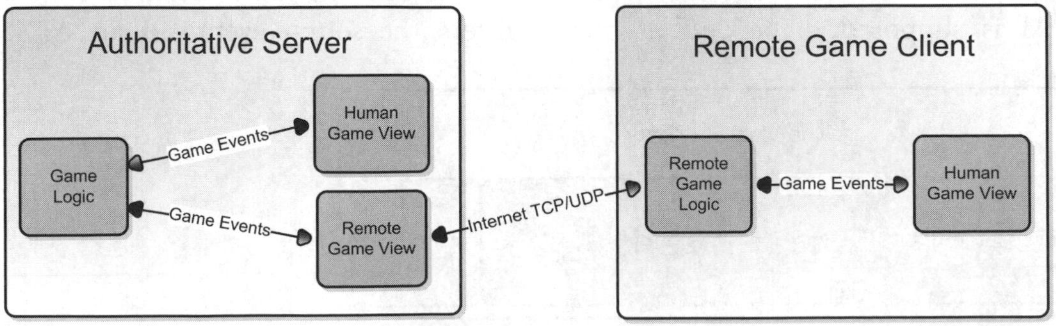


**Figure 2.7**
Client/server networked game architecture.

You'll see the same game logic/game view architecture, but there is a new implementation of the game logic and a new implementation of the game view. Both are needed to create remote versions of their single-player brethren.

## Remote Game View

On the server machine, the remote player should appear just like an AI agent. The remote view receives game events from the game logic and responds with commands back to the game logic. What happens inside the remote view is completely different from the AI agent view or the human view.

Game events received from the game logic are packaged up and sent via TCP or UDP to a client computer across the network. Since game events on a local machine can be somewhat bloated, there should be some processing of the event data before it is sent out. First, redundant messages should be removed from the message stream. It makes no sense to send two "Object Move" events when the only one that matters is the last one. Second, multiple events should be sent together as one packet. If the packet is large enough, it should be compressed to save bandwidth.

The remote game view also receives IP traffic from the remote machine, namely the game commands that result from the controller input. One difference in the remote game view is that it should never trust this command data entirely. The game logic should be smart enough to do some sanity checking on impossible commands, but the remote view can take a front-line approach and attempt to short-circuit any hacking attempts, such as detecting badly formed packets or packets that come in with an unusual frequency. Once the game commands have gone through some kind of anti-hacking filter, they are sent on to the game logic.

## Remote Game Logic

In this model, the game logic is an authoritative server; its game state is the final word on what is happening in the game. Of course, the client machines need a copy of the game state and a way to manage delays in Internet traffic. This is the job of the remote game logic.

The remote game logic is quite similar to the authoritative game logic. It contains everything it needs to simulate the game, even code that can simulate decisions when it must. It has two components that the authoritative game logic doesn't have: something to predict authoritative decisions, and something to handle corrections in those decisions. This is easier to see with a concrete example.

Imagine playing *Halo,* and imagine you are about to shoot an RPG at your best friend. If your friend is playing over the Internet and has a bad lag, your friend's machine might not get the message that you fired the RPG until a few hundred milliseconds after you fired it. If you could watch both screens at the same time, you'd see your RPG rocketing over to blow up your friend, but your friend wouldn't see anything at all, for just a short time.

Some 500ms later, your friend's machine gets the message that you fired an RPG. Since there was no way to predict this message, it must show the fired RPG but begin to move the rocket fast enough to "catch up" to the rocket on the authoritative server, or *host.*

That's why playing shooter games is impossible when you have bad lag and you're not running the host! That's also why no one will play with you when you run the host over a slow connection, because it gives you an unfair advantage. The remote machines simply don't get the messages fast enough.

What this means to the remote game logic is that it has to make corrections in its game state, perhaps breaking the "rules" in order to get things back in sync. In the previous example, the rule that had to be bent a bit was the acceleration and speed of an RPG. If you've ever seen an RPG turn a corner and kill you dead, you've experienced this firsthand.

Other than that, the remote game logic interacts with the game view in pretty much exactly the same way as the authoritative view; it sends the game view events and changes in game state and accepts game commands from the view. Those commands are then packaged and forwarded on to the server machine, specifically the remote game view mentioned in the previous section.

**You Need Multiplayer? Give Me a Few Hours...**

We designed our last card game for Microsoft using a rigorous implementation of the game logic/game view system. When we started working on the game, Microsoft wanted us to code it such that we could create a multiplayer version of the game in as short a time as possible even though we weren't shipping a multiplayer game. Believe me, it wasn't easy, and all the programmers had to take some time to learn how to deal with this very different architecture. After we shipped the project, I was curious how well we'd done in creating something that was multiplayer-aware, even though we'd never actually used the feature. One of our programmers spent about two days and had our card game playing over the Internet. If that's not proof, I don't know what is.

# Do I Have to Use DirectX?

If your platform of choice is the PC, you have to consider whether to use DirectX in your game or try an alternative API for graphics, sound, and input.

Just to be perfectly clear, this section has nothing to do with how to draw a shaded polygon under Direct3D. This section is going to enlighten you about why you would choose something like OpenGL over Direct3D. Believe it or not, the choice isn't clear cut no matter what your religious beliefs.

**All Roads Lead to Rome**

It's not possible for me to be more tired of the religious nature of the OpenGL/DirectX debate. Any good programmer should understand what's under the hood of every API if you have to make a choice between them. Disregarding DirectX simply because Microsoft made it is asinine.

## Design Philosophy of DirectX

DirectX was designed to sit between the application and the hardware. If the hardware was capable of performing an action itself, DirectX would call the driver and be done with it. If the hardware wasn't there, DirectX would emulate the call in software. Clearly, that would be much slower.

One thing that was gained by this design philosophy was a single API for every hardware combination that supported DirectX. Back in the old days (that would be the early 1990s), programmers weren't so lucky. A great example was all the work that needed to be done for sound systems. Origin supported Adlib, Roland, and SoundBlaster with separate bits of code. Graphics were similar; the old EGA graphics standard was completely different than Hercules. Yes, there was a graphics system called Hercules. It was a pain to support all this stuff!

Of course, DirectX isn't the simplest API to learn. COM is a weird thing to look at if you aren't used to it. It also seems weird to have 50 lines of code to initialize a 3D rendering surface when OpenGL does it so much easier. Herein lies one basis for religious argument: old-time C versus newfangled COM. Get over it long enough to understand it and then make an informed choice.

DirectX exposes a lot more about what the hardware is capable of doing. Those CAPS bits can tell you if your video card can support nothing, hardware transform and lighting (T&L), or the latest shaders. Perhaps that means you'll load up denser geometry or simply bring up a dialog box telling some loser that he needs a better video card. Your customer service people will thank you if you decide to leave the word "loser" out of the error message.

## Direct3D or OpenGL

I'm not going to preach to you about why DirectX is unusable and why OpenGL is God's gift. Instead, I hope to give you enough knowledge about how and why you would judge one against the other with the goal of making the best choice for your game, your team, and the good people who will throw money at you to play your latest game. I'm sure to get lovely emails about this section. Bring it on. I'm going to take a weirder tack on this argument anyway. Both APIs will get you a nice-looking game. There are plenty of middleware rendering engines that support both. What does that tell you? It tells me that while there may be interesting bits and pieces here and there that are unique, the basic job of pushing triangles to the video card is essentially equivalent.

There was a time when there were marked differences in quality between OpenGL and DirectX drivers, but those days are thankfully gone. Given that, perhaps the best choice you can make is to go with the API that you and your fellow coders are most comfortable with. Learning a new graphics system can be a special kind of "fun" for some, but it is probably best to spend the time making your game fun rather than sweating over learning DirectX if you happen to be an OpenGL guru.

## DirectSound or What?

For years, I never looked farther than RAD Game Tools, Inc., for sound and video technology. The Miles Sound System includes full source code, has a flat license fee, and works on every platform in existence today. The Bink Video tools are cross platform and support all the latest consoles, Win32, and Macintosh. Check out the latest at www.radgametools.com. It doesn't hurt that RAD has been in business since 1988 and has licensed their technology for thousands of games. They are probably the most used middleware company in the industry.

Miles can use DirectSound as a lower layer. This is quite convenient if you want to do some odd thing that Miles can't. One nail in the coffin for DirectSound is that it doesn't include the ability to decode MP3 files. Part of your license fee for Miles pays for a license to decode MP3s, which are a fantastic alternative to storing bloated WAV files or weird-sounding MIDIs. You could use OGG files, which are completely open source and unencumbered by an expensive license—in fact, the audio chapter shows you how to do this. There is one great thing Miles gets you—and that's streaming. You don't have to load the entire sound file in memory at once if you don't want to, and believe me, Miles makes this easy. Bottom line, do yourself a favor and get Miles for your game.

Other audio technologies, like FMod or WWise, take playing sound buffers to the next step and allow tighter control over sound in your game: how sounds are mixed, which sounds have higher priority, and what tunable parameters your game can tweak to make different effects in real time. WWise is more expensive than Miles, but it is more capable. The audio team used by Red Fly Studios, GL33k, swears by WWise, and they make the best sounds in the game industry. FMod is a good choice since it is free for noncommercial software development.

### DirectInput or Roll Your Own

DirectInput encapsulates the translation of hardware-generated messages to something your game can use directly. This mapping isn't exactly rocket science, and most programmers can code the most used portions of DirectInput with their eyes closed. The weirder input devices, like the force feedback joysticks that look like an implement of torture, plug right into DirectInput. DirectInput also abstracts the device so that you can write one body of code for your game, whether or not your players have the weirdest joystick on the block.

## Other Bits and Pieces

There are tons of other bits and pieces to coding games, many of which you'll discover throughout this book. These things defy classification, but they are every bit as important to games as a good random number generator.

Beyond that, you'll find some things important to game coding such as how to convince Microsoft Windows to become a good platform for your game—a more difficult task than you'd think. Microsoft makes almost all of its income from the sales of business software like Microsoft Office, and the operating system reflects that. Sure, DirectX is supposed to be the hard-core interface for game coders, but you'll find that it's something of a black sheep even within Microsoft. Don't get me wrong, it works and works surprisingly well, but you can't ever forget that you are forcing a primarily business software platform to become a game platform, and sometimes you'll run into dead-ends.

Debugging games is much more difficult than other software, mostly because there's a lot going on in real time, and there are gigabytes of data files that can harbor nasty bugs. Combine that with the menagerie of game hardware like video cards, audio cards, user input devices, and even operating systems, and it's a wonder that games work as well as they do. It's no secret that games are considered to be the most unstable software on the market, and it reflects the difficulty of the problem.

Now that you know what's in a game, let's discuss how game code needs a certain style.

## Further Reading

*Design Patterns: Elements of Reusable Object-Oriented Software,* Erich Gamma, Richard Helm, and Ralph E. Johnson

*Antipatterns: Refactoring Software, Architectures, and Projects in Crisis,* William H. Brown, Raphael C. Malveau, and Hays W. "Skip" McCormick

*Modern C++ Design: Applied Generic and Design Patterns,* Andrei Alexandrescu

# Chapter 3

*by David "Rez" Graham*

# Coding Tidbits and Style That Saved Me

On December 5, 2005, I walked onto the fifth floor of an old office building in downtown San Francisco. There was a door near the elevator with a simple piece of paper taped to it that said "Super-Ego Games." The entire office held less than a dozen people, almost all of them programmers. This was my first day as a professional video game programmer. I had been making my own games for about nine years at that point so I figured I had a major leg up. I was completely wrong. Being able to render 3D models on the screen, play sound effects, read input devices, and implement gameplay features are all extremely important parts of making video games, but there's another more subtle beast lurking in the shadows that is just as important: architecture.

Architecture refers to the structure of your game code and how all of the little pieces fit together. An engine with good architecture can be reused over and over to make games that are somewhat similar to the games that came before it. There are certain problems that every game faces, such as loading assets from the hard drive and rendering objects onto the screen efficiently. These problems are often tailored to the specific type of game you're making. For example, culling out objects from rendering in a scene efficiently often requires different techniques, depending on how your level geometry is laid out. Worlds that are mostly indoors tend to use different techniques from worlds that are mostly outdoors. Most of the time, different engines tailor their architecture toward a specific type of game. If you grew up in the 80s and 90s, you might remember the old *Sierra* adventure games when they started using the point-and-click interface. There have been dozens of games that have used that same game engine. The engineers didn't have to worry about how things were rendered or how to display a text box, they just used the tools in the engine to make it work.

I've been an engineer in the video games industry for nearly seven years as of the writing of this book. I've worked on a number of different games, from tiny iPhone apps with only a few people to huge triple-A games with nearly 200 people, each using a number of different game engines. Some of those games used a commercially available engine as the core, while others were developed from scratch. All of these different game engines had their strengths and weaknesses. Over the years, I've found a number of universal patterns, both good and bad, that have cropped up in nearly every game I've worked on. Before we dig into the meat of rendering, sound effects, AI, and other juicy game development topics, I'd like to provide a foundation of core architectural principles. These are the things to keep in mind when you are developing large systems. Trust me, they'll save your butt in the end.

One thing worth noting is that are as many ways of doing things as there are programmers. The techniques and philosophies presented in this chapter are the result of my own experiences. You will probably find things in this chapter (and book, for that matter) that you disagree with. That's great! It just means you're a programmer. You and I can debate endlessly on the Internet about the best ways of doing things. Just remember, neither of us is wrong—just different and opinionated.

Let's start by looking at design practices that you should consider when writing a game, and then we'll move on and look at specific programming techniques such as working with pointers, memory management, how to avoid memory leaks, and other goodies. In the last part of this chapter, I'll provide you with a few coding tools taken from my own personal toolbox.

## General Coding Styles

If you walk into a room full of programmers and ask them about how they name their variables or where to place braces, you'll find the conversation soon turning into an all-out holy war. Programmers are *very* opinionated about coding style. It makes sense—we spend the vast majority of our time staring at code. In the end, there is little difference between all the various styles you see. I have a particular style I use for my own projects that works very well for me. You might hate how I name my variables or how I use camel-casing for function and class names, and that's just fine. You should do whatever works for you; however, there are a few pitfalls I've come across that I'd like to share with you.

## Bracing

Bracing is one of those things I do feel strongly about. I have fixed actual logic bugs due to poor bracing on more than one occasion. There are three styles I've run into in the past. The first is lining up all the braces:

```
void FindObject (unsigned int id, std::list& found)
{
  for (int i = 0; i < m_max; ++i)
  {
    if (m_map[i].id == id)
    {
      found.push_back(m_map[i]);
      GCC_LOG("Objects", "Found");
    }
    else
    {
      GCC_LOG("Objects", "Not Found");
    }
  }
  GCC_LOG("Objects", "Next");
}
```

The second is called K&R bracing:

```
void FindObject (unsigned int id, std::list& found) {
  for (int i = 0; i < m_max; ++i) {
    if (m_map[i].id == id) {
      found.push_back(m_map[i]);
      GCC_LOG("Objects", "Found");
    }
    else {
      GCC_LOG("Objects", "Not Found");
    }
  }
  GCC_LOG("Objects", "Next");
}
```

The third is just arbitrarily placing braces where they make sense at the time:

```
void FindObject (unsigned int id, std::list& found)
{
  for (int i = 0; i < m_max; ++i)
    {
    if (m_map[i].id == id)
    {
```

```
        found.push_back(m_map[i]);
        GCC_LOG("Objects", "Found");
        }
          else { GCC_LOG("Objects", "Not Found");
        }
    }
    GCC_LOG("Objects", "Next");
}
```

Which one is the most readable? In my opinion, the first style is much more readable than the other two. The second style is preferred by some programmers I know because it saves space and creates more compact code, and they feel that K&R bracing is just as readable. I strongly disagree with this and have fixed a couple of bugs due to braces getting out of alignment in K&R bracing. By contrast, I have never fixed a bug due to bad bracing using the first method. Still, it's considered to be a valid style at some companies. The most important thing here is that you never, ever use the third method. Arbitrarily placing braces and tabs is a sure-fire ticket to creating incredibly hard-to-read code.

**5,000 Lines of Pure Horror**

During development of *Barbie Diaries,* there were a number of complaints about the architecture of the camera code. The original author had left the company, so once the game shipped, I was tasked with refactoring that whole system before we started production on the next game. When I opened up *SeCameraMgr.cpp,* I was horrified to find that the entire camera system was a series of nested switch/case statements with completely arbitrary indentation and bracing. This complete lack of style and organization made the code pretty much unusable. I spent about an hour just lining up the braces and tabbing so I could even *read* the code, much less refactor it. It took me two weeks to refactor the camera system into something usable and extendable.

## Consistency

Which of these function names is best?

```
Action* FindBestAction(void);
Action* findBestAction (void);
Action* find_best_action( void );
```

Honestly, it doesn't really matter. I prefer the first one, but that's just my opinion. It makes very little difference how you handle capitalization, whether you put a space between the identifiers and braces, whether you use underscores, and so on. The key is that you're *consistent*. If you choose method #1, I should never see a function in your code base that doesn't conform to that style. You might think it's a relatively minor topic, but when you have a code base with millions of lines of code written by dozens of different people, consistency becomes extremely important.

One important exception to this is when integrating code written by a third party. You don't want to change every single line to match your style because every time you update that code, you'll have to make those changes all over again. Make sure that all such code is isolated from your main code base. If you look at the source code for this book, you can see a really good way of doing this. All third-party code and libraries live in the *Source/GCC4/3rdParty* directory.

Another very important place to be consistent is in general API and function naming conventions. For example, if you have a number of classes that require an update every frame, the update function should be named the same thing across all of these classes and probably have the same signature. For example, here's the signature for the update function in the `Process` class you'll see later:

```
virtual void VOnUpdate(const int deltaMilliseconds);
```

Here's the update for the `HumanView` class:

```
virtual void VOnUpdate(const int deltaMilliseconds);
```

The function signatures are exactly the same even though the two classes are not related in any way. This can be important when you're in a large code base and looking at a class you've never seen before. This kind of consistency lets you be reasonably sure of what a function does. At Super-Ego Games, all trivial getter functions started with the word "Get," while non-trivial getters started with the word "Find." It was a simple mechanism that alerted the programmer to a possible performance hit on what might seem like a simple operation.

You can see a good example of this kind of consistency by looking at the interface for the STL. Ordered containers use `push_back()` to append an object to the container. You can be reasonably certain that any ordered container that supports appending will use a function named `push_back()`. Notice how unordered containers like `std::map` or `std::set` name their function `insert()`. Since these containers make no guarantees as to which order the objects exist in the container, the behavior is fundamentally different than it is for ordered containers. This is a good paradigm to follow in your own code.

Consistency goes beyond naming conventions; it also applies to class layout and code organization. For example, I prefer to put all of the member variables of a class at the top, followed by initialization and destruction functions like the constructor and destructor. After that, I have my public interface followed by protected and private internal function definitions. You don't have to follow my scheme, of course, but you should come up with something that you like and stick with it.

## Smart Code Design Practices

One of the keys to writing good software is designing robust systems that can stand the test of time. Game programming is extremely volatile. A designer can change the whole game out from under you, requiring you to rewrite large chunks of your game. There's no way around this, because it's simply the nature of the beast. You can mitigate the effect of these kinds of changes by having a strong, flexible architecture.

Isaac Asimov's Foundation series invented an interesting discipline called *psychohistory*, a social science that could predict societal trends and macro events with great certainty. Each historian in the story was required to contribute new formulas and extend the science. As a programmer, your job is similar. Every new module or class that you create gives you the opportunity to extend the capabilities and usefulness of the code base. But to do this effectively, you must learn how to think ahead and design code with the goal of keeping it in use for many projects and many years.

Designing good code in an object-oriented language can be more difficult than in a procedural language such as C or PASCAL. The power and flexibility of an object-oriented language like C++, for example, allows you to create extremely complicated systems that look quite simple. This is both good and bad. Simplicity is good, but the down side is that it's easy to get yourself into trouble without realizing it. A great example of this is the C++ constructor. Some programmers create code in a constructor that can fail—maybe they tried to read data from an initialization file, and the file doesn't exist. A failed constructor doesn't return any kind of error code, so the badly constructed object still exists and might get used. While you can use structured exception handling to catch a failure in a constructor, it is a much better practice to write constructors that can't fail. Another example is the misuse of virtual functions. For example, a naive programmer might make every method in the class virtual, thinking that future expandability for everything was good. Well, he'd be wrong. On some platforms, virtual functions can be very expensive. A well thought through design is more important than blind application of object-oriented programming constructs.

You can make your work much more efficient by improving how you design your software. With a few keystrokes, you can create interesting adaptations of existing systems. There's nothing like having such command and control over a body of code. It makes you more of an artist than a programmer.

A different programmer might view your masterpiece entirely differently, however. For example, intricate relationships inside a class hierarchy could be difficult or impossible to understand without your personal guidance. Documentation, usually written in haste, is almost always inadequate or even misleading.

To help you avoid some of the common design practice pitfalls, I'm going to spend some time in this chapter up-front discussing how you can do the following:

- Avoid hidden code that performs nontrivial operations.
- Keep your class hierarchies as flat as possible.
- Be aware of the difference between inheritance and composition.
- Avoid abusing virtual functions.
- Use interface classes and factories.
- Encapsulate the components of your system that are most likely to change.
- Use streams in addition to constructors to initialize objects.

## Avoiding Hidden Code and Nontrivial Operations

Copy constructors, operator overloads, and destructors are all party to the "nasty" hidden code problems that plague game developers. This kind of code can cause you a lot of problems when you least expect. The best example is a destructor because you never actually call it explicitly. It is called when the memory for an object is being deallocated or the object goes out of scope. If you do something really crazy in a destructor, like attach it to a remote computer and download a few megabytes of MP3 files, your teammates are going to have you drawn and quartered.

My advice is that you should try to avoid copy constructors and operator overloads that perform nontrivial operations. If something looks simple, it should be simple and not deceptive. For example, most programmers would assume that if they encountered some code that contained a simple equals sign or multiplication symbol that it would not invoke a complicated formula, like a Taylor series. They would assume that the code under the hood would be as straightforward as it looked—a basic assignment or calculation between similar data types like `floats` or `doubles`.

Game programmers love playing with neat technology, and sometimes their sense of elegance drives them to push nontrivial algorithms and calculations into C++ constructs, such as copy constructors or overloaded operators. They like it because the high-level code performs complicated actions in a few lines of code, and on the surface, it seems like the right design choice. Don't be fooled.

*Any operation with some meat to it should be called explicitly*. This might annoy your sense of cleanliness if you are the kind of programmer who likes to use C++ constructs at each and every opportunity. Of course, there are exceptions. One is when every operation on a particular class is comparatively expensive, such as a 4 × 4 matrix class. Overloaded operators are perfectly fine for classes like this because the clarity of the resulting code is especially important and useful.

One thing to watch out for is that the C++ compiler will magically generate functions in your class. It will silently generate a copy constructor, copy assignment operator, and destructor for you if you don't create them yourself. If you don't create any constructors, it will also generate a default constructor. These will all be public functions. This can cause unintended side effects if you're not aware of what's happening under the covers. To get around this, you can make copy constructors and assignment operators private, which keeps programmers from assuming the object can be duplicated in the system. A good example of this is an object in your resource cache, such as an ambient sound track that could be tens of megabytes. You clearly want to disable making blind copies of this thing, because an unwary programmer might believe all he's doing is copying a tiny sound buffer.

A recurring theme throughout this book is that you should always try to avoid surprises. Most programmers don't like surprises because most surprises are bad ones. Don't add to the problem by tucking some crazy piece of code away in a destructor or similar mechanism. It's important to remember that you're not writing code for the compiler, you're writing code for other programmers. The compiler will be just as happy with clean code as it will with sloppy code. The same is not true for another programmer.

## Class Hierarchies: Keep Them Flat

One of the most common mistakes game programmers make is that they either overdesign or underdesign their classes and class hierarchies. Getting your class structure well designed for your particular needs takes real practice.

A good rule of thumb is that each class should have a single responsibility in your code base and should have inheritance trees that are no more than two or three levels deep. As with anything, there are always exceptions to this rule, but you should strive to flatten your hierarchy as much as possible.

On the opposite end of the spectrum, a common problem found in C++ programs is the Blob class, as described in the excellent book *Antipatterns* by Brown et al. This is a class that has a little bit of everything in it and comes from the reluctance on the programmer's part to make new, tightly focused classes. In the source code that accompanies this book, the `GameCodeApp` class is probably the one that comes closest to this, but if you study it a bit you can find some easy ways to factor it.

When I was working on *The Sims Medieval*, there was a class that fell very neatly into the Blob category. Our Sim class became a dumping ground for every little extra timer, variable, and tracking bit that could be remotely tied to a Sim. Entire systems would be written inside this one class. By the end of the project, the Sim.cs file was 11,491 lines of code, and it was nearly impossible to find anything.

I try always to use a flat class hierarchy. Whenever possible, it starts with an interface class and has at most two or three levels of inheritance. This class design is usually much easier to work with and understand. Any change in the base class propagates to a smaller number of child classes, and the entire architecture is something normal humans can follow.

Try to learn from my mistakes. Good class architecture is *not* like a Swiss Army knife; it should be more like a well-balanced throwing knife.

## Inheritance Versus Composition

Game programmers love to debate the topics of inheritance and composition. Inheritance is used when an object has evolved from another object, or when a child object *is* a version of the parent object. Composition is used when an object is composed of multiple discrete components, or when an aggregate object *has* a version of the contained object.

A good example of this relationship is found in user interface code. You might have a base control class to handle things like mouse and keyboard events, positioning, and anything else that all controls need to know how to do. When you create a control such as a button or check box, you will inherit from this control. A check box *is a* control. Then you might create a window that can contain a bunch of these controls. The window *has a* control or, in this case, many controls. You window is most likely a valid UI control as well, so it might be fair to say that that your window *is a* control, too. When you make a choice about inheritance or composition, your goal is to communicate the right message to other programmers. The resulting assembly code is almost exactly the same, barring the oddities of virtual function tables. This means that the CPU doesn't give a damn if you inherit or compose. Your fellow programmers will care, so try to be careful and clear.

## Virtual Functions Gone Bad

Virtual functions are powerful creatures that are often abused. Programmers often create virtual functions when they don't need them, or they create long chains of overloaded virtual functions that make it difficult to maintain base classes. I did this for a while when I first learned how to program with C++.

Take a look at MFC's class hierarchy. Most of the classes in the hierarchy contain virtual functions, which are overloaded by inherited classes or by new classes created by application programmers. Imagine for a moment the massive effort involved if some assumptions at the top of the hierarchy were changed. This isn't a problem for MFC because it's a stable code base, but your game code isn't a stable code base. Not yet.

An insidious bug is often one that is created innocently by a programmer mucking around in a base class. A seemingly benign change to a virtual function can have unexpected results. Some programmers might count on the oddities of the behavior of the base class that, if they were fixed, would actually break any child classes. Maybe one of these days someone will write an IDE that graphically shows the code that will be affected by any change to a virtual function. Without this aid, any programmer changing a base class must learn (the hard way) for himself what hell he is about to unleash. One of the best examples of this is by changing the parameter list of a virtual function. If you're unlucky enough to change only an inherited class and not the base class, the compiler won't bother to warn you at all; it will simply break the virtual chain, and you'll have a brand new virtual function. It won't ever be called by anything, of course.

If you're using Visual Studio 2010 or above, you can take advantage of the keywords `override` and `sealed`. The `override` keyword tells the compiler that you are overriding a virtual function from the base class. It will generate an error if it can't find that function. The `sealed` keyword tells the compiler that subclasses aren't allowed to override the virtual function anymore. If you have a subclass that attempts to override it, it will generate an error. Here's a quick example of their usage:

```
class Base
{
public:
   virtual void Go(void);
};

class Sub1 : public Base
{
public:
   // If Base didn't declare this function with this exact signature,
   // the compiler would kick out an error.
   virtual void Go(void) override;
};
```

```
class Sub2 : public Sub1
{
public:
   // If you create a new subclass inheriting from Sub2 and attempt
   // to override this method, the compiler will kick out an error.
   virtual void Go(void) sealed;
};
```

C# and other languages have been doing this for a long time now. I'm happy to see C++ starting to do the same.

**Let the Compiler Help You**

If you ever change the nature of anything that is currently in wide use, virtual functions included, I suggest you actually change its name. The compiler will find each and every use of the code, and you'll be forced to look at how the original was put to use. It's up to you if you want to keep the new name. I suggest you do, even if it means changing every source file.

When you decide to make a function virtual, what you are communicating to other programmers is that you intend for your class to be inherited from by other classes. The virtual functions serve as an interface for what other programmers can change. By overriding your virtual functions and choosing whether or not to call your implementations, they are changing the behavior of your class. Sometimes this is exactly what you intend. The `Process` class you'll see in Chapter 7, "Controlling the Main Loop," has a virtual `VOnUpdate()` method that is meant to be overridden to allow you to define the behavior of your specific process.

Oftentimes, making an `Update()` function virtual is not the best way of doing things. For example, say you have a class that processes a creature. You have an update function that runs some AI, moves the creature, and then processes collisions. Instead of making your update function virtual, you could make three separate protected virtual functions: one for AI, one for movement, and one for collision processing, each with a default implementation. The subclass can override one or more of these functions, but not the update function. So subclasses can't change the order of operations, they can only change what happens at each step. This is called the *template method design pattern* and is very handy. In fact, I used it recently at work to allow subclasses to redefine how interactions are chosen and scored.

If you're on the other side and trying to extend a class by deriving a subclass from it and overriding some virtual functions, you should make sure that you're doing it for the right reasons. If you find yourself significantly altering its behavior, you should step back and consider if inheritance is the right solution. One solution might be composition, where you write a new class that has the other class as a member.

*Try to look at classes and their relationships like appliances and electrical cords.* Always seek to minimize the length of the extension cords, minimize the appliances that plug into one another, and don't make a nasty tangle that you have to figure out every time you want to turn something on. This metaphor is put into practice with a flat class hierarchy—one where you don't have to open 12 source files to see all the code for a particular class.

## Use Interface Classes

Interface classes are those that contain nothing but pure virtual functions. They form the top level in any class hierarchy. Here's an example:

```
class IAnimation
{
public:
  virtual void VAdvance(const int deltaMilliseconds) = 0;
  virtual bool const VAtEnd() const = 0;
  virtual int const VGetPosition() const = 0;
};

typedef std::list<IAnimation *> AnimationList;
```

This sample interface class defines simple behavior that is common for a timed animation. You could add other methods, such as one to tell how long the animation will run or whether the animation loops; that's purely up to you. The point is that any system that contains a list of objects inheriting and implementing the `IAnimation` interface can animate them with a few lines of code:

```
AnimationList::iterator end = animList.end();
for(AnimationList::iterator itr = animList.begin(); itr != end; ++itr)
{
  (*itr).VAdvance( delta );
}
```

Whenever possible, you should have systems depend on these interfaces instead of the implementation classes. Two different systems should never know about each other's implementation classes. Interface classes act like a gate into a particular system in the engine. Outsiders are only able to call the interface functions to interact with the system; they don't know or care how it gets done.

**Rewriting Your Graphics Engine Without Killing Your Game**

When I was at Super-Ego Games, we landed a deal with Sony to make *Rat Race* on the then-unreleased PlayStation 3. None of us had ever made a console game, and the engine was very PC-centric. We devised a scheme we called the Render Skin. This was a layer of abstraction where all graphics and sound functionality would live. The entire thing was made up of a series of interface classes that wrapped some piece of functionality. The appropriate implementation classes were instantiated at runtime based on compiler flags. Once we got this system working, we were able to replace our old DirectX rendering system with a new rendering system that worked on the PS3 without keeping the designers or gameplay programmers blocked. None of the code that called into the Render Skin knew or cared which engine it was using, so the graphics programmers could port everything over without stepping on anyone's toes.

Another great benefit of using interface classes is they reduce compile time dependencies. The interfaces can be defined in a single `#include` file, or a very small number of them, and because they hide all the disgusting guts of implementation classes, there's very little for the compiler to do but register the class and move on.

## Consider Using Factories

Games tend to build complex objects, such as controls or sprites, and store them in lists or other collections. A common way to do this is to have the constructor of one object, say a certain implementation of a screen class, "new up" all the sprites and controls. In many cases, many types of screens are used in a game, all having different objects inheriting from the same parents.

In the book *Design Patterns: Elements of Reusable Object-Oriented Software* by Erich Gamma et al., one of the object creation patterns is called a *factory*. An abstract factory can define the interface for creating objects. Different implementations of the abstract factory carry out the concrete tasks of constructing objects with multiple parts. Think of it this way—a constructor creates a single object. A factory creates and assembles these objects into a working mechanism.

Imagine an abstract factory that builds screens. The fictional game engine in this example could define screens as components that have screen elements, a background, and a logic class that accepts control messages. Here's an example:

```
class SaveGameScreenFactory : public IScreenFactory
{
public:
  SaveGameScreenFactory();
```

```
  virtual IScreenElements * const BuildScreenElements() const;
  virtual ScreenBackground * const BuildScreenBackground() const;
  virtual IScreenLogic * const BuildScreenLogic() const;
};
```

The code that builds screens will call the methods of the `IScreenFactory` interface, each one returning the different objects that make the screen, including screen elements like controls, a background, or the logic that runs the screen. As all interface classes tend to enforce design standards, factories tend to enforce orderly construction of complicated objects. Factories are great for screens, animations, AI, or any nontrivial game object.

What's more, factories can help you construct these mechanisms at the right time. One of the neatest things about the factory design pattern is a delayed instantiation feature. You could create factory objects, push them into a queue, and delay calling the `BuildXYZ()` methods until you were ready. In the screen example, you might not have enough memory to instantiate a screen object until the active one was destroyed. The factory object is tiny, perhaps a few tens of bytes, and can easily exist in memory until you are ready to fire it.

Factories and interfaces work hand-in-hand. In the previous example, each of the objects being returned by the factory is an interface, so the calling code is decoupled from the implementation of these objects. In other words, the system that's using the `IScreenElements` object doesn't need to know which specific screen element is being instantiated. All it needs to know is what the interface is. You can freely swap this with any other object that comforms to the same interface.

## Encapsulate Components That Change

Whenever I'm designing a new system, I'm always looking for the parts that are the most likely to change. I try to isolate those pieces as much as I can so that when they change, it has little or no effect on the rest of the engine. Your goal is make it easy to modify and extend functionality so that when a designer comes to you and says "let's change this feature so that it does something else instead," you don't go insane rewriting huge chunks of your game.

For example, let's say I want to build an AI system. I want to create a number of different creatures with different behaviors. I could simply write all of these bahaviors in a big hard-coded function, or I could encapsulate these different behaviors into objects that can be reused on different creatures. Each creature can have some set of behaviors that defines its overall AI. Since you have your behaviors separate from each other, you can modify each one without worrying about how it will affect the other ones.

You can take this concept a step further and separate the code that chooses which behavior to run next. Not only can you mix and match behaviors, but you can also mix and match the transitions between those behaviors. Any of these components can change without affecting any other component in your system. This is exactly what I did on *Drawn to Life* for the enemy AI.

Another thing that often changes is your rendering system. We've chosen to use Direct3D in this book because of its accessibility, but that doesn't mean you can't use OpenGL. In a real game engine, you typically have multiple build configurations for different platforms, each with a different renderer. That's exactly what we did for *The Sims Medieval*. It used DirectX for the PC build and OpenGL for the Mac build.

Learning to spot the things that are likely to change is something that comes with experience. In general, any major system you build should be as decoupled as possible from every other major system. Interfaces, factories, and other techniques are the tools to enable you to do this.

There is an amazing book called *Design Patterns: Elements of Reusable Object-Oriented Software* by Erich Gamma et al., which I mentioned previously in this chapter. Many of these design patterns, such as the Observer pattern and the Strategy pattern, are aimed at decoupling different components in software. I highly recommend that you check this book out. It's one of those books that should be on every programmer's bookshelf.

## Use Streams to Initialize Objects

Any persistent object in your game should implement a method that takes a stream as a parameter and reads the stream to initialize the object. If the game is loaded from a file, objects can use the stream as a source of parameters. Here's an example to consider:

```
class AnimationPath
{
public:
  AnimationPath();
  Initialize (std::vector<AnimationPathPoint> const & srcPath);
  Initialize (InputStream & stream);
  //Of course, lots more code follows.
};
```

This class has a default constructor and two ways to initialize it. The first is through a classic parameter list, in this case, a list of `AnimationPathPoints`. The second initializes the class through a stream object. This is cool because you can initialize objects from a disk, a memory stream, or even the network. If you want to load game objects from a disk, as you would in a save game, this is exactly how you do it.

Some programmers try to do stream initialization inside an object's constructor:

```
AnimationPath (InputStream & stream);
```

Here's why this is a bad idea—a bad stream will cause your constructor to fail, and you'll end up with a bad object. You can never trust the content of a stream. It could be coming from a bad disk file or hacked network packets. Ergo, construct objccts with a default constructor you can rely on and create initialization methods for streams.

**Exercise Your Load/Save System**

Test your stream initializers by loading and saving your game automatically in the DEBUG build at regular intervals. It will have the added side effect of making sure that programmers keep the load/save code pretty fast.

## Smart Pointers and Naked Pointers

All smart pointers wear clothing.

If you declare a pointer to another object, you've just used a naked pointer. Pointers are used to refer to another object, but they don't convey enough information. Anything declared on the heap must be referenced by at least one other object, or it can never be freed, causing a memory leak. It is common for an object on the heap to be referred to multiple times by other objects in the code. A good example of this is a game object like a clock. A pointer to the clock will exist in the game object list, the physics system, the graphics system, and even the sound system.

If you use naked pointers, you must remember which objects implicitly own other objects. An object that owns other objects controls their existence. Imagine a ship object that owns everything on the ship. When the ship sinks, everything else is destroyed along with it. If you use naked pointers to create these relationships, you have to remember who owns who. Depending on the system, this might be perfectly reasonable or nearly impossible. If you choose to use a naked pointer, make sure that you know exactly who can access it and when, or you'll quickly find yourself going down with the ship.

Smart pointers, on the other hand, hold extra information along with the address of the distant object. This information can count references, record permanent or temporary ownership, or perform other useful tasks. In a sense, an object controlled by a smart pointer "knows" about every reference to itself.

Why not use smart pointers for everything? There are two major pitfalls to using smart pointers. First, maintaining those internal reference counts adds a small memory and CPU overhead. This is rarely noticeable, but if you have thousands of objects to manage and want to process them each frame, it can really start to add up. The other problem is that smart pointers tend to take away some of your control over the memory. For example, you may not have a clear understanding of which systems could be holding a reference to any particular game object. When you "destroy" that object by removing the reference, another reference may keep the object alive longer than you intended. If I had a dollar for every smart pointer bug I fixed over the years, I'd be a rich man.

So which one do you choose? It depends on the purpose. If you have a pointer to an object that is not visible outside of the owner, a naked pointer is just fine. An example of this is the `m_pProcessManager` member of `BaseGameLogic`. This pointer is never accessed outside of the class or its children so there's no risk for another system to hold onto it. It can safely be destroyed without affecting any other systems. Notice that the only access to this pointer is through the `BaseGameLogic::AttachProcess()` method. This is a great pattern to follow because it means that no one outside of the `BaseGameLogic` even has any idea that the `ProcessManager` class exists. You could create multiple `ProcessManager` classes or remove it entirely without having to touch any other code.

By contrast, if you look at the event system, all events are stored as smart pointers. This is because it's never clear who might be hanging on to a reference to these objects. This is by design; the event receiver can hold on to the event without fear of it being destroyed, or it cannot hold on to it and the event will be happily destroyed after the event is handled.

## Reference Counting

Reference counting stores an integer value that counts how many other objects are currently referring to the object in question. Reference counting is a common mechanism in memory management. DirectX objects implement the COM-based `IUnknown` interface, which uses reference counting. Two methods that are central to this task are `AddRef()` and `Release()`. The following code shows how this works:

```
MySound *sound = new MySound;
sound->AddRef();              // reference count is now 1
```

After you construct a reference-counted object, you call the `AddRef()` method to increase the integer reference counter by one. When the pointer variable goes out of scope, by normal scoping rules or by the destruction of the container class, you must call `Release()`. `Release()` will decrement the reference counter and destroy the object if the counter drops to zero. A shared object can have multiple references safely without fear of the object being destroyed, leaving bad pointers all over the place.

**Use `AddRef()` and `Release()` with Caution**

Good reference counting mechanisms automatically delete the object when the reference count becomes zero. If the API leaves the explicit destruction of the object to you, it's easy to create memory leaks—all you have to do is forget to call `Release()`. You can also cause problems if you forget to call `AddRef()` when you create the object. It's likely that the object will get destroyed unexpectedly, not having enough reference counts.

Any time you assign a pointer variable to the address of the reference-counted object, you'll do the same thing. This includes any calls inside a local loop:

```
for (int i=0; i<m_howMany; ++i)
{
  MySound *s = GoGrabASoundPointer(i);
  s->AddRef();

  DangerousFunction();

  if (s->IsPlaying())
  {
    DoSomethingElse();
  }

  s->Release();
}
```

This kind of code exists all over the place in games. The call to `DangerousFunction()` goes deep and performs some game logic that might attempt to destroy the instance of the `MySound` object. Don't forget that in a release build the deallocated memory retains the same values until it is reused. It's quite possible that the loop will work just fine even though the `MySound` pointer is pointing to unallocated memory. What's more likely to occur is a terrible corruption of memory, which can be extremely difficult to track down.

Reference counting keeps the sound object around until `Release()` is called at the bottom of the loop. If there was only one reference to the sound before the loop started, the call to `AddRef()` will add one to the sound's reference count, making two references. `DangerousFunction()` does something that destroys the sound, but through a call to `Release()`. As far as `DangerousFunction()` is concerned, the sound is gone forever. It still exists because one more reference to it, through `MySound *s`, kept the reference count from dropping to zero inside the loop. The final call to `Release()` causes the destruction of the sound.

## C++'s shared_ptr

If you think calling AddRef() and Release() all over the place might be a serious pain in the rear, you're right. It's really easy to forget an AddRef() or a Release() call, and your memory leak will be almost impossible to find. It turns out that there are plenty of C++ templates out there that implement reference counting in a way that handles the counter manipulation automatically. One of the best examples is the shared_ptr template class in the standard TR1 C++ library.

Here's an example of how to use this template:

```
#include <memory>

using std::tr1::shared_ptr;

class IPrintable
{
public:
  virtual void VPrint()=0;
};

class CPrintable : public IPrintable
{
  char *m_Name;
public:
  CPrintable(char *name)  { m_Name = name; printf("create %s\n",m_Name); }
  virtual ~CPrintable()   { printf("delete %s\n",m_Name); }
  void VPrint()           { printf("print %s\n",m_Name); }
};

shared_ptr<CPrintable> CreateAnObject(char *name)
{
  return shared_ptr<CPrintable>(new CPrintable(name));
}

void ProcessObject(shared_ptr<CPrintable> o)
{
  printf("(print from a function) ");
  o->VPrint();
}

void TestSharedPointers(void)
{
  shared_ptr<CPrintable> ptr1(new CPrintable("1"));  // create object 1
  shared_ptr<CPrintable> ptr2(new CPrintable("2"));  // create object 2
```

```
    ptr1 = ptr2;              // destroy object 1
    ptr2 = CreateAnObject("3");  // used as a return value
    ProcessObject(ptr1);      // call a function

    // BAD USAGE EXAMPLES....
    //
    CPrintable o1("bad");
    //ptr1 = &o1;     // Syntax error! It's on the stack....
    //
    CPrintable *o2 = new CPrintable("bad2");
    //ptr1 = o2;     // Syntax error! Use the next line to do this...

    ptr1 = shared_ptr<CPrintable>(o2);

    // You can even use shared_ptr on ints!

    shared_ptr<int> a(new int);
    shared_ptr<int> b(new int);

    *a = 5;
    *b = 6;

    const int *q = a.get();  // use this for reading in multithreaded code

    // this is especially cool - you can also use it in lists.
    std::list< shared_ptr<int> > intList;
    std::list< shared_ptr<IPrintable> > printableList;
    for (int i=0; i<100; ++i)
    {
      intList.push_back(shared_ptr<int>(new int(rand())));
      printableList.push_back(shared_ptr<IPrintable>(new CPrintable("list")));
    }

    // No leaks!!!! Isn't that cool...
}
```

The template classes use overloaded assignment operators and copy operators to keep track of how many references point to the allocated data. As long as the `shared_ptr` object is in scope and you behave yourself by avoiding the bad usage cases, you won't leak memory, and you won't have to worry about objects getting destroyed while you are still referencing them from somewhere else.

This smart pointer even works in multithreaded environments, as long as you follow a few rules. First, don't write directly to the data. You can access the data through const operations such as the `.get()` method. As you can also see, the template works fine even if it is inside an STL container such as `std::list`.

**Be Careful Using Threads and Sharing Memory**

Don't ignore multithreaded access to shared memory blocks. You might think that the chances of two threads accessing the shared data are exceedingly low and convince yourself that you don't need to go to the trouble of adding multithreaded protection. You'd be wrong every time.

There are a couple of safety tips with smart pointers.

- You can't have two different objects manage smart pointers for each other.
- When you create a smart pointer, you have to make sure it is created straight from a raw pointer `new` operator.

I'll show you examples of each of these abuses. If two objects have smart pointers to each other, neither one will ever be destroyed. It may take your brain a moment to get this, since each one has a reference to the other.

```
class Jelly;
class PeanutButter
{
public:
   shared_ptr<Jelly> m_pJelly;
   ~PeanutButter(void) { cout << "PeanutButter destructor\n"; }
};

class Jelly
{
public:
   shared_ptr<PeanutButter> m_pPeanutButter;
   ~Jelly(void) { cout << "Jelly destructor\n"; }
};

void PleaseLeakMyMemory(void)
{
   shared_ptr<PeanutButter> pPeanutButter(new PeanutButter);
   shared_ptr<Jelly> pJelly(new Jelly);

   pPeanutButter->m_pJelly = pJelly;
   pJelly->m_pPeanutButter = pPeanutButter;

   // Both objects are leaked here....
}
```

If you copied this code into the compiler, you would never see the messages printed out in the destructors. Following the code, you'll find that `Jelly` has a reference to `PeanutButter` and `PeanutButter` has a reference to `Jelly`. Since they both point to each other, neither one can ever have its reference count decremented. Basically, because they point to each other, it's almost like two stubborn gentlemen saying, "No, sir, after you" and "Please, I insist" when trying to go through a single door—because they point to each other, they will never be destroyed.

The solution to this is usually some kind of "owned" pointer or "weak referenced" pointer, where one object is deemed the de facto owner and therefore won't use the multiply referenced `shared_ptr` mechanism. The `weak_ptr` template is used exactly for this purpose:

```
class Jelly;
class PeanutButter
{
public:
   shared_ptr<Jelly> m_pJelly;
   ~PeanutButter(void) { cout << "PeanutButter destructor\n"; }
};

class Jelly
{
public:
   weak_ptr<PeanutButter> m_pPeanutButter; // this is a weak pointer now!
   ~Jelly(void) { cout << "Jelly destructor\n"; }
};

void PleaseDontLeakMyMemory(void)
{
   shared_ptr<PeanutButter> pPeanutButter(new PeanutButter);
   shared_ptr<Jelly> pJelly(new Jelly);

   pPeanutButter->m_pJelly = pJelly;
   pJelly->m_pPeanutButter = pPeanutButter;

   // No memory is leaked!
}
```

In this version of the code, `PeanutButter` is the owner, and `Jelly` has a weak reference back to `PeanutButter`. If you execute this code, both objects will be destroyed, and you will see the destructor messages printed in the console.

The other gotcha is constructing two smart pointers to manage a single object:

```
int *z = new int;
shared_ptr<int> bad1(z);
shared_ptr<int> bad2(z);
```

Remember that smart pointers work with a reference count, and each of the smart pointer objects only has one reference. If either of them goes out of scope, the memory for the object will be deallocated, and the other smart pointer will point to garbage.

# Using Memory Correctly

Did you ever hear the joke about the programmer trying to beat the devil in a coding contest? Part of his solution involved overcoming a memory limitation by storing a few bytes in a chain of sound waves between the microphone and the speaker. That's an interesting idea, and I'll bet there's someone out there who has already done it.

Memory comes in very different shapes, sizes, and speeds. If you know what you're doing, you can write programs that make efficient use of these different memory blocks. If you believe that it doesn't matter how you use memory, you're in for a real shock. This includes assuming that the standard memory manager for your operating system is efficient; it usually isn't, and you'll have to think about writing your own.

## Understanding the Different Kinds of Memory

The system RAM is the main warehouse for storage, as long as the system has power. Video RAM (or VRAM) is usually much smaller and is specifically used for storing objects that will be used by the video card. Some platforms, such as Xbox and Xbox360, have a unified memory architecture that makes no distinctions between RAM and VRAM. Desktop PCs run operating systems like Windows 7 and have virtual memory that mimics much larger memory space by swapping blocks of little-used RAM to your hard disk. If you're not careful, a simple `memcpy()` could cause the hard drive to seek, which to a computer is like waiting for the sun to cool off.

### *System RAM*

Your system RAM is a series of memory sticks that are installed on the motherboard. Memory is actually stored in nine bits per byte, with the extra bit used to catch memory parity errors. Depending on the OS, you get to play with a certain addressable range of memory. The operating system keeps some to itself. Of the parts you get to play with, it is divided into three parts when your application loads:

- **Global memory:** This memory never changes size. It is allocated when your program loads and stores global variables, text strings, and virtual function tables.
- **Stack:** This memory grows as your code calls deeper into core code, and it shrinks as the code returns. The stack is used for parameters in function calls

and local variables. The stack has a fixed size that can be changed with compiler settings.

- **Heap:** This memory grows and shrinks with dynamic memory allocation. It is used for persistent objects and dynamic data structures.

Old-timers used to call global memory the DATA segment, harkening back to the days when there used to be near memory and far memory. It was called that because programmers used different pointers to get to it. What a disgusting practice! Everything is much cleaner these days because each pointer is a full 32 or 64 bits. (Don't worry, I'm not going to bore you with the "When I went to school I only had 640k of memory to play with" story.)

Your compiler and linker will attempt to optimize the location of anything you put into the global memory space based on the type of variable. This includes constant text strings. Many compilers, including Visual Studio, will attempt to store text strings only once to save space:

```
const char *error1 = "Error";
const char *error2 = "Error";

int main()
{
  printf ("%x\n", (int)error1);
  // How quaint. A printf.
  printf ("%x\n", (int)error2);
  return 0;
}
```

This code yields interesting results. You'll notice that under Visual C++, the two pointers point to the same text string in the global address space. Even better, the text string is one that was already global and stuck in the CRT libraries. It's as if we wasted our time typing "Error." This trick only works for constant text strings, since the compiler knows they can never change. Everything else gets its own space. If you want the compiler to consolidate equivalent text strings, they must be constant text strings.

Don't make the mistake of counting on some kind of rational order to the global addresses. You can't count on anything the compiler or linker will do, especially if you are considering crossing platforms.

On most operating systems, the stack starts at high addresses and grows toward lower addresses. C and C++ parameters get pushed onto the stack from right to left—the last parameter is the first to get pushed onto the stack in a function call. Local parameters get pushed onto the stack in their order of appearance:

```
void testStack(int x, int y)
{
  int a = 1;
  int b = 2;

  printf("&x= %-10x &y= %-10x\n", &x, &y);
  printf("&a= %-10x &b= %-10x\n", &a, &b);
}
```

This code produces the following output:

```
&x= 12fdf0    &y= 12fdf4
&a= 12fde0    &b= 12fdd4
```

Stack addresses grow downward to smaller memory addresses. Thus, it should be clear that the order in which the parameters and local variables were pushed was: y, x, a, and b, which turns out to be exactly the order in which you read them—a good mnemonic. The next time you're debugging some assembler code, you'll be glad to understand this, especially if you are setting your instruction pointer by hand.

C++ allows a high degree of control over the local scope. Every time you enclose code in a set of braces, you open a local scope with its own local variables:

```
int main()
{
  int a = 0;

  {         // start a local scope here...
    int a = 1;
    printf("%d\n", a);
  }

  printf("%d\n", a);
}
```

This code compiles and runs just fine. The two integer variables are completely separate entities. I've written this example to make a clear point, but I'd never actually write code like this. Doing something like this is likely to get you shot. The real usefulness of this kind of code is for use with C++ objects that perform useful tasks when they are destroyed—you can control the exact moment a destructor is called by closing a local scope.

### *Video Memory (VRAM)*

Video RAM is the memory installed on your video card, unless we're talking about an Xbox. Xbox hardware has unified memory architecture (or UMI), so there's no difference between system RAM and VRAM. It would be nice if the rest of the world worked that way. Other hardware, such as the Intel architecture, must send any data between VRAM and system RAM over a bus. The PS3 has even more different kinds of memory. There are quite a few bus architectures and speeds out there, and it is wise to understand how reading and writing data across the bus affects your game's speed.

As long as the CPU doesn't have to read from VRAM, everything clicks along pretty fast. If you need to grab a piece of VRAM for something, the bits have to be sent across the bus to system RAM. Depending on your architecture, your CPU and GPU must argue for a moment about timing, stream the bits, and go their separate ways. While this painful process is occurring, your game has come to a complete halt.

This problem was pretty horrific back in the days of fixed function pipelines when anything not supported by the video card had to be done with the CPU, such as the first attempts at motion blur. With programmable pipelines, you can create shaders that can run directly on the bits stored in VRAM, making this kind of graphical effect extremely efficient.

The hard disk can't write straight to VRAM, so every time a new texture is needed, you'll need to stop the presses, so to speak. The smart approach is to limit any communication needed between the CPU and the video card. If you are going to send anything to it, it is best to send it in batches.

If you've been paying attention, you'll realize that the GPU in your video card is simply painting the screen using the components in VRAM. If it ever has to stop and ask system RAM for something, your game won't run as fast as it could.

## Optimizing Memory Access

Every access to system RAM uses a CPU cache. If the desired memory location is already in the cache, the contents of the memory location are presented to the CPU extremely quickly. If, on the other hand, the memory is not in the cache, a new block of system RAM must be fetched into the cache. This takes a lot longer than you'd think.

A good test bed for this problem uses multidimensional arrays. C++ defines its arrays in row major order. This ordering puts the members of the right-most index next to each other in memory.

`TestData[0][0][0]` and `TestData[0][0][1]` are stored in adjacent memory locations.

**Row Order or Column Order?**

Not every language defines arrays in row order. Some versions of PASCAL define arrays in column order. Don't make assumptions unless you like writing slow code.

If you access an array in the wrong order, it will create a worst-case CPU cache scenario. Here's an example of two functions that access the same array and do the same task. One will run much faster than the other:

```
const int g_n = 500;
float TestData[g_n][g_n][g_n];

inline void column_ordered()
{
  for (int k=0; k<g_n; k++)           // K
    for (int j=0; j<g_n; j++)         // J
      for (int i=0; i<g_n; i++)       // I
        TestData[i][j][k] = 0.0f;
}

inline void row_ordered()
{
  for (int i=0; i<g_n; i++)           // I
    for (int j=0; j<g_n; j++)         // J
      for (int k=0; k<g_n; k++)       // K
        TestData[i][j][k] = 0.0f;
}
```

The timed output of running both functions on my test machine showed that accessing the array in row order was over 10 times faster:

```
Column Ordered: 3531 ms
Row Ordered: 297 ms
Delta: 3234 ms
```

Any code that accesses any largish data structure can benefit from this technique. If you have a multistep process that affects a large data set, try to arrange your code to perform as much work as possible in smaller memory blocks. You'll optimize the use of the L2 cache and make a much faster piece of code. While you surely won't have any piece of runtime game code do something this crazy, you might very well have a game editor or production tool that does.

## Memory Alignment

The CPU reads and writes memory-aligned data much faster than other data. Any N-byte data type is memory aligned if the starting address is evenly divisible by *N*. For example, a 32-bit integer is memory aligned on a 32-bit architecture if the starting address is 0x04000000. The same 32-bit integer is unaligned if the starting address is 0x04000002, since the memory address is not evenly divisible by 4 bytes.

You can perform a little experiment in memory alignment and how it affects access time by using example code like this:

```
#pragma pack(push, 1)
struct ReallySlowStruct
{
  char c : 6;
  __int64 d : 64;
  int b : 32;
  char a : 8;
};

struct SlowStruct
{
  char c;
  __int64 d;
  int b;
  char a;
};

struct FastStruct
{
  __int64 d;
  int b;
  char a;
  char c;
  char unused[2];
};

#pragma pack(pop)
```

I wrote a piece of code to perform some operations on the member variables in each structure. The difference in times is as follows:

```
Really Slow: 609 ms
Slow: 422 ms
Fast: 406 ms
```

Your penalty for using the SlowStruct over FastStruct is about 5 percent on my test machine. The penalty for using ReallySlowStruct is code that runs 1.5 times as slowly.

The first structure isn't even aligned properly on bit boundaries, hence the name ReallySlowStruct. The definition of the 6-bit char variable throws the entire structure out of alignment. The second structure, SlowStruct, is also out of alignment, but at least the byte boundaries are aligned. The last structure, FastStruct, is completely aligned for each member. The last member, unused, ensures that the structure fills out to an 8-byte boundary in case someone declares an array of FastStruct.

Notice the #pragma pack(push, 1) at the top of the source example? It's accompanied by a #pragma pack(pop) at the bottom. Without them, the compiler, depending on your project settings, will choose to spread out the member variables and place each one on an optimal byte boundary. When the member variables are spread out like that, the CPU can access each member quickly, but all that unused space can add up. If the compiler were left to optimize SlowStruct by adding unused bytes, each structure would be 24 bytes instead of just 14. Seven extra bytes are padded after the first char variable, and the remaining bytes are added at the end. This ensures that the entire structure always starts on an 8-byte boundary. That's about 40 percent of wasted space, all due to a careless ordering of member variables.

*Don't let the compiler waste precious memory space. Put some of your brain cells to work and align your own member variables.* You don't get many opportunities to save memory and optimize CPU at the same time.

## Virtual Memory

Virtual memory increases the addressable memory space by caching unused memory blocks to the hard disk. The scheme depends on the fact that even though you might have a 500MB data structure, you aren't going to be playing with the whole thing at the same time. The unused bits are saved off to your hard disk until you need them again. You should be cheering and wincing at the same time. Cheering because every programmer likes having a big memory playground, and wincing because anything involving the hard disk wastes a lot of time.

**Cache Misses Can Cost You Dearly**

Any time a cache is used inefficiently, you can degrade the overall performance of your game by many orders of magnitude. This is commonly called "thrashing the cache," and it is your worst nightmare. If your game is thrashing cache, you might be able to solve the problem by reordering some code, but most likely you will need to reduce the size of the data.

Try not to rely on virtual memory systems. Game consoles typically don't have any kind of virtual memory, so you're stuck with the amount of memory the system gives you. If you allocate one byte more, the system crashes. This can be especially deadly if you're allocating and deallocating a lot during runtime because it will be nearly impossible to determine your peak memory usage for any given situation.

#### Memory Insurance

When I worked at Planet Moon, we made an educational game for the Gameboy DS called *Brain Quest*. The DS only has 4MB of RAM, and toward the end of the project, we were running right up against that limit. When the final assets came in and were added to the package, we were *just* over the 4MB limit. One of the engineers grinned and walked over to his computer. He opened up *main.cpp* and commented out the following line:

```
unsigned char insurance[10240];
```

## Writing Your Own Memory Manager

Most games extend the provided memory management system. The biggest reasons to do this are performance, efficiency, and improved debugging. Default memory managers in the C runtime are designed to run fairly well in a wide range of memory allocation scenarios. They tend to break down under the load of computer games, where allocations and deallocations of relatively tiny memory blocks can be fast and furious.

A standard memory manager, like the one in the C runtime, must support multithreading. Each time the memory manager's data structures are accessed or changed, they must be protected with critical sections, allowing only one thread to allocate or deallocate memory at a time. All this extra code is time consuming, especially if you use `malloc()` and `free()` very frequently. Most games are multithreaded but don't necessarily need a multithreaded memory manager for every part of the game. A single-threaded memory manager that you write yourself might be a good solution.

Simple memory managers can use a doubly linked list as the basis for keeping track of allocated and free memory blocks. The C runtime uses a more complicated system to reduce the algorithmic complexity of searching through the allocated and free blocks that could be as small as a single byte. Your memory blocks might be either more regularly shaped, fewer in number, or both. This creates an opportunity to design a simpler, more efficient system.

Default memory managers must assume that deallocations happen approximately as often as allocations, and they might happen in any order and at any time.

Their data structures have to keep track of a large number of blocks of available and used memory. Any time a piece of memory changes state from used to available, the data structures must be traversed quickly. When blocks become available again, the memory manager must detect adjacent available blocks and merge them to make a larger block. Finding free memory of an appropriate size to minimize wasted space can be extremely tricky. Since default memory managers solve these problems to a large extent, their performance isn't as high as another memory manager that can make more assumptions about how and when memory allocations occur.

If your game can allocate and deallocate most of its dynamic memory space at once, you can write a memory manager based on a data structure no more complicated than a singly linked list. You'd never use something this simple in a more general case, of course, because a singly linked list has O(n) algorithmic complexity. That would cripple any memory management system used in the general case.

A good reason to extend a memory manager is to add some debugging features. Two features that are common include adding additional bytes before and after the allocation to track memory corruption or to track memory leaks. The C runtime adds only one byte before and after an allocated block, which might be fine to catch those pesky `x+1` and `x-1` errors but doesn't help for much else. If the memory corruption seems pretty random, and most of them sure seem that way, you can increase your odds of catching the culprit by writing a custom manager that adds more bytes to the beginning and ending of each block. In practice, the extra space is set to a small number, even one byte, in the release build.

**Different Build Options Will Change Runtime Behavior**

Anything you do differently from the debug and release builds can change the behavior of bugs from one build target to another. Murphy's Law dictates that the bug will only appear in the build target that is hardest, or even impossible, to debug.

Another common extension to memory managers is leak detection. It is a common practice to redefine the new operator to add `__FILE__` and `__LINE__` information to each allocated memory block in debug mode. When the memory manager is shut down, all the unfreed blocks are printed out in the output window in the debugger. This should give you a good place to start when you need to track down a memory leak.

If you decide to write your own memory manager, keep the following points in mind:

- **Data structures:** Choose the data structure that matches your memory allocation scenario. If you traverse a large number of free and available blocks very frequently, choose a hash table or tree-based structure. If you hardly ever traverse it to find free blocks, you could get away with a list. Store the data structure separately from the memory pool; any corruption will keep your memory manager's data structure intact.
- **Single/multithreaded access:** Don't forget to add appropriate code to protect your memory manager from multithreaded access if you need it. Eliminate the protections if you are sure that access to the memory manager will only happen from a single thread, and you'll gain some performance.
- **Debug and testing:** Allocate a little additional memory before and after the block to detect memory corruption. Add caller information to the debug memory blocks; at a minimum, you should use `__FILE__` and `__LINE__` to track where the allocation occurred.

One of the best reasons to extend the C runtime memory manager is to write a better system to manage small memory blocks. The memory managers supplied in the C runtime or MFC library are not meant for tiny allocations. You can prove it to yourself by allocating two integers and subtracting their memory addresses as shown here:

```
int *a = new int;
int *b = new int;

int delta1 = ((int)b - (int)a) - sizeof(int);
```

The wasted space for the C runtime library was 28 bytes for a release build and 60 bytes for the debug build under Visual Studio. Even with the release build, an integer takes eight times as much memory space as it would if it weren't dynamically allocated.

Most games overload the `new` operator to allocate small blocks of memory from a reserved pool set aside for smaller allocations. Memory allocations that are larger than a set number of bytes can still use the C runtime. I recommend that you start with 128 bytes as the largest block your small allocator will handle and tweak the size until you are happy with the performance. I'll show you a simple memory pool class later in this chapter in the "Memory Pools" section.

## Grab Bag of Useful Stuff

Every programmer I know has a collection of gems that they use in nearly every project. As you grow in your programming abilities, you'll find yourself doing the same thing. I want to share a few of the ones I've found or developed over the years to hopefully give you a head start on making your own. First, I'll show you a cool random number generator, and then I'll show you a neat algorithm to traverse any set in random order without visiting the same member twice. Finally we'll end with a memory pool class I wrote a while back.

## An Excellent Random Number Generator

There are as many good algorithms for generating random numbers as there are pages in this book. Most programmers will soon discover that the ANSI `rand()` function is completely inadequate because it can only generate a single stream of random numbers. Most games need multiple discrete streams of random numbers.

Unless your game comes with a little piece of hardware that uses the radioactive decay of cesium to generate random numbers, your random number generator is only pseudo random. A pseudo-random number sequence can certainly appear random, achieving a relatively flat distribution curve over the generation of billions of numbers mapped to a small domain, like the set of numbers between 1 and 100. Given the same starting assumption, commonly called a *seed*, the sequence will be exactly the same. A truly random sequence could never repeat like that.

This might seem bad because you might feel that a hacker could manipulate the seed to affect the outcome of the game. In practice, all you have to do is regenerate the seed every now and then using some random element that would be difficult or impossible to duplicate. In truth, a completely predictable random number generator is something you will give your left leg for when writing test tools or a game replay system.

**Even Old Code Can Be Useful**

Every *Ultima* from *Ultima I* to *Ultima VIII* used the same random number generator, originally written in 6502 assembler. In 1997, this generator was the oldest piece of continuously used code at Origin Systems. Finally, this RNG showed its age and had to be replaced. Kudos to Richard Garriott (aka Lord British) for making the longest-lived piece of code Origin ever used.

Here's a cool little class to keep track of your random numbers. You'll want to make sure you save this code and stuff it into your own toolbox. The RNG core is called a *Mersenne Twister pseudorandom number generator*, and it was originally developed by Takuji Nishimura and Makoto Matsumoto:

```
class GCCRandom
{
```

```
private:
    // DATA
    unsigned int    rseed;
    unsigned int    rseed_sp;
    unsigned long mt[CMATH_N]; /* the array for the state vector */
    int mti; /* mti==N+1 means mt[N] is not initialized */

    // FUNCTIONS
public:
    GCCRandom(void);

    unsigned int  Random( unsigned int n );
    float           Random( );
    void           SetRandomSeed(unsigned int n);
    unsigned int  GetRandomSeed(void);
    void            Randomize(void);
};
```

The original code has been modified to include a few useful bits, one of which was to allow this class to save and reload its random number seed, which can be used to replay random number sequences by simply storing the seed. Here's an example of how you can use the class:

```
GCCRandom r;
r.Randomize();
unsigned int num = r.Random(100);  // returns a number from 0-99, inclusive
```

You should use a few instantiations of this class in your game, each one generating random numbers for a different part of your game. Here's why: Let's say you want to generate some random taunts from AI characters. If you use a different random number sequence from the sequence that generates the contents of treasure chests, you can be sure that if the player turns off character audio, the same RNG sequence will result for the treasure chests, which nicely compartmentalizes your game. In other words, your game becomes predictable and testable.

**Your Random Number Generator Can Break Automation**

I was working on an automation system for some Microsoft games, and the thing would just not work right. The goal of the system was to be able to record game sessions and play them back. The system was great for testers and programmers alike. It's hard, and boring, to play a few million hands of blackjack. Our programming team realized that since the same RNG was being called for every system of the game, small aberrations would occur as calls to the RNG went out of sync. This was especially true for random character audio, since the timing of character audio was completely dependent on another thread, which was impossible to synchronize. When we used one `CRandom` class for each subsystem of the game, the problem disappeared.

## Pseudo-Random Traversal of a Set

Have you ever wondered how the "random" button on your CD player works? It will play every song on your CD randomly without playing the same song twice. That's a really useful solution for making sure players in your games see the widest variety of features like objects, effects, or characters before they have the chance of seeing the same ones over again.

The following code uses a mathematical feature of prime numbers and quadratic equations. The algorithm requires a prime number larger than the ordinal value of the set you want to traverse. If your set had 10 members, your prime number would be 11. Of course, the algorithm doesn't generate prime numbers; instead, it just keeps a select set of prime numbers around in a lookup table. If you need bigger primes, there's a convenient website for you to check out.

Here's how it works. A skip value is calculated by choosing three random values greater than zero. These values become the coefficients of the quadratic, and the domain value (x) is set to the ordinal value of the set:

```
Skip = RandomA * (members * members) + (RandomB * members) + RandomC
```

Armed with this skip value, you can use this piece of code to traverse the entire set exactly once, in a pseudo-random order:

```
nextMember += skip;
nextMember %= prime;
```

The value of skip is so much larger than the number of members of your set that the chosen value seems to skip around at random. Of course, this code is inside a `while` loop to catch the case where the value chosen is larger than your set but still smaller than the prime number. Here's the class definition:

```
class PrimeSearch
{
  static int prime_array[];

  int skip;
  int currentPosition;
  int maxElements;
  int *currentPrime;
  int searches;
```

```
public:
  PrimeSearch(int elements);
  int GetNext(bool restart=false);
  bool Done() { return (searches==*currentPrime); }
  void Restart() { currentPosition=0; searches=0; }
};
```

I'll show you a trivial example to make a point.

```
void FadeToBlack(Screen *screen)
{
  int w = screen.GetWidth();

  int h = screen.GetHeight();

  int pixels = w * h;

  PrimeSearch search(pixels);

  int p;
  while((p=search.GetNext())!=-1)
  {
    int x = p % w;
    int y = h / p;
    screen.SetPixel(x, y, BLACK);
  }
}
```

The example sets random pixels to black until the entire screen is erased. I should warn you now that this code is completely stupid, for two reasons. First, you wouldn't set one pixel at a time. Second, you would likely use a pixel shader to do this. I told you the example was trivial: use `PrimeSearch` for other cool things like spawning creatures, weapons, and other random stuff.

## Memory Pools

I mentioned memory pools earlier in this chapter when I covered different types of memory management. They are incredibly useful for frequent, small allocations and deallocations because they are lightning fast. The idea is that you allocate a large block of memory up front, which is then divided into chunks of even sizes. Each chunk has a small header that points to the next element. This creates a singly linked list of memory chunks, as shown in Figure 3.1.

When an allocation request comes in, it simply removes the chunk at the front of the list and returns it, making the next chunk the making the next chunk the new front (see Figure 3.2).

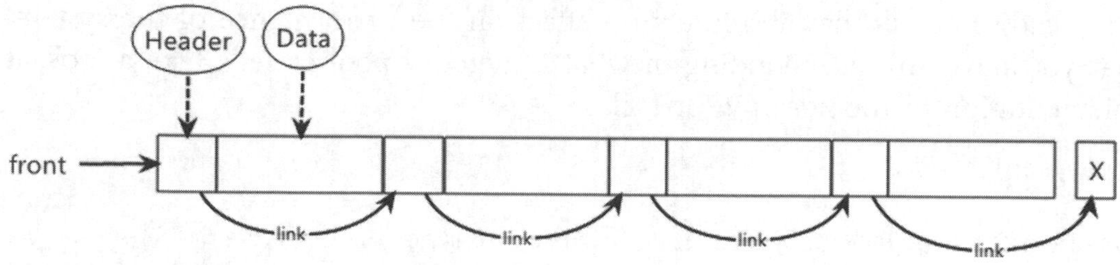


**Figure 3.1**
Memory pool block.

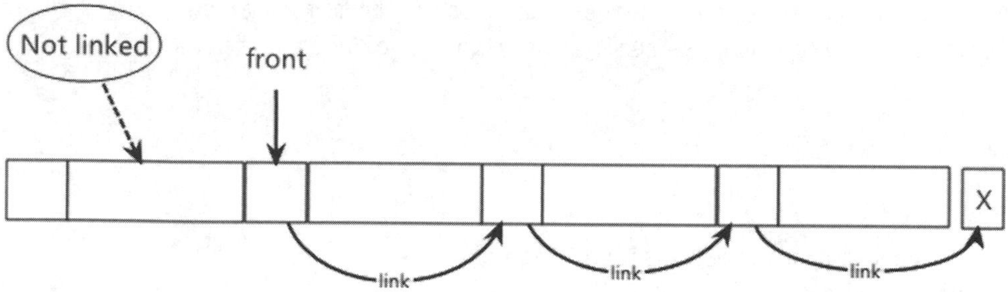


**Figure 3.2**
Memory pool chunk allocated.

When a chunk of memory is destroyed, it simply returns it to the list. It may seem like an unnecessarily complex system to use this linked list, but it's not. You can't guarantee the order in which things will be freed, so having this linked list structure allows you to find the next free chunk in constant time. It also allows for deallocation in constant time since the chunks are returned to the front of the list. After a while, your nice clean array will start to look a bit messy with chunks being requested and freed all the time. Figure 3.3 shows what your block might end up looking like.

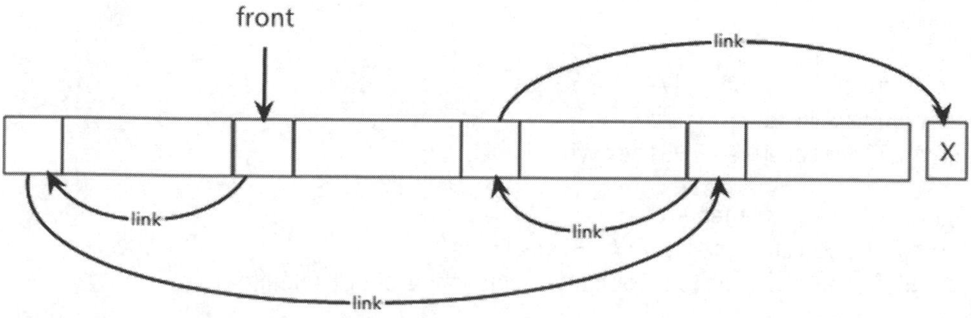


**Figure 3.3**
Memory pool usage.

This is perfectly fine and has absolutely no effect on the performance of the system. Now that you have an understanding of what a memory pool is, let's take a look at the implementation of the `MemoryPool` class:

```
class MemoryPool
{
  unsigned char** m_ppRawMemoryArray;  // an array of memory blocks, each
                                       // split up into chunks
  unsigned char* m_pHead;  // the front of the memory chunk linked list
  unsigned int m_chunkSize, m_numChunks;  // the size of each chunk and
                                          // number of chunks per array
  unsigned int m_memArraySize;  // the number elements in the memory array
  bool m_toAllowResize;  // true if we resize the memory pool when it fills

public:
  // construction
  MemoryPool(void);
  ~MemoryPool(void);
  bool Init(unsigned int chunkSize, unsigned int numChunks);
  void Destroy(void);

  // allocation functions
  void* Alloc(void);
  void Free(void* pMem);
  unsigned int GetChunkSize(void) const { return m_chunkSize; }

  // settings
  void SetAllowResize(bool toAllowResize)
  {
    m_toAllowResize = toAllowResize;
  }

private:
  // resets internal vars
  void Reset(void);

  // internal memory allocation helpers
  bool GrowMemoryArray(void);
  unsigned char* AllocateNewMemoryBlock(void);

  // internal linked list management
  unsigned char* GetNext(unsigned char* pBlock);
  void SetNext(unsigned char* pBlockToChange, unsigned char* pNewNext);

  // don't allow copy constructor
  MemoryPool(const MemoryPool& memPool) {}
};
```

To use this class, instantiate it and call the `Init()` function. The `chunkSize` is the size of each atomic memory chunk, and `numChunks` is the number of chunks that are created for each set of chunks. Collectively, this set of chunks is called a *block*. If you go over your limit of memory chunks, the memory pool will allocate another block for you. This isn't catastrophic, but you don't want to make a habit of going over your limit because it's very time consuming to set up a new memory block. If `Init()` returns `true`, your memory pool is ready to go! You can call `Alloc()` and `Free()` to allocate and free a chunk, respectively.

The `Init()` function just sets some member variables and calls the `GrowMemoryArray()` function to allocate the new block of memory. Let's take a look inside `GrowMemoryArray()` to see how the magic happens:

```
bool MemoryPool::GrowMemoryArray(void)
{
    // allocate a new array
    size_t allocationSize = sizeof(unsigned char*) * (m_memArraySize + 1);
    unsigned char** ppNewMemArray = (unsigned char**)malloc(allocationSize);

    // make sure the allocation succeeded
    if (!ppNewMemArray)
        return false;

    // copy any existing memory pointers over
    for (unsigned int i = 0; i < m_memArraySize; ++i)
    {
        ppNewMemArray[i] = m_ppRawMemoryArray[i];
    }

    // Allocate a new block of memory. Indexing m_memArraySize here is
    // safe because we haven't incremented it yet to reflect the new size
    ppNewMemArray[m_memArraySize] = AllocateNewMemoryBlock();

    // attach the block to the end of the current memory list
    if (m_pHead)
    {
        unsigned char* pCurr = m_pHead;
        unsigned char* pNext = GetNext(m_pHead);
        while (pNext)
        {
            pCurr = pNext;
            pNext = GetNext(pNext);
        }
        SetNext(pCurr, ppNewMemArray[m_memArraySize]);
    }
```

```
    else
    {
        m_pHead = ppNewMemArray[m_memArraySize];
    }

    // destroy the old memory array
    if (m_ppRawMemoryArray)
        free(m_ppRawMemoryArray);

    // assign the new memory array and increment the size count
    m_ppRawMemoryArray = ppNewMemArray;
    ++m_memArraySize;

    return true;
}

unsigned char* MemoryPool::AllocateNewMemoryBlock(void)
{
    // calculate the size of each block and the size of the
    // actual memory allocation
    size_t blockSize = m_chunkSize + CHUNK_HEADER_SIZE;  // chunk + linked list
     // overhead
    size_t trueSize = blockSize * m_numChunks;

    // allocate the memory
    unsigned char* pNewMem = (unsigned char*)malloc(trueSize);
    if (!pNewMem)
        return NULL;

    // turn the memory into a linked list of chunks
    unsigned char* pEnd = pNewMem + trueSize;
    unsigned char* pCurr = pNewMem;
    while (pCurr < pEnd)
    {
        // calculate the next pointer position
        unsigned char* pNext = pCurr + blockSize;

        // set the next pointer
        unsigned char** ppChunkHeader = (unsigned char**)pCurr;
        ppChunkHeader[0] = (pNext < pEnd ? pNext : NULL);

        // move to the next block
        pCurr += blockSize;
    }

    return pNewMem;
}
```

This function starts by allocating a new array of pointers. This array will hold all of the blocks of memory chunks that are allocated. It starts with only one element and adds more if the memory pool needs to grow. After that, it copies any existing blocks to the new array. Now that the array is in order, a new block of memory is allocated by calling `AllocateNewMemoryBlock()` and assigned to the end of the array. Inside `AllocateNewMemoryBlock()`, a new block of memory is allocated. Notice that the true size of each chunk is the size requested, plus the `CHUNK_HEADER_SIZE`, which is defined as follows:

```
const static size_t CHUNK_HEADER_SIZE = (sizeof(unsigned char*));
```

This is the header data that will point to the next element. After the block has been allocated, the function walks through each chunk in the block and points the header to the next block. This sets up the singly linked list. After that, you're ready to go, and the new block is returned to `GrowMemoryArray()`.

Now that the `GrowMemoryArray()` function has the newly constructed block, it checks to see if `m_pHead` is valid. This is the pointer to the front of the list. If it's valid, it must walk through the list of chunks to find the end and append it there. If not, the new block can be attached right there. Currently, `GrowMemoryArray()` is only called when you're initializing the memory pool or when you've run out of chunks. In both of these cases, `m_pHead` will be `NULL`. The extra clause is there in case you want the ability to grow the memory at any time.

That's pretty much it. Once `GrowMemoryArray()` returns, you'll have a brand new block of memory ready to be dished out. Now that all the heavy lifting is done, the `Alloc()` and `Free()` functions become very simple:

```
void* MemoryPool::Alloc(void)
{
   // If we're out of memory chunks, grow the pool. This is very expensive.
   if (!m_pHead)
   {
      // if we don't allow resizes, return NULL
      if (!m_toAllowResize)
         return NULL;

      // attempt to grow the pool
      if (!GrowMemoryArray())
         return NULL; // couldn't allocate anymore memory
   }

   // grab the first chunk from the list and move to the next chunks
   unsigned char* pRet = m_pHead;
```

```
    m_pHead = GetNext(m_pHead);
    return (pRet + CHUNK_HEADER_SIZE);  // make sure we return a pointer to
                                        // the data section only
}

void MemoryPool::Free(void* pMem)
{
  // Calling Free() on a NULL pointer is perfectly valid C++ so
  // we have to check for it.
  if (pMem != NULL)
  {
      // The pointer we get back is just to the data section of
      // the chunk. This gets us the full chunk.
      unsigned char* pBlock =
        ((unsigned char*)pMem) - CHUNK_HEADER_SIZE;

      // push the chunk to the front of the list
      SetNext(pBlock, m_pHead);
      m_pHead = pBlock;
  }
}
```

The first thing the `Alloc()` function checks is whether or not the block has been fully allocated. If it has, it has to allocate a new block. You can disallow this by setting `m_toAllowResize` to `false`. This is handy for games that have a limited memory budget, like console or mobile games. After that, it returns the front of the list:

```
return (pRet + CHUNK_HEADER_SIZE);
```

Notice how it adds the `CHUNK_HEADER_SIZE`? This is necessary because you only want to return the actual data section and not include the header section.

The `Free()` function is pretty much the reverse. If the chunk is valid, the function subtracts `CHUNK_HEADER_SIZE` to get the full chunk, including the header. Then it sets the header to point to the current front of the list and assigns the `m_pHead` pointer to itself. This pushes the freed chunk to the front of the list.

In practice, the best way to use this memory pool is to figure out which objects you'll be constructing and destroying extremely often and make them use a memory pool. The best way to do this is to override the `new` and `delete` operators for that class so that they call into the memory pool for allocation and deallocation. This keeps it nice and contained within the class so that the calling code doesn't have to know anything about whether the class is pooled or not—it just calls `new` and `delete` as normal.

There are a number of ways you can add to this memory system. For example, you might want to create a simple distributor that creates a number of memory pools of different sizes and routes memory allocation requests through it. It can return memory chunks for anything smaller than the size of the largest pool and default to the global `new` operator for everything larger. This is exactly what we did on *BrainQuest*.

Another improvement would be to create a series of macros that would generate the necessary code required to have a class use a memory pool. That way, you could have a class use a memory pool with only a couple of lines of code. This is exactly what I did for the sample code. If you look in `MemoryMacros.h`, you'll see the macro definitions. An example of their use is in `Pathing.h` where I pool all of the pathing nodes. I'll talk more about this in Chapter 18, "An Introduction to Game AI."

## Developing the Style That's Right for You

Throughout this chapter, I've tried to point out a number of coding techniques and pitfalls that I've learned over the years. I've tried to focus on the ones that seem to cause the most problems and offer the best results. Of course, keep in mind that there is no single best approach or one magic solution for writing a game.

I wish I had more pages because there are tons of gems out there. Most of them you'll beg or borrow from your colleagues. Some of them you'll create for yourself after you solve a challenging problem.

However you find them, don't forget to share.

## Further Reading

*C++ Templates: The Complete Guide*, Nicolai M. Josuttis and David Vandevoorde

*Effective C++*, Scott Meyers

*More Effective C++*, Scott Meyers

*Effective STL*, Scott Meyers

*Design Patterns: Elements of Reusable Object-Oriented Software*, Erich Gamma et al.

*AntiPatterns: Refactoring Software, Architectures, and Projects in Crisis, William Brown et al.*

*Game Programming Gems* series, various authors

*Thinking in C++* Vol. 1, Bruce Eckel

*Thinking in C++* Vol. 2, Bruce Eckel and Chuck Allison

# Chapter 4

*by Mike McShaffry*

## Building Your Game

Do you ever freeze up just before starting a new project? I do, and I'm not afraid to admit it. I get hung up thinking about the perfect directory structure, where the art and sound data should be stored, how the build process should work, and mostly how I will keep my new game from becoming a horrible mess. By the end of a project, it usually turns out to be a mess anyway! So I'm always thankful I plan out a directory structure, employ good version control tools, and incorporate automation scripts that all keep entropy just low enough for a human like me to be able to keep track of what I'm doing.

In this chapter, I'm going to tell you everything you need to know to get your game projects organized from the start and how to configure project files and use version control tools effectively. This is an area where many game developers try to cut corners, so my advice is to invest a little time and ensure that your projects go together smoothly and stay that way. Hopefully, they'll stay organized right to the day you ship.

As you read through this chapter, you might feel that you are getting an education in software engineering. Try not to feel overwhelmed. These techniques are very critical to the process of successfully developing games, and they are used by real game developers on teams that are big, small, and even single developers.

## A Little Motivation

Games are much more than source code. A typical game includes raw and optimized art and sound data, map levels, event scripts, test tools, and more. Don't forget the project documentation—both the docs that ship with your project, such as the user guide, and the internal documents, such as the technical design document (TDD), general design document (GDD), and test plans.

There are two essential problems that all these files create. First, the sheer number of game files for art, sound, music, and other assets need to have some rational organization—there can be hundreds of thousands of these files. Games like *Age of Empires Online* and *Battlefield 3* easily have many hundreds of thousands of asset files in production. Some online games like *Star Wars: The Old Republic* may have breached one million asset files. With this many files, it can be really easy to lose track of one, or a few hundred. The second problem is the difficulty of ensuring that sensitive debug builds and other internal files are kept separate from the stuff that will be shipped to consumers. The last thing you need is to release your debug build, with all its symbols, to the public at large. The best setup lets you segregate your release files from everything else so you can burn a single directory tree to a DVD without worrying about culling a weird list of files. Over the last few years, I've settled on a project organization that solves these two problems.

The process of building a project should be as automatic as possible. You should be able to automatically build your game every night so that you can check your latest work. A game that can't build every day is in big trouble. If you want an easy way to get a project cancelled, just make it impossible to fulfill a build request at a moment's notice.

The directory structure, project settings, and development scripts you use should make building, publishing, and rebuilding any previously published build a snap. If your source code repository supports branching, like SVN or Perforce do, you'll be ahead of the game because you can support multiple lines of development simultaneously. For those of you who haven't used source code repositories, they are server-based archives files that can be checked out to developers like a person might check out a book from a library. When the developer is finished with that file, he checks the file back into the server, and it makes the most recent version available to everyone. Unlike a library, source code repositories are good at allowing the same file to be modified by multiple developers and allowing all their changes to merge together when they are done. Branches are "copies" of groups of these files, typically meant for developers to sequester them as a group for a specific purpose, such as walling them off from rapid changes or doing research without affecting other programmers. Branches can even be merged together, such as when mass changes in one branch need to be brought to another—this might be done after installing a new physics system or renderer. There's a whole section about this later in this chapter called "Source Code Repositories and Version Control."

Everyone does things differently, but the project organization, build scripts, and build process you'll learn in this chapter are hard to beat. I figure that if they're good enough for Microsoft, and they got our projects out the door on time, I'll keep them.

## Creating a Project

This might sound a little hokey, but every project I work on has its own code word. I picked this up from Microsoft, and I love it. You should let your project team choose the code word, but try to make sure that the name chosen is somewhat cryptic. It's actually really convenient if you end up at the bar with a bunch of software developers from other companies. You can talk all day about finishing a build for "Slickrock" or that "Rainman" needs another programmer. Cloak and dagger aside, there's a real utilitarian reason to use short code words for projects.

You can use this code word for your top-level project directory and the Visual Studio solution file (SLN file) that builds your game and tools. It is an easy step from there to create a standard build script that can find your key project files, build the game, and even test it. If you work in a studio with multiple projects, a master build server can easily build every project in development every night and take very little maintenance to add or remove projects.

Beyond that, a code word for a project has one other use. If you end up making multiple versions of the same product, you can use different code words to refer to them instead of version numbers. You are ready to start your project, so choose a code word and create your top-level directory. May whatever gods you believe in have mercy on your soul:

```
mkdir <codeword>
```

### Build Configurations

Every project should have two build targets at a minimum: debug and release. The release build will enable optimizations critical for a product the customer will actually use. Many projects also have a profile build, which usually disables enough optimizations to allow for debugging but disables code inside `#ifdef DEBUG` constructs to allow it to actually run in real time. It's a good idea to have all three targets because they serve different purposes. Mostly, programmers will run and develop with a profile build target, and they will use the debug target only when something really nasty is in their bug list.

**Don't Go Too Long Between Builds**

Try to keep all your build targets alive and working every day. If you ignore any build configuration, especially the release build, it could take a very long time to figure out why it's not working properly. Build it nightly, if you can, and make sure any problems get handled the very next day.

## Create a Bullet-Proof Directory Structure

Over the years of developing complex projects, I've experimented with different directory structures trying to find the ideal structure. I've learned that it is important to have a good working directory structure from the start. It will help you work your way through all the stages of developing a project—from writing your first lines of source code to testing and debugging your project. You also need to keep in mind that you'll likely need to share aspects of your project with others during the development process, even if you are the only one writing all the source code. For example, you might need to hire an independent testing team to work over your game. If you organize your project well, you'll be able to share files when necessary with a minimum of hassle.

Keeping all of this in mind, here is my recommended directory structure where you should store each project you develop, including your game engine:

- *Docs*
- *Assets*
- *Source*
- *Temp*
- *Lib*
- *Game*

The *Docs* directory is a reference for the development team. It should have an organized hierarchy to store both design documents and technical specifications. I always put a copy of the contract exhibits and milestone acceptance criteria in it for my team, since these documents specify our obligations to the publisher or investor. (You don't want to ever forget who is paying the bills!) While I'm developing a project, it's not unusual to find detailed character scripts, initial user interface designs, and other works in progress in the *Docs* directory.

The *Assets* directory is going to store all your art, animation, and sound assets in their raw, naked form. This directory is likely going to get huge, so make sure the source control system is configured to filter it out for people who don't care about it. I say "raw" and "naked" not just because I enjoy putting it in print—these assets are those *not* used by the game directly, but those that are used by artists, designers, or sound engineers while they are working on them. Think of it as the same kind of directory that programmers use for their code. When the assets get imported or packed into game files that are used by the game directly, they'll be inside the *Game* directory where all the distributable stuff lives. One more thing—the *Assets* directory will be a huge, complicated hierarchy that will most likely be created to appease the whims of artists or sound engineers, so don't expect to have much control over it.

The source code lives in the *Source* directory. It should be organized by the programmers in whatever manner they see fit. The project's solution file or makefile should also reside in the *Source* directory and be named according to the code word for the project. The rest of the source code should be organized into other directories below *Source*.

When a project is being built, each build target will place temporary files into the *Temp* directory.

Each build project, building configuration, and platform can be segregated into their own directories underneath *Temp*. For example, the OBJ and other temporary files for the Debug configuration of the GameCode4 project compiled with Visual Studio 2010 for Win32 can be stored in *Temp\GameCode4_2010Win32Debug*. Doing it this way makes it very easy to create a directory structure that supports multiple compiled targets, multiple compilers, multiple platforms, and multiple build configurations. If you think you might not need this, think about building a project for both Android and iOS—because being able to store the results of a build on a server might be very convenient, and if you don't give each build flavor a safe place to live, they might overwrite each other.

**Visual Studio Defaults Aren't Always So Great**

Visual Studio does a really bad thing by assuming that software engineers want their build targets to clutter up the *Source* directory. I find this annoying, since I don't want a single byte of the *Source* directory to change when I build my project. Why, you ask? First, I like to be able to copy the entire *Source* directory for publishing or backup without worrying about large temporary files. Second, I can compare two different *Source* directories from version to version to see only the deltas in the source code, instead of wading through hundreds of useless .OBJ, .SBR, and other files. Third, I know I can always delete files in the *Temp* directory to force a new build of the entire project, a particular platform, or a particular build configuration of all platforms. I also know that I never have to back up or publish the *Temp* directory.

The *Game* directory should hold the release build and every game data file your game needs to run and anything that will get distributed to your players. You should be able to send the contents of the *Game* directory to a separate testing group or to someone in the press, and they'd have everything they would need to run and test the game. You also want to ensure that they don't get anything you want to keep to yourself, such as confidential project documentation or your crown jewels—the source code. Generally, you'll place release executables and DLLs in *Game* and store all your game data and config files in *Game/Data*. If you take the time to set up a directory that stores the files that you may be providing to others from time to time, you'll likely avoid sending out your source code or internal project design documents. Documentation that will get sent to your players on disc or downloaded, like help files, also should be stored here. Printed documentation should be stored separately; I'd suggest in its own hierarchy inside the *Assets* directory.

The *Test* directory should hold special files only for the test team. It usually contains test scripts, files that unlock cheats, and test utilities. Some games have a logging feature that writes diagnostic, warning, and error messages to a text file—the *Test* directory is a great place for them. Most importantly, it should contain the release notes for the latest build. The release notes are a list of features that work, or don't work, in the latest build. They also contain quick instructions about anything the test team needs to know, such as how to expose a certain feature or a part of your game that needs special attention. As you are developing your project, I strongly encourage you to keep the release notes up-to-date. If you hand your game over to a testing team, they won't have to pull out their hair trying to figure out how to get your project to work. You'll discover that Visual Studio has to be convinced to use this directory structure, and it takes a little work to create projects under this standard. Visual Studio assumes that everything in the project lives underneath the directory that stores the solution file. It may be a pain to get Visual Studio to conform to this structure, but trust me, it is worth it.

**C# Projects Are Tougher to Reorganize**

While you can tweak the directory structure of C++ projects under Visual Studio, C# projects are tougher. There is a way to reconfigure the solution files to make my recommended directory structure work, but it isn't exactly supported by Microsoft. Perhaps Microsoft will in their great wisdom figure this out someday, but don't hold your breath. For more on this topic, visit the companion website for this book.

The directory structure I propose is useful because it caters to all the different people and groups that need access to your game development files. The development team gets access to the whole thing. Executives and press looking for the odd demo can copy the *Game* directory whenever they want. The test group grabs *Game* and *Test*, and they have everything they need.

If you store the build targets in the *Source* directory, like Visual Studio wants you to, you'll have to write complicated batch files to extract the build target, clean temporary files, and match game data with executables. Those batch files are a pain to maintain and are a frequent source of bad builds. If you pound Visual Studio for a little while to get a better directory structure started, you won't have to worry about a nasty batch file during the life of your product.

## Where to Put Your Game Engine and Tools

In case it wasn't clear, your game engine should get its own directory, with the same directory structure in parallel with your game. On one project I worked on, our game engine had a pretty uncreative code name: Engine. It was stored in an *Engine* directory with *Source*, *Docs*, *Temp*, and *Lib* instead of *Game*, since the output of the build was a library. There was some debate about separating the `#include` files into an *Inc* directory at the top level. That's a winner of an idea because it allows the game engine to be published with only the `#include` files and the library. The source code would remain safely in our hands. The source code that is a companion to this book is divided into *GameCode4*, which can be considered the engine, and *Teapot Wars*, the game that uses this engine. *GameCode4* compiles into a library, which is linked to game-specific files to create the final executable, so the final result of a complete rebuild is stored in *Game*. You could have the engine compile itself into a DLL, in which case a post-build step would copy the DLL into the *Game* directory. To play the game, you should be able to copy only the contents of the *Game* directory to a player's computer, and the game should run as expected.

Tools can be a little fuzzier and depend somewhat on whether the tool in question is one that is a custom tool for the project or something that everyone on every project uses. As you might expect, a tool for one project would go into the source tree for the project, and one that everyone uses would go into the same directory hierarchy as your shared game engine. If neither seems to fit, such as a one-off tool to convert some wacky file format to another, and it would never need to change or undergo any further development, perhaps you should install it into a special directory tree for those oddballs. Basically, the rule of thumb is that any directory tree should be under the same kind of development: rapid, slow, or completely static.

If your game needs any open source or third-party libraries to build, I suggest putting them in a *3rdParty* directory inside your *Source* directory. This makes it easy to keep all the right versions of each library with your code base, and it is convenient for other programmers who need to grab your code and work with it. After all, it might be tough to find an old version of something if your source code requires it.

One thing I'd suggest is to massage the output targets of third-party libraries and SDKs, especially the PDB files that are used for debugging. Most third-party libraries are pretty good at having directory structures that support a vast array of compiler versions, operating systems, and platforms. They typically do this by naming their LIB files using the library name, platform, and configuration. Some libraries, however, do not do that and keep exactly the same name no matter what platform or build target is being used. This can cause all manner of confusion and make it difficult to debug a project where important PDB files from different libraries all have the same name, causing one or more of them to be overwritten. In reorganizing the source code for the fourth edition of this book, I had to wrestle with this very problem, and I wanted a solution that minimized any changes to the build scripts of the third-party libraries.

Here's the solution I settled on to clean up this mess. First, I made sure that I only changed the third-party builds to create PDB files that were named exactly the same as the LIB file in question. *BulletCollision.LIB* would have a companion *BulletCollision.PDB*. The default PDB filename in most Visual Studio build targets is *vc100.PDB*, which can't be used if another library is doing that too! Next, I created a small batch file inside the *3rdParty* directory to run through all the build targets and platform-specific versions to copy them into a special *Lib* directory. Inside the *Lib* directory, I created platform and configuration specific spots where all the *3rdParty* targets could live in harmony, without stepping on one another (see Figure 4.1).

One important suggestion I can give you: Don't bother putting all the different LIB files into the solution settings; instead, use `#pragma comment (lib, "foo.lib")` in the source files that will be needing them and surround the #pragmas with #if defined blocks that can include the right LIB file for your target and platform. This is a Microsoftian thing, I know, but it is convenient because you don't have to sweat over setting each build target and platform's library dependencies. Keeping the project build settings from diverging drastically can save you a ton of headaches down the road.

## Setting Visual Studio Build Options

I mentioned that you have to coax Visual Studio to move its intermediate and output files outside the directory that stores the solution file. To do this, open your solution, right-click the solution in your solution explorer, and select Properties. Click the

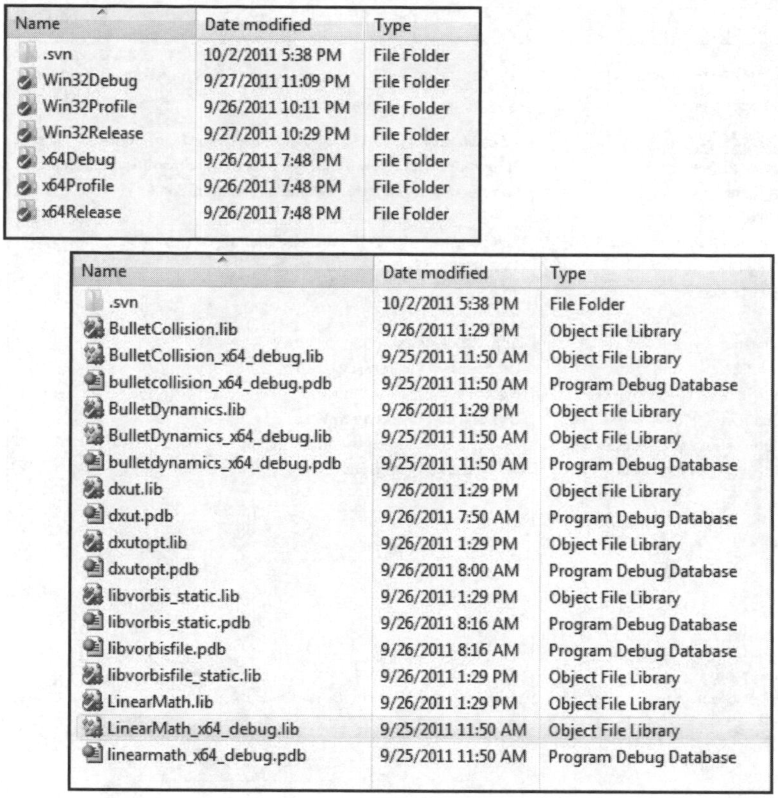


**Figure 4.1**
How to manage third-party build targets.

General group under Configuration Properties (see Figure 4.2), and you'll be able to select the *Output* and *Intermediate* directories.

The *Intermediate* directory is set to where you want all of your OBJ and other intermediate build files to be saved. Visual Studio has defined the macro $(ConfigurationName) to separate intermediate files in directories with the configuration name, such as *Debug* or *Release*, but there's an important improvement. I also like to add the macro $(ProjectName)$(PlatformName)$(Configuration) to separate the compile results of each project, platform, and configuration.

#### Include The Compiler Version In Your Project File Names

Since this book has been in constant publication since 2003, I also like to name the Visual Studio projects to include the compiler version, such as GameCode4_2008 for Visual Studio 2008 or GameCode4_2010 for Visual Studio 2010. That enables me to use the same directory structure to hold simultaneous builds from multiple compilers, which can be extremely convenient if you are making engine code.

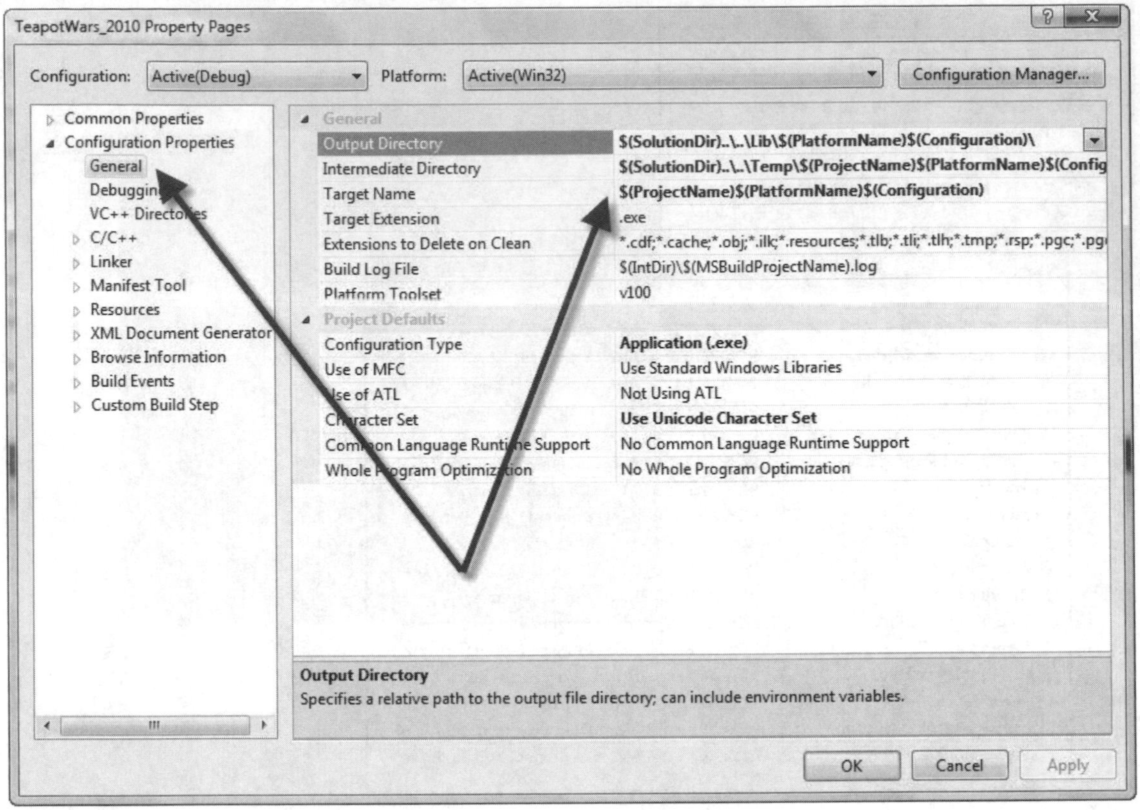


**Figure 4.2**
Visual Studio 2010 configuration properties.

In these property settings, you can use the $(IntDir) macro to identify the entire path defined in the *Intermediate* directory setting, which makes it useful for placing other build-specific files, such as your build log.

The *Output* directory is where the linked result, such as your EXE file will go. You should set that to your *Game* directory for the release configuration and the *Test* directory for other configurations. There is one alternative suggestion I like as well, which stores the final build result in a directory named for the build configuration and platform. You do have to set the working directory for debugging, and you might want to create a post-build step for your release build so that your *Game* directory always has what it needs to be instantly published, but that's a minor inconvenience. The $(OutDir) macro can then be used to store any build output file you want to live in your *Output* directories.

Since you store the final build result in separate directories for each platform and build configuration, you can set the output filename in the linker settings to $(OutDir)/$(TargetName)$(TargetExt) for all build configurations and all platforms.

**Rename Your Build Targets So They Exist in the Same Directory**

You can distinguish the debug, profile, and release files by adding a "d" or a "p" to the end of any final build target. You could also use the $(ConfigurationName) macro if you wanted absolute clarity. If for any reason the files need to coexist in the same directory, you don't have to worry about copying them or creating temporary names.

With the target directories set right, Visual Studio has some macros you can use in your project settings.

- **$(IntDir):** The path to intermediate files
- **$(OutDir):** The path to the output directory
- **$(TargetDir):** The path to the primary output file
- **$(TargetName):** The name of the primary output file of the build without the extension
- **$(TargetPath):** The fully qualified path and filename for the output file
- **$(Configuration):** Set to the name of your current configuration, such as Debug or Release

Use these macros for the following settings for all build configurations:

- **Debugging/Debugging Command:** $(TargetPath) will call the right executable for each build target
- **Debugging/Working Directory:** Should be set to your *Game* directory
- **C/C++/Precompiled Headers/Precompiled Header File:** $(IntDir)$(TargetName).pch
- **C/C++/Output Files:** $(IntDir) for the ASM list location, object filename, and program database filename
- **Linker/Debug Settings/Generate Program Database File:** $(TargetDir)$(TargetName).pdb
- **Linker/Debug Settings/Map File:** $(TargetDir)$(TargetName).map

**Some Notes About Changing Default Directories in Visual Studio**

There are plenty of third-party tools that work with Visual Studio. Most of them make the same assumptions about project default directories that Visual Studio does. They'll still work with my suggested directory structure, but you'll have to tweak the search directories for source code and symbol files.

The macros also help to keep the differences between the build targets to a minimum. For example, $(IntDir) can stand for *..\Temp\x64Debug* or *..\Temp \Win32Release* because they are the same in all build targets, and they don't disappear when you choose All Configurations in the project settings dialog.

## Multiplatform Projects

If you happen to be lucky enough, or unlucky enough, to work on a multiplatform project, you'll see that the previous strategy works great for multiplatform projects. Multiplatform projects usually have files that are common to all platforms and platform-specific files, too. The general idea is to keep all the common files together and create parallel directories for the platform-dependent stuff.

You'll need to install the platform-specific SDK before Visual Studio will recognize the new project platform. Your platform SDK will usually have instructions for this if it is compatible with Visual Studio, but most of the console manufacturers have SDKs that are compatible, so even if you are working on the Nintendo Wii you can still use Visual Studio to do your work.

Once the platform SDK is installed, you can add the platform to your solution by opening the Configuration Manager from the Build menu. Then for each project, drop down the platform choice and choose New. You should be able to select the new platform (see Figure 4.3).

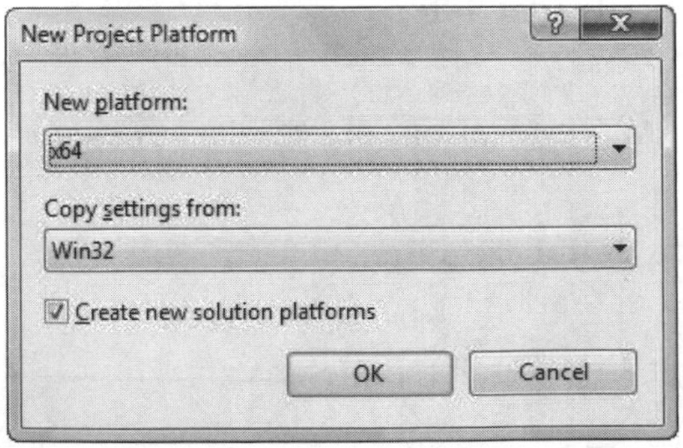


**Figure 4.3**
Adding a new platform configuration to your project.

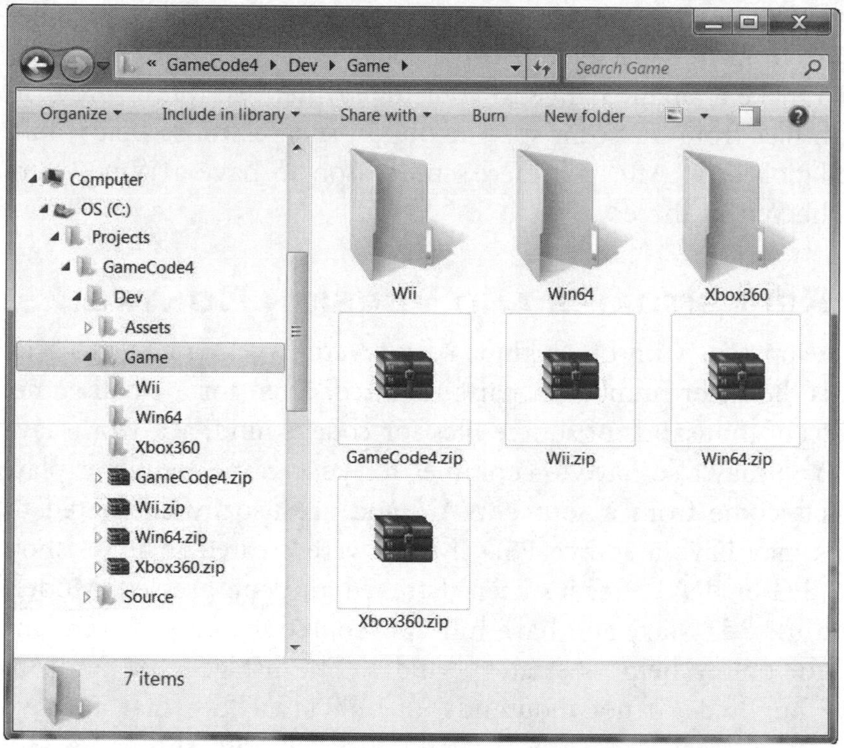


**Figure 4.4**
Platform Directory V2.

You can use the $(PlatformName) macro in your properties settings to keep platform-specific intermediate and output files nice and neat.

As far as how you should change your directory structure, Figure 4.4 shows how to set up a Win32/Xbox360/Wii multiplatform structure.

Take a look at Figure 4.4. The project root is *C:\Projects\GameCode4\Dev*. That directory stores the familiar *Game*, *Assets*, *Source*, and *Test* directories I mentioned earlier. There are two accommodations for platform-dependent files and directories. First, there is a special platform-dependent directory for each platform. These directories will hold executables and DLLs. The *Game* directory holds both the common files and platform-dependent files, named for what they contain. *GameCode4.zip* stores cooked game assets common to all platforms, and there are platform-specific files as well. Basically, you follow the same rules as before—make it easy to find and filter your files based on what you want—in this case, by platform.

During development you'll want the convenience of having all the platforms side-by-side, which keeps you from making tons of copies of the common files for every platform. You'll need to make a small change to your deployment script, in order to strip unwanted platform files from platform-specific builds, such as those that would get burned to an installation disk. After all, there's no reason to have a Win32 version of your game on the Wii, is there?

## Source Code Repositories and Version Control

In comparing game development with other kinds of software development projects, what really stands out is the sheer number of parts required. Even for a small game, you may have many tens of thousands of source files for code, sound, art, world layout, scripts, and more. You may also have to cook files for your game engine or platform. Most sound effects come from a source WAV and are usually converted to OGG or MP3. Textures may have a source PSD if they were created in Photoshop and have a companion JPG or PNG after it's been flattened and compressed. Models have a MAX file (if you use 3ds Max) and have multiple source textures. You might also have HTML files for online help or strategy guides. The list goes on and on. Even small games have hundreds, if not thousands, of individual files that all have to be created, checked, fixed, rechecked, tracked, and installed into the game. Big games will frequently have hundreds of thousands of files, or even millions

Back in the old days, the source files for a big project were typically spread all over the place. Some files were stored on a network (if you knew where to look), but most were scattered in various places on desktop computers, never to be seen again after the project finished. Unfortunately, these files were frequently lost or destroyed while the project was in production. The artist or programmer would have to grudgingly re-create his work, a hateful task at best.

### The Flame

When I first arrived at Origin Systems, I noticed some odd labels taped to people's monitors. One said, "The Flame of the Map" and another "The Flame of Conversation." I thought these phrases were Origin's version of Employee of the Month, but I was wrong. This was source control in the days of "sneaker net," when Origin didn't even have a local area network. If someone wanted to work on something, he physically walked to the machine that was the "Flame of Such and Such" and copied the relevant files onto a floppy disk, stole the flame label, and went back to his machine. Then he became the "Flame." When a build was assembled for QA, everyone carried his floppy disks to the build computer and copied all the flames to one place. Believe it or not, this system worked fairly well.

Many years later, I was working on a small project, and one afternoon a panicked teammate informed me that our development server went down and no one could work. We were only two days away from a milestone, and the team thought we were doomed. "Nonsense!" I said, as I created a full list of our development files and posted them outside my office. I reintroduced our team to SneakerNet—and they used a pencil to "check out" a file from the list and a diskette to move the latest copy of the file from my desktop to theirs where they could work on it.

We made our milestone, and no files were lost or destroyed. Sometimes an old way of doing something isn't so bad after all.

---

Source control management is a common process used by game development teams everywhere. Game development is simply too hard and too risky to manage without it. Nonprogrammers find source control systems unwieldy and will complain for a while, but they will get used to it pretty quickly. Even 3ds Max has plug-ins for source control systems so everyone on the team can use it.

Outside of source control, many companies choose to track these bits and pieces with the help of a database, showing what state the asset is in and whether it is ready to be installed in the game. Source control repositories can help you manage who is working on something, but they aren't that good at tracking whether something is "good enough" to be in the game. For that, you don't need anything more than an Excel spreadsheet to keep a list of each file, who touched it last, what's in the file, and why it is important to your game. You could also write a little PHP/MySQL portal site and put a complete content management intranet up on your local network to track files.

To help you put your own version control process in place, I'll introduce you to some of the more popular version control tools that professional game developers use in their practices, I'll also tell you which ones to avoid. Of course, keep in mind that there is no perfect, one-size-fits-all tool or solution. The important thing is that you put some type of process together and that you do it at the beginning of any project.

## A Little History—Visual SourceSafe from Microsoft

Visual SourceSafe is the source repository that was distributed with Microsoft's Visual Studio until the 2010 release, and it is an excellent example of "You get what you pay for." What attracted most people to this product was an easy-to-use GUI interface and an extremely simple setup. You can be up and running on SourceSafe in 10 minutes if you don't type slowly.

The biggest problem with SourceSafe is how it stores the source repository. If you dig a bit into the shared files where the repository is stored, you'll find a data directory with a huge tree of files with odd names like *AAAAAAAB.AAA* and

*AAACCCAA.AAB*. The contents of these files are clear text, or nearly, so this wacky naming scheme couldn't have been for security reasons. If anyone out there knows why they did it this way, drop me an email. I'm completely stumped.

Each file stores information of how the file changed from revision to revision. Specifically, the information was in "reverse delta" form, so that if you had the most recent file, you could apply the next most recent reverse delta to re-create the previous revision. Every revision of a file will create a new SourceSafe file with one of those wacky names. For those of you paying attention, you'll remember that many of these files will be pretty small, given that some source changes could be as simple as a single character change. The amount of network drive space taken up by SourceSafe is pretty unacceptable in my humble opinion.

There's also a serious problem with speed. Even small projects get to be a few hundred files in size, and large projects can be tens or even hundreds of thousands of files. Because SourceSafe stores its data files in the repository directory structure, access time for opening and closing all these files is quite long, and programmers can wait forever while simply checking to see if they have the most recent files. Source-Safe doesn't support branching (see my discussion on branching a little later) unless you make a complete copy of the entire tree you are branching. Ludicrous!

Forget attempting to access SourceSafe remotely. Searching thousands of files over a pokey Internet connection is murder. Don't even try it over a high-bandwidth line. Finally, SourceSafe's file index database can break down, and even the little analyzer utility will throw up its hands and tell you to start over. I've finished projects under a corrupted database before, but it just happened that the corruption was affecting a previous version of a file that I didn't need. I was lucky.

SourceSafe also has a habit of corrupting itself, making your entire repository a useless pile of unfathomable files. This is especially true when you store large binary assets like sounds, textures, and video.

If I haven't convinced you to try something other than SourceSafe, let me just say it: Don't use it. I've heard rumors that Microsoft doesn't use it, so why should you?

## Subversion and TortoiseSVN

Subversion is a free source repository available at http://subversion.tigris.org. It uses a command-line interface, which can give some nonprogrammers heartburn when using it. Luckily, you can also download TortoiseSVN, a GUI that integrates with Windows Explorer. It is available at http://tortoisesvn.tigris.org. Both are free, easy to set up and administer, and a great choice for a development team on a budget.

The system stores the file state on the local machine, which makes it trivial to work on files even if you have no network access. You just work on them and tell the Subversion server when you are ready to commit them to the server. If anyone else made modifications with you in parallel, the system will let you merge the changes so that everyone's changes will be present in the file, preserving everyone's work. This is typically done automatically when the changes are far apart in the file, but a special editor can be used to see all the changes in parallel so that conflicting changes can be integrated by hand.

Complaints about the system generally fall into the speed and scalability category. If you are working on a large game with a huge directory structure and tens of thousands of assets, you would be wise to consider something else, such as Perforce.

I developed this edition of the book, and all the source code in it, under Subversion. So if you are reading this now and can play with the source code, I guess Subversion worked just fine. Google Code also uses Subversion—and they store plenty.

## Perforce by Perforce Software

My favorite commercial product in this category is Perforce. I've used this product for years, and it's never let me down. For any of you lucky enough to move from SourceSafe to Perforce, the first thing you'll notice is its speed. It's damn fast.

Perforce uses a client/server architecture and a Btrieve-based database for storing the repository. Btrieve is an extremely efficient data storage and retrieval engine that powers Pervasive's SQL software. That architecture simply blows the pants off anything that uses the network directory hierarchy. More than storing the current status of each version of each file, it even stores the status of each file for everyone who has a client connection. That's why most SourceSafe slaves freak out when they use Perforce the first time; it's so fast they don't believe it's actually doing anything. Of course, this makes remote access as fast as it can possibly be.

**Don't Forget to Ask Perforce's Permission**

Since Perforce "knows" the status of any file on your system, you have to be careful if you change a file while you are away from your network connection and you can't connect to the Perforce server to "check out" a file. Since Perforce knows nothing of the change, it will simply complain later that a local file is marked read/write, so while it won't blow away your changes, it also doesn't go out of its way to remind you that you've done anything. SourceSafe actually does local data/time comparisons, so it will tell you that the local file is different than the network copy. Subversion stores your local file status locally, so it is much faster than SourceSafe.

Perforce has a nice GUI for anyone who doesn't want to use the command line. The GUI will perform about 99 percent of the tasks you ever need to perform, so you can leave the command line to someone who knows what they're doing. Even better, Perforce integrates with Windows Explorer, and you can edit and submit files just by right-clicking them. Artists love that kind of thing.

The branching mechanisms are extremely efficient. When you create a branch from your main line of development to a test line, Perforce only keeps the deltas from the original branch to the new branch. Network space is saved, and merging branches is also very fast. Subversion and others make a completely new copy of the branch, taking up enormous network storage space.

You'll find almost as many third-party tools that work with Perforce as with some of the free repositories. Free downloads are available, including tools that perform graphical merges, C++ APIs, conversion tools from other products like SourceSafe, Subversion, and tons of others.

**Perforce + Visual SourceSafe = Chaos**

When I worked for Ion Storm, the programmers used Perforce, but everyone else used Visual SourceSafe. What a fiasco! The content tree that stored art, game levels, and sounds would always be a little "off" from the source code in Perforce. If you even had to check in a change that required a parallel change to content, you had to practically halt the entire team and tell everyone to do this massive refresh from the network. This was simply horrible and wasted an amazing amount of time. Don't screw around—make sure that you get source code control licenses for everyone on your development team: Programmers, artists, and everyone else who touches your game should all use the same source control software

## AlienBrain from Avid

For those of you with really serious asset tracking problems and equally serious budgets, there's a pretty good solution out there that will track your source code and other assets: AlienBrain from Avid. They have a huge client list that looks like a who's who of the computer game industry. Their software integrates with nearly every tool out there: CodeWarrior, Visual Studio, 3ds Max, Maya, Photoshop, and many others.

AlienBrain is somewhat more expensive than Perforce, but it has some features Perforce doesn't have. AlienBrain is used by game developers, filmmakers, and big iron simulation developers who have to track much more than source code. They've also made some serious strides in the last few versions to improve performance and bring better branching to their software that better matches other software. They also have some excellent production pipeline helpers in their software, so files can be reviewed and approved after they are checked in.

Programmers and "build gurus" will like the fact that AlienBrain has sophisticated branching and pinning mechanisms just like the more advanced source code repositories on the market. (I'll discuss the importance of branching in the next section.) Artists and other contributors will actually use this product, unlike others that are mainly designed to integrate well with Visual Studio and not creative applications such as Photoshop and 3D Studio Max. One of the big drawbacks of other products is their rather naive treatment of nontext files. AlienBrain was written with these files in mind. They have some great features to track peer review in art files, for example.

## Using Source Control Branches

I freely admit that up until 2001 I didn't use branching. I also admit that I didn't really know what it was for, but it also wasn't my fault. I blame Microsoft. Their Visual SourceSafe tool is distributed with Visual Studio, and some engineers use it without question, as I did for many years. Microsoft software, like Office, has hundreds of thousands of source files and many hundreds of engineers. It turns out that SourceSafe was never designed to handle repositories of that size and certainly wasn't designed to account for the tricky problem of trying to get each one of those engineers and the files they changed every day to be ready at a moment's notice to build the entire, massive project without any errors caused by incompatibilities. Those readers who have worked on even a modest-size project will know that, on any given morning, when you grab the latest code from everyone's work the previous day, more often than not it doesn't even compile, much less link and run. This problem is compounded when the test department needs a build to test and needs it right away. Luckily, there's a solution.

*Branching* is a process where an entire source code repository is copied so that parallel development can proceed unhindered on both copies simultaneously. Sometimes the copies are merged back into one tree. It is equally possible that after being branched, the branched versions diverge entirely and are never merged. Why is branching so important? Branches of any code imply a fundamental change in the development of that code. You might branch source code to create a new game. You might also branch source code to perform some heavy research where your changes won't affect anyone else's. Sometimes a fundamental change, such as swapping out one rendering engine for another or coding a new object culling mechanism, is too dangerous to attempt where everyone else is working. If you make a new branch, you'll wall off your precious main code line, usually called the "trunk."

You'll have a nice sandbox to play in and get the benefits of source control for every source file.

SourceSafe's branching mechanism, and I use that term loosely, makes a complete copy of the entire source tree. That's slow and fat. Most decent repositories keep track of only the deltas from branch to branch. This approach is much faster, and it doesn't penalize you for branching the code.

Here are the branches I use and why:

- **Trunk:** Normal development branch
- **Sandbox:** A "playground" branch where anything goes, including trashing it entirely—the branch typically includes the name of the person or team that owns it—so you might see *Sandbox-MrMike* or *Sandbox-NewPhysicsEngine*
- **Gold:** The branch submitted for milestone approvals or release

The Sandbox and Gold branches originate from the Trunk branch. Changes in these branches may or may not be merged with the Trunk branch, depending on what happens to the code. The Trunk branch supports the main development effort; almost all of your development effort will happen in the Trunk branch.

The Sandbox branch supports experimental efforts. It's a great place to make some core API changes, swap in new middleware, or make any other crazy change without damaging the Trunk or slowing development there. The Gold branch is the stable branch that has your last, or next, milestone submission. Programmers can code fast and furious in the Trunk, while minor tweaks and bug fixes needed for milestone approval are tucked into the Gold branch.

Perhaps the best evidence for branching code can be found in how a team works under research and release scenarios. Consider a programming team about to reach a major milestone. The milestone is attached to a big chunk of cash, which is only paid out if the milestone is approved. Say this team is old-fashioned and doesn't know anything about branching.

Just before the build, the lead programmer runs around and makes everyone on the team promise not to check on any code while the build is compiling. Everyone promises to keep their work to themselves, and everyone continues to work on their own machines.

Most likely the build doesn't even compile the first time. One of the programmers might have forgotten to check in some new files or simply gotten sloppy and checked in work that didn't compile. By the time the lead programmer figures out who can fix the build, the programmer at fault may have already started work on other things, which now may have to be reverted to get the build working again. This is a big waste of time. While all of this is going on, another programmer is frustrated because he can't begin making major changes to the AI code since it might need a tweak to make the build work, too. Getting the build to become stable with everyone working in one branch basically shuts everyone down until the build is complete, which can take more than a day in some cases.

But the problems don't stop there. Let's assume the completed build is going to be tested by a remote test team, and the build takes hours to upload to their FTP site. By the time the build is uploaded and then grabbed by the test team, it could be two days. If the test team finds a problem that halts testing, the whole process starts again, with the whole development team hobbled until testing gives the green light. This whole process could take two to three days or more.

If you don't think this is that bad, you are probably working without branches and have trained yourself to enjoy this little hellish scenario. You've probably developed coping mechanisms that you call "process" instead of what they are, which is crazy. I used to do the same thing because I thought branches were too much trouble and too confusing. Until I tried them myself.

Let's look at the same scenario from the perspective of a team that uses branches.

The lead programmer walks around and makes sure the team has all the milestone changes checked in. She goes to the build machine and launches a milestone build. The first thing that happens is the Gold branch gets refreshed with the very latest of everything in the Trunk branch. The build finishes with the same failure as before—compile errors due to missing files. The programmer responsible simply checks the missing files into both the Trunk branch and the Gold branch, and everything continues without delay. The AI programmer mentioned previously continues working without worry, since all of his changes will happen in the Trunk branch, safely away from the Gold branch.

The finished build is checked and sent to the testing group via the same FTP site, and it still takes almost eight hours. When the build gets just as hosed as before, the lead programmer makes a small tweak directly in the Gold branch to get it working, and she uploads a small patch. The test team gets to work and reports a few issues, which are then fixed directly in the Gold branch and merged back into the Trunk branch. When the milestone is approved, the Gold branch has the latest and greatest version of the game, and the development team never lost a second during the entire process. They even have the bug fixes that were made in the Gold branch.

Every minute of lost development time means your game is a little less fun or a little less polished than it could be. Given the above—which team do you think is going to make the best game? My money and Metacritic are going with the team that used branches.

### Silver, Gold, and Live

A friend of mine who worked at Microsoft was in the build lab for Microsoft Office. At the time, they used three branches: a Trunk, a Silver, and a Gold. The teams would publish from Trunk to Silver when a milestone was about to be delivered, but because of the vast number and speed of changes that happened even in the Silver branch, they also published Silver to Gold when a real "version" was ready to go into final testing.

This same strategy is also used by my friends working on online games—they usually have three branches, too: Trunk, Gold, and Live. Sometimes you have to make a change directly in the Live branch to fix a critical issue right on the live servers and then propagate that change back to the Gold and Trunk branches.

### Sandbox Development

In the Sims division at EA, we all work out of sandboxes. This means that all engineers have their own branches that they do major development in. When you complete a feature, you begin the process of integrating up to the main development line. First, you publish a code review that shows the diff of every file you modified and allows other engineers on the team to comment on your work and identify potential issues. Once you've been approved to check in, you grab "the lychee," which is essentially a mutex that keeps anyone else from being able to check in. You can only have one person checking in at a time. Then you run the various unit tests followed by a smoke test, which is a series of in-game tests to ensure that you didn't break some core functionality inadvertently. (I'd be a rich man if I had a dollar for every time someone accidentally broke Sim autonomy.) Finally, you can actually submit your changes into the development line and release the lychee. This might seem like an overly complex system, but breaking the build on a Sims game means you've just stopped the productivity of 180+ people. Working sandboxes also allow multiple programmers to collaborate in their own little world and have QA run vigorous testing without worrying about affecting the rest of the team.

## Building the Game: A Black Art?

You can't build a testable version of your game by simply grabbing the latest source code and launching the compiler. Most games have multiple gigabytes of data, install programs, multiple languages, game editors, special tools, and all manner of components that have nothing at all to do with the executable. All of these components come together in one way or another during the build. Every shred of code and data must make it onto the install image on one or more discs or on the network for the test team. Frequently, these components don't come together without a fight. On some teams, building the game is something of a black art, assigned to the most senior code shamans. There is a much better and safer way, which you'll learn shortly.

*Ultima VIII* had a build process that was truly insane. It went something like this:

1. Grab the latest source code: editor, game, and game scripts.
2. Build the game editor.
3. Run the game editor and execute a special command that nukes the local game data files and grab the latest ones from the shared network drive.
4. Build the game.
5. Run the UNK compiler (*Ultima*'s game scripting language) to compile and link the game scripts for English. Don't ask me what UNK stands for, I really can't remember....
6. Run the UNK compiler twice more and compile the French and German game scripts.
7. Run the game and test it. Watch it break and loop back to Step 1 until the game finally works.
8. Copy the game and all the game data into a *Temp* directory.
9. Compress the game data files.
10. Build the install program.
11. Copy the English, French, and German install images to 24 floppy disks.
12. Copy the CD-ROM image to the network. (The only CD burner was on the first floor, and I worked on the third floor.)
13. Go to the first floor media lab and make three copies of each install: 72 floppy disks and three CDs. And hope like hell there are enough floppy disks.

Before you ask, I'll just tell you that the fact that the build process for *Ultima VIII* had 13 steps never sat very well with me. Each step generally failed at least twice for some dumb reason, which made building *Ultima VIII* no less than a four-hour process—on a good day.

The build was actually fairly automated with batch files. The game editor even accepted command-line parameters to perform the task of grabbing the latest map and other game data. Even so, building *Ultima VIII* was so difficult and fraught with error that I was the only person who ever successfully built a testable version of the game. That wasn't an accomplishment, it was a failure.

On one of my trips to Microsoft, I learned something about how they build Office. The build process is completely automatic. The build lab for Office has a fleet of servers that build every version of Office in every language, and they never stop. The moment a build is complete, they start again, constantly looking for compile errors introduced by someone in the last few minutes. If they find an error, the programmer is contacted via email by the build machine. Once the build is complete, automated testing begins, and if any of the automated tests fail, the build system emails the programmer responsible for the errant check-in. Office is a huge piece of software. If Microsoft can automate a build as big and complex as this, surely you can automate yours.

## Automate Your Builds

My experience has taught me that every project can and should have an automatic build. No exceptions. It's far easier (and safer) to maintain build scripts that automate the process instead of relying on a build master, whose knowledge is so arcane he might better be called a witch doctor. My suggestion is that you should try to create Microsoft's build lab in miniature on your own project. Here is what's needed:

- A build machine, or even multiple machines, if your project is big enough
- Good tools for automatic building, both from third-party sources or made on your own
- Time invested creating and maintaining automation scripts

## The Build Machine

Don't try to save a buck and use a programmer's development box as your build machine. Programmers are always downloading funky software, making operating system patches, and installing third-party development tools that suit their needs and style. A build machine should be a pristine environment that has known versions and updates for each piece of software: the operating system, compiler, internal tools, SDKs, install program, and anything else used to build the game.

#### After You Go Gold, Back Up Your Build Machine

A complete backup of the build machine is good insurance. The physical machine itself, preserved for eternity, is even better. If you need to build an old project, the backup of the build machine will have the right versions of the compiler, operating system, and other tools. New versions and patches come out often, and even a project just 12 months old can be impossible to build, even if the source code is readily available in the source code repository. Just try to build something 10 or 12 years old, and you'll see what I mean. If anyone out there has a good copy of Turbo Pascal and IBM DOS 3.3, let me know!

The build machine should be extremely fast, have loads of RAM, and have a high performance hard disk, preferably multiple hard disks with high RPM and configured with at least RAID 0 for ultimate speed. Compiling is RAM- and hard-disk–intensive, so try to get the penny-pinchers to buy a nice system. If you ever used the argument about how much money your company could save by buying fast computers for the programmers, imagine how easy it would be to buy a nice build machine. The entire test team might have to wait on a build. How much is that worth?

## Automated Build Scripts

Automated builds have been around as long as there have been makefiles and command-line compilers. I admit that I've never been good at the cryptic syntax of makefiles, which is one reason I put off automating builds. If you use Visual Studio, you might consider using the prebuild or postbuild settings to run some custom batch files or makefiles. I wouldn't, and here's why: You'll force your programmers to run the build scripts every time they build. That's probably wasteful at best, completely incorrect at worst.

Prebuild and postbuild steps should run batch files, makefiles, or other utilities that are required every time the project is built. Build scripts tend to be a little different and skew toward getting the build ready for the test department or burning to disc. As an example, the build script will always grab the latest code from the source repository and rebuild the entire project from scratch. If you forced your programmers to do that for every compile, they'd lynch you.

Batch files and makefiles are perfectly fine solutions for any build script you need. You can also write great batch files or shell scripts, since Visual Studio builds can be run from the command line. There are some better tools for those who like GUIs, such as Visual Build Pro from Kinook Software (see Figure 4.5).

This tool is better than batch files or makefiles. The clean GUI helps you understand and maintain a complicated build process with multiple tools and failure steps. The build script is hierarchical, each group possibly taking different steps if a component of the build fails. Visual Build also integrates cleanly with a wide variety of development tools and source code repositories.

Every internal tool you create should have a command-line interface. Whether the tool creates radiosity maps for your levels, calculates visibility sets, analyzes map

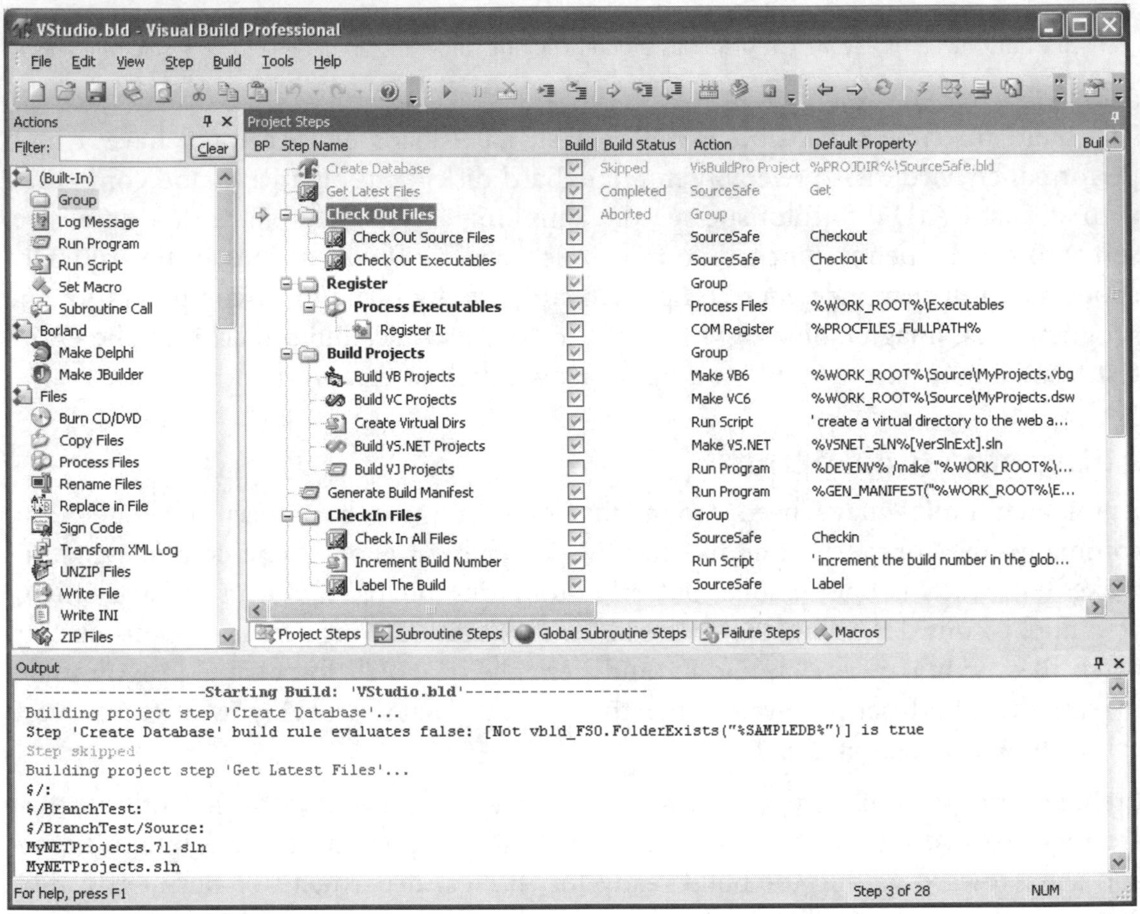


**Figure 4.5**
Visual Build from Kinook software.

data, or runs a proprietary compression technology, it must be able to take input from the command line, or you won't be able to automate your build process.

Another clever piece of software I've used at multiple companies is called Incredibuild by Xoreax Software. It takes the long process of a build and distributes it to idle machines across your network. It can take some time to set up, but you can often get up to a 20-fold decrease in your build times!

## Creating Build Scripts

You'll want to create a few build scripts for your project. Most builds will simply grab the latest code, build it, and copy the results somewhere on the network. The milestone build is a little more complicated and involves branching and merging the source code repository.

## Normal Build

The normal build script builds a clean version of the game and copies the results somewhere useful. It is run as a part of the milestone build process, but it can also run automatically at regular intervals. I suggest you run a normal build at least once per day, preferably in the wee hours of the morning, to check the code on the network for any errors. The normal build script is also useful for building ad-hoc versions of the game for the test team.

The normal build script performs the following steps:

- **Clean the build machine.** If you use the directory structure I suggested at the beginning of this chapter, you can just delete the *Temp* directory.
- **Get the latest source code and game media.** I used to recommend cleaning everything and starting from nothing, but on most games this simply takes too long. Just grab the recent files.
- **Grab the latest version number and label the build.** You can decide when to change the version number—each build or even each night. You can use the version number to specify the ultimate destination on your build server, so every build you've ever made can be available. Visual Build Pro has a utility to grab or even change the version number of Visual Studio resource files, but it's pretty easy to write one yourself. At Red Fly, the build number was increased every day and even included the changelist number of the last check-in. Bugs that are found in a particular build can be entered into the bug database, and even if a programmer sees it days later, he can know fairly reliably if the bug is a new one or the fix just didn't make it into the latest build.
- **Compile and link every build target: debug, profile, and release.** The project settings will make sure that everything goes into the right place.
- **Run automatic test scripts.** If you have automated testing, have the build machine run the test scripts to see if the build is a good one. This is more reliable than a bleary-eyed programmer attempting to test the game at 4 a.m.
- **Process and copy the build results.** The *destination* directory should use the code name of the project and the version number to distinguish it from other projects or other versions of the same project. For example, version 2.0.8.25 of the Rainman project might go into *E:\Builds\Rainman\2.0.8.25.* The nightly build of the same project might go into *E:\Builds\Rainman\Nightly.* If you have multiple platforms to worry about, stick them in directories that are easy to find —*\E:\Builds\Rainman\Nightly\3DS.*

**Scripts Can't Update Themselves While They Are Running**

If you're paying attention, you'll realize that the build scripts themselves should be checked to make sure they haven't changed. If the build script is running, how can it clean itself off the build machine and get itself from the source code repository? It can't, at least not easily. If you standardize your projects with a single directory structure, it's better to create a master build script that works for any project. Project-specific build commands are put into a special build script that lives in the same directory as the project files. The master build script should only change when the build process for every project is changed—something that should be extremely rare.

A nightly build process is actually trivial to set up if you have your automated build working—just set up a scheduled task on the build machine. For Windows, you can create a scheduled task by going into the Control Panel, run Administrative Tools, and run the Task Scheduler. The wizard will take you through the steps of defining when and how often to run it. If you happen to be a Linux person, look up the cron command. Usually, it's a good idea to copy the results of the build to your network where everyone can grab it.

## Milestone Build

Milestone builds add more steps to the beginning and end of the build since they involve branching the code. They also involve an approval process that takes days or weeks instead of minutes, so the build process has an "open," a "create," and a "close" script to manage the branches and make sure that any changes that happen during approval get back into the Trunk branch.

**No Build Automation = Madness**

At Origin Systems, we didn't do anything special for milestone builds on the *Ultima* projects. Some unlucky programmer, usually me, launched the build on his desktop machine, and after plenty of cursing and a few hours, the new version was ready to test. The other programmers kept adding features and bugs as fast as the test team could sign off old features. New code and features would break existing code—stuff the test team approved. The bugs would pile up, and it was difficult to figure out if the project was making any progress. To minimize the pain of this process, it was usually done in the middle of the night when most of the developers had gone home.

The projects I've been on since then were entirely different, mostly due to ditching SourceSafe and using branches. Our source code repository, Perforce, had excellent branching and merging capabilities. The programming team resisted at first, but they quickly saw that milestone builds were linked directly to their paychecks. A few milestones later, everyone wondered how we ever developed projects without branching.

Every project should have a Trunk branch and a Gold branch. Every source code repository does this a little differently. When a milestone build is launched, the first thing that happens is the Gold branch gets a fresh copy of the Main branch. The branches are synchronized without merging, which means that the entire Main branch is simply copied to the Gold branch, making them identical. Make sure that the Gold branch doesn't have any unintegrated changes you want to keep! That usually requires a little human supervision—that is one bit that you probably shouldn't automate. The build machine runs the build scripts from the Gold branch to make the milestone build. This implies that the Trunk and Gold branches can exist on the same machine at the same time. This is true.

Most source code repositories allow a greater degree of freedom for each client to configure how it views the contents of the repository. It's pretty easy to configure the client to put all the Trunk branches of the Rainman project into a *D:\Projects\Rainman\Trunk* directory and all the Gold branches into *D:\Projects\Rainman\Gold*. The build scripts can even use a branch macro to figure out which branch needs building.

After the milestone build is assembled, it should be packaged and sent to testing. In our case, this meant ZIPing up the entire build and putting it on our FTP site so Microsoft's test department could grab it.

### Old Advice Turned Out to Be Dumb Advice

In the first and second editions of this book, I advised readers to use monolithic ZIP or RAR files to package their entire build and FTP that one file. This turns out to be a horrible idea. I was working on a project that had to upload a multigigabyte file, and when the FTP failed seven hours into the upload, we had to start all over. Contrary to intelligence, some top 20 publishers use old-fashioned FTP systems with no ability to restart bad transfers. Instead of monolithic files, use volumed RAR/PAR files. Most RAR tools can split a monolithic RAR file into smaller volumes, each of which may only be a few hundred megabytes. The PAR files can be used to actually rebuild a corrupted file on the receiving end, saving both parties a ton of time.

Teams almost never submit milestone builds that are approved with no changes. Most of the time, testing will require some changes, both major and minor. Any of these changes should happen in your Gold branch. You can then rebuild the Gold branch and resubmit it to your testing group. This process continues until the test team is satisfied. The Gold branch is then merged to the Trunk branch. This is usually an automatic process, but sometimes merge conflicts force a human to stare at the changes and merge them.

The two additional scripts you'll need to build and manage your changes in a multi-branch environment are Open and Close. Here's an outline of what you'll want in the Open script:

- Get the latest files in the Trunk branch.
- Unlock the Gold branch and revert any modified files.
- Force-integrate from Trunk to Gold.
- Submit the Gold branch.

You may notice a command to unlock the Gold branch. More on that in a moment. Take a look at the Close script:

- Get the latest files in the Gold branch.
- Integrate from Gold to Trunk.
- Resolve all changes.
- Submit the Trunk branch and the Gold branch.
- Lock the Gold branch from all changes.

The integration commands are expected, but if you look at the last two lines of the Close phase, you'll see that the Gold branch is locked so that no one can change it. The Open phase unlocks the files and reverts any changes. Why bother? This makes absolutely sure that the Gold branch is only open for changes during milestone approval. If no milestone build is in test, there should be no reason to change the Gold branch.

This has an added side effect: Anyone who wants the latest approved milestone build can simply grab the code in the Gold branch and build the game. This is especially useful if the odd executive or representative of the press wants to see a demo. Even if the last build is missing from the network, you can always re-create it by building the Gold branch.

### Builds Were Tough on *Thief: Deadly Shadows*

On *Thief: Deadly Shadows*, there was an unfortunate problem in the build process that no automation could possibly fix. Since the project was really large, and there was no automated testing, the test team would only get new builds every couple of days. It would take them that long just to be sure they could send the latest version to the entire test team. The problem was that the new build was launched at fairly random times, and the development team was never given much if any notice.

Now, I know what you're thinking. If every submission to the source repository were individually checked, then a new build should be able to launch at any time without error. Wrong! The builds took days to perform because there was little, if any, integration testing on the part of programmers—mostly because doing so really took a very long time, and not every programmer had an Xbox development kit to test with. They simply tested their own stuff in quick, isolated tests on whichever platform they had handy. This rarely caught the odd problems due to integration flaws, and these problems accumulated between builds. The solution? Give the developers a little notice—at least a few hours—and get them to run some more serious integration tests of their own before the build. That, and for goodness sake, create some automated testing and run it nightly.

## Multiple Projects and Shared Code

It's difficult to share code between multiple projects if the shared code is still under rapid development. Two different teams will eventually be in different stages of development because it is unlikely they both will have the same project schedule. Eventually, one team will need to make a change to the shared code that no one else wants.

There are a couple of different cases you should consider:

- One team needs to put a "hack" in the shared code to make a milestone quickly, and the other team wants to code the "real" solution.
- One team is close to shipping and has started a total code lockdown. No one can change anything. The other team needs to make modifications to the shared code to continue development.

How do you deal with this sticky problem? Branching, of course.

In the case of the scenario where two project teams need to share a common game engine, the game engine has three branches:

- **Trunk:** The normal development branch
- **Gold_Project_A:** The Gold branch for the first project
- **Gold_Project_B:** The Gold branch for the second project

While both projects are in normal development, they both make changes to the shared engine code in the Trunk branch. If either project goes into a milestone approval phase, they fix milestone blockers in the Gold branch for their project. Since they each get their own Gold branch, both projects can be in approval simultaneously without worrying about each other. If they happen to be broken in exactly the same way, you can always make the change in the Trunk branch and integrate that single change forward to both Gold branches—it's totally up to you. After their milestone has been approved, the changes get merged back into the Trunk. When either project hits code lockdown, meaning that only a few high-priority changes are being made to the code, the project stays in the Gold branch until it ships.

All this work assumes the two teams are motivated to share the game engine and continually contribute to its improvement. There might be a case for one project permanently branching the shared code, in which case it should get its own code line apart from the Trunk branch of the original shared code. If the changes are minor, and they should be, it's trivial to merge any two arbitrary code lines, as long as they originated from an original source. Even if you got unlucky and the changes were overhauls, the difficulty of the merge is preferable to making huge changes in your Trunk while trying to satisfy a milestone. Best to leave this activity in its own branch.

## Some Parting Advice

This chapter has likely shown you that there is a lot of drudgery on any software project, and games are no exception. Back in the dark ages, I built game projects by typing in commands at the command prompt and checking boxes on a sheet of paper. Since most of this work happened way after midnight, I made tons of mistakes. Some of these mistakes wasted time in heroic amounts—mostly because the test team had a broken build on their hands, courtesy of a decaffeinated or just exhausted Mike McShaffry.

Without using branching techniques, the whole development team had to tiptoe around their changes during a build. Moving targets are much harder to hit. Every game developer takes a long time to get in a good zone. If you break anyone's concentration by halting progress to do a build, you lose valuable time.

My parting advice: Always automate the monkey work, give the test team a good build every time, and never ever get in the way of a developer in the zone.

# Chapter 5

*by Mike McShaffry*

# Game Initialization and Shutdown

There are a million little details about writing games that no one talks about. Lots of books and websites can teach you how to draw textured polygons in Direct3D. But when it comes to figuring out your initialization sequence, you'll find little discussion. Most programmers hack something together over time that eventually turns into a horrible mess.

I've written this chapter to show you the ins and outs of the entire initialization and shutdown sequence. As you check out the code in this chapter, keep in mind that every game is different and may require a different initialization sequence. Hopefully, you'll gain an understanding of the approach presented here and be able to adapt it to your particular situation. Truly elegant solutions and algorithms rarely just fall out of the sky. They usually come to you after seeing some code that is close to what you need, and you push it the rest of the way yourself.

Every piece of software, including games, has initialization, the core or main loop, and shutdown. Initialization prepares your canvas for painting pixels. The main loop accepts and translates user input, changes the game state, and renders the game state until the loop is broken. This loop is broken by a user quitting the game or some other kind of failure. The cleanup code releases key system resources, closes files, and exits back to the operating system.

This chapter deals with initialization and shutdown. Chapter 7, "Controlling the Main Loop," will dig a little deeper and show you how to control the main loop of your game.

## Initialization 101

Initializing games involves performing setup tasks in a particular order, especially on Windows platforms. Initialization tasks for Windows games are a superset of console games due to more unpredictable hardware and OS configuration. Of course, every platform will be different, and to cover even a few of them is beyond the scope of this book. If you see how this is done in a more complicated system such as Windows, you'll have a jump start on doing this for other platforms.

There are some tasks you must perform before creating your window, and others that must have a valid window handle (or `HWND`) and therefore happen after you create your window. Initialization tasks for a Windows game should happen in this order:

- Check system resources: hard drive space, memory, input and output devices.
- Check the CPU speed.
- Initialize your main random number generator (this was covered in Chapter 3).
- Load programmer's options for debugging purposes.
- Initialize your memory cache.
- Create your window.
- Initialize the audio system.
- Load the player's game options and saved game files.
- Create your drawing surface.
- Perform initialization for game systems: physics, AI, and so on.

## Some C++ Initialization Pitfalls

Before we work through our initialization checklist, let's get some critical initialization pitfalls out of the way, starting with the misuse of C++ constructors. I've heard that power corrupts, and absolute power corrupts absolutely. You might get some disagreement from Activision's executives on this point. I'll prove it to you by showing you some problems with going too far using C++ constructors to perform initialization. It turns out that C++ constructors are horrible at initializing game objects, especially if you declare your C++ objects globally.

Programming in C++ gives you plenty of options for initializing objects and subsystems. Since the constructor runs when an object comes into scope, you might believe that you can write your initialization code like this:

```
// Main.cpp - initialization using globals
//
```

```
DataFiles g_DataFiles;
AudioSystem g_AudioSystem;
VideoSystem g_VideoSystem;

int main(void)
{
  bool done = false;
  while (! done)
  {
    // imagine a cool main loop here
  }
  return 0;
}
```

The global objects in this source code example are all complicated objects that could encapsulate some game subsystems. The fledgling game programmer might briefly enjoy the elegant look of this code, but that love affair will be quite short lived. When any of these initialization tasks fail, and they will, there's no easy way to recover.

I'm not talking about using exception handling as a recovery mechanism. Rather, I'm suggesting that any problem with initialization should give the player a chance to do something about it, such as wiping the peanut butter off the DVD. To do this, you need a user interface of some kind, and depending on where the failure happens, your user interface might not be initialized yet.

Global objects under C++ are initialized before the entry point, in this case `main(void)`. One problem with this is ordering; you can't control the order in which global objects are instantiated. Sometimes the objects are instantiated in the order of the link, but you can't count on that being the case with all compilers, and even if it were predictable, you shouldn't count on it. What makes this problem worse is that since C++ constructors have no return value, you are forced to do something ugly to find out if anything went wrong. The wise programmer will inform his game players about what has gone wrong so they can have some possibility of fixing the problem. The simpler alternative of failing and dropping back to the operating system with some lame error message is sure to provoke a strong reaction.

If you want to inform the player, you might want to do it with a simple dialog box. This assumes that you've already initialized the systems that make the dialog box function: video, user interface, data files that contain the button art, font system, and so on. This is certainly not always possible. What if your nosey game player hacked into the art data files and screwed them up? You won't have any button art to display your nice dialog box telling hackers they've screwed themselves. You have no choice but to use the system UI, such as the standard message box under Windows. It's better than nothing.

**Initialize Your String Subsystem Early**

Initialize your text cache, or whatever you use to store text strings, very early. You can present any errors about initialization failures in the right language. If the initialization of the text cache fails, present an error with a number. It's easier for foreign language speakers almost anywhere in the world to use the number to find a solution from a customer service person or a website.

Global object pointers are much better than global objects. Singleton objects, such as the instantiation of the class that handles the audio system or perhaps your application object, are naturally global, and if you're like me, you hate passing pointers or references to these objects in every single method call from your entry point to the lowest-level code. Declare global pointers to these objects, initialize them when you're good and ready, and free them under your complete control. Here's an example of a more secure way to initialize:

```
// Main.cpp - initialization using pointers to global objects
//
// A useful macro
#define SAFE_DELETE(p)  { if (p) { delete (p); (p)=NULL; } }

DataFiles *gp_DataFiles = NULL;
AudioSystem *gp_AudioSystem = NULL;
VideoSystem *gp_VideoSystem = NULL;

int main(void)
{
  gp_DataFiles = new DataFiles();
  if ( (NULL==gp_DataFiles) || (!gp_DataFiles->Initialized() ) )
  {
    printf("The data files are somehow screwed.");
    return 1;
  }
  gp_AudioSystem = new AudioSystem();
  if ( (NULL==gp_AudioSystem) || (!gp_AudioSystem ->Initialized() ) )
  {
    printf("The audio system is somehow screwed.")
    return 1;
  }
  gp_VideoSystem = new VideoSystem();
  if ( (NULL==gp_VideoSystem) || (!gp_VideoSystem ->Initialized() ) )
  {
```

```
    printf("The video system is screwed.");
    return 1;
  }
  bool done = false;
  while (! done)
  {
    // imagine a cool main loop here
  }

  SAFE_DELETE(gp_VideoSystem);      // AVOID DEADLOCK!!!
  SAFE_DELETE(gp_AudioSystem);
  SAFE_DELETE(gp_DataFiles);
  return 0;
}
```

Note that the objects are released in the reverse order in which they were instantiated. This is no mistake, and it is a great practice whenever you need to grab a bunch of resources of different kinds in order to do something. In multithreaded operating systems with limited resources, *deadlock* occurs when two threads can't do their work because each has a resource the other needs. You can avoid deadlock by allocating and deallocating your resources in this way. You'll learn more about deadlock in Chapter 20, "Introduction to Multiprogramming." Computers are very patient and will happily wait until the sun explodes. Get in the habit of programming with that problem in mind, even if your code will never run on an operating system where that will be a problem. It's a great habit, and you'll avoid some nasty bugs.

## The Game's Application Layer

We're now ready to work our way through the initialization checklist. We'll create the class for your application layer, a very Windows-specific thing. The application layer would be completely rewritten for different operating systems, such as Linux, or consoles like the Wii. The application layer class is instantiated as a global singleton object and is referred to throughout your code through a pointer. It is constructed globally, too, since it has to be there from the entry point to the program termination.

### `WinMain`: The Windows Entry Point

The GameCode4 framework sets its Windows entry point to the function below; this is the code that will begin executing after any global constructor code is finishing running. It sets up calls for DirectX to work properly, runs the initialization sequence, enters the main loop, and runs any shutdown code after the main loop exits.

I've decided to use the DirectX Framework for rendering, mostly because it handles all of the pain and suffering of dealing with running a DirectX-based application under Windows, especially drawing fonts and dialog boxes. Take a quick look at the code in one of the source files in the DirectX Framework, *DXUT.cpp*, sometime, and you'll see exactly what I mean! The following code can be found in *Source\GameCode.cpp*:

```
INT WINAPI GameCode4(HINSTANCE hInstance,
                     HINSTANCE hPrevInstance,
                     LPWSTR    lpCmdLine,
                     int       nCmdShow)
{
  // Set up checks for memory leaks.
  int tmpDbgFlag = _CrtSetDbgFlag(_CRTDBG_REPORT_FLAG);
  // always perform a leak check just before app exits.
  tmpDbgFlag |= _CRTDBG_LEAK_CHECK_DF;
  _CrtSetDbgFlag(tmpDbgFlag);

  Logger::Init("logging.xml");
  g_pApp->m_Options.Init("PlayerOptions.xml", lpCmdLine);

  DXUTSetCallbackD3D11DeviceAcceptable(GameCodeApp::IsD3D11DeviceAcceptable);
  DXUTSetCallbackD3D11DeviceCreated(GameCodeApp::OnD3D11CreateDevice);
  DXUTSetCallbackD3D11SwapChainResized(GameCodeApp::OnD3D11ResizedSwapChain);
  DXUTSetCallbackD3D11SwapChainReleasing(
    GameCodeApp::OnD3D11ReleasingSwapChain );
  DXUTSetCallbackD3D11DeviceDestroyed( GameCodeApp::OnD3D11DestroyDevice );
  DXUTSetCallbackD3D11FrameRender( GameCodeApp::OnD3D11FrameRender );

  // Show the cursor and clip it when in full screen
  DXUTSetCursorSettings( true, true );

  // Perform application initialization
  if (!g_pApp->InitInstance (hInstance, lpCmdLine, 0,
    g_pApp->m_Options.m_ScreenSize.x,
    g_pApp->m_Options.m_ScreenSize.y))
  {
    return FALSE;
  }

  DXUTMainLoop();
  DXUTShutdown();

  //_CRTDBG_LEAK_CHECK_DF is used at program initialization
  // to force a leak check just before program exit. This
```

```
    // is important because some classes may dynamically
    // allocate memory in globally constructed objects.
    //
    //_CrtDumpMemoryLeaks();  // Reports leaks to stderr
    // Destroy the logging system at the last possible moment
    Logger::Destroy();

    return g_pApp->GetExitCode();
}
```

These calls to the `DXUTSetCallbackEtc` functions allow the DirectX Framework to notify the application about device changes, user input, and Windows messages. You should always handle the callbacks for device reset/lost, or your game won't be able to withstand things like fast user task switching under Windows.

The calls to the `CrtDumpMemory` functions set up your game to detect memory leaks, something discussed at length in Chapter 23, "Debugging Your Game."

Player options are stored in an XML file and are loaded into the `GameOptions` class. This class can store whatever you like, but in this example it simply stores the desired screen width and height of the game window. Extensions of this class could store sound volume settings, how many players the game supports, and other important data.

`g_pApp` points to a global object that stores the game's application layer. Let's take a look at the base class, `GameCodeApp`.

## The Application Layer: `GameCodeApp`

The game's application layer handles operating system–specific tasks, including interfacing with the hardware and operating system, handling the application life cycle including initialization, managing access to localized strings, and initializing the game logic. This class is meant to be inherited by a game-specific application class that will extend it and define some game-specific things, such as title, but also implementations for creating the game logic and game views and loading the initial state of the game.

The class acts as a container for other important members that manage the application layer:

- A handle to the text resource, which is initialized with an XML file. It contains all of the user-presented strings, such as "Do you want to quit?," so the game can easily be localized into other languages.
- The game logic implementation.
- A data structure that holds game options, usually read from an XML file.

- The resource cache, which is responsible for loading textures, meshes, and sounds from a resource file.
- The main Event Manager, which allows all the different game subsystems to communicate with each other.
- The network communications manager.

All of these members are initialized in `GameCodeApp::InitInstance()`.

## `InitInstance()`: Checking System Resources

Checking system resources is especially important for Windows games, but console developers don't get off scot-free. Permanent storage, whether it is a hard disk or a memory card, should be checked for enough space to store game data before the player begins. Windows and console games that support special hardware, like steering wheels or other input devices, must check for their existence and fall back to another option, like the gamepad, if nothing is found. Checking system RAM and calculating the CPU speed can be important, too, even if the platform isn't Windows.

The code inside `InitInstance()` is particularly sensitive to order, so be careful if you decide to change this method. You should also keep your shutdown code in sync, or rather reverse sync, with the order of initialization. Always release systems and resources in the reverse order in which you requested or created them.

Here's what this method does:

- Detects multiple instances of the application.
- Checks secondary storage space and memory.
- Calculates the CPU speed.
- Loads the game's resource cache.
- Loads strings that will be presented to the player.
- Creates the LUA script manager.
- Creates the game's Event Manager.
- Uses the script manager to load initial game options.
- Initializes DirectX, the application's window, and the D3D device.
- Creates the game logic and game views.
- Sets the directory for save games and other temporary files.
- Preloads selected resources from the resource cache.

```
  m_screenSize = CPoint(screenWidth, screenHeight);
  DXUTCreateDevice( D3D_FEATURE_LEVEL_10_1, true, screenWidth, screenHeight);
  m_Renderer = shared_ptr<IRenderer>(GCC_NEW D3DRenderer11());
  m_Renderer->VSetBackgroundColor(255, 20, 20, 200);
  m_Renderer->VOnRestore();

  m_pGame = VCreateGameAndView();
  if (!m_pGame)
    return false;
  // now that all the major systems are initialized, preload resources
  m_ResCache->Preload("*.ogg", NULL);
  m_ResCache->Preload("*.dds", NULL);
  m_ResCache->Preload("*.jpg", NULL);
  m_ResCache->Preload("*.sdkmesh", NULL);
```

You have to make sure that everything is initialized before some other subsystem needs it to exist. Inevitably, you'll find yourself in a catch-22 situation, and you'll see that two subsystems depend on each other's existence. The way out is to create one in a hobbled state, initialize the other, and then notify the first that the other exists. It may seem a little weird, but you'll probably run into this more than once.

The next sections tell you more about how to do these tasks and why each is important.

## Checking for Multiple Instances of Your Game

If your game takes a moment to get around to creating a window, a player might get a little impatient and double-click the game's icon a few times. If you don't take the precaution of handling this problem, you'll find that users can quickly create a few dozen instances of your game, none of which will properly initialize. You should create a splash screen to help minimize this problem, but it's still a good idea to detect an existing instance of your game.

```
bool IsOnlyInstance(LPCTSTR gameTitle)
{
  // Find the window. If active, set and return false
  // Only one game instance may have this mutex at a time...

  HANDLE handle = CreateMutex(NULL, TRUE, gameTitle);

  // Does anyone else think 'ERROR_SUCCESS' is a bit of an oxymoron?
  if (GetLastError() != ERROR_SUCCESS)
  {
    HWND hWnd = FindWindow(gameTitle, NULL);
    if (hWnd)
    {
```

```
      // An instance of your game is already running.
      ShowWindow(hWnd, SW_SHOWNORMAL);
      SetFocus(hWnd);
      SetForegroundWindow(hWnd);
      SetActiveWindow(hWnd);
      return false;
    }
  }
  return true;
}
```

The Windows `CreateMutex()` API is used to gate only one instance of your game to the window detection code, the `FindWindow()` API. You call it with your game's title, which uniquely identifies your game. A mutex is a process synchronization mechanism and is common to any multitasking operating system. It is guaranteed to create one mutex with the identifier `gameTitle` for all processes running on the system. If it can't be created, then another process has already created it. You'll learn more about these in Chapter 20.

## Checking Hard Drive Space

Most games need a bit of free secondary storage space for saving games, caching data from the DVD-ROM drive, and other temporary needs. Here's a bit of code you can use to find out if your player has enough storage space for those tasks:

```
bool CheckStorage(const DWORDLONG diskSpaceNeeded)
{
  // Check for enough free disk space on the current disk.
  int const drive = _getdrive();
  struct _diskfree_t diskfree;

  _getdiskfree(drive, &diskfree);

  unsigned __int64 const neededClusters =
    diskSpaceNeeded /
    ( diskfree.sectors_per_cluster * diskfree.bytes_per_sector );

  if (diskfree.avail_clusters < neededClusters)
  {
    // if you get here you don't have enough disk space!
    GCC_ERROR("CheckStorage Failure: Not enough physical storage.");
    return false;
  }
  return true;
}
```

If you want to check free disk space, you'll use the `_getdrive()` and `_getdiskfree()` utility functions, which work on any ANSI-compatible system. The return value from the `_getdiskfree()` function is in clusters, not in bytes, so you have to do a little math on the results.

## Checking Memory

Checking for system RAM under Windows is a little trickier; sadly, you need to leave ANSI compatibility behind. You should check the total physical memory installed, as well as the available virtual memory, using Windows calls. Virtual memory is a great thing to have on your side as long as you use it wisely. You'll learn more about caching in Chapter 8, "Loading and Caching Game Data," but until then you can think of it as having a near infinite bank account with a very slow bank. If your game uses virtual memory in the wrong way, it will slow to a crawl. You might as well grab a pencil and sketch a storyboard of the next few minutes of your game; you'll see it faster.

```
bool CheckMemory(
  const DWORDLONG physicalRAMNeeded, const DWORDLONG virtualRAMNeeded)
{
  MEMORYSTATUSEX status;
  GlobalMemoryStatusEx(&status);
  if (status.ullTotalPhys < physicalRAMNeeded)
  {
    // you don't have enough physical memory. Tell the player to go get a
    // real computer and give this one to his mother.
    GCC_ERROR("CheckMemory Failure: Not enough physical memory.");
    return false;
  }
  // Check for enough free memory.
  if (status.ullAvailVirtual < virtualRAMNeeded)
  {
    // you don't have enough virtual memory available.
    // Tell the player to shut down the copy of Visual Studio running in the
    // background, or whatever seems to be sucking the memory dry.
    GCC_ERROR("CheckMemory Failure: Not enough virtual memory.");
    return false;
  }

  char *buff = GCC_NEW char[virtualRAMNeeded];
  if (buff)
    delete[] buff;
  else
  {
```

```
    // even though there is enough memory, it isn't available in one
    // block, which can be critical for games that manage their own memory
    GCC_ERROR("CheckMemory Failure: Not enough contiguous memory.");
    return false;
  }
}
```

This function relies on the `GlobalMemoryStatusEx()` function, which returns the current state of the physical and virtual memory system. In addition, this function allocates and immediately releases a huge block of memory. This has the effect of making Windows clean up any garbage that has accumulated in the memory manager and double-checks that you can allocate a contiguous block as large as you need. If the call succeeds, you've essentially run the equivalent of a Zamboni machine through your system's memory, getting it ready for your game to hit the ice. Console programmers should nuke that bit of code—it simply isn't needed in a system that only runs one application at a time.

## Calculating CPU Speed

Since Windows XP, the CPU speed can be read from the system registry with this code:

```
DWORD ReadCPUSpeed()
{
  DWORD BufSize = sizeof(DWORD);
  DWORD dwMHz = 0;
  DWORD type = REG_DWORD;
  HKEY hKey;

  // open the key where the proc speed is hidden:
  long lError = RegOpenKeyEx(HKEY_LOCAL_MACHINE,
     L"HARDWARE\\DESCRIPTION\\System\\CentralProcessor\\0",
     0, KEY_READ, &hKey);

     if(lError == ERROR_SUCCESS)
  {
    // query the key:
    RegQueryValueEx(hKey, L"~MHz", NULL, &type, (LPBYTE) &dwMHz, &BufSize);
  }
  return dwMHz;
}
```

If you want to calculate the CPU speed, there's a great bit of code written by Michael Lyons at Microsoft that does the job nicely. You can find it in the companion source code to this book in *Dev\Source\GCC4\Mainloop\CPUSpeed.cpp*.

## Do You Have a Dirtbag on Your Hands?

If you are lucky (or probably unlucky) enough to be working on a mass-market title, or even a title that will be distributed worldwide, you should support computers and devices that have a wide range of capabilities. Everyone wants a game to look really good, but when you have to support devices that don't support the right graphics system, something has to give. Choose a benchmark for your game that makes sense to determine what makes a computer a dirtbag and what doesn't. Whatever you use, it is important to set your standards and determine if the computer the player is using is at the shallow end of the hardware pool.

**What to Do with Your Dirtbag**

Once you figure out that the computer is at the bottom end, you should set your game defaults for new players accordingly. A good start would be to turn off any CPU-intensive activities like decompressing MP3 streams, scaling back skeletal detail, animations, and physics, or reducing the cycles you spend on AI. If the player decides to bring up the options screen and turn some of these features back on, my suggestion is to let him do it if it's possible. Maybe he'll be inclined to retire his old machine.

## Initialize Your Resource Cache

You read about general memory management in Chapter 3 and resource caching is covered in Chapter 8. Initializing the resource cache will be a gateway to getting your game data from the media into memory. The size of your resource cache is totally up to your game design and the bottom-end hardware you intend to support. It's a good idea to figure out if your player's computer is a dirtbag or flamethrower and set your resource cache memory accordingly.

**No Room Even for the Basics?**

You can't impress a player with fantastic graphics until you reserve a nice spot in system and video memory for your textures, models, and animations. If your resource cache allocation fails, you can't even bring up a nice dialog box telling a loser player he is low on memory. The game should fail as elegantly as possible and maybe print out a coupon for some memory sticks.

In this book, we'll use Zip files to store game resources. It's reasonably speedy, especially if no decompression is necessary. Here's the code to initialize the resource cache:

```
new ResCache(50, new ResourceZipFile(_T("Assets.zip")));
if (!m_ResCache->Init())
{
```

```
    GCC_ERROR("Failed to initialize resource cache! Are your paths set up
        correctly?");
    return false;
  }

  m_ResCache->RegisterLoader(CreateWAVResourceLoader());
  m_ResCache->RegisterLoader(CreateOGGResourceLoader());
  m_ResCache->RegisterLoader(CreateDDSResourceLoader());
  // Note a few more loaders continue past here...
```

This code creates the `ResCache` object and initializes the resource cache to 50 megabytes. It also creates an object that implements the `IResource` interface.

Choosing the size of your resource cache has everything to do with what kind of computer you expect your players to have. Players of the latest game from Crytek are going to have way more memory than my mother-in-law's computer—an old laptop I gave her about four years ago. After you choose the size of your cache, you should be cautious about how that memory is being used as you stuff in more textures, sounds, animations, and everything else. Once you run out, your game will stop performing like it should as it suffers cache misses. Console programmers have a harsher climate—if they run one byte over, their game will simply crash.

You'll notice the calls to `RegisterLoader()`. A resource cache can contain many different types of resources, such as sounds, music, textures, and more. The resource cache needs to know how each one of these files types is read and converted into something the game engine can use directly. The process of registering a loader associates a specific loader class with a file type. You'll learn more about how that works in the Chapter 8 and see how each of these loaders is coded throughout the book.

**How Much Longer?!?**

It seems like every game I work on has the same cycle when it comes to load optimization. At first, things are just fine because we're loading small sets of artwork and parsing small XML files. As artists and designers add content to the game, the load times start to grind to a halt, and before too long, our game is taking 5–10 minutes just to load the test level! Some programmers usually spend a few days optimizing the data loading to get it to a decent time again, but it will inevitably creep back up. It's an interesting dance.

## Loading Text Strings

Text strings that are presented to the player should never be hardcoded. Whatever language you speak, there are more people out there who speak other languages! This is handled easily by putting all your text strings into a data file that is easy to edit and load. In this case, the data format is XML, read easily by the TinyXML SDK, available freely under the zlib license. Here's an example of what this might look like:

```
<?xml version="1.0" encoding="UTF-8"?>
<strings>
  <string value="Alert" id="IDS_ALERT"/>
  <string value="Question" id="IDS_QUESTION"/>
  <string value="Initializing" id="IDS_INITIALIZING"/>
  <string value="Ok" id="IDS_OK"/>
  <string value="Yes" id="IDS_YES" hotkey="Y"/>
</strings>
```

One note: the identifier should be representative of what the string stands for and named to group strings together into categories. For example, if you had a string "You are out of hard drive space," you could define that as `IDS_INITCHECK_LOW_DISK_SPACE`.

Reading this file is a piece of cake. First, an STL map is declared that will map a string key to the actual string resource:

```
std::map<std::wstring,std::wstring> m_textResource;
```

Then two methods are defined—the first to load the strings from the XML file from the resource cache and the next to access the string given the key value:

```
bool GameCodeApp::LoadStrings(std::string language)
{
  std::string languageFile = "Strings\\";
  languageFile += language;
  languageFile += ".xml";

  TiXmlElement* pRoot =
    XmlResourceLoader::LoadAndReturnRootXmlElement(languageFile.c_str());
  if (!pRoot)
  {
    GCC_ERROR("Strings are missing.");
    return false;
  }
  // Loop through each child element and load the component
  for (TiXmlElement* pElem = pRoot->FirstChildElement(); pElem; pElem =
      pElem->NextSiblingElement())
  {
    const char *pKey=pElem->Attribute("id");
    const char *pText=pElem->Attribute("value");
    if (pKey && pText)
    {
```

```
        wchar_t wideKey[64];
        wchar_t wideText[1024];
        AnsiToWideCch(wideKey, pKey, 64);
        AnsiToWideCch(wideText, pText, 1024);
        m_textResource[std::wstring(wideKey)] = std::wstring(wideText);
      }
    }
  return true;
}
std::wstring GameCodeApp::GetString(std::wstring sID)
{
  auto localizedString = m_textResource.find(sID);
  if(localizedString == m_textResource.end())
  {
    GCC_ASSERT(0 && "String not found!");
    return L"";
  }
  return localizedString->second;
}
```

## Your Script Manager and the Events System

The next section of the initialization sequence creates the script parser and event system. The GameCode4 code base uses Lua, which is fairly easy to learn and popular.

```
  if (!LuaStateManager::Create())
  {
    GCC_ERROR("Failed to initialize Lua");
    return false;
  }

  // Register functions exported from C++
  ScriptExports::Register();
  ScriptProcess::RegisterScriptClass();
```

Once it is created, you could actually use a Lua initialization script to control the rest of the initialization sequence. This can be a fantastic idea, as the script doesn't add very much additional time to the initialization sequence. What the programmer gets in return is the capability to change the initialization sequence without recompiling the game. The only other way to do this would be to throw some crazy options on the command line, which can be unwieldy, even in a trivial case. A Lua script has control mechanisms for evaluating expressions and looping—something you'll come to enjoy very quickly.

The Event Manager is initialized next with these few lines of code:

```
m_pEventManager = GCC_NEW EventManager("GameCodeApp Event Mgr", true );
if (!m_pEventManager)
  return false;
```

## Initialize DirectX and Create Your Window

Windows programmers can't put off the task of creating their window any longer. Creating a game window is easy enough, especially since the DirectX Framework does the whole thing for you. Here's the code that does this job inside `InitInstance()`:

```
DXUTInit( true, true, lpCmdLine, true );
DXUTCreateWindow( VGetGameTitle(), hInstance, VGetIcon());
if (!GetHwnd())
  return FALSE;
SetWindowText(GetHwnd(), VGetGameTitle());
```

Notice the calls to the virtual methods `VGetGameTitle()` and `VGetIcon()`. They are overloaded to provide this game-specific information to the `GameCodeApp` base class. You'll see exactly how to do this in Chapter 21, "A Game of *Teapot Wars,*" when we create a game of *Teapot Wars* with this code.

Since this code is using the DirectX Framework, the next line of code creates the Direct3D device:

```
DXUTCreateDevice( D3D_FEATURE_LEVEL_10_1, true, screenWidth, screenHeight);
```

The constant, `D3D_FEATURE_LEVEL_10_1`, will be discussed more in the 3D chapters, but basically it sets the minimum 3D feature level required by your game.

## Create Your Game Logic and Game View

After the game window is ready, you can create the game logic and all the views that attach to the game logic. This is done by calling `VCreateGameAndView()`, which is a pure virtual function in the `GameCodeApp` class. Here's an example of what it might look like in the inherited class:

```
BaseGameLogic *TeapotWarsApp::VCreateGameAndView()
{
  BaseGameLogic *game = GCC_NEW TeapotWarsLogic();
  shared_ptr<IGameView> gameView(GCC_NEW TeapotWarsHumanView());
  game->VAddView(gameView);
  return game;
}
```

## Set Your Save Game Directory

Finding the right directory for user-settable game options used to be easy. A programmer would simply store user data files close to the EXE and use the `GetModuleFileName()` API. Starting with Windows XP Home, the *Program Files* directory is off limits by default, and applications are nevermore allowed to write directly to this directory tree. Instead, applications must write user data to the *C:\Documents and Settings\{User name}\Application Data* directory for XP, *C:\Users\{User Name}\Application Data* directory for Vista, and *C:\Users\{User Name}\AppData* for Windows 7. Not only can this directory be completely different from one version of Windows to another, but some users also store these on a drive other than the C: drive. You can use a special API to deal with this problem: `SHGetSpecialFolderPath()`.

If you open Windows Explorer to your application data directory, you'll see plenty of companies who play by the rules, writing application data in the spot that will keep Windows XP from freaking out. Usually, a software developer will create a hierarchy, starting with his company name, maybe adding his division, then the product, and finally the version. A Microsoft product I worked on used this path:

```
GAME_APP_DIRECTORY = "Microsoft\\Microsoft Games\\Bicycle Casino\\2.0";
```

**`GAME_APP_DIRECTORY` = Your Registry Key**

The value for your `GAME_APP_DIRECTORY` is also a great value for a registry key. Don't forget to add the version number at the end. You might as well hope for a gravy train: 2.0, 3.0, 4.0, and so on.

It's up to you to make sure you create the directory if it doesn't exist. This is made easier with a call to `SHCreateDirectoryEx()`, which will create the entire directory hierarchy if it doesn't already exist:

```
const TCHAR *GetSaveGameDirectory(HWND hWnd, const TCHAR *gameAppDirectory)
{
  HRESULT hr;
  static TCHAR m_SaveGameDirectory[MAX_PATH];
  TCHAR userDataPath[MAX_PATH];
  hr = SHGetSpecialFolderPath(hWnd, userDataPath, CSIDL_APPDATA, true);

  _tcscpy_s(m_SaveGameDirectory, userDataPath);
  _tcscat_s(m_SaveGameDirectory, _T("\\"));
  _tcscat_s(m_SaveGameDirectory, gameAppDirectory);

  // Does our directory exist?
  if (0xffffffff == GetFileAttributes(m_SaveGameDirectory))
  {
```

```
    if (SHCreateDirectoryEx(hWnd, m_SaveGameDirectory, NULL)
      != ERROR_SUCCESS)
      return false;
  }

  _tcscat_s(m_SaveGameDirectory, _T("\\"));
  return m_SaveGameDirectory;
}
```

**Developers Have Different Needs Than Your Players**

Make sure that you have two different game option files—one for users and one for developers. For example, it can be very convenient to have some way to override the full-screen option in the user settings to open in window mode for a debug session. Debugging a full-screen application with a single monitor is sure to send you on a killing spree. While you are at it, make sure that you allow gamers to set which monitor your game will be displayed on in a multimonitor configuration, which is becoming much more common.

## Preload Selected Resources from the Cache

Most games preload much, if not all, of the resources they'll need during the game, or at the very least the level that is currently loaded. Even open world games will typically preload as much of the game as makes sense, given the player's current location in the game world. The resource cache has methods that you can call to preload resources, based on file type:

```
m_ResCache->Preload("*.ogg", NULL);
m_ResCache->Preload("*.dds", NULL);
m_ResCache->Preload("*.jpg", NULL);
m_ResCache->Preload("*.sdkmesh", NULL);
```

Preloading these resources will take some time, but players expect a pause during game initialization. What they don't expect is a big hitch right after they fire a weapon, which might happen if the sound effect for the weapon isn't loaded yet.

# Stick the Landing: A Nice Clean Exit

Your game won't run forever. Even the best games will take a back seat to food and water. There may be a temptation to simply call `exit(0)` and be done with it. This isn't a wise choice because your DirectX drivers might be left in a bad state, and it could be difficult to tell if your game is leaking resources.

If you don't have a decent exit mechanism, you'll also find it impossible to determine where your game is leaking memory or other resources. After all, a hard exit is basically a huge memory leak, even though the operating system cleans it up. A tight exit mechanism will show you a single byte of leaked memory before returning control to the operating system. This is important for all games, Windows or console.

**Always Fix Leaks, Fast**

Games should never leak memory. Period. The reality of it is that some Windows API calls leak resources, and you just have to live with it. That's no reason your game code should be sloppy; hold yourself to a higher standard, and you won't get a reputation for crappy software.

## How Do I Get Out of Here?

There are two ways to stop a game from executing without yanking the power cord:

- The player quits the game on purpose.
- The operating system shuts the application down.

If the player chooses to stop playing, the first thing you should do is ask the player if he wants to save his game. The last thing someone needs is to lose six hours of progress only to hit the wrong button by accident. One standard detects if the current state of the game has changed since the last time the user saved, and only if the state is different does the system ask if the player wants to save his game. It is equally annoying to save your game, select quit, and have the idiot application ask if the game needs saving all over again.

Console programmers can stop here and simply run their exit code, destroying all the game systems generally in the reverse order in which they were created. Windows programmers, as usual, don't get off nearly that easy.

When Windows decides your game has to shut down, it sends a different message. Windows apps should intercept the `WM_SYSCOMMAND` message and look for `SC_CLOSE` in the `wParam`. This is what Windows sends to applications that are being closed, perhaps against their will. This can happen if the machine is shut down, runs low on battery power, or if the player hits Alt-F4.

The problem with this message is that Alt-F4 should act just like your normal exit, asking you if you want to quit. If you can save to a temporary location and load that state the next time the player starts, your players will thank you. Most likely, they were just getting to the boss encounter, and the batteries on their laptop finally ran out of motivated electrons.

You have to double-check for multiple entries into this code with a Boolean variable. If your players hit Alt-F4 and bring up a dialog box in your game asking if they want to quit, nothing is keeping them from hitting Alt-F4 again. If your players are like the folks at Microsoft's test labs, they'll hit it about 50 times. Your game is still pumping messages, so the WM_SYSCOMMAND will get through every time a player presses Alt-F4. Make sure you handle that by filtering it out.

If your game is minimized, you have to do something to catch the player's attention. If your game runs in full-screen mode and you've tabbed away to another app, your game will act just as if it is minimized. If your player uses the system menu by right-clicking on the game in the Start bar, your game should exhibit standard Windows behavior and flash. This is what well-behaved Windows applications do when they are minimized but require some attention from a human being.

```
void GameCodeApp::FlashWhileMinimized()
{
  // Flash the application on the taskbar
  // until it's restored.
  if ( ! GetHwnd() )
    return;

  // Blink the application if we are minimized,
  // waiting until we are no longer minimized
  if (IsIconic(GetHwnd()) )
  {
    // Make sure the app is up when creating a new screen
    // this should be the case most of the time, but when
    // we close the app down, minimized, and a confirmation
    // dialog appears, we need to restore
    DWORD now = timeGetTime();
    DWORD then = now;
    MSG msg;

    FlashWindow( GetHwnd(), true );

    while (true)
    {
      if ( PeekMessage( &msg, NULL, 0, 0, 0 ) )
      {
        if ( msg.message != WM_SYSCOMMAND || msg.wParam != SC_CLOSE )
        {
          TranslateMessage(&msg);
          DispatchMessage(&msg);
        }

        // Are we done?
        if ( ! IsIconic(GetHwnd()) )
```

```
          {
            FlashWindow( GetHwnd(), false );
            break;
          }
        }
        else
        {
          now = timeGetTime();
          DWORD timeSpan = now > then ? (now - then) : (then - now);
          if ( timeSpan > 1000 )
          {
            then = now;
            FlashWindow( GetHwnd(), true );
          }
        }
      }
    }
  }
```

Doing this is a little tricky. You basically have to run your own message pump in a tight loop and swallow the `WM_SYSCOMMAND` and `SC_CLOSE` messages until your game isn't minimized anymore, all the while calling `FlashWindow()` at regular time intervals.

## Forcing Modal Dialog Boxes to Close

When your game is closed by something external, such as a power down due to a low battery condition, you might have some tricky cleanup to do if you are inside one of your modal dialogs we'll be discussing in Chapter 9, "Programming Input Devices." Since you are running a special version of the message pump, the "real" message pump won't get the message.

The solution lies in forcing the modal dialog to close with its default answer and then resending the `WM_SYSCOMMAND` with the `SC_CLOSE` parameter back into the message pump. If you happen to have nested dialogs up, this will still work because each dialog will get a forced close until the normal message pump can process the close message.

Here's the pseudo-code for the code inside the `SC_CLOSE` message handler:

```
If (you want to prompt the user)
{
  If (m_bQuitRequested)
    Return early - user is spamming Alt-F4
```

```
    Set your m_bQuitRequested = true
    Call the model dialog box: "Are you sure you want to quit?"
    If (user said no)
    {
      Abort the quit request - return here.
    }
}

// By here we are quitting the game, by request or by force.
Set you m_bQutting = true
If (a modal dialog box is up)
{
  Force the dialog to close with a default answer
  Repost the WM_SYSCOMMAND message again to close the game
  Set m_bQuitRequested = false
}
```

You'll want to take a closer look at the source code to see more, but this code will allow the game to bring up a quit dialog even if the player presses Alt-F4 or another app, like an install program, and attempts to shut down your game by force.

## Shutting Down the Game

With some exceptions, you should shut down or deallocate game systems in the reverse order of which they were created. This is a good rule of thumb to use whenever you are grabbing and releasing multiple resources that depend on each other. Each data structure should be traversed and freed. Take care that any code that is run inside destructors has the resources it needs to execute properly. It's pretty easy to imagine a situation where the careless programmer has uninitialized something in the wrong order and a destructor somewhere fails catastrophically. Be extremely aware of your dependencies, and where multiple dependencies exist, lean on a reference counting mechanism, such as smart pointers, to hold on to resources until they really aren't needed anymore.

The message pump, `GameCodeApp::MsgProc`, will receive a `WM_CLOSE` message when it is time for you to shut down your game, and you'll handle it by calling the nonstatic `GameCodeApp::OnClose` method:

```
case WM_CLOSE:
{
  result = g_pApp->OnClose();
  break;
}
```

The application layer will delete things in the reverse order in which they were created. The creation order was resource cache first, the game window second, and the game logic object third. We'll release them in the reverse order.

```
LRESULT GameCodeApp::OnClose()
{
  // release all the game systems in reverse order from which they
  // were created

  SAFE_DELETE(m_pGame);
  DestroyWindow(GetHwnd());
  VDestroyNetworkEventForwarder();
  SAFE_DELETE(m_pBaseSocketManager);
  SAFE_DELETE(m_pEventManager);
  ScriptExports::Unregister();
  LuaStateManager::Destroy();
  SAFE_DELETE(m_ResCache);
  return 0;
}
```

If you extended the `GameCodeApp` application layer into your own class, you'll want to do exactly the same thing with the custom objects there and release them in the reverse order. When the game logic is deleted, it will run a destructor that releases its objects, including its process manager and all the views attached to it.

After the `WM_CLOSE` message is processed, the main message pump exits, and control will eventually return to the `WinMain` function, which calls `DXUTShutdown()` to release the DirectX Framework.

## What About Consoles?

This book has a decidedly Windows bend, mostly because Windows is a very accessible programming platform. But that doesn't mean you can't be exposed to some discussion about how to perform certain tasks with the constraints imposed by console and mobile platforms—and shutdown is no exception.

Consoles run one program at a time and essentially don't have to worry about being left in a weird state. The shutdown solution used on *Thief: Deadly Shadows* could have been documented in a single page—we simply rebooted the machine. Is this a good idea or not?

From the player's point of view, it's a great idea. Shutdown doesn't have to take any time whatsoever, simply unrolling the data structures and cleaning up allocated memory. It just exits—and BAM!—you are back to the launch window.

From a programmer's point of view, it is easier, but you don't have to clean up your mess, so to speak. A lazy programmer can create systems that are so entangled they can't be torn down in an orderly manner, and that can be a bad thing. If something can't be torn down during runtime, you have no choice but to allow it to exist whether it is being actively used or not, and console resources are so tight you still want every byte. Also, if you ever want to be able to load a new level into memory, something has to exist in your codebase to remove all the resources in that level and return the system to a pristine state.

I propose a dual solution—the release build should reboot, exit the game all at once, and take as little time as possible. This is for the player's convenience. The debug build should attempt a clean exit, and any problems with a clean exit should be addressed before they become a cancer in the rest of your system—especially memory leaks.

## Getting In and Getting Out

Games have a lot of moving parts and use every bit of hardware in the system. Getting all the green lights turned on in the right order can be a real pain, as you saw in initialization. It's really easy to have dependent systems, so much so that you have "chicken and egg" problems—where more than one system has to be first in the initialization chain. I don't think I've ever worked on a game where we didn't have to hack something horribly to make initialization work correctly. Start with a good organization, and hopefully your problems in this area will be minimal at best.

Shutting down cleanly is critical under any multitasking operating system like Windows, not only to make sure system resources like video memory are released, but it also helps the engineering team to know that the underlying technologies can be torn down in an orderly manner. It doesn't guarantee good technology, but it is a good sign of clean code.

# Chapter 6

*by David "Rez" Graham*

# Game Actors and Component Architecture

Games are full of objects that bring your world to life. A World War II game might be full of tanks and planes, while a futuristic science fiction game might have robots and starships. Like actors on a stage, these objects are at the heart of the gameplay. It seems fitting that we call them "game actors" because that's exactly what they are.

A game actor is an object that represents a single entity in your game world. It could be an ammo pickup, a tank, a couch, an NPC, or anything you can think of. In some cases, the world itself might even be an actor. It's important to define the parameters of game actors and to ensure that they are as flexible and reusable as possible.

There are as many ways for defining a game actor as there are games. Like everything else in computer programming, there is rarely a perfect solution.

## A First Attempt at Building Game Actors

A common approach to building game actors is to start with an `Actor` base class that defines things that every actor needs to know, which could just be an ID and a position.

```
class Actor
{
  ActorId m_id;

protected:
  Vec3 m_position;
```

```
public:
  const Vec3& GetPosition(void) const { return m_position; }
  const ActorId GetId(void) const { return m_id; }
};
```

Then you define subclasses for specific actor types. Each subclass adds some new piece of functionality that builds on the last. For example, you might have a subclass for actors that could be rendered:

```
class RenderableActor : public Actor
{
  Model* m_pModel;
  Texture* m_pTexture;
public:
  virtual bool VDraw(void);
};
```

Underneath that, you could have a subclass for actors that requires physics, pickups, characters, and so on. Eventually, you'd probably end up with a big inheritance tree like the one in Figure 6.1.

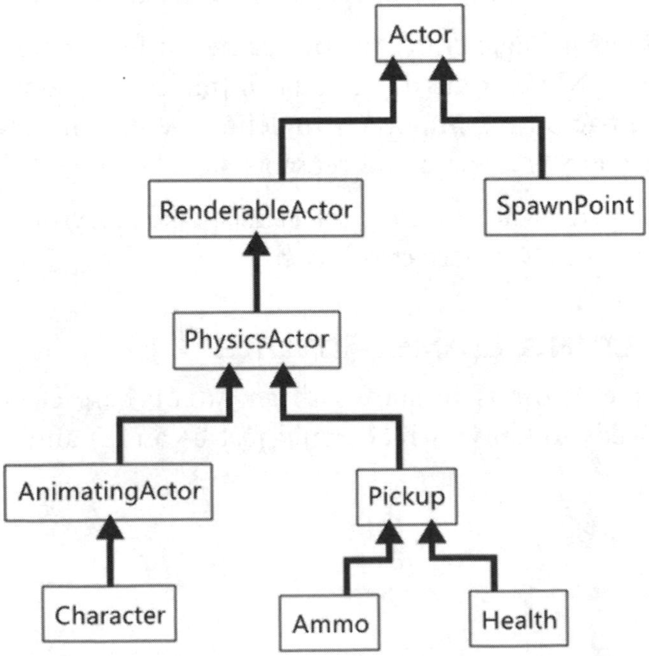


**Figure 6.1**
A possible actor inheritance tree.

The arrows show inheritance, so `RenderableActor` inherits from `Actor`. On the surface, this looks okay. You can instantiate an object from anywhere in this tree to provide the functionality you want. If you just need a boulder to fall on the player, it can be a `PhysicsActor` object. If you want a new type of pickup, you just write a new subclass and instantiate that. It's perfect, right?

Nope, it's not perfect by any stretch of the imagination. If you recall my advice from Chapter 3, "Coding Tidbits and Style That Saved Me," looking at this diagram should raise a red flag. I spoke about keeping class hierarchies nice and flat, which this fails at completely. Why does it matter?

Let's say you build the previous system for your first-person shooter game. It would probably work just fine for a while. Now let's say the designer comes up to you and asks you to make a new kind of pickup, a mana pickup that has an animation. You can't derive from `Pickup` since it doesn't include any of the animation code, and you can't derive from `AnimatingActor` since that doesn't include any of the functionality needed for pickups.

One option would be to derive from both classes via multiple inheritance, but that would be disastrous. You would have to use a virtual base class to avoid the dreaded diamond of death, as shown in Figure 6.2.

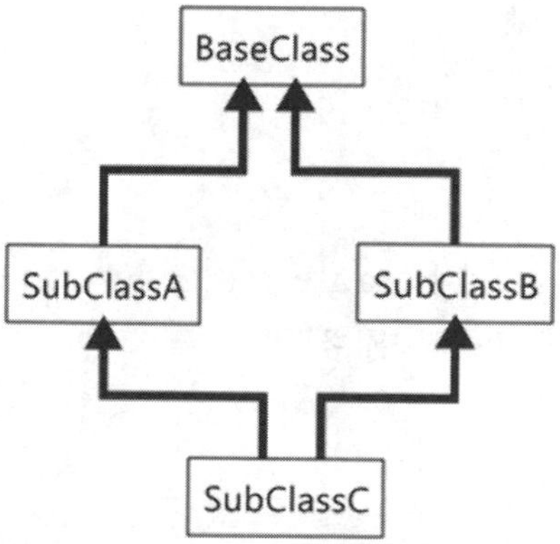


**Figure 6.2**
The diamond of death.

The problem with the diamond of death is that it's not clear what happens when members are inherited from the base class. Let's say you have the following declaration for the previous diagram:

```
class BaseClass
{
protected:
```

```
    int m_num;
    explicit BaseClass(int num)
    {
        m_num = num;
    }
};

class SubClassA : public BaseClass
{
public:
    explicit SubClassA(void) : BaseClass(1) { }
};

class SubClassB : public BaseClass
{
public:
    explicit SubClassB(void) : BaseClass(2) { }
};

class SubClassC : public SubClassA, public SubClassB
{
public:
    void Print(void)
    {
        cout << m_num << endl;
    }
};
```

In this example, the `Print()` function can't even be called because the code won't get past the compiler. Visual Studio 2010 generates the following error:

```
error C2385: ambiguous access of 'm_num'
```

The problem is that both `SubClassA` and `SubClassB` inherit the `m_num` member, so `SubClassC` has two copies of `m_num`, and the compiler doesn't know which one you're referring to. You could solve the issue by explicitly choosing one like this:

```
cout << SubClassA::m_num << endl;
```

Of course you still have the problem of an unused `SubClassB::m_num` variable floating around just asking for trouble. Someone is bound to accidentally access that particular `m_num`. This duplication is made even worse when you realize that in our use case for the actor tree, you'd be doubling up on the `PhysicsActor` class. That means potentially duplicating large objects.

**Multiple Inheritance Is Evil**

If at all possible, try to never use multiple inheritance unless every base class you're deriving from has nothing but pure virtual functions. You can have one exception to this and inherit from a single base class with data members, but every other base class should only contain pure virtual functions. This is so important that some languages, like Java, actually enforce it.

Clearly, this is not an option. Another possibility is to shuffle around the hierarchy and make `Pickup` inherit from `AnimatingActor`. This would solve the problem, but it means that all pickups have to carry around the weight of the animation system, which is most likely nontrivial. What about if you want to have a ghost character that ignores physics? They still need to animate and render, but you don't want the physics system to even have to know about them.

These kinds of problems give rise to the dreaded blob class. You keep shuffling around functionality until it all ends up living in one or two gigantic classes. Each change you make is like trying to untangle a web. You'll be lucky if you can make any of these changes without breaking half of the actors in the game. Obviously, this kind of architecture is fundamentally flawed.

## Component Architecture

Go back and take a look at Figure 6.1 again and notice how all of those subclasses are really just trying to add a new feature to the actor. If you can encapsulate each of those features into a component and compose a final object made up of those components, you can get the same functionality as the old class hierarchy but still have the flexibility to make changes. The `Actor` class becomes nothing more than a place to store components. What's even better is that these components are built up at runtime, so you can add and remove them during the course of the game. You can't do that with the old inheritance model!

The components have a base class that the actor maintains a reference to as well as a subclass interface that represents the responsibility of that component. Each subclass of that interface is an implementation of that responsibility. For example, you might have one interface class called `AiComponent`, which has several different implementations for different kinds of AI. The important thing to note is that each component interface has a unique identifier, and each actor is only allowed to have one class of a particular responsibility. That means you could have two `AiComponent` subclasses, but you could replace an existing one with a new one, allowing you to change the actor's behavior at runtime.

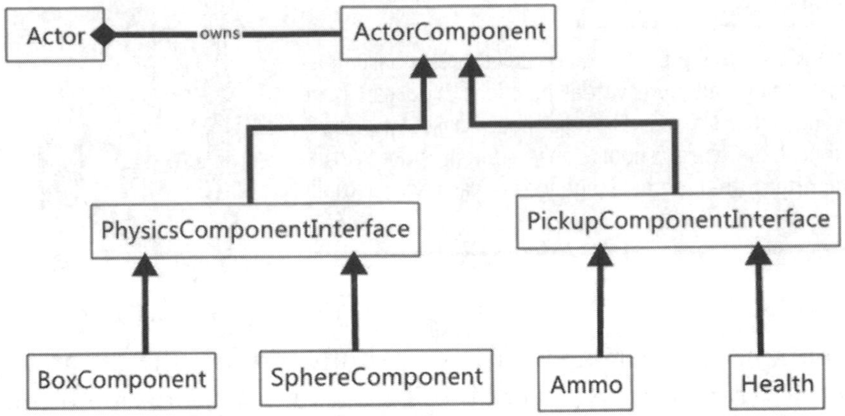


**Figure 6.3**
The actor component system.

Figure 6.3 highlights the new class diagram, showing how these components interact.

In this model, the actor owns a bunch of components (as represented by the diamond), which in turn serves as the base class for the component interfaces. Whenever a system needs access to a component, it asks the actor for that interface and gets a pointer to the appropriate interface object. The lowest level of the tree defines the behavior for that component. It's important to note that no outside system ever gets a pointer directly to the concrete class. You would never have a system know about `Ammo` or `Health` directly. You'll learn more about this in Chapter 11, "Game Event Management," when you see the event system.

**Blobs Can Exist Anywhere**

I mentioned earlier how having a deep class hierarchy for game objects can create blob classes and how components can help mitigate that. Components are the answer to all of your problems, and it's really easy to create blob components. At SuperEgo Games, we had a component called `SeClump`, which was a class that contained all the rendering info, geometry, textures, shaders, effects, and positioning for an actor. This really should have been split into several different components that had the ability to work together. Not all things with position need to be rendered, and not everything that needs to be rendered needs a shader. Try to have each component handle exactly one thing.

## Creating Actors and Components

All actors are created using a factory. The factory's job is to take an XML resource, parse it, and return a fully initialized actor complete with all the appropriate components. It's important to understand how actors are built, so let's take a look at this process before diving into the `Actor` and `ActorComponent` classes.

All actors are defined with an XML data file. This data file allows you to define a component configuration and any default values for that component. Here's some sample XML for an actor:

```
<Actor>
  <CubePhysicsComponent>
    <InitialTransform>
      <Position x="0" y="5" z="0"/>
      <Orientation degrees="-90"/>
    </InitialTransform>
    <Shape>
      <Dimensions x="1" y="1" z="1"/>
    </Shape>
    <Density>castIron</Density>
    <PhysicsMaterial>Normal</PhysicsMaterial>
  </CubePhysicsComponent>
  <TeapotRenderComponent>
    <Color r="0" g="0" b="1.0" a="1.0"/>
  </TeapotRenderComponent>
</Actor>
```

This XML file defines an actor with two components, a `CubePhysicsComponent` and a `TeapotRenderComponent`. If you decide later on that the density of the physics material needs to change, you can do that right here. If you decide that this actor needs to have a brain, you can easily add an AI component without changing a single line of code. That's the power of data-driven development.

Keep in mind that these actor XML files define the template for a type of actor, *not* a specific actor instance. There can be many instances of this actor running around, each with completely different sets of data within their components. The XML file only defines the definition. You can think of it as defining a class for this type of actor.

Now that you've seen how to define types of actors, let's take a look at the factory class that's responsible for parsing this data and creating the actor instance.

```
typedef ActorComponent *(*ActorComponentCreator)(void);
typedef std::map<std::string, ActorComponentCreator> ActorComponentCreatorMap;

// some actor typedefs to make our life easier
typdef unsigned long ActorId;
typedef shared_ptr<Actor> StrongActorPtr;
typedef shared_ptr<ActorComponent> StrongActorComponentPtr;

class ActorFactory
{
  ActorId m_lastActorId;
```

```
protected:
  ActorComponentCreatorMap m_actorComponentCreators;

public:
  ActorFactory(void);
  StrongActorPtr CreateActor(const char* actorResource);

protected:
  virtual StrongActorComponentPtr CreateComponent(TiXmlElement* pData);

private:
  ActorId GetNextActorId(void) { ++m_lastActorId; return m_lastActorId; }
};
```

The `typedef` at the very top defines the function pointer signature for instantiating component objects. These functions are stored in the `m_actorComponentCreators` map, which is keyed by the string name of the component. This string comes from the XML.

Everything starts with the `CreateActor()` function, which is the only public method.

```
StrongActorPtr ActorFactory::CreateActor(const char* actorResource)
{
  // Grab the root XML node
  TiXmlElement* pRoot =
    XmlResourceLoader::LoadAndReturnRootXmlElement(actorResource);
  if (!pRoot)
  {
    GCC_ERROR("Failed to create actor from resource: " +
      std::string(actorResource));
    return StrongActorPtr();
  }

  // create the actor instance
  StrongActorPtr pActor(GCC_NEW Actor(GetNextActorId()));
  if (!pActor->Init(pRoot))
  {
    GCC_ERROR("Failed to initialize actor: " + std::string(actorResource));
    return StrongActorPtr();
  }

  // Loop through each child element and load the component
  for (TiXmlElement* pNode = pRoot->FirstChildElement(); pNode;
      pNode = pNode->NextSiblingElement())
```

```
    {
        StrongActorComponentPtr pComponent(CreateComponent(pNode));
        if (pComponent)
        {
            pActor->AddComponent(pComponent);
            pComponent->SetOwner(pActor);
        }
        else
        {
            return StrongActorPtr();
        }
    }

    // Now that the actor has been fully created, run the post init phase
    pActor->PostInit();

    return pActor;
}
```

First, this function loads the resource, gets the root XML node, and does a little error checking. Then it instantiates the actor object, generating and passing in the next actor ID. The actor ID is important because it allows you to represent the actor uniquely as a single primitive value (in this case, an unsigned long). It's generally faster and easier to pass this value around, especially when you start dealing with other systems and languages. You'll see this ID used quite a bit in Chapter 12, "Scripting with Lua." Lua doesn't have to know anything about the internals of the actor system; it just knows that it has a value it can use to tell the actor system to do something with a specific actor.

The actor's `Init()` function is called to do any base-level initialization before adding components. If this succeeds, the next step is to loop through all the components defined in the XML file and load each one. This is done by calling the `CreateComponent()` function, passing in the XML node for that component. The component returned is then added to the actor's component map, and the component is told of its new owner. If this process fails, the function aborts. Having no actor is better than having a partially constructed one. Once the components have all been added, the actor's `PostInit()` function is run. The `PostInit()` function takes care of any initialization that needs to occur after the actor and all components have been fully created. That's it, the newly composed actor is returned to the caller.

The `CreateComponent()` function is relatively simple.

```
StrongActorComponentPtr ActorFactory::CreateComponent(TiXmlElement* pData)
{
```

```
    std::string name(pData->Value());

    StrongActorComponentPtr pComponent;

    auto findIt = m_actorComponentCreators.find(name);
    if (findIt != m_actorComponentCreators.end())
    {
        ActorComponentCreator creator = findIt->second;
        pComponent.reset(creator());
    }
    else
    {
        GCC_ERROR("Couldn't find ActorComponent named " + name);
        return StrongActorComponentPtr();  // fail
    }

    // initialize the component if we found one
    if (pComponent)
    {
        if (!pComponent->Init(pData))
        {
            GCC_ERROR("Component failed to initialize: " + name);
            return StrongActorComponentPtr();
        }
    }

    // pComponent will be NULL if the component wasn't found. This isn't
    // necessarily an error since you might have a custom CreateComponent()
    // function in a subclass.
    return pComponent;
}
```

**C++0x/C++ 11 Redefines the `auto` Keyword**

What is the `auto` keyword doing in that function? There's a new standard being published called C++0x, or C++ 11. This new standard adds a huge amount of really cool features to the C++ language, some of which were covered in Chapter 3. If you have Visual Studio 2010, you can take advantage of a few of them.

One of these features is the newly overloaded `auto` keyword. The original usage of this keyword was to declare the variable in the automatic storage class. In other words, make the variable behave normally. This made it the single most useless (and redundant) keyword in the C++ language. In C++0x, the `auto` keyword now defines a variable whose type can be deduced at compile time. In the above code, I use it to declare an iterator so that if the data structure changes in the future, I don't have to update this code. It also makes the code a bit easier to read. Since the variable type is deduced statically (at compile time), there's no runtime cost at all. In fact, if you hover over the variable itself in Visual Studio 2010, a tooltip will even tell you what the type is.

First, this function grabs the name of the component from the XML node passed in. Then it searches the component creator map to find the specific creator function and calls it to instantiate the component. If it can't find the creator, it tosses up an error message and returns in disgrace. The creator functions are trivially simple. They just return the appropriate instantiated object.

```
ActorComponent* CreateCubePhysicsComponent()
{
  return GCC_NEW BoxPhysicsComponent;
}
```

Back to the `CreateComponent()` function, the newly created component is then initialized by calling its `Init()` function. Assuming this succeeds, the newly initialized component is returned back to the `CreateActor()` function.

And there you have it! That's the process for creating and initializing an actor from a data file.

## Defining Actors and Components

Now that you have an understanding of how actors get into the game, it's time to show you what an actor really looks like. Here's the `Actor` class:

```
class Actor
{
  friend class ActorFactory;

  typedef std::map<ComponentId, StrongActorComponentPtr> ActorComponents;

  ActorId m_id;                     // unique id for the actor
  ActorComponents m_components;  // all components this actor has

public:
  explicit Actor(ActorId id);
  ~Actor(void);

  bool Init(TiXmlElement* pData);
  void PostInit(void);
  void Destroy(void);
```

```
    void Update(int deltaMs);

    // accessors
    ActorId GetId(void) const { return m_id; }

    // template function for retrieving components
    template <class ComponentType>
    weak_ptr<ComponentType> GetComponent(ComponentId id)
    {
      ActorComponents::iterator findIt = m_components.find(id);
      if (findIt != m_components.end())
      {
        StrongActorComponentPtr pBase(findIt->second);
        // cast to subclass version of the pointer
        shared_ptr<ComponentType> pSub(
          std::tr1::static_pointer_cast<ComponentType>(pBase));
        weak_ptr<ComponentType> pWeakSub(pSub);  // convert strong pointer
                                                  // to weak pointer
        return pWeakSub;  // return the weak pointer
      }
      else
      {
        return weak_ptr<ComponentType>();
      }
    }

private:
    // This is called by the ActorFactory; no one else should be
    // adding components.
    void AddComponent(StrongActorComponentPtr pComponent);
};
```

The `m_components` member is the map of all components that this actor has. Notice that they're keyed off the component ID. This ID is unique for each component interface.

The `Init()` and `PostInit()` functions are called by the factory as the actor is being created and were covered in the `CreateActor()` function previously.

The `Destroy()` function is called when you want to destroy the actor. The actor holds onto strong references to each of its components, but the components also need to hold onto strong references to the actor. If you recall from my peanut butter and jelly example in Chapter 3, having a circular reference can potentially cause memory leaks. It's not easily avoided since some components may still need to access the actor during destruction time. If weak pointers were used instead, it would cause a crash whenever the component destructor tried to access the actor. The actor gets destroyed when all strong references are released, which means all weak references are immediately made invalid. The result is that the component's weak reference to the actor is no longer valid and can't be used. Since both references need to be strong references, the circular reference chain has to be explicitly broken. The `Destroy()` function takes care of this by explicitly clearing out the component map.

The `Update()` function is called every time the game updates. You'll see how this works in Chapter 7, "Controlling the Main Loop," when you learn about the main game loop.

`GetComponent()` is a template function that enables you to get any component by passing in the component ID. It takes care of the smart pointer casting and returns a weak reference to the component, which allows the caller to safely store this pointer while still allowing the component to be destroyed. Just be sure to check the validity of the pointer before using it.

Looking back at the class declaration, you might notice something a bit odd. There are no virtual functions whatsoever, because this class is not meant to be subclassed. All the variation comes from the components you attach to this actor. That's called composition, which is in action here (see Chapter 3).

Another key thing to notice is that the `Actor` class does absolutely nothing by itself. Its entire purpose in life is to manage and maintain components. An actor without components is just an empty box.

**Simple Functions Can Be More Expensive Than You Think**

The `GetComponent()` function is extremely simple—it just searches a map that's typically very small and returns a value. By itself, this is certainly fast enough, but this function has the possibility of being called hundreds or even thousands of times *each frame*. It's important to make sure that functions like this are lightning fast. The previous implementation is the simplest way but not the fastest.

On *The Sims Medieval,* our component maps for actors are laid out in a contiguous block of memory and are accessed by offset. When a system asks for a component, it's a simple pointer add to find the correct component. Another solution could be to cache certain components. One project I worked on had a transform component that was so commonly accessed, we just had a pointer to it directly on the `Actor` class.

Here's a look at the `ActorComponent` base class:

```
class ActorComponent
{
  friend class ActorFactory;
```

```
protected:
  StrongActorPtr m_pOwner;

public:
  virtual ~ActorComponent(void) { }

  // These functions are meant to be overridden by the implementation
  // classes of the components.
  virtual bool VInit(TiXmlElement* pData) = 0;
  virtual void VPostInit(void) { }
  virtual void VUpdate(int deltaMs) { }

  // This function should be overridden by the interface class.
  virtual ComponentId VGetComponentId(void) const = 0;

private:
  void SetOwner(StrongActorPtr pOwner) { m_pOwner = pOwner; }
};
```

This is the interface for all components. The `m_pOwner` member is the link back to the actor, which is necessary to allow components to communicate with each other. Other than that, there are no member variables. The rest of the class serves as an interface for individual components to override and implement.

You already saw the `VInit()` and `VPostInit()` functions in the factory's `Create-Component()` method. The `VUpdate()` function is called by the actor's `Update()` function. The `VGetComponentId()` function is overridden by the component interface classes that derive from this class. Every component interface has a unique ID, and this accessor is used to retrieve it. A component must have an ID, which is why this is a pure virtual function.

## Storing and Accessing Actors

There are a number of ways to store actors and even components. The method used in this book is an STL map where the key is the actor ID.

```
typedef std::map<ActorId, StrongActorPtr> ActorMap;
ActorMap m_actors;
```

Maps allow for relatively fast lookups, insertions, and removals (which, for the mathematically inclined, are all `O(log n)`). All actors live in this map on the `BaseGameLogic` class, which has a public API for retrieving actors.

```
virtual weak_ptr<Actor> VGetActor(const ActorId id);
```

Note that `VGetActor()` returns a weak pointer to the actor so that systems can hold on to this pointer for as long as they want without keeping the actor from being destroyed. In fact, the only thing that should maintain a strong pointer to the actor is the `m_actors` map and the `m_pOwner` pointer on components owned by the actor. Having only two strong pointers to the actor ensures that an actor is truly destroyed when you call its `Destroy()` method.

Having this direct control over the lifetime of actors (or really any object) is *very* important. Actors are used to represent complex objects like characters. A character has geometry information, textures, shaders, scripts, maybe an inventory that links to even more actors, and so on. All of these things together amount to a ton of data, which means a ton of memory. You need to have the ability to destroy these actor objects at any time to free up memory. If you allowed other systems to hold onto strong pointers to actors, you'd have a tough time ensuring that the actor was destroyed at all. Even worse, since actors are composites of multiple objects, you could get actors that lie around in completely broken states. Fixing these types of issues was my fulltime job for about a month toward the end of *The Sims Medieval.*

There are many other ways of storing actors. You could put them all in a single STL vector and have the index be the ID. This could be very wasteful if you're often deleting actors, unless you account for the reuse of actor IDs. The advantage here is in the ultra-fast lookups, which are `O(1)`, or constant time. It's lightning fast because you can just index into an array. This type of data structure would work well on a game where your actors tend to stick around, like an adventure game. It wouldn't work as well in an FPS due to the constant deletions.

Another possible solution is to break up your game world into chunks where each chunk represents some part of the world. If your whole world is a grid of chunks, it becomes trivial to find out which actors belong to what chunks by taking their position and dividing it by the width and height of the grid cells. This kind of spatial partitioning is crucial in FPS or RTS games. Let's say I throw a grenade that explodes in a 15-foot radius. Which actors are affected? With the implementation above, you'd have to loop through the entire map to find your actor. If you had a cell-based partitioning system, you could figure out which cells were affected by the grenade and just loop through the actors in those cells.

Looping through the entire map isn't a big deal when you have a couple dozen actors. When you have hundreds or even thousands of actors, it becomes way too costly. Spatial partitioning gives you a way to cut down the number of actors you have to consider.

This is just the tip of the iceberg in how to store actors. I could probably write an entire book on the subject! The simple STL map solution we use here makes for a good starting point, but just keep in mind that you'll have some work to do when you start thinking about taking this engine to the next level and making a real game.

## Putting It All Together

Now that you've seen how actors are built up with components and you understand the definitions for the `Actor` and `ActorComponent` classes, it's time to see how it all works together with a simple example showing you how to implement a simple component for different kinds of pickups in the game. First, we need to define the pickup interface that all pickups will derive from.

```
class PickupInterface : public ActorComponent
{
public:
  const static ComponentId COMPONENT_ID; // unique ID for this component type
  virtual ComponentId VGetComponentId(void) const
  {
    return COMPONENT_ID;
  }

  // Pickup interface
  virtual void VApply(WeakActorPtr pActor) = 0;
};
```

At the top is the ID that must be unique for all component interfaces, as well as the override for the `VGetComponentId()` function. This is the bare-minimum requirement for all components. Then the pickup interface itself is defined with declaring the `VApply()` pure virtual function. All pickup implementations must override and define this function.

Now let's write the actual implementation classes. This example will use an ammo pickup and a health pickup.

```
class AmmoPickup : public PickupInterface
{
public:
  virtual bool VInit(TiXmlElement* pData);
  virtual void VApply(WeakActorPtr pActor);
};

class HealthPickup : public PickupInterface
{
```

```
public:
  virtual bool VInit(TiXmlElement* pData);
  virtual void VApply(WeakActorPtr pActor);
};
```

The next thing to do is to define new creator factory methods:

```
ActorComponent* CreateAmmoPickup()
{
  return GCC_NEW AmmoPickup;
}

ActorComponent* CreateHealthPickup()
{
  return GCC_NEW HealthPickup;
}
```

These methods need to be added to the creator map, so the following lines need to be added to the `ActorFactory` constructor:

```
  m_actorComponentCreators["AmmoPickup"] = CreateAmmoPickup;
  m_actorComponentCreators["HealthPickup"] = CreateHealthPickup;
```

That's it! Now you can create ammo and health pickup definitions in the XML and create them by calling the actor factory `CreateActor()` method.

## Data Sharing

Inevitably, components are going to need to talk to each other. You may have a component that stores and manipulates the position of an actor. Your AI component will need to know this position in order to determine where it is, and your render component will need to know where to draw the actor. There are two main ways to do this, and many games use a combination of both.

#### Who Owns the Transform?

The component system at Planet Moon tried to minimize communication between components by having each component cache important information about other components. One such piece of information was the transform, which described the position, orientation, and scaling of the actor. There were no less than three transforms for any given actor: one for the render component, one for the game logic component, and the other for the physics component. These three transforms all had to be kept in sync with each other. If something got out of sync, you'd see very strange behavior, where the actor might get rendered in a different position from its physical transform.

One common debugging practice was to set a breakpoint on the actor's update function and examine all three transforms to see if they were all correct. Another common practice was to force a call to the sync function to ensure that everything was in sync during a given code path. These were all terrible practices and didn't really work in the long run. One engineer was fed up with it; by the end of the project, he refactored the whole system to use only a single transform for each actor, which had the interesting side effect of providing a decent performance boost since we didn't have all those sync calls everywhere.

## Direct Access

The first way to share data is by directly accessing the component interface. Each component stores a pointer back to the owning actor, so it's a simple matter of asking the actor for the component.

```
weak_ptr<Pickup> pWeakPickup =
  pActor->GetComponent<Pickup>(Pickup::COMPONENT_ID);
shared_ptr<Pickup> pPickup = MakeStrongPtr(pWeakPickup);
```

`pPickup` will now either contain a strong reference to the `Pickup` component for `pActor` or it will be empty. If it's empty, it means `pActor` doesn't have a `Pickup` component. It's important to always run this check and never make assumptions.

Notice the extra step in there to convert the `weak_ptr` returned by `GetComponent()` into a `shared_ptr` by calling `MakeStrongPtr()`. The reason for this is that a `weak_ptr` cannot be dereferenced directly; it must always be converted to a `shared_ptr` before being used. `MakeStrongPtr()` is a helper function I wrote to handle dead `weak_ptrs`.

```
template <class Type>
shared_ptr<Type> MakeStrongPtr(weak_ptr<Type> pWeakPtr)
{
  if (!pWeakPtr.expired())
    return shared_ptr<Type>(pWeakPtr);
  else
    return shared_ptr<Type>();
}
```

It's important to note that systems should never hold onto this `shared_ptr` longer than they have to because it keeps that component from getting destroyed when the actor is destroyed. You can hold onto `weak_ptr` as long as you want, however. A common strategy is to get a `weak_ptr` to the component you need and hold onto it so that you don't have to look it up every frame. Just make sure you test and that the component is still valid. If it becomes invalid, it means the actor was destroyed, and you need to handle that.

The advantage of this method is that it's very easy to access the component you want: You just grab the pointer, test it, and go. The disadvantage is that you can begin to couple multiple components tightly together. After a while, you'll realize that every actor needs to have a position somewhere because every other component asks for it. As long as you make sure to always gracefully handle the case where no component exists, this scenario shouldn't be too bad.

## Events

If you really want to decouple your components, another method is to use an event system. The actor acts as a messaging service that its components (and other systems) can use to post messages about important events. Each component registers which events it cares about, and when the actor receives a message, it distributes it to the appropriate components.

For example, let's say the AI component wants to move the actor. It just posts a message requesting the move to a new position, and the actor tells the appropriate components. The AI component doesn't have to know, nor does it care, which components receive the message.

This situation certainly keeps components from being decoupled from one another, but it also raises a few concerns. Sometimes it's important to know which component is answering the message and in which order. Say you post a move message, and the renderable component receives it first. It updates its internal positions, and everything is fine. Then the physics component receives the new position and detects it as being invalid. Now what? The physics system could send an event to disregard the old position and give the new position, but this could cause an oscillation where the AI component and physics component are battling each other trying to move the actor. The actor will mostly appear to vibrate, jumping back and forth between two positions.

There are certainly ways around this issue. You could (and probably should) have all message registration defined in data, which allows a great deal of control on a per-actor basis.

Game events are covered in detail in Chapter 11.

## The Best of Both Worlds

The best solution to these problems is to use a mixture of the two communication methods. Events are great for broadcasting things that other components may or may not care about, and direct access is great when you need to directly tell something to a specific component. Why not use both? Many games do.

In the sample game of *Teapot Wars,* I've chosen to use the first method of directly accessing components because it's a lot more readable and easier to understand exactly what's happening. If you were take this actor system to the next level so it could be used in a professional game, you would want to apply the concepts from Chapter 11 and add a simple messaging system as I described in the previous section. Other than that, this component system is very similar to the one we used on *Rat Race* at Super-Ego Games.

# Chapter 7

*by David "Rez" Graham*

# Controlling the Main Loop

Every game has a series of operations that run over and over to present and update the game to the player. This is the heartbeat that lets you know the game is alive. Games are unlike many forms of software in that even if the player does absolutely nothing, the game still needs to be constantly thinking and processing. A typical main loop may receive and process player input, run creature AI, update animations, update the physics system, run any world simulation that needs to happen, render the scene, and play music and sound effects. Every main loop is different and tailored for each individual game. All of these operations occur in one giant loop that can't take longer than 33ms per iteration (or 30 iterations per second) at a minimum. When you exit the main loop, your game shuts down

This is very different than your typical Windows program. Most Windows programs run a message pump designed to sit there doing nothing until the application receives an event. It does absolutely no processing until the user triggers something. This won't work for a game, which will happily go about processing and rendering regardless of player input. Even a chess game needs to be allowed to run its AI while the player is considering his move.

## Organizing the Main Loop

There are many ways to organize the main loop, and each game has its own technique. In this chapter, we'll look at a number of different possibilities.

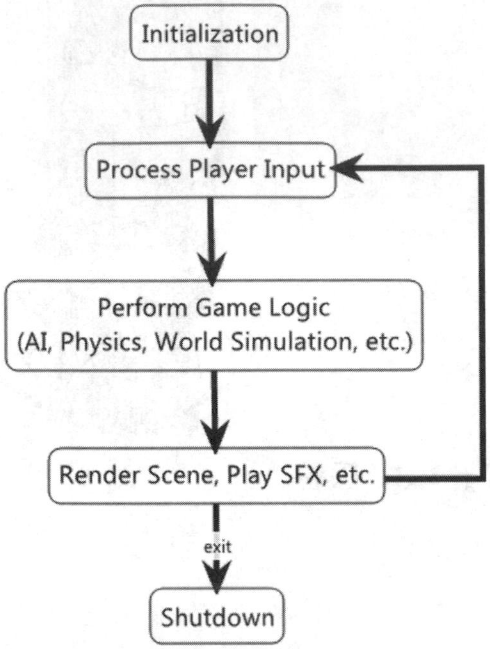


**Figure 7.1**
A simple main loop.

## Hard-Coded Updates

The easiest way to create a main loop is to simply update every system once each frame, as shown in Figure 7.1.

This is the easiest method to actually write since all you need to do is directly call a bunch of update functions, but it tends to be very inflexible. What happens if you want the AI to update at a different frequency? On *Rat Race,* we used a complex heuristic utility function to determine what action an NPC wanted to do next. We had code in there to ensure that it only ran once every second. At EA, we have even more complex timing functions to determine which Sim gets to run AI, for how long, and at what level of detail. Conversely, you'll want to render as quickly as humanly possible to avoid hitches in the visual presentation of the game.

As inflexible as this method is, it's still certainly valid. Early games from the Stone Age (for example, the late 80s and early 90s) all used this method. Some games still do. I worked at a game company called PlayFirst on casual iPhone and iPad games for a time. They all used this hard-coded method.

## Multithreaded Main Loops

Another method of building the main loop is to divide your update into major sections that can run concurrently. The classic split is between game logic and

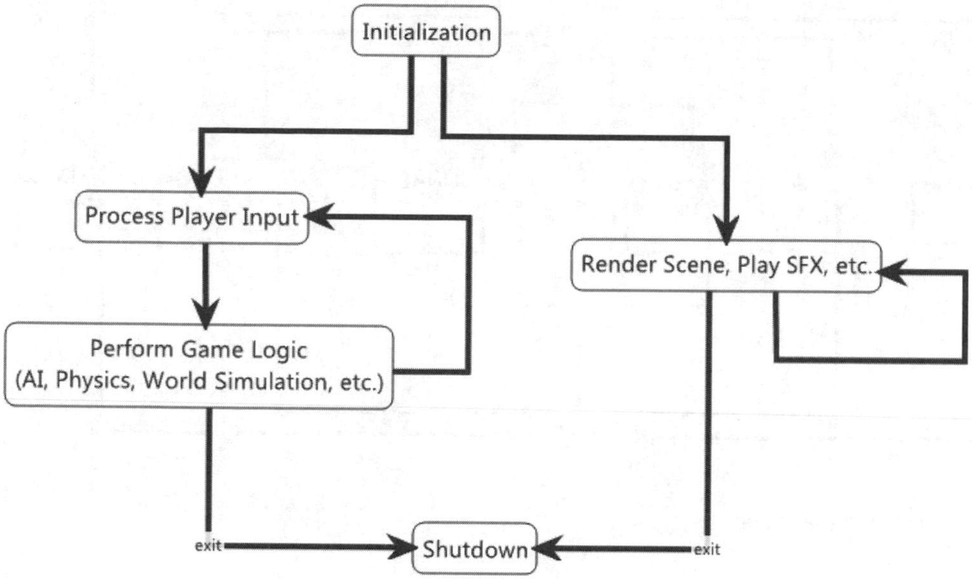


**Figure 7.2**
A multithreaded main loop.

rendering. One problem with rendering is that on modern hardware, your CPU spends most of its time waiting for the video card to process what it just sent. By putting the rendering system on another thread, you free up the CPU while the GPU is working its magic (see Figure 7.2).

This is a great technique for squeezing more out of your processor, especially considering that modern processors aren't really getting faster clock cycles, they're getting more cores.

Why not put everything on its own thread? You could have an architecture like the one in Figure 7.3, where every system gets its own separate thread of execution.

One problem with using a multithreaded architecture is communication between threads. When you have multiple threads all running at the same time and trying to communicate with each other, you have to take steps to ensure thread safety. Furthermore, threads tend to be pretty heavyweight objects, so it's inefficient to use threads for everything.

I'm not going to get too deep into the details here, since multithreaded architecture is beyond the scope of this chapter. You'll learn more about these exact issues and how you can work around them in Chapter 19, "An Introduction to Game AI."

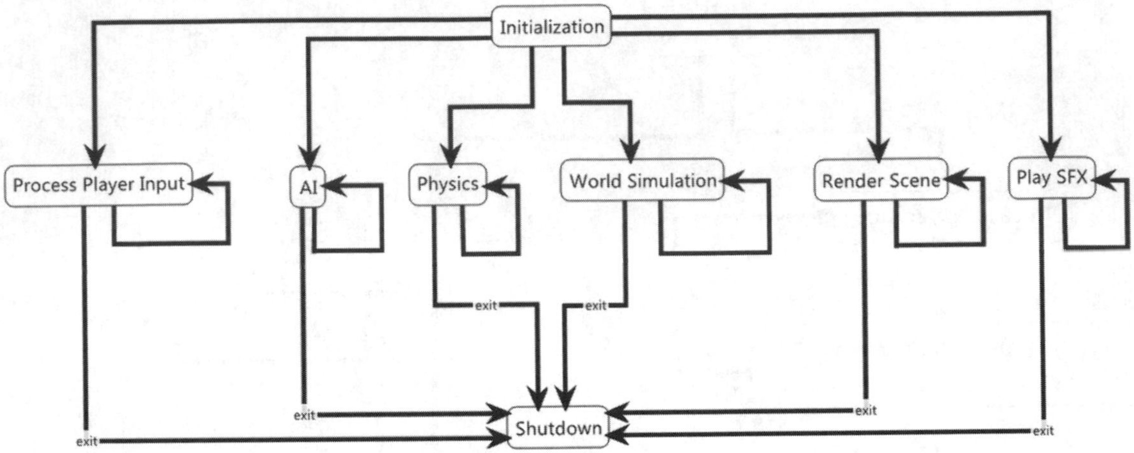


**Figure 7.3**
A cooperative multithreaded main loop.

## A Hybrid Technique

What if we take the idea of putting multiple systems in their own discrete execution modules but throw away all the problems with true concurrent execution? This gives us the best of both worlds, keeping all of our different systems nice and decoupled from each other and allowing them the illusion of being run simultaneously while avoiding race conditions and other nasty threading issues. This technique is called *cooperative multitasking.*

Cooperative multitasking is a mechanism where each process gets a little CPU time in a round-robin fashion. It's called *cooperative* because each process is responsible for releasing control back to the calling entity. If a process goes into an infinite loop, the entire system will hang. The trade-off for that weakness is that the system is simple to design and extremely efficient.

Imagine a simple base class called `Process` with a single virtual method, `VOnUpdate()`:

```
class Process
{
public:
  virtual void VOnUpdate(unsigned long deltaMs) = 0;
};
```

You could create objects inheriting from this class and stick them in a master process list. Every game loop, your code could traverse this list and call `VOnUpdate()` for each object:

```
typedef std::list<Process*> ProcessList;
ProcessList g_processList;
```

```
void UpdateProcesses(unsigned long deltaMs)
{
  ProcessList::iterator i = m_processList.begin();
  ProcessList::iterator end = m_processList.end();

  while (i != end)
  {
    Process* pProcess = *i;
    pProcess->VOnUpdate(deltaMs);
    ++i;
  }
}
```

The contents of the `VOnUpdate()` overload could be anything. It could move the object on a spline, it could monitor the contents of a buffer stream and update it accordingly, and it could run some AI code. It could monitor user interface objects like screens and buttons. If everything in your game were run by a process, you could actually get away with a main function that looked like this:

```
void main()
{
  if (CreateProcesses())
  {
    RunProcesses();
  }
  ShutdownProcesses();
}
```

It may sound crazy, but *Ultima VIII*'s main loop looked almost exactly like that, give or take a few lines.

**Think Like a Sim**

On *The Sims Medieval,* every Sim had two processes that were constantly running. One process handled the AI and ran any interactions on the Sim (like eating, sword fighting, and so on). The other thread was the SimUpdate, which mostly dealt with the simulation of the Sim itself. This process took care of things like decaying commodities, moods, and any other noninteraction updates the Sim needed to make. This system worked remarkably well. You could actually Ctrl-Alt-Shift-click on a Sim and break the execution of its specific interaction process! This made debugging the internals of a particular Sim a *lot* easier.

There are a few wrinkles to this wonderful design that you should know. If creating a system to handle your main loop were as easy as all that, I wouldn't bother devoting so much time to it. The first big problem comes when one process's `VOnUpdate()`

can destroy other processes, or even worse cause a recursive call to indirectly cause itself to be destroyed. Think of the likely code for a hand grenade exploding. The `VOnUpdate()` would likely query the game object lists for every object in a certain range, and then cause all those objects to be destroyed in a nice fireball. The grenade object would be included in the list of objects in range, wouldn't it?

The solution to this problem involves some kind of reference counting system or maybe a smart pointer. The `shared_ptr` template class in Chapter 3, "Coding Tidbits and Style That Saved Me," solves this problem well, and it will be used in the next section.

## A Simple Cooperative Multitasker

A good process class should contain some additional data members and methods to make it interesting and flexible. There are as many ways to create this class as there are programmers, but this should give you a good start. There are two classes in this nugget of code:

- `class Process`: A base class for processes. You'll inherit from this class and redefine the `VOnUpdate()` method.
- `class ProcessManager`: This is a container and manager for running all your cooperative processes.

Here's the definition for `Process`:

```
// some smart pointer typedef's
class Process;
typedef shared_ptr<Process> StrongProcessPtr;
typedef weak_ptr<Process> WeakProcessPtr;

class Process
{
  friend class ProcessManager;

public:
  enum State
  {
   // Processes that are neither dead nor alive
   UNINITIALIZED = 0, // created but not running
   REMOVED, // removed from the process list but not destroyed; this can
         // happen when a process that is already running is parented
         // to another process.
   // Living processes
   RUNNING, // initialized and running
```

```
    PAUSED,  // initialized but paused
    // Dead processes
    SUCCEEDED, // completed successfully
    FAILED,    // failed to complete
    ABORTED,   // aborted; may not have started
  };
  private:
  State m_state;            // the current state of the process
  StrongProcessPtr m_pChild;  // the child process, if any
public:
  // construction
  Process(void);
  virtual ~Process(void);

  protected:
  // interface; these functions should be overridden by the subclass as needed
  virtual void VOnInit(void) { m_state = RUNNING; }
  virtual void VOnUpdate(unsigned long deltaMs) = 0;
  virtual void VOnSuccess(void) { }
  virtual void VOnFail(void) { }
  virtual void VOnAbort(void) { }

public:
  // Functions for ending the process.
  inline void Succeed(void);
  inline void Fail(void);

  // pause
  inline void Pause(void);
  inline void UnPause(void);

  // accessors
  State GetState(void) const { return m_state; }
  bool IsAlive(void) const {return (m_state == RUNNING || m_state == PAUSED);}
  bool IsDead(void) const
  {
    return (m_state == SUCCEEDED || m_state == FAILED || m_state == ABORTED);
  }
  bool IsRemoved(void) const { return (m_state == REMOVED); }
  bool IsPaused(void) const { return m_state == PAUSED; }

  // child functions
  inline void AttachChild(StrongProcessPtr pChild);
  StrongProcessPtr RemoveChild(void); // releases ownership of the child
  StrongProcessPtr PeekChild(void) { return m_pChild; } // doesn't release
                                                        // ownership of child
```

```
private:
  void SetState(State newState) { m_state = newState; }
};
```

At the very top of this class is the `State` enum. There are a number of different states a process could potentially be in. Its current state determines how the `ProcessManager` handles it during the update loop. Processes start in the `UNINITIALIZED` state.

Along with its state, every process can have a child process (the `m_pChild` member). The child is a suspended process that's attached to this process. If this process completes successfully, the `ProcessManager` will attach the child and process it in the next frame. This is a very simple yet powerful technique, allowing you to create chains of processes. For example, if you wanted an NPC to walk to the water cooler and take a drink, you could create one process for path finding and another for running an animation. You would then instantiate the path-finding process and attach the animation process as a child. When you ran it, the character would path up to the water cooler and run the animation. This was exactly how *Rat Race* worked. Actions were built up by the AI and then pushed as a single-chained process.

There are five virtual functions that subclasses are allowed to override. The only function you *have* to override is `VOnUpdate()` since that's where the magic happens. This function defines what your process does and gets run once every loop. The only parameter is the delta time between this frame and the last.

`VOnInit()` is called once during the very first update. All of your process initialization should go here. It's important to remember to call the base class version of this function at the top of your override to ensure that the process state correctly gets set to `RUNNING`.

`VOnSuccess()`, `VOnFail()`, and `VOnAbort()` are exit functions. One of them is called when your process ends, depending on how it ended. The `Succeed()` and `Fail()` public member functions are used to end a process and tell it if it succeeded or failed. A process is typically only aborted due to an internal issue. It is perfectly valid to call `Succeed()` or `Fail()` from inside `VOnInit()`. This is a fairly common case since initialization can fail. If this happens, the process will never have its `VOnUpdate()` function called.

If a process is successful and it has a child process attached, that child will be promoted into the `ProcessManager`'s list. It will get initialized and run the next frame. If a process fails or is aborted, the child will *not* get promoted.

Note the use of the `StrongProcessPtr typedef` throughout. This is an excellent example of using smart pointers in a class that uses an STL list. Any reference to a

StrongProcessPtr is managed by the smart pointer class, ensuring that the process object will remain in memory as long as there is a valid reference to it. The moment the last reference is cleared or reassigned, the process memory is finally freed. That's why the ProcessManager has a list of StrongProcessPtr's instead of a list of Process pointers.

### A Seriously Nasty Bug on *Ultima VIII*

One of the trickiest bugs I ever had to find had to do with a special kind of process in *Ultima VIII*. *Ultima VIII* processes could attach their OnUpdate() calls to a real-time interrupt, which was pretty cool. Animations and other events could happen smoothly without worrying about the exact CPU speed of the machine. The process table was getting corrupted somehow, and no one was sure how to find it as the bug occurred completely randomly—or so we thought. After tons of QA time and late nights, we eventually found that jumping from map to map made the problem happen relatively frequently. We were able to track the bug down to the code that removed processes from the main process list. It turned out that the real-time processes were accessing the process list at the same moment that the list was being changed. Thank goodness, we weren't on multiple processors; we never would have found it.

Here is the definition of the ProcessManager class:

```
class ProcessManager
{
  typedef std::list<StrongProcessPtr> ProcessList;
  ProcessList m_processList;

public:
  // construction
  ~ProcessManager(void);

  // interface
  unsigned int UpdateProcesses(unsigned long deltaMs);
  WeakProcessPtr AttachProcess(StrongProcessPtr pProcess);
  void AbortAllProcesses(bool immediate);

  // accessors
  unsigned int GetProcessCount(void) const { return m_processList.size(); }

private:
  void ClearAllProcesses(void);  // should only be called by the destructor
};
```

The ProcessManager class is pretty small. At the very top is a typedef for a list of pointers to Process objects. Note how they are all StrongProcessPtr types, which in turn are of type shared_ptr<Process>. This allows you to create a process and safely hold on to your own reference without worrying about when the object is actually destroyed. It will be destroyed when the final strong reference is removed.

When you want to run a new process, you instantiate the specific Process subclass you want and then call AttachProcess() to attach it to the Process Manager. This queues it up to be initialized and run the next time the Process Manager updates.

To update the Process Manager, you call UpdateProcesses(). Let's take a look at that function:

```
unsigned int ProcessManager::UpdateProcesses(unsigned long deltaMs)
{
  unsigned short int successCount = 0;
  unsigned short int failCount = 0;

  ProcessList::iterator it = m_processList.begin();
  while (it != m_processList.end())
  {
    // grab the next process
    StrongProcessPtr pCurrProcess = (*it);

    // save the iterator and increment the old one in case we need to remove
    // this process from the list
    ProcessList::iterator thisIt = it;
    ++it;

    // process is uninitialized, so initialize it
    if (pCurrProcess->GetState() == Process::UNINITIALIZED)
      pCurrProcess->VOnInit();

    // give the process an update tick if it's running
    if (pCurrProcess->GetState() == Process::RUNNING)
      pCurrProcess->VOnUpdate(deltaMs);

    // check to see if the process is dead
    if (pCurrProcess->IsDead())
    {
      // run the appropriate exit function
      switch (pCurrProcess->GetState())
      {
        case Process::SUCCEEDED :
```

```
        {
          pCurrProcess->VOnSuccess();
          StrongProcessPtr pChild = pCurrProcess->RemoveChild();
          if (pChild)
            AttachProcess(pChild);
          else
            ++successCount;  // only counts if the whole chain completed
          break;
        }
        case Process::FAILED :
        {
          pCurrProcess->VOnFail();
          ++failCount;
          break;
        }
        case Process::ABORTED :
        {
          pCurrProcess->VOnAbort();
          ++failCount;
          break;
        }
      }
      // remove the process and destroy it
      m_processList.erase(thisIt);
    }
  }
  return ((successCount << 16) | failCount);
}
```

This function loops through every process in the list. If the process is in the `UNINITIALIZED` state, it calls `VOnInit()` on the process. Then, if the process is in the `RUNNING` state, it calls `VOnUpdate()`. Note that `VOnInit()` typically sets the state to `RUNNING`, so the process will get initialized and run its first update in the same frame, assuming `VOnInit()` succeeded.

The next block checks to see if the process has died. If so, it checks the exact state and calls the appropriate exit function, allowing the process to perform any exit logic. A successful process will have its child attached to the process list before being removed. Failed processes will simply be removed, causing their children to be destroyed.

Recall that nearly 100 percent of the game code could be inside various overloads of `Process::VOnUpdate()`. This game code can, and will, cause game processes and objects to be deleted, all the more reason that this system uses smart pointers.

**Round Robin Scheduling Gone Bad**

This system was used extensively to control the login servers of *Ultima Online*. When it was initially deployed, customer service began to receive complaints that some users were waiting more than five minutes for the login process to finish, and that didn't agree with the login server metrics, which measured over 2,000 logins per minute and an average login time of 15 seconds or so. The problem was identified after a little digging. I had bailed early from serving all the processes in the list in an attempt to poll network sockets and database activity, and in so doing, I left a few processes at the end of the list completely out in the cold.

## Very Simple Process Example: DelayProcess

A very simple example of a useful process using this cooperative design is a delay process. This process is useful for inserting timed delays, such as the fuse on an explosive. Here's how it works:

```
class DelayProcess : public Process
{
  unsigned long m_timeToDelay;
  unsigned long m_timeDelayedSoFar;

  public:
  explicit DelayProcess(unsigned long timeToDelay);

protected:
  virtual void OnUpdate(unsigned long deltaMs);
};

DelayProcess::DelayProcess(unsigned long timeToDelay)
{
  m_timeToDelay = timeToDelay;
  m_timeDelayedSoFar = 0;
}
void DelayProcess::OnUpdate(unsigned long deltaMs)
{
  m_timeDelayedSoFar += deltaMs;
  if (m_timeDelayedSoFar >= m_timeToDelay)
    Succeed();
}
```

Here's how you create an instance of DelayProcess:

```
StrongProcessPtr pDelay(new DelayProcess(3000)); // delay for 3 seconds
processManager.AttachProcess(pDelay);
```

Take note of two things. First, you don't just "new up" a `DelayProcess` and attach it to the `ProcessManager`. You have to use the `StrongProcessPtr` `typedef` (or the `shared_ptr` template directly) to manage `Process` objects. This fixes problems when processes get deleted, but other objects may still point to them. Second, you must call the `Attach()` method of `ProcessManager` to attach the new process to the Process Manager.

As the main loop is processed and `ProcessManager::UpdateProcesses()` is called, the `DelayProcess` counts the elapsed time, and once it has passed the wait period, it calls `Succeed()`. By itself, it's a little underwhelming—it just uses up a little CPU time and goes away. But if you define another process, such as `KaboomProcess`, things get a little more interesting. You can then create a nuclear explosion with a three-second fuse without a physics degree:

```
// The delay process will stay alive for three seconds
StrongProcessPtr pDelay(new DelayProcess(3000));
processManager.AttachProcess(pDelay);

// The KaboomProcess will wait for the DelayProcess
//  Note - kaboom will be attached automatically
StrongProcessPtr pKaboom(new KaboomProcess());
pDelay->AttachChild(pKaboom);
```

The `Process::AttachChild()` method sets up a simple dependency between the `DelayProcess` and the `KaboomProcess`. `KaboomProcess` will remain inactive until the `DelayProcess` succeeds. If the `DelayProcess` fails or is aborted for some reason (maybe the level ended before it finished), then the `KaboomProcess` is simply removed and never actually updates.

**Data-Driven Processes**

If you plan on using processes as the core of your game, you should have a data format that lets you define chains of processes and dependencies. At Super-Ego Games, we used XML to define our process chains and how they all fit together. It allowed us to set up complex game logic without having to touch a single line of code. An even better way would be to use a visual editor so designers would be able to move around nodes and create complex game logic without involving engineers at all. This is basically what the quest system did in *The Sims Medieval*.

## More Uses of `Process` Derivatives

Every updatable game object can inherit from `Process`. User interface objects such as buttons, edit boxes, or menus can inherit from `Process`. Audio objects such as sound effects, speech, or music make great use of this design because of the dependency and timing features.

## Playing Nicely with the OS

Now that we've seen what goes on inside the main loop and some techniques for managing your various processes, let's take a step out of that and look at how the game loop fits into the operating system. This is especially important if you're making a game for a multitasking platform like Windows. You need to learn how to play nicely with the operating system and the other applications running on it. For example, this code would cause Windows to think your program has stalled:

```
while (true)
{
  RunLogic();
  RenderScene();
}
```

The problem here is that the code is completely ignoring all messages being sent to it. You can't click the X button at the top right, because none of the mouse messages get through, and Windows considers the program to be unresponsive. It will eventually say "not responding" next to your app in the Task Manager. It's important to respond to messages being sent from the operating system, even if you just pass them through to the default handler:

```
return DefWindowProc(hwnd, msg, wparam, lparam);
```

Another problem with working on a multitasking platform like Windows is that you sometimes have to yield resources to those applications. For example, games typically acquire exclusive access to system resources like the video card, which allows them to render in full screen at custom resolutions. If the user Alt-tabs, you will lose that exclusive control and need to be able to handle that situation. You'll learn more about this later in this chapter when we talk about the DirectX 11 Framework.

On Windows, you typically have a message pump like this:

```
int WINAPI WinMain(HINSTANCE hInstance, HINSTANCE hPrevInstance,
          LPSTR lpCmdLine, int nCmdShow)
{
  MSG msg;
  while(GetMessage(&msg, NULL, 0, 0) > 0)
  {
   TranslateMessage(&msg);
   DispatchMessage(&msg);
```

```
    }
    return msg.wParam;
}
```

The `GetMessage()` function will block execution until the application has at least one message pending, and then it will run the inner block of the `while` loop. This in turn calls the Windows procedure callback function you registered when creating the window. If that function blocks the execution of `GetMessage()` by locking the application in a loop, it won't receive any messages. Have you ever clicked on a Windows program and had it gray itself out, followed by a message saying something like "this program is not responding"? What's happening is that the program is never getting back to the `GetMessage()` call.

The problem here is that we can't stop execution if there are no messages pending, nor can we ignore messages that come in. The solution here is the `PeekMessage()` function, which is just like `GetMessage()` except that it doesn't block execution. That leaves us with the following loop:

```
while (msg.message != WM_QUIT)
{
  if (PeekMessage( &msg, NULL, 0U, 0U, PM_REMOVE))
  {
    TranslateMessage(&msg);
    DispatchMessage(&msg);
  }
  else
  {
   MainGameLoop();
  }
}
```

This is much better! First, if the application receives a quit message, it breaks out of the loop. Then it checks to see if there's a Windows message. If there is, it handles it in the usual way. If not, it allows the game loop to process one iteration.

## Using the DirectX 11 Framework

The code in this chapter is written to integrate with the DirectX Framework, which handles many nasty problems, such as detecting when a player switches screen resolutions or Alt-tabs to another full-screen application. If you code on other platforms, you'll likely be spared these issues. Windows can run multiple applications simultaneously, and the user can change hardware configurations, like screen size, while your game is running. On consoles you can't do that, and you avoid all of those hellish little problems.

## Rendering and Presenting the Display

The DirectX 11 Framework provides a pretty good routine to render and present the display. It is called from the `DXUTMainLoop()` function when the game is not processing messages, in exactly the way the `MainGameLoop()` function was mentioned earlier. The function is `DXUTRender3DEnvironment11()` inside *Source\GCC4\3rdParty\DX11\Core\DXUT.cpp* around line 3816. Let's pick it apart so you can understand what's going on. Since I don't have permission to reprint this method, you should launch Visual Studio and load either a DirectX sample or the Game Coding Complete 4 source code and follow along.

The first thing you should notice about this function is how much can go wrong, and that it can pretty much go wrong after nearly every single line of code. The reason for this is a quirk of Windows games—players have an annoying tendency to actually have other applications up, like Firefox or something, while playing your game! Any kind of task switching, or user switching under XP or later, can cause DirectX to lose its devices.

After getting a bunch of a DirectX objects and making sure they still exist, the function checks to see if rendering is paused, if the window is occluded, or if it's inactive. If any of these conditions is true, it calls `Sleep()` to relinquish time back to other applications. This is just part of being a nice Windows application, and even silly Windows tools that have similar message pumps should do this. You might decide to tweak the amount of time you sleep. Your mileage with the sleep values in the framework could vary from game to game.

After all that, the code handles issues related to timers and timing. This is the section of code that starts with `DXUTGetGlobalTimer()->GetTimeValues()`. Almost every game needs to track how many milliseconds have elapsed since the last frame so that animations and object movement can be kept in sync with reality. The alternative is to ignore time altogether and just render things based on each frame that renders, but that would mean that faster computers would literally play the game faster—not in the "gamer" sense but in an actual sense. If you keep track of time, then objects on faster computers will still fall to the ground at the same rate as slower computers, but the faster computers will look smooth as silk.

The next section of code retrieves and calls the application's frame move callback function. This callback is set to `GameCodeApp::OnUpdateGame()`, which controls the game logic and how the game state changes over each pass of the main loop. Control passes to the game logic's `VOnUpdate()` method, which will update all the running game processes and send updates to all the game views attached to the game logic.

The next bit of code retrieves and calls the application's frame render callback, which will call VOnRender() methods of views attached to the game. After the rendering is complete, the screen must be presented, which is when things can go awry. Back in the good old days, this was called "slamming" because the back buffer was copied byte-by-byte to the front buffer in one memory copy. Now this is handled by a simple pointer change in the video hardware and is generally called "flipping" because nothing is really copied at all.

The call to Present() will cause the scene to actually be presented onto the monitor. The next step is to check the return code from this function because there may be more work to do. The user might have to change video modes, requiring that the device be reset, or perhaps it was removed or the window became fully occluded. These edge cases must all be handled gracefully.

After all that, the frame counter is updated, and a little status bit is checked to see if the game should exit after one frame. This is actually a quite handy thing to have, whether you write your own frame counter or use the one in the framework, because you can use it to smoke test your game. An amazing amount of code runs when you initialize, update, and render your game, and any problems during this process could be written out to a log file for later analysis. This is a great thing to do, and it can be an important part of a simple smoke test where you can be somewhat sure that the game can at least get to the first frame.

## Your Callback Functions for Updating and Rendering

Luckily, the DirectX Framework has done most of the major work for you, even to the point of splitting updates in your game logic from the rendering of the game. This matches well with the architecture I'm pushing in this book. If you recall the _tWinMain() implementation from the previous chapter, among the code were these two calls:

```
DXUTSetCallbackD3D11FrameMove( GameCodeApp::OnUpdateGame );
DXUTSetCallbackD3D11FrameRender( GameCodeApp::OnRender );
```

The first is a callback where you can update your game, and the second is a callback where your game can render. Let's take a look at the implementation of those two methods:

```
void CALLBACK GameCodeApp::OnUpdateGame(double fTime, float fElapsedTime,
                              void* pUserContext)
{
  if (g_pApp->HasModalDialog())
  {
    // don't update the game if a modal dialog is up.
```

```
    return;
  }
  if (g_pApp->m_bQuitting)
  {
    PostMessage(g_pApp->GetHwnd(), WM_CLOSE, 0, 0);
  }
  if (g_pApp->m_pGame)
  {
    // allow event queue to process for up to 20 ms
    IEventManager::Get()->VTick(20);

    if (g_pApp->m_pBaseSocketManager)
      g_pApp->m_pBaseSocketManager->DoSelect(0);  // pause 0 microseconds

    g_pApp->m_pGame->VOnUpdate(float(fTime), fElapsedTime);
  }
}
```

This method updates your game logic, but only if there isn't a modal dialog box up and if the application isn't quitting.

This code implies that you shouldn't perform any quit mechanism while you are pumping messages. Quitting takes a good amount of time, and a player worried about getting caught playing your game while he is supposed to be doing something else can press Alt-F4 to close your game about 20 times in a single second. If you send all those quit messages into the message pump, you've got to filter them out, which is why you check to see if you're actually quitting so you can post a WM_CLOSE message. The user interface control that receives the quit button click event or the hot key event should simply set a Boolean variable to true, which will be checked after the last message in the queue has been handled.

This function is a member of GameCodeApp, but since this method is a callback, it must be declared static, which means that you have to use the global g_pApp pointer to get to the instance of the GameCodeApp class. The same is true for the GameCodeApp::OnRender call:

```
void CALLBACK GameCodeApp::OnD3D11FrameRender(ID3D11Device* pd3dDevice,
    ID3D11DeviceContext* pd3dImmediateContext, double fTime,
    float fElapsedTime, void* pUserContext )
{
  BaseGameLogic *pGame = g_pApp->m_pGame;
  for(GameViewList::iterator i=pGame->m_gameViews.begin(),
    end=pGame->m_gameViews.end(); i!=end; ++i)
  {
    (*i)->VOnRender(fTime, fElapsedTime);
```

```
  }
  g_pApp->m_pGame->VRenderDiagnostics();
}
```

This method simply iterates through all the views attached to the game logic, `g_pApp->m_pGame`, and calls `VOnRender()` for each one. After that, the game logic calls a special method for rendering debug information, `VRenderDiagnostics()`. This is a convenience for programmers who would rather not adhere to the separation between logic and view just to draw some debug lines on the screen.

A good example of how I use `VRenderDiagnostics()` is drawing physics information, such as mesh wireframe of any objects moving on the screen. The physics system is purely a game logic object, and the renderer really belongs to the game view. If you wanted to religiously follow the separation of game logic and game view, you'd have to do something like have the game logic create special "line" objects and send messages to the game view that it needs to draw these lines.

That's just dumb, in my opinion. A game logic should be able to use the application layer—in this case, DirectX's renderer—to draw debug data onto the screen. Yes, it breaks the rules, but yes, you should do it.

## Can I Make a Game Yet?

By now you've learned a lot about some of the hidden superstructure of game code, most notably about `GameCodeApp`, `BaseGameLogic`, `Process`, and `ProcessManager`. You've probably figured out that most of the subsystems discussed so far can benefit from cooperative multitasking: animated objects, user interface code, and more. If you're like me, you've already played with writing your own games, and you're itching to put everything together in a tight little game engine. At this point, you know just enough to be dangerous and could probably strike out on your own to write a few very simple games. However, there are still quite a few important bits and pieces you should know if you want to take it to the next level.

For example, you probably never thought about how game engines stuff a few gigabytes of game art and sounds through a much smaller memory space. Read the next chapter and find out.

CHAPTER 8

*by Mike McShaffry*

# Loading and Caching Game Data

Once you get a nice 3D model or sound, how do you actually get it into your game? Most game books present code examples where the game loads X, WAV, or MP3 files directly. This doesn't work in real games. Real games have tens of thousands of these files and other bits of data. They might not fit into memory at the same time, either. When you see a detailed environment in *Gears of War,* you can bet that it fills memory nearly to the last bit, and the act of walking into another room or building needs some way of kicking out unused assets and bringing in the new, and doing it in a way that seems completely transparent to the player. So how does this really work? Take a look at Figure 8.1.

Games usually pack selected bits of game data into a small number of files, often called a *resource file.* By the way, just in case I haven't mentioned it, I tend to use the terms *game assets* and *game resources* to mean the same thing—they are all *game data.* Art, animations, sounds, 3D meshes, and map levels are all game assets. These files usually map one-to-one with an entire game level. When you see a loading screen, you are likely witnessing the game reading just enough of the resource files to begin playing the game.

Each game resource you use must be converted to the smallest possible format that is supported by the hardware, taking care to keep the quality at the right level. This is pretty easy for sounds, since you can easily predict the quality and size delta of a 44KHz stereo WAV versus an 11KHz mono WAV stream. Textures are trickier to

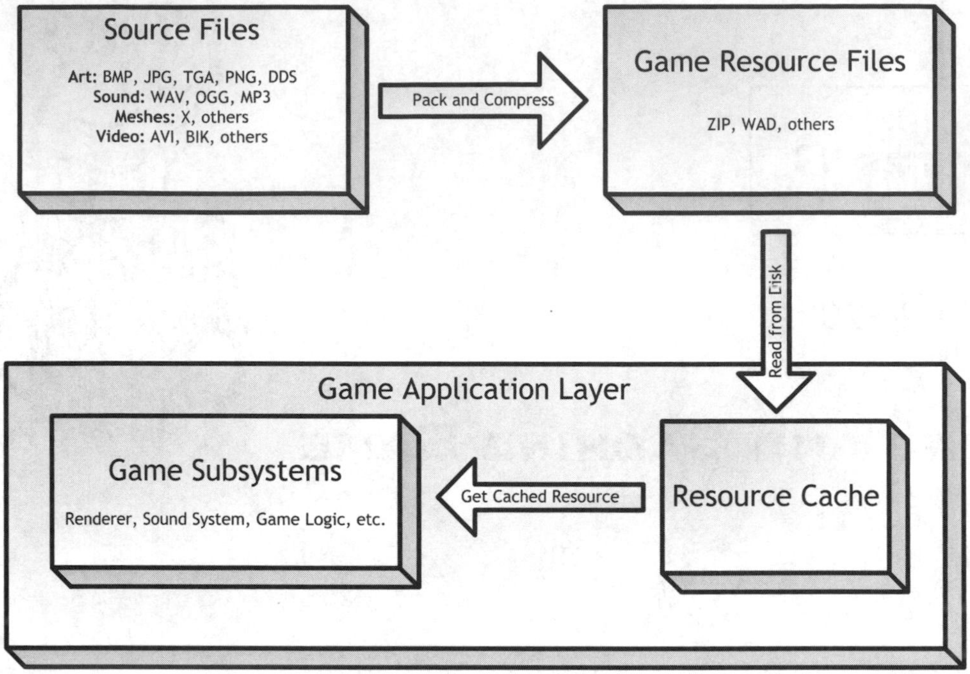


**Figure 8.1**
This is how data flows from game resource files to your game subsystems.

work with, on the other hand, because the best storage format is completely dependent on its use in the game and what it looks like.

These conversions are also dependent on the hardware platform. You can count on the fact that the Sony PS3 and the Microsoft Xbox360 will want sounds and textures presented in two completely different formats. This process will result in different resource files for each platform you support.

Most everyone is familiar with the Zip file, originally created back in 1989 by Phil Katz, first implemented in PKWARE's PKZIP utility. There might be better compression and storage formats for storing particular bits of game data, but for our purposes it will do nicely as a general-purpose resource file. Later in this chapter, I'll show you how this is implemented in code, packing all your game assets into one neat file format.

If your game is more of an open world design, your technology has to be more complicated and manage resources streaming from disc into memory and being released as the player moves through the game world.

More likely than not, you'll be streaming resources not from disc, but from the Web. The concepts are exactly the same, but the bandwidth can be extremely variable and certainly less than grabbing resources from the local hardware. Predicting what the player needs, and finding ways to stream those bits, is a key part of any nontrivial game that runs over the Web.

Both of those subjects are beyond the scope of this book to present detailed solutions, but you will be introduced to basic ideas behind resource caching so you can become familiar with the basic concepts.

## Game Resources: Formats and Storage Requirements

Modern games have gigabytes of data. A single-layer DVD can hold 4.7GB, and a single layer of a Blu-ray disc can hold up to 25GB. For PC games, you can browse the install directories and get an idea of what they store and how much storage they need. I'll go over the big stuff and give you an idea of how the data is stored, what formats you can use, how you can compress it, and what that does to the final product. I'll cover the following game data file types:

- **3D Object Meshes and Environments:** This usually requires a few tens of megabytes and stores all the geometry for your game.
- **3D Mesh/Object Animation Data:** This is much smaller than you'd think, but lots of in-game cinematics can blow this up to many tens of megabytes.
- **Map/Level Data:** This is a catchall for components like trigger events, object types, scripts, and others. Together, they take up very little space and are usually easy to compress.
- **Sprite and Texture Data:** These get pretty big very fast and can take many hundreds of megabytes, even on a Wii game.
- **Sound, Music, and Recorded Dialogue:** Recorded dialogue usually takes more space on games than any other data category, especially when the games have a strong story component.
- **Video and Prerendered Cinematics:** Minute-per-minute, these components take up the most space, so they are used sparingly in most games. They are essentially the combination of sprite animation and stereo sound.

### 3D Object Meshes and Environments

3D object and environment geometry takes up a lot less space than you'd think. A 3D mesh, whether it is for an object, a character, or an environment, is a collection of points in 3D space with accompanying data that describes how these points are organized into polygons and how the polygons should be rendered.

The points in 3D space are called *vertices*. They are stored as three floating-point numbers that represent the location of the point (X,Y,Z) from the origin. Individual triangles in this mesh are defined by three or more indices into the point list. Here's an example of the mesh for a cube that has been pushed around so that it isn't symmetrical in any axis (a useful object you'll use later in the 3D graphics chapter):

```
Vec3 TestObject::g_SquashedCubeVerts[] =
{
  Vec3( 0.5,0.5,-0.25),     // Vertex 0.
  Vec3(-0.5,0.5,-0.25),     // Vertex 1.
  Vec3(-0.5,0.5,0.5),       // And so on.
  Vec3(0.75,0.5,0.5),
  Vec3(0.75,-0.5,-0.5),
  Vec3(-0.5,-0.5,-0.5),
  Vec3(-0.5,-0.3,0.5),
  Vec3(0.5,-0.3,0.5)
};

WORD TestObject::g_TestObjectIndices[][3] =
{
  { 0,1,2 }, { 0,2,3 }, { 0,4,5 },
  { 0,5,1 }, { 1,5,6 }, { 1,6,2 },
  { 2,6,7 }, { 2,7,3 }, { 3,7,4 },
  { 3,4,0 }, { 4,7,6 }, { 4,6,5 }
};
```

Feel free to plot it out on graph paper if you want, or you can take my word for it. The eight vertices are stored in an array, and the triangles are defined by groups of three indices into that array. A cube has eight points in space and six faces, but those faces are each comprised of two triangles. Twelve groups of three indices each are needed to define twelve triangles that make a cube.

If you have some experience with 3D programming, you might know that there are ways to save some space here. Instead of storing each triangle as a group of three points, you can store a list of connected triangles with fewer indices. These data structures are called *triangle lists* or *triangle fans*. Either of these stores the first triangle with three indices and each following triangle with only one additional index. This technique is a little like drawing a shape without picking up your pencil, since each extra triangle requires only one additional vertex rather than an entire set of

**Table 8.1 Raw Geometry Sizes**

| Object | Members | Size |
|---|---|---|
| Vertices | 2,000 points @ (3 floating-point numbers x 4 bytes each). | 24,000 bytes |
| Each triangle group | 300 triangles @ (302 indices x 2 bytes each). | 604 bytes |
| All triangle groups | 100 groups @ 604 bytes = 60,400 bytes. Vertices @ 24,000 bytes + Triangles @ 60,400 bytes. | 84,400 bytes |

three vertices. This way you can store *n* triangles with only *n* + *2* indices instead of *n**3 vertices—quite a savings.

Let's assume you have an object with 2,000 vertices: 300 triangles stored in 100 triangle groups. Take a look at Table 8.1 to see how much space this data takes.

It looks like you can store the raw geometry in about 82KB. But wait, there's a little more data to consider. The data doesn't tell you anything about how to texture the object. Renderers will assume that each triangle group has the same material and textures. For each group, you'll need to store some additional data.

A material describing the diffuse map is going to define the color of an object and how it reflects light. The size of the material can vary, depending on what the graphics chip and renderer can handle. The renderer can also apply one or more textures to the object. This data can vary in size. If the object is unaffected by lighting and has a solid color, it will require only a few bytes. If the object is affected by lighting and has a base texture, a decal texture, a normal map, a specular map, an environment map, and stores color information for ambient, diffuse, and specular lighting, then it could require almost 100 bytes per vertex. This information is stored for each index in each triangle group.

Let's look at two cases, shown in Table 8.2. The first has a simple textured, colored object, and the second has an additional 64 bytes per index in each triangle group to store material and lighting data.

Notice the staggering difference. The more complicated object is quite a bit larger, but it also looks amazing. So what have you learned? The complexity of the geometry can be made much smaller if your 3D models make good use of triangle strips and fans, but most of the savings comes from being frugal with complicated material

**Table 8.2 Storing Simple versus Complicated Objects**

| Object | Members | Size |
|---|---|---|
| Simple textured and lit object (30 bytes per vertex): | 302 indices per group x 100 groups @ 30 bytes | 906,000 bytes |
| Complicated material info (80 bytes per vertex): | 302 indices per group x 100 groups @ 80 bytes | 2,416,000 bytes |

models. This savings comes at a cost to the visual fidelity of the object, which affects the player's gameplay experience.

One thing you should note: The actual textures are stored separately from the mesh data, and we haven't even talked about those yet. They are orders of magnitude larger, too.

## Animation Data

Animations are stored as changes in position and orientation over time. You already know that a position in 3D space takes 12 bytes—4 bytes each for X, Y, and Z coordinates. Orientation is usually stored as a 12-byte or 16-byte data structure, depending on the rendering engine. This is the difference between storing the orientation as angles of yaw, pitch, and roll (Euler angles) or a mathematical entity known as a *quaternion*, which is a 4-vector (X, Y, Z, W). (You'll learn all about the quaternion in Chapter 14, "3D Graphics Basics.") For now, we'll assume the orientation takes 12 bytes.

One way to store animations is by recording a stream of position and orientation data at fast intervals, say 30 times per second. For each second and each object, you have the following:

12 bytes for position + 12 bytes for orientation = 24 bytes per sample

30 samples per second × 24 bytes per sample = 720 bytes/second

An object like a character is represented by a lot of discrete objects. Assuming you have a very simple character with only 30 separate movable parts (called *bones*), this gets pretty big very fast:

720 bytes/second × 30 bones = 21,600 bytes per second

Of course, there are ways to cheat. Games never store this much data for animations—it is like storing an uncompressed TGA file for every frame of an entire movie. First, most motions don't need 30 samples per second to look good. Actually, even complicated motions can usually get by with 15 samples per second or less, and not every bone is typically in motion at the same time, at maximum speed. Your mileage may vary with different motions, so your code might need to store different motions sampled at different rates. One thing you can be sure of, not every animation can look good with the same sampling rate, so your engine should be sophisticated enough to use animation data at different sampling rates.

Sometimes objects don't need to change position and orientation every frame. This implies you could store a stream of changes in position or orientation when they happen and store nothing at all but a time delay when the object or bone is still. Starting in the middle of or reversing an animation can be a little tricky, since you have to start at a known position and reapply the position and orientation deltas until you get to the position you want—something like finding the right spot in a track on a DJ's turntable. Every second or so, you should store the full position and orientation information. These snapshots are usually called *keyframes*. They can be very useful for jumping quickly to somewhere in the middle of an animation, and they can also reduce small errors that can accumulate.

Finally, since the position and orientation changes are small, you can usually get away with storing them in something other than floating-point numbers. You can convert them to 2-byte integers, for example. The Unreal Engine does exactly this—storing Euler angles as mapped values from 0 to 65536. You might wonder if this is a good idea, but think about how humans perceive angles. I'd defy most people to discern the difference between a 127-degree angle and a 128-degree one—and that's just $1/360^{th}$ of a circle. Take those deltas down to $1/65536^{th}$ of a circle, and you'll see the Unreal engineers were pretty clever indeed. These compression techniques can dramatically reduce the size of animation data down to a few tens of kilobytes per second for an animated character. For example, the animation data for a main character like Garrett in *Thief: Deadly Shadows*, who can use different weapons, climb on walls, crouch, crawl, and perform other activities, should be in the 5MB to 7MB range. The size of these animations increases linearly with the number of bones and the nature of their movement, so as characters get more complicated and active, the size of the animations increases, too.

Assuming that your game has a big storyline and you want to store lots of in-game cinematics, you can estimate the size of your in-game movies, minus the audio, like this:

- Assume the average of two characters moving simultaneously per cinematic
- Each cinematic averages 30 seconds
- 50KB per second (25KB per character per second) × 30 seconds = 1.53MB

Don't get too excited yet; the animation data is the least of your problems. Just wait until you see how much storage your digital audio is going to take.

## Map/Level Data

Most game object data is stored in a proprietary format, which is often determined by the type of data and the whim of the programmer. There is no standard format for storing game object data, AI scripts, dialogue, and other components. This data is usually packed in a binary format for the game, but during development it is usually stored in a format that is easy to work with, such as XML. There's a good public domain XML parser called TinyXML, and it is included as a part of the third-party SDKs with the companion source code.

Either way, this data is usually the least of your problems as far as storage is concerned. Your textures, audio, and animation data will overshadow this stuff by a long, long way.

## Texture Data

Left to their own devices, artists would hand you every texture they create in a TIF or TGA file. The uncompressed 32-bit art would look exactly like the artist envisioned. When you consider that a raw 32-bit 1024 × 768 bitmap tips the scales at just over 3MB, you'll quickly decide to use a more efficient format when your artists are demanding a few thousand of these.

As always, you'll generally need to trade quality for size. Load time will also need to be considered. The best games choose the right format and size for each asset. You'll be better at doing this if you understand how bitmaps, textures, and audio files are stored and processed and what happens to them under different compression scenarios.

## Bitmap Color Depth

Different bitmap formats allocate a certain number of bits for red, green, blue, and alpha channels. Some formats are indexed, meaning that the pixel data is actually an index into a color table that stores the actual RGBA values. Here's a list of the most common formats:

- **32-bit (8888 RGBA):** The least compact way to store bitmaps, but retains the most information.
- **24-bit (888 RGB):** This format is common for storing backgrounds that have too much color data to be represented in either 8-bit indexed or 16-bit formats and have no need for an alpha channel.

- **24-bit (565 RGB, 8 A):** This format is great for making nice-looking bitmaps with a good alpha channel. Green gets an extra bit because the human eye is more sensitive to changes in green than red or blue.
- **16-bit (565 RGB):** This compact format is used for storing bitmaps with more varieties of color and no alpha channel.
- **16-bit (555 RGB, 1 A):** This compact format leaves one bit for translucency, which is essentially a chroma key.
- **8-bit indexed:** A compact way to store bitmaps that have large areas of subtly shaded colors; some of the indexes can be reserved for different levels of translucency.

Many renderers, including DirectX, support a wide variety of pixel depth in each red, blue, green, and alpha channel.

**Support Tools Your Content Creators Will Actually Use**

Avoid writing oddball tools to try to save a few bits here and there. Try to write your game so that your content creators, such as artists, can use the same art formats used by popular art tools like Photoshop. They will be able to easily manipulate their work in a common and well-known tool, and your game will look exactly the way the artists intended it to look. You'll also be able to find artists who can work on your game if you stick to the standard formats and tools. If you must, you can write some great compression methods to process the results into something really small.

### *Which Is Better: 24-, 16-, or 8-Bit Art?*

It's virtually impossible to choose a single format to store every bitmap in your game and have all your bitmaps come through looking great. In fact, I can assure you that some of your bitmaps will end up looking like they should be in your laundry pile.

Figure 8.2 shows three different bitmaps that were created by drawing a grayscale image in Photoshop. The bitmap on the far left uses 8 bits per channel, the center bitmap is stored using 5 bits per channel, while the one on the right is stored using 4 bits. If you attempt to store a subtly shaded image using too few colors, you'll see results closer to the right bitmap, which looks crummy.

If you can use 8 bits for each channel, you'll see the best result, but you'll trade this quality for a much larger size. Needless to say, if your artist storms into your office and wonders why her beautiful bitmaps are banded all to hell, you've likely forced them into a bad color space. If your artists can choose the format that reproduces the image reliably in the best possible compression, great! But you'll tend to find

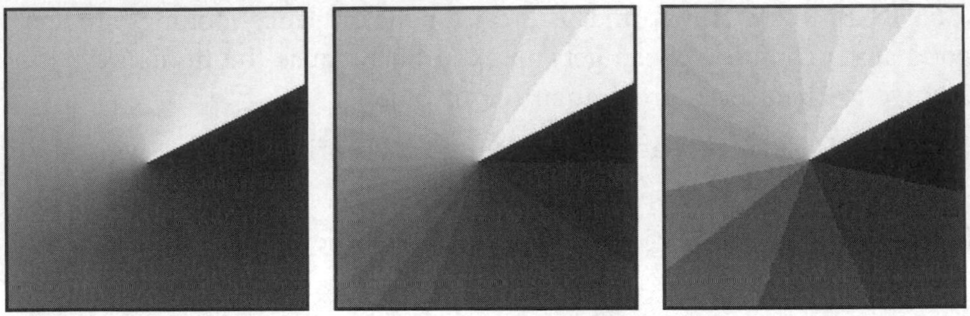

**Figure 8.2**
Grayscale banding patterns for 24-bit, 16-bit, and 8-bit depths.

that artists will choose the biggest format every time, so some gentle incentives might be needed to get them to optimize their art along the way. Just like programmers, artists tend to be perfectionists in their craft.

### *Using Lossy Compression*

A discussion of art storage wouldn't be complete without taking a look at the effects of using a lossy compression scheme such as JPG. The compression algorithm tweaks some values in the original art to achieve a higher compression ratio, hence the term "lossy." It's not a mistake that if you spell-check the word lossy you get "lousy" as one of your choices. Beyond a certain threshold, the art degrades too much to get past your QA department, and it certainly won't get past the artist who spent so much time creating it.

Perhaps the best approach is to get artists to decide how they'll save their own bitmaps using the highest lossiness they can stand. It still won't be enough, I guarantee you, because they are much more sensitive to subtle differences than a consumer, but it's a start.

### *Data Sizes for Textures*

Texture storage is one of the big budget areas for games. They take up the most space second only to audio and streaming video. Character textures for high-definition console games like *Gears of War* can be as large as 2048 × 2048. They also have multiple layered maps for specular and emissive effects that weigh in at 512 × 512 or 1024 × 1024. This starts to add up extremely quickly.

An uncompressed 1024 × 1024 texture is going to take 2MB to 4MB in memory, depending on whether it is a 16-bit or 32-bit texture. Most of your level geometry and game objects won't need that kind of density; they'll usually use different textures in layers to create interesting effects.

A single object, such as a wall, might have a 16-bit 512 × 512 texture on it taking 1MB of memory, but add to that a couple of 128 × 128 decals and a 128 × 128 normal map and you start eating up some memory. This one object with these three textures will take almost 2MB of texture memory. Your game might have a few hundred objects of various detail, eating your memory faster than you expect. The Nintendo Wii only has 64MB in the first place, which means you have to budget your textures more than almost any other game asset.

Even the best video cards don't perform well when you have to swap textures in and out of video memory. If your game is expected to run well on a 512MB video card, you'd better be careful and take that into account when building levels. A few hundred objects and 10 unique characters will chew up that 512MB in a real hurry, and you'll have to scramble to fix the problem. Believe me, you won't be able to ask your customers to simply buy new video cards, unless of course you are Valve and are publishing the latest *Half-Life*.

Finally, most textures need some additional storage for their mip-maps. A textured object with a mip-map will look good no matter how far away the viewer is from the textured object. If you've ever seen a really cheap 3D game where the object textures flashed or scintillated all the time, it's because the game didn't use mip-mapped textures. A mip-map precalculates the image of a texture at different distances. For example, a 128 × 128 texture that is fully mip-mapped has a 64 × 64, 32 × 32, 16 × 16, 8 × 8, 4 × 4, 2 × 2, and 1 × 1 version of itself. The renderer will choose one or even blend more than one of these mip-maps to render the final pixels on the polygon. This creates a smooth textured effect, no matter how the viewpoint is moving.

A full mip-map for a texture takes 33 percent more space than the texture does by itself. So don't forget to save that texture space for your mip-maps. One interesting bit—games almost always pregenerate their mip-maps and store them in the resource file rather than generating them on the fly. There are two reasons for this. First, a good mip-map takes a long time to generate, and the second reason is that even a crappy mip-map takes longer to generate on the fly than it takes to load from disc. Improving loading speed can be a much bigger problem than media storage.

## Sound and Music Data

Sound formats in digital audio are commonly stored in either mono or stereo, sampled at different frequencies, and accurate to either 8 or 16 bits per sample. The effect of mono or stereo on the resulting playback and storage size is obvious. Stereo sound takes twice as much space to store but provides left and right channel waveforms. The different frequencies and bit depths have an interesting and quite drastic effect on the sound.

Digital audio is created by sampling a waveform and converting it into discrete 8- or 16-bit values that approximate the original waveform. This works because the human ear has a relatively narrow range of sensitivity: 20Hz to 20,000Hz. It's no surprise that the common frequencies for storing WAV files are 44KHz, 22KHz, and 11KHz.

It turns out that telephone conversations are 8-bit values sampled at 8KHz, after the original waveform has been filtered to remove frequencies higher than 3.4MHz. Music on CDs is first filtered to remove sounds higher than 22KHz and then sampled at 16-bit 44KHz. Just to summarize, Table 8.3 shows how you would use the different frequencies in digital audio.

Use lower sampling rates for digital audio in your game to simulate telephone conversations or talking over shortwave radio.

## Video and Prerendered Cinematics

Animated sequences in games go as far back as *Pac Man*, where after every few levels you'd see a little cartoon featuring the little yellow guy and his friends. The cartoons had little or nothing to do with the game mechanics, but they were fun to watch and gave players a reward and a short break. One of the first companies to use large amounts of video footage in games was Origin Systems in the *Wing Commander* series. More than giving players a reward, they actually told a story. Epic cinematics are not only common in today's big-budget games, but they are also expected.

There are two techniques worth considering for incorporating cinematic sequences. Some games like *Wing Commander III* will shoot live video segments and simply

**Table 8.3 Using Different Audio Frequencies with Digital Formats**

| Format | Quality | Size per Second | Size per Minute |
|---|---|---|---|
| 44.1KHz 16-bit stereo WAV | CD quality | 172KB/second | 10MB/minute |
| 128Kbps stereo MP3 | Near CD quality | 17KB/second | 1MB/minute |
| 22.05KHz 16-bit stereo WAV | FM Radio | 86KB/second | 5MB/minute |
| 64Kbps stereo MP3 | FM Radio | 9KB/second | 540KB/minute |
| 11.025KHz 16-bit mono WAV | AM Radio | 43KB/second | 2.5MB/minute |
| 11.025KHz 8-bit mono WAV | Telephone | 21KB/second | 1.25MB/minute |

play them back. The file is usually an enormous AVI file that would fill up a good portion of your optical media. That file is usually compressed into something more usable by the game.

The second approach uses the game engine itself. Most games create their animated sequences in 3ds Max or Maya and export the animations and camera motion. The animations can be played back by loading a relatively tiny animation file and pumping the animations through the rendering engine. The only media you have to store beyond that is the sound and 3D models for the characters and environment. If you have tons of cinematic sequences, doing them in-game like this is the way to go. Lots of story-heavy games are going this direction because it is more efficient than storing that much prerendered video.

The biggest difference your players will notice is in the look of the cinematic. If an animation uses the engine, your players won't be mentally pulled out of the game world. The in-game cut-scenes will also flow perfectly between the action and the narrative, as compared to the prerendered cut-scenes, which usually force some sort of slight delay and interruption as the game engine switches back and forth between in-game action and retrieving the cut-scene from the disc or hard drive. If the player has customized the look of his character, that customization is still visible in the cinematic because it is being rendered on the fly. As a technologist, the biggest difference you'll notice is the smaller resulting cinematic data files. The animation data is tiny compared to digital video. One bit of advice: You should make sure the AI characters hold for the cinematic moment and attack you only after it is over!

**Motion Comics in *Thor: The God of Thunder* Were a Good Idea, but...**

Everyone knows that licensed movie tie-in titles tend to get the short shrift from a budget and schedule perspective—and the games tend to suffer in the 40 Metacritic zone as a result. On *Thor*, we had hoped to save some money and increase quality at the same time by doing all of the cinematic sequences as motion comics. After all, wouldn't it be cheaper to draw some 3D graphic panels, slide them around, and add a few particle effects? It turned out that they cost about the same per minute as typical in-game cinematics. Ah well—they didn't save us any money or time, but they looked super cool.

Sometimes you'll want to show a cinematic that simply can't be rendered in real time by your graphics engine—perhaps something you need Maya to chew on for a few hours in a huge render farm. In that case, you'll need to understand a little about streaming video and compression.

### *Streaming Video and Compression*

Each video frame in your cinematic should pass through compression only once. Every compression pass will degrade the art quality. Prove this to yourself by compressing a piece of video two or three times, and you'll see how bad it gets even with the second pass.

**USB Hard Drives and FedEx**

If you need to move a large data set like uncompressed video from one network to another, use a stand-alone Ethernet or high-speed USB-capable hard drive. It might make security-conscious IT guys freak out, but it's a useful alternative to burning a stack of DVDs or worse, trying to send a few hundred gigabytes over the Internet. This is modern day "Sneakernet."

Don't waste your time backing up uncompressed video files. Instead, make sure that you have everything you need to re-create them, such as a 3ds Max scene file or even raw videotape. Make sure the source is backed up and the final compressed files are backed up. If you need to regenerate them, just press the "animate" button and wait a few hours.

Compression settings for streaming video can get complicated. Predicting how a setting will change the output is also tricky. Getting a grasp of how it works will help you understand which settings will work best for your footage. Video compression uses two main strategies to take a 5GB two-minute uncompressed movie and boil it down into a 10MB or so file. Just because the resolution drops doesn't mean you have to watch a postage stamp-sized piece of video. Most playback APIs will allow a stretching parameter for the height, width, or both.

The first strategy for compressing video is to simply remove unneeded information by reducing the resolution or interlacing the video. Reducing resolution from 800 × 600 to 400 × 300 would shave 3GB from a 4GB movie, a savings of 75 percent. An interlaced video alternates drawing the even and odd scanlines every other frame. This is exactly how television works; the electron gun completes a round trip from the top of the screen to the bottom and back at 60Hz, but it only draws every other scanline. The activated phosphors on the inside of a CRT persist longer than 1/30th of a second after they've been hit with the electron gun and can therefore be refreshed or changed at that rate without noticeable degradation in the picture. Modern displays aren't so forgiving, but remember that the human eye generally perceives continuous movement between 30 and 60fps, but since human vision is not frame based, this is highly dependent on the content being reproduced. As always, removing data will result in a degradation of perceived quality. Interlacing the video will drop the data set down to one-half of its original size. Using interlacing and resolution reduction can make a huge difference in your video size, even before the compression system kicks in.

**Table 8.4 Matching Bit Rates with CD-ROM/DVD Speeds**

| Technology | Bit Rate |
|---|---|
| 1x CD | 150 Kbps |
| 1x DVD | 1,385 Kbps |
| 32x CD | 4,800 Kbps |
| 16x DVD | 2.21 Mbps |
| 1x Blu-ray | 36 Mbps |
| 8x Blu-ray | 288 Mbps |

Video compression can be lossless, but in practice you should always take advantage of the compression ratios even a small amount of lossiness can give you. If you're planning on streaming the video from optical media, you'll probably be forced to accept some lossiness simply to get your peak and average data rates down low enough for your needs, whether that be streaming from the Web or disc. In any case, you'll want to check the maximum bit rate you can live with. Most compression utilities give you the option of entering your maximum bit rate. The resulting compression will attempt to satisfy your bit-rate limitations while keeping the resulting video as accurate to the original as possible. Table 8.4 shows the ideal bit rate that should be used for different CD-ROM, DVD, and Blu-ray speeds. Web streaming speeds are too unpredictable to list, but from the table you can get a general idea. At least on the Web, you can vary the content; it's hard to get the player to install a new Blu-ray player for a specific cinematic.

**Save Video Compression Settings—They're Hard to Remember!**

Getting the video compression settings just right can be a black art and very time consuming to reproduce later. Make sure that you record these settings in a convenient place so you can get to them again. When the writers change the dialogue, or the Hollywood actor featured in your game decides his cheekbones aren't prominent enough, you'll be happy these settings are at your fingertips.

## Resource Files

When I wrote the first edition of this book in 2003, many hard disks rotated as fast as 7,200rpm. By the second edition, the fast drives were already up to 15,000rpm. At the writing of the third edition, there was talk of a 20,000rpm hard disk. By the fourth edition, storing games in memory rather than hard disk was becoming more popular. That's fine with me because I don't want anything sitting in my lap spinning at 20,000rpm. For a 15,000rpm device, the CPU must wait an average of 2ms for a desired piece of data to be located in the right position to be read, assuming the read/write head doesn't have to seek to a new track. For a modern day processor operating at 3GHz or more, this time is interminable. It's a good thing processors aren't conscious because they'd go mad waiting for hard disks all the time. Seeking time is much slower. The read/write head must accelerate, move, stop, and become stable enough to accurately read the magnetic media. For a CPU, that wait is an eternity.

Optical media is even worse. Their physical organization is a continuous spiral from the inside of the disc to the outside, and the read laser must traverse this spiral at a constant linear velocity. This means that not only does the laser read head have to seek an approximate location instead of an exact location, but also the rotational velocity of the disc must change to the right speed before reading can begin. If the approximate location was wrong, the head will re-seek. All this mechanical movement makes optical media much slower that their magnetic brethren.

The only thing slower than reading data from a hard drive or optical media is to have an intern actually type the data in manually from the keyboard.

Needless to say, you want to treat data in your files like I treat baubles in stores like Pier One. I do everything in my power to stay away from these establishments (my wife loves them) until I have a big list of things to buy. When I can't put it off any longer, I make my shopping trip a surgical strike. I go in, get my stuff, and get out as fast as I can, avoiding as many candles as possible. When your game needs to grab data from the hard drive or optical media, it should follow the same philosophy.

The best solution would completely compartmentalize game assets into a single block of data that could be read in one operation with a minimum of movement of the read/write head. Everything needed for a screen or a level would be completely covered by this single read. This is usually impractical because some common data would have to be duplicated in each block. A fine compromise factors the common data in one block and the data specific to each level or screen in their own blocks. When the game loads, it is likely you'll notice two seeks—one for the common data block and one for the level-specific block. Once the common data is in memory, you leave it there and only load data for new levels or streamed areas as needed.

**Know Your Hardware**

Knowing how hardware works is critical to writing any kind of software. You don't have to be a guru writing device drivers to crack the books and learn exactly how everything works and how you can take advantage of it. This same lesson applies to the operating system and how the hardware APIs work under the hood. Learn about the memory and how it is organized. See how the secondary storage works. Get a basic clue about the graphics chipset. Most importantly, learn how data flows to and from all these systems, and how it can be stalled. This knowledge can turn a hobbyist into a professional.

## Packaging Resources into a Single File

It's a serious mistake to store every game asset, such as a texture or sound effect, in its own file. Separating thousands of assets in their own files wastes valuable storage space and makes it impossible to get your load times faster.

Hard drives are logically organized into blocks or clusters that have surprisingly large sizes. Most hard drives in the gigabit range have cluster sizes of 16KB–32KB. File systems like FAT32 and NTFS were written to store a maximum of one file per cluster to enable optimal storage of the directory structure. This means that if you have 500 sound effect files, each ½-second long and recorded at 44KHz mono, you'll have 5.13MB of wasted space on the hard disk:

0.5 seconds * 44KHz mono = 22,000 bytes

32,768 bytes minimum cluster size –22,000 bytes in each file = 10,768 bytes wasted per file

10,768 bytes wasted in each file * 500 files = 5.13MB wasted space

You can easily get around this problem by packing your game assets into a single file. If you've ever played with DOOM level editors, you're familiar with WAD files; they are a perfect example of this technique. These packed file formats are file systems in miniature, although most are read only. *Ultima VIII* and *Ultima IX* had a read/write version (FLX files) that had multiuser locking capabilities for development. Almost every game on the market uses some custom packing scheme for more reasons than saving hard drive space.

## Other Benefits of Packaging Resources

The biggest advantage of combining your resources by far is load time optimization. Opening files is an extremely slow operation on most operating systems. The full filename must be parsed, the directory structure traversed, the hardware must locate and read a number of blocks into the operating system read cache, and more. This can cause multiple seeks, depending on the organization of the media. Another advantage is security. You can use a proprietary logical organization of the file that will hamper armchair hackers from getting to your art and sounds. While this security is quite light, and serious hackers will usually break it before the sun sets the first day your game is on the shelves, it's better than nothing. Of course, you can always publish the format of your files and get the mod community going. Either way, it is your choice.

**Hard Drive Ticking? Maybe You Should Listen**

During development on any platform with a hard drive or optical disc, keep your ear tuned to the sounds your drive makes while you play your game. At worst, you should hear it seek or "tick" every few seconds or so as new data is cached in. This would be common in an open world game, where the player could walk anywhere on an enormous outdoor map. At best, your game will have a level design that grabs all the data in one read, and you'll play an entire level without going back to the disc.

A great trick is to keep indexes or file headers in memory while the resource file is open. These are usually placed at the beginning or end of a file, and on large files the index might be a considerable physical distance away from your data. Read the index once and keep it around to save yourself that extra, and very time consuming, media seek.

## Data Compression and Performance

Compression is a double-edged sword. Every game scrambles to store as much content on the distribution media and secondary storage as possible. Compression can achieve some impressive space ratios for storing text, graphics, and sound at the cost of increasing the load on the CPU and your RAM budget to decompress everything. The actual compression ratios you'll get from using different utilities are completely dependent on the algorithm and the data to be compressed. Use algorithms like Zlib or LZH for general compression that can't afford lossiness. Use JPG, OGG, or MPEG compression for anything that can stand lossiness, such as graphics and sound.

Consider the cost of decompressing MP3 files for music, speech, or sound effects. On the upper end, each stream of 128KB stereo MP3 can suck about 25MHz from your CPU budget, depending on your processor. If you design your audio system to handle 16 simultaneous streams, a 2GHz desktop will only have 1.6GHz left, losing 400MHz to decompressing audio. Of course, you can be clever about decompressing them only when needed and trade some memory for CPU time.

**Keep an Eye on Your Message Queue During Callbacks**

If you are working on a Windows game and your decompressor API uses a callback, it is quite likely that the decompression will forward Windows system messages into your message pump. This can create a real nightmare since mouse clicks or hot keys can cause new art and sounds to be recursively sent into the decompression system. Callbacks are necessary for providing user feedback like a progress bar, but they can also wreak havoc with your message pump. If this is happening to your application, trap the offending messages and hold them in a temporary queue until the primary decompression is finished.

## Zlib: Open Source Compression

If you need a lossless compression/decompression system for your game, a good choice that has stood the test of time is Zlib, which can be found at www.zlib.net. It's free, open source, legally unencumbered, and simple to integrate into almost any platform or compiler. Typical compression ratios with Zlib are 2:1 to 5:1, depending on the data stream.

Zlib was written by Jean-Loup Gailly and Mark Adler and is an abstraction of the DEFLATE compression algorithm. A Zip file uses Zlib to compress many files into a single file. An overview of the basic structure of a Zip file is shown in Figure 8.3. I'll show you the basic structure first, and then we'll look at the code that can read it.

Zip files store their table of contents, or file directory, at the end of the file. If you read the file, the `TZipDirHeader` at the very end of the file contains data members such as a special signature and the number of files stored in the Zip file. Just before the `TZipDirHeader`, there is an array of structures, one for each file, which stores data members such as the name of the file, the type of compression, and the size of

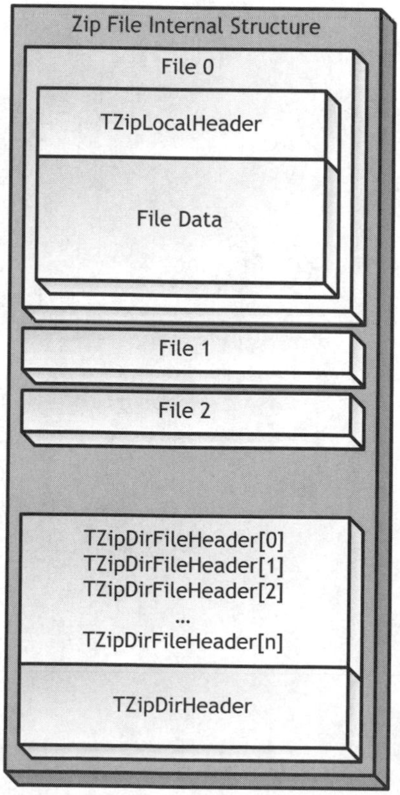


**Figure 8.3**
The internal structure of a Zip file.

the file before and after compression. Each file in the Zip file has a local header stored just before the compressed file data. It stores much of the same data as the `TZipDirFileHeader` structure.

One fine example of reading a Zip file comes from Javier Arevalo. I've modified it only slightly to work well with the rest of the source code in this book. The basic premise of the solution is to open a Zip file, read the directory into memory, and use it to index the rest of the file. Here is the definition for the `ZipFile` class:

```
// This maps a path to a zip content id
typedef std::map<std::string, int> ZipContentsMap;

class ZipFile
{
public:
  ZipFile() { m_nEntries=0; m_pFile=NULL; m_pDirData=NULL; }
  Virtual ~ZipFile() { End(); fclose(m_pFile); }

  bool Init(const std::wstring &resFileName);
  void End();

  int GetNumFiles()const { return m_nEntries; }
  std::string GetFilename(int i) const;
  int GetFileLen(int i) const;
  bool ReadFile(int i, void *pBuf);

  // Added to show multi-threaded decompression
  bool ReadLargeFile(int i, void *pBuf, void (*progressCallback)(int, bool &));
  optional<int> Find(const std::string &path) const;

  ZipContentsMap m_ZipContentsMap;

private:
  struct TZipDirHeader;
  struct TZipDirFileHeader;
  struct TZipLocalHeader;

  FILE *m_pFile;        // Zip file
  char *m_pDirData;    // Raw data buffer.
  int m_nEntries;      // Number of entries.

  // Pointers to the dir entries in pDirData.
  const TZipDirFileHeader **m_papDir;
};
```

```
// ---------------------------------------------------------------------------
// Basic types.
// ---------------------------------------------------------------------------
typedef unsigned long dword;
typedef unsigned short word;
typedef unsigned char byte;

// ---------------------------------------------------------------------------
// ZIP file structures. Note these have to be packed.
// ---------------------------------------------------------------------------

#pragma pack(1)
// ---------------------------------------------------------------------------
struct ZipFile::TZipLocalHeader
{
  enum
  {
    SIGNATURE = 0x04034b50
  };
  dword  sig;
  word   version;
  word   flag;
  word   compression;    // COMP_xxxx
  word   modTime;
  word   modDate;
  dword  crc32;
  dword  cSize;
  dword  ucSize;
  word   fnameLen;       // Filename string follows header.
  word   xtraLen;        // Extra field follows filename.
};

struct ZipFile::TZipDirHeader
{
  enum { SIGNATURE = 0x06054b50 };
  dword  sig;
  word   nDisk;
  word   nStartDisk;
  word   nDirEntries;
  word   totalDirEntries;
  dword  dirSize;
  dword  dirOffset;
  word   cmntLen;
};
```

```
// -----------------------------------------------------------------------
struct ZipFile::TZipDirFileHeader
{
  enum { SIGNATURE  = 0x02014b50 };
  dword  sig;
  word   verMade;
  word   verNeeded;
  word   flag;
  word   compression;    // COMP_xxxx
  word   modTime;
  word   modDate;
  dword  crc32;
  dword  cSize;          // Compressed size
  dword  ucSize;         // Uncompressed size
  word   fnameLen;       // Filename string follows header.
  word   xtraLen;        // Extra field follows filename.
  word   cmntLen;        // Comment field follows extra field.
  word   diskStart;
  word   intAttr;
  dword  extAttr;
  dword  hdrOffset;

  char *GetName   () const { return (char *)(this + 1);  }
  char *GetExtra  () const { return GetName() + fnameLen; }
  char *GetComment() const { return GetExtra() + xtraLen; }
};
// -----------------------------------------------------------------------
#pragma pack()
```

You should notice a couple of interesting things about the definition of these structures. First, there is a `#pragma pack` around the code. This disables anything the C++ compiler might do to optimize the memory speed of these structures, usually by spreading them out so that each member variable starts on a 4-byte boundary. Anytime you define a structure that will be stored onto a disk or in a stream, you should pack them. Another thing is the definition of a special signature for each structure. The `sig` member of each structure is set to a known, constant value, and it is written out to disk. When it is read back in, if the signatures don't match the known constant value, you can be sure that you have a corrupted file. It won't catch everything, but it is a good defense.

When a Zip file is opened, the class reads the `TZipDirHeader` structure at the end of the file. If the signatures match, the file position is set to the beginning of the array of TZipDirFileHeader structures. Note that there is a length of this array already stored in the TZipDirHeader. This is important because there's actually a little extra data stored in between each TZipDirFileHeader. It is variable length data and contains the filename, comments, and other extras.

Enough memory is allocated to store the directory, and it is read in one chunk. The data is then processed a bit. All the signatures are checked, the UNIX slashes are converted to backslashes, and the pointers to each entry in the directory are set for quick access. The filenames are also stored in an STL map for quick lookup. The ReadFile method takes the index number of the file you want to read and a pointer to the memory you've preallocated. Prior to calling this method, you'll call GetFileLen to find the size of the buffer and allocate enough memory to hold the file. It reads and decompresses the entire file at once in a blocking call, which could be bad if you have a large compressed file inside the Zip file. If you want to decompress something larger, use the ReadLargeFile method. It has the same parameters as ReadFile has, and it adds a function pointer to a callback method. This lets you show a progress bar as the file is loaded, and it also allows a cancel button to stop the decompression midstream.

One thing is a matter of taste for Windows programmers: Under UNIX operating systems, filenames are case sensitive, which means that you could have two filenames in the same directory that differ only in case. The same thing is true of Zip files, and while it is not exactly perfect form to convert all filenames to lowercase before you compare names, it sure makes it easier on you and the development team. An artist might name a file *Allbricks.bmp*, and a programmer might expect it to be named *Allbricks.bmp*. If you don't force the names to lowercase, the class will think the file doesn't exist.

With this class, you can iterate through all of the files packed in the Zip, find their names, read and decompress the file data, and use the data in your game. Here's an example:

```
char *buffer = NULL;
ZipFile zipFile;
if (zipFile.Init(resFileName))
{
  optional<int> index = zipFile.Find(path);
  if (index.valid())
  {
    int size = zipFile->GetFileLen(*index);
    buffer = new char[size];
```

```
      if (buffer)
      {
        zipFile.ReadFile(*index, buffer);
      }
    }
  }
  return buffer;
```

This is about as easy as it gets. After the Zip file is initialized, you find the index to the name of the file inside the Zip, grab the size, allocate the memory buffer, and read the bits.

Zip files are a good choice for the base file type of a general purpose resource file—something you can open once and read sounds, textures, meshes, and pretty much everything else. It's a common practice to load all of the resources you'll use for a given level in a single Zip file. Even doing this, you might soon discover that the Zip file for any one level is much bigger than your available memory. Some resources, like the sounds for your character's footsteps, will need to be in memory all the time. Others are used more rarely, like a special sound effect for a machine that is only activated once.

This problem calls for a cache, and luckily you're about to find out how one works.

## The Resource Cache

If your game has a modest set of graphics and sounds small enough to exist completely in memory for the life of your game, you don't need a cache. It's still a good idea to use resource files to pack everything into one file; you'll save disk space and speed up your game's load time.

Most games are bigger. If your game is going to ship on optical media, you'll have almost five gigabytes on a DVD and over 25GB on Blu-ray. Optical media will be larger than the RAM you have. You almost certainly won't have enough memory to load this all at once, but even if you do, you don't want players to wait while the entire thing is streamed in. What you need is a resource cache—a piece of technology that will sit on top of your resource files and manage the memory and the process of loading resources when you need them. Even better, a resource cache should be able to predict resource requirements before you need them.

Resource caches work on similar principles as any other memory cache. Most of the bits you'll need to display the next frame or play the next set of sounds are probably ones you've used recently. As the game progresses from one state to the next, new resources are cached in. They might be needed, for example, to play sound effects for the first time. Since memory isn't available in infinite quantities, eventually your game will run out of memory, and you'll have to throw something out of the cache.

A cache miss occurs when a game asks for the data associated with a resource and it isn't there. The game has to wait while the hard drive or the optical media wakes up and reads the data. Cache misses can come in three types, as categorized by Mark Hill, professor of Computer Sciences at the University of Wisconsin. The first is a compulsory miss, one that happens when the desired data is first requested and now has its first opportunity to load. The second is a capacity miss, which happens when the cache is out of space and must throw something out to load in the desired data. A conflict miss is the third type, which is a miss that could have been avoided, but the system was given hints that the data was no longer needed, and it was preemptively thrown out. Thrashing is a worst-case condition when the data required from the cache in a single game loop is larger than the cache can store and the resource cache gets into a state where it is constantly trying to make room for more data. Thrashing, as you might expect, is fatal for your frame rate, and you must either make your cache bigger or you must optimize or reduce your data.

Cache thrashing occurs when your game consistently needs more resource data than can fit in the available memory space. The cache is forced to throw out resources that are still frequently referenced by the game. The disk drives spin up and run constantly, and your game goes into semi-permanent hibernation.

The only way to avoid thrashing is to decrease the memory needed or increase the memory requirements. On console platforms, you don't get to ask for more RAM—it is what it is. On PC projects, it's rare that you'll get the go-ahead to increase the memory requirements, so you're left with slimming down the game data. You'll probably havc to use smaller textures, fewer sounds, or break up your levels into smaller sections to get things to fit.

Most of the interesting work in resource cache systems involves predictive analysis of your game data in an attempt to avoid cache misses. There are some tricks to reduce this problem, some of which reach into your level design by adding pinch points such as doors, elevators, or elbow hallways. Some games with open maps, like flight simulators, can't do this and have to work a lot harder. I'll show you a very simple resource cache so you can get your bearings. Then I'll discuss why this problem generally gets its own programmer—and a good one.

For the sake of simplicity, I'm going to assume that the cache only handles one resource file. It's easy enough to make the modifications to track resources across multiple files. You'll need to attach a file identifier of some sort to each resource to track which resources came from which file. There's no need to create a monolithic file that holds all the game assets. You should just break them up into manageable chunks. Perhaps you'll put assets for a given level into one resource file and assets common to all levels in another. It's totally up to you.

Resources might not exist in memory if they've never been loaded or if they've been thrown out to make room for other resources. You need a way to reference them whether they are loaded or not, and these references need to uniquely identify each resource. This resource reference enables the cache to match a particular resource identifier with its data. For our simple resource system, an easy assumption is to simply use the filename of the original resource—it is easy to read in code and guaranteed to be unique. Some games might use something that doesn't require parsing a file path —a typical scheme uses unique identifiers like `const char *ART_TEXTURE_GRID_DDS = "art\\grid.dds"` in a header file. This can work, but it is something of a hassle because you'll need a place to define the constants or GUIDs, and this file will probably change constantly and be referenced throughout your game code. The recompiles this solution causes on even modest sized teams can bring programmers to a crawl. The trade-off is a little processor time during resource loads as opposed to a ton of convenience during development, which ultimately makes for a better game.

**You Might Have Multiple Resource Caches in Your Game**

Different assets in your game require different resource caching. Level data, such as object geometry and textures, should be loaded in one chunk when the level is loaded. Audio and cinematics can be streamed in as needed. Most user interface screens should be loaded before they are needed, since you don't want players to wait while you cache something in. If you are going to load something, make sure that you load it when the player isn't going to notice. Some games just load everything they need when you begin playing and never hit the disk for anything else at all, so a resource cache isn't something every game uses.

The resource cache needs a way to define the identifier of each resource in a unique way. As discussed previously, a good solution is to just use the name of the file that points to the resource in the Zip file:

```
class Resource
{
public:
  std::string m_name;
  Resource(const std::string &name)
  {
```

```
    m_name=name;
    std::transform(m_name.begin(), m_name.end(),
        m_name.begin(), (int(*)(int)) std::tolower);
  }
};
```

You might wonder why a string-based identifier is used here rather than some kind of defined ID. The reason is that game assets tend to change incredibly fast during development, and you don't want to have a huge list of IDs that will be changing constantly, perhaps forcing a recompile of your game every time an artist adds a new texture. Speed is typically not a big problem here, since string lookups will likely not happen that often after a resource is loaded, which you can control. In short, this is one of those cases where a little CPU time is traded for a huge development convenience.

Another quick nod to development convenience is to convert the resource name to lowercase. Doing so keeps you from having to set up rules for artists and other content providers that they probably won't remember to follow anyway!

Two phases are involved in using a resource cache: creating the resource and using it. When you create a resource, you are simply creating an identifier for the resource. It doesn't really do much of anything. The heavy lifting happens when you send the resource into the resource cache to gain access to the bits or a resource handle. Handles should always be managed by a `shared_ptr` so the bits are guaranteed to be good as long as you need them. Here's an example of how to use the `Resource` class to grab a handle and get to the bits:

```
Resource resource("Brick.bmp");
shared_ptr<ResHandle> texture = g_pApp->m_ResCache->GetHandle(&resource);
int size = texture->GetSize();
char *brickBitmap = (char *) texture->Buffer();
```

If the resource is already loaded in the cache, these lines of code execute extremely quickly. If the resource is not loaded, you have a cache miss on your hands, and the resource cache will make room if necessary, allocate memory for the resource, and finally load the resource from the resource file. The bits are available as long as the `ResHandle` remains in scope, since it is managed by a `shared_ptr`. Once the `ResHandle` structure goes out of scope, the resource cache may retain the bits if there's room to keep them.

Now you're ready to see how the resource cache is coded. You've already seen how a resource is defined through the `Resource` structure. There are a few other parts of a resource cache, and I'll go over each one in detail:

- `IResourceFile` interface and `ResourceZipFile`, the resource file

- ResHandle, a handle to track loaded resources
- ResCache, a simple resource cache

## IResourceFile Interface

A resource file should be able to be opened and closed and provide the application programmer access to resources. Here's a simple interface that defines just that:

```
class IResourceFile
{
public:
  virtual bool VOpen()=0;
  virtual int VGetRawResourceSize(const Resource &r)=0;
  virtual int VGetRawResource(const Resource &r, char *buffer)=0;
  virtual int VGetNumResources() const = 0;
  virtual std::string VGetResourceName(int num) const = 0;
  virtual ~IResourceFile() { }
};
```

There are only five pure virtual functions to implement. I told you it was simple. The implementation of VOpen() should open the file and return success or failure based on the file's existence and integrity. VGetRawResourceSize() should return the size of the resource based on the name of the resource, and VGetRawResource() should read the resource from the file. The VGetNumResources() method should tell you how many resources are in the file, and the VGetResourceName() method should tell you the name of the nth resource. The last two methods enable you to iterate through every resource by number or by name.

The accompanying source code implements the IResourceFile interface with a ZipFile implementation. This is a convenient file format since it is supported by so many off-the-shelf and open source tools on many platforms. This is a great example of using interfaces to hide the technical implementation of something while maintaining a consistent API. If you wanted to, you could implement this interface using a completely different file structure, like CAB or WAD.

## ResHandle: Tracking Loaded Resources

For the cache to do its work, it must keep track of all the loaded resources. A useful class, ResHandle, encapsulates the resource identifier with the loaded resource data:

```
class ResHandle
{
```

```
    friend class ResCache;

protected:
    Resource m_resource;
    char *m_buffer;
    unsigned int m_size;
    shared_ptr<IResourceExtraData> m_extra;
    ResCache *m_pResCache;

public:
    ResHandle ( Resource & resource,
            char *buffer,
            unsigned int size,
            ResCache *pResCache);
    virtual ~ResHandle();

    unsigned int Size() const { return m_size; }
    char *Buffer() const { return m_buffer; }
    char *WritableBuffer() { return m_buffer; }
    shared_ptr<IResourceExtraData> GetExtra() { return m_extra; }
    void SetExtra(shared_ptr<IResourceExtraData> extra) { m_extra = extra; }
};

ResHandle::ResHandle(
    Resource & resource, char *buffer, unsigned int size, ResCache *pResCache)
    : m_resource(resource)
{
    m_buffer = buffer;
    m_size = size;
    m_extra = NULL;
    m_pResCache = pResCache;
}

ResHandle::~ResHandle()
{
    SAFE_DELETE_ARRAY(m_buffer);
    m_pResCache->MemoryHasBeenFreed(m_size);

}
```

When the cache loads a resource, it dynamically creates a ResHandle, allocates a buffer of the right size, and reads the resource from the resource file. The ResHandle class exists in memory as long as the resource caches it in, or as long as any consumer of the bits keeps a shared_ptr to a ResHandle object. The ResHandle also tracks the size of the memory block. If the resource cache gets full, the resource handle is discarded and removed from the resource cache.

The destructor of `ResHandle` makes a call to a `ResCache` member, `MemoryHasBeenFreed()`. `ResHandle` objects are always managed through a `shared_ptr` and can therefore be actively in use at the moment the cache tries to free them. This is fine, but when the `ResHandle` object goes out of scope, it needs to inform the resource cache that it is time to adjust the amount of memory actually in use.

There's a useful side effect of holding a pointer to the resource cache in the `ResHandle`: it is possible to have multiple resource caches in your game. One may control a specific type of resource, such as sound effects, whereas another may control level geometry and textures.

Most resources can be used exactly as they exist in the Zip file; they can be loaded into memory and sent to whatever game subsystem needs them. Other resources need to be processed when they are loaded. A resource might need a special decompression method or processing to extract some important data from it. A good example of this might be to store the length and format of a sound file. This is the reason that the resource file defines loaders—classes that implement the `IResourceLoader` interface.

## `IResourceLoader` Interface and the `DefaultResourceLoader`

Here's the definition of the `IResourceLoader` interface:

```
class IResourceLoader
{
public:
  virtual std::string VGetPattern()=0;
  virtual bool VUseRawFile()=0;
  virtual unsigned int VGetLoadedResourceSize(
    char *rawBuffer, unsigned int rawSize)=0;
  virtual bool VLoadResource(char *rawBuffer, unsigned int rawSize,
    shared_ptr<ResHandle> handle)=0;
};
```

The first method returns a wildcard pattern that the resource cache uses to distinguish which loaders are used with which files. You might define a loader for all OGG files, if you wanted to decompress the music file, or all XML files, to parse the XML data as the resource was loaded. The next method, `VUseRawFile()` returns true if the resource loader can use the bits stored in the raw file, no extra processing needed. The next two methods define the size of the loaded resource if it is different from the size stored in the file, and then how the resource is actually loaded from the file.

Many resources in the Zip file require no processing at all, so it is convenient to load them exactly as-is. This requires the definition of a `DefaultResourceLoader`.

```
class DefaultResourceLoader : public IResourceLoader
{
public:
  virtual bool VUseRawFile() { return true; }
  virtual unsigned int VGetLoadedResourceSize(char *rawBuffer, unsigned int rawSize) {
return rawSize; }
   virtual bool VLoadResource(char *rawBuffer, unsigned int rawSize, shared_ptr<Re-
sHandle> handle) { return true; }
  virtual std::string VGetPattern() { return "*"; }
};
```

There's not much to this class. Since the resource is loaded exactly as it exists in the file, there's not really anything to do. The `IResourceFile` interface has already loaded the bits into memory, and the `ResHandle` already stores those bits. You'll see a more interesting implementation of the `IResourceLoader` interface in Chapter 13, "Game Audio," which loads WAV and OGG files.

## ResCache: A Simple Resource Cache

Since most of the players are already on the stage, it's time to bring out the `ResCache` class, an ultra-simple resource cache.

First, a few type definitions. While the resource is in memory, a pointer to the `ResHandle` exists in two data structures. The first, a linked list, is managed such that the nodes appear in the order in which the resource was last used. Every time a resource is used, it is moved to the front of the list, so you can find the most and least recently used resources.

The second data structure, an STL map, provides a way to quickly find resource data with the unique resource identifier. The third defines a map to store the resource loaders.

```
typedef std::list< shared_ptr <ResHandle > > ResHandleList;
typedef std::map<std::string, shared_ptr < ResHandle > > ResHandleMap;
typedef std::list< shared_ptr < IResourceLoader > > ResourceLoaders;

class ResCache
{
```

```
protected:
  ResHandleList m_lru;          // LRU (least recently used) list
  ResHandleMap m_resources;     // STL map for fast resource lookup
  ResourceLoaders m_resourceLoaders;

  IResourceFile *m_file;        // Object that implements IResourceFile

  unsigned int  m_cacheSize;    // total memory size
  unsigned int  m_allocated;    // total memory allocated

  shared_ptr<ResHandle> Find(Resource * r);
  const void *Update(shared_ptr<ResHandle> handle);
  shared_ptr<ResHandle> Load(Resource * r);
  void Free(shared_ptr<ResHandle> gonner);

  bool MakeRoom(unsigned int size);
  char *Allocate(unsigned int size);
  void FreeOneResource();
  void MemoryHasBeenFreed(unsigned int size);

public:
  ResCache(const unsigned int sizeInMb, IResourceFile *resFile);
  ~ResCache();

  bool Init();
  void RegisterLoader( shared_ptr<IResourceLoader> loader );

  shared_ptr<ResHandle> GetHandle(Resource * r);
  int Preload(const std::string pattern, void (*progressCallback)(int, bool &));
  void Flush(void);
};
```

The first three members of the class have already been introduced. They are the least recently used (LRU) list to track which resources are less frequently used than others, the STL map, which is used to quickly find resources by name, and another STL list of the resource loaders that match resource types with the loader that can process them. There is a pointer to the resource file and two unsigned integers that track the maximum size of the cache and the current size of the cache.

The `m_file` member points to an object that implements the `IResourceFile` interface.

The two unsigned integers, `m_cacheSize` and `m_allocated`, keep track of the cache size and how much of it is currently being used.

The constructor is pretty basic. It simply sets a few member variables. The destructor frees every resource in the cache by making repeated calls to `FreeOneResource` until there's nothing left in the cache.

```
ResCache::ResCache(const unsigned int sizeInMb, IResourceFile *resFile )
{
  m_cacheSize = sizeInMb * 1024 * 1024;      // total memory size
  m_allocated = 0;                           // total memory allocated
  m_file = resFile;
}

ResCache::~ResCache()
{
  while (!m_lru.empty())
  {
    FreeOneResource();
  }
  SAFE_DELETE(m_file);
}
```

To initialize the resource cache, call the `Init()` method:

```
bool ResCache::Init()
{
  bool retValue = false;
  if ( m_file->VOpen() )
  {
    RegisterLoader(shared_ptr<IResourceLoader>(GCC_NEW DefaultResourceLoader()));
    retValue = true;
  }
  return retValue;
}
```

Besides opening the resource file, a default resource loader is created and registered. The `RegisterLoader` method simply pushes the loader onto the front of the loader list. The idea is that the most generic loaders come last in the list and the most specific loaders come first. This scheme allows you to define a specific loader for a given file but still use another loader of other files with the same extension.

To get the bits for a resource, you call `GetHandle()`:

```
shared_ptr<ResHandle> ResCache::GetHandle(Resource * r)
{
  shared_ptr<ResHandle> handle(Find(r));
  if (handle==NULL)
    handle = Load(r);
```

```
    else
      Update(handle);
    return handle;
}
```

ResCache::GetHandle() is brain-dead simple. If the resource is already loaded in the cache, update it. If it's not there, you have to take a cache miss and load the resource from the file.

The process of finding, updating, and loading resources is easy.

- ResCache::Find() uses an STL map, m_resources, to locate the right ResHandle given a Resource.
- ResCache::Update() removes a ResHandle from the LRU list and promotes it to the front, making sure that the LRU is always sorted properly.
- ResCache::Free() finds a resource by its handle and removes it from the cache.

The other members, Load(), Allocate(), MakeRoom(), and FreeOneResource(), are the core of how the cache works:

```
shared_ptr<ResHandle> ResCache::Load(Resource *r)
{
  shared_ptr<IResourceLoader> loader;
  shared_ptr<ResHandle> handle;

  for (ResourceLoaders::iterator it = m_resourceLoaders.begin();
      it != m_resourceLoaders.end(); ++it)
  {
    shared_ptr<IResourceLoader> testLoader = *it;
    if (WildcardMatch(testLoader->VGetPattern().c_str(), r->m_name.c_str()))
    {
      loader = testLoader;
      break;
    }
  }

  if (!loader)
  {
    assert(loader && _T("Default resource loader not found!"));
    return handle;      // Resource not loaded!
  }

  unsigned int rawSize = m_file->VGetRawResourceSize(*r);
```

```
char *rawBuffer = loader->VUseRawFile() ?
  Allocate(rawSize) : GCC_NEW char[rawSize];

if (rawBuffer==NULL)
{
  // resource cache out of memory
  return shared_ptr<ResHandle>();
}
m_file->VGetRawResource(*r, rawBuffer);
char *buffer = NULL;
unsigned int size = 0;

if (loader->VUseRawFile())
{
  buffer = rawBuffer;
  handle = shared_ptr<ResHandle>(
    GCC_NEW ResHandle(*r, buffer, rawSize, this));
}
else
{
  size = loader->VGetLoadedResourceSize(rawBuffer, rawSize);
  buffer = Allocate(size);
  if (rawBuffer==NULL || buffer==NULL)
  {
    // resource cache out of memory
    return shared_ptr<ResHandle>();
  }
  handle = shared_ptr<ResHandle>(
    GCC_NEW ResHandle(*r, buffer, size, this));
  bool success = loader->VLoadResource(rawBuffer, rawSize, handle);
  SAFE_DELETE_ARRAY(rawBuffer);

  if (!success)
  {
    // resource cache out of memory
    return shared_ptr<ResHandle>();
  }
}

if (handle)
{
  m_lru.push_front(handle);
  m_resources[r->m_name] = handle;
```

```
  }

  assert(loader && _T("Default resource loader not found!"));
  return handle;      // ResCache is out of memory!
}
```

The first thing that happens in Load() is the right resource loader is located in the STL list. The utility function WildcardMatch() returns true if the loader's pattern matches the resource name. WildcardMatch() uses the same matching rules as the CMD window in Microsoft Windows, so * matches everything, *.JPG matches all JPG files, and so on. If a loader isn't found, an empty ResHandle is returned. Then the method grabs the size of the raw resource from the resource file and allocates memory for the raw resource. If the resource doesn't need any processing, the memory is allocated from the cache through the Allocate() method; otherwise, a temporary buffer is created. If the memory allocation is successful, the raw resource bits are loaded with the call to VGetRawResource(). If no further processing of the resource is needed, a ResHandle object is created using the pointers to the raw bits and the raw resource size.

Other resources need processing and might even be a different size after they are loaded. This is the job of a specially defined resource loader, which loads the raw bits from the resource file, calculates the final size of the processed resource, allocates the right amount of memory in the cache, and finally copies the processed resource into the new buffer. You'll learn more about this in Chapter 13, which discusses using the resource system to create sound resources.

After the resource is loaded, the newly created ResHandle is pushed onto the LRU list, and the resource name is entered into the resource name map.

Next up is the Allocate() method, which makes more room in the cache when it is needed.

```
char *ResCache::Allocate(unsigned int size)
{
  if (!MakeRoom(size))
    return NULL;

  char *mem = GCC_NEW char[size];
  if (mem)
    m_allocated += size;

  return mem;
}
```

Allocate() is called from the Load() method when a resource is loaded. It calls MakeRoom() if there isn't enough room in the cache and updates the member variable to keep track of all the allocated resources.

```
bool ResCache::MakeRoom(unsigned int size)
{
  if (size > m_cacheSize)
  {
    return false;
  }
  // return null if there's no possible way to allocate the memory
  while (size > (m_cacheSize - m_allocated))
  {
    // The cache is empty, and there's still not enough room.
    if (m_lru.empty())
      return false;

    FreeOneResource();
  }

  return true;
}
```

After the initial sanity check, the while loop in MakeRoom() performs the work of removing enough resources from the cache to load the new resource by calling FreeOneResource(). If there's already enough room, the loop is skipped.

```
void ResCache::FreeOneResource()
{
  ResHandleList::iterator gonner = m_lru.end();
  gonner--;

  shared_ptr<ResHandle> handle = *gonner;

  m_lru.pop_back();
  m_resources.erase(handle->m_resource.m_name);
}
```

ResCache::FreeOneResource() removes the oldest resource and updates the cache data members. Note that the memory used by the cache isn't actually modified here—that's because any active shared_ptr<ResHandle> in use will need the bits until it actually goes out of scope.

Here's an example of how this class is used. You construct the cache with a size in mind, in our case 50MB, and an object that implements the `IResourceFile` interface. You then call `Init()` to allocate the cache and open the file.

```
ResourceZipFile zipFile("Assets.zip");
ResCache resCache (50, zipFile);
if (m_ResCache.Init())
{
  Resource resource("art\\brick.bmp");
  shared_ptr<ResHandle> texture = g_pApp->m_ResCache->GetHandle(&resource);
  int size = texture->GetSize();
  char *brickBitmap = (char *) texture->Buffer();
  // do something cool with brickBitmap !
}
```

If you want to use this in a real game, you've got more work to do. First, there's hardly a line of defensive or debugging code in `ResCache`. Resource caches are a significant source of bugs and other mayhem. Data corruption from buggy cache code or something else trashing the cache internals will cause your game to simply freak out.

A functional cache will need to be aware of more than one resource file. It's not reasonable to assume that a game can stuff every resource into a single file, especially since it makes it inconvenient for teams. If every resource were stuffed into a single file, then even the change of a minor texture in the options screen would cause every person on the team to grab a new copy of the entire resource file for the game, which could be multiple gigabytes. Break your game up into some reasonable number of resource files, and you'll be happier for it.

**Write a Custom Memory Manager**

Consider implementing your own memory allocator. Many resource caches allocate one contiguous block of memory when they initialize and manage the block internally. Some even have garbage collection, where the resources are moved around as the internal block becomes fragmented. A garbage collection scheme is an interesting problem, but it is extremely difficult to implement a good one that doesn't make the game stutter. *Ultima VIII* used a scheme like this.

That brings us to the idea of making the cache multithreading compliant. Why not have the cache defrag itself if there's some extra time in the main loop, or perhaps allow a reader in a different thread to fill the cache with resources that might be used in the near future? With high-definition consoles like the PS3 and Xbox360, this area of game programming is getting a lot of attention. The new multiprocessor systems have tons of CPU horsepower, and resource management can certainly get its own thread. The problem is going to be synchronization and keeping all the CPUs from stalling.

## Caching Resources into DirectX et al.

Luckily for you, DirectX objects such as sound effects, textures, and even meshes can all load from a memory stream. For example, you can load a DirectX texture using the `D3DXCreateTextureFromFileInMemory()` API, which means loading a texture from your resource cache is pretty easy:

```
Resource resource(m_params.m_Texture);
shared_ptr<ResHandle> texture = g_pApp->m_ResCache->GetHandle(&resource);
if ( FAILED (
  D3DXCreateTextureFromFileInMemory(
    DXUTGetD3D9Device(),
    texture->Buffer(),
    texture->Size(),
    &m_pTexture ) ) )
{
    return E_FAIL;
}
```

There are some SDKs out there that don't let you do this. They require you to send filenames into their APIs, and they take complete control of loading their own data. While it's unfortunate, it simply means that you can't use the resource cache for those parts of your game.

## World Design and Cache Prediction

Perhaps you've just finished a supercharged version of `ResCache`—good for you. You're not done yet. If you load resources the moment you need them, you'll probably suffer a wildly fluctuating frame rate. The moment your game asks for resources outside of the cache, your game will suffer a major stutter—even a few tens of milliseconds in a platformer or first-person shooter can frustrate a player.

First, classify your game design into one of the following categories:

- **Load Everything at Once:** This is for any game that caches resources on a screen-by-screen basis or level-by-level. Each screen of *Myst* is a good example, as well as *Grim Fandango*. Most fighting games work under this model for each event.
- **Load Only at Pinch Points:** Almost every shooter utilizes this design, where resources are cached in during elevator rides or in small barren hallways.

- **Load Constantly:** This is for open-map games where players can go anywhere they like. Examples include flight simulators, racing games, massively multiplayer games, and action/adventure games like Rockstar's *Red Dead Redemption.*

The first scheme trades one huge loading pause for lightning fast action during the game. These games have small levels or arenas that can fit entirely in memory. Thus, there's never a cache miss. The game designers can count on every CPU cycle being spent on the game world instead of loading resources. The downside is that, since your entire playing area has to fit entirely in memory, it can't be that big.

Shooters like *Halo* on the Xbox360 load resources at pinch points. The designers add buffer zones in between the action when relatively little is happening in the game. Elevators and hallways with a few elbow turns are perfect examples of this technique. The CPU spends almost no time rendering the tiny environment in these areas, and it uses the leftover cycles to load the next hot zone. In elevators, players can't change their minds in the middle of the trip until the elevator gets to the right floor, which happens to be timed to open exactly when the next area is loaded. Elbow hallways are constructed so that the loading time will always be less than the maximum running speed of the player. The more loading is needed, the longer the hallway will be.

One thing you may notice is that with each of these designs, the `ResCache` needs to load in the background while the rest of the game continues to run. This turns out to be pretty tricky stuff.

**Buffer Zones in Your Game Affect Pacing and Player Tension**

These buffer zones will exist in many places throughout the game, providing the player with a brief moment to load weapons and rest happy trigger fingers. The designers at Bungie took advantage of this and placed a few surprise encounters in these buffer zones, something that always made me freak out when I was playing *Halo.*

Even better, the folks at Bungie were wise enough to use the hallways to set the tone for the next fight with Covenant forces or the Flood. Sometimes it was as simple as painting the walls with enemy blood or playing some gruesome sound effects.

**Gamers Don't Want to Read, They Want to Play**

Don't make the player read a bunch of text in between levels just to give yourself time to cache resources. Players figure this out right away and want to click past the text they've read five or six times. They won't be able to do so since you've got to spend a few more seconds loading resources, and they'll click like mad and curse your name. If you're lucky, the worst thing they'll do is return your game. Don't open any suspicious packages you receive in the mail.

Open-mapped games such as flight simulators, fantasy role-playing games, or action/adventure games have a much tougher problem. The maps are huge and relatively open, and the game designers have little or no control over where the player will go next. Players also expect an incredible level of detail in these games. They want to read the headlines in newspapers or see individual leaves on the trees, while tall buildings across the river are in plain view. Players like that alternate reality. One of the best games that uses this open world design is *Grand Theft Auto*.

Modern operating systems have more options for multithreading, especially for caching in game areas while the CPU has some extra time. They use the player's direction of travel to predict the most likely areas that will be needed shortly and add those resources to a list that is loaded on an ad hoc basis as the cache gets some time to do extra work. This is especially beneficial if the game designers can give the cache some hints, such as the destination of a path or the existence of pinch points, such as a tunnel. These map elements almost serve as pinch points, similar to the hallways in *Halo*, although players can always turn around and go the other direction.

**Batch Your Cache Reads if You Can**

Create your cache to load multiple resources at one time and sort your cache reads in the order in which they appear in the file. This will minimize any seeking activity on the part of the drive's read head. If your resource file is organized properly, the resources used together will appear next to each other in the file. It will then be probable that resource loads will be accomplished in a single read block with as few seeks as possible.

A good example of this is to use a method to preload resources into your cache:

```
int ResCache::Preload(const std::string pattern,
            void (*progressCallback)(int, bool &))
{
  if (m_file==NULL)
    return 0;

  int numFiles = m_file->VGetNumResources();
  int loaded = 0;
  bool cancel = false;
  for (int i=0; i<numFiles; ++i)
  {
    Resource resource(m_file->VGetResourceName(i));

    if (WildcardMatch(pattern.c_str(), resource.m_name.c_str()))
    {
```

```
      shared_ptr<ResHandle> handle =
        g_pApp->m_ResCache->GetHandle(&resource);
      ++loaded;
    }

    if (progressCallback != NULL)
    {
      progressCallback(i * 100/numFiles, cancel);
    }
  }
  return loaded;
}
```

This method uses a simple scheme of wildcard pattern matching that you've seen previously. The resources are iterated as they are ordered in the file, and if they match the pattern, they are loaded. During the load, a progress callback function can be called to animate a progress bar, or it can be set to NULL and ignored. With this method, you could preload a number of resources based on a wildcard pattern, which could be set to a named area or room of a level, for example. If all the resources were very small, this method could be used to load resources asynchronously.

If you want to find out how your resources are being used, you should instrument your build. That means you should create a debug build with special code that creates a log file every time a resource is used. Use this log as a secondary data file to your resource file creator, and you'll be able to sequence the file to your game's best advantage.

In open world games, the maximum map density should always leave a little CPU time to perform some cache chores. Denser areas will spend most of their CPU time on game tasks for rendering, sound, and AI. Sparse areas will spend more time preparing the cache for denser areas about to reach the display. The trick is to balance these areas carefully, guiding the player through pinch points where it's possible, and never overloading the cache.

If the CPU can't keep up with cache requests and other game tasks, you'll probably suffer a cache miss and risk the player detecting a stutter in the game. Not all is lost, however, since a cache miss is a good opportunity to catch up on the entire list of resources that will be needed all at once. This should be considered a worst-case scenario, because if your game does this all the time, it will frustrate players. If you do this in a first-person shooter, you'll end up with a lot of bad reviews.

A better solution is a fallback mechanism for some resources that suffer a cache miss. Flight simulators and other open architecture games can sometimes get away with keeping the uncached resource hidden until the cache can load it. Imagine a flight simulator game that caches in architecture as the plane gets close. If the game attempts to draw a building that hasn't been cached in, then the building simply won't show up. Think for a moment what is more important to the player: a piece of architecture that will likely show up in 100ms or so anyway, or a frustrating pause in the action?

**Not All Resources Are Equally Important**

It's a good idea to associate a priority with each resource. Some resources are so important to the game that it must suffer a cache miss rather than fail to render it. This is critical for sound effects, which must often be timed exactly with visual events, such as explosions.

The really tough open-map problems are those games that add a level of detail on top of an open-map design. This approach is common with flight simulators and action adventure games. Each map segment has multiple levels of detail for static and dynamic objects. It's not a horrible problem to figure out how to create different levels of detail for each segment. The problem is how to switch from one level of detail to another without the player noticing. This is much easier in action/adventure games where the player is on the ground and most objects are obscured from view when they flip to a new level of detail.

Flight simulators don't have that luxury. Players want the experience of flying high enough to see the mountains on the horizon and diving low enough to see individual trees and ground clutter whiz by at Mach 1. This requires a delicate balance between the resource cache and the renderer, and it is one of the most difficult problems in modern flight simulators that provide a truly realistic experience with supersonic aircraft.

This subject is way beyond the scope of this book, but I won't leave you hanging. There is some amazing work done in this area, not the least of which was published in *Level of Detail for 3D Graphics* by D. Luebke, M. Reddy, J. Cohen, A. Varshney, B. Watson, and R. Huebner. They also have a website at http://lodbook.com.

## I'm Out of Cache

Smart game programmers realize early on that some problems are harder than others. If you thought that creating a good flight simulator was a piece of cake, I'd tell you that the hard part isn't simulating the airplane but simulating the ground and everything on it. The newbie game programmer could spend all his time creating a great flight model, and when he started the enormous task of representing undulating terrain with smooth detail levels, he would fold like laundry.

Games need enormous amounts of data to suspend disbelief on the part of players. No one, not even Epic, can set their system RAM requirements to hold the entire contents of even one disk of current day optical media. It's also not enough to simply assume that a game will load resources as needed, and the game designers can do what they want. That is a tragic road traveled by many games that never shipped and a few that have. Most games that suffer frame stutter issues ignored their cache constraints.

It's up to programmers to code the best cache they can and figure out a way to get game level designers, artists, and sound engineers to plan the density of game areas carefully. If everyone succeeds in his task, you get a smooth game that plays well. If you succeed, you'll get a game that can almost predict the future.

# Chapter 9

*by Mike McShaffry*

# Programming Input Devices

Even though user interface programming seems easy, it's actually quite tricky, which is ironic since most game companies assign the user interface code to their greenest programmers. It's a simple matter under almost any platform to read a keyboard, mouse, or gamepad. Most programmers take this input, like the X,Y coordinate of a mouse, and use it to directly modify the game state, such as where the player is looking in a first-person shooter. This technique works all too well until you want to do something like switch out that mouse for a USB gamepad or perhaps change how the controls are interpreted by the game. Maybe your player wants to switch the up/down or Y-axis of the camera controls from normal to inverted, like I prefer.

The framework presented in this book puts reading the hardware input devices squarely inside the application layer, which is the layer that handles any and all operating system or machine-dependent code. Once the application layer handles the raw input, it is handed off to the game view layer, usually a game view written specifically for a human player, to interpret the raw input and translate it into a command for your game. This chapter deals with the hardware and the raw messages, and you'll learn how these messages are handled in a game view in the next chapter, on user interface programming.

Because input devices are typically very hardware specific, this chapter has a decidedly Windows feel to it. While that is true, the concepts used in the chapter regarding what you do with the data coming from those devices are universal. While it can be a big headache to rewrite a hardware support layer for a new platform, it falls into the "mind numbing" category a bit more than "interesting." For that reason, I focus on Windows since it is an easy platform to own and experiment with.

First, we'll play with the hardware.

## Getting the Device State

No matter what platform you are on or what type of device you use—keyboard, mouse, joystick, and so on—you'll need to understand the techniques and subtleties of getting and controlling the state of your input devices. We'll start by working at the lowest level, and then we'll work our way up the input device food chain. The interfaces to input devices are completely dependent on the platforms you use and to some extent any middleware you might be using. Many 3D graphics engines also provide APIs to all the input hardware. Regardless of the API used or devices they control, there are two schemes for processing user input:

- **Polling:** This method minimizes the layers of code between you and the hardware, and it requires an application to query each device to find out its state. Your code should react to the state accordingly, usually comparing it against a previous state and calling an input handler if anything changed. The APIs to accomplish this are typically unique to the hardware.
- **Callbacks or messages:** This method is more common in advanced game engines that handle the low level stuff for you. Here you just register input device callbacks based on which devices you care about, and when they change state, your callback will get control. They poll at the low level just like DirectX would, but state changes are detected for you, which launches your callback.

Meaningful changes in hardware state should be translated into a game event, whether you use a polling method or callback method. With a little work you can structure your code to do this.

Of course, every platform operates a little differently, but the code looks very similar; mouse buttons still go up and down, and the entire device moves on a two-dimensional plane. It's not crazy to assume that most device-handling code reflects the nature of the specific device.

- **Buttons:** They will have up and down states. The down state might have an analog component. Most game controllers support button pressure as an 8-bit value.
- **One-axis controllers:** They will have a single analog state, with zero representing the unpressed state. Game controllers usually have analog triggers for use in features such as accelerators in driving games.

- **Two-axis controllers:** A mouse and joystick are 2D controllers. Their status can be represented as integers or floating-point numbers. When using these devices, you shouldn't assume anything about their coordinate space. The coordinate (0,0) might represent the upper left-hand corner of the screen, or it might represent the device center.
- **Three-axis controllers:** This would be typical of an accelerometer in a Wii-style controller or smart phone. The status is typically represented as a three-dimensional vector of floating-point numbers.
- **Others:** There are more controllers and input devices out there, such as gyrometers, microphones, cameras, multitouch screens, GPS devices, and more.

Game controllers, even complicated ones, are typically built from assemblies of these component types. The tricked-out joysticks that the flight simulator fans go for are simply buttons and triggers attached to a 2D controller. A Wii Remote has multiple buttons, a trigger, and an accelerometer. To support these devices, you need to write a custom handler function for each component. Depending on the way your handler functions get the device status, you might have to factor the device status for each component out of a larger data structure. Eventually, you'll call your handler functions and change the game state.

#### Choose Controls with Fidelity in Mind

When you choose a control scheme for your game, be mindful of the fidelity of each control. For example, a gamepad thumbstick has a low fidelity because the entire movement from one extreme to another is only a few centimeters. The mouse, on the other hand, has a very high fidelity since its movement is perhaps 10 times as far. This is a fundamental difference between games that use the gamepad, where targets are large and few in number, versus games that require a mouse, where targets require speed and precision, such as a headshot.

If you attempt to force a gamepad thumbstick into the same role as a mouse control, your players will be extremely frustrated and likely will stop playing your game. For games that are gamepad based, the players using gamepads will certainly need a little help aiming, as do most console shooters such as *Halo*. The players still need a high degree of skill, and its design cleverly balances the movement of the AI, the aiming help, and the control scheme to be fun. Also, don't think for a second that a game that requires the precision of a mouse can work on a tablet like the iPad—the typical human finger is far from pixel accurate.

You can create some interface classes for each kind of device that takes as input the translated events that you received from messages, callbacks, or even polling.

You can write these any way you want, but here are some examples to help you get started:

```
class IKeyboardHandler
{
  virtual bool VOnKeyDown(unsigned int const kcode)=0;
  virtual bool VOnKeyUp(unsigned int const kcode)=0;
};

class IPointerHandler
{
public:
  virtual bool VOnPointerMove(const CPoint &mousePos)=0;
  virtual bool VOnPointerButtonDown(const CPoint &mousePos,
                                    const std::string &buttonName)=0;
  virtual bool VOnPointerButtonUp(const CPoint &mousePos,
                                    const std::string &buttonName)=0;
  virtual int VGetPointerRadius()=0;
};

class IJoystickHandler
{
  virtual bool VOnButtonDown(const std::string &buttonName,
                             int const pressure)=0;
  virtual bool VOnButtonUp(const std::string &buttonName)=0;
  virtual bool VOnJoystick(float const x, float const y)=0;
};

class IGamepadHandler
{
  virtual bool VOnTrigger(const std::string &triggerName,
                          float const pressure)=0;
  virtual bool VOnButtonDown(const std::string &buttonName,
                             int const pressure)=0;
  virtual bool VOnButtonUp(const std::string &buttonName)=0;
  virtual bool VOnDirectionalPad(const std::string &direction)=0;
  virtual bool VOnThumbstick(const std::string &stickName,
                             float const x, float const y)=0;
};
```

Most functions represent an action taken by a control when something happens to an input device, such as when a button is pressed or a thumbstick is moved. Here's how the return values work: If the message is handled, the functions return `true`; otherwise, they return `false`.

You'll implement these interfaces in control classes to convert input from devices to commands that can change the game state. Control objects in your game are guaranteed to receive device input in a standard and predictable way. Thus, it should be a simple matter to modify and change the interface of your game by attaching new control objects that care about any device you've installed.

The interface classes described previously are simple examples, and they should be coded to fit the unique needs of your game. You can easily remove or add functions at will, and not every game will use input exactly the same way.

**Map Controls Directly to Controlled Objects**

Don't add parameters to distinguish between multiple joysticks or gamepads. A better solution is to create controls that map directly to the object they are controlling. For example, if multiple gamepads control multiple human drivers, the control code shouldn't need to be aware of any other driver but the one it is controlling. You could set all this up in a factory that creates the driver and the controller and informs the input device code where to send the input from each gamepad.

If you follow a modular design, your game objects can be controlled via the same interface, whether the source of that control is a gamepad or an AI character. For example, the AI character could send commands like "brake 75%" or "steer 45%" into a car controller, where the human player touches a few gamepad keys, generating translated events that eventually result in exactly the same calls but to a different car.

This design should always exist in any game where AI characters and humans are essentially interchangeable. If humans and AI characters use completely different interfaces to game objects, it becomes difficult to port a single-player game to multiplayer. You'll soon discover that none of the "plugs" fit.

You'll see in Chapter 10, "User Interface Programming," how to attach a mouse handler and keyboard handler to a game view class, and you'll also see in Chapter 14, "3D Graphics Basics," how to implement a user interface using both the mouse and the keyboard to move about a 3D scene.

## Using XInput or DirectInput

DirectInput was the de facto DirectX API for input devices such as the mouse, keyboard, joystick, game controllers, and force-feedback devices. It hasn't seen any major development since DirectX 8, however. DirectX sits in between your application and a physical device like a gamepad, video card, or sound card. For video and sound systems, many things are handled directly by the hardware, such as a video card's ability to texture map a polygon. If the hardware doesn't have that feature, it is simulated in software. This architecture is usually called a *hardware abstraction layer*, or

HAL. While there is nothing for DirectInput to hardware accelerate, it does provide an important service, which is to expose the capabilities of the user input hardware. For example, a USB game controller might have a rumble or force-feedback feature. If it does, DirectInput will give your game a way to detect it and use it to make your game more interesting.

XInput is Microsoft's answer to DirectInput, but it is a simpler and somewhat less capable system. It has a few limitations that DirectInput never had, such as only supporting certain controllers, a four controller limit, limited support for force feedback, no support for keyboards or mice, and others. While I'm certainly for simplification of APIs, I never like to lose functionality, even if I have to dig into the lower layers a bit more.

Windows can certainly grab user input with DirectInput or XInput. Mouse and keyboard messages are well understood by a Win32 programmer the moment he creates his first Win32 application. You might not be aware that the Win32 Multimedia Platform SDK has everything you need to accept messages from your joystick. You don't even need DirectInput for that, so why bother? Straight Win32 code does not expose every feature of all varieties of joysticks or PC game controller pads. For example, you can grab input from a Logitech PC gamepad without DirectInput with this code:

```
bool CheckForJoystick(HWND hWnd)
{
  JOYINFO joyinfo;
  UINT wNumDevs, wDeviceID;
  BOOL bDev1Attached, bDev2Attached;
  if((wNumDevs = joyGetNumDevs()) == 0)
     return false;
  bDev1Attached = joyGetPos(JOYSTICKID1,&joyinfo) != JOYERR_UNPLUGGED;
  bDev2Attached = joyGetPos(JOYSTICKID2,&joyinfo) != JOYERR_UNPLUGGED;
  if(bDev1Attached)
     joySetCapture(hWnd, JOYSTICKID1, 1000/30, true);
  if (bDev2Attached)
     joySetCapture(hWnd, JOYSTICKID2, 1000/30, true);

  return true;
}
```

After this code runs, Windows will begin sending messages to your game such as `MM_JOY1MOVE` and `MM_JOY2BUTTONDOWN`. You might feel that this simple code is preferable to the much larger initialization and required polling needed by DirectInput, but DirectInput gives you access to the entire device—all the buttons, the rumble, force feedback, and so on. The Windows Multimedia Platform SDK only gives you the most basic access to joystick messages.

Beyond this, another feature of DirectInput that's pretty useful is called *action mapping*. This is a concept that binds actions to virtual controls. Instead of looking at the X-axis of the joystick to find the direction of a car's steering wheel, DirectInput can map the action of steering the car to a virtual control. The actual controls can be mapped to the virtual controls at the whim of the player and are the basis for providing a completely configurable control system. Some gamers really love this. DirectInput isn't the only way to make that work, however, but it does buy you a few other things like a standard way to tweak the force-feedback system.

**Remappable Controls Are Expected by Your Players**

Whether you use DirectInput or not, this action-mapping idea is something every game should have, even if you have to code it yourself. If you can easily switch your controls from right-handed to left-handed or from normal camera movement to inverted camera movement, you'll automatically get more people to play your game. Actually, you'll keep people from throwing your game in the garbage. Most players expect a customizable interface, and you'll find more players giving your game great reviews if they can adopt a control scheme they are comfortable with. Even more importantly, PC gamepads from different manufacturers may map input completely differently—for example, one may switch the thumbsticks from left-handed to right-handed or give you negative values when you expect positive values. A configurable input scheme lets you easily remap these wacky values to a standard your game will use.

Mass market games that don't use any advanced features of joysticks or don't have insanely configurable controls can work just fine with Windows messages and the Windows Multimedia Platform SDK. You don't have to learn to use DirectInput to make games, and Windows messages are easy and familiar. There are plenty of DirectInput samples in the DirectX SDK for you to look at, so I'm not going to waste your time or any trees on the subject. What I want to work on is the fact that there's plenty to talk about in terms of user interface code, regardless of the API you use or on what platform your game ships.

## A Few Safety Tips

I've probably spent more of my programming time on user interface tasks than almost anything else. The design for the early *Ultima* games loaded tons of control on the mouse—the idea being that the player could play the whole game without ever touching the keyboard. As good an idea as it seemed at the time, this was a horrible idea because it ignored simple physiology and the nature of the hardware. Remember that any input scheme should be designed around how players physically manipulate the device, and that they tend to do this for hours at a time.

There are plenty of standard conventions for input devices, from Microsoft Windows to first-person shooters on the PC. When you sit down to write your interface code, consider your control scheme carefully and make a conscious decision whether you want to stay with a well-known convention or go in a totally new direction. You take a risk with going rogue on user interface controls, but it can pay off, too. After all, before the shooter-style game was popular, how many games used the mouse as a model for a human neck? This idea worked well in a case like this for two reasons: It solved a new problem, and the solution was intuitive.

**If It Ain't Broke, Don't Fix It**

If you're solving an interface problem that has a standard solution and you choose a radically different approach, you take a risk of annoying players. If you think their annoyance will transition into wonder and words of praise as they discover (and figure out) your novel solution, then by all means give it a try. Make sure that you test your idea first with some people you trust. They'll tell you if your idea belongs on the garbage heap.

After them, try the idea out on real players you've never met. Be careful with interfaces, though. A friend of mine once judged the many entrants into the Indie Games Festival (www.indiegames.com), and he said the biggest mistake he saw that killed promising entrants was poor interface controls. He was amazed to see entries with incredible 3D graphics not make the cut because they were simply too hard to control.

What's worse, even game professionals get caught in this problem. The big retail buyers will give your game just a few minutes, and if they can't figure out your control scheme, they won't buy your game. Believe me, if someone like Walmart or Best Buy doesn't buy your game, you are destined for the unemployment line. In short, don't be afraid to use a good idea just because it's already been done.

**Be cautious with overloading simple controls with complicated results.** Context sensitivity in controls can be tough to deal with as a player. It's easy to make the mistake of loading too much control onto too little a device. The *Ultima* games generally went a little too far, I think, in how they used the mouse. A design goal for the games was to have every conceivable action be possible from the mouse, so every click and double-click was used for something. In fact, the same command would do different things if you clicked on a person, a door, or a monster. I'm sometimes surprised that we never implemented a special action for the "shave and a haircut, two bits" click.

**Give the player some feedback.** One thing I think the *Ultima* games did well, and many others since, was how they used the cursor, or reticle image. As it floated over different objects, it would change shape to give the player feedback about what things were and whether they could be activated by a button press. This is especially useful when your screens are very densely populated. When the reticle changes shape to signify that the player can perform an action, players immediately understand that they can use it to explore the screen. In *Thief: Deadly Shadows*, the gamepad controls did very different things when the player was shooting an arrow or picking a lock. The very first tutorial mission exposed these differences with specific tasks the player had to complete during the tutorial mission, and the screens were very different for both modes. On *Mushroom Men: The Spore Wars* for the Wii, the changing icon told the player what special power was possible on any object being pointed to by the Wii Remote.

**Players won't use it if they don't know about it.** A great term in games is "discoverability." It describes how easy it is for a player to figure things out on his own. Power-user moves are sometimes hidden on purpose, such as a special button combo in a fighting game, and that's a fine thing to hide. A special shortcut to page through equipped weapons is different—it is something that more advanced players will use to shorten the time between their desire to do something and having it actually happening. Make sure that you expose anything like this in a tutorial or in hints during loading screens. Documenting it isn't good enough since players almost never read documentation.

**Watch and learn.** When you finish any work on any kind of interface, bring some people in and watch them try to use it. Stand behind them and give them a task to perform, but don't give them any hints. An interface should be self evident to players, and they should be able to figure it out in 30 seconds or less on their own. A really good tip: Watch what your impromptu testers do first, and most likely they'll all do something similar. If they struggle with your solution, consider carefully whether you should consider changing your design.

**Avoid pixel perfect accuracy.** It's a serious mistake to assume that players of all ages can target a screen area with pixel perfect accuracy. Even with a high-fidelity control like a mouse, this task is very difficult; on a very low-fidelity control like the Wii Remote or pad touch controls, this is simply impossible. An example of this might be a small click target on an item or a small drop point on the screen. High requirements for accuracy can create tons of player frustration, even with a high-fidelity input device like a mouse. Instead, consider creating a sloppy buffer zone that effectively widens the active target area. On *Thief: Deadly Shadows,* these "sloppy" targeting areas would sometimes overlap on-screen, and the code had to choose which item was the most likely one targeted. The solution was to choose the closest one to the viewer, but that doesn't necessarily work all the time.

Anyone who has attempted to cast spells in the original version of *Ultima VIII* will agree. The reagents that made some of the spells work had to be placed exactly. This requirement made spell casting frustrating and arbitrary. Even though the QA department complained about it early on, after some time they learned how to cast spells with no problem. But real players are not hired to deal with your bad interface, so don't expect them to just tolerate it until they finally learn it.

**Targeting Is Always a Little Sloppy**

The *Ultima VII* mouse code detected objects on the screen by performing pixel collision testing with the mouse (X,Y) position and the images that made up the objects in the world. Most of these sprites were chroma keyed and therefore had spots of the transparent color all through them. This was especially true of objects like jail cell bars and fences. *Ultima VII*'s pixel collision code ignored the transparent color, allowing players to click through fences and jail cell bars to examine objects on the other side. That was a good feature, and it was used in many places to advance the story. The problem it created, however, was that sometimes the transparent colored pixels actually made it harder for players to click on an object. For example, double-clicking the door of the jail cell was difficult. If you use an approach like this, take some care in designing which objects are active and which are simply scenery, and make sure you make this clear to your players.

This is an extremely important issue with casual games or kids' games. Very young players or older gamers find games with forgiving interfaces much easier to play. Making your game easier to play tends to broaden the appeal of the game, but it also narrows the skill gap between first-time players and elite players. This balance is sometimes hard to gauge. The best advice I can give you on that front is try to know your audience. If the game is something families of all ages will play, make the game fairly forgiving. If the game is targeted more toward a hard-core audience, ramp up the difficulty quickly and give the elite players something that will challenge them. It isn't impossible, but typically you can't do both.

**A Fine Use of a Piece of Tape**

With *Ultima VIII,* the left mouse button served as the "walk/run" button. As long as you held it down, the avatar character would run in the direction of the mouse pointer. Ultima games require a lot of running; your character will run across an entire continent only to discover that the thingamajig that will open the gate of *whosiz* is back in the city you just left, so you go running off again. By the time I'd played through the game the umpteenth time, my index finger was so tired of running I started using tape to hold the mouse button down. One thing people do in a lot of FPS games when playing online is set them to "always run" mode. I wish we'd done that with *Ultima VIII.*

**Accelerometers Sometimes Don't Know Which Way Is Up**

Being at Red Fly for a few years gave me a special appreciation for coders who had to deal with motion controls, especially those on the Wii Remote. All of our games, most recently including *Star Wars: The Force Unleashed II* and *Thor: God of Thunder* on the Wii had quick-time sequences where you finished off bosses with a slam to the left, right, up, or down. If you play these games, you'll quickly realize that left and right are equivalent, as are up and down. The reason why we did this has to do with how different players move the Wii Remote.

Watch someone when he performs a "slam left" movement, and you'll see that more often than not, he'll begin with a slight leftward motion, then go toward the right as he builds up speed, and end with a big slam back to the left. This creates quite a bit of madness for the coder trying to recognize this motion, especially since not all players will do it the same way. It turned out that the best course of action was to simply watch the left-right accelerometer and just register the slam correctly if they didn't move it (much) in a vertical direction and did so within the time limit.

## Working with Two-Axis Controls

Two-axis controls include the mouse, touch screen, or joystick. I'm not going to talk about basic topics like grabbing `WM_MOUSEMOVE` and pulling screen coordinates out of the `LPARAM`. Many books have been written to cover these programming techniques. If you need a primer on Win32 and GDI, I suggest you read Charles Petzold's classic book *Programming Windows: The Definitive Guide to the Win32 API*. Instead, what follows are things you'll need to do after you get those coordinates.

### Capturing the Mouse on Desktops

I'm always surprised that programming documentation doesn't make inside jokes about capturing the mouse. At least we can still laugh at it. If you've never programmed a user interface before, you probably don't know what capturing the mouse means or why any programmer in his right mind would want to do this. Catching a mouse isn't probably something that's high on your list.

To see what you've been missing, go to a desktop machine right now and bring up a dialog box. A Windows or Mac will do. Move the mouse over a button, hopefully not one that will erase your hard drive, and click the mouse button that will activate the button and hold it down. You should see the button graphic depress. Move the mouse pointer away from the button, and you'll notice the button graphic pop back up again. Until you release the mouse button, you can move the mouse all you want, but only the button on the dialog will get the messages. If you don't believe me, open

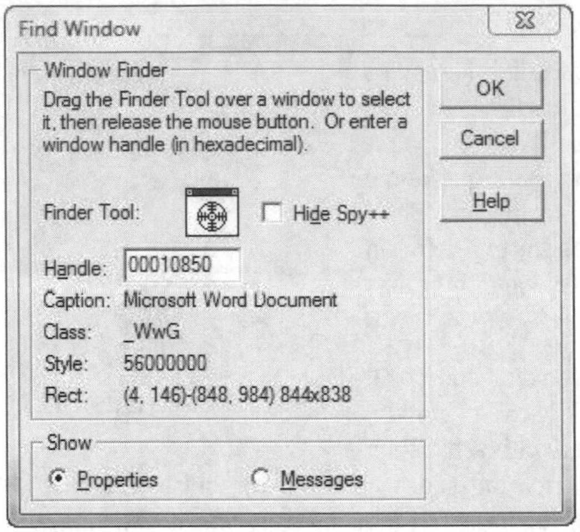


**Figure 9.1**
The Find window with Spy++.

up Microsoft Spy++ on a Windows desktop and see for yourself. Microsoft Spy++ is a tool that you use to figure out which Windows messages are going to which window, and it's a great debugging tool if you are coding a standard GDI-based application. Here's a quick tutorial:

1. If you are running Visual Studio, select Spy++ from the Tools menu. You can also launch it from the Tools section of the Visual Studio area of your Start menu.
2. Close the open default window and select Find Window from the main menu or press Ctrl-F.
3. You'll then see a little dialog box that looks like the one shown in Figure 9.1.
4. Click and drag the little finder tool to the window or button you are interested in and then click the Messages radio button at the bottom of the dialog. You'll get a new window in Spy++ that shows you every message sent to the object.

Perform the previous experiment again, but this time use Spy++ to monitor the Windows messages sent to the button. You'll find that as soon as you click on the button, every mouse action will be displayed, even if the pointer is far away from the button in question. That might be interesting, but why is it important? If a user interface uses the boundaries of an object like a button to determine whether it should receive mouse events, capturing the mouse is critical. Imagine a scenario where you can't capture mouse events:

1. The mouse button goes down over an active button.
2. The button receives the event and draws itself in the down position.

3. The mouse moves away from the button, outside its border.
4. The button stops receiving any events from the mouse since the mouse isn't directly over the button.
5. The mouse button is released.

The result is that the button will still be drawn in the down position, awaiting a button release event that will never happen. If the mouse events are captured, the button will continue to receive mouse events until the button is released.

To better understand this, take a look at a code snippet that shows some code you can use to capture the mouse and draw lines:

```
LRESULT APIENTRY MainWndProc(HWND hwndMain, UINT uMsg, WPARAM wParam,
                             LPARAM lParam)
{
  static POINTS ptsBegin;           // beginning point

  switch (uMsg)
  {
    case WM_LBUTTONDOWN:
      // Capture mouse input.
      SetCapture(hwndMain);
      bIsCaptured = true;
      ptsBegin = MAKEPOINTS(lParam);
      return 0;

    case WM_MOUSEMOVE:
      // When moving the mouse, the user must hold down
      // the left mouse button to draw lines.
      if (wParam & MK_LBUTTON)
      {
        // imaginary code - you write this function
        pseudocode::ErasePreviousLine();

        // Convert the current cursor coordinates to a
        // POINTS structure, and then draw a new line.
        ptsEnd = MAKEPOINTS(lParam);

        // also imaginary
        pseudocode::DrawLine(ptsEnd.x, ptsEnd.y);
      }
      break;
```

```
    case WM_LBUTTONUP:
      // The user has finished drawing the line. Reset the
      // previous line flag, release the mouse cursor, and
      // release the mouse capture.

      fPrevLine = FALSE;
      bIsCaptured = false;
      ReleaseCapture();
      break;
  }

    case WM_ACTIVATEAPP:
    {
      if (wParam == TRUE)
      {
        // got focus again - regain our mouse capture
        if (bIsCaptured)
          SetCapture(hwndMain);
      }
      break;
    }
  return 0;
}
```

If you were to write functions for erasing and drawing lines, you'd have a nice rubber band line-drawing mechanism, which mouse capturing makes possible. By using it, your lines will continue to follow the mouse, even if you leave the window's client area.

One thing to note: If your application loses focus, you'll also lose the mouse capture, which can be handled easily by listening to the `WM_ACTIVATEAPP` message.

## Making a Mouse Drag Work

You might wonder why a mouse drag is so important. Drags are important because they are prerequisites to much of the user interface code in a lot of PC games. When you select a group of combatants in RTS games like good old *Command & Conquer*, for example, you drag out a rectangle. When you play *Freecell* in Windows, you use the mouse to drag cards around. It is quite likely that you'll have to code a mouse drag at some point.

Dragging the mouse adds a little complexity to the process of capturing it. Most user interface code distinguishes a single-click, double-click, and drag as three separate actions, and therefore will call different game code. Dragging also relates to the notion of legality; it's not always possible that anything in your game can be dragged to anywhere. If a drag fails, you'll need a way to set things back to the way they were. This issue might seem moot when you consider that dragging usually affects the look of the game—the dragged object needs to appear like it is really moving around, and it shouldn't leave a copy of itself in its original location. That might confuse the player big-time.

The code to support dragging requires three phases:

- Detect and initiate a drag event.
- Handle the mouse movement and draw objects accordingly.
- Detect the release and finalize the drag.

The actions that define a drag are typically a mouse press (button down) followed by a mouse movement, but life in the mouse drag game is not always that simple. Also, during a double-click event, a slight amount of mouse movement might occur, perhaps only a single pixel coordinate. Your code must interpret these different cases.

In Windows, a drag event is only allowed on objects that are already selected, which is why drags usually follow on the second "click and hold" of the mouse button. The first click of the left mouse button always selects objects. Many games differ from that standard, but it's one of the easier actions to code since only selected objects are draggable.

Since a drag event involves multiple trips around the main loop, you must assume that every mouse button down event could be the beginning of a drag event. I guess an event is assumed draggable until proven innocent. In your mouse button down handler, you need to look at the mouse coordinates and determine if they are over a draggable object. If the object is draggable, you must create a temporary reference to it that you can find a few game loops later. Since this is the first button down event, you can't tell if it's a bona fide drag event just yet.

The only thing that will make the drag event real is the movement of the mouse, but only movement outside of a tiny buffer zone. On most screen resolutions, a good choice is five pixels in either the X or Y coordinate. This is large enough to indicate that the drag was real, but small enough that small shakes in the mouse during a double-click won't unintentionally initiate a drag. If you were to create a drag on a Wii game, you'd want a much sloppier buffer zone since the Wii Remote pointer can shake quite a bit. If you can set this buffer size while the game is running, like with a hack or a cheat, you'll be able to tune this to suit a majority of players quickly.

Here's the code that performs this dirty work of the drag:

```
// Place this code at the top of your mouse movement handler
if (m_aboutToDrag)
{
  CPoint offset = currentPoint - dragStartingPoint;
  if (abs(offset.x) > DRAG_THRESHOLD || abs(offset.y) > DRAG_THRESHOLD)
  {
    // We have a real drag event!
    bool dragOK =
      pseudocode::InitiateDrag(draggedObject, dragStartingPoint);
    SetCapture( GetWindow()->m_hWnd );
    m_dragging = TRUE;
  }
}
```

The call to `pseudocode::InitiateDrag()` is something you write yourself. Its job is to set the game state to remove the original object from the display and draw the dragged object in some obvious form, such as a transparent ghost object.

Until the mouse button is released, the mouse movement handler will continue to get mouse movement commands, even those that are outside the client area of your window if you are running in windowed mode. Make sure that your draw routines don't freak out when they see these odd coordinates.

While the drag is active, you must direct all the mouse input to the control that initiated the drag. Other controls should essentially ignore the input. The best way to do this is to keep a pointer to the control that initiated the drag and send all input directly to it, essentially bypassing any code that sends messages to your control list. It's a little like masking all the controls in your control list, rendering them deaf to all incoming messages until the drag is complete.

What must go down must finally come up again. When the mouse button is released, your drag is complete, but the drag location might not be in a legal spot, so you might have to reset your game back to the state before the drag started, like this:

```
// Place this code at the top of your mouse button up handler
if ( m_dragging )
{
  ReleaseCapture();
  m_bDragging = false;

  if (!pseudocode::FinishDrag(point))
  {
```

```
    pseudocode::AbortDrag(dragStartingPoint);
  }
}
```

This bit of code would exist in your handler for a mouse button up event. The call to `ReleaseCapture()` makes sure that mouse events get sent to all their normal places again. `pseudocode::FinishDrag()` is a function you'd write yourself. It should detect if the destination of the drag was legal and perform the right game state manipulations to make it so. If the drag is illegal, the object has to snap back to its previous location as if the drag never occurred. This function can be trickier to write than you'd think, since you can't necessarily use game state information to send the object back to where it came from.

**Game Editors Are All Powerful**

In *Ultima VII* and *Ultima VIII,* we created a complicated system to keep track of object movement, specifically whether or not an object could legally move from one place to another. It was possible for a game designer to use the all-powerful game editor to force objects into any location, whether it was legal or not. If these objects were dragged to another illegal location by the player, the object had to be forced back into place. Otherwise, the object would exist in limbo. What we learned was that the drag code could access the game state at a low enough level to run the abort code.

You can have exactly the same problem with modern games that use modern physics systems. These days when you place an actor like a candle inside a table or something, the physics system can't solve for a legal place for the candle to exist. It's best course of action is to remove the candle completely from the collision detector, causing it to fall through the table and plummet downward, perhaps forever. It may just fall to the floor, but either way the candle won't stay on the table when the physics simulator begins running on the candle, which usually happens when it is moved. This can make dragging objects with real physics somewhat painful. The best course of action is to require the world editor to place dynamic objects in proper positions where they can be moved by the player later. This means the physics system is actually solving for legal support under the candle when it is placed.

## Working with a Game Controller

Working on Ion Storm's *Thief: Deadly Shadows* game was my first experience with console development and my first experience with writing code for a gamepad. It was much more of an eye-opener than I thought it would be. Until I actually had one of these things in my hot little hands and the code saturating my overcaffeinated brain, I thought these devices were little more than a collection of buttons and joysticks. Boy, was I wrong!

Having played tons of console games, I already had a pretty good feel for a good control scheme, but I'd never had the chance to write one myself. The basics of the gamepad interface code are really quite the same as a mouse, keyboard, or joystick, but subtle differences between interface design and interpreting the device inputs warrant some additional explanation. I'll talk a little about dead zones, normalizing input, input acceleration, and the design impact of one-stick versus two-stick control schemes.

## Dead Zones

A dead zone is any area of a control interface that has no input effect. This keeps small errors in hand movement from adversely affecting game input. You know you need a dead zone in a control when you watch players make mistakes because the controls were too sensitive and interpreted their input in a way that they didn't expect.

A great example of this was on the *Thief: Deadly Shadows* camera control for the Xbox gamepad. It used a two-stick control scheme like *Halo* or *Splinter Cell*, which meant that the character moved with the left thumbstick and the camera moved with the right thumbstick.

The first iteration of the camera movement code was pretty simple; the right thumbstick controlled the camera. Up/down movement caused the camera to pitch, and left/right movement caused the camera to yaw. The speed of movement was coded directly to how far the thumbstick was moved. But when I went to QA and watched them play, I noticed something really strange happening. As the QA person would spin the camera left or right, the camera would also pitch a few degrees up or down. This happened every time in QA, but not with me as I tested the code.

I watched QA play more to try to figure out what was happening, and I realized that when they were actually playing the game, they'd jam the left thumbstick left or right to see if something was behind them, and it was a pretty fast movement. Once the thumbstick hit the extreme position, it would stop, of course, but it would usually also be in a slightly up or down angle as well as all the way left or right. In my tests, I wasn't jamming the controller, and thus I never had the slight up/down position. Even though it was small, the up/down error in the thumbstick movement always resulted in the camera pitching up/down, just as I wrote the code.

Figure 9.2 shows the movement area of a thumbstick controller on a gamepad. By convention, gamepads, joysticks, and other two-axis controllers usually have raw output ranges from [–1.0f, 1.0f], and the neutral position returns a raw output value of (0.0f, 0.0f). Every now and then, you might find a control device returning odd

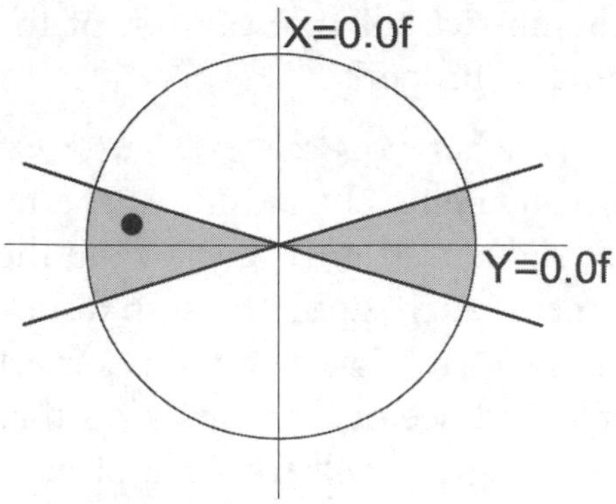


**Figure 9.2**
Dealing with a dead zone for pitch control.

values, like integers from [0, 255] or something like that. If you ever see this happening, it's a good idea to remap the output range back to [–1.0f, 1.0f]. Standardizing these ranges helps keep the code that interprets these values nice and clean.

If the thumbstick were positioned at the location of the black spot, you'd expect an X, Y value of (–0.80, 0.15) or thereabouts. That small positive Y input would be the cause of my previous trouble; the camera would slowly pitch until it was looking straight up or down, depending on the control scheme.

You might not think this is a serious problem—until you watch players play the game. Many first-person shooter players like to twitch-look—where they snap the thumbstick quickly to the left or right and pause for a second or two. If there's no dead zone, the camera will always begin to pitch a little up or down, depending on how the player is holding the gamepad. At some point, the player has to stop and correct the camera pitch, usually with a snort of disgust. Many players and game critics complain about bad cameras, but it seems that what they are really complaining about is bad camera *control.*

The answer to my problem, and yours if you are coding thumbstick controls, is a dead zone for pitch control. The dead zone is represented by the darkened area in Figure 9.2. Inside this area, all Y values are forced to zero. The values of our block spot become (–0.80, 0.0), and our camera pitch stays mercifully still.

You might be wondering why the dead zone has a bowtie shape instead of just a simple dead area all the way across the middle of the circle. There's a really good reason: When the thumbstick is close to the center and being moved about with a fine degree of control, the player is probably doing something like aiming a sniper rifle. A dead zone in this situation would be really annoying, since any up/down movement would require the player to push the thumbstick all the way out of the dead zone. That would make it almost impossible to aim properly.

The dead zone shape also doesn't have to be exactly what you see in Figure 9.2. Depending on your game and how people play it, you might change the shape by making the angle shallower or even pull the left and right dead areas away from the center, giving the player complete control over camera pitch until the thumbstick is closer to the extreme right or left side. The only way to figure out the perfect shape is by watching a lot of people play your game and seeing what they do that frustrates them. Controls that are too sensitive or too sluggish will frustrate players, and you'll want to find a middle ground that pleases a majority of people.

There's one additional trick to this solution. Think about what happens when the thumbstick moves away from the dead zone into the active, clear zone. One thing players expect in all control schemes is continuous, predictive movement. This means that you can't just force the Y value to zero in the dead zone and use regular values everywhere else; you have to smoothly interpolate the Y values outside of the dead zone from 0.0 to 1.0, or the player will notice a pop in the movement of the camera pitch. The code to do this is not nearly as bad as you might think:

```
float Interpolate(float normalizedValue, float begin, float end)
{
  // first check input values
  assert(normalizedValue>=0.0f);
  assert(normalizedValue<=1.0f);
  assert(end>begin);

  return ( normalizedValue * (end - begin) ) + begin;
}

void MapYDeadZone(Vec3 &input, float deadZone)
{
  if (deadZone>=1.0f)
    return;

  // The dead zone is assumed to be zero close to the origin
  // so we have to interpolate to find the right dead zone for
  // our current value of X.
  float actualDeadZone = Interpolate(fabs(input.x), 0.0f, deadZone);

  if (fabs(input.y) < actualDeadZone)
  {
```

```
        input.y = 0.0f;
        return;
    }

    // Y is outside of the dead zone, but we still need to
    // interpolate it so we don't see any popping.

    // Map Y values [actualDeadZone, 1.0f] to [0.0f, 1.0f]
    float normalizedY = (input.y - actualDeadZone) / (1.0f - actualDeadZone);
    input.y = normalizedY;
}
```

## Normalizing Input

Even though the game controller thumbsticks have a circular area of movement, the inputs for X and Y only reach 1.0 at the very top, bottom, left, and right of the circle. In other words, X and Y are mapped to a Cartesian space, not a circular space. Take a look at Figure 9.3, and you'll see what I mean.

Imagine what happens when a player pushes a control diagonally up and to the left. On some controllers, you'll get values for X and Y that are close to their maximum range and probably look something like (–0.95f, 0.95). The reason for this is how the

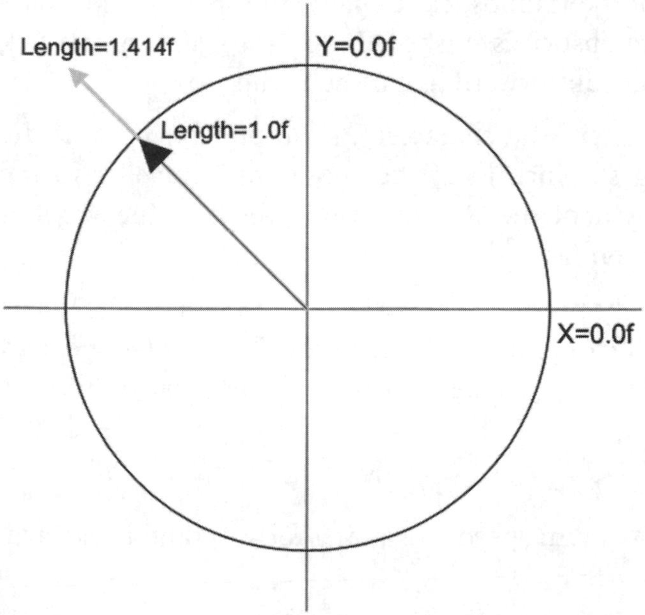


**Figure 9.3**
Normalized input from a two-axis controller.

controllers are built. Remember the two-axis controller I mentioned earlier? X and Y are both analog electrical devices called *potentiometers*. They measure electrical resistance along an analog dial and are used for things like volume controls on stereos and, of course, joysticks and thumbsticks. On two-axis controllers like these, you have two potentiometers: one for each axis.

You can see from Figure 9.3 that the Y potentiometer can reach 1.0 or –1.0 if you push the controller all the way up or down. You can get the same values for the X potentiometer. You might think that all you need to do to calculate the input speed is find the length of the combined vector. That's just classic geometry, the Pythagorean Theorem.

$$a^2 + b^2 = c^2$$
$$\sqrt{a^2 + b^2} = \pm c$$
$$\sqrt{1^2 + 1^2} = \pm\sqrt{2} = \pm 1.414$$

This length is represented by the gray arrow in Figure 9.3. The problem is that the new input vector is 1.414f units long, and if you feed it right into the game, you'll be able to move diagonally quite a bit faster than in the cardinal directions. The direction of the new vector is correct, but it is too long.

For character movement, the forward/back motion of the character is mapped to the up/down movement of the thumbstick, and the left/right motion of the character is mapped to the left/right movement of the thumbstick. Usually, the speed of the character is controlled by how far the thumbstick is pushed. If you push the thumbstick all the way forward, the character will run forward as fast as it can.

But look at what happens when you want the character to run and turn left at the same time, as Figure 9.3 would suggest. Since I have to move the controller to the left, I automatically increase the length of the X input while the Y value stays at 1.0f, and the character begins to run too fast.

The solution to this problem is actually pretty simple: The speed of the character is mapped to the length of the X/Y 2D vector, not the value of the Y control alone, and you have to cap the speed at 1.0f. All you do is take the capped length and multiply it by the maximum speed:

```
int speed = maxSpeed * min(1.0f, sqrt((x * x) + (y * y)));
```

Of course, you may have different maximum speeds for going forward and backward, or even side to side.

You might not realize it, but you also want to use this normalizing scheme on keyboard input. Consider the classic WASD scheme used by most first-person shooters on the PC. W and S move the player forward and back. A and D strafe the player from side to side. If you press W and A together, your character should move diagonally forward and to the left. If you don't normalize the input, your character will move faster diagonally than in the cardinal directions, because the combined forward and left inputs add together to create a longer vector, just as it does on the gamepad.

## One Stick, Two Stick, Red Stick, Blue Stick

It's never a bad thing to invoke Dr. Seuss, is it? One of the huge design decisions you'll make in your game is whether to follow a one-stick or two-stick control scheme. You'll attract different players for either one, and depending on your level design, you might be much better off going with one over the other.

A one-stick design lets the player control the character movement with one thumbstick, and the camera is usually controlled completely by the computer. There might be a camera control, but it is usually relegated to the D-pad instead of the other thumbstick. Lots of games do this, such as racing games like *Project Gotham 4* on the Xbox360 and *Mario Galaxies* on the Wii. It's generally seen by game designers and players as the easiest interface to control.

The two-stick design puts complete control of camera movement in the other thumbstick. This is done in games like *Halo*, *Thief: Deadly Shadows*, and *Gears of War*. This control scheme is harder to learn and is generally reserved for a hard-core audience.

How do you decide which one to use for your game? The best thing to do in my mind is try to compare your game design to others that have succeeded with a particular control scheme. We chose the control scheme in *Thief* by looking at *Halo* and *Splinter Cell* and decided that the gameplay was quite close to those two products. We also realized that because the game was first and third person, the same control interface would work exactly the same way in both modes.

## Ramping Control Values

*Ramping* is another way of saying *accelerating*. The raw control values are usually not sent directly into things like camera rotation because the movement can be quite jarring. You can jam a thumbstick control from the center to the edge of the control area extremely quickly, perhaps less than 80ms. If you take a little extra time to accelerate the movement of whatever it is you are controlling, you'll get a smoother acceleration, which adds a finer degree of control and looks much better to boot.

The input parameters for this calculation are the current elapsed time, the current speed, the maximum speed, and the number of seconds you want to accelerate.

```
// Ramp the acceleration by the elapsed time.
float numberOfSeconds = 2.0f;
m_currentSpeed += m_maxSpeed * ( (elapsedTime*elapsedTime) / numberOfSeconds);
if (m_currentSpeed > m_maxSpeed)
  m_currentSpeed = m_maxSpeed;
```

The elapsed time should be a floating-point number measuring the number of seconds it has been since the last time this code was called. It turns out that humans have a keen sense of how things should accelerate, probably because we watch things fall under the acceleration of gravity all the time. If those things are coconuts and we happen to be standing beneath them, this skill becomes quite life saving. Whenever you accelerate anything related to a control in your game, always accelerate it with a time-squared component so that it will "feel" more natural.

## Working with the Keyboard

There are many ways to grab keyboard input from Win32. They each have their good and bad points, and to make the right choice, you need to know how deep you need to pry into keyboard input data. Before we discuss these various approaches, let's get a few vocabulary words out of the way so that we're talking the same language:

- **Character code:** Describes the ASCII or UNICODE character that is the return value of the C function, `getchar()`.
- **Virtual scan code:** Macros defined in *Winuser.h* that describe the components of data sent in the `wParam` value of `WM_CHAR`, `WM_KEYDOWN`, and `WM_KEYUP` messages.
- **OEM scan code:** The scan codes provided by OEMs. They are useless unless you care about coding something specific for a particular keyboard manufacturer.

Those definitions will resonate even more once you've seen some data, so let's pry open the keyboard and do a little snooping.

### Mike's Keyboard Snooper

I wrote a small program to break out all the different values for Windows keyboard messages, and as you'll see shortly, this tool really uncovers some weird things that take place with Windows. Taken with the definitions we just discussed, however, you'll soon see that the different values will make a little more sense. Each line in the tables below contains the values of `wParam` and `lParam` for Windows keyboard messages. I typed the following sequence of keys: `1 2 a b`, to produce the first table.

Look closely at the different values that are produced for the different Windows messages:

WM_KEYDOWN, WM_CHAR, WM_KEYUP, and so on:

```
WM_KEYDOWN   Code:49 '1' Repeat:1 Oem: 2 Ext'd:0 IsAlt:0 WasDown:0 Rel'd:0
WM_CHAR      Code:49 '1' Repeat:1 Oem: 2 Ext'd:0 IsAlt:0 WasDown:0 Rel'd:0
WM_KEYUP     Code:49 '1' Repeat:1 Oem: 2 Ext'd:0 IsAlt:0 WasDown:0 Rel'd:1
WM_KEYDOWN   Code:50 '2' Repeat:1 Oem: 3 Ext'd:0 IsAlt:0 WasDown:0 Rel'd:0
WM_CHAR      Code:50 '2' Repeat:1 Oem: 3 Ext'd:0 IsAlt:0 WasDown:0 Rel'd:0
WM_KEYUP     Code:50 '2' Repeat:1 Oem: 3 Ext'd:0 IsAlt:0 WasDown:0 Rel'd:1
WM_KEYDOWN   Code:65 'A' Repeat:1 Oem:30 Ext'd:0 IsAlt:0 WasDown:0 Rel'd:0
WM_CHAR      Code:97 'a' Repeat:1 Oem:30 Ext'd:0 IsAlt:0 WasDown:0 Rel'd:0
WM_KEYUP     Code:65 'A' Repeat:1 Oem:30 Ext'd:0 IsAlt:0 WasDown:0 Rel'd:1
WM_KEYDOWN   Code:66 'B' Repeat:1 Oem:48 Ext'd:0 IsAlt:0 WasDown:0 Rel'd:0
WM_CHAR      Code:98 'b' Repeat:1 Oem:48 Ext'd:0 IsAlt:0 WasDown:0 Rel'd:0
WM_KEYUP     Code:66 'B' Repeat:1 Oem:48 Ext'd:0 IsAlt:0 WasDown:0 Rel'd:1
```

You'll first notice that the message pipe gets the sequence of WM_KEYDOWN, WM_CHAR, and WM_KEYUP for each key pressed and released. The next thing you'll notice is that the code returned by WM_CHAR is different from the other messages when characters are lowercase.

This should give you a clue that you can use WM_CHAR for simple character input when all you care about is getting the right character code. What happens if a key is held down? Let's find out. The next table shows the output I received by first pressing and holding an "a" and then the left Shift key:

```
WM_KEYDOWN   Code:65 'A' Repeat:1 Oem:30 Ext'd:0 IsAlt:0 WasDown:0 Rel'd:1
WM_CHAR      Code:97 'a' Repeat:1 Oem:30 Ext'd:0 IsAlt:0 WasDown:0 Rel'd:1
WM_KEYDOWN   Code:65 'A' Repeat:1 Oem:30 Ext'd:0 IsAlt:0 WasDown:0 Rel'd:1
WM_CHAR      Code:97 'a' Repeat:1 Oem:30 Ext'd:0 IsAlt:0 WasDown:0 Rel'd:1
WM_KEYDOWN   Code:65 'A' Repeat:1 Oem:30 Ext'd:0 IsAlt:0 WasDown:0 Rel'd:1
WM_CHAR      Code:97 'a' Repeat:1 Oem:30 Ext'd:0 IsAlt:0 WasDown:0 Rel'd:1
WM_KEYDOWN   Code:65 'A' Repeat:1 Oem:30 Ext'd:0 IsAlt:0 WasDown:0 Rel'd:1
WM_CHAR      Code:97 'a' Repeat:1 Oem:30 Ext'd:0 IsAlt:0 WasDown:0 Rel'd:1
WM_KEYDOWN   Code:65 'A' Repeat:1 Oem:30 Ext'd:0 IsAlt:0 WasDown:0 Rel'd:1
WM_CHAR      Code:97 'a' Repeat:1 Oem:30 Ext'd:0 IsAlt:0 WasDown:0 Rel'd:1
WM_KEYUP     Code:65 'A' Repeat:1 Oem:30 Ext'd:0 IsAlt:0 WasDown:0 Rel'd:1
WM_KEYDOWN   Code:16 '_' Repeat:1 Oem:42 Ext'd:0 IsAlt:0 WasDown:0 Rel'd:0
WM_KEYDOWN   Code:16 '_' Repeat:1 Oem:42 Ext'd:0 IsAlt:0 WasDown:0 Rel'd:1
WM_KEYDOWN   Code:16 '_' Repeat:1 Oem:42 Ext'd:0 IsAlt:0 WasDown:0 Rel'd:1
WM_KEYDOWN   Code:16 '_' Repeat:1 Oem:42 Ext'd:0 IsAlt:0 WasDown:0 Rel'd:1
WM_KEYDOWN   Code:16 '_' Repeat:1 Oem:42 Ext'd:0 IsAlt:0 WasDown:0 Rel'd:1
WM_KEYUP     Code:16 '_' Repeat:1 Oem:42 Ext'd:0 IsAlt:0 WasDown:0 Rel'd:1
```

It seems that I can't count on the repeat value as shown here. It is completely dependent on your equipment manufacturer and keyboard driver software. You may get repeat values and you may not. You need to make sure your code will work either way.

For the next sequence, I held the left Shift key and typed the same original sequence—1 2 a b:

```
WM_KEYDOWN   Code:16 '_' Repeat:1 Oem:42 Ext'd:0 IsAlt:0 WasDown:0 Rel'd:0
WM_KEYDOWN   Code:16 '_' Repeat:1 Oem:42 Ext'd:0 IsAlt:0 WasDown:0 Rel'd:1
WM_KEYDOWN   Code:16 '_' Repeat:1 Oem:42 Ext'd:0 IsAlt:0 WasDown:0 Rel'd:1
WM_KEYDOWN   Code:16 '_' Repeat:1 Oem:42 Ext'd:0 IsAlt:0 WasDown:0 Rel'd:1
WM_KEYDOWN   Code:16 '_' Repeat:1 Oem:42 Ext'd:0 IsAlt:0 WasDown:0 Rel'd:1
WM_KEYDOWN   Code:49 '1' Repeat:1 Oem: 2 Ext'd:0 IsAlt:0 WasDown:0 Rel'd:0
WM_CHAR      Code:33 '!' Repeat:1 Oem: 2 Ext'd:0 IsAlt:0 WasDown:0 Rel'd:0
WM_KEYUP     Code:49 '1' Repeat:1 Oem: 2 Ext'd:0 IsAlt:0 WasDown:0 Rel'd:1
WM_KEYDOWN   Code:50 '2' Repeat:1 Oem: 3 Ext'd:0 IsAlt:0 WasDown:0 Rel'd:0
WM_CHAR      Code:64 '@' Repeat:1 Oem: 3 Ext'd:0 IsAlt:0 WasDown:0 Rel'd:0
WM_KEYUP     Code:50 '2' Repeat:1 Oem: 3 Ext'd:0 IsAlt:0 WasDown:0 Rel'd:1
WM_KEYDOWN   Code:65 'A' Repeat:1 Oem:30 Ext'd:0 IsAlt:0 WasDown:0 Rel'd:0
WM_CHAR      Code:65 'A' Repeat:1 Oem:30 Ext'd:0 IsAlt:0 WasDown:0 Rel'd:0
WM_KEYUP     Code:65 'A' Repeat:1 Oem:30 Ext'd:0 IsAlt:0 WasDown:0 Rel'd:1
WM_KEYDOWN   Code:66 'B' Repeat:1 Oem:48 Ext'd:0 IsAlt:0 WasDown:0 Rel'd:0
WM_CHAR      Code:66 'B' Repeat:1 Oem:48 Ext'd:0 IsAlt:0 WasDown:0 Rel'd:0
WM_KEYUP     Code:66 'B' Repeat:1 Oem:48 Ext'd:0 IsAlt:0 WasDown:0 Rel'd:1
WM_KEYUP     Code:16 '_' Repeat:1 Oem:42 Ext'd:0 IsAlt:0 WasDown:0 Rel'd:1
```

There's nothing too surprising here; the Shift key will repeat until the next key is pressed. Note that the repeats on the Shift key don't continue. Just as in the first sequence, only the `WM_CHAR` message gives you your expected character.

You should realize by now that if you want to use keys on the keyboard for hot keys, you can use the `WM_KEYDOWN` message and you won't have to care if the Shift key (or even the Caps Lock key) is pressed. Pressing the Caps Lock key gives you this output:

```
WM_KEYDOWN Code: 20 '_' Repeat:1 Oem:58 Ext'd:0 IsAlt:0 WasDown:0 Rel'd:0
WM_KEYUP   Code: 20 '_' Repeat:1 Oem:58 Ext'd:0 IsAlt:0 WasDown:0 Rel'd:1
```

The messages that come through for `WM_CHAR` will operate as if the Shift key were pressed down.

Let's try some function keys, including F1, F2, F3, and the shifted versions also:

```
WM_KEYDOWN   Code:112 'p' Repeat:1 Oem:59 Ext'd:0 IsAlt:0 WasDown:0 Rel'd:0
WM_KEYUP     Code:112 'p' Repeat:1 Oem:59 Ext'd:0 IsAlt:0 WasDown:0 Rel'd:1
WM_KEYDOWN   Code:113 'q' Repeat:1 Oem:60 Ext'd:0 IsAlt:0 WasDown:0 Rel'd:0
```

```
WM_KEYUP      Code:113 'q' Repeat:1 Oem:60 Ext'd:0 IsAlt:0 WasDown:0 Rel'd:1
WM_KEYDOWN    Code:114 'r' Repeat:1 Oem:61 Ext'd:0 IsAlt:0 WasDown:0 Rel'd:0
WM_KEYUP      Code:114 'r' Repeat:1 Oem:61 Ext'd:0 IsAlt:0 WasDown:0 Rel'd:1
WM_KEYDOWN    Code: 16 '_' Repeat:1 Oem:42 Ext'd:0 IsAlt:0 WasDown:0 Rel'd:0
WM_KEYDOWN    Code:112 'p' Repeat:1 Oem:59 Ext'd:0 IsAlt:0 WasDown:0 Rel'd:0
WM_KEYUP      Code:112 'p' Repeat:1 Oem:59 Ext'd:0 IsAlt:0 WasDown:0 Rel'd:1
WM_KEYDOWN    Code:113 'q' Repeat:1 Oem:60 Ext'd:0 IsAlt:0 WasDown:0 Rel'd:0
WM_KEYUP      Code:113 'q' Repeat:1 Oem:60 Ext'd:0 IsAlt:0 WasDown:0 Rel'd:1
WM_KEYDOWN    Code:114 'r' Repeat:1 Oem:61 Ext'd:0 IsAlt:0 WasDown:0 Rel'd:0
WM_KEYUP      Code:114 'r' Repeat:1 Oem:61 Ext'd:0 IsAlt:0 WasDown:0 Rel'd:1
WM_KEYUP      Code: 16 '_' Repeat:1 Oem:42 Ext'd:0 IsAlt:0 WasDown:0 Rel'd:1
```

There's a distinct lack of WM_CHAR messages, isn't there? Also, notice that the code returned by the F1 key is the same as the lowercase "p" character. So, what does "p" look like?

```
WM_KEYDOWN    Code: 80 'P' Repeat:1 Oem:25 Ext'd:0 IsAlt:0 WasDown:0 Rel'd:0
WM_CHAR       Code:112 'p' Repeat:1 Oem:25 Ext'd:0 IsAlt:0 WasDown:0 Rel'd:0
WM_KEYUP      Code: 80 'P' Repeat:1 Oem:25 Ext'd:0 IsAlt:0 WasDown:0 Rel'd:1
```

Isn't that interesting? The virtual scan code for "p" as encoded for WM_CHAR is exactly the same as the code for WM_KEYUP and WM_KEYDOWN. This funky design leads to some buggy misinterpretations of these two messages if you are looking at nothing but the virtual scan code. I've seen some games where you could use the function keys to enter your character name!

**Function Keys Require Special Handling**

You can't use WM_CHAR to grab function key input or any other keyboard key not associated with a typeable character. It is confusing that the ASCII value for the lowercase "p" character is also the VK_F1. If you were beginning to suspect that you couldn't use the wParam value from all these messages in the same way, you're right.

If you want to figure out the difference between keys, you should use the OEM scan code. There's a Windows helper function to translate it into something useful:

```
// grab bits 16-23 from LPARAM
unsigned int oemScan = int(lParam & (0xff << 16))>>16;
UINT vk = MapVirtualKey(oemScan, 1);
if (vk == VK_F1)
{
  // we've got someone pressing the F1 key!
}
```

The `VK_F1` is a `#define` in *WinUser.h*, where you'll find definitions for every other virtual key you'll need: `VK_ESCAPE`, `VK_TAB`, `VK_SPACE`, and so on.

Processing different keyboard inputs seems messy, doesn't it? Hold on, it gets better. The next sequence shows the left Shift key, right Shift key, left Ctrl key, and right Ctrl key:

```
WM_KEYDOWN   Code: 16 '_' Repeat:1 Oem:42 Ext'd:0 IsAlt:0 WasDown:0 Rel'd:0
WM_KEYUP     Code: 16 '_' Repeat:1 Oem:42 Ext'd:0 IsAlt:0 WasDown:0 Rel'd:1
WM_KEYDOWN   Code: 16 '_' Repeat:1 Oem:54 Ext'd:0 IsAlt:0 WasDown:0 Rel'd:0
WM_KEYUP     Code: 16 '_' Repeat:1 Oem:54 Ext'd:0 IsAlt:0 WasDown:0 Rel'd:1
WM_KEYDOWN   Code: 17 '_' Repeat:1 Oem:29 Ext'd:0 IsAlt:0 WasDown:0 Rel'd:0
WM_KEYUP     Code: 17 '_' Repeat:1 Oem:29 Ext'd:0 IsAlt:0 WasDown:0 Rel'd:1
WM_KEYDOWN   Code: 17 '_' Repeat:1 Oem:29 Ext'd:1 IsAlt:0 WasDown:0 Rel'd:0
WM_KEYUP     Code: 17 '_' Repeat:1 Oem:29 Ext'd:1 IsAlt:0 WasDown:0 Rel'd:1
```

The only way to distinguish the left Shift key from the right Shift key is to look at the OEM scan code. On the other hand, the only way to distinguish the left Ctrl key from the right Ctrl key is to look at the extended key bit to see if it is set for the right Ctrl key. This insane cobbler of aggregate design is the best example of what happens if you have a mandate to create new technology while supporting stuff as old as my high school diploma (or is that my grade school one?).

**You Might Need Your Own Keyboard Handler**

To get around the problems of processing keyboard inputs that look the same as I've outlined in this section, you'll want to write your own handler for accepting the `WM_KEYDOWN` and `WM_KEYUP` messages. If your game is going to have a complicated enough interface to distinguish between left and right Ctrl or Shift keys and will use these keys in combination with others, you've got an interesting road ahead. My best advice is to try to keep things as simple as possible. It's a bad idea to assign different actions to both Ctrl or Shift keys anyway. If your game only needs some hot keys and no fancy combinations, `WM_KEYDOWN` will work fine all by itself.

Here's a summary of how to get the right data out of these keyboard messages:

- `WM_CHAR`: Use this message only if your game cares about printable characters: no function keys, Ctrl keys, or Shift keys as a single input.
- `WM_KEYDOWN/WM_KEYUP`: Grabs each key as you press it, but makes no distinction between upper- and lowercase characters. Use this to grab function key input and compare the OEM scan codes with `MapVirtualKey()`. You won't get upper- and lowercase characters without tracking the status of the Shift keys yourself.

It's almost like this system was engineered by a congressional conference committee.

### `GetAsyncKeyState()` and Other Evils

There's a Windows function that will return the status of any key. It's tempting to use, especially given the morass of weirdness you have to deal with going a more traditional route with Windows keyboard messages. Unfortunately, there's a dark side to these functions and other functions that poll the state of device hardware outside of the message loop.

Most testing scripts or replay features pump recorded messages into the normal message pump, making sure that actual hardware messages are shunted away. Polling functions like `GetAsyncKeyState()` aren't easily trapped in the same way. They also make debugging and testing more difficult, since timing of keyboard input could be crucial to re-creating a weird bug.

There are other polled functions that can cause the same issues. One of them is the polled device status functions in DirectInput, such as `IDirectInputDevice::GetDeviceState()`. The only way I'd consider using these functions is if I wrote my own mini-message pump, where polled device status was converted into messages sent into my game logic. That, of course, is a lot more work.

### Handling the Alt Key Under Windows

If I use the same program to monitor keyboard messages related to pressing the right and left Alt keys, I get nothing. No output at all. Windows keeps the Alt key for itself and uses it to send special commands to your application. You should listen to `WM_SYSCOMMAND` to find out what's going on. You could use the polling functions to find out if the Alt keys have been pressed, but not only does that go against some recent advice, it's not considered "polite" Windows behavior. Microsoft has guidelines that well-behaved applications should follow, including games. The Alt key is reserved for commands sent to Windows. Users will not expect your game to launch missiles when all they want to do is switch over to Excel and try to look busy for the boss.

## What, No Dance Pad?

I freely admit that I'm still a *Dance Dance Revolution* junkie, and anyone who knows me is probably wondering why I didn't spend a few pages on dance pad controls. At first blush, you might say that the dance pad is programmed exactly the same way as the game controller—it has buttons that get pressed just like the controller you hold in your hand.

Now that you've read this chapter, you probably realize that the programming for a dance pad is quite different, simply because the player is using his feet and not his hands. You still use the same code to get button down and up messages. But think for a moment about how your feet are different from your hands. They move slower, for one thing—at least mine do. You have two feet moving on four buttons, which is different than a handheld controller where only your right thumb can press those four buttons. Tuning for timing is probably really different, too, especially since there is a vast skill difference between people like my Mom and the kids in the arcades who can move so fast you can't even see their feet.

Input devices are physiological, and you can't ever forget that when defining how your game gets mouse movement events or thumbstick events. One is controlled with the arm and wrist, the other the thumb. This one fact is a key issue when working with input devices.

Here's my best example. Why do you think the WASD control scheme became so popular in first-person shooters on the PC? I'll take an educated guess—fine movements like aiming, firing, and looking are mapped to the mouse, which are usually in a player's right hand. The movement keys, which are W, A, S, and D, are easily controllable with the player's left hand. The physical nature of the keyboard and the mouse and the fact that most people are right-handed made this interface so popular.

One thing deserves mentioning more than any other—even though it is more geared toward game design than the technology that makes games possible. Players interact with your game through the hardware—whether it is a plastic guitar, a touch screen, or a Wii Remote. Designing your control systems can create an intense sense of "being there" more than almost anything else. This is one of the reasons why *Guitar Hero*, *Rock Band,* and *Wii Sports* were so incredibly popular. It is also one of the reasons the iPhone was so revolutionary: It simplified the physical interaction between human and machine, leaving nothing more than the experience of interacting with the software. Think about this as you make your game and try to find that perfect "touch" that players will love.

## Chapter 10

*by Mike McShaffry*

# User Interface Programming

After exploring input devices in the previous chapter, we're ready to move a little deeper and see what happens when the raw input messages are passed from the application layer to your game.

Games usually have a small set of user interface components, and they are almost always custom coded. Games don't use the operating system's native user interface API, like Windows GDI, to create their menus, dialogs, or radar screens. These special controls are almost always home grown. Sure, the number of controls you can attach to dialog boxes and screens is overwhelming, but most games don't need rich text editors, grid controls, tree controls, property pages, and so on. Rather, the lack of control over position, animation, and sounds usually compels game programmers to roll their own simple user interface or perhaps layer on a Flash-based one.

If you roll your own, a simple interface breaks the job into two parts: controls and containers for controls. Some user interface designs, such as Windows, don't distinguish between controls and control containers. Everything in the Win32 GDI has an `HWND`, which is a handle for a window. This might seem a little weird because it would be unlikely that a button in your game would have other little buttons attached to it, but it does standardize how these structures are referenced.

Instead of proposing any specific design, it's best to discuss some of the implementation issues and features any game will need in a user interface. I'll talk about the human game view, screens, and dialog boxes and end up with a discussion about controls.

## DirectX's Text Helper and Dialog Resource Manager

Since the low level details of implementing user interface objects like a button, slider, or font renderer are beyond the scope of this book, I'm going to cheat and use some DirectX utility classes.

If you've seen any of DirectX Foundation, found in the *Samples\C++\DXUT11* directory in the DirectX SDK, you've probably noticed that Microsoft implemented an entire GUI system that uses the DirectX rendering pipeline and yet has most of the functionality of traditional Windows controls. This is a nice place to start, but it does have its drawbacks. I'll show you how you can integrate this GUI system with the game logic/game view architecture in this book, and I will suggest some future directions. First, there's a wrapper class I'll use to manage the life and access of these two helpers. It uses the Direct3D 11 renderer to draw, which you'll learn more about in the 3D chapter. There's a little more to this class that you see here, but for now these members are all you need to see to get your user interface working:

```
class D3DRenderer11
{
public:
  // You should leave this global - it does wacky things otherwise.
  static CDXUTDialogResourceManager g_DialogResourceManager;
  static CDXUTTextHelper* g_pTextHelper;

  virtual HRESULT VOnRestore()
  virtual ~D3DRenderer11() { SAFE_DELETE(g_pTextHelper); }
  virtual bool VPreRender();          // more on this later!
  virtual bool VPostRender();         // more on this later!
};

// You should leave this global - it does wacky things otherwise.
CDXUTDialogResourceManager D3DRenderer::g_DialogResourceManager;
CDXUTTextHelper *D3DRenderer::g_pTextHelper = NULL;

HRESULT D3DRenderer11::VOnRestore()
{
  HRESULT hr;
  V_RETURN ( D3DRenderer::VOnRestore() );
  SAFE_DELETE(D3DRenderer::g_pTextHelper);
  D3DRenderer::g_pTextHelper = GCC_NEW CDXUTTextHelper(
    DXUTGetD3D11Device(), DXUTGetD3D11DeviceContext(),
    &g_DialogResourceManager, 15 );
  return S_OK;
}
```

The CDXUTDialogResourceManager is a class that helps you draw all of the UI gizmos you need—buttons, sliders, text boxes, and so on. Later in this chapter, you will see calls to this class to create and place them on the screen. The CDXUTTextHelper class is nearly indispensable to those programmers who want to draw text on a Direct3D 11 screen.

The reason for this is that Direct3D 11 does not support the very easy-to-use ID3DXFont interface you may have seen before. Instead, Microsoft is pushing DirectWrite, which pushes font rendering or glyph rendering to new levels of complexity. When writing this book, I nearly panicked thinking how I was going to condense this huge subject into this chapter, until I found that the CDXUTTextHelper class essentially hid all that complexity from me. Thank goodness!

## The Human's Game View

Recall from Chapter 2, "What's in a Game?," that the game interface should be completely separate from the game logic. A game view receives game events, such as "object was created" or "object was moved," and does whatever it needs to present this new game state. In return, the view is responsible for interpreting inputs from controllers and other hardware into commands that will get sent back to the game logic, such as "request throw grenade." It would be up to the game logic to determine whether this was a valid request.

I'm about to show you a base class that creates a game view for a human player. As you might expect, it's pretty heavy on user interface. I think it's a good idea to take somewhat of a top-down approach, showing you major components and how they fit together.

As you might expect, a class that implements the game view for a human player is going to be tied very closely to how input devices are read and how the view is actually presented to the player. This crossroads is a great intersection between the operating system, which will let you get the state of the input devices, and the graphics system, which will draw the game world. Oh, and I can't forget the audio system either, which is a renderer in its own right—one for the player's ears. I could abstract all this into platform-independent classes with the right interfaces, etc., but in the interest of making things a little easier for me to present and for you to understand, I'll leave that improvement as an exercise for you. OK, enough excuses—here's the class definition for the HumanView.

```
typedef std::list<shared_ptr<IScreenElement> > ScreenElementList;
```

```
class HumanView : public IGameView
{
protected:
  GameViewId   m_ViewId;
  ActorId      m_ActorId;

  // this ProcessManager is for things like button animations, etc.
  ProcessManager *m_pProcessManager;

  DWORD m_currTick;       // time right now
  DWORD m_lastDraw;       // last time the game rendered
  bool m_runFullSpeed;    // set to true if you want to run full speed

  virtual void VRenderText() { };

public:
   bool LoadGame(TiXmlElement* pLevelData);
protected:
   virtual bool VLoadGameDelegate(TiXmlElement* pLevelData) { return true; }

public:
  // Implement the IGameView interface
  virtual HRESULT VOnRestore();
  virtual void VOnRender(double fTime, float fElapsedTime );
  virtual void VOnLostDevice();
  virtual GameViewType VGetType() { return GameView_Human; }
  virtual GameViewId VGetId() const { return m_ViewId; }

  virtual void VOnAttach(GameViewId vid, optional<ActorId> aid)
  {
    m_ViewId = vid;
    m_ActorId = aid;
  }

  virtual LRESULT CALLBACK VOnMsgProc( AppMsg msg );
  virtual void VOnUpdate( int deltaMilliseconds );

  // Virtual methods to control the layering of interface elements
  virtual void VPushElement(shared_ptr<IScreenElement> pElement);
  virtual void VRemoveElement(shared_ptr<IScreenElement> pElement);

  void TogglePause(bool active);

  ~HumanView();
  HumanView(D3DCOLOR background);

  ScreenElementList m_ScreenElements;
```

```
    // Interface sensitive objects
    shared_ptr<IPointerHandler> m_PointerHandler;
    int m_pointerRadius;
    shared_ptr<IKeyboardHandler> m_KeyboardHandler;

    // Audio
    bool InitAudio();

    //Camera adjustments.
    virtual void VSetCameraOffset(const Vec4 & camOffset ) { }

protected:
     virtual bool VLoadGameDelegate(TiXmlElement* pLevelData) { return true; }

};
```

Let's take a quick look at the data members of this class. The first two members store the view ID and the actor ID, if it exists. This makes it easy for the game logic to determine if a view is attached to a particular actor in the game universe.

The `ProcessManager` was presented in Chapter 7, "Controlling the Main Loop." This class is a convenient manager for anything that takes multiple game loops to accomplish, such as playing a sound effect or running an animation.

The next four members deal with drawing the frame. The first three keep track of when the view was rendered last and whether or not to limit the frame rate. It is typically a good idea to set your game to a constant frame rate, typically 60 frames per second, leaving the rest of the time for other operations like AI, physics, and other game-specific things. The last member stores the background color the view is cleared to every frame. If your game is guaranteed to draw every pixel each frame, you could set the color to RGB 255,0,255, and if for some reason some pixels were missed, you would see a hot pink flash. In the release build, you could save a few cycles by simply not clearing the frame at all. It's totally up to you.

The next member, `VRenderText()`, is stubbed out. This member, once overloaded in an inherited class, is what is called when text-specific elements need to be drawn by the view. In a DirectX supported game, this would eventually wind up in calls to the `CDXUTTextHelper` class. I'm sure all you OpenGL fans can easily swap in your own equivalents if you like.

The next two methods, `LoadGame()` and the protected `VLoadGameDelegate()`, are called when the game loads. `LoadGame()` is responsible for creating view-specific elements from an XML file that defines all the elements in the game. This might include a background music track, something that could be appreciated by the human playing but is inconsequential for the game logic.

The next set of virtual methods starting with VOnRestore() and ending with VOnUpdate() completes the implementation of the IGameView interface originally discussed back in Chapter 2. You'll see what each of these methods is responsible for shortly.

The next two virtual methods, VPushElement() and VRemoveElement(), control the ordering and layering of screen interface elements.

The next data member is an STL list of pointers to objects that implement the IScreenElement interface. A screen element is a strictly user interface thing and is a container for user interface controls like buttons and text edit boxes. You could have a number of these components attached to do different things, and because they are separate entities, you could hide or show them individually. A good example of this kind of behavior is modular toolbars in the Window GUI.

The next two members are a generic pointer handler and a keyboard handler. You'll create pointer and keyboard handlers to interpret device messages into game commands. Notice the member m_pointerRadius? Even on Windows games, you can't count on the pointer device having pixel perfect accuracy anymore. With tablet computers and cameras detecting human input in the place of a mouse, it makes sense for your pointer interface to also keep track of a pointer radius along with its location. This way you can do hit detection with an area instead of a single X,Y coordinate.

The next member is InitAudio(), which does exactly what is says—initializes the audio system. After that is a stubbed utility method for setting the camera offset, which will be implemented by a child class in Chapter 21, "A Game of Teapot Wars," at the end of the book.

Let's take a look at some of the more interesting bits of the HumanView class, starting with the VOnRender() method. The render method is responsible for rendering the view at either a clamped maximum refresh rate or at full speed, depending on the value of the local variables.

```
void HumanView::VOnRender(double fTime, float fElapsedTime )
{
  m_currTick = timeGetTime();

  // early out - we've already drawn in this tick
  if (m_currTick == m_lastDraw)
    return;

  HRESULT hr;

  // It is time to draw ?
  if( m_runFullSpeed ||
    ( (m_currTick - m_lastDraw) > SCREEN_REFRESH_RATE) )
```

```
  {
    // Render the scene
    if(g_pApp->m_Renderer->VPreRender())
    {
      VRenderText();
      m_ScreenElements.sort(
         SortBy_SharedPtr_Content<IScreenElement>());

      for(ScreenElementList::iterator i=m_ScreenElements.begin();
        i!=m_ScreenElements.end(); ++i)
      {
        if ( (*i)->VIsVisible() )
        {
          (*i)->VOnRender(fTime, fElapsedTime);
        }
      }

      // record the last successful paint
      m_lastDraw = m_currTick;
    }
    g_pApp->m_Renderer->VPostRender();
  }
}
```

If the view is ready to draw, it calls the application renderer's `VPreRender()` method, which is called to get the Direct3D 11 device ready for rendering. The `VRenderText()` method is next, which will render any text applied directly to the screen. In this class, the method has a null implementation. In Chapter 21, a human view class will overload this to display some debug text.

The `for` loop iterates through the screen layers one-by-one, and if it is visible, it calls `IScreenElement::VOnRender()`. This implies that the only thing the view really draws for itself is the text in `VRenderText()`, and that's exactly correct. Everything else should be drawn because it belongs to the list of screens. The last thing that happens is a call to the renderer's `VPostRender()` method, which finalizes the render and presents the screen to the viewer.

Notice that the screen list is drawn from the beginning of the list to the end of the list. That's important because screens can draw on top of one another in layers, such as when a modal dialog box draws on top of everything else in your game.

```
HRESULT HumanView::VOnRestore()
{
  HRESULT hr;
  for(ScreenElementList::iterator i=m_ScreenElements.begin();
```

```
    i!=m_ScreenElements.end(); ++i)
  {
    V_RETURN ( (*i)->VOnRestore() );
  }
  return hr;
}

void HumanView::VOnLostDevice()
{
  HRESULT hr;
  for(ScreenElementList::iterator i=m_ScreenElements.begin();
    i!=m_ScreenElements.end(); ++i)
  {
    V_RETURN ( (*i)->VOnLostDevice() );
  }
}
```

The `HumanView::VOnRestore()` method is responsible for re-creating anything that might be lost while the game is running. This kind of thing typically happens as a result of the operating system responding to something application wide, such as restoring the application from a sleep mode or changing the screen resolution while the game is running. Also remember that `VOnRestore()` gets called just after the class is instantiated, so this method is just as useful for initialization as it is for restoring lost objects. These objects include all of the attached screens. The `HumanView::VOnLostDevice()` method will be called prior to `VOnRestore()`, so it is used to chain the "on lost device" event to other objects or simply release the objects so they'll be re-created in the call to `VOnRestore()`. This is a common theme in DirectX applications on the PC, since any number of things can get in the way of a game, such as a change of video resolution or even Alt-Tabbing away to another application that makes exclusive use of DirectX objects. Being able to reinitialize your UI could come in extremely handy, no matter what operating system or platform your game uses. For example, smart phone and tablet games might need to completely change their UI layout when players reorient their devices from a landscape format to a portrait style format.

The view is called once per frame by the application layer so that it can perform nonrendering update tasks. The `VOnUpdate()` chain is called as quickly as the game loops and is used to update any object attached to the human view. In this case, the Process Manager is updated, as well as any of the screen elements attached to the human view. As you will see in Chapter 16, "3D Scenes," this includes updating the objects in the 3D scene, which is itself a screen element.

```
void HumanView::VOnUpdate( int deltaMilliseconds )
{
  m_pProcessManager->UpdateProcesses(deltaMilliseconds);
  for(ScreenElementList::iterator i=m_ScreenElements.begin();
    i!=m_ScreenElements.end(); ++i)
  {
    (*i)->VOnUpdate(deltaMilliseconds);
  }
}
```

This code deserves a little clarity, perhaps, since there are a number of potentially confusing things about it. A game object that exists in the game universe and is affected by game rules, like physics, belongs to the game logic. Whenever the game object moves or changes state, events are generated that eventually make their way to the game views, where they update their internal representations of these objects. A good example of this are the ever-present crates in games like *Thief: Deadly Shadows*—you can knock them downstairs and break them open.

There is a different set of objects that only exist visually and have no real effect on the world themselves, such as particle effects. The `VOnUpdate()` that belongs to the human view is what updates these objects. Since the game logic knows nothing about them, they are completely contained in the human view and need some way to be updated if they are animating.

Another example of something the human perceives but the game logic does not is the audio system. Background music and ambient sound effects have no effect on the game logic per se and therefore can safely belong to the human view. The audio system is actually managed as a `Process` object that is attached to the `ProcessManager` contained in the human view.

But wait—you might ask, didn't *Thief: Deadly Shadows* have systems that allowed the AI characters to respond to sounds? Well, yes and no. The AI in *Thief* didn't respond directly to what was being sent out of the sound card, but rather it responded to collision events detected by the game logic. These collision events were sent by the game logic and were separately consumed by both the sound manager *and* the AI manager. The sound manager looked at the type of collision and determined which sound effect was most suitable. The AI manager looked at the proximity and severity of the collision to determine if it was inside the AI's motivational threshold. So the AIs actually responded to collision events, not sounds.

The real meat of the human view is processing device messages from the application layer. Somewhere in the application layer of all Windows games is the main message processor, where you get `WM_CHAR`, `WM_MOUSEMOVE`, and all those messages. Any conceivable message that the game views would want to see should be translated into the generic message form and passed on to all the game views. The following is a code fragment from GameCodeApp::MsgProc(), which is the main message handling callback that was set up with DXUTSetCallbackMsgProc( GameCodeApp::MsgProc ):

```
switch (uMsg)
{
  case WM_KEYDOWN:
  case WM_KEYUP:
  case WM_MOUSEMOVE:
  case WM_LBUTTONDOWN:
  case WM_LBUTTONUP:
  case WM_RBUTTONDOWN:
  case WM_RBUTTONUP:
  case MM_JOY1BUTTONDOWN:
  case MM_JOY1BUTTONUP:
  case MM_JOY1MOVE:
  case MM_JOY1ZMOVE:
  case MM_JOY2BUTTONDOWN:
  case MM_JOY2BUTTONUP:
  case MM_JOY2MOVE:
  case MM_JOY2ZMOVE:
  {
    // translate the Windows message into the 'generic' message.
    AppMsg msg;
    msg.m_hWnd = hWnd;
    msg.m_uMsg = uMsg;
    msg.m_wParam = wParam;
    msg.m_lParam = lParam;

    for ( GameViewList::reverse_iterator i=m_gameViews.rbegin();
          i!=m_gameViews.rend(); ++i)
    {
      if ( (*i)->VOnMsgProc( msg ) )
      {
        return true;
      }
    }
  }
  break;
}
```

I completely admit that I'm cheating by taking the Windows message parameters and sticking them into a structure. Call me lazy and unable to be truly platform agnostic; I can live with that. It is a valuable exercise for you to generalize these messages into something that will work on many platforms. If a game view returns `true` from `VOnMsgProc()`, it means that it has completely consumed the message, and no other view should see it.

This architecture will still work with a multiple player, split-screen type of game—here's how. The `HumanView` class can contain multiple screens, but instead of being layered, they will sit side by side. The `HumanView` class will still grab input from all the devices and translate it into game commands, just as you are about to see, but in this case, each device will be treated as input for a different player.

Back to the implementation of `HumanView::VOnMsgProc()`. Its job is to iterate through the list of screens attached to it, forward the message on to the visible ones, and if they don't eat the message, then ask the pointer and keyboard handler if they can consume it.

```
LRESULT CALLBACK HumanView::VOnMsgProc( AppMsg msg )
{
  // Iterate through the screen layers first
  // In reverse order since we'll send input messages to the
  // screen on top
  for(ScreenElementList::reverse_iterator i=m_ScreenElements.rbegin();
     i!=m_ScreenElements.rend(); ++i)
  {
    if ( (*i)->VIsVisible() )
    {
      if ( (*i)->VOnMsgProc( msg ) )
      {
        return 1;
      }
    }
  }

  LRESULT result = 0;
  switch (msg.m_uMsg)
  {
    case WM_KEYDOWN:
      if (m_KeyboardHandler)
      {
        result = m_KeyboardHandler->VOnKeyDown(
          static_cast<const BYTE>(msg.m_wParam));
      }
      break;

  case WM_KEYUP:
      if (m_KeyboardHandler)
```

```
        {
          result = m_KeyboardHandler->VOnKeyUp(
            static_cast<const BYTE>(msg.m_wParam));
        }
        break;

      case WM_MOUSEMOVE:
        if (m_PointerHandler)
          result = m_PointerHandler->VOnPointerMove(
            CPoint(LOWORD(msg.m_lParam), HIWORD(msg.m_lParam)),
            m_PointerRadius);
        break;

      case WM_LBUTTONDOWN:
        if (m_PointerHandler)
        {
          SetCapture(msg.m_hWnd);
          result = m_PointerHandler->VOnPointerButtonDown(
            CPoint(LOWORD(msg.m_lParam), HIWORD(msg.m_lParam)),
            m_PointerRadius, "PointerLeft");
        }
        break;

      case WM_LBUTTONUP:
        if (m_PointerHandler)
        {
          SetCapture(NULL);
          result = m_PointerHandler->VOnPointerButtonUp(
            CPoint(LOWORD(msg.m_lParam), HIWORD(msg.m_lParam)),
            m_PointerRadius, "PointerUp");
        }
        break;

      case WM_RBUTTONDOWN:
        if (m_PointerHandler)
        {
          SetCapture(msg.m_hWnd);
          result = m_PointerHandler->VOnPointerButtonDown(
            CPoint(LOWORD(msg.m_lParam), HIWORD(msg.m_lParam)),
            m_PointerRadius, "PointerRight");
        }
        break;

      case WM_RBUTTONUP:
        if (m_PointerHandler)
```

```
      {
        SetCapture(NULL);
        result = m_PointerHandler->VOnPointerButtonUp(
          CPoint(LOWORD(msg.m_lParam), HIWORD(msg.m_lParam)),
          m_PointerRadius, "PointerRight");
      }
      break;

    default:
      return 0;
  }

  return 0;
}
```

Did you notice that I used a reverse iterator for the screens? Here's why: If you draw them using a normal forward iterator, the screen on top is going to be the last one drawn. User input should always be processed in order of the screens from top to bottom, which in this case would be the reverse order.

If none of the screen elements in the list processed the message, we can ask the input device handlers, in this case `m_KeyboardHandler` and `m_PointerHandler`, to process the messages. Of course, you could always write and add your own input device handler, perhaps for a dance pad or gamepad—if you do, here's where you would hook it in.

Notice that the existence of the handler is always checked before the message is sent to it. There's nothing that says you have to have a keyboard for every game you'll make with this code, so it's a good idea to check it.

## A WASD Movement Controller

You might be wondering how you use this system to create a WASD movement controller, since this interface requires the use of a mouse and a keyboard combined. In Chapter 9, "Programming Input Devices," you read about the `IPointerHandler` and `IKeyboardHandler` interface classes. You can use these to create a single controller class that can respond to both devices.

```
class MovementController : public IPointerHandler, public IKeyboardHandler
{
protected:
  Mat4x4 m_matFromWorld;
  Mat4x4 m_matToWorld;
  Mat4x4 m_matPosition;
```

```
  CPoint    m_lastMousePos;
  BYTE      m_bKey[256];       // Which keys are up and down

  // Orientation Controls
  float      m_fTargetYaw;
  float      m_fTargetPitch;
  float      m_fYaw;
  float      m_fPitch;
  float      m_fPitchOnDown;
  float      m_fYawOnDown;
  float      m_maxSpeed;
  float      m_currentSpeed;

  shared_ptr<SceneNode> m_object;

public:
  MovementController(shared_ptr<SceneNode> object,
                     float initialYaw, float  initialPitch);
  void SetObject(shared_ptr<SceneNode> newObject);
  void OnUpdate(DWORD const elapsedMs);

public:
  bool VOnPointerMove(const CPoint &mousePos, const int radius);
  bool VOnPointerButtonDown(const CPoint &mousePos, const int radius,
                            const std::string &buttonName);
  bool VOnPointerButtonUp(const CPoint &mousePos, const int radius,
                          const std::string &buttonName);
  bool VOnKeyDown(const BYTE c) { m_bKey[c] = true; return true; }
  bool VOnKeyUp(const BYTE c) { m_bKey[c] = false; return true; }

  const Mat4x4 *GetToWorld() { return &m_matToWorld; }
  const Mat4x4 *GetFromWorld() { return &m_matFromWorld; }
};
```

I'm giving you something of a sneak peak into Chapter 14, "3D Graphics Basics," with the introduction of the `Mat4x4` member variables. I won't explain them in detail here, but suffice it to say that these members track where an object is in relation to the game world and how it is oriented.

Since this WASD controller doesn't have any weapons to fire, we'll simply return `false` from the mouse button up and down handlers. Notice that the `VOnKeyUp()` and `VOnKeyDown()` methods simply set members of a Boolean array to be `true` or `false` to match the state of the key. Now, take a look at `VOnPointerMove()`:

```
bool MovementController::VOnPointerMove(const CPoint &mousePos)
```

```
{
  if(m_lastMousePos!=mousePos)
  {
    m_fTargetYaw = m_fTargetYaw + (m_lastMousePos.x - mousePos.x);
    m_fTargetPitch = m_fTargetPitch + (mousePos.y - m_lastMousePos.y);
    m_lastMousePos = mousePos;
  }
  return true;
}
```

This method was probably simpler than you expected. All it does is set the target yaw and pitch of the controller to match the mouse movement. Here's the real meat of the controller, `OnUpdate()`:

```
void MovementController::OnUpdate(DWORD const deltaMilliseconds)
{
  if (m_bKey['W'] || m_bKey['S'])
  {
    // code here will calculate movement forward & backward
  }

  if (m_bKey['A'] || m_bKey['D'])
  {
    // code here will calculate movement left & right
  }

  {
    // code here will set object rotation based on
    // previously calculated pitch and yaw values.

    // then, the movements forward, backward, left or
    // right will be used to send a movement command
    // to the game logic, which will evaluate them
    // for legality and actually move the object
  }
}
```

The full code of this routine requires some deeper knowledge of 3D transformations. To avoid sending you into convulsions, I'll postpone those discussions until Chapter 14.

## Screen Elements

You've seen how the human view works; its big job is managing the list of screen elements, drawing them, sending them input, and managing a couple of things like the audio system and the Process Manager. The audio system is discussed in detail in

Chapter 13, "Game Audio," and you should remember the Process Manager from Chapter 7, "Controlling the Main Loop."

A screen element is anything that draws and accepts input. It could be anything from a button to your rendered 3D world. In Chapter 15, "3D Vertex and Pixel Shaders," we create a screen element that can draw 3D objects and accept mouse and keyboard input to move the camera through the 3D world. In this chapter, we'll concentrate on user interface components like buttons and dialog boxes.

Screen elements can be hierarchical—for example, a dialog box can have buttons attached to it. A Windows-style scroll bar has lots of moving parts: a background, two buttons, and a dynamically sized, movable bit in the middle to represent where the scrolled data is positioned and how much data is represented off screen.

Screen elements in various configurations create the user interface for your game, such as a menu, inventory screen, scoreboard, radar, or dialog box. Some run on top of the main game screen, such as a radar or minimap, but others might completely overlay the main view and even pause the game, such as an options screen. Throughout this chapter, I'll generally refer to a screen as something that contains screen elements and a control as the leaf nodes of this hierarchy. In addition to acting as a container for controls, screens parse user input messages from the application layer and translate them into game messages.

**Screens Need Transition Management**

If your game has multiple screens, and even simple games have many, it's wise to manage them and the transitions between them in a high-level API. This might seem a little strange to Windows programmers, but it's a little like programming multiple applications for the same window, and you can freely move from one screen to another by selecting the right controls.

If your screens are fairly small "memory-wise," consider preloading them. Any transitions that happen will be blazingly fast, and players like responsive transitions. If your screens have tons of controls, graphics, and sounds, you won't necessarily be able to preload them because of memory constraints, but you might consider loading a small transition screen to give your players something to look at while you load your bigger screens. Lots of console games do this, and they usually display a bit of the next mission in the background while a nice animation plays showing the load progress. The animation during the load is important, because all console manufacturers require animations during loading screens beyond some small threshold, such as 10 seconds. They do this not to make your job harder, but they want to communicate to the player that something is still happening in the background.

Lots of kids' games and mass-market titles use a screen architecture like the one shown in Figure 10.1 throughout the entire game. When the right controls are activated in the right order, the current screen is replaced by a new one with different controls.

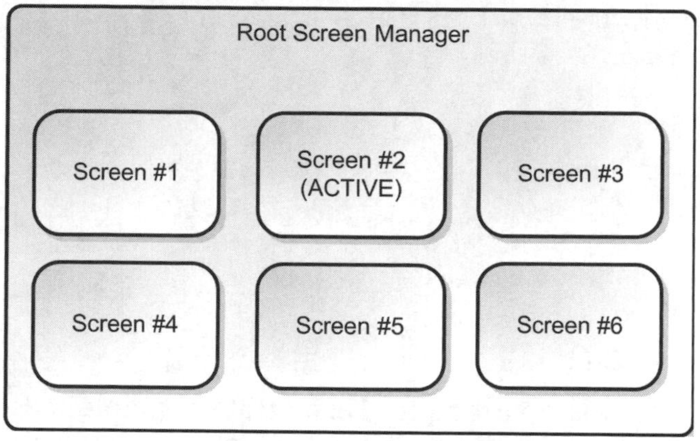


**Figure 10.1**
Screens need a screen manager.

Other games use multiple screens to set up the characters or missions. When everything is set up for the player, the game transitions to the game screen where most, if not all, of the game is played. Almost every console game uses this model. Let's look at a simple interface design for a screen:

```
class IScreenElement
{
public:
  virtual HRESULT VOnRestore() = 0;
  virtual HRESULT VOnRender(double fTime, float fElapsedTime) = 0;
  virtual void VOnUpdate(int deltaMilliseconds) = 0;
  virtual int VGetZOrder() const = 0;
  virtual void VSetZOrder(int const zOrder) = 0;
  virtual bool VIsVisible() const = 0;
  virtual void VSetVisible(bool visible) = 0;

  virtual LRESULT CALLBACK VOnMsgProc( AppMsg msg )=0;

  virtual ~IScreenElement() { };
  virtual bool const operator <(IScreenElement const &other)
    { return VGetZOrder() < other.VGetZOrder(); }
};
```

This interface shows that a screen knows how to restore itself when it needs to be rebuilt, render itself when it's time to draw, how it should be ordered in the master draw list, and whether it is visible. The `VOnMsgProc()` method accepts Windows messages from the application layer, but translates them into a structure to simplify the call signature of anything that will accept these messages:

```
struct AppMsg
{
  HWND m_hWnd;
  UINT m_uMsg;
  WPARAM m_wParam;
  LPARAM m_lParam;
};
```

## A Custom MessageBox Dialog

The best way to show you how this works is by example. Let's create a simple message box that your game can call instead of the MessageBox API. The code for this uses the DirectX GUI framework that is defined in DXUTgui.h. Word to the wise: The DirectX GUI framework is a great start for a game interface, but it does make some assumptions about how you want to load textures and some other quirks. On the other hand, it sure keeps you from having to write a text edit control from scratch. If you simply hate DirectX, and you are sufficiently motivated, just surgically remove the DirectX components and roll your own.

This message box class conforms pretty well with the Windows MessageBox API. You send in a text message and what kind of buttons you want, and the dialog will store the ID of the control that was pressed:

```
class BaseUI : public IScreenElement
{
protected:
  int           m_PosX, m_PosY;
  int           m_Width, m_Height;
  optional<int> m_Result;
  bool m_bIsVisible;
public:
  BaseUI()
    { m_bIsVisible = true; m_PosX = m_PosY = 0; m_Width = 100; m_Height = 100; }
  virtual void VOnUpdate(int) { };
  virtual bool VIsVisible() const { return m_bIsVisible; }
  virtual void VSetVisible(bool visible) { m_bIsVisible = visible; }
};

class CMessageBox : public BaseUI
{
protected:
  CDXUTDialog m_UI;  // DirectX dialog
  int m_ButtonId;
```

```
public:
  MessageBox(std::wstring msg, std::wstring title, int buttonFlags=MB_OK);
  ~MessageBox();

  // IScreenElement Implementation
  virtual HRESULT VOnRestore();
  virtual HRESULT VOnRender(double fTime, float fElapsedTime);
  virtual int VGetZOrder() const { return 99; }
  virtual void VSetZOrder(int const zOrder) { }
  virtual bool VIsVisible() const { return true; }
  virtual void VSetVisible(bool visible) { }

  virtual LRESULT CALLBACK VOnMsgProc( AppMsg msg );
  static void CALLBACK OnGUIEvent(
    UINT nEvent, int nControlID, CDXUTControl* pControl );
  static int Ask(MessageBox_Questions question);
};
```

The class design is pretty simple. It inherits from a base implementation of the IScreenElement interface, which has a few member variables to keep track of the size, position, and dialog result. The MessageBox class adds a DXUT member, CDXUT-Dialog, to manage the rendering and messaging for the dialog box. The constructor sets the callback routine and creates controls for the static text message and the buttons:

```
MessageBox::MessageBox(std::wstring msg, std::wstring title, int buttonFlags)
{
  // Initialize dialogs
  m_UI.Init( &DirectXHumanView::g_DialogResourceManager );
  m_UI.SetCallback( OnGUIEvent );

  // Find the dimensions of the message
  RECT rc;
  SetRect( &rc, 0,0,0,0);
  m_UI.CalcTextRect( msg.c_str(),
                     m_UI.GetDefaultElement(DXUT_CONTROL_STATIC,0), &rc );
  int msgWidth = rc.right - rc.left;
  int msgHeight = rc.bottom - rc.top;

  int numButtons = 2;
  if ( (buttonFlags == MB_ABORTRETRYIGNORE) ||
       (buttonFlags == MB_CANCELTRYCONTINUE) ||
       (buttonFlags == MB_CANCELTRYCONTINUE) )
  {
    numButtons = 3;
  }
```

```
else if (buttonFlags == MB_OK)
{
  numButtons = 1;
}

int btnWidth = (int)((float) g_pApp->GetScreenSize().x * 0.15f);
int btnHeight = (int)((float) g_pApp->GetScreenSize().y * 0.037f);
int border = (int)((float) g_pApp->GetScreenSize().x * 0.043f);

m_Width = std::max(msgWidth + 2 * border, btnWidth + 2 * border);
m_Height = msgHeight + (numButtons * (btnHeight+border) ) + (2 * border);

m_PosX = (g_pApp->GetScreenSize().x -m_Width)/2;
m_PosY = (g_pApp->GetScreenSize().y -m_Height)/2;
m_UI.SetLocation( m_PosX, m_PosY );

m_UI.SetSize( m_Width, m_Height );
m_UI.SetBackgroundColors(g_Gray40);

int iY = border;
int iX = (m_Width - msgWidth) / 2;

m_UI.AddStatic( 0, msg.c_str(), iX, iY, msgWidth, msgHeight);

iX = (m_Width - btnWidth) / 2;
iY = m_Height - btnHeight - border;

buttonFlags &= 0xF;
if ( (buttonFlags == MB_ABORTRETRYIGNORE) ||
     (buttonFlags == MB_CANCELTRYCONTINUE) )
{
  // The message box contains three push buttons:
  // Cancel, Try Again, Continue.
  // This is the new standard over Abort,Retry,Ignore

  m_UI.AddButton( IDCONTINUE, g_pApp->GetString(IDS_CONTINUE).c_str(),
                  iX, iY - (2*border), btnWidth, btnHeight );
  m_UI.AddButton( IDTRYAGAIN, g_pApp->GetString(IDS_TRYAGAIN).c_str(),
                  iX, iY - border, btnWidth, btnHeight );
  m_UI.AddButton( IDCANCEL, g_pApp->GetString(IDS_CANCEL).c_str(),
                  iX, iY, btnWidth, btnHeight );
}
else if (buttonFlags == MB_OKCANCEL)
{
  //The message box contains two push buttons: OK and Cancel.
```

```
    m_UI.AddButton( IDOK, g_pApp->GetString(IDS_OK).c_str(),
                    iX, iY - border, btnWidth, btnHeight );
    m_UI.AddButton( IDCANCEL, g_pApp->GetString(IDS_CANCEL).c_str(),
                    iX, iY, btnWidth, btnHeight );
  }
  else if (buttonFlags == MB_RETRYCANCEL)
  {
    //The message box contains two push buttons: Retry and Cancel.
    m_UI.AddButton( IDRETRY, g_pApp->GetString(IDS_RETRY).c_str(),
                    iX, iY - border, btnWidth, btnHeight );
    m_UI.AddButton( IDCANCEL, g_pApp->GetString(IDS_CANCEL).c_str(),
                    iX, iY, btnWidth, btnHeight );
  }
  else if (buttonFlags == MB_YESNO)
  {
    //The message box contains two push buttons: Yes and No.
    m_UI.AddButton( IDYES, g_pApp->GetString(IDS_YES).c_str(),
                    iX, iY - border, btnWidth, btnHeight );
    m_UI.AddButton( IDNO, g_pApp->GetString(IDS_NO).c_str(),
                    iX, iY, btnWidth, btnHeight );
  }
  else if (buttonFlags == MB_YESNOCANCEL)
  {
    //The message box contains three push buttons: Yes, No, and Cancel.
    m_UI.AddButton( IDYES, g_pApp->GetString(IDS_YES).c_str(),
                    iX, iY - (2*border), btnWidth, btnHeight );
    m_UI.AddButton( IDNO, g_pApp->GetString(IDS_NO).c_str(),
                    iX, iY - border, btnWidth, btnHeight );
    m_UI.AddButton( IDCANCEL, g_pApp->GetString(IDS_CANCEL).c_str(),
                    iX, iY, btnWidth, btnHeight );
  }
  else //if (buttonFlags & MB_OK)
  {
    // The message box contains one push button: OK. This is the default.
    m_UI.AddButton( IDOK, g_pApp->GetString(IDS_OK).c_str(),
                    iX, iY, btnWidth, btnHeight );
  }
}
```

DXUT needs two bits of homework to get started. First, the `m_UI` member is initialized with a pointer to the global dialog resource manager. Next, a callback function is set. On every game user interface I've ever worked on, there's some mechanism for a control to send a message to the screen that it has been clicked on or otherwise messed with. The `OnGuiEvent()` will trap those events so you can see which button was clicked.

The next bit of code figures out how big the text message is. After that, you start laying out the controls and positioning the dialog in the center of the screen. The idea here is to find the number of buttons you're going to add, place them in a vertical stack at the bottom of the dialog box, and add up all the space you're going to need to make sure there's enough room to have the buttons and the text. The button width, height, and border of the dialog box are given sizes relative to the overall screen. This automatically scales your dialog box with the pixel width and height of the game screen. A more complicated but better system would be one that takes screen aspect ratio into account—which is especially useful for games that run in 4:3 or 16:9 screens, which are typical of console games. Smart phone games can even do 9:16 if they run in portrait orientation.

One good solution to this tricky problem is to write some code that lets you specify how you want user interface controls anchored. Instead of anchoring them as you see here, by the upper-left corner only, you could anchor them from the center of the screen, top left, bottom left, and so on. This gives your user interface some flexibility to have members float and adjust themselves to multiple screen configurations. I could probably write a whole book about those problems alone. For now, we'll stick to the basics and go with a less flexible but easier to understand system.

**16:9 Does *Not* Equal 16:10**

Red Fly was working on a cooking game for The Food Network and Namco Bandai called *The Food Network Presents: Cook or Be Cooked.* As we were going through our final testing, we received word from Namco that the screens that pop up at the beginning of all Wii games warning you not to throw Wii remotes through your nice new plasma TV weren't correct, and they were stretched slightly. Red Fly's user interface programmer looked hard at the problem, and after many hours of searching for the problem realized with horror that the display he was using, a nice Dell monitor, wasn't actually 16:9 at all. It, as every other monitor at Red Fly, was actually 16:10. It turned out that Namco's test team found something that every other game publisher and Nintendo missed until then.

If you are positioning user interface controls by the upper left-hand corner, centering is done by subtracting the inner width from the outer width and dividing by two:

```
m_PosX = (g_pApp->GetScreenSize().x -m_Width)/2;
m_PosY = (g_pApp->GetScreenSize().y -m_Height)/2;
```

If you subtract the width of the dialog from the width of the screen and divide by two, you've got the X position that will center the dialog. Switch all the parameters for heights, and you'll have the correct Y position. You see that kind of thing a lot, and it works a hell of a lot better than hard-coded positions and widths. Now we're ready to add controls to the dialog member, and you'll see that in the calls to AddStatic() for the message text and AddButton() for the buttons.

One thing you should notice right away in the call to add buttons is no hard-coded text:

```
m_UI.AddButton( IDOK, g_pApp->GetString(IDS_OK).c_str(),
                iX, iY - border, btnWidth, btnHeight );
```

I mentioned this back in the application layer discussion. Instead of seeing the naked text "OK," you see a call into the application layer to grab a string identified by IDOK. The application layer is responsible for grabbing text for anything that will be presented to the player because you might have multiple foreign language versions of your game. You could create this text grabber in any number of ways, but for PC games I prefer using an XML file with all the strings and their hot keys defined. The cool thing about XML files is they are easy for translators to edit, and you can easily add XML files to your game as you support more languages. They even support Asian languages like Chinese.

In the event of a device restoration event like a full-screen/windowed mode swap, it's a good idea to tell the DirectX dialog how big it is and where it is on the screen, which you can do through the VOnRestore API:

```
HRESULT MessageBox::VOnRestore()
{
  m_UI.SetLocation( m_PosX, m_PosY );
  m_UI.SetSize( m_Width, m_Height );
  return S_OK;
}
```

The render method for our screen class simply calls CDXUTDialog::OnRender. If you create your own GUI system, this is where you'd iterate through the list of controls and draw them:

```
HRESULT MessageBox::VOnRender(double fTime, float fElapsedTime)
{
  m_UI.OnRender( fElapsedTime );
  return S_OK;
};
```

You feed Windows messages to the DirectX GUI controls through the VOnMsgProc() method. If you create your own GUI, you'd have to iterate through your controls and have them process messages. A good example of that would be to highlight the control if the mouse moved over it or change the graphic to depress the control if the mouse went down over the control's area:

```
LRESULT CALLBACK MessageBox::VOnMsgProc( AppMsg msg )
{
  return m_UI.MsgProc( msg.m_hWnd, msg.m_uMsg, msg.m_wParam, msg.m_lParam );
}
```

The only thing left to handle is the processing of the control messages. In the case of a message box, the only thing you need to do is send the button result back to a place so that you can grab it later. We'll do that by posting a custom Windows message into the message pump:

```
void CALLBACK CMessageBox::OnGUIEvent( UINT nEvent, int nControlID,
                                       CDXUTControl* pControl )
{
  PostMessage(g_pApp->GetHwnd(), G_MSGENDMODAL, 0, nControlID);
}
```

This might seem confusing at first. Why not just set the member variable in the dialog box class that holds the last button the player selected? The answer lies in how you have to go about creating a modal dialog box in games, which is our very next subject.

## Modal Dialog Boxes

Modal dialog boxes usually present the player with a question, such as "Do you really want to quit?" In most cases, the game stops while the dialog box is displayed so the player can answer the question (see Figure 10.2). The answer is usually immediately accepted by the game.

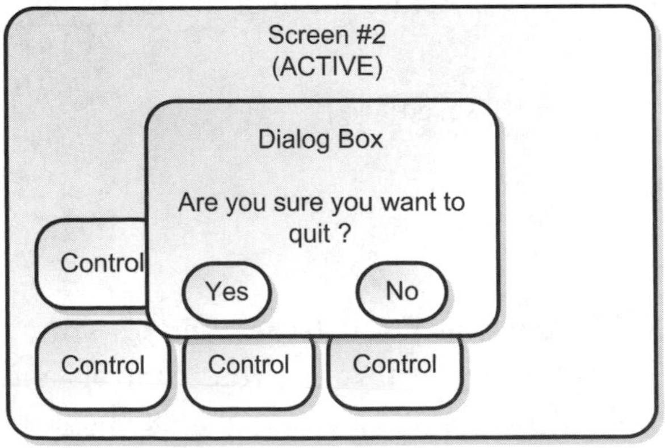


**Figure 10.2**
A modal dialog box.

This might seem easy to code, but it can be a lot trickier than you think. Why? Let's look at the anatomy of the "quit" dialog. If you were coding a Windows application, the code to bring up a message box looks like this:

```
int answer = MessageBox(_T("Do you really want to quit?"),
                        _T("Question"), MB_YESNO | MB_ICONEXCLAMATION);
```

When this code is executed, a message box appears over the active window and stays there until one of the buttons is pressed. The window disappears, and the button ID is sent back to the calling code. If you haven't thought about this before, you should realize that the regular message pump can't be working, but clearly some message pump is active, or the controls would never get their mouse and mouse button messages. How does this work? The trick is to create another message pump that runs in a tight loop and manage that within a method that handles the life cycle of a modal dialog box:

```
#define G_QUITNOPROMPT MAKELPARAM(-1,-1)
#define G_MSGENDMODAL (WM_USER+100)

int GameCodeApp::Modal(
  shared_ptr<IScreenElement> pModalScreen, int defaultAnswer)
{
  // If we're going to display a dialog box, we need a human view
  // to interact with.
  HumanView *pView;
  for(GameViewList::iterator i=m_pGame->m_gameViews.begin();
     i!=m_pGame->m_gameViews.end(); ++i)
  {
    if ((*i)->VGetType()==GameView_Human)
    {
      shared_ptr<IGameView> pIGameView(*i);
      pView = static_cast<HumanView *>(&*pIGameView);
      break;
    }
  }

  if (!pView)
  {
    // Whoops! There's no human view attached.
    return defaultAnswer;
  }

  assert(GetHwnd() != NULL && _T("Main Window is NULL!"));
  if ( ( GetHwnd() != NULL ) && IsIconic(GetHwnd()) )
  {
    FlashWhileMinimized();
  }
```

```
  if (m_HasModalDialog & 0x10000000)
  {
    assert(0 && "Too Many nested dialogs!");
    return defaultAnswer;
  }

  m_HasModalDialog <<= 1;
  m_HasModalDialog |= 1;

  pView->VPushElement(pModalScreen);

  LPARAM lParam = 0;
  int result = PumpUntilMessage(G_MSGENDMODAL, NULL, &lParam);
  if (lParam != 0)
  {
    if (lParam==G_QUITNOPROMPT)
      result = defaultAnswer;
    else
      result = (int)lParam;
  }

  pView->VRemoveElement(pModalScreen);
  m_HasModalDialog >>= 1;

  return result;
}
```

The first thing that `GameCodeApp::Modal()` method does is find an appropriate game view to handle the message. You can imagine a case where you have nothing but AI processes attached to the game, and they couldn't care less about a dialog box asking them if they want to quit. Only a human view can see the dialog and react to it, so you iterate through the list of game views and find a view that belongs to the human view type. If you don't find one, you return a default answer.

If the entire game is running in a window and that window is minimized, the player will never see the dialog box. The player needs a clue that the game needs interaction with the player, and a good way to do this under Windows is to flash the window until the player maximizes the window again, which is what `FlashWhileMinimized()` accomplishes.

The next thing you see is a dirty trick, and I love it. You can imagine a situation where you have a modal dialog on the screen, such as something to manage a player inventory, and the player presses Alt-F4 and wants to close the game. This requires an ability to nest modal dialog boxes, which in turn means you need some way to detect this nesting and if it has gone too deep. This is required because the modal dialogs are managed by the game application. I use a simple bit field to do this, shifting the bits each time you nest deeper.

The next thing that happens is you push the modal screen onto the view you found earlier, and you call a special method that acts as a surrogate Windows message pump for the modal dialog:

```
int GameCodeApp::PumpUntilMessage (UINT msgEnd,
                                   WPARAM* pWParam, LPARAM* pLParam)
{
  int currentTime = timeGetTime();
  MSG msg;
  for ( ;; )
  {
    if ( PeekMessage( &msg, NULL, 0, 0, PM_NOREMOVE ) )
    {
      if ( PeekMessage( &msg, NULL, 0, 0, 0 ) )
      {
        if ( msg.message != WM_SYSCOMMAND ||
             msg.wParam != SC_CLOSE )
        {
          TranslateMessage(&msg);
          DispatchMessage(&msg);
        }

        // Are we done?
        if ( ! IsIconic(GetHwnd()) )
        {
          FlashWindow( GetHwnd(), false );
          break;
        }
      }
    }
    else
    {
      // Update the game views, but nothing else!
      // Remember this is a modal screen.
      if (m_pGame)
      {
        int timeNow = timeGetTime();
        int deltaMilliseconds = timeNow - currentTime;
        for(GameViewList::iterator i=m_pGame->m_gameViews.begin();
             i!=m_pGame->m_gameViews.end(); ++i)
        {
          (*i)->VOnUpdate( deltaMilliseconds );
        }
        currentTime = timeNow;
        DXUTRender3DEnvironment();
```

```
      }
    }
  }
  if (pLParam)
    *pLParam = msg.lParam;
  if (pWParam)
    *pWParam = msg.wParam;

  return 0;
}
```

The PumpUntilMessage function works similarly to the message pump in your main loop, but it is a special one meant for modal dialog boxes. One message, WM_CLOSE, gets special treatment since it must terminate the dialog and begin the game close process. Other than close, the loop continues until the target message is seen in the message queue. I define this custom message myself:

```
#define G_MSGENDMODAL   ( WM_USER + 100 )
```

If there are no messages in the queue, the pump calls the right code to make the game views update and render. Without this, you wouldn't be able to see anything, especially if you drag another window over your game.

As soon as the modal dialog wants to kill itself off, it will send the G_MSGENDMODAL into the message queue, and the PumpUntilMessage method will exit back out to the Modal method you saw earlier. G_MSGENDMODAL is a special user-defined message, and Win32 gives you a special message range starting at WM_USER. I usually like to start defining application-specific Windows messages at WM_USER+100 instead of starting right at WM_USER, since I'll be able to tell them apart in the message queue.

The trick to this is getting the answer back to the calling code, which is done with the parameters to the G_MSGENDMODAL. In this case, we look at the ID of the control that was clicked on. Recall CMessageBox::OnGUIEvent():

```
void CALLBACK CMessageBox::OnGUIEvent(
      UINT nEvent, int nControlID, CDXUTControl* pControl, void *pUserContext )
{
  PostMessage(g_pApp->GetHwnd(), G_MSGENDMODAL, 0, nControlID);
}
```

This posts G_MSGENDMODAL to the message queue, which is what the PumpUntilMessage method was looking for all along. This breaks the tight loop, and the GameCodeApp::Modal() method can extract the answer the player gave to the modal dialog box.

You might be asking yourself two things at this point. First, this seems an awful lot of trouble to implement a modal dialog box that can be called with one line of code. Second, how would I do this on non-Windows platforms? There is another way—easier in some ways to implement, but a little more hassle to call and ask the player a simple yes or no question. The answer is to do this asynchronously.

First, you set up a dialog box as a screen just like we did above. You instantiate it and launch it and set up a flag in your application to basically pause the game while this screen is active. When the player presses the button and registers a response, it sends a message to the subsystem that needed the player to answer a question. You'll see more about how game messages can be created, sent, and interpreted in the next chapter.

## Controls

Controls have lots of permutations, but most of them share similar properties. I've seen push buttons, radio buttons, check boxes, combo boxes, edit boxes, expandable menus, and all sorts of stuff. I've also coded quite a few of them, I'm sad to say.

Luckily, the DirectX Framework has already implemented most of the standard GUI controls for you:

- `CDXUTButton`: A simple push button, like "OK" or "Cancel"
- `CDXUTStatic`: A static text control for putting non-active text on a dialog
- `CDXUTCheckBox`: A check box control for selecting on/off status for different items
- `CDXUTRadioButton`: A radio button control for selecting one thing out of many choices
- `CDXUTComboBox`: A combo box uses one line but can drop down a list box of choices
- `CDXUTSlider`: A simple slider to do things like volume controls
- `CDXUTEditBox`: A text edit box for doing things like entering your name or a console command
- `CDXUTIMEEditBox`: A foreign language edit box
- `CDXUTListBox`: A list of choices displayed with a scroll bar
- `CDXUTScrollBar`: A vertical or horizontal scroll bar

You can attach any of these controls to a `CDXUTDialog` object to create your own user interface, and as you saw in the `CMessageBox` example in the previous section, these interfaces can be modal or modeless.

The tough thing about implementing a new kind of control in your game isn't how to draw a little "x" in the check box. If you want to learn how to do that, you can trace through the source code in the CDXUTCheckBox and find out how it works. Rather, the tough thing is knowing what features your controls will need beyond these simple implementations. You also need to be aware of the important "gotchas" you'll need to avoid. Let's start with the easy stuff first.

- **Identification:** How is the control distinguished from others on the same screen?
- **Hit Testing/Focus Order:** Which control gets messages, especially if they overlap graphically?
- **State:** What states should controls support?

I suggest you approach the first problem from a device-centric point of view. Each device is going to send input to a game, some of which will be mapped to the same game functions. In other words, you might be able to select a button with the mouse to perform some game action, like firing a missile. You might also use a hot key to do the same thing.

## Control Identification

Every control needs an identifier—something the game uses to distinguish it from the other controls on the screen. The easiest way to do this is define an enum, and when the controls are created, they retain the unique identifier they were assigned in their construction:

```
enum MAINSCREEN_CONTROL_IDS
{
  CID_EXIT,
  CID_EXIT_DESKTOP,
  CID_PREVIOUS_SCREEN,
  CID_MAIN_MENU,
  CID_OPTIONS
};

void CALLBACK CGameScreen::OnGUIEvent( UINT nEvent, int nControlID, MyControl*
pControl )
 {
  switch(pControl->GetID())
  {
    case CID_EXIT:
      // exit this screen
      break;
```

```
    case CID_EXIT_DESKTOP:
      // exit to the desktop
      break;

    // etc. etc.
  }
}
```

This is very similar to the way Windows sends messages from controls to windows via the WM_COMMAND message, but simplified. The only problem with defining control IDs in this manner is keeping them straight, especially if you create screen classes that inherit from other screen classes, each with its own set of controls.

**Flatten Your Screen Class Hierarchies**

There's almost no end to the religious arguments about creating new screens by inheriting from existing screen classes. Object-oriented coding techniques make it easy to extend one class into another, but there is a risk of confusion and error when the new class is so different from the original that it might as well be a completely new class. This is why it's better to define functionality in terms of interfaces and helper functions and flatten your class hierarchy into functional nuggets. A deep inheritance tree complicates the problems of changing something in a base class without adversely affecting many classes that inherit from it.

**Measure Twice, Cut Once**

Many game companies don't consider UI to be a particularly complex system, and thus it tends to be delegated to junior engineers. This is also why most UI systems are generally very difficult to maintain. When I worked at Slipgate, we were making an MMO game that had very hefty UI requirements, so they assigned a very senior engineer to create a UI architecture. He created a system called *COG,* which allowed people to trivially create UI elements, piece them together, and allow the gameplay team to hook into UI events for button presses. It's the best system I've used. A single engineer was able to prototype complex UI screens in a matter of days or even hours while the same screen at another company might take five times as long (literally). This just goes to show you that UI can easily be just as complex as any other system. Make sure you think through your architecture before jumping in there, and don't underestimate the amount of work you'll have to do.

Some games define controls in terms of text strings, assigning each control a unique string. But there is a downside to using strings to identify controls—you have to do multiple string compares every time a control sends a message to your string class. You'll learn about a more efficient and interesting solution for this problem in Chapter 11, "Game Event Management." It does make things easier to debug, but there's nothing stopping you from including a string member in the debug build of the class. You can solve this problem by writing a bit of debug code that detects multiple controls with the same ID. Your code should simply assert so you can go find the problem and redefine the offending identifier.

## Hit Testing and Focus Order

There are two ways that controls know they are the center of your attention. The first way is via a hit test. This is where you use a pointer or a cursor and position it over the control by an analog device such as a mouse. This method is prevalent in desktop games, especially games that have a large number of controls on the screen.

The second method uses a focus order. Only one control has the focus at any one time, and each control can get the focus by an appropriate movement of the input device. If the right key or button is pressed, the control with focus sends a message to the parent screen. This is how most console games are designed, and it clearly limits the number and density of controls on each screen.

Hit testing usually falls into three categories: rectangular hit testing, polygonal hit testing, and bitmap collision testing. Bitmap collision isn't too hard, but it is a little beyond the scope of this chapter. The other two are really easy. The rectangle hit test is brain-dead simple. You just make sure your hit test includes the entire rectangle, not just the inside. If a rectangle's coordinates were (15,4) and (30,35), then a hit should be registered both at (15,4) and (30,35).

The hit test for a 2D polygon is not too complicated. The following algorithm was adapted from Graphics Gems and assumes the polygon is closed. This adaptation uses a `point` structure and STL to clarify the original algorithm. It will work on any arbitrary polygons, convex or concave:

```
#include <vector>
struct Point
{
  int x, y;
  Point() { x = y = 0; }
  Point(int _x, int _y) { x = _x; y = _y; }
};

typedef std::vector<Point> Polygon;

bool PointInPoly( Point const &test, const Polygon & polygon)
{
  Point newPoint, oldPoint;
  Point left, right;
```

```
  bool inside=false;

  size_t points = polygon.size();

  // The polygon must at least be a triangle
  if (points < 3)
        return false;

  oldPoint = polygon[points-1];

  for (unsigned int i=0 ; i < points; i++)
  {
    newPoint = polygon[i];
    if (newPoint.x > oldPoint.x)
    {
      left = oldPoint;
      right = newPoint;
    }
    else
    {
      left = newPoint;
      right = oldPoint;
    }

    // A point exactly on the left side of the polygon
    // will not intersect - as if it were "open"
    if ((newPoint.x < test.x) == (test.x <= oldPoint.x)
      && (test.y-left.y) * (right.x-left.x)
        < (right.y-left.y) * (test.x-left.x) )
    {
      inside=!inside;
    }

    oldPoint = newPoint;
  }
  return(inside);
}
```

## Control State

Controls have four states: active, highlighted, pressed, and disabled, as shown in Figure 10.3. An active control is able to receive events, but it isn't the center of attention. When the control gets the focus or passes a hit test from the pointing device, its state changes to highlighted. It's common for highlighted controls to have separate art or even a looping animation that plays as long as it has focus.

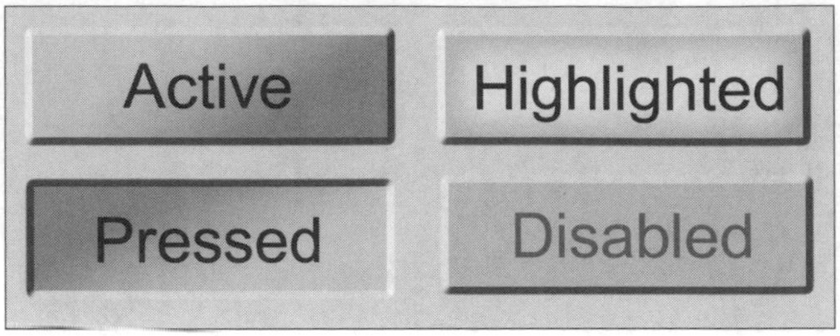


**Figure 10.3**
Four control states used with controls.

When the player presses a button on the mouse or controller, the control state changes from active to pressed. The art for this state usually depicts the control as pressed downward so that the player can tell what's going on. If the cursor moves away from the control, it will change state to active again, giving the player a clue that if the activation button is released, nothing will happen.

Disabled controls are usually drawn darkened or grayed out, giving the impression that no one is home. I know that Windows does this all over the place, but there is one thing about it that really bothers me: I can never tell *why* the control is disabled. It's fine to have a disabled state, but make sure that the player can figure out why it's disabled, or you'll just cause a lot of frustration.

**Use the Mouse Cursor for User Feedback**

If your interface uses a mouse, change the mouse cursor to something different, like a hand icon, when you are over an active control. This approach will give the player another clue that something will happen when he clicks the button. Use the Windows `LoadCursor()` API to grab a handle to the right mouse cursor and call `SetCursor()` with the cursor handle. If you want a good package to create animated mouse pointers, try Microangelo by Impact Software at www.impactsoftware.com.

Don't get confused about the control states mentioned here and control activation. Control activation results in a command message that propagates through to the screen's `OnControl()` function. For a standard push button control, this only happens if the mouse button is pressed and released over the button's hit area.

## More Control Properties

There are some additional properties you can attach to controls, mostly to give the player a more flexible and informative interface. These properties include hot keys, tooltips, context-sensitive help, draggability, sounds, and animation.

## Hot Keys

An excellent property to attach to any control on a desktop game is a hot key. As players become more familiar with the game, they'll want to ditch the pointer control in favor of pressing a single key on the keyboard. It's faster, which makes hard-core players really happy. You can distinguish between a hot key command and a normal keyboard input by checking the keyboard focus. The focus is something your screen class keeps track of itself, since it is an object that moves from control to control. Let's assume that you have a bunch of button controls on a game screen, as well as a chat window. Normally, every key down and up event will get sent to the controls to see if any of their hot keys match. If they do match, the `OnControl()` method of the screen will get called. The only way to enable the chat window is to click it with the mouse or provide a hot key for it that will set the keyboard focus for the screen.

As long as the keyboard focus points to the chat control, every keyboard event will be sent there, and hot keys are essentially disabled. Usually, the focus is released when the edit control decides it's done with keyboard input, such as when the Enter key is pressed. The focus can also be taken away by the screen, for example, if a different control were to be activated by the mouse.

## Tooltips

Tooltips are usually controlled by the containing screen, since it has to be aware of moving the tooltip around as different controls are highlighted. Tooltips are trickier than you'd think, because there's much more to enabling them than creating a bit of text on your screen for each control.

For one thing, every tooltip needs to have a good position relative to the control it describes. You can't just assume that every tooltip will look right if you place it in the same relative position to every control. If you decide that every tooltip will be placed in the upper-right area of every control, what happens when a control is already at the upper-right border of the screen? Also, you'll want to make sure that tooltips don't cover other important information on the screen when they appear. You don't want to annoy the heck out of your users.

#### Tooltips Don't Do Much Good Off-Screen

Even if you provide a placement hint, such as above or beside a control, you'll still need to tweak the placement of the tooltip to make sure it doesn't clip on the screen edge. Also, make sure that screens can erase tooltips prematurely, such as when a dialog box appears or when a drag begins.

### Context-Sensitive Help

Context-sensitive help is useful if you have a complicated game with lots of controls. If the player presses a hot key to launch the help window when a control is highlighted, the help system can bring up help text that describes what the control will do. An easy way to do this is to associate an identifier with each control that has context-sensitive help. In one game, this identifier was the name of the HTML file associated with that control. When the screen gets the hot key event for help, it first finds any highlighted control and asks it if it has an associated help file.

### Dragging

Controls can initiate a drag event or accept drag events. Drag initiation is simply a Boolean value that is used to indicate if a drag event can start on top of the control or not. Drag acceptance is a little more complicated. Most drag events have a source type, as discussed at the beginning of this chapter. Some controls might accept drags of different types, given only particular game states. An example of this might be dragging items around in a fantasy role-playing game. A character in the game might not be able to accept a dragged object because he's already carrying too much, and thus not be a legal target for the drag event.

One thing you should be careful of is the discoverability of dragging. Interfaces are becoming much more point and click, rather than click and hold, drag around, and release. If dragging is important to your game, as it frequently is in RTS games, just make sure your players have a good tutorial when the game starts.

### Sounds and Animation

Most controls have a sound effect that launches when the button changes state. Some games associate a single sound effect for every button, but it's not crazy to give each control its own sound effect. Animation frames for buttons and other controls are usually associated with the highlighted state. Instead of a single bitmap, you should use a bitmap series that loops while the control is highlighted.

## Some Final User Interface Tips

As parting advice, there are a few random but important tips I can give you on user interface work.

- All rectangular interfaces are boring.
- Localization can make a mess of your UI.

- You don't have to roll your own UI code anymore.
- UI code is easy to write, but making a good UI is an art form.

If your interface code doesn't use polygonal hit testing or bitmap collision, you are destined to have legions of square buttons and other controls populating your interface. That's not only a dull and uncreative look, but your artists will probably strangle you before you ever finish your game. Artists need the freedom to grow organic shapes in the interface and will resist all those vertical and horizontal lines.

Localization is a huge subject, but a significant part of that subject is interface design. You may hear things like, "make all your buttons 50 percent wider for German text," as the be-all end-all for localization. While that statement is certainly true, there's a lot more to it than that. It's difficult to achieve an excellent interface using nothing but icons instead of clear text labels. One of the casino games I worked on at Compulsive Development used this approach, and the team was completely stymied with the problem of choosing an international icon for features like blackjack insurance and placing a repeat bet on a roulette table. The fact is that international symbols are used and recognized for men's and women's bathrooms and locating baggage claim, but they are only recognized because they are extremely common and follow international standards—hardly something you should expect with a random icon in your game. If you use icons, more power to you, but you'd better provide some tooltips to go along with them.

A truly international application has to conform to much more than left-to-right, top-to-bottom blocks of text. Asian and Middle Eastern languages don't always follow Western European "sensibility." All you can really count on is being able to print text to a definable rectangle. If you have to print lots of text, consider using a well-known format like HTML or Flash and be done with it.

Since the first edition of this book was published, there has been a lot of good work done in user interface systems you can grab from the open source community or license. Scaleform is probably the most well known, implementing a Flash-based UI in almost any platform on the market. RADGameTools has also entered the fray with their Iggy product. There's even an open source library, gameswf, that you can use, but be very careful with it. The gameswf library might seem like a great way to save money, but you'll quickly realize that it allocates and frees memory hundreds of times per frame, and that's not good for your game and will fragment your memory like nothing you thought possible. You'll spend just as much time fixing it as licensing something. Also, it stands to reason that if you license a Flash-based UI system, you need someone who knows something about making user interfaces in Flash.

When you design your user interface, know your audience. Older players are more comfortable with menus and labeled buttons. Younger players enjoy the experience of exploring a graphical environment with their mouse and clicking where they see highlights. This is extremely problematic if you are a youngish programmer writing games for little kids or your parents. They simply don't think the same way you do, and nothing you do in your interface code will change that. Mimic proven solutions if you can, but always get a random sample of your target audience by taking your interface design for a test drive.

There's nothing more humbling than when you stand behind someone playing your game and silently watch that person struggle with the simplest task. You want to scream at the top of your lungs, "Simpleton! How do you find enough neurons to respirate?" In a calmer moment, perhaps you'll realize that the one with missing neurons looks back at you from mirrors. Take a deep breath, go back to your drawing board, and make things better. You'll be glad you did.

## Chapter 11

*by David "Rez" Graham*

# Game Event Management

So far, you've learned about actors, the resource cache, the main loop, and a number of other systems. Communication between these various systems can get very complicated and even start to break down completely if you're not careful. Consider this example: A game script wants to create an object, such as a ticking time bomb. The game logic needs to insert the time bomb into the game object list, and the various view objects need to know that a new object has been created. The human view will need to render it, while the AI views need to know it exists so that NPCs will react appropriately, such as running away in a panic. You'll also need to schedule future explosion events.

A naive programmer might code this complicated system by using a series of API calls to various subsystems of the game engine. This approach could get extremely messy and could require a morass of `#includes` at the top of every CPP file. I'm sure that you have come across code like this before. Each system would have to know about the public API of every other system that it interacted with. I've worked on a number of games that were built this way, and each experience was pretty horrible. Whenever even a trivial modification was made to a subsystem, it seemed that the whole game would have to be recompiled. This can also be the source of hard-to-find bugs.

In this chapter, you'll learn that you can solve the problems of communications between game subsystems and how they interact with game objects by using a general-purpose game event system. We'll start first by exploring game events, and then we'll build a basic Event Manager that you can use as a building block for your own games.

## Game Events

Whenever some authoritative system in your game makes something important happen, such as destroying an actor, it fires off an event. Your game must then notify all the appropriate subsystems that the event has occurred so that they can handle the event in their own way. A good example of an authoritative system is the game logic, which is responsible for all the actors in the game. An example of a subsystem that consumes events is the game renderer (or human view). The view needs to know the actor's correct position. It also needs to know when the actor is destroyed so that it can destroy its own internal representation of the actor and remove it from the scene.

The game logic could try to keep track of all the systems that need to know about actors, such as the renderer, and call each system's API to tell each one that an actor has been destroyed. If there are a number of systems that need to know about actors, the game logic must call into each one, probably using a slightly different API and parameter list. Yuck!

Fortunately, there's a much better way to do this. Instead of calling each system every time an actor is destroyed, the game logic could create a game event and send it into a system that knows how to distribute the event to any subsystem that wants to listen. One side effect of this solution is that it cleans up the relationship between game subsystems. Mostly, they don't care about anything but themselves and the event management system.

A system such as an audio system already knows what events it should listen to. In this case, it would listen to "object collided" or "object destroyed." On the other hand, there might be tons of other messages that the audio system could safely ignore, such as an event that signals the end of an animation.

In a well-designed game, each subsystem should be responsible for subscribing to and handling game events as they pass through the system. The game event system is global to the application and therefore makes a good candidate to sit in the application layer. It manages all communications going on between the game logic and game views. If the game logic moves or destroys an actor, an event is sent, and all the game views will receive it. If a game view wants to send a command to the game logic, it does so through the event system. The game event system is the glue that holds the entire game logic and game view architecture together.

**Death in the Kingdom**

The death code in *The Sims Medieval* works more or less like it did in *The Sims 3*, but we had a number of new systems that had to respond to a sim dying. There was a quest system, for example, that had to ensure the sim was properly removed from the quest and potentially fail the quest if this was an important NPC (or the player). We also had to ensure that the role system knew about the death. If it was a town guard, blacksmith's apprentice, or some other "role sim" that died, the role system had to generate a new one to replace the dead sim. This could have been a major hassle if it weren't for the event system. When a sim died, the death system sent an event. All we had to do was make our new systems handle this event appropriately. The death system didn't have to know anything about the new systems, and the new systems didn't have to know anything about the death system. They just knew that Garvin the Town Crier was dead.

The game event system is organized into three basic parts:

- Events and event data
- Event handler delegates
- Event Manager

Events and event data are generated by authoritative systems when an action of any significance occurs, and they are sent into the Event Manager, sometimes also called a *listener registry*. The Event Manager matches each event with all the subsystems that have subscribed to the event and calls each event listener delegate function in turn so it can handle the event in its own way.

## Events and Event Data

A classic problem in computer games is how to define types of data or objects. The easiest way to define different types of elements, such as event types, is to put them all into a single enumeration like this:

```
Enum EventType
{
  Event_Object_Moved,
  Event_Object_Created,
  Event_Object Destroyed,
  Event_Guard_Picked_Nose,
  // and on and on....
};
```

With this type of solution, each subsystem in your game would likely need this enumeration because each probably generates one or more of these events. In coding this approach, you would need to have every system `#include` this enumeration. Then, every time you add to it or change it, your entire game would need to be recompiled, clearly a bad thing.

**Build Times on *Thief: Deadly Shadows***

When I was working on *Thief: Deadly Shadows* at Ion Storm, we had a few systems like this, including the event system. Each event type was defined in a huge enumeration, and creating a new event or deleting a deprecated one caused us to recompile everything, and I mean everything. *Thief: Deadly Shadows* had nine build targets: PC Game, Xbox Game, and Editor, with each having Debug, Profile, and Release build flavors. Even on a fast desktop workstation, it would take us 15 minutes or more to build just one, and building everything took more than an hour. Screams of anguish could be heard when someone checked in one of these core header files without sending a warning email with plenty of advance notice. The moment someone had to get code off the Net, that person might as well go take a prolonged break. Believe me, we didn't want the break either because it would just turn a 12-hour day into a 13-hour day.

Fortunately, there's a better way to do this. Instead of creating a massive enumeration in a core header file, you can create a bunch of GUIDs (globally unique identifiers) for each event. These GUIDs are defined on the event itself so if something gets added or removed, you only need to recompile the effected files. It's fast and saves your team from the terrible monolithic enumeration that everyone has to reference.

You can create GUIDs in Visual Studio by going to the Tools menu and clicking on Create GUID, which will bring up a dialog box with several new options. The one I always choose is "DEFINE_GUID that(…)." Then you can press the Copy button, which copies the GUID to your clipboard. When you paste this into your code or a text file somewhere, you'll get something like this:

```
// {6A873D78-508D-4AC0-AC79-1D73B3FF1A0A}
DEFINE_GUID(<<name>>,
0x6a873d78, 0x508d, 0x4ac0, 0xac, 0x79, 0x1d, 0x73, 0xb3, 0xff, 0x1a, 0xa);
```

Then grab the first number, 0x6a873d78 in this case, and use that as your 32-bit GUID. Now you have an easy way to create as many event types as you want. Here's how to create events and data that can ride along with the event:

```
class IEventData
{
public:
```

```
    virtual const EventType& VGetEventType(void) const = 0;
    virtual float VGetTimeStamp(void) const = 0;
    virtual void VSerialize(std::ostrstream& out) const = 0;
    virtual IEventDataPtr VCopy(void) const = 0;
    virtual const char* GetName(void) const = 0;
};

class BaseEventData : public IEventData
{
    const float m_timeStamp;

public:
    explicit BaseEventData(const float timeStamp = 0.0f) :
        m_timeStamp(timeStamp) { }
    virtual ~BaseEventData(void) {}

    // Returns the type of the event
    virtual const EventType& VGetEventType(void) const = 0;

    float VGetTimeStamp(void) const { return m_timeStamp; }

    // Serializing for network out.
    virtual void VSerialize(std::ostrstream &out) const   { }
};
```

### Choose Your Stream Implementation Carefully

Did you note the use of `std::ostrstream` in the previous code snippet? This was chosen to make the stream human readable, which can be very useful during development, but a big mistake for any shipping game. For one thing, a human-readable stream is trivial to hack. More importantly, the stream is large and takes much longer to load and parse than a binary stream. Try using `std::ostream` instead or your own custom stream class.

An event encapsulates the event type, the event data, and the time the event occurred. Event data is defined by you, the programmer, and you are free to create ad hoc data that will accompany your event. It's a little easier to see what's going on with a concrete example. Recall from Chapter 6, "Game Actors and Component Architecture," that every actor has an ID that's used for tracking purposes. Now, if an actor is ever destroyed, this `ActorId` would get sent along with an event so other subsystems could remove the actor from their lists. The event data class for an "actor destroyed" event would look like this:

```
typedef unsigned long EventType;

class EvtData_Destroy_Actor : public BaseEventData
```

```
{
  ActorId m_id;

public:
  static const EventType sk_EventType;

  explicit EvtData_Destroy_Actor(ActorId id)
    : m_id(id) { }
  explicit EvtData_Destroy_Actor(std::istrstream& in)
  {
    in >> m_id;
  }

  virtual const EventType& VGetEventType(void) const
  {
    return sk_EventType;
  }

  virtual IEventDataPtr VCopy(void) const
  {
    return IEventDataPtr(GCC_NEW EvtData_Destroy_Actor(m_id));
  }

  virtual void VSerialize(std::ostrstream &out) const
  {
    out << m_id;
  }
  virtual const char* GetName(void) const
  {
    return "EvtData_Destroy_Actor";
  }

  ActorId GetId(void) const { return m_id; }
};
```

The event data inherits from the `BaseEventData` so it can be wired into the event system. When an actor is destroyed, its `ActorId` is sent along with the event.

The `sk_EventType` variable is the GUID, which is initialized like this:

```
const EventType EvtData_Destroy_Actor::sk_EventType(0x77dd2b3a);
```

This is how the event is uniquely identified across the entire application. Listeners register for events using this ID.

## The Event Listener Delegates

Events and event data need to go somewhere, and they always go to event listener delegate functions. A delegate function is basically a function pointer that can be coupled with an object pointer and used as a callback. They are used quite extensively in C# and other .NET applications. C++ can do C-style function pointers as well as C++ functor objects, but it tends to fall apart when you try to encapsulate pointers to member functions. The problem is that the C++ compiler needs to know the type of the function pointer, which defeats our purposes. What we really want is a C#-style delegate where we can define a function signature and not care where the function comes from, as long as it conforms to our signature. C++ can't do this without a *lot* of template magic.

Fortunately, someone has already solved this problem for us! Don Clugston wrote a great article on *The Code Project* about fast C++ delegates and was kind enough to publish the code for public use. It has no license whatsoever, so you can use it in commercial applications. The article itself is fantastic and worth a read, although I warn you that it covers some pretty advanced C++ stuff. It's not for the feint of heart:

http://www.codeproject.com/KB/cpp/FastDelegate.aspx

All event listener delegate functions must conform to the following function prototype:

```
typedef shared_ptr<IEventData> IEventDataPtr; // smart ptr to IEventData
void Delegate(IEventDataPtr pEventData);
```

The name of the function doesn't matter, nor does the name of the parameter or even what class it comes from. It could be a virtual function, a static function, a global function, or just a regular member function. That's the beauty of the fast delegate library! To declare this function signature as a delegate, we `typedef` it like so:

```
typedef fastdelegate::FastDelegate1<IEventDataPtr> EventListenerDelegate;
```

Everything in the fast delegate library is under the `fastdelegate` namespace. The `FastDelegate1` template is the help class used to bind the runtime object (if it exists) with the appropriate function pointer. The "1" you see there is because there is one parameter. If there were two parameters, you would use `FastDelegate2`, and so on. This is required mostly for compiler compatibility. The template parameter is the parameter type you want to pass into the function. There is an optional additional parameter for the return value, which we're not using here. `EventListenerDelegate` is now a `typedef` of the delegate type.

To use the delegate, you instantiate it and call the `bind()` method. This overloaded method will bind your function (or object pointer and function pair) to the delegate object. If you're binding C++ functions, the easiest thing to do is to use the global `MakeDelegate()` function. This function takes in the object pointer and member function pointer and returns a newly constructed delegate object.

There's a lot more to the fast delegates library, but these are the core features we'll be using for the event system presented in this chapter. If you want to see some examples of how to use this system, download the source code for this book and check out the following file:

*Source\GCC4\3rdParty\FastDelegate\Demo.cpp*

This file comes with the fast delegates source bundle and exists to show off the functionality and interface.

You now know how to create an event and write a delegate method that listens for events, but you still lack a crucial piece of this puzzle. The Event Manager is the nexus of events in your game. It receives them from practically anywhere and calls any registered delegate functions.

## The Event Manager

As you might expect, the Event Manager is more complicated than the events or the delegate methods. It has a tough job matching events with listeners and doing it in a manner that is pretty fast. First, you'll see the `IEventManager` interface. The Event Manager class is set up to be a global singleton, and it manages its own global pointer. This is pretty useful, since virtually every system in your game will need access to the Event Manager object.

The interface defines the following methods:

- `VAddListener`: Matches a delegate function with an event type, so anytime the event type is sent, the delegate will be called.
- `VRemoveListener`: Removes a delegate. You must call this when the registering object is destroyed.
- `VTriggerEvent`: Immediately fires an event to listeners that care about it.
- `VQueueEvent`: Puts an event in a queue to be fired later.
- `VAbortEvent`: Removes an event from the queue.
- `VUpdate`: Processes the events in the queue. This is called every game loop.

```
class IEventManager
{
public:

  enum eConstants { kINFINITE = 0xffffffff };

  explicit IEventManager(const char* pName, bool setAsGlobal);
  virtual ~IEventManager(void);

  // Registers a delegate function that will get called when the event type is
  // triggered. Returns true if successful, false if not.
  virtual bool VAddListener(const EventListenerDelegate& eventDelegate,
                            const EventType& type) = 0;

  // Removes a delegate / event type pairing from the internal tables.
  // Returns false if the pairing was not found.
  virtual bool VRemoveListener(const EventListenerDelegate& eventDelegate,
                               const EventType& type) = 0;

  // Fires off event NOW. This bypasses the queue entirely and immediately
  // calls all delegate functions registered for the event.
  virtual bool VTriggerVTriggerEvent(const IEventDataPtr& pEvent) const = 0;

  // Fires off event. This uses the queue and will call the delegate function
  // on the next call to VTickVUpdate(), assuming there's enough time.
  virtual bool VQueueEvent(const IEventDataPtr& pEvent) = 0;

  // Finds the next-available instance of the named event type and remove it
  // from the processing queue. This may be done up to the point that it is
  // actively being processed ... e.g.: is safe to happen during event
  // processing itself.
  //
  // If allOfType is true, then all events of that type are cleared from the
  // input queue.
  //
  // returns true if the event was found and removed, false otherwise
  virtual bool VAbortEvent(const EventType& type, bool allOfType = false) = 0;

  // Allows for processing of any queued messages, optionally specify a
  // processing time limit so that the event processing does not take too
  // long. Note the danger of using this artificial limiter is that all
  // messages may not in fact get processed.
  //
  // returns true if all messages ready for processing were completed, false
  // otherwise (e.g. timeout).
```

```
  virtual bool VTickVUpdate(unsigned long maxMillis = kINFINITE) = 0;

  // Getter for the main global event manager. This is the event manager that
  // is used by the majority of the engine, though you are free to define your
  // own as long as you instantiate it with setAsGlobal set to false.
  // It is not valid to have more than one global event manager.
  static IEventManager* Get(void);
};
```

You can take a look at the comments above each method to see what it is supposed to do. The implementation of `IEventManager` manages two sets of objects: event data and listener delegates. As events are processed by the system, the Event Manager matches them up with subscribed listener delegate functions and calls each one with events they care about.

There are two ways to send events—by queue and by trigger. By *queue* means the event will sit in line with other events until the game processes `IEventManager::VUpdate()`. By *trigger* means the event will be sent immediately—almost like calling each delegate function directly from your calling code.

Now you're ready to see how an Event Manager class implements the interface:

```
const unsigned int EVENTMANAGER_NUM_QUEUES = 2;

class EventManager : public IEventManager
{
  typedef std::list<EventListenerDelegate> EventListenerList;
  typedef std::map<EventType, EventListenerList> EventListenerMap;
  typedef std::list<IEventDataPtr> EventQueue;

  EventListenerMap m_eventListeners;
  EventQueue m_queues[EVENTMANAGER_NUM_QUEUES];
  int m_activeQueue;  // index of actively processing queue; events
                      // enque to the opposing queue

public:
  explicit EventManager(const char* pName, bool setAsGlobal);
  virtual ~EventManager(void) { }

  virtual bool VAddListener(const EventListenerDelegate& eventDelegate,
                            const EventType& type);
  virtual bool VRemoveListener(const EventListenerDelegate& eventDelegate,
                               const EventType& type);

  virtual bool VTriggerVTriggerEvent(const IEventDataPtr& pEvent) const;
  virtual bool VQueueEvent(const IEventDataPtr& pEvent);
```

```
  virtual bool VAbortEvent(const EventType& type, bool allOfType = false);

  virtual bool VTickVUpdate(unsigned long maxMillis = kINFINITE);
};
```

EventListenerList is a list of EventDelegate objects. EventListenerMap is a map where the key is an EventType and the data is the EventListenerList. This is the data structure used to register listener delegate functions. Each event has a list of delegates to call when the event is triggered. The third typedef, EventQueue, defines a list of smart pointers to IEventData objects.

The next block declares the actual data members. The first is the map, and the second is an array of event queues. There are two event queues here so that delegate methods can safely queue up new events. You can imagine an infinite loop where two events queue up each other. Without two queues, the program would hang in an infinite loop and never break out of the event VTickVUpdate() function. The m_activeQueue member is the index of the currently active queue.

The constructor is pretty bare bones:

```
EventManager::EventManager(char const * const pName, bool setAsGlobal)
  : IEventManager(pName, setAsGlobal)
{
  m_activeQueue = 0;
}
```

Here's the code for adding a new delegate function:

```
bool EventManager::VAddListener(const EventListenerDelegate& eventDelegate,
                                const EventType& type)
{
  // this will find or create the entry
  EventListenerList& eventListenerList = m_eventListeners[type];
  for (auto it = eventListenerList.begin(); it != eventListenerList.end();
       ++it)
  {
    if (eventDelegate == (*it))
    {
      GCC_WARNING("Attempting to double-register a delegate");
      return false;
    }
  }

  eventListenerList.push_back(eventDelegate);
  return true;
}
```

First, the code grabs (or creates) the event listener list. It walks through the list to see if the listener has already been registered and kicks out a warning if it has been. Registering the same delegate for the same event more than once is definitely an error, since processing the event would end up calling the delegate function multiple times.

If the delegate has never been registered for this event, it's added to the list.

Here's how you remove a listener:

```
bool EventManager::VRemoveListener(const EventListenerDelegate& eventDelegate,
                                   const EventType& type)
{
  bool success = false;

  auto findIt = m_eventListeners.find(type);
  if (findIt != m_eventListeners.end())
  {
    EventListenerList& listeners = findIt->second;
    for (auto it = listeners.begin(); it != listeners.end(); ++it)
    {
      if (eventDelegate == (*it))
      {
        listeners.erase(it);
        success = true;
        // We don't need to continue because it should be impossible for
        // the same delegate function to be registered for the same event
        // more than once.
        break;
      }
    }
  }

  return success;
}
```

This function gets the event listener list for the event type that was passed in. If the list is valid, it walks through it, attempting to find the delegate. The `FastDelegate` classes all implement an overloaded == operator, so this works really well. If the delegate is found, it's removed from the list, `success` is set to `true`, and the loop is broken. That's all there is to it.

**Always Clean Up After Yourself**

The fast delegate library uses raw pointers on the inside and binds the object pointer you give it to the function pointer. That means that if you destroy the object without removing the delegate, you'll get a crash when an event that delegate is set to receive is fired. You should always remember to clean up after yourself and remove any delegate listeners in the destructor of your listener class.

While the situation is certainly not the norm, it is occasionally necessary to fire an event and have all listeners respond to it immediately, without using the event queue. That's where the `VTriggerVTriggerEvent()` function comes in. In all honesty, this method breaks the paradigm of remote event handling, as you will see done in Chapter 18, "Network Programming for Multiplayer Games," but it's still necessary for certain operations. A good example of a valid use is in the game startup code when you don't want to wait a frame just to ensure that something started before continuing to the next stage. Here's the `VTriggerVTriggerEvent()` method:

```
bool EventManager::VTriggerVTriggerEvent(const IEventDataPtr& pEvent) const
{
  bool processed = false;

  auto findIt = m_eventListeners.find(pEvent->VGetEventType());
  if (findIt != m_eventListeners.end())
  {
    const EventListenerList& eventListenerList = findIt->second;
    for (EventListenerList::const_iterator it = eventListenerList.begin();
       it != eventListenerList.end(); ++it)
    {
      EventListenerDelegate listener = (*it);
      listener(pEvent); // call the delegate
      processed = true;
    }
  }
    return processed;
}
```

This function is relatively simple. It tries to find the event listener list associated with this event type and then, if found, iterates through all the delegates and calls each one. It returns `true` if any listener handled the event.

The most common (and correct) way of sending events is by using the `VQueueEvent` method:

```
bool EventManager::VQueueEvent(const IEventDataPtr& pEvent)
{
  GCC_ASSERT(m_activeQueue >= 0);
  GCC_ASSERT(m_activeQueue < EVENTMANAGER_NUM_QUEUES);

  auto findIt = m_eventListeners.find(pEvent->VGetEventType());
  if (findIt != m_eventListeners.end())
  {
    m_queues[m_activeQueue].push_back(pEvent);
    return true;
  }
  else
  {
    return false;
  }
}
```

This function is also pretty simple. First, it finds the associated event listener list. If it finds this list, it adds the event to the currently active queue. This keeps the Event Manager from processing events for which there are no listeners.

Of course, you could change your mind about a queued message and want to take it back, like some of those emails I sent to my boss.

```
bool EventManager::VAbortEvent(const EventType& inType, bool allOfType)
{
  GCC_ASSERT(m_activeQueue >= 0);
  GCC_ASSERT(m_activeQueue < EVENTMANAGER_NUM_QUEUES);

  bool success = false;
  EventListenerMap::iterator findIt = m_eventListeners.find(inType);

  if (findIt != m_eventListeners.end())
  {
    EventQueue& eventQueue = m_queues[m_activeQueue];
    auto it = eventQueue.begin();
    while (it != eventQueue.end())
    {
      // Removing an item from the queue will invalidate the iterator, so
      // have it point to the next member. All work inside this loop will
      // be done using thisIt.
      auto thisIt = it;
      ++it;
```

```
        if ((*thisIt)->VGetEventType() == inType)
        {
          eventQueue.erase(thisIt);
          success = true;
          if (!allOfType)
            break;
        }
      }
    }

    return success;
}
```

The `VAbortEvent()` method is a simple case of looking in the active queue for the event of a given type and erasing it. Note that this method can erase the first event in the queue of a given type or all events of a given type, depending on the value of the second parameter. You could use this method to remove redundant messages from the queue, such as two "move object" events for the same object.

All those queued messages have to be processed sometime. Somewhere in the game's main loop, the Event Manager's `VUpdate()` method should be called, and the queued messages will get distributed like so many pieces of mail.

```
bool EventManager::VTickVUpdate(unsigned long maxMillis)
{
  unsigned long currMs = GetTickCount();
  unsigned long maxMs = ((maxMillis == IEventManager::kINFINITE) ?
                        (IEventManager::kINFINITE) :
                        (currMs + maxMillis));

  // swap active queues and clear the new queue after the swap
  int queueToProcess = m_activeQueue;
  m_activeQueue = (m_activeQueue + 1) % EVENTMANAGER_NUM_QUEUES;
  m_queues[m_activeQueue].clear();

  // Process the queue
  while (!m_queues[queueToProcess].empty())
  {
    // pop the front of the queue
    IEventDataPtr pEvent = m_queues[queueToProcess].front();
    m_queues[queueToProcess].pop_front();

    const EventType& eventType = pEvent->VGetEventType();

    // find all the delegate functions registered for this event
```

```
        auto findIt = m_eventListeners.find(eventType);
        if (findIt != m_eventListeners.end())
        {
          const EventListenerList& eventListeners = findIt->second;

          // call each listener
          for (auto it = eventListeners.begin(); it != eventListeners.end();
              ++it)
          {
            EventListenerDelegate listener = (*it);
            listener(pEvent);
          }
        }

        // check to see if time ran out
        currMs = GetTickCount();
        if (maxMillis != IEventManager::kINFINITE && currMs >= maxMs)
        {
          GCC_LOG("EventLoop", "Aborting event processing; time ran out");
          break;
        }
      }
      // If we couldn't process all of the events, push the remaining events to
      // the new active queue.
      // Note: To preserve sequencing, go back-to-front, inserting them at the
      // head of the active queue.
      bool queueFlushed = (m_queues[queueToProcess].empty());
      if (!queueFlushed)
      {
        while (!m_queues[queueToProcess].empty())
        {
          IEventDataPtr pEvent = m_queues[queueToProcess].back();
          m_queues[queueToProcess].pop_back();
          m_queues[m_activeQueue].push_front(pEvent);
        }
      }
        return queueFlushed;
    }
```

The `VUpdate()` method takes all of the queued messages and calls the registered delegate methods. As I said before, there are actually two queues. This is almost like double buffering in a renderer. Sometimes handling events creates new events; in fact, it happens all the time. Colliding with an object might cause it to move and collide with another object. If you always added events to a single queue, you might never run out of events to process. This problem is handled easily with two queues: one for the events being actively processed and the other for new events.

The code is very much like what you saw in the `VTriggerEvent()` method, with one more difference than the fact the events are being pulled from one of the queues. It also can be called with a maximum time allowed. If the amount of time is exceeded, the method exits, even if there are messages still in the queue.

This can be pretty useful for smoothing out some frame rate stutter if you attempt to handle too many events in one game loop. If your game events start to pile up and your queue always seems to stay full, perhaps you'd better work on a little optimization.

## Example: Bringing It All Together

Let's look at a simple example to bring it all together. In this case, we'll look at what happens when you destroy an actor. The first step is to define the event data by writing a new class that inherits from `BaseEventData`. You've already seen this class; it's `EvtData_Destroy_Actor` event above, so let's use that. Flip back to earlier in this chapter if you need a refresher on that class.

The next step is to define the delegate methods that need to handle this event. Here's what it might look like:

```
void RoleSystem::DestroyActorDelegate(IEventDataPtr pEventData)
{
  // cast the base event pointer to the actual event data we need
  shared_ptr<EvtData_Destroy_Actor> pCastEventData =
    static_pointer_cast<EvtData_Destroy_Actor>(pEventData);

  // Remove the actor from the map of roles. Assume the role map is
  // defined as follows:
  // std::map<ActorId, RoleData> m_roleMap;
  m_roleMap.erase(pCastEventData->GetActorId());
}
```

Somewhere in the initialization of the role system, you also need to register the delegate:

```
bool RoleSystem::VInit(void)
{
  // create the delegate function object
  EventListenerDelegate delegateFunc =
    MakeDelegate(this, &RoleSystem::DestroyActorDelegate);

  // register the delegate with the event manager
```

```
  IEventManager::Get()->VAddListener(delegateFunc,
    EvtData_Destroy_Actor::sk_EventType);
}
```

You also need to remember to remove it in the destructor:

```
RoleSystem::~RoleSystem(void)
{
  // Create a delegate function object. This will have the same value as
  // the one previously registered in VInit(). Another way to do this would
  // be to cache the delegate object. This is a memory vs performance trade-
  // off. Since the performance gain would only be during shut-down, memory
  // is the better way to go here.
  EventListenerDelegate delegateFunc =
    MakeDelegate(this, &RoleSystem::DestroyActorDelegate);

  // remove the delegate from the event manager
  IEventManager::Get()->VRemoveListener(delegateFunc,
    EvtData_Destroy_Actor::sk_EventType);
}
```

That's all you need to do in order to register events. Here's the code to send the event:

```
// Instantiate the event. The event system tracks all events with smart
// pointers, so you must instantiate the event using a smart pointer.
shared_ptr<EvtData_New_Actor> pDestroyEvent(
  GCC_NEW EvtData_Destroy_Actor(pActor->GetId());

// Queue the event.
IEventManager::Get()->VQueueEvent(pDestroyEvent);

// Or, if you prefer, force the event to resolve immediately with VTrigger()
// with VTriggerEvent()
IEventManager::Get()->VTriggerVTriggerEvent(pDestroyEvent);
```

And there you have it, a simple event system!

## What Game Events Are Important?

It's a little something of a cop-out, but it completely depends on your game, doesn't it? A game like *Tetris* might care about a few simple events such as "Brick Created," "Brick Moved," "Brick Rotated," and "Brick Collision." A game like *The Sims Medieval* had dozens, if not hundreds, of different game events. Table 11.1 shows an example of the kind of game events you might send in just about any game:

**Table 11.1 Common Types of Events**

| Game Events | Description |
|---|---|
| ActorMove | A game object has moved. |
| ActorCollision | A collision has occurred. |
| AICharacterState | Character has changed states. |
| PlayerState | Player has changed states. |
| PlayerDeath | Player is dead. |
| GameOver | Player death animation is over. |
| ActorCreated | A new game object is created. |
| ActorDestroy | A game object is destroyed. |
| **Map/Mission Events** | |
| PreLoadLevel | A new level is about to be loaded. |
| LoadedLevel | A new level is finished loading. |
| EnterTriggerVolume | A character entered a trigger volume. |
| ExitTriggerVolume | A character exited a trigger volume. |
| PlayerTeleported | The player has been teleported. |
| **Game Startup Events** | |
| GraphicsStarted | The graphics system is ready. |
| PhysicsStarted | The physics system is ready. |
| EventSystemStarted | The event system is ready. |
| SoundSystemStarted | The sound system is ready. |
| ResourceCacheStarted | The resource system is ready. |
| NetworkStarted | The network system is ready. |
| HumanViewAttached | A human view has been attached. |
| GameLogicStarted | The game logic system is ready. |
| GamePaused | The game is paused. |
| GameResumedResumed | The game is resumed. |
| PreSave | The game is about to be saved. |
| PostSave | The game has been saved. |

(*Continues*)

**Table 11.1 Common Types of Events (*Continued*)**

| Game Events | Description |
|---|---|
| **Animation and Sound Events** | |
| AnimationStarted | An animation has begun. |
| AnimationLooped | An animation has looped. |
| AnimationEnded | An animation has ended. |
| SoundEffectStarted | A new sound effect has started. |
| SoundEffectLooped | A sound effect has looped back to the beginning. |
| SoundEffectEnded | A sound effect has completed. |
| VideoStarted | A cinematic has started. |
| VideoEnded | A cinematic has ended. |

## Distinguishing Events from Processes

If you recall the `Process` class from Chapter 7, "Controlling the Main Loop," you might wonder if there is a significant difference between a game event and a process. The difference is easy—a *game event* is something that has happened in the most recent frame, such as an actor has been destroyed or moved. A *process* is something that takes more than one frame to process, such as an animation or monitoring a sound effect.

These two systems are quite powerful by themselves and can easily create a game of significant complexity with surprisingly little code in your game logic or view classes.

Events are the main tool used for communicating to other systems. Using the event system presented in this chapter, you can design complex systems that are nice and decoupled from each other while still allowing them to talk to one another. This decoupling allows these systems to grow and change organically without affecting any of the other systems they are attached to, as long as they still send and respond to the same events as before. As you can see, events are crucial tools to have in your programming toolbox.

## Further Reading

*Algorithms in C++*, Robert Sedgewick

*Beyond the C++ Standard Library*, Björn Karlsson

*Effective STL*, Scott Meyers

*Introduction to Algorithms*, Thomas Cormen

The Code Project article: *Member Function Pointers and the Fastest Possible C++ Delegates*, by Don Clugston: http://www.codeproject.com/KB/cpp/FastDelegate.aspx

# Chapter 12

*by David "Rez" Graham*

## Scripting with Lua

In the past decade or so, games have started to become much more data driven. For example, the Actor system lets you create whole classes of different actors by just mixing and matching different components. You can even add and remove components at runtime, making it possible to completely change an actor's definition, behavior, and properties without having to recompile and relaunch the game. The days of having hard-coded constants that affect gameplay are coming to a close, being replaced by tuning hierarchies that are completely in the hands of the designers.

As a programmer, my job is becoming more about enabling the designers, artists, and musicians to be creative. I spend my days creating tuning hooks for them to play with the simulation. This is an incredibly powerful concept because it means that once a system is working, the designers can iterate on it without having to talk to me at all. On *The Sims,* a programmer doesn't need to be involved in creating every single television, he just needs to figure out the first one. And with a bit of cleverness, he may not need to be involved in *any* television objects at all since they can be defined entirely in data. The available channels, the amount of fun it provides, and so on can all be set by the designers.

This chapter is much more than just coverage of Lua syntax and how to embed a scripting language into your game. I want to take you back to the very early days of computer programming and talk about how languages evolved from machine code up to the high-level languages we have today. With a little background, I hope to give you a better context for why you might want to use a scripting language at all and how it fits into the grand scheme of things. After that, I'll talk about strategies for using a scripting language, including comparing two of the most popular ones. Then the time will be right to dig into the internals of the Lua scripting language. I'll also show you not only the mechanics of how to get it up and running in your game, but also some best practices in using a scripting language, including how to decouple your engine code from your scripting code and figure out what should live in C++ and what should live in the script. This is done by extending systems you've already worked with in previous chapters.

## A Brief History of Game Programming Languages

Way back in 1946, the ENIAC was completed at the University of Pennsylvania. This is considered the first general-purpose electronic computer, able to be reprogrammed to solve any number of complex operations. The process of programming this massive machine involved setting a series of switches and changing cables, which often took days even for simple tasks. Input and output were handled with punch cards, a far cry from the modern keyboard and monitor we all know and love. There are a few pieces of the ENIAC on display at various museums. It's worth the trip to get an appreciation of our programming forefathers.

One of the very first video games was called *Tennis for Two* and was first seen in 1958 at the Brookhaven National Laboratory. It was created on an oscilloscope screen and showed a tennis court on its side. The brightly lit ball bounced from one end to the other, simulating the physics of a ball bouncing in real time. Players would use controllers with buttons and rotating dials to control the angle of an invisible racquet. If you do a quick search online, you can find video of this grandfather of modern gaming. It's quite remarkable.

*Tennis for Two* was created on a small analog computer. By using resistors, capacitors, and relays, it was possible to generate various curves on the oscilloscope. In fact, the computer was made to perform tasks like calculating trajectories for bullets, missiles, and yes, even a ball. The programming for the game was largely done by building the actual circuitry for it, which sent input to the analog computer, received the output, and displayed it on the oscilloscope.

The dawn of video games as an industry occurred in 1972 with the release of the Magnavox Odyssey and, shortly afterwards, the Atari VCS (renamed the Atari 2600). I'm sure many of you have never even heard of the Magnavox Odyssey. It was only marginally successful, but it undoubtedly shaped the video games industry as we know it today by being the first dedicated home video game console you could hook up to your TV.

## Assembly Language

All of these first-generation video games were programmed in some flavor of assembly language. Assembly language is a very low-level language that sits right on top of the processor. It's one step above inputting the machine code (for example, the actual hex instructions sent to the CPU), though it's not a very big step. Each instruction translates directly to a series of machine code instructions. For example, here's an instruction written in ×86 assembler:

```
mov byte ptr [eax],61h
```

This instruction translates to the following machine code:

```
C6 00 61
```

As you can see, assembly language is quite a step up from machine code. It's typically just as fast, too, since the instructions translate directly into small sets of machine code instructions, although there are certain machine code optimizations a programmer might want to do. For the most part, this was the way games were developed for quite some time.

#### Learn Assembly Language

Nothing will help you truly understand what's happening inside the processor better than learning assembly language. Simply reading a book or Web page doesnt count. You need to actually do something useful with it, like get yourself an Atari 2600 emulator and an assembler capable of building Atari ROMs and make a simple game. You will be incredibly frustrated just trying to render a single line, but I guarantee that you will learn more by doing this than learning just about any other language. As a bonus, you'll also be forced to learn the extreme importance of commenting your code. It will also vastly increase your debugging skills.

Assembly language worked well enough for older games since they were smaller and simpler than the games we have today. The typical working model at Atari was to lock one programmer in a room for several months to create a game. Contrast that with the 100 or so people we had on *The Sims Medieval* at its peak. If we had written *The Sims Medieval* entirely in assembly language, we'd still be working on it. As games got more complex and processors got even faster, it was time to move up to the next level.

## C/C++

The C programming language was originally created by the late Dennis Ritchie at Bell Labs in the early 70s. It was originally designed for use with the UNIX operating system, but it had the capability of being platform independent. That's a big one—assembly language is completely dependant on the instruction set of the CPU.

C compilers had the ability to build different executables from the same code for different platforms.

While assembly language has a one-to-one correlation with machine code, C is compiled into object code. This is a translation from the C code to machine code for that particular platform. Those object files are then linked with each other and other libraries to form a final, platform-specific executable. This is one major difference between C and assembly language. Assembly language is tied directly to the machine architecture, while the same C program can be compiled onto multiple platforms with completely different architectures.

Another huge difference between assembly language and C is that C is *much* easier for a human to understand. As an example, here's a bubble sort function implemented in 6502 Assembly, which is what the Atari 2600 and NES used:

```
;DOWNLOADED FROM: http://6502.org/source/sorting/bubble8.htm
;THIS SUBROUTINE ARRANGES THE 8-BIT ELEMENTS OF A LIST IN ASCENDING
;ORDER.  THE STARTING ADDRESS OF THE LIST IS IN LOCATIONS $30 AND
;$31.  THE LENGTH OF THE LIST IS IN THE FIRST BYTE OF THE LIST.  LOCATION
;$32 IS USED TO HOLD AN EXCHANGE FLAG.
SORT8  LDY #$00      ;TURN EXCHANGE FLAG OFF (= 0)
       STY $32
       LDA ($30),Y   ;FETCH ELEMENT COUNT
       TAX           ; AND PUT IT INTO X
       INY           ;POINT TO FIRST ELEMENT IN LIST
       DEX           ;DECREMENT ELEMENT COUNT
NXTEL  LDA ($30),Y   ;FETCH ELEMENT
       INY
       CMP ($30),Y   ;IS IT LARGER THAN THE NEXT ELEMENT?
       BCC CHKEND
       BEQ CHKEND
                     ;YES. EXCHANGE ELEMENTS IN MEMORY
       PHA           ; BY SAVING LOW BYTE ON STACK.
       LDA ($30),Y   ; THEN GET HIGH BYTE AND
       DEY           ; STORE IT AT LOW ADDRESS
       STA ($30),Y
       PLA           ;PULL LOW BYTE FROM STACK
       INY           ; AND STORE IT AT HIGH ADDRESS
       STA ($30),Y
       LDA #$FF      ;TURN EXCHANGE FLAG ON (= -1)
       STA $32
CHKEND DEX           ;END OF LIST?
       BNE NXTEL     ;NO. FETCH NEXT ELEMENT
       BIT $32       ;YES. EXCHANGE FLAG STILL OFF?
```

```
        BMI SORT8      ;NO. GO THROUGH LIST AGAIN
        RTS            ;YES. LIST IS NOW ORDERED
```

And here's a bubble sort in C:

```
void BubbleSort(int numbers[], int array_size)
{
  int i, j, temp;
  for (i = (array_size - 1); i > 0; i--)
  {
    for (j = 1; j <= i; j++)
    {
      if (numbers[j-1] > numbers[j])
      {
        temp = numbers[j-1];
        numbers[j-1] = numbers[j];
        numbers[j] = temp;
      }
    }
  }
}
```

As you can see, assembly language is much more difficult to understand and parse than C. As technology marched forward and processors became faster and more efficient, it finally started to become feasible to write large parts of the game in C and leave assembly language for the performance-intensive stuff. Using C allowed developers to save huge amounts of development time.

As processor speeds and compilers continued to improve, C was eventually replaced by C++ in most game studios, although there is at least one studio I know of that still uses straight C. C++ has the power of C with all the cool object-oriented bits added on top. It's a great language for performance because it still sits pretty close to the hardware while offering relatively straightforward syntax. The semantics of many languages used today owe their roots to C and C++.

As great as C++ is, it still has many flaws and is really beginning to show its age. For example, you have to deal with memory management yourself. Every `new` must have a matching `delete`, which isn't the case in many higher-level languages. This can be a blessing or a curse, depending on the problem you're trying to solve. I can write a C++ program that only allocates memory once during the entire program. This would be impossible in many scripting languages.

With even faster computers and more complex games, the time was right to start looking into scripting languages.

## Scripting Languages

What is a scripting language? This may seem like a simple question, but the term "script" has become somewhat ambiguous as more complex programs are written in what are traditionally thought of as scripting languages. Simply put, a scripting language is a high-level programming language that is interpreted by another program at runtime. It is often embedded within a native application. If you think about it, this is a rather broad definition. Is C# a scripting language? It certainly meets the criteria. C# is compiled into byte-code that's interpreted at runtime by NET, yet most people don't consider it a scripting language.

For purposes of this chapter, I'm going to consider anything higher level than C++ that is embedded into the core game engine to be a scripting language. I'm sure the time will come when even C# and Python are considered archaic relics of the past, and programming is done entirely visually.

As far as I can tell, the first scripting language used in a game was the SCUMM engine by LucasArts. SCUMM stands for *Script Creation Utility for Maniac Mansion.* It was a custom language created during the development of *Maniac Mansion* to make it easy to create locations, dialogue, objects, puzzles, and other high-level gameplay constructs without having to the touch the 6502 Assembly code at all. This was an incredibly powerful tool that allowed them to iterate on gameplay incredibly quickly. In a talk at GDC in 2011, Ron Gilbert (one of the creators of the SCUMM system) recalled one particular sequence where the player could take a hamster, put it in the microwave, turn it on, and watch it explode. This was all done in just a few minutes with the power of the SCUMM system. If you were to do something like this in 6502 Assembly, it would take 10–20 times as long. This is the power of scripting and why you should absolutely use it for all of your high-level game logic.

# Using a Scripting Language

There are a number of benefits to using scripting languages for your gameplay, but there are also a lot of pitfalls that I see developers fall into over and over again. I've made a number of these mistakes myself, and I hope that you can learn from them.

## Rapid Prototyping

One of the coolest things about using a scripting language is the rapid prototyping. You can build complex interactions and systems extremely quickly and get them running in the game without a lot of effort (at least compared to C++). A great example is the delegate system used in the Event Manager. It took me a full Saturday to rewrite the event system using delegate functions, and that's not including the `FastDelegate` stuff, which was written by a third party. There's a lot of code there just to allow you to pass in an arbitrary function that matches a particular signature. In most scripting languages, such a system would be trivial. Functions are usually first-class objects, which means they are treated like any other variable. You can pass them around, assign them to other variables, and so on. An event system implemented purely in Python or Lua probably wouldn't take me more than an hour to write.

Another big advantage to scripts is that they can usually be reloaded at runtime. Scripts are loaded from the resource cache just like any other asset and interpreted at runtime. It's pretty easy to imagine a system that would let you change a script while the game was running and type a console command that would reload your script right there. You wouldn't even have to shut down the game! When I was developing the minigames in *Rat Race,* this is exactly what we did. It made iterating on those games extremely easy. I could play the minigame and fix issues as I found them and then reload the script and do it again.

**The Poster Child for Rapid Prototyping**

When I worked at Planet Moon, there was a programmer who was in charge of the camera system for *Drawn to Life.* He implemented the entire thing in Lua very quickly, moving the math functions to C++ as needed. This allowed him to iterate with the designers very quickly, often making changes and reloading the scripts while they were sitting right there. I think we went through a dozen different camera schemes, all very different from each other. When the design finally solidified, he moved most of it down to C++ for performance reasons. This is a great example of what rapid prototyping buys you. If he had started in C++, he wouldn't have been able to iterate nearly as quickly.

## Design Focused

An interesting side effect to scripting languages is that they tend to be a bit more designer friendly. At Planet Moon, we had special scripts that designers were allowed to modify. All of the AI on *Drawn to Life,* for instance, was configured through these designer-facing scripts. This is a very powerful concept. By giving your designers access to the scripting system, you give them the ability to prototype things in the game without having to involve you directly.

The nature of most scripting languages enables you to take this a step further and attach snippets of code to objects. For example, you could load up a creature and pass in an AI script. You could even expose the scripts to the end-users and allow them to mod your game. *World of Warcraft* does this with their HUD layout; with some simple Lua script and XML, you can write your own custom UI.

## Speed and Memory Costs

All of this power comes at a cost. Scripts are generally very slow when compared to C++, and they take up more memory, which is one of the main disadvantages to using a scripting language. When you load a script, the interpreter typically parses the actual text right then and there and then executes the instructions found within. Many languages give you a way to speed this up by allowing you to compile the script into a binary form as an offline process, but a script's execution is always going to be slower. Crossing the boundary between C++ and script is also very slow, especially if you're marshalling a large amount of data. For these reasons, you would never want to attempt to write a high performance graphics engine or physics engine using a scripting language; these systems are best saved for C++.

## Where's the Line?

One of the pitfalls I see a lot of developers make is trying to do too much in the scripting language. Scripting languages are extremely powerful, and it can be tempting to try to write huge, complex systems entirely in script. In the end, I've found that this doesn't really buy you anything. By their very nature, scripts tend to be more difficult to maintain than a language like C++. For example, take a look at the process system you saw in Chapter 7, "Controlling the Main Loop." It would have been possible to implement that entire system in Lua or Python much faster than C++, but this is the kind of system that can potentially do a lot of work every single frame. Furthermore, once it's built, it's pretty unlikely that you'll need to iterate on it. You don't lose very much by having it in C++, and you gain a considerable amount of performance. You could certainly prototype it in script, but this is the kind of system that you'd eventually want to move out to C++.

As a counter example, let's suppose you want to make an RPG similar to *Dragon Age* or *Skyrim*. You decide that you'll need a quest system that can manage what quests the player is on, the state of each quest, all the flags and items associated with them, etc. This entire quest system can and should be implemented completely in script. This is the kind of thing that you will be constantly iterating on and will want to have the ability to tweak on the fly. It's also not a system that needs to be constantly updating every frame because it will most likely just respond to events or potentially timers, so the performance gain of having this type of system in C++ doesn't really buy you anything.

So where's the line between systems that should live in the script and systems that should live in C++? The answer to this really depends on who you ask. I know developers who think only truly time-critical things should ever be in C++, and everything else should be in script. I also know developers who think script should be more for defining data, like you might use in XML. I personally tend to fall somewhere in the middle. I think that large systems that tend to remain relatively static and time-critical code should be in C++, while volatile code or code that's not time-critical should be in the script. No matter what, it's always a judgment call. We had to move all of the AI processing for *Drawn to Life* out to C++ because it was taking too long to process.

## Scripting Language Integration Strategies

Scripting languages come in all shapes and sizes, each with its own strengths and weaknesses that complement the things I've already mentioned. When choosing a scripting language, there are two general strategies you can follow. You can either write your own, or you can integrate an existing language.

### Writing Your Own

In the early days of scripting languages, writing your own was really the only viable choice, as other high-level languages either weren't available or weren't up to the task. Most early scripting languages were very specific to the engine they were developed for. Examples of such languages include SCUMM, used by many of the LucasArts adventure titles, SCI, used by Sierra On-Line for many of their early point-and-click adventure games, and UNK and AGIL for the *Ultima* games at Origin Systems, QuakeC, and UnrealScript.

The real advantage to creating a custom scripting language is that engine-specific constructs can be integrated directly into the language. With an existing general-purpose language, you must write all these layers yourself. You can also cut out all the things you don't need that many languages include directly.

Writing your own scripting language is an incredibly daunting task. If you choose to walk down this path, expect to spend the first year or so just getting the language up and running, assuming you're targeting a high level of polish. The first year of development for *Maniac Mansion* was just getting the SCUMM language up and running.

There are entire books dedicated to writing your own programming language. You have to write an interpreter that can read a source file, decompose it into its core structure, and then process that structure to actually execute the instructions. Doing this is far beyond the scope of this book, but if you're interested in it, you should check out LEX and YACC. They can give a leg up in your endeavor. Good luck.

### Using an Existing Language

Using an existing scripting language is relatively common these days. In fact, the Lua programming language was designed from the ground up to be embedded within a native application.

There are a number of advantages to using an existing language—the most important being the incredible amount of time you'll save. I integrated Lua into this engine in about a day, with another day for writing some glue code and a bunch of testing. In a professional game, it might take 10 times as long, but if you compare that to the numbers above for writing your own, the savings are obvious.

Another advantage is the huge amount of testing already done. You know that Python's `if` statement and `for` loops work, and you can be pretty sure that their data structures are relatively optimized. The same will never be said about your own scripting language. The reason is sheer numbers; there are thousands upon thousands of people using Python and Lua every day, so the developers have had a lot of users flushing out all the bugs. Your language will have considerably fewer users. On top of that, there are a number of resources already available for existing languages. Do you need a very fast math module for Lua? You can probably find one with a bit of searching. There are thousands of people who can tell you how to call a function in Lua. By contrast, there are maybe half a dozen people in this world who could tell you how to call a function in the custom Action System scripting language we made at Super-Ego Games.

One disadvantage of using an existing scripting language is that you're locked into their environment model. It's typically harder to control things like memory allocation, garbage collection, memory footprint, execution overhead, and so on. In a custom scripting language, you have complete control over all of those things.

Unless you have a really good reason not to do so, I strongly recommend using an existing language instead of creating your own. The advantages almost always outweigh the disadvantages. This is the method I have chosen for this book.

## Choosing a Scripting Language

The two most common general-purpose scripting languages used in game development are Python and Lua. UnrealScript is also fairly common, but only because the Unreal engine itself is fairly common. C# is a relatively new contender with XNA and Unity3D entrenching themselves on the scene. They tend to be used more in independent games rather than professional games, but that's been changing. C# was used on *The Sims 3* as well as *The Sims Medieval* for scripting.

## Python

Python is a very popular scripting language with a huge support community. It is fully object-oriented and has tons of tools and support. Here's some sample Python code:

```
# This is a comment in python
def process_actors(actors):
```

```
  for actor in actors:
    if actor.is_alive():
      actor.process()
```

The syntax is easy to follow for the most part, although Python does have certain constructs that throw new users for a loop, like list comprehensions:

```
pruned_list = [x for x in actors if x.is_alive()]
```

This will generate a list of living actors and will run very fast (the bulk of it actually runs in C). Another odd thing with Python that some users (including me) dislike is that Python uses whitespace to determine scope. When you indent in Python, you are creating a scope, and when you unindent, you step out of that scope. For an old crusty C++ programmer like me, it can be tough to get used to. I wonder if that's how old assembly language programmers felt about the `goto` statement.

Overall, Python is a great language with a rich feature set. It's been used on a number of professional games, including *Eve Online*, *Star Trek Bridge Commander*, and the later games in the Civilization series. We used it at Slipgate for our core gameplay language.

## Lua

As I said earlier, Lua is another popular scripting language that was designed from the ground up to be an embedded language for use with native applications. It's fast, small, and an overall great language. Here's some sample Lua code:

```
-- This is a comment in Lua
function process_actors(actors)
  for index, actor in ipairs(actors) do
    if actor:is_alive() then
      actor.process()
    end
  end
end
```

As you can see, the syntax is relatively simple. It's a bit more verbose than a compact language like Python, which tends to bother some people. Lua is also much more bare bones than Python.

The language itself has a number of very simple features and a rather sparse series of optional libraries for math, IO, etc. Many people see this as an advantage to Lua. Most of the code you write with your scripting language will be game or engine specific. It's rare that you'll need a network socket API or even file IO, especially since those things can easily be exposed from the engine. A lack of these libraries means that Lua runs in a much smaller memory space than other languages like Python. This makes it a viable language even for console games. We successfully used Lua on *Drawn to Life* for the Wii and even on *Wedding Dash* for the iPhone.

It is the simplicity and elegance of the language that won me over several years ago when I started working with it. For these reasons and more, Lua is the language I have chosen for this book.

## A Crash Course in Lua

Before I get into the details of how to integrate Lua into the game, I'd like to give you a crash course in the language itself. This is by no means a complete language reference, but we'll explore the core language features.

### Comments

Lua comments begin with two dashes:

```
-- This is a comment
```

There is also a block comment for commenting out across multiple lines. It uses double square brackets, like this:

```
--[[
This is a single comment
that takes multiple lines.
--]]
```

As with any programming language, commenting your code is extremely important. Since Lua is dynamically typed, it's often hard to tell what an object is just by looking at the code.

### Variables

Lua is a dynamically typed language. That means that a variable can change its type just by assigning something new to it:

```
x = 3     -- x is an integer
x = 3.14  -- now it's a float
x = "PI"  -- now it's a string
```

Unlike C, variables aren't declared until they are used. In the above code, `x` doesn't exist until the first line. The second line overwrites the contents of the variable, as does the third line. There are eight basic types that Lua recognizes: `number`, `string`, `Boolean`, `table`, `function`, `nil`, `userdata`, and `thread` (more on these later).

The `nil` type is a special type that is equivalent in concept to C++'s `NULL` value, although it behaves a bit differently. Any name that has never been used before is considered to have a value of `nil`. This is also how you can delete objects from Lua.

```
print(type(y))  -- this will print "nil"
y = 20
print(type(y))  -- this will print "number"
y = nil  -- This effectively deletes y, causing the memory to be marked
      -- for garbage collection
```

### Attempting to Use a nil Value

C++'s `NULL` and Lua's `nil` are conceptually the same, but they behave very differently. Most C++ compilers define NULL as 0. In Lua, `nil` has no value, it only has a type. Be careful attempting to use `nil` as a valid value.

Like most other programming languages, variables in Lua have scope. Unlike most other programming languages, the default scope for Lua variables is global. That means that even if you declare a variable inside of a function or `if` statement, it is still considered a global variable. In order to make a variable local, you must explicitly use the `local` keyword:

```
local x = 10  -- this is a local variable
```

### Variable Scoping in Lua

These scoping issues can really bite you if you're not careful. You should always declare a variable as local unless there is a real reason not to; otherwise, you will find yourself with hard-to-fix bugs.

### Variable Naming Conventions

Lua is a dynamically typed language, which means that it's not always clear what type a variable is intended to be. If you see a variable named `position`, what do you think it is? Maybe it's a 3D vector or a matrix or even a custom table. It's impossible to know without running the code and inspecting the value. For these types of ambiguous variables, it's often a good idea to bake the type into the name. For example, the above variable could be named `positionVec3` or `positionMat` instead. This will save you a lot more time than you might think.

## Functions

Functions are self-contained chunks of execution, much like they are in C or C++. One big difference is that functions are also first-class objects in Lua, which means they are treated like any other variable. You can assign them to other variables, pass them as parameters to other functions, and so on.

Functions are declared using the `function` keyword, followed by the function name. Parentheses are used to enclose any variables the function expects. Functions can return anything or nothing at all. They can return multiple values as well. If a function doesn't explicitly return, it returns `nil` by default. If you call a function without enough parameters, the extra parameters will all be `nil`. If you call a function with too many parameters, the extra parameters passed in are ignored.

Here's a simple function:

```
function Square(val)
  return val * val
end
```

This function returns the square of the number you pass in. In reality, what this statement is really doing is creating a function and assigning a pointer to that function to a variable called `Square`. You call the function like you would call a function in C.

```
x = Square(5)
print(x) --> prints 25
```

Since `Square` is really just a variable pointing to a function, you can treat it like any other variable.

```
x = Square  -- no parentheses; x is now pointing to the same function
print(type(x)) --> prints "function"
Square = x(5)
print(Square) --> prints 25
```

In fact, the syntax you've seen thus far for writing functions is just syntax sugar to make it a bit more readable. The more explicit way a function is defined is as follows:

```
Square = function(val) return val * val end
```

As far as the Lua interpreter is concerned, there's no difference between the two. The first form is a bit more readable, but the second form can be handy when assigning functions to a table or generating anonymous functions as parameters to other functions.

You can overwrite any function (including any Lua system function) by simply assigning a new version of that function to the variable. For example, the following code overwrites the `print()` function to add "[Lua] " in front of every `print()` statement.

```
oldprint = print;  -- save the old version of print
print = function(string)
  local newString = "[Lua] " .. string
  oldprint(newString)
end
```

This is a very important property of functions, as you will see later on in this chapter.

**Save Old Functions**

If you choose to overwrite existing Lua library functions, it's a good practice to save the old one in a global variable somewhere. If you don't, you won't have any way to call upon the original behavior.

As I said before, functions can return multiple values. These values are separated with a comma:

```
function MultiReturn()
  return 2, 4
end
x, y = MultiReturn();  -- x will contain 2 and y will contain 4
```

## Tables

Tables are Lua's basic (and only) data structure. They are arrays and generic dictionaries all in one. Here's a simple table:

```
prime = { 2, 3, 5, 7, 11 }
```

This statement declares a table with the first five prime numbers. A table is created through the use of curly braces, which will actually instantiate a table object under the covers. You can access the table using square brackets, just like in C.

```
print(prime[2])  -- > prints out 3
```

**Lua Tables Are 1-Indexed!**

If you're paying attention, you might think there's a typo in the above code sample. Surely `prime[2]` should point to 5, right? Not in Lua! Lua is 1-indexed, meaning that all arrays start at the index of 1, as opposed to C++, which is 0-indexed. I guarantee that this rather unfortunate decision by the developers of Lua will cause bugs in your code. This becomes especially messy when you pass array indexes between C++ and Lua.

It's important to note that in the above example, `prime` is just a reference to the real table object. If you assign `prime` to another variable, Lua does a simple pointer copy, and both variables will contain references to the same table.

```
prime = { 2, 3, 5, 7, 11 } -- the original table
prime2 = prime -- this is just a simple pointer copy
print(prime, prime2) --> this prints out "table: 02D76278 table: 02D76278"
prime2[1] = 10
print(prime[1]) --> prints out "10"
```

Tables don't have to be indexed using a number, that's just the default. You can index tables using anything, including numbers, strings, other tables, functions, or anything else you want.

```
messyTable = {} -- an empty table

-- index by string
messyTable["string"] = 20
messyTable["another string"] = "data" -- the data doesn't have to
                                      -- be consistent either

-- index by table
anotherTable = {}
messyTable[anotherTable] = 5

-- index by function
Function X() end
messyTable[X] = anotherTable -- this time the data is another table
```

As you can see, tables have the ability to get very messy. In practice, you probably wouldn't have a table that was so inconsistent with its keys and data. One interesting property of Lua tables is that they treat integer-indexed items separately from everything else. Under the covers, tables actually have two sections. One section behaves like a resizable array and the other like a map. As the programmer, you rarely have to worry about the differences between these. When you create a table like the `prime` table above, you are using the array section. When you create one like `messyTable`, you are using the map section. This is done mostly for optimization reasons, as Lua uses a true array for the array section and a hash map for everything else. This typically only comes into play when you want to loop through all the elements of a table, which you'll see below. Note that all tables have these sections, so there's nothing stopping you from using both in a single table.

In the first example, a table was initialized with the first five prime numbers. You can also initialize tables that use non-integer keys by wrapping the key in square brackets and using the assignment operator. The messy table above could be created like this, assuming that `anotherTable` and `X` were already defined:

```
messyTable = { ["string"] = 20, ["another string"] = "data",
               [anotherTable] = 5, [X] = anotherTable }
```

You can actually do both:

```
temp = { ["hat"] = "blue", 5, "purple", ["ninja"] = 3 }
```

This is equivalent to:

```
temp = {}
temp["hat"] = "blue"
temp[1] = 5
temp[2] = "purple"
temp["ninja"] = 3
```

Indexing a table by string is so common that Lua provides a bit of syntax sugar to make it a little cleaner. First, you don't have to surround string keys with square brackets or quotes when initializing the table. Second, you can access the value by using the "." operator with no quotes. These two tables are identical, and the two print statements show two different ways to access them:

```
v1 = { ["x"] = 13.5, ["y"] = 1, ["z"] = 15.4 }
v2 = { x = 13.5, y = 1, z = 15.4 }
print(v1["x"])  -- > prints 13.5
print(v1.x)  - > prints 13.5
v1.y = 3  -- you can set values using the '.' operator as well
```

Lua provides a special table named "table" that contains a number of helper functions for table manipulation. I'm not going to go into detail on these functions, since you can look them up pretty easily, but here's the one-line description for each:

- `insert()`: Inserts elements into the table.
- `remove()`: Removes elements from the table.
- `getn()`: Returns the number of elements in the array section of the table (not including the map section).

- `setn()`: Sets the number of elements in the array section of the table (not the map section). This is useful to allow `nil` to exist in a table.
- `maxn()`: Returns the highest positive numerical index of the table by doing a O(n) search.
- `sort()`: Sorts the array portion of the table.
- `concat()`: Joins the elements of a table together to form a string.

Tables are extremely powerful, especially when you factor in the idea that everything in Lua is a first-class object, including functions. You can create tables that contain data and functions indexed by strings using the "." operator. At that point, it starts looking like a real object-oriented language. Once you add in metatables, you have everything you need to create a fully object-oriented system very easily. I'll revisit this concept later on in the chapter after I show you more of the basic operations in Lua.

## Flow Control

Lua supports a number of control structures that are common in most programming languages, like `if`, `while`, and `for`.

### `if`

The structure of an `if` statement looks like this:

```
if exp then
  -- do something
end
```

Unlike C, Lua doesn't use curly braces for scoping blocks of code. In this case, it uses the `then` keyword to define the beginning of the block and the `end` keyword to end it. You can also have `else` and `elseif` statements, which work like they do in C:

```
if exp then
  -- do something
elseif exp2 then  -- note that elseif is all one word
  -- do something else
else
  -- otherwise, do this other thing
end  -- note how end will end the whole chain and is omitted above
```

### `while`

`while` loops work much like they do in C. Here's the basic form:

```
i = 5
while i > 0 do
```

```
  print(i)
  i = i - 1
end
```

There's nothing fancy here. As with `if` statements, there are no curly braces. The loop block is between the `do` and `end` keywords.

### for

Lua has two flavors of `for` loop. The first is the numeric form, which is very similar to what you'd find in C. The second is the generic form, which is a handy shorter form typically used for tables. The numeric form looks like this:

```
for i = 1, 10, 1 do
  -- do stuff here
end
```

As with the `while` loop, the `do` and `end` keywords define where the inner scope of this loop is. The first part of the `for` declaration sets a local variable to the value of 1. (Note that the `local` keyword is not required in this specific case; `for` loop counter variables are always local.) The second part of the declaration is the limit and will cause the loop to exit once it's reached. The third part of the declaration is the step, which adds that value to the variable. If you omit the third statement entirely, Lua will assume you want to increment the variable by 1, so this part is unnecessary unless you want something else. This loop will do exactly the same thing:

```
for i = 1, 10 do
  -- do stuff here
end
```

Note that Lua evaluates the limit inclusively. In other words, it checks to see if `i` is less than or equal to the value. The above loop will execute 10 times.

The generic form of the `for` loop works using iterator functions. On each iteration, the function is called to produce a new value and breaks out when the function returns `nil`.

```
prime = { 2, 3, 5, 7, 11 }  -- the first five prime numbers
for index, value in ipairs(prime) do
  print(index, value)
end
```

This chunk will loop through the `prime` table and print out the index and value for each element in the table. The `ipairs()` function is a built-in Lua iterator function that returns the next index/value pair until the end of the table is reached. Note that this function only works for the array portion of the table. If you need to see the hash table portion, you have to use the `pairs()` function. This will loop through the entire table.

```
test = { x = 5, y = 10, z = 15, 20, 25 }

-- This block will print out:
-- 1  20
-- 2  25
for index, value in ipairs(test) do
  print(index, value)
end

-- This block will print out:
-- 1  20
-- 2  25
-- y  10
-- x  5
-- z  15
for key, value in pairs(test) do
  print(key, value)
end
```

Did you notice the odd ordering in the second version of the loop? The reason is because the non-array part of the table is a hash map, so the ordering is not defined. You get similar behavior looping through an STL map. Use `ipairs()` to loop over the array part of the table and use `pairs()` to loop over everything in the table.

## Operators

Lua supports a number of operators like you'd expect in any language. For basic mathematics, it supports addition (+), subtraction (–), multiplication (*), division (/), modulo (%), exponentiation (^), and unary negation (-). These all work like the ones in C++, except for the exponentiation operator, which C++ doesn't have. This operator takes the value on the left and raises to the power of the value on the right. For example:

```
x = 2 ^ 4  -- x = 16, or 2-to-the-4th power.
```

You may notice a few missing operators here. Lua doesn't support increment (++) or decrement (--) operators, nor does it support the combo assignment operators that also perform a mathematical operation (+=, -=, *=, etc.).

Lua's relational operators are also rather similar to C++. It has equality (==), inequality (~=), less-than (<), greater-than (>), less-than or equal-to (<=), and greater-than or equal-to (>=). Note that the inequality operator is not the typical one you may be used to. They all work like you would expect from other languages.

Lua provides three logical operators: and, or, and not. They are analogous to C++'s logical and (&&), or (||) and not (!) operators and generally behave like you would expect them to.

One very handy operator Lua provides is the string concatenation operator (..). This concatenates two strings and returns the results, like so:

```
x = "the brown " .. "dog went home. "
print(x) --> prints "the brown dog went home. "

-- It works on numbers as well
y = 10
print(x .. y) --> prints "the brown dog went home. 10"
```

## What's Next?

The goal of this section was to familiarize you with basic Lua syntax. As I said previously, this is nowhere near the full breadth of the language, and I strongly urge you to check out some resources online. I've provided a few helpful links at the end of this chapter that should help. If there were some things you didn't quite understand, now would be a good time to go reread those sections or check out online samples. The rest of this chapter talks about some pretty advanced stuff and from this point on, I'll assume you are relatively comfortable with the basics of Lua programming.

# Object-Oriented Programming in Lua

Lua doesn't have any direct support for object-oriented programming, although it's possible to plug it in using tables. Tables give you a way to group data together and map chunks of data to names (string keys). Since functions are really just another form of data, you can easily group them all together to create encapsulation. Let's start by attempting to make a vector object in Lua.

```
-- Note how the table is defined across multiple lines, just like you might do
-- for a C array or parameter list.  Lua doesn't care.  This is much more
-- readable for our purposes.
vector =
{
  -- This is the vector data
  x = 0, y = 0, z = 0,

  -- Here's the first attempt at a Length() function.  Note the use of the
  -- math table for math.sqrt().  This works exactly like the table functions
  -- you saw above.
```

```
  Length = function(vec)
    return math.sqrt((vec.x * vec.x) + (vec.y * vec.y) + (vec.z * vec.z));
  end
}
```

This technically works:

```
vector.x = 10
vector.y = 20
vector.z = 15
print(vector.Length(vector))  --> prints 26.92582321167
```

There are several things wrong with this object. One glaring issue is that the `Length()` function requires the table it is on as a parameter. This idea isn't completely unreasonable from a technical point of view; after all, C++ passes the `this` pointer as a hidden first parameter to all member functions. Fortunately, Lua offers this same functionality. By replacing the "." with a ":", Lua passes in the table as the first parameter and calls it `self`.

```
print(vector:Length())  --> prints 26.92582321167
```

This works when defining the function, too:

```
vector =
{
  x = 0, y = 0, z = 0
}

-- Note the lack of parameter; since the colon operator is used, self
-- is implied.
function vector:Length()
  return math.sqrt((self.x * self.x) + (self.y * self.y) + (self.z * self.z));
end
```

As you can see, the function is defined using the colon operator. This implies a first parameter called `self`, which is implicitly passed in when function is called with the colon operator. Note that the colon operator is just syntax sugar, because it doesn't actually change anything except to supply that hidden first parameter. It's perfectly valid to define a function using the colon operator and call it by explicitly passing the table or vice versa. Another side effect of using the colon operator is the need to declare the function outside the table. This is the preferred method for assigning functions to tables.

Now we have a vector object that has what appears to be a member function on it. This is nice, but it doesn't get us what we really want. We need a way to define classes of data and functionality that we can then instantiate objects from. We need a way to write a class.

## Metatables

One of the most powerful concepts of Lua is its ability to modify the behavior of tables. For example, it is typically illegal to attempt to add two tables together. Using metatables, you could define behavior where this is valid.

A metatable is just another table. There's nothing particularly special about it. Any table may be the metatable for any other table. Metatables may have metatables themselves, and multiple tables can have the same metatable that defines a set of common behaviors. A table can even be its own metatable! By default, tables have no metatable.

Metatables are use by Lua when it encounters certain situations. For example, when Lua attempts to add two tables, it first checks to see if either table has a metatable. If so, it checks to see if one of them defines a variable named `__add`. It then calls this variable (which should be a function). The `__add` field is a *metamethod*, which is a predefined field that Lua looks for in that situation. There are many such metamethods, several of which you'll see below.

You can get and set the metatable of a table with `getmetatable()` and `setmetatable()`.

```
x = {} -- empty table
print(getmetatable(x)) -- > nil; tables don't have metatables by default
y = {}
setmetatable(x, y) -- y is now the metatable for x

-- This block will print "Success"
if getmetatable(x) == y then
  print("Success")
else
  print("Fail")
end
```

In order to be useful, you need to set metamethod fields on the metatable. The metamethod we're interested in is `__index`, which is used when Lua can't find a field you are attempting to read. For example, say you have the following code:

```
x = {}
print(x.y)
```

The output of the `print` statement will be `nil`. What's really happening is that Lua looks at the `x` table and checks to see if it has a field called `y`. If it does, it returns this. If not, it checks to see if the table has a metatable. If it does, it checks to see if that metatable has the `__index` metamethod and, if it does, calls it, returning the result as the value for `y`. If the `__index` field is another table, Lua attempts the same access on it. It checks the new table for a field called `y`, followed by a metatable, and so on until it either finds a valid value or can't find anything valid, in which case it returns `nil`.

It's important to note that this only affects the reading of a value, not the writing of one. There's a separate metamethod, `__newvalue`, that's invoked when attempting to write a new value. This is invoked first, before writing the value, to allow you to change how the table deals with new values. This could be used to implement a read-only table, for example.

For our vector example, we want to create a template of functionality. We do this by creating the vector table just as before. This will be our class. To instantiate an object from this class, a new table is created with a metatable that has an `__index` field pointing to the vector class. Here's the new version with an example:

```
-- Renaming this table to make it look more like a class
Vec3 =
{
  -- These values now represent defaults
  x = 0, y = 0, z = 0
}

-- This function is unchanged
function Vec3:Length()
  return math.sqrt((self.x * self.x) + (self.y * self.y) + (self.z * self.z));
end

-- Create an instance of this class. v is initialized with an __index
-- field set to the Vec3 table.

v = { __index = Vec3 }
setmetatable(v, v)  -- v is now its own metatable

-- This will cause Lua to search v for the x field. It won't find it, so
-- Lua will check for a metatable. It will find out that v is the metatable
-- for v, so it will look for an __index field. It will find one that points
-- to the Vec3 table. Lua will then search Vec3 for an x field, which it finds
-- and returns. The below line will print 0.
print(v.x)

-- This assignment will cause Lua to search v for a metatable, which is has.
-- It will then search for a __newindex field, which doesn't exist. Lua will
-- set the value of v.x to 10 without affecting the Vec3 table.
v.x = 10

-- This will cause Lua to search v for the x field, which it finds and returns.
-- It will print 10.
print(v.x)
```

Now we have a very simple 3D vector class! You can extend this class with more metamethods for addition, multiplication, etc. Check out Assets/Scripts/PreInit.lua in the *Teapot Wars* code base for the complete `Vec3` listing, including a number of these metamethods defined.

Incidentally, inheritance works exactly the same way. If you want `Vec3` to inherit from something, simply set up a metatable and point the `__index` field to the base class. Lua doesn't distinguish between classes and objects; they're all just tables, which may or may not have metatables.

It's worth noting that metatables are very similar to C++ virtual tables, which are the tables used by C++ to store virtual functions. When you call a virtual function, C++ looks it up in the virtual table to find the actual implementation. Lua metatables with the `__index` field behave much the same way. With all the other meta fields available to Lua, it makes the language itself extremely flexible.

## Creating a Simple Class Abstraction

As you can see, with a little legwork, Lua fully supports object-oriented programming techniques. There's still one thing missing. The `Vec3` class will work very well, but it's still not as easy as defining a class in C++, C#, Python, or any other truly object-oriented language. Our ultimate goal is something like this:

```
class SomeClass : public BaseClass {};
```

What we really need is to abstract away all the metatable stuff into a function you can call that generates the class table and allows you to instantiate objects from it.

```
function class(baseClass, body)
  local ret = body or {};

  -- if there's a base class, attach our new class to it
  if (baseClass ~= nil) then
    setmetatable(ret, ret);
    ret.__index = baseClass;
  end

  -- Add the Create() function
  ret.Create = function(self, constructionData, originalSubClass)
    local obj;
    if (self.__index ~= nil) then
      if (originalSubClass ~= nil) then
        obj = self.__index:Create(constructionData, originalSubClass);
      else
        obj = self.__index:Create(constructionData, self);
      end
```

```
    else
      obj = constructionData or {};
    end

    setmetatable(obj, obj);
    obj.__index = self;

    -- copy any operators over
    if (self.__operators ~= nil) then
      for key, val in pairs(self.__operators) do
        obj[key] = val;
      end
    end

    return obj;
  end

  return ret;
end
```

This is probably one of the most complex Lua functions you've seen so far, so let's walk through it step by step. The function takes two parameters. The `baseClass` parameter is the base class for this class. It is expected to be a table that also creates with the `class()` function. If this class has no base class, you must explicitly pass in `nil`. The `body` parameter is the body of the class. It is expected to be a table where all of the member variables live.

The first line of the function creates the return value `ret` as a local variable that is initialized to either the body table (if there is one) or an empty table. This variable will be the class table itself, much like `Vec3` was earlier. If a base class is passed in, `ret` will be set up as its own metatable with the `__index` field pointing to the base class. This sets up the inheritance hierarchy.

The next section defines and creates the `Create()` member function, which is used to instantiate objects from this class. Since the class table is generated by the function, this function needs to be defined inline like this.

The `Create()` function takes in three parameters. The first parameter is `self`, which is the class table we're instantiating the object from. This is passed in automatically by using the colon operator when calling it. Since this function is being defined with the assignment operator, this parameter needs to be explicitly put here. The second parameter is `constructionData`, which is a table that can be sent in as extra data. Think of it like a constructor: any extra data that's sent in will be added to the instance data, overriding any values from the class. The third parameter, `originalSubClass`, is a special parameter used for recursion. It must be `nil`. This parameter is used internally in some cases when accessing the leaf table is necessary. It's currently used by the ScriptProcess class in C++, which you'll see later in this chapter.

The first thing the Create() function does is declare a local variable called obj. This will be the instance table of the class. The next section will recursively call into the Create() function of each base class in the inheritance chain, passing in the construction data and the original leaf class (which is self the first time). When it finally reaches the top base class, obj is initialized with either the constructionData table or an empty table if there is no construction data. After that, the metatable is set up, and any overloaded operators defined in a special __operators table are copied over. Finally, the object is returned.

Using the class() function is a breeze. Here's how you would define the Vec3 class above:

```
Vec3 = class(nil,
{
  x = 0, y = 0, z = 0
})

function Vec3:Length()
  return math.sqrt((self.x * self.x) + (self.y * self.y) + (self.z * self.z));
end

-- Create an instance of this class
V = Vec3:Create()

-- This version initializes the values
V2 = Vec3:Create({x = 10, y = 10, z = 10})
```

It doesn't get much easier than that! Later in this chapter, I'll even show you how you can inherit from C++ classes.

**Public/Private Variable Naming Conventions**

One thing you can't easily get in Lua is a way to represent public, private, and protected variables. A typical convention in many scripting languages is to put an underscore in front of variable and function names that are meant to be private, so seeing _var would let the programmer know that this variable is meant to be private. Similarly, a function named _Update() would be a private function. It's good to have this kind of convention, or it quickly becomes confusing what the public interface is. Refactoring can be a nightmare.

## Memory Management

Like most scripting languages, Lua uses automatic memory management and garbage collection. This works very much like TR1's `shared_ptr` construct. Every variable you create is reference counted, and when all references go away, the object is marked for garbage collection. Lua periodically runs a garbage collection cycle where it walks through the garbage list and frees up memory. You don't have to do this manually; it's done automatically by Lua. If you do want to force a garbage collection cycle, you can call the `collectgarbage()` function.

**Global Variables Are Here to Stay**

Global variables are never garbage collected until the program shuts down. They can be accessed by any part of the program at any time, so Lua has no way of knowing when you don't need them anymore. When you're done with a global variable, it's good to assign `nil` to it. Assuming there are no other references, this will cause Lua to mark it as collectable.

## Binding Lua to C++

Hopefully by now you have a pretty good understanding of Lua and how it works. The remainder of this chapter will build upon this foundation and create a working relationship between Lua script and the C++ engine we've been creating throughout this entire book. First, we'll look at some integration strategies and third-party libraries to make the process of embedding Lua into the C++ engine easier. Then we'll go over some of the glue to get Lua to play nicely with the Process Manager and event system. Finally, I'll bring it all together with a couple of examples.

### The Lua C API

As I said earlier in this chapter, Lua was built from the ground up to be integrated into an existing system. (Its original intent was to be an embedded configuration language.) To facilitate this, there is a core C API for integrating Lua into your codebase. Unfortunately, this API is rather lacking in terms of usability. You have to manually deal with the Lua stack and language internals. Binding C functions to the Lua API is not particularly easy, and calling Lua functions from C is equally difficult. Good luck trying to bind a C++ class or function!

With a bit of work, you can get the Lua C API to function in your programs, but it's certainly not ideal. There are a large number of binding libraries that make this job a lot easier. They are typically built on top of the core C API, although that's not always the case.

## tolua++

This library attempts to solve the problem of registering functions and classes to Lua so they can be used in script. First, you go into your C++ code and tag the things you want to expose with special comments. When you build your game, you run a simple pre-process that scans your source tree and generates the binding C file that exports these functions and classes for Lua. When your program compiles, these are all visible to Lua. We used this at Super-Ego Games very successfully.

The advantage of this system is that it's trivial to export any function or class to the script. You literally just tag the line with a `// tolua_export` comment, and the pre-process does the rest. There are a few disadvantages, though. One of the biggest disadvantages is that tolua++ is a one-way street. It's not easy to call a Lua function from within C++ code and read a Lua-specific data structure like a table. You can return simple types like numbers and strings, but tables are much more difficult to work with.

## luabind

luabind solves a lot of the problems of two-way communication that tolua++ has by wrapping a lot of the Lua C API functionality into classes. You can grab any Lua variable, read it, iterate across its elements if it's a table, call it if it's a function, and so on. You can expose C++ class, functions, and other objects to Lua, going back and forth relatively easily. Overall, it's a great system.

One big disadvantage of luabind is its reliance on boost, which includes a lot of overhead. Some people don't mind this much, but for others it's a deal breaker.

## LuaPlus

LuaPlus was created by Josh Jensen and has a lot of the same core functionality as luabind, but it has absolutely no reliance on other libraries. It tends to run faster and adds wide-string support to the core Lua library. Many of the same class and function binding capabilities exist in LuaPlus as well. For these reasons, it is the binding system I have chosen for this book.

LuaPlus does have a few disadvantages. First, it modifies the core Lua implementation. This is done for performance reasons and to add wide-string support. For some people, modifying the core library is a deal breaker. Another slight flaw when compared to luabind is that LuaPlus doesn't include all of the same functionality, although LuaPlus has more than enough for most purposes.

## A Crash Course in LuaPlus

Unfortunately, I don't have the page count to go in-depth into LuaPlus. This will be a whirlwind tour of what it has to offer. Hang on!

### LuaState

Everything in Lua begins with the Lua state. The Lua state represents an execution environment for Lua. You can have as many states as you want; each will be totally separate with its own set of global variables, functions, etc. There are many reasons you might want multiple states. One example might be allowing each C++ thread to have its own state. For the purposes of this book, we only create a single state for the program.

In the Lua C API, the `lua_State struct` contains all the data necessary to access the state. Nearly all Lua functions require the `lua_State` object as their first parameter. This looks suspiciously like C trying to act like C++, doesn't it? LuaPlus removes this entirely and wraps the whole thing in a single C++ class called `LuaState`.

To create a `LuaState` object, call the static `Create()` function. Call `Destroy()` to destroy it. Do *not* use `new` or `delete` on these objects.

```
// All LuaPlus objects are under this namespace. I will omit it from future
// code listings.
using namespace LuaPlus;

// This is called during the initialization of your application.
LuaState* pLuaState = LuaState::Create();

// This is done during the destruction of your application.
LuaState::Destroy(pLuaState);
pLuaState = NULL;
```

`LuaState` has a number of very useful functions for accessing the Lua execution unit as a whole. Two key functions are `DoString()` and `DoFile()`, both of which take a string as an argument. `DoString()` will parse and execute an arbitrary string as Lua code. `DoFile()` will open, parse, and execute a file.

```
pLuaState->DoFile("test.lua");  // execute the test.lua file
pLuaState->DoString("x = {}");  // after this line, there will be a new global
                                // variable called x, which is an empty table.
```

### LuaObject

The `LuaObject` class represents a single Lua variable. This can be a number, string, table, function, `nil`, or any other object Lua supports. This is the main interface for dealing with Lua variables. Note that a `LuaObject` is considered a strong reference to the underlying data. In other words, you don't have to worry about the Lua garbage collector coming to clean up the object out from under you, even if all the references in Lua go away. On the flip side, make sure you get rid of any references to `LuaObject` variables that you want Lua to garbage collect.

You can check the type of an object by using the `Type()` function, which returns a value from the `Types enum` in `LuaState`. There are also a number of `Is*()` functions:

- `bool IsNil()`
- `bool IsTable()`
- `bool IsUserData()`
- `bool IsCFunction()`
- `bool IsNumber()`
- `bool IsString()`
- `bool IsWString()`
- `bool IsConvertibleToNumber()`
- `bool IsConvertibleToString()`
- `bool IsConvertibleToWString()`
- `bool IsFunction()`
- `bool IsNone()`
- `bool IsLightUserData()`
- `bool IsBoolean()`

These functions return `true` if the variable type matches. To retrieve a value, call one of the `Get*()` functions:

- `int GetInteger()`
- `float GetFloat()`
- `double GetDouble()`
- `const char* GetString()`
- `const wchar_t* GetWString()`
- `void* GetUserData()`
- `void* GetLightUserData()`
- `bool GetBoolean()`

To assign a value to a value to a LuaObject, use the Assign*() functions:

- void AssignNil(LuaState* state)
- void AssignBoolean(LuaState* state, bool value)
- void AssignInteger(LuaState* state, int value)
- void AssignNumber(LuaState* state, double value)
- void AssignString(LuaState* state, const char* value)
- void AssignWString(LuaState* state, const wchar_t* value)
- void AssignUserData(LuaState* state, void* value)
- void AssignLightUserData(LuaState* state, void* value)
- void AssignObject(LuaState* state, LuaObject& value)
- void AssignNewTable(LuaState* state, int narray = 0, int nhash = 0)

Notice that the various assignment functions require a LuaState pointer. This is because every valid value must be attached to a state in Lua, so when you create a new value, you tell LuaPlus where to attach it.

## Tables

LuaObject has a number of functions and operators specifically written to help deal with tables. The easiest way to look up a value on a table is to use the overloaded array access operator. You can also use the GetByName(), GetByObject(), or GetByIndex() functions to retrieve a value from the table. For example, let's say we have the following table in Lua:

```
positionVec = { x = 10, y = 15 }
```

Let's also say that this value is stored in a LuaObject called positionTable. We can access fields on this table like so:

```
GCC_ASSERT(positionTable.IsTable());        // safety first
LuaObject x = positionTable["x"];           // this is one way
LuaObject y = positionTable.GetByName("y"); // here's another

// let's fill up a Vec2:
GCC_ASSERT(x.IsNumber() && y.IsNumber()); // more type checking
Vec2 vec(x.GetFloat(), y.GetFloat());
```

That's all there is to it. Of course, without any type safety, you need to handle all the error checking yourself.

You can also set a field on a table with the various Set*() functions:

- void SetNil(const char* key)
- void SetBoolean(const char* key, bool value)
- void SetInteger(const char* key, int value)
- void SetNumber(const char* key, double value)
- void SetString(const char* key, const char* value)
- void SetWString(const char* key, const wchar_t* value)
- void SetUserData(const char* key, void* value)
- void SetLightUserData(const char* key, void* value)
- void SetObject(const char* key, LuaObject& value)

To add a z field to the table above, you would do the following:

```
positionTable.SetNumber("z", 0);
```

Iterating through tables is possible with the use of LuaPlus's LuaTableIterator. It's somewhat similar in form to STL iterators, but it is not STL compliant. Here's an example that loops through an entire table:

```
// set up a test table in Lua and read it into a LuaObject
pLuaState->DoString("birthdayList = { John = 'Superman', Mary = 'Batman' }");
LuaObject table = pLuaState->GetGlobals().GetByName("globalPosition");

// loop through the table, printing out the pair
for (LuaTableIterator it(table); it; it.Next())
{
  LuaObject key = it.GetKey();
  LuaObject value = it.GetValue();
  // do whatever you want with the objects...
}
```

As you can see, looping through a table is relatively straightforward. This is a *huge* improvement from the Lua C API with the various lua_next() and lua_pop() calls.

## Globals

The previous example had a glaring hole in it. I showed you a table in Lua and how to get values from the C++ representation, but I didn't show you how to actually read a Lua variable in C++. In order to do that, I need to pull the curtain back a bit and show you how global variables are actually stored in Lua.

In Lua, tables are used for just about everything. A variable is really just a field in a table indexed by a string. That string is the variable name. When you define a global variable in Lua, what really happens is that Lua inserts it into a special table where all global variables live. There's nothing special about this table; you can even access it directly.

```
-- These two lines are equivalent
x = 10
_G["x"] = 10

-- This will print out all global variables
for key, val in pairs(_G) do
  print(key, val)
end
```

In fact, if you're feeling really crazy, you can even change the behavior of global variables by assigning a metatable to `_G` with `__index` or `__newindex` defined! You could completely forbid new global variables or call a function whenever a global is accessed or set.

**Don't Do That**

Just because you can modify the behavior of the globals table doesn't mean you should. Leave it alone unless you have a really, really, ***really*** good reason. I've shipped five professional games with Lua, and we never once had to mess with the behavior of this table. Chances are, neither will you.

To access a global variable in LuaPlus, you grab the globals table from the `LuaState` object and access it like any other member. Here's the missing code from the example above that gets the `positionVec` global:

```
LuaObject globals = pLuaState->GetGlobals();
LuaObject positionTable = globals.GetByName("positionVec");
```

Once you have this globals table, you can assign values as well:

```
globals.SetString("programName", "Teapot Wars");
```

This creates a global variable called `programName` and sets it to the value of `"Teapot Wars."` You can access it in Lua as normal:

```
print(programName) -- > prints "Teapot Wars"
```

## Functions

LuaPlus provides a few ways to call Lua functions from C++. The easiest way is to use the overloaded template `LuaFunction` functor class, which makes calling Lua functions look a lot like calling any C++ function. It takes care of all the parameter and return value conversions as well. For example, let's say we have the following Lua function:

```
function Square(val)
  return val * val
end
```

To call this function from C++, you would do the following:

```
LuaPlus::LuaState* pLuaState; // assume this is valid
LuaPlus::LuaFunction<float> LuaSquare = pLuaState->GetGlobal("Square");
float result = LuaSquare(5);
cout << result; // this will print out 25
```

The `LuaFunction` template parameter defines the return value. The parameters are determined by what you pass when you call the functor. There are a number of overloaded templated call operators so that nearly every combination is supported, up to and including eight different parameters. If you need more than that, you'll need to use another method for calling Lua functions.

## Calling C++ Functions from Lua

Calling a C++ function from Lua requires you to bind that function to the Lua state. If you were just using the Lua C API, it would require writing a wrapper function that took the arguments off the stack, translated them into the correct types, and called the C++ function directly. If you want to bind a C++ instance method, it's even trickier.

Fortunately, LuaPlus takes care of a lot of the headaches for you. All you need to do is bind your function to a variable in Lua. That variable becomes a Lua function that can be accessed directly in your Lua code. Simple types are automatically converted, though there's still a little translation that needs to happen in the case of tables.

There are several ways to perform this binding with LuaPlus. The simplest way is to call the `RegisterDirect()` function on the table you want the function bound to:

```
float Square(float val)
{
   return val * val;
}
```

```
LuaState* pState; // assume this is a valid LuaState pointer
LuaObject globals = pState->GetGlobals();
globals.RegisterDirect("Square", &Square);
```

That's all there is to it. This binds the global C++ function Square() to the name "Square" in the globals table in Lua. That means anywhere in your Lua code, you can do this:

```
x = Sqaure(5) -- x will be 25
```

This works for static functions as well. This is how you would bind a static function to a global Lua function:

```
globals.RegisterDirect("SomeFunction", &SomeClass::SomeStaticFunction);
```

Notice how the arguments are deciphered and sent through to the function automatically. This is one of the really nice things about using systems like LuaPlus; it takes care of a lot of the overhead of marshalling data across the C++/Lua boundary.

You can use an overloaded version of RegisterDirect() to bind member functions of C++ classes. If you have an object you know isn't going to be destroyed while the script has access to it, you can bind the pointer and function pair directly by providing a reference to the object as the second parameter.

```
class SingletonClass
{
public:
  void MemberFunction(int param);
  virtual VirtualMemeberFunction(char* str);
};

SingletonClass singletonInst;

LuaState* pLuaState; // once again, assume this is valid

// Register the member function
pLuaState->GetGlobals().RegisterDirect("MemberFunction", singletonInst,
                                      &SingletonClass::MemberFunction);

// You can register virtual functions too, it doesn't matter. The correct
// version will get called.
pLuaState->GetGlobals().RegisterDirect("VirtualMemberFunction", singletonInst,
                                      &SingletonClass::VirtualMemberFunction);
```

In the example above, two member functions along with their instances are bound to global Lua functions. This still only gets us part of the way there since the reference you bind with RegisterDirect() never changes. What we really need is a way to bind C++ member functions to a special table in Lua without having to specify the object instance at registration time. This table can serve as the metatable for other tables that represent instances of the object. It only needs to be created once. When a new object is sent to the script, a new table is created with that metatable applied. This new table has a special `__object` field that contains a `lightuserdata` pointer back to the C++ instance. This is how LuaPlus know which C++ instance to invoke the function on. In Lua, `lightuserdata` is a type that is ignored by the Lua interpreter. It's a raw pointer that is effectively equivalent to a `void*` in C++. In fact, when you retrieve a `lightuserdata` object in C++, a `void*` is returned.

Creating this table and binding methods to it are relatively straightforward. You create the table as you would any other variable and call `RegisterObjectDirect()` for each method you want to bind. As an example, let's say you have a very simple class you want to expose to the script.

```
class Ninja
{
  Vec3 m_position;
public:
  void SetPosition(float x, float y, float z);
};
```

The `SetPosition()` method is the one you want to expose to the script. Somewhere in the initialization code, the metatable needs to be created, and the function needs to be registered.

```
LuaState* pLuaState; // assume this is valid

// create the metatable under the global variable name NinjaMetaTable
LuaObject metaTable = pLuaState->GetGlobalVars().CreateTable("NinjaMetaTable");
metaTable.SetObject("__index", metaTable); // it's also its own metatable

// register the SetPosition() function
metaTable.RegisterObjectDirect("SetPosition", (Ninja*)0, &Ninja::SetPosition);
```

The metatable now exists in Lua and has the `SetPosition()` method bound to it. It can't be called, of course, since it's missing the instance pointer. When the object itself is created, that pointer needs to be bound to a new table, which will serve as the instance of that object in Lua. One way to do this is to create a new static method that will instantiate the object, take care of the binding, and return the table with the C++ instance pointer bound to it.

```
class Ninja
{
  Vec3 m_position;
```

```
public:
  void SetPosition(float x, float y, float z);
  static LuaObject CreateFromScript(void);  // new function on the Ninja class
};

LuaObject Ninja::CreateFromScript(void)
{
  // create the C++ instance
  Ninja* pCppInstance = new Ninja();

  // create the Lua instance
  LuaObject luaInstance;
  luaInstance.AssignNewTable(pLuaState);

  // assign the C++ instance pointer to the lua instance
  luaInstance.SetLightUserData("__object", pCppInstance);

  // assign the metatable to the new Lua instance table
  LuaObject metaTable =
    pLuaState->GetGlobalVars().GetByName("NinjaMetaTable");
  luaInstance.SetMetaTable(metaTable)

  return luaObject;
}
```

The `CreateFromScript()` function also needs to be registered to Lua.

```
LuaObject globals = pLuaState->GetGlobals();
globals.RegisterDirect("CreateNinja", &Ninja::CreateFromScript);
```

Now you can create instances of the `Ninja` class in Lua and call the `SetPosition()` function just like you would any other Lua object.

```
ninja = CreateNinja()
ninja:SetPosition(10, 20, 30)
```

These two methods of function and object registration form the basis of the glue between C++ and Lua.

## Bringing It All Together

In this next section, I'll show you how to bring all of these components together to form a cohesive scripting system. I'll show you how to manage the `LuaState` object and initialize the scripting system, how to send events to and receive events from the Event Manager, and how to write your own processes that run inside Lua. This section builds on everything you've learned in this book so far.

## Managing the Lua State

The Lua state is managed through a singleton that encapsulates construction and destruction and exposes a few useful methods. It also handles some error checking. Here's the class declaration:

```
class LuaStateManager : public IScriptManager
{
  static LuaStateManager* s_pSingleton;
  LuaPlus::LuaState* m_pLuaState;
  std::string m_lastError;

public:
  // Singleton functions
  static bool Create(void);
  static void Destroy(void);
  static LuaStateManager* Get(void)
    { GCC_ASSERT(s_pSingleton); return s_pSingleton; }

  // IScriptManager interface
  virtual bool VInit(void) override;
  virtual void VExecuteFile(const char* resource) override;
  virtual void VExecuteString(const char* str) override;

  LuaPlus::LuaObject GetGlobalVars(void);
  LuaPlus::LuaState* GetLuaState(void) const;

  // public helpers
  LuaPlus::LuaObject CreatePath(const char* pathString,
                                 bool toIgnoreLastElement = false);
  void ConvertVec3ToTable(const Vec3& vec,
                          LuaPlus::LuaObject& outLuaTable) const;
  void ConvertTableToVec3(const LuaPlus::LuaObject& luaTable,
                          Vec3& outVec3) const;

private:
  void SetError(int errorNum);
  void ClearStack(void);

  // Private constructor & destructor; call the static Create() and Destroy()
  // functions instead.
  explicit LuaStateManager(void);
  virtual ~LuaStateManager(void);
};
```

This class inherits from `IScriptManager`, a pure virtual interface. This is what you'd override to implement a new scripting system. As stated before, this is a singleton class. It's created and destroyed explicitly through the static `Create()` and `Destroy()` methods. The `Get()` method gets the singleton pointer.

The `ExecuteFile()` function opens and runs a Lua script while the `ExecuteString()` function parses an arbitrary string as Lua code. These two functions just wrap `LuaState::DoFile()` and `LuaState::DoString()`, respectively.

The `Init()` function is called from the `Create()` function and initializes the Lua state and registers a couple of functions. Here's the definition:

```
bool LuaStateManager::Init(void)
{
  m_pLuaState = LuaPlus::LuaState::Create(true);
  if (m_pLuaState == NULL)
    return false;

  // register functions
  m_pLuaState->GetGlobals().RegisterDirect("ExecuteFile", (*this),
                                          &LuaStateManager::ExecuteFile);
  m_pLuaState->GetGlobals().RegisterDirect("ExecuteString", (*this),
                                          &LuaStateManager::ExecuteString);

  return true;
}
```

`GetGlobalVars()` and `GetLuaState()` are both simple wrappers. `CreatePath()` is a handy function that takes a string and creates a table path to it. For example, if you pass in `A.B.C`, it will create a table called `A` with a single element named `B`, which has a single element named `C`. This can be handy when exposing methods to specific tables in script. You'll see it used below when we talk about the `Script` component.

`ConvertVec3ToTable()` and `ConvertTableToVec3()` are both helpers for converting vectors between C++ and Lua.

## Script Exports

All global script exports are placed into an internal class for organizational purposes. This allows for a single place to export functions from. Here's the initial implementation of the class:

```
class InternalScriptExports
{
public:
  // initialization
  static bool Init(void);
  static void Destroy(void);
```

```
  // These are exported to Lua
  static bool LoadAndExecuteScriptResource(const char* scriptResource);
};
```

The static functions that are exported to Lua are done in the typical manner. These functions are wrappers for engine functionality and typically just send the request to that system. For example, here's the `LoadAndExecuteScriptResource()` function:

```
bool InternalScriptExports::LoadAndExecuteScriptResource(
  const char* scriptResource)
{
  Resource resource(scriptResource);
  shared_ptr<ResHandle> pResourceHandle =
    g_pApp->m_ResCache->GetHandle(&resource);
  if (pResourceHandle)
    return true;
  return false;
}
```

The functions are registered with the global `ScriptExports::Register()` function:

```
namespace ScriptExports
{
  void Register(void);
  void Unregister(void);
}
```

And the implementation:

```
void ScriptExports::Register(void)
{
  LuaPlus::LuaObject globals = LuaStateManager::Get()->GetGlobalVars();

  // init
  InternalScriptExports::Init();

  // resource loading
  globals.RegisterDirect("LoadAndExecuteScriptResource",
  InternalScriptExports::LoadAndExecuteScriptResource);
}

void ScriptExports::Unregister(void)
{
  InternalScriptExports::Destroy();
}
```

This is just the initial implementation. As more systems are integrated and exposed to Lua later in this chapter, the `InternalScriptExports` class will grow. You can see the final version of this class and how it all fits together in source code in the *ScriptExports.cpp* source file, located at *Source/GCC4/LUAScripting/ScriptExports.cpp*.

## Process System

The Lua system needs a heartbeat—a way to update over multiple frames. Fortunately, the process system introduced in Chapter 7 works perfectly for this. It just needs to be extended and exposed to Lua. One possibility would be to attach some Lua information to the `ProcessManager` and `Process` classes, but this would be a bad idea. We want to leave the original system intact and not add references to Lua where we don't have to.

A better approach would be to create a special type of process that has knowledge of the scripting system. This special process is created from Lua with a parameter to a table containing methods that are called at the appropriate times. The idea is to create the illusion that the Lua table is inheriting from this special process so that it looks pretty much the same in Lua or C++. We can do all of this without modifying or even extending the Process Manager whatsoever; we just need to write a special script process that inherits from `Process`. This subclass will override each of the `Process` virtual functions to call the Lua versions of those functions

Here's the `ScriptProcess` class:

```
class ScriptProcess : public Process
{
  unsigned long m_frequency, m_time;
  LuaPlus::LuaObject m_scriptInitFunction, m_scriptUpdateFunction;
  LuaPlus::LuaObject m_scriptSuccessFunction, m_scriptFailFunction;
  LuaPlus::LuaObject m_scriptAbortFunction;
  LuaPlus::LuaObject m_self;

public:
  static void RegisterScriptClass(void);

protected:
  // Process interface
  virtual void VOnInit(void);
  virtual void VOnUpdate(unsigned long deltaMs);
  virtual void VOnSuccess(void);
  virtual void VOnFail(void);
  virtual void VOnAbort(void);
```

```
private:
  // private helpers
  static void RegisterScriptClassFunctions(void);
  static LuaPlus::LuaObject CreateFromScript(LuaPlus::LuaObject self,
    LuaPlus::LuaObject constructionData,
    LuaPlus::LuaObject originalSubClass);
  virtual bool VBuildCppDataFromScript(LuaPlus::LuaObject scriptClass,
    LuaPlus::LuaObject constructionData);

  // These are needed because the base-class version of these functions are
  // all const and LuaPlus can't deal with registering const functions.
  bool ScriptIsAlive(void) { return IsAlive(); }
  bool ScriptIsDead(void) { return IsDead(); }
  bool ScriptIsPaused(void) { return IsPaused(); }

  // This wrapper function is needed so we can translate a Lua script object
  // to something C++ can use.
  void ScriptAttachChild(LuaPlus::LuaObject child);

  // don't allow construction outside of this class
  explicit ScriptProcess(void);

  // static create function so Lua can instantiate it; only used internally
  static ScriptProcess* Create(const char* scriptName = NULL);
  static void Destroy(ScriptProcess* pObj);
};
```

The `m_frequency` and `m_time` members are used for timing. They allow the Lua update function to be called at a set frequency. This can be important because crossing the C++ / Lua boundary can be expensive. You should only call the update function as often as you have to.

The next several member variables hold the various Lua functions that are treated as overrides. The `m_self` member holds onto the Lua instance of the class. This is passed into the Lua overrides as the first parameter, which mimics calling the function using Lua's colon operator. It allows the functions to access the appropriate member variables.

The static `RegisterScriptClass()` function must be called during the application initialization to set up the initial metatable to allow the `ScriptProcess` class to be accessible from Lua. Here's the function:

```
const char* SCRIPT_PROCESS_NAME = "ScriptProcess";

void ScriptProcess::RegisterScriptClass(void)
{
```

```
  LuaPlus::LuaObject metaTableObj =
    LuaStateManager::Get()->GetGlobalVars().CreateTable(SCRIPT_PROCESS_NAME);
  metaTableObj.SetObject("__index", metaTableObj);
  metaTableObj.SetObject("base", metaTableObj);
  metaTableObj.SetBoolean("cpp", true);
  RegisterScriptClassFunctions();
  metaTableObj.RegisterDirect("Create", &ScriptProcess::CreateFromScript);
}
```

First, the metatable itself is created and assigned as a global object. The `__index` field of the metatable is set to point to itself. A special base variable is also set to the parent class. This allows the instance or subclass to force a call to a parent class member, even if the subclass already defines that member. Another member, `cpp`, is also set. This allows queries to see if a particular class comes from C++ or not. All script class functions are registered with the call to the private function `RegisterScriptClassFunctions()`, after which the `CreateFromScript()` static function is registered to the new metatable.

The `RegisterScriptClassFunctions()` function is a helper that registers all the member functions with the metatable object.

```
void ScriptProcess::RegisterScriptClassFunctions(void)
{
  metaTableObj.RegisterObjectDirect("Succeed",(Process*)0,&Process::Succeed);
  metaTableObj.RegisterObjectDirect("Fail", (Process*)0, &Process::Fail);
  metaTableObj.RegisterObjectDirect("Pause", (Process*)0, &Process::Pause);
  metaTableObj.RegisterObjectDirect("UnPause",(Process*)0, &Process::UnPause);
  metaTableObj.RegisterObjectDirect("IsAlive", (ScriptProcess*)0,
                                    &ScriptProcess::ScriptIsAlive);
  metaTableObj.RegisterObjectDirect("IsDead", (ScriptProcess*)0,
                                    &ScriptProcess::ScriptIsDead);
  metaTableObj.RegisterObjectDirect("IsPaused", (ScriptProcess*)0,
                                    &ScriptProcess::ScriptIsPaused);
  metaTableObj.RegisterObjectDirect("AttachChild",(ScriptProcess*)0,
                                    &ScriptProcess::ScriptAttachChild);
}
```

These are all the functions that are exposed to Lua through this metatable. Any Lua class that inherits from `ScriptProcess` will be able to call these C++ functions. Notice that some of these functions come from the base `Process` class while others are defined directly on the `ScriptProcess` class. The reason is because Lua doesn't necessarily know anything about the actual C++ class. For example, `AttachChild()` can't be directly exposed because Lua has no idea what a `Process` is, so it has no idea how to translate the Process* parameter. A special ScriptAttachChild() is written to manually perform the translation:

```
void ScriptProcess::ScriptAttachChild(LuaPlus::LuaObject child)
{
  if (child.IsTable())
  {
    LuaPlus::LuaObject obj = child.GetByName("__object");
    if (!obj.IsNil())
    {
      // Casting a raw ptr to a smart ptr is generally bad, but Lua has no
      // concept of what a shared_ptr is. There's no easy way around it.
      shared_ptr<Process> pProcess(
        static_cast<Process*>(obj.GetLightUserData()));
      GCC_ASSERT(pProcess);
      AttachChild(pProcess);
    }
    else
    {
      GCC_ERROR("Attempting to attach child with no valid object");
    }
  }
  else
  {
    GCC_ERROR("Invalid object type passed into \
      ScriptProcess::ScriptAttachChild(); type = " +
      std::string(child.TypeName()));
  }
}
```

This function first makes sure the child parameter is a table. Then it tries to find the __object field in that table (or the table's metatable). Remember that the __object field is a light userdata field that contains the pointer to the C++ Process object. This is the object that needs to actually be attached. This pointer is cast into a Process smart pointer and attached. Casting a raw pointer into a smart pointer isn't ideal since Lua still holds onto the raw pointer, but it should be safe since the __object field is destroyed when the C++ Process object is destroyed.

Functions like IsAlive() and IsDead() are declared as const, which LuaPlus doesn't know how to handle. Simple non-const wrappers are created.

The CreateFromScript() function is registered as a function on the metatable that is exported to Lua. This function creates the actual C++ and Lua instances and binds them together through the __object field:

```
LuaPlus::LuaObject ScriptProcess::CreateFromScript(LuaPlus::LuaObject self,
  LuaPlus::LuaObject constructionData,
  LuaPlus::LuaObject originalSubClass)
{
  // Note: The self parameter is not used in this function but it allows us
  // to be consistent when calling Create(). The Lua version of this function
  // needs self.
  ScriptProcess* pObj = GCC_NEW ScriptProcess;

  pObj->m_self.AssignNewTable(LuaStateManager::Get()->GetLuaState());
  if (pObj->BuildCppDataFromScript(originalSubClass, constructionData))
  {
    LuaPlus::LuaObject metaTableObj =
      LuaStateManager::Get()->GetGlobalVars().Lookup(SCRIPT_PROCESS_NAME);
    GCC_ASSERT(!metaTableObj.IsNil());

    pObj->m_self.SetLightUserData("__object", pObj);
    pObj->m_self.SetMetaTable(metaTableObj);
  }
  else
  {
    pObj->m_self.AssignNil(LuaStateManager::Get()->GetLuaState());
    SAFE_DELETE(pObj);
  }

  return pObj->m_self;
}
```

The first parameter is just to allow consistency so the function can be called in Lua with the colon operator, just like the `Create()` functions for other Lua classes using the `class()` function. The second parameter is the construction data, and the third parameter is the original subclass this object is being instantiated from. These parameters are exactly the same as the three parameters in the `Create()` function attached to classes through the `class()` function you saw earlier in this chapter. This is no coincidence; the functions should be completely interchangeable so that the caller has no idea if it's creating a C++ object or a pure Lua object.

Inside the function, the C++ object is instantiated, followed by the creation of the Lua table that will serve as the instance object. It's created on the `m_self` member so that the C++ object always has a reference to the Lua object, just like the Lua object has a reference to the C++ object through the `__object` field. Next, the function calls `BuildCppDataFromScript()`, which mines the `constructionData` and `originalSubClass` tables for any functions and configuration data that are appropriate (see below). If this succeeds, the function finds the metatable that was created with RegisterScriptClass() function. Then it binds the C++ instance to the Lua instance by setting the __object field. Then it sets the metatable. If BuildCppDataFromScript() fails, both the table and the C++ object are destroyed. The m_self parameter is returned, which, if successful, will contain the Lua instance. If the function failed, the return value will be nil.

The BuildCppDataFromScript() function is responsible for finding all the appropriate functions defined in the Lua class table:

```
bool ScriptProcess::BuildCppDataFromScript(LuaPlus::LuaObject scriptClass,
                                           LuaPlus::LuaObject constructionData)
{
  if (scriptClass.IsTable())
  {
    // OnInit()
    LuaPlus::LuaObject temp = scriptClass.GetByName("OnInit");
    if (temp.IsFunction())
      m_scriptInitFunction = temp;

    // OnUpdate()
    temp = scriptClass.GetByName("OnUpdate");
    if (temp.IsFunction())
    {
      m_scriptUpdateFunction = temp;
    }
    else
    {
      GCC_ERROR("No OnUpdate() found in script process; type == " +
           std::string(temp.TypeName()));
      return false;
    }

    // OnSuccess()
    temp = scriptClass.GetByName("OnSuccess");
    if (temp.IsFunction())
      m_scriptSuccessFunction = temp;

    // OnFail()
    temp = scriptClass.GetByName("OnFail");
    if (temp.IsFunction())
      m_scriptFailFunction = temp;

    // OnAbort()
    temp = scriptClass.GetByName("OnAbort");
    if (temp.IsFunction())
```

```
        m_scriptAbortFunction = temp;
    }
    else
    {
      GCC_ERROR("scriptClass is not a table in \
                ScriptProcess::BuildCppDataFromScript()");
      return false;
    }
    if (constructionData.IsTable())
    {
      for (LuaPlus::LuaTableIterator constructionDataIt(constructionData);
          constructionDataIt; constructionDataIt.Next())
      {
        const char* key = constructionDataIt.GetKey().GetString();
        LuaPlus::LuaObject val = constructionDataIt.GetValue();

        if (strcmp(key, "frequency") == 0 && val.IsInteger())
          m_frequency = val.GetInteger();
        else
          m_self.SetObject(key, val);
      }
    }

    return true;
}
```

The first parameter to this function is `scriptClass`, which is the Lua table that represents the class we're trying to instantiate. The `originalScriptClass` parameter from `CreateFromScript()` is passed in as this parameter. This ensures that when the function looks for a function called `OnInit()` or `OnUpdate()`, it's looking at the right class. The second parameter, `constructionData`, is used for any extra configuration.

The first part of this function ensures that `scriptClass` is a valid table. Everything within that `if` block has the same format; its entire purpose is to find the Lua versions of the various `Process` virtual functions. Since it's looking for functions that have the same name, it gives the illusion that Lua is overriding C++ virtual functions. Any found functions are placed in the appropriate member variables. The only required function is `OnUpdate()`, which will cause the function to fail if it's not found. The `OnUpdate()` function in `Process` is a pure virtual function, so this makes sense.

The second part of the function processes the `constructionData` parameter. It loops through each element on the table and tests to see if the key is frequency and the value is an integer. If it is, the `m_frequency` member is set. If not, the value is set on the m_self table. This keeps the constructionData parameter sent to the Create-FromScript() function acting like the constructor of the Create() function on Lua classes generated with the class() function. Consistency is important to ensure that the calling code never has to care whether this is a C++ or Lua object.

The overridden virtual methods from Process call the functions found by BuildCppDataFromScript(). They all behave essentially the same way. They check to see if the appropriate Lua variable was defined and call the function if it was. Here's the OnInit() function as an example:

```
void ScriptProcess::VOnInit(void)
{
  Process::VOnInit();
  if (!m_scriptInitFunction.IsNil())
  {
    LuaPlus::LuaFunction<void> func(m_scriptInitFunction);
    func(m_self);
  }
}
```

OnSuccess(), OnFail(), and OnAbort() behave the same way. The only function that behaves a bit differently is OnUpdate().

```
void ScriptProcess::VOnUpdate(unsigned long deltaMs)
{
  m_time += deltaMs;
  if (m_time >= m_frequency)
  {
    LuaPlus::LuaFunction<void> func(m_scriptUpdateFunction);
    func(m_self, m_time);
    m_time = 0;
  }
}
```

This function updates the m_time variable with the current delta and doesn't call the Lua OnUpdate() function until the appropriate amount of time has passed. As I said earlier, this is important to keep from constantly crossing over the C++ / Lua boundary if it's not necessary. Of course, if no frequency was provided, the Lua OnUpdate() function will happily call every frame. This isn't a huge deal, it's just an extra performance cost that may or may not be necessary, depending on the process.

That's everything you need to define a process in Lua, but what about the Process Manager? We still need a way to attach processes to the Process Manager. Instead of trying to expose the ProcessManager class, the best thing to do in this case to write a global wrapper function and export it through the ScriptExports interface you saw earlier. This is just a simple wrapper to the `ProcessManager::AttachProcess()` function:

```
void InternalScriptExports::AttachScriptProcess(
  LuaPlus::LuaObject scriptProcess)
{
  LuaPlus::LuaObject temp = scriptProcess.Lookup("__object");
  if (!temp.IsNil())
  {
    shared_ptr<Process> pProcess(
      static_cast<Process*>(temp.GetLightUserData()));
    g_pApp->m_pGame->AttachProcess(pProcess);
  }
  else
  {
    GCC_ERROR("Couldn't find __object in script process");
  }
}
```

Let's put all this together and see it in action with an example. This is a complete process written entirely in Lua:

```
TestScriptProcess = class(ScriptProcess,
{
  count = 0;
});

function TestScriptProcess:OnInit()
  print("OnInit()");
end

function TestScriptProcess:OnUpdate(deltaMs)
  self.count = self.count + 1;
  print("Count: " .. self.count);

  if self.count >= 5 then
    self:Succeed();
  end
end

function TestScriptProcess:OnSuccess()
  print("Success!!");
end

-- run some tests
parent = TestScriptProcess:Create({frequency = 1000});
```

```
child = TestScriptProcess:Create({frequency = 500});
parent:AttachChild(child);
AttachProcess(parent);
```

First, the `TestScriptProcess` class is created with the `class()` function. It defines three methods: `OnInit()`, `OnUpdate()`, and `OnSuccess()`. The `OnUpdate()` method counts to five and then calls `Succeed()`—a C++ method—to end the process. The test code for this class creates two objects, one with an update frequency of 1,000 and the other with an update frequency of 500. It then attaches the child to the parent and attaches the parent to the Process Manager. You'll see the count from 1–5, each taking 1 second in between, followed by another count of 1–5, taking half a second each, before terminating.

As you can see, this class looks very much like any other class that inherits from `Process`, which is the whole idea. Remember at the beginning of the chapter when I said that one of the biggest reasons for using a scripting language is for fast iteration? This is exactly how you achieve it. You can write processes very quickly in Lua, test them out, and iterate very quickly. In many cases, you can update a process without even restarting the game. You just edit the code, reload the script (probably by calling `ExecuteFile()`, which is exposed to Lua), and then trigger the process again.

If you decide that you need to move the process to C++ for performance reasons, the Lua class is already laid out like the C++ version. You just create the same class in C++, port the code from Lua to C++, and set up the triggering calls. This is an extremely powerful and flexible system, and you should use it wherever you can.

**Inheriting from C++ Classes**

The `ScriptProcess` class gives us one more thing that's extremely powerful: the ability to inherit from C++ classes in Lua. Without too much trouble, you should be able to create a system that allows you to expose any arbitrary class to Lua and enable Lua classes to inherit from them. I chose not to do this here because such a system tends to make the details much more obscure and harder to understand. My goal here is not to give you the best engine I possibly can, but to teach you how you can build it yourself. I leave this as an exercise to the reader. If you get stuck, you can always post in the forums, and I'll be happy to help.

By the way, you should always be on the lookout for these types of abstractions. They can make the difference between an okay engine and an amazing one.

## Event System

Communication between C++ and Lua is inevitable, and there needs to be a system to facilitate that communication. A naive approach might be to expose all the methods you need to Lua and allow them to be called directly. This would probably work just fine, but it would end up being very messy. You'll have dozens or even hundreds of methods exposed to Lua, and this tightly couples your engine to the Lua script. If one of those methods changes, you'll have to update all the appropriate places in the script as well.

A much better approach is to use the event system we already created in Chapter 11, "Game Event Management," and extend it in a similar way that we extended the process system. Unfortunately, this won't be as easy. It's one thing to create a self-contained process with very little data that needs to cross the C++ / Lua boundary, and it's quite another to facilitate that communication.

The first thing you need is a special type of event that can be sent to or from Lua. This event should take care of all the data translation as well. The goal is for the receiver of the event to have no idea where it came from. You should be able to send an event that's received by both Lua and C++ without either knowing of the source. This keeps it all nice and decoupled, which is the whole point of the event system.

Here's the `ScriptEvent` class, which serves as the base class for all events that need to cross the C++ / Lua boundary:

```
#define REGISTER_SCRIPT_EVENT(eventClass, eventType) \
  ScriptEvent::RegisterEventTypeWithScript(#eventClass, eventType); \
  ScriptEvent::AddCreationFunction(eventType, \
                                   &eventClass::CreateEventForScript)

#define EXPORT_FOR_SCRIPT_EVENT(eventClass) \
  public: \
    static ScriptEvent* CreateEventForScript(void) \
    { \
      return new eventClass; \
    }

// function ptr typedef to create a script event
typedef ScriptEvent* (*CreateEventForScriptFunctionType)(void);

class ScriptEvent : public BaseEventData
{
  typedef std::map<EventType, CreateEventForScriptFunctionType>
    CreationFunctions;
  static CreationFunctions s_creationFunctions;
    bool m_eventDataIsValid;
```

```
protected:
  LuaPlus::LuaObject m_eventData;

public:
  // construction
  ScriptEvent(void) { m_eventDataIsValid = false; }

  // script event data, which should only be called from the appropriate
  // ScriptExports functions
  LuaPlus::LuaObject GetEventData(void);  // called when event is sent from
                                          // C++ to script
  bool SetEventData(LuaPlus::LuaObject eventData);  // called when event is
                                                    // sent from script to C++

  // Static helper functions for registering events with the script.
  static void RegisterEventTypeWithScript(const char* key, EventType type);
  static void AddCreationFunction(EventType type,
    CreateEventForScriptFunctionType pCreationFunctionPtr);
  static ScriptEvent* CreateEventFromScript(EventType type);

protected:
  virtual void VBuildEventData(void);
  virtual bool VBuildEventFromScript(void) { return true; }
};
```

The macros at the top are used for registering the event and exporting it to Lua. `REGISTER_SCRIPT_EVENT()` is called during the initialization of the application, passing in the class and the event type guid as parameters. It calls the static `RegisterEventTypeWithScript()` and `AddCreationFunction()` functions, which you'll see below. The reason this needs to be a macro is so that the `RegisterEventTypeWithScript()` function can use the name of the class as the first parameter with the # operator, which places quotes around the token. The `EXPORT_FOR_SCRIPT_EVENT()` macro is called inside the subclass declaration to generate the `CreateEventForScript()` function. This is a macro so that you have one central place to change any of this code should you need to do so without having to go to every single subclass.

Inside the `ScriptEvent` class is a static map variable that maps event type guids to creation functions. Whenever an event needs to be created by guid, it looks up the appropriate function in the map and calls it to create the appropriate subclass instance.

The `m_eventData` member is the Lua representation of the data used by the event. It is typically a table, but it can be anything you like. This data is manipulated by the protected virtual functions VBuildEventData() and VBuildEventFromScript(). All subclasses of this event should implement one or both of these functions. VBuildEventData() must be overridden if you want to fire this event from C++ and have it be received by Lua. The VBuildEventFromScript() must be overridden by events that are sent from Lua and received by C++. If you want both, then both functions must be overridden.

Thcsc two functions perform the translation between C++ and Lua. Inside VBuild EventData(), you are expected to fill out the m_eventData member with any data you want passed to Lua. Inside VBuildEventFromScript(), you do the opposite. You read the m_eventData member and fill out any C++ members you want. Although you could just read the table when the event is received, it's better to do it here because VBuildEventFromScript() is only called once. The performance costs are the same, regardless of how many receivers listen for the event.

The RegisterEventTypeWithScript() function registers the event type guid with Lua. This guid maps the ScriptEvent subclass name to that guid. It does this by adding to a global EventType table in Lua. This ensures that C++ and Lua can refer to the same event using the same identifier.

```
void ScriptEvent::RegisterEventTypeWithScript(const char* key, EventType type)
{
  // get or create the EventType table
  LuaPlus::LuaObject eventTypeTable =
    LuaStateManager::Get()->GetGlobalVars().GetByName("EventType");
  if (eventTypeTable.IsNil())
    eventTypeTable =
      LuaStateManager::Get()->GetGlobalVars().CreateTable("EventType");

  // error checking
  GCC_ASSERT(eventTypeTable.IsTable());
  GCC_ASSERT(eventTypeTable[key].IsNil());

  // add the entry
  eventTypeTable.SetNumber(key, (double)type);
}
```

First, this function gets or creates the EventType table and then it does some simple error checking. After that, it assigns the guid to the table. Since this function is called from the REGISTER_SCRIPT_EVENT() macro, it's able to turn the ScriptProcess subclass into a string and use that as the key.

The AddCreationFunction() function is trivial, as it just inserts the EventType/function pair into the static map. This is called automatically by the

REGISTER_SCRIPT_EVENT() macro. CreateEventFromScript() finds the creation function pointer and calls it.

Now that we have a nice little class that can translate C++ and Lua data, we need a system to be able to queue up and receive events on the Lua side. Events coming from C++ don't need anything special, they can just call VQueueEvent() or VTriggerEvent() as normal.

The easiest problem to tackle is that of queuing events from Lua. We'll use the same scheme used for attaching processes from Lua, using ScriptExports to expose a couple of wrapper functions.

```
bool InternalScriptExports::QueueEvent(EventType eventType,
                                       LuaPlus::LuaObject eventData)
{
  shared_ptr<ScriptEvent> pEvent(BuildEvent(eventType, eventData));
  if (pEvent)
  {
    IEventManager::Get()->VQueueEvent(pEvent);
    return true;
  }
  return false;
}

bool InternalScriptExports::TriggerEvent(EventType eventType,
                                         LuaPlus::LuaObject eventData)
{
  shared_ptr<ScriptEvent> pEvent(BuildEvent(eventType, eventData));
  if (pEvent)
    return IEventManager::Get()->VTriggerEvent(pEvent);
  return false;
}
```

Both of these functions are very simple; they just call BuildEvent() to create the event instance and then call into the Event Manager. BuildEvent() is a helper function.

```
shared_ptr<ScriptEvent> InternalScriptExports::BuildEvent(EventType eventType,
                                                     LuaPlus::LuaObject& eventData)
{
  // create the event from the event type
  shared_ptr<ScriptEvent> pEvent(
    ScriptEvent::CreateEventFromScript(eventType));
  if (!pEvent)
    return shared_ptr<ScriptEvent>();
```

```
  // set the event data that was passed in
  if (!pEvent->SetEventData(eventData))
  {
    return shared_ptr<ScriptEvent>();
  }

  return pEvent;
}
```

This function creates the event by calling `CreateEventFromScript()`, which in turn calls the factory method to instantiate the appropriate subclass. Then it calls `SetEventData()`, which will call your implementation of `BuildEventFromScript()`. If this succeeds, it returns the newly created event. That's all there is to it. Using these two methods, you can send events from Lua and have them received by C++ listeners. In C++, you create those listeners as normal.

Allowing Lua to receive events is a little trickier. We want to create a system where you can register a Lua function to receive a C++ event. Doing this requires a special `ScriptEventListener` class that finds the event type guid with the Lua callback function. We also need a place to store these listener objects, so a `ScriptEventListenerMgr` class is created as well. First, we'll look at the `ScriptEventListener` class.

```
class ScriptEventListener
{
  EventType m_eventType;
  LuaPlus::LuaObject m_scriptCallbackFunction;

public:
  explicit ScriptEventListener(const EventType& eventType,
    const LuaPlus::LuaObject& scriptCallbackFunction);
  ~ScriptEventListener(void);
  EventListenerDelegate GetDelegate(void)
  {
    return MakeDelegate(this, &ScriptEventListener::ScriptEventDelegate);
  }
  void ScriptEventDelegate(IEventDataPtr pEventPtr);
};
```

The first member is the event type guid, and the second member is the Lua function that will act as the listener delegate. These are both set in the constructor. `ScriptEventDelegate()` is the true C++ listener delegate that acts as the proxy to the Lua delegate.

```
void ScriptEventListener::ScriptEventDelegate(IEventDataPtr pEvent)
{
```

```
  // call the Lua function
  shared_ptr<ScriptEvent> pScriptEvent =
    static_pointer_cast<ScriptEvent>(pEvent);
  LuaPlus::LuaFunction<void> callback = m_scriptCallbackFunction;
  callback(pScriptEvent->GetEventData());
}
```

All this function does is calls the Lua delegate function with the results of `GetEventData()` as the only parameter. `GetEventData()` calls your script event's `BuildEventData()` function if necessary and returns `m_eventData`. The Lua delegate then does whatever it wants with the data.

These event listeners take care of all the overhead for binding the Lua listener delegate to a C++ delegate. The `ScriptEventListenerMgr` manages these objects.

```
class ScriptEventListenerMgr
{
  typedef std::set<ScriptEventListener*> ScriptEventListenerSet;
  ScriptEventListenerSet m_listeners;

public:
  ~ScriptEventListenerMgr(void);
  void AddListener(ScriptEventListener* pListener);
  void DestroyListener(ScriptEventListener* pListener);
};
```

This class maintains a set of `ScriptEventListener` objects, which are added and removed through the `AddListener()` and `DestroyListener()` functions, respectively. These functions are just wrappers to insert or remove/delete objects from the set.

The final piece we need is a function for registering a Lua event listener, which is a function that is exposed to Lua.

```
unsigned long InternalScriptExports::RegisterEventListener(EventType eventType,
                                              LuaPlus::LuaObject callbackFunction)
{
  GCC_ASSERT(s_pScriptEventListenerMgr);

  if (callbackFunction.IsFunction())
  {
    // create the C++ listener proxy and set it to listen for the event
    ScriptEventListener* pListener = GCC_NEW ScriptEventListener(eventType,
                                                        callbackFunction);
    s_pScriptEventListenerMgr->AddListener(pListener);
    IEventManager::Get()->VAddListener(pListener->GetDelegate(), eventType);
```

```
    // convert the pointer to an unsigned long to use as the handle
    unsigned long handle = reinterpret_cast<unsigned long>(pListener);
    return handle;
  }

  GCC_ERROR("Attempting to register script event listener with \
            invalid callback function");
  return 0;
}
```

After a bit of error checking, this function creates a new `ScriptEventListener` object and adds it to the `ScriptEventListenerMgr` instance. Then it registers the newly created C++ delegate proxy with the Event Manager.

With all the pieces in place, it is now possible to create events that can be sent across the C++/Lua boundary. To do this, create a new event class that inherits from `ScriptEvent`. Then implement the `BuildEventData()` and `BuildEventFrom-Script()` virtual methods as necessary. Call the `EXPORT_FOR_SCRIPT_EVENT()` macro in the event subclass declaration and call the `REGISTER_SCRIPT_EVENT()` macro in the initialization code for the application.

To test out this functionality, we create two simple events. One is sent from C++ and received by Lua, the other is sent from Lua and received by C++. Both of these events inherit from `ScriptEvent` and override the appropriate virtual functions. Here are the overridden functions:

```
// This is for the event being sent from C++ to Lua
void EvtData_ScriptEventTest_ToLua::BuildEventData(void)
{
  m_eventData.AssignNumber(LuaStateManager::Get()->GetLuaState(), m_num);
}

// This is for the event being sent from Lua to C++
bool EvtData_ScriptEventTest_FromLua::BuildEventFromScript(void)
{
  if (m_eventData.IsInteger())
  {
    m_num = m_eventData.GetInteger();
    return true;
  }

  return false;
}
```

In the application initialization, the REGISTER_SCRIPT_EVENT() macro must be called:

```
REGISTER_SCRIPT_EVENT(EvtData_ScriptEventTest_ToLua,
                      EvtData_ScriptEventTest_ToLua::sk_EventType);
REGISTER_SCRIPT_EVENT(EvtData_ScriptEventTest_FromLua,
                      EvtData_ScriptEventTest_FromLua::sk_EventType);
```

Now the events are ready for Lua:

```
function TestEventHandler(eventData)
  print("Event Received in Lua: " .. eventData)
  eventData = eventData + 1
  QueueEvent(EventType.EvtData_ScriptEventTest_FromLua, eventData)
end

RegisterEventListener(EventType.EvtData_ScriptEventTest_ToLua,TestEventHandler)
```

This code creates a listener function and registers it to listen for an event. The listener adds a number and then queues a new event, which is received by C++. The event chain can be tested by firing off the C++ event.

```
shared_ptr<EvtData_ScriptEventTest_ToLua> pEvent(
  GCC_NEW EvtData_ScriptEventTest_ToLua);
IEventManager::Get()->VQueueEvent(pEvent);
```

That will send an event from C++ that's received by Lua, which in turn will send an event from Lua that is received by C++.

Using events is a great way to communicate between C++ and Lua. It keeps Lua and C++ nicely decoupled by ensuring that the listener doesn't care about the source of the event. That means you can move events freely from Lua to C++ or vice versa without having to change any of the code on the listeners.

## Script Component

So far, we've created a way to deal with script processing over multiple frames as well as communicating between C++ and Lua using events. Another crucial piece to this puzzle is the ability to manipulate actors through Lua. It wouldn't be a good idea to start exposing tons of different components since that can get really messy, so instead, a new type of component is created. This component knows how to access the other components on the actor and call whatever functions are appropriate to expose.

The implementation of the script component is fairly trivial compared to everything you've seen so far. Here's the class declaration:

```
class BaseScriptComponent : public ScriptComponentInterface
{
  std::string m_scriptObjectName;
  std::string m_constructorName;
  std::string m_destructorName;

  LuaPlus::LuaObject m_scriptObject;
  LuaPlus::LuaObject m_scriptConstructor;
  LuaPlus::LuaObject m_scriptDestructor;

public:
  BaseScriptComponent(void);
  virtual ~BaseScriptComponent(void);
  virtual bool VInit(TiXmlElement* pData);
  virtual void VPostInit(void);
  virtual TiXmlElement* VGenerateXml(void);

  static void RegisterScriptFunctions(void);
  static void UnregisterScriptFunctions(void);

private:
  void CreateScriptObject(void);

  // component script functions
  LuaPlus::LuaObject GetActorId(void);

  // physics component script functions
  LuaPlus::LuaObject GetPos(void);
  void SetPos(LuaPlus::LuaObject newPos);
  LuaPlus::LuaObject GetLookAt(void) const;
  float GetYOrientationRadians(void) const;
  void RotateY(float angleRadians);
};
```

The XML definition for this component allows you to define a script object, a constructor, and a destructor. The script object is the name of a Lua variable where a Lua instance of this object will live. The constructor is the name of a Lua function that is called when the actor has been created, while the destructor is the name of a Lua function that is called when the actor is destroyed. Both the constructor and destructor Lua functions are of the form `func(scriptObject)`, where `scriptObject` is the Lua instance of this component.

Since there's nothing particularly new, I'm not going to cover it in depth. This class follows the same basic pattern the others have. The idea behind this class is that it represents the actor as far as Lua is concerned. All actor-specific functions should either go through here or use script events. You can see the full implementation of the class in the source code in the *Source/GCC4/Actors/* directory. The files you want are *ScriptComponentInterface.h*, *BaseScriptComonent.h*, and *BaseScriptComponent.cpp*.

## Lua Development and Debugging

As your scripts become more complex, you will invariably need tools in order to manage and debug them. The `print()` statement and debug logs will only get you so far, so you need a way to set breakpoints in Lua functions, inspect the values of variables and tables, and single-step through your scripts. Lua does provide a number of debug hooks to be able to do this, but they can be tedious to use. What you really need is a full IDE (Integrated Development Environment) made for Lua. There are a few of them out there of varying levels of quality.

**C++ for Debugging**

I've worked at two separate companies that used Lua without having a debugger. At Super-Ego Games, we just used print debugging, and any complex code was written in C++ whether it belonged there or not. At PlayFirst, we only used Lua for UI configurations, so a debugger wasn't necessary. If we had a debugger at either of these companies, we would have gotten a lot more from Lua than we did. This was proven to me when I worked at Planet Moon, where we had a fully featured Lua debugger. Trust me, you can get away without a debugger for a little while, but not long.

The best I've used by far is Decoda, by Unknown Worlds. It's fast, easy to use, and has a large set of features for managing projects and debugging your Lua scripts. The only down side is that it's not free, although it still costs less than the price of a typical console game. If you're at all serious about integrating Lua into your games, I highly recommend this program.

## Final Thoughts

This Lua integration is relatively simple, but it's enough for you play around with. It's important to note that I really only scratched the surface of Lua in this chapter. There are a lot more things you can do with Lua and LuaPlus that I simply didn't have the page count to cover, like co-routines, threads, and more. Make sure you go through the reading section below and check out some of the material there. Remember to experiment!

You'll see this system really put to use later on in Chapter 19, "An Introduction to Game AI," when you learn about artificial intelligence, as well as Chapter 21, "A Game of *Teapot Wars*," when you see the sample *Teapot Wars* game.

## Further Reading

*Programming in Lua*, Roberto Ierusalimschy

www.lua.org

www.lua.org/manual/5.1/

*Lua Programming Gems*, various authors

*C++ Templates: The Complete Guide,* Nicolai M. Josuttis und David Vandevoorde

CHAPTER 13

*by Mike McShaffry*

# GAME AUDIO

If you have any doubt about how important sound is in games, try a little experiment. First, find a home theater system that can turn off all the sound except for the center channel. The center channel is almost always used for dialogue, and everything else is for music and sound effects. Pop a movie in and feel for yourself how flat the experience is without music and sound.

The same is true for games. Done well, sound and music convey critical information to the player as well as incite powerful emotional reactions. One of my favorite examples of powerful music in any game is the original *Halo* from Bungie. When the music segues into a driving combat tune, you can tell what is coming up—lots of carnage, hopefully on the Covenant side of things!

I'm biased, of course, but an excellent example of sound design and technology comes from *Thief: Deadly Shadows* by Ion Storm. This game integrated the physics, portal, and AI subsystems with the sound system. AI characters would receive propagated sound effect events that happened anywhere near them, and they would react accordingly. If you got clumsy and stumbled Garrett, the main character in *Thief*, into a rack of swords, AI characters around the corner and down the hall would hear it, and they'd come looking for you.

Another great example is from *Mushroom Men: The Spore Wars* for the Wii by Red Fly Studio. In this game, the sound system was actually integrated into the graphics and particles system, creating a subtle but effective effect that had each sparkle of a particle effect perfectly timed with the music. They called this the "Metronome."

In this chapter, I'll take you as far as I can into the world of sound. We'll explore both sound effects and music. With a little work and imagination, you should be able to take what you learn here and create your own sound magic.

## How Sound Works

Imagine someone on your street working with a hammer. Every time the hammer strikes a nail, or perhaps the poor schmuck's finger, a significant amount of energy is released, causing heat, deformation of the hammer, deformation of whatever was hit, and vibrations in all the objects concerned as they return to an equilibrium state. A more complete description of the situation would also include high-amplitude vibration of Mr. Schmuck's vocal cords. Either way, those vibrations are propagated through the air as sound waves.

When these sound waves strike an object, sometimes they make the object vibrate at the same frequency. This only happens if the object is resonant with the frequency of the sound waves. Try this: Go find two guitars and make sure they are properly tuned. Then hold them close together and pluck the biggest, fattest string of one of them. You should notice that the corresponding string on the second guitar will vibrate, too, and you never touched it directly.

The experiment with the guitars is similar to how the mechanical parts of your ear work. Your ears have tiny hairs, each having a slightly different length and resonant frequency. When sound waves get to them and make different sets of them vibrate, they trigger chemical messages in your brain, and your conscious mind interprets the signals as different sounds. Some of them sound like a hammer striking a nail, and others sound more like words you'd rather not say in front of little kids.

The tone of a sound depends on the sound frequency, or how fast the vibrations hit your ear. Vibrations are measured in cycles per second, or Hertz (abbreviated Hz). The lowest tone a normal human ear can hear is 20Hz, which is so low you almost feel it more than you hear it! As the frequency rises, the tone of the sounds gets higher until you can't hear it anymore. The highest frequency most people can hear is about 20,000Hz, or 20 kiloHertz (KHz).

The intensity of a sound is related to the number of air molecules pushed around by the original vibration. You can look at this as the "pressure" applied to anything by a sound wave. A common measurement of sound intensity is the decibel, or dB. This measurement is on a logarithmic scale, which means that a small increase in the dB level can be a dramatic increase in the intensity of the sound. Table 13.1 shows the dB levels for various common sounds.

**Table 13.1 Decibel Levels for Different Sounds**

| dB Level | Description |
|---|---|
| 0 | The softest sound a person can hear with normal hearing |
| 10 | Normal breathing |
| 20 | Whispering at five feet |
| 30 | Soft whisper |
| 50 | Rainfall |
| 60 | Normal conversation |
| 110 | Shouting in ear |
| 120 | Thunder |
| 150 | Mr. Mike screaming when he beats his nephew Chris at *Guitar Hero* |

The reason the scale is a logarithmic one has to do with the sensitivity of your ears. Normal human hearing can detect sounds over an amazing range of intensity, with the lowest being near silence and the highest being something that falls just shy of blowing your eardrums out of your head. The power difference between the two is over one million times. Since the range is so great, it is convenient to use a nonlinear, logarithmic scale to measure the intensity of sound.

Did you ever wonder why the volume knob on expensive audio gear is marked with negative dB? This is because volume is actually attenuation, or the level of change of the base level of a sound. Decibels measure relative sound intensity, not absolute intensity, which means that negative decibels measure the amount of sound reduction. Turning the volume to 3dB lower than the current setting reduces the power to your speakers by half. Given that, and I can put this in writing, all the stereo heads out there will be happy to know that if you set your volume level to 0dB, you'll be hearing the sound at the level intended by the audio engineer. This is, of course, usually loud enough to get complaints from your neighbors.

## Digital Recording and Reproduction

If you happen to have some speakers with the cones exposed, like my nice Boston Acoustics setup, you can watch these cones move in and out in a blur when you crank the music. It turns out that the speakers are moving in correlation to the plot of the sound wave recorded in the studio.

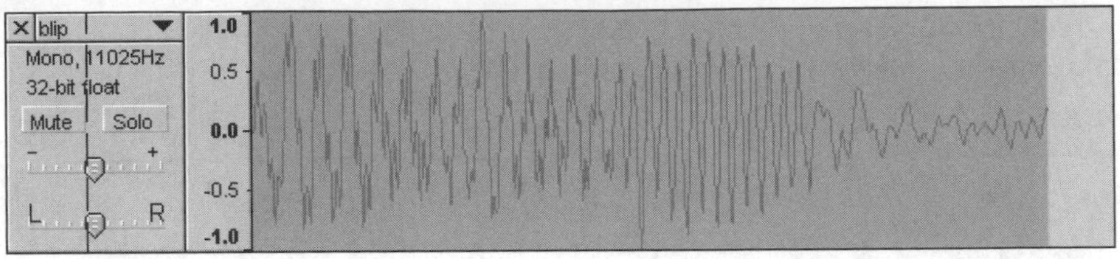


**Figure 13.1**
A typical sound wave.

You've probably seen a graphic rendering of a sound wave; it looks like some random up-and-down wiggling at various frequencies and amplitudes (see Figure 13.1).

This scratching is actually a series of values that map to an energy value of the sound at a particular moment in time. This energy value is the power level sent into a speaker magnet to get the speaker cone to move, either in or out. The frequency, or tone, of the sound is directly related to the number of up/down wiggles you see in the graphic representation of the waveform. The speaker is reproducing, to the best of its ability, the identical waveform of the sound that was recorded in the studio.

If you zoom into the waveform, you'll see these energy values plotted as points above and below the X-axis (see Figure 13.2).

If all the points were in a straight line at value 0.0f, there would be complete silence. The odd thing is, if all the points were in a straight line at 1.0, you would get a little "pop" at the very beginning and silence thereafter. The reason is the speaker cone would sit at the maximum position of its movement, making no vibrations at all.

The amplitude, or height, of the waveform is a measure of the sound's intensity. Quiet sounds only wiggle close to the 0.0 line, whereas loud noises wiggle all the way from 1.0f to -1.0f. You can also imagine a really loud noise, like an explosion, has an energy level that my Boston Acoustics can't reproduce and can't be accurately recorded anyway because of the energies involved. Figure 13.3 shows what happens to a sound wave that fails to record the amplitude of a high-energy sound.

Instead of a nice waveform, the tops and bottoms are squared off. This creates a nasty buzzing noise because the speaker cones can't follow a nice smooth waveform.

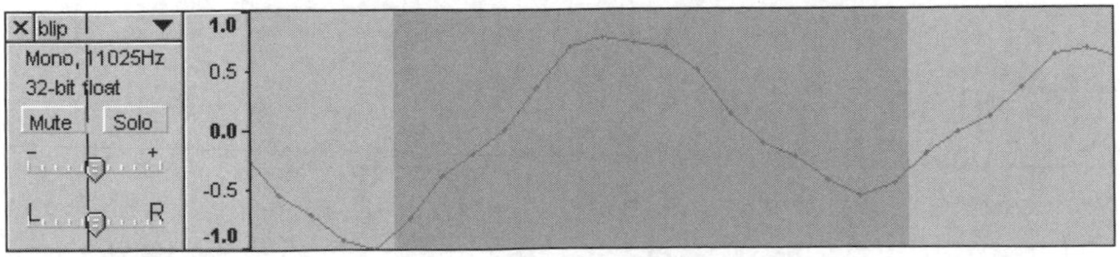


**Figure 13.2**
A closer view of a sound wave.

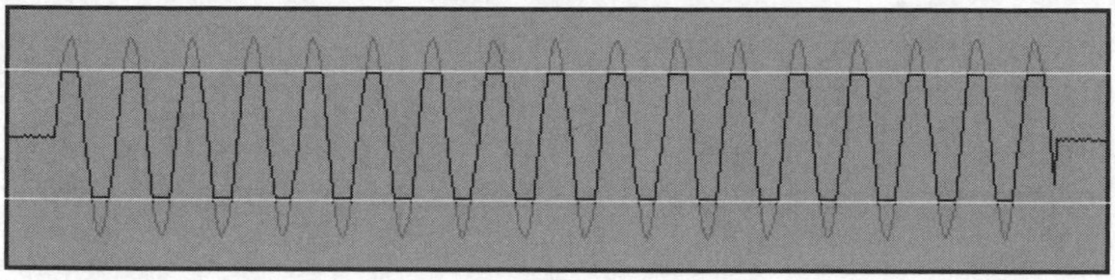

**Figure 13.3**
A clipped sound wave.

Audio engineers say that a recording like this had the "levels too hot," and they had to re-record it with the input levels turned down a bit. If you ever saw those recording meters on a mixing board, you'd notice that the input levels jumped into the red when the sound was too hot, creating the clipped waveforms. The same thing can happen when you record sounds straight to your desktop with a microphone, so keep an eye on those input levels.

**Crusty Geezers Say the Wildest Things**

On the *Microsoft Casino* project, the actors were encouraged to come up with extemporaneous barks for their characters. Not surprisingly, some of them had to be cut from the game. One was cut by Microsoft legal because they thought it sounded too much like the signature line, "I'll be back," from Arnold Schwarzenegger. Another was cut because it made disparaging remarks toward the waitresses at the Mirage Resorts. My favorite one of all time, though, was a bit of speech from a crusty old geezer, "You know what I *REALLY* love about Vegas??? The hookers!!!"

## Sound Files

Sound files have many different formats, the most popular being WAV, MP3, OGG, and MIDI. The WAV format stores raw sound data, the aural equivalent of a BMP or TGA file, and is therefore the largest. MP3 and OGG files are compressed sound file formats and can achieve about a 10:1 compression ratio over WAV, with only a barely perceptible loss in sound quality. MIDI files are almost like little sound programs and are extremely tiny, but the sound quality is completely different—it sounds like those video games from the 1980s. So why would you choose one over the other?

MIDI was popular for downloadable games and games on handheld platforms because they were so small and efficient. These days MIDI is more a choice for style than anything else, since even handheld devices are fully capable of playing most sound formats. The WAV format takes a lot of memory, but it is incredibly easy on your CPU budget. MP3s and OGGs will save your memory budget but will hit your CPU for each stream you decompress into a hearable sound.

If you're short on media space, you can store everything in MP3 or OGG and decompress the data in memory at load time. This is a pretty good idea for short sound effects that you hear often, like weapons fire and footsteps. Music and background ambiance can be many minutes long and are almost always played in their compressed form.

**Always Keep Your Original High-Fidelity Audio Recordings**

Make sure that all of your original sound is recorded in high-resolution WAV format, and plan to keep it around until the end of the project. If you convert all your audio to a compressed format such as MP3, you'll lose sound quality, and you won't be able to reconvert the audio stream to a higher bit-rate if the quality isn't good enough. This is exactly the same thing as storing all your artwork in high-resolution TGAs or TIFFs. You'll always have the original work stored in the highest possible resolution in case you need to mess with it later.

## A Quick Word About Threads and Synchronization

Sound systems run in a multithreaded architecture. I'm talking about real multithreading here and not the cooperative multitasking. What's the difference? You should already be familiar with the `Process` and `ProcessManager` classes from Chapter 7, "Controlling the Main Loop." These classes are cooperative, which means it is up to them to decide when to return control to the calling routine. For those of you who remember coding in the old DOS or Windows 3.x days, this is all we had without some serious assembly level coding. In a way, it was a lot safer, for reasons you'll see in a minute, but it was a heck of a lot harder to get the computer to accomplish many tasks at once.

A classic task in games is to play some neat music in the background while you are playing the game. Like I said at the start of this chapter, sound creates emotion in your game. But what is really going on in the background to make sound come out of your speakers?

Sound data is pushed into the sound card, and the sound card's driver software converts this data into electric signals that are sent to your speakers. The task of reading new data into the sound card and converting it into a usable format takes some CPU time away from your computer. While modern sound cards have CPUs of their own, getting the data from the digital media into the sound card still takes your main CPU.

Since sound data is played at a linear time scale, it's critical to push data into the sound card at the right time. If it is pushed too early, you'll overwrite music that is about to be played. If it is pushed too late, the sound card will play some music you've already heard, only to skip ahead when the right data gets in place.

This is the classic reader/writer problem, where you have a fixed memory area with a writer that needs to stay ahead of the reader. If the reader ever overtakes the writer or vice versa, the reader reads data that is either too old or too new. When I heard about this in college, the example presented was always some horribly boring data being read and written, such as employee records or student class enrollment records. I would have paid a lot more attention to this class if they had told me the same solutions could be applied to computer game sound systems.

What makes this problem complicated is there must be a way to synchronize the reader and writer to make sure the writer process only writes when it knows it is safely out of the reader's way. Luckily, the really nasty parts of this problem are handled at a low level in DirectSound, but you should always be aware of it so you don't pull the rug out from the sound system's feet, so to speak. Let me give you an example.

In your game, let's assume there's a portable stereo sitting on a desk, and it is playing music. You take your gun and fire an explosive round into the radio and destroy the radio. Hopefully, the music the radio is playing stops when the radio is destroyed, and the memory used by the music is returned to the system. You should be able to see how order-dependent all this is. If you stop the music too early, it looks like the radio was somehow self-aware and freaked out just before it was sent to radio nirvana. If you release all the radio's resources before you notify the sound system, the sound system might try to play some sound data from a bogus area of memory.

Worse still, because the sound system runs in a different thread, you can't count on a synchronous response when you tell the sound system to stop playing a sound. Granted, the sound system will respond to the request in a few milliseconds, far shorter than any human can perceive, but far longer than you could count on using the memory currently allocated to the sound system for something that is still active.

All these complications require a little architecture to keep things simple for programmers who are attaching sounds to objects or music to a game.

## Game Sound System Architecture

Just like a graphics subsystem, audio subsystems can have a few different implementations. DirectSound, Miles Audio, WWise, and FMod are a few examples. It's a good idea to create an implementation-agnostic wrapper for your sound system so that you are free to choose the implementation right for your game. The audio system presented in this chapter can use DirectSound or Miles, and the only change you have to make for your high-level game code is one line of code. Figure 13.4 shows the class hierarchy for our sound system.

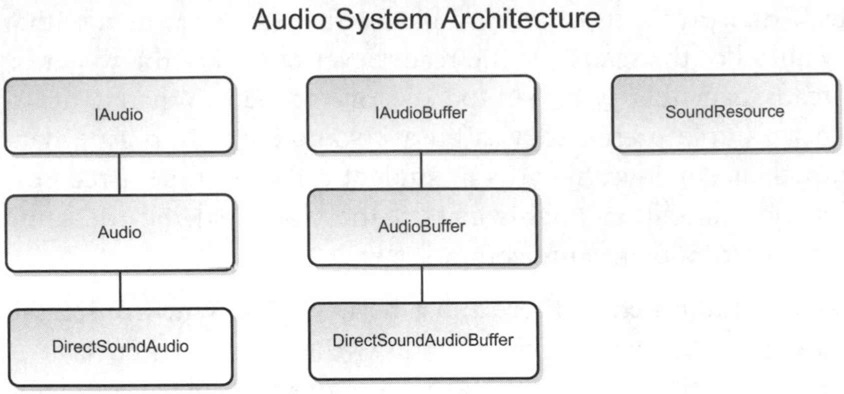


**Figure 13.4**
Sound system class hierarchy.

The sound system inherits from `IAudio`. This object is responsible for the list of sounds currently active. As you might predict, you only need one of these for your game. The `Audio` base class implements some implementation-generic routines, and the `DirectSoundAudio` class completes the implementation with DirectSound-specific calls.

The sound system needs access to the bits that make up the raw sound. The `IAudioBuffer` interface defines the methods for an implementation-generic sound buffer. `AudioBuffer` is a base class that implements some of the `IAudioBuffer` interface, and the `DirectSoundAudioBuffer` completes the implementation of the interface class using DirectSound calls. Each instance of a sound effect will use one of these buffer objects.

A `Resource` encapsulates sound data, presumably loaded from a file or your resource cache. If you had five explosions going off simultaneously, you'd have one `Resource` object and five `DirectSoundAudioBuffer` objects.

## Sound Resources and Handles

If you want to play a sound in your game, the first thing you do is load it. Sound resources are loaded exactly the same as other game resources; they will likely exist in a resource file. Sound effects can be tiny or quite long. Your game may have thousands of these things, or tens of thousands as many modern games have. Just as you saw in Chapter 8, "Loading and Caching Game Data," you shouldn't store each effect in its own file; rather, you should pull it from a resource cache.

A resource cache is convenient if you have many simultaneous sounds that use the same sound data, such as weapons fire. You should load this resource once, taking up only one block of memory, and have the sound driver create many "players" that will use the same resource.

The concept of streaming sound, compressed or otherwise, is beyond the scope of this chapter. The sound system described here uses the resource cache to load the sound data from a resource file, decompresses it if necessary, and manages DirectSound audio buffers if you happen to have the same sound being played multiple times. As usual, I'm exchanging clarity for performance, specifically memory usage, so take this into account when looking at this system. A commercial grade sound system would only load the compressed sound into memory and use a thread to decompress bits of it as it is played, saving a ton of memory. With that caveat in mind, the first thing to do is define three classes to help the resource cache load and decompress WAV and OGG files::

```
class SoundResourceExtraData : public IResourceExtraData
{
  friend class WaveResourceLoader;
  friend class OggResourceLoader;

public:
  SoundResourceExtraData();
  virtual ~SoundResourceExtraData() { }
  virtual std::string VToString() { return "SoundResourceExtraData"; }
  enum SoundType GetSoundType() { return m_SoundType; }
  WAVEFORMATEX const *GetFormat() { return &m_WavFormatEx; }
  int GetLengthMilli() const { return m_LengthMilli; }

protected:
  enum SoundType m_SoundType;      // is this an Ogg, WAV, etc.?
  bool m_bInitialized;             // has the sound been initialized
  WAVEFORMATEX m_WavFormatEx;      // description of the PCM format
  int m_LengthMilli;               // how long the sound is in milliseconds
};

class WaveResourceLoader : public IResourceLoader
{
public:
  virtual bool VUseRawFile() { return false; }
  virtual unsigned int VGetLoadedResourceSize(char *rawBuffer,
    unsigned int rawSize);
  virtual bool VLoadResource(char *rawBuffer, unsigned int rawSize,
    shared_ptr<ResHandle> handle);
  virtual std::string VGetPattern() { return "*.wav"; }

protected:
  bool ParseWave(char *wavStream, size_t length,
    shared_ptr<ResHandle> handle);
};
```

```
class OggResourceLoader : public IResourceLoader
{
public:
  virtual bool VUseRawFile() { return false; }
  virtual unsigned int VGetLoadedResourceSize(char *rawBuffer,
    unsigned int rawSize);
  virtual bool VLoadResource(char *rawBuffer, unsigned int rawSize,
    shared_ptr<ResHandle> handle);
  virtual std::string VGetPattern() { return "*.ogg"; }

protected:
  bool ParseOgg(char *oggStream, size_t length, shared_ptr<ResHandle> handle);
};
```

The `SoundResourceExtraData` class stores data that will be used by DirectSound. It is initialized when the resource cache loads the sound. Take a look at the protected members first. The `m_SoundType` members store an enumeration that defines the different sound types you support: WAV, OGG, and so on. The next Boolean stores whether the sound has been initialized, which is to say that the sound is ready to play.

The next data member, `m_wavFormatEx`, stores information about the sound so that DirectSound can play it. This includes how many channels are included in the sound, its sample rate, its bits per sample, and other data. The last member is a convenience member used to grab the length of the sound in milliseconds, which is nice to have if you are timing something, like an animation, to coincide with the end of the sound.

A real game would keep compressed sounds in memory and send bits and pieces of them into the audio hardware as they were needed, saving precious memory space. For longer pieces such as music, the system might even stream bits of the compressed music from digital media and then uncompress those bits as they were consumed by the audio card. As you can see, that system could use its own book to describe it thoroughly.

The resource cache will use implementations of the `IResourceLoader` interface to determine what kind of resource the sound is and the size of the loaded resource and to actually load the resource into the memory the resource cache allocates.

**Stream Your Music**

A better solution for music files, which tend to be huge in an uncompressed form, is to stream them into memory as the sound data is played. This is a complicated subject, so for now we'll simply play uncompressed sound data that is loaded completely into memory. Notice that even though a multimegabyte OGG file is loaded into a decompressed buffer, taking up perhaps 10 times as much memory, it loads many times faster. As you might expect, the Vorbis decompression algorithm is much faster than your hard drive.

#### *Loading the WAV Format with* `WaveResourceLoader`

WAV files are what old-school game developers call a *chunky* file structure. Each chunk is preceded by a unique identifier, which you'll use to parse the data in each chunk. The chunks can also be hierarchical; that is, a chunk can exist within another chunk. Take a quick look at the code below, and you'll see what I'm talking about. The first identifier, `RIFF`, is a clue that the file has an IFF, or Indexed File Format, basically the same thing as saying a chunky format. If the next identifier in the file is `WAVE`, you can be sure the file is a WAV audio file.

You'll notice the identifier is always four bytes and is immediately followed by a 4-byte integer that stores the length of the chunk. Chunky file formats allow parsing code to ignore chunks they don't understand, which is a great way to create extensible file formats. As you'll see next, we're only looking for two chunks from our WAV file, but that doesn't mean that other chunks aren't there:

```
bool WaveResourceLoader::ParseWave(char *wavStream, size_t bufferLength,
  shared_ptr<ResHandle> handle)
{
shared_ptr<SoundResourceExtraData> extra =
  static_pointer_cast<SoundResourceExtraData>(handle->GetExtra());

  DWORD     file = 0;
  DWORD     fileEnd = 0;
  DWORD     length = 0;
  DWORD     type = 0;
  DWORD     pos = 0;

  // mmioFOURCC -- converts four chars into a 4 byte integer code.
  // The first 4 bytes of a valid .wav file is 'R','I','F','F'

  type = *((DWORD *)(wavStream+pos));     pos+=sizeof(DWORD);
  if(type != mmioFOURCC('R', 'I', 'F', 'F'))
    return false;

  length = *((DWORD *)(wavStream+pos));   pos+=sizeof(DWORD);
  type = *((DWORD *)(wavStream+pos));     pos+=sizeof(DWORD);

  // 'W','A','V','E' for a legal .wav file
  if(type != mmioFOURCC('W', 'A', 'V', 'E'))
    return false;     //not a WAV

  // Find the end of the file
  fileEnd = length - 4;

  memset(&extra->m_WavFormatEx, 0, sizeof(WAVEFORMATEX));
```

```
bool copiedBuffer = false;

// Load the .wav format and the .wav data
// Note that these blocks can be in either order.
while(file < fileEnd)
{
  type = *((DWORD *)(wavStream+pos));  pos+=sizeof(DWORD);
  file += sizeof(DWORD);

  length = *((DWORD *)(wavStream+pos));  pos+=sizeof(DWORD);
  file += sizeof(DWORD);

  switch(type)
  {
    case mmioFOURCC('f', 'a', 'c', 't'):
    {
      GCC_ERROR"We don't handle compressed wav files");
      break;
    }

    case mmioFOURCC('f', 'm', 't', ' '):
    {
      memcpy(&extra->m_WavFormatEx, wavStream+pos, length);
      pos+=length;
      extra->m_WavFormatEx.cbSize = (WORD)length;
      break;
    }

    case mmioFOURCC('d', 'a', 't', 'a'):
    {
      copiedBuffer = true;
      if (length != handle->Size())
      {
        GCC_ERROR"Wav resource size does not equal buffer size"));
        return 0;
      }
      memcpy(handle->WritableBuffer(), wavStream+pos, length);
      pos+=length;
      break;
    }
  }

  file += length;

  // If both blocks have been seen, we can return true.
  if( copiedBuffer )
```

```
    {
      extra->m_LengthMilli = ( handle->Size() * 1000 ) /
        extra->GetFormat()->nAvgBytesPerSec;
      return true;
    }

    // Increment the pointer past the block we just read,
    // and make sure the pointer is word aligned.
    if (length & 1)
    {
      ++pos;
      ++file;
    }
  }

  // If we get to here, the .wav file didn't contain all the right pieces.
  return false;
}
```

The `ParseWave()` method has two parts. The first part initializes local and output variables and makes sure the WAV file has the right beginning tag, `RIFF`, signifying that the file is the IFF type, and the identifier immediately following is `WAVE`. If either of these two checks fails, the method returns `false`.

The code flows into a `while` loop that is looking for two blocks: `fmt` and `data`. They can arrive in any order, and there may be other chunks interspersed. That's fine, because we'll just ignore them and continue looking for the two we care about. Once they are found, we return with success. If for some reason we get to the end of the file and we didn't find the two chunks we were looking for, we return `false`, indicating a failure.

### Loading the OGG Format

The `ParseOgg()` method decompresses an OGG stream already in memory. The `OggVorbis_File` object can load from a normal file or a memory buffer. Loading from a memory buffer is a little trickier since you have to "fake" the operations of an ANSI `FILE *` object with your own code.

This first task is to create a structure that will keep track of the memory buffer, the size of this buffer, and where the "read" position is:

```
struct OggMemoryFile
{
  unsigned char* dataPtr;  // Pointer to the data in memory
  size_t   dataSize;       // Size of the data
  size_t   dataRead;       // Bytes read so far
```

```
  OggMemoryFile(void)
  {
    dataPtr = NULL;
    dataSize = 0;
    dataRead = 0;
  }
};
```

The next task is to write functions to mimic `fread`, `fseek`, `fclose`, and `ftell`:

```
size_t VorbisRead(void* data_ptr, size_t byteSize,
  size_t sizeToRead, void* data_src)
{
  OggMemoryFile *pVorbisData = static_cast<OggMemoryFile *>(data_src);
  if (NULL == pVorbisData)
  {
    return -1;
  }

  size_t actualSizeToRead, spaceToEOF =
    pVorbisData->dataSize - pVorbisData->dataRead;
  if ((sizeToRead*byteSize) < spaceToEOF)
  {
    actualSizeToRead = (sizeToRead*byteSize);
  }
  else
  {
    actualSizeToRead = spaceToEOF;
  }

  if (actualSizeToRead)
  {
   memcpy(data_ptr,
    (char*)pVorbisData->dataPtr + pVorbisData->dataRead, actualSizeToRead);
   pVorbisData->dataRead += actualSizeToRead;
  }

  return actualSizeToRead;
}

int VorbisSeek(void* data_src, ogg_int64_t offset, int origin)
{
  OggMemoryFile *pVorbisData = static_cast<OggMemoryFile *>(data_src);
  if (NULL == pVorbisData)
  {
    return -1;
  }
```

```
  switch (origin)
  {
    case SEEK_SET:
    {
      ogg_int64_t actualOffset;
      actualOffset = (pVorbisData->dataSize >= offset) ?
        offset : pVorbisData->dataSize;
      pVorbisData->dataRead = static_cast<size_t>(actualOffset);
      break;
    }

    case SEEK_CUR:
    {
      size_t spaceToEOF =
        pVorbisData->dataSize - pVorbisData->dataRead;

      ogg_int64_t actualOffset;
      actualOffset = (offset < spaceToEOF) ? offset : spaceToEOF;

      pVorbisData->dataRead += static_cast<LONG>(actualOffset);
      break;
    }

   case SEEK_END:
    pVorbisData->dataRead = pVorbisData->dataSize+1;
    break;

   default:
    assert(false && "Bad parameter for 'origin', requires same as fseek.");
    break;
  };

  return 0;
}

int VorbisClose(void *src)
{
   // Do nothing - we assume someone else is managing the raw buffer
   return 0;
}

long VorbisTell(void *data_src)
{
  OggMemoryFile *pVorbisData = static_cast<OggMemoryFile *>(data_src);
  if (NULL == pVorbisData)
```

```
    {
      return -1L;
    }

    return static_cast<long>(pVorbisData->dataRead);
}
```

You might notice that the method that fakes the `fclose()` doesn't do anything. Ordinarily, you might free the memory in the buffer, but since the raw sound data is managed by the resource cache, nothing needs to be done. Here's what the `ParseOgg()` method looks like:

```
bool OggResourceLoader::ParseOgg(char *oggStream, size_t length,
shared_ptr<ResHandle> handle)
{
  shared_ptr<SoundResourceExtraData> extra =
   static_pointer_cast<SoundResourceExtraData>(handle->GetExtra());

  OggVorbis_File vf;        // for the vorbisfile interface
  ov_callbacks oggCallbacks;

  OggMemoryFile *vorbisMemoryFile = new OggMemoryFile;
  vorbisMemoryFile->dataRead = 0;
  vorbisMemoryFile->dataSize = length;
  vorbisMemoryFile->dataPtr = (unsigned char *)oggStream;

  oggCallbacks.read_func = VorbisRead;
  oggCallbacks.close_func = VorbisClose;
  oggCallbacks.seek_func = VorbisSeek;
  oggCallbacks.tell_func = VorbisTell;

  int ov_ret =
    ov_open_callbacks(vorbisMemoryFile, &vf, NULL, 0, oggCallbacks);
  assert(ov_ret>=0);

  // ok now the tricky part
  // the vorbis_info struct keeps the most of the interesting format info
  vorbis_info *vi = ov_info(&vf,-1);

  memset(&extra->m_WavFormatEx, 0, sizeof(extra->m_WavFormatEx));

  extra->m_WavFormatEx.cbSize          = sizeof(extra->m_WavFormatEx);
  extra->m_WavFormatEx.nChannels       = vi->channels;
  // ogg vorbis is always 16 bit
  extra->m_WavFormatEx.wBitsPerSample  = 16;
  extra->m_WavFormatEx.nSamplesPerSec  = vi->rate;
```

```
  extra->m_WavFormatEx.nAvgBytesPerSec =
    extra->m_WavFormatEx.nSamplesPerSec* extra->m_WavFormatEx.nChannels*2;
  extra->m_WavFormatEx.nBlockAlign      = 2* extra->m_WavFormatEx.nChannels;
  extra->m_WavFormatEx.wFormatTag       = 1;

  DWORD  size = 4096 * 16;
  DWORD  pos = 0;
  int    sec = 0;
  int    ret = 1;

  // get the total number of PCM samples
  DWORD bytes = (DWORD)ov_pcm_total(&vf, -1);
  bytes *= 2 * vi->channels;

  if (handle->Size() != bytes)
  {
    GCC_ERROR("The Ogg size does not match the memory buffer size");
    ov_clear(&vf);
    SAFE_DELETE(vorbisMemoryFile);
    return false;
  }
  // now read in the bits
  while(ret && pos<bytes)
  {
    ret = ov_read(&vf, handle->WriteableBuffer()+pos, size, 0, 2, 1, &sec);
    pos += ret;
    if (bytes - pos < size)
    {
      size = bytes - pos;
    }
  }

  extra->m_LengthMilli = 1000.f * ov_time_total(&vf, -1);
  ov_clear(&vf);
  delete vorbisMemoryFile;
  return true;
}
```

This method shows you how to decompress an OGG memory buffer using the Vorbis API. The method will decompress the OGG stream into a PCM buffer that is essentially identical to the results you saw earlier with the `WaveResourceLoader`. The first part of the method initializes the `OggMemoryFile` structure and sets up the callback functions for Vorbis. Then a structure called `vorbis_info` is used to initialize the members of the `WAVEFORMATEX`, stored with the resource handle.

After the memory buffer is double-checked to be big enough to handle the decompressed OGG stream, the `ov_read` function is called in a loop to decompress it.

If you feel sufficiently energetic one weekend, this is where you'll want to play around if you'd like to implement decompression of the OGG stream in real time. Instead of decompressing the entire buffer, you'll decompress a part of it, save the stream where you left off, and let DirectSound play the buffer. Before DirectSound finishes playing the buffer, you'll run the decompression loop again into a different buffer. If your timing is right, DirectSound will be playing from one buffer while you are decompressing into another. If you think this is touchy work, you are right; it is for this reason that sound systems were typically fraught with weird bugs and instability. Imagine what would happen if the source OGG stream were thrown out of the resource cache, causing a cache miss and a huge delay in providing DirectSound with the data it needs to create the illusion of a continuous sound from a single uncompressed stream.

**Always Show Something Moving**

Any time you have a `while` loop that might take some time, such as decompressing a large OGG file, it's a good idea to create a callback function that your game can use to monitor the progress of the routine. This might be important for creating a progress bar or some other animation that will give your players something to look at other than a completely stalled screen. Console games are usually required to have on-screen animations during loads, but this is a good idea for PC games, too.

If you are just lifting this OGG code into your game and ignoring the rest of this chapter, don't forget to link the Vorbis libraries into your project. Since there's no encoding going on here, you can just link the following libraries: *libvorbisfile_static.lib, libvorbis_static.lib, and libogg_static.lib*. If you are compiling your code under Visual Studio, you can add the following lines of code to one of your CPP files. In the GameCode4 source, they are in *GameCode4.cpp*, where all of the other `#pragma comment()` statements are.

```
#pragma comment(lib, "libogg_static.lib")
#pragma comment(lib, "libvorbis_static.lib")
#pragma comment(lib, "libvorbisfile_static.lib")
```

To learn more about the OGG format, go to www.xiph.org/. The technology is open source, the sound is every bit as good as MP3, and you don't have to worry about paying expensive license fees. In other words, unless you have money to burn, use OGG for sound data compression. Lots of audio tools support OGG, too. You can go to the Xiph website to find out which ones.

## IAudioBuffer Interface and AudioBuffer Class

Now that you've got a sound in memory, it's time to play it. IAudioBuffer exposes methods such as volume control, pausing, and monitoring individual sounds while they are in memory. IAudioBuffer, and a partial implementation AudioBuffer, are meant to be platform agnostic. You'll see the DirectSound specific implementation shortly. Here's the interface class:

```
class IAudioBuffer
{
public:
  virtual ~IAudioBuffer() { }

  virtual void *VGet()=0;
  virtual shared_ptr<ResHandle> const VGetResource()=0;
  virtual bool VRestore()=0;

  virtual bool VPlay(int volume, bool looping)=0;
  virtual bool VPause()=0;
  virtual bool VStop()=0;
  virtual bool VResume()=0;

  virtual bool VTogglePause()=0;
  virtual bool VIsPlaying()=0;
  virtual bool VIsLooping() const=0;
  virtual void VSetVolume(int volume)=0;
  virtual int VGetVolume() const=0;
  virtual float VGetProgress() const=0;
};
```

The first method is a virtual destructor, which will be overloaded by classes that implement the interface. If this destructor weren't virtual, it would be impossible to release audio resources grabbed for this sound effect.

The next method, VGet(), is used to grab an implementation-specific handle to the allocated sound. When I say implementation-specific, I'm talking about the piece of data used by the audio system implementation to track sounds internally. In the case of a DirectSound implementation, this would be a LPDIRECTSOUNDBUFFER. This is for internal use only, for whatever class implements the IAudio interface to call. Your high-level game code will never call this method unless it knows what the implementation is and wants to do something really specific.

The next method, VRestore(), is primarily for Windows games since it is possible for them to lose control of their sound buffers, requiring their restoration. The audio system will double-check to see if an audio buffer has been lost before it sends commands to the sound driver to play the sound. If it has been lost, it will call the `VRestore()` method, and everything will be back to normal. Hopefully, anyway.

The next four methods can control the play status on an individual sound effect. `VPlay()` gets a volume from 0–100 and a Boolean `looping`, which you set to `true` if you want the sound to loop. `VPause()`, `VStop()`, `VResume()`, and `VPause()` let you control the progress of a sound.

The volume methods do exactly what you'd think they do: set and retrieve the current volume of the sound. The method that sets the volume will do so instantly, or nearly so. If you want a gradual fade, on the other hand, you'll have to use something a little higher level. Luckily, we'll do exactly that later on in this chapter.

The last method, `VGetProgress()`, returns a floating-point number between 0.0f and 1.0f and is meant to track the progress of a sound as it is being played. If the sound effect is one-fourth of the way through playing, this method will return 0.25f.

**All Things Go from 0.0 to 1.0**

Measuring things like sound effects in terms of a coefficient ranging from 0.0 to 1.0 instead of a number of milliseconds is a nice trick. This abstraction gives you some flexibility if the actual length of the sound effect changes, especially if it is timed with animations, or animations are tied to sound, which is very frequently the case. If either the sound changes or the animation changes, it is easy to track one versus the other.

With the interface defined, we can write a little platform-agnostic code and create the `AudioBuffer` class. The real meat of this class is the management of the smart pointer to a `SoundResource`. This guarantees that the memory for your sound effect can't go out of scope while the sound effect is being played.

```
class AudioBuffer : public IAudioBuffer
{
public:
  virtual shared_ptr<ResHandle> VGetResource() { return m_Resource; }
  virtual bool VIsLooping() const { return m_isLooping; }
  virtual int VGetVolume() const { return m_Volume; }
protected:
  AudioBuffer(shared_ptr<ResHandle >resource)
  {
    m_Resource = resource;
    m_isPaused = false;
```

```
    m_isLooping = false;
    m_Volume = 0;
  } // disable public construction

  shared_ptr<ResHandle> m_Resource;

  // Is the sound paused
  bool m_isPaused;

  // Is the sound looping
  bool m_isLooping;

  //the volume
  int m_Volume;
};
```

This class holds the precious smart pointer to your sound data managed by the resource cache and implements the `IAudioBuffer` interface. `VIsLooping()` and `VGetVolume()` tell you if your sound is a looping sound and the current volume setting. `VGetResource()` returns a smart pointer to the sound resource, which manages the sound data.

We're nearly to the point where you have to dig into DirectSound. Before that happens, take a look at the classes that encapsulate the system that manages the list of active sounds: `IAudio` and `Audio`.

## `IAudio` Interface and `Audio` Class

`IAudio` has three main purposes: create, manage, and release audio buffers.

```
class IAudio
{
public:
  virtual bool VActive()=0;

  virtual IAudioBuffer *VInitAudioBuffer(shared_ptr<ResHandle> soundResource)=0;
  virtual void VReleaseAudioBuffer(IAudioBuffer* audioBuffer)=0;

  virtual void VStopAllSounds()=0;
  virtual void VPauseAllSounds()=0;
  virtual void VResumeAllSounds()=0;

  virtual bool VInitialize()=0;
  virtual void VShutdown()=0;
};
```

`VActive()` is something you can call to determine if the sound system is active. As rare as it may be, a sound card might be disabled or not installed. It is also likely that during initialization or game shutdown, you'll want to know if the sound system has a heartbeat.

The next two methods, `VInitAudioBuffer()` and `VReleaseAudioBuffer()`, are called when you want to launch a new sound or tell the audio system you are done with it and it can release audio resources back to the system. This is important, so read it twice. You'll call these for each instance of a sound, even if it is exactly the same effect. You might want to play the same sound effect at two different volumes, such as when two players are firing the same type of weapon at each other, or you have multiple explosions going off at the same time in different places.

You'll notice that the only parameter to the initialize method is a shared pointer to a `ResHandle` object. This object contains the single copy of the actual decompressed PCM sound data. The result of the call, assuming it succeeds, is a pointer to an object that implements the `IAudioBuffer` interface. What this means is that the audio system is ready to play the sound.

The next three methods are system-wide sound controls, mostly for doing things like pausing and resuming sounds when needed, such as when the player on a Windows game Alt-Tabs away from your game. It's extremely annoying to have game sound effects continue in the background if you are trying to check email or convince your boss you aren't playing a game.

The last two methods, `VInitialize()` and `VShutdown()`, are used to create and tear down the sound system. Let's take a look at a platform-agnostic partial implementation of the `IAudio` interface:

```
class Audio : public IAudio
{
public:
  Audio();
  virtual void VStopAllSounds();
  virtual void VPauseAllSounds();
  virtual void VResumeAllSounds();

  virtual void VShutdown();

  static bool HasSoundCard(void);
  bool IsPaused() { return m_AllPaused; }

protected:
  typedef std::list<IAudioBuffer *> AudioBufferList;
```

```
  AudioBufferList m_AllSamples;  // List of all currently allocated buffers
  bool m_AllPaused;              // Has the sound system been paused?
  bool m_Initialized;            // Has the sound system been initialized?
};
```

We'll use STL to organize the active sounds in a linked list called `m_AllSamples`. This is probably good for almost any game because you'll most likely have only a handful of sounds active at one time. Linked lists are great containers for a small number of objects. Since the sounds are all stored in the linked list, and each sound object implements the `IAudioBuffer` interface, you can define routines that perform an action on every sound in the system.

```
void Audio::VShutdown()
{
  AudioBufferList::iterator i=m_AllSamples.begin();

  while (i!=m_AllSamples.end())
  {
    IAudioBuffer *audioBuffer = (*i);
    audioBuffer->VStop();
    m_AllSamples.pop_front();
  }
}

//Stop all active sounds, including music
void Audio::VPauseAllSounds()
{
  AudioBufferList::iterator i;
  AudioBufferList::iterator end;
  for(i=m_AllSamples.begin(), end=m_AllSamples.end(); i!=end; ++i)
  {
    IAudioBuffer *audioBuffer = (*i);
    audioBuffer->VPause();
  }
  m_AllPaused=true;
}

void Audio::VResumeAllSounds()
{
  AudioBufferList::iterator i;
  AudioBufferList::iterator end;
  for(i=m_AllSamples.begin(), end=m_AllSamples.end(); i!=end; ++i)
  {
    IAudioBuffer *audioBuffer = (*i);
    audioBuffer->VResume();
```

```
  }
  m_AllPaused=false;
}

void Audio::VStopAllSounds()
{
  IAudioBuffer *audioBuffer = NULL;

  AudioBufferList::iterator i;
  AudioBufferList::iterator end;
  for(i=m_AllSamples.begin(), end=m_AllSamples.end(); i!=end; ++i)
  {
    audioBuffer = (*i);
    audioBuffer->VStop();
  }

  m_AllPaused=false;
}
```

The code for each of these routines iterates the list of currently playing sounds and calls the appropriate stop, resume, or pause method of the `IAudioBuffer` object.

## DirectSound Implementations

The `Audio` and `AudioBuffer` classes are useless on their own; we must still create the platform-specific code. Since DirectSound is completely free to use by anyone, we'll create our platform-specific code around that technology.

You'll need to extend this code if you want to play MP3 or MIDI. Still, DirectSound can make a good foundation for a game's audio system. Let's take a look at the implementation for `DirectSoundAudio` first, which extends the `Audio` class we just discussed:

```
class DirectSoundAudio : public Audio
{
public:
  DirectSoundAudio()    { m_pDS = NULL; }
  virtual bool VActive() { return m_pDS != NULL; }
  virtual IAudioBuffer *VInitAudioBuffer(
    shared_ptr<ResHandle> soundResource);
  virtual void VReleaseAudioBuffer(IAudioBuffer* audioBuffer);
  virtual void VShutdown();
  virtual bool VInitialize(HWND hWnd);

protected:
  IDirectSound8* m_pDS;
```

```
    HRESULT SetPrimaryBufferFormat(
      DWORD dwPrimaryChannels,
      DWORD dwPrimaryFreq,
      DWORD dwPrimaryBitRate );
};
```

The only piece of data in this class is a pointer to an `IDirectSound8` object, which is DirectSound's gatekeeper, so to speak. Initialization, shutdown, and creating audio buffers are all done through this object. One way to look at this is that `DirectSoundAudio` is a C++ wrapper around `IDirectSound8`. Let's look at initialization and shutdown first:

```
bool DirectSoundAudio::VInitialize(HWND hWnd)
{
  if ( m_Initialized )
    return true;
  m_Initialized=false;
  m_AllSamples.clear();

  SAFE_RELEASE( m_pDS );

  HRESULT hr;

  // Create IDirectSound using the primary sound device
  if( FAILED( hr = DirectSoundCreate8( NULL, &m_pDS, NULL ) ) )
    return false;

  // Set DirectSound coop level
  if( FAILED( hr = m_pDS->SetCooperativeLevel( hWnd, DSSCL_PRIORITY) ) )
    return false;

  if( FAILED( hr = SetPrimaryBufferFormat( 8, 44100, 16 ) ) )
    return false;

  m_Initialized = true;
  return true;
}
```

This code is essentially lifted straight from the DirectX sound samples, so it might look pretty familiar. When you set the cooperative level on the DirectSound object, you're telling the sound driver you want more control over the sound system, specifically how the primary sound buffer is structured and how other applications run at the same time. The `DSSCL_PRIORITY` level is better than `DSSCL_NORMAL` because you can change the format of the output buffer. This is a good setting for games that still want to allow background applications like Microsoft Messenger or Outlook to be able to send something to the speakers.

Why bother? If you don't do this, and set the priority level to DSSCL_NORMAL, you're basically informing the sound driver that you're happy with whatever primary sound buffer format is in place, which might not be the same sound format you need for your game audio. The problem is one of conversion. Games use tons of audio, and the last thing you need is for every sound to go through some conversion process so it can be mixed in the primary buffer. If you have 100,000 audio files and they are all stored in 44KHz, the last thing you want is to have each one be converted to 22KHz, because it's a waste of time. Take control and use DSSCL_PRIORITY.

The call to SetPrimaryBufferFormat() sets your primary buffer format to a flavor you want; most likely, it will be 44KHz, 16-bit, and some number of channels that you feel is a good trade-off between memory use and the number of simultaneous sound effects you'll have in your game. For the purposes of this class, I'm choosing eight channels, but in a commercial game you could have 32 channels or even more. The memory you'll spend with more channels is dependent on your sound hardware, so be cautious about grabbing a high number of channels—you might find some audio cards won't support it.

```
HRESULT DirectSoundAudio::SetPrimaryBufferFormat(
  DWORD dwPrimaryChannels,
  DWORD dwPrimaryFreq,
  DWORD dwPrimaryBitRate )
{
  // !WARNING! - Setting the primary buffer format and then using this
  // for DirectMusic messes up DirectMusic!
  //
  // If you want your primary buffer format to be 22KHz stereo, 16-bit
  // call with these parameters:  SetPrimaryBufferFormat(2, 22050, 16);

  HRESULT          hr;
  LPDIRECTSOUNDBUFFER pDSBPrimary = NULL;

  if( ! m_pDS )
    return CO_E_NOTINITIALIZED;

  // Get the primary buffer
  DSBUFFERDESC dsbd;
  ZeroMemory( &dsbd, sizeof(DSBUFFERDESC) );
  dsbd.dwSize        = sizeof(DSBUFFERDESC);
  dsbd.dwFlags       = DSBCAPS_PRIMARYBUFFER;
  dsbd.dwBufferBytes = 0;
  dsbd.lpwfxFormat   = NULL;
```

```
    if( FAILED( hr = m_pDS->CreateSoundBuffer( &dsbd, &pDSBPrimary, NULL ) ) )
      return DXUT_ERR( L"CreateSoundBuffer", hr );

    WAVEFORMATEX wfx;
    ZeroMemory( &wfx, sizeof(WAVEFORMATEX) );
    wfx.wFormatTag      = (WORD) WAVE_FORMAT_PCM;
    wfx.nChannels       = (WORD) dwPrimaryChannels;
    wfx.nSamplesPerSec  = (DWORD) dwPrimaryFreq;
    wfx.wBitsPerSample  = (WORD) dwPrimaryBitRate;
    wfx.nBlockAlign     = (WORD) (wfx.wBitsPerSample / 8 * wfx.nChannels);
    wfx.nAvgBytesPerSec = (DWORD) (wfx.nSamplesPerSec * wfx.nBlockAlign);

    if( FAILED( hr = pDSBPrimary->SetFormat(&wfx) ) )
      return DXUT_ERR( L"SetFormat", hr );

    SAFE_RELEASE( pDSBPrimary );

    return S_OK;
}
```

You have to love DirectSound. This method essentially makes two method calls, and the rest of the code simply fills in parameters. The first call is to `CreateSoundBuffer()`, which actually returns a pointer to the primary sound buffer where all your sound effects are mixed into a single sound stream that is rendered by the sound card. The second call to `SetFormat()` tells the sound driver to change the primary buffer's format to one that you specify.

The shutdown method, by contrast, is extremely simple:

```
void DirectSoundAudio::VShutdown()
{
  if(m_Initialized)
  {
    Audio::VShutdown();
    SAFE_RELEASE(m_pDS);
    m_Initialized = false;
  }
}
```

The base class's `VShutdown()` is called to stop and release all the sounds still active. The `SAFE_RELEASE` on `m_pDS` will release the `IDirectSound8` object and shut down the sound system completely.

The last two methods of the `DirectSoundAudio` class allocate and release audio buffers. An audio buffer is the C++ representation of an active sound effect. In our platform-agnostic design, an audio buffer is created from a sound resource, presumably something loaded from a file or more likely a resource file.

```
IAudioBuffer *DirectSoundAudio::VInitAudioBuffer(shared_ptr<ResHandle> resHandle)
{
  shared_ptr<SoundResourceExtraData> extra =
   ::static_pointer_cast<SoundResourceExtraData>(resHandle->GetExtra());

  if( ! m_pDS )
    return NULL;

  switch(soundResource->GetSoundType())
  {
    case SOUND_TYPE_OGG:
    case SOUND_TYPE_WAVE:
      // We support WAVs and OGGs
      break;

    case SOUND_TYPE_MP3:
    case SOUND_TYPE_MIDI:
      // If it's a midi file, then do nothing at this time...
      // maybe we will support this in the future
      GCC_ERROR("MP3s and MIDI are not supported");
      return NULL;
      break;

    default:
      GCC_ERROR("Unknown sound type");
      return NULL;
  }
  LPDIRECTSOUNDBUFFER sampleHandle;
  // Create the direct sound buffer, and only request the flags needed
  // since each requires some overhead and limits if the buffer can
  // be hardware accelerated
  DSBUFFERDESC dsbd;
  ZeroMemory( &dsbd, sizeof(DSBUFFERDESC) );
  dsbd.dwSize             = sizeof(DSBUFFERDESC);
  dsbd.dwFlags            = DSBCAPS_CTRLVOLUME;
  dsbd.dwBufferBytes      = resHandle->Size();
  dsbd.guid3DAlgorithm = GUID_NULL;
  dsbd.lpwfxFormat        = const_cast<WAVEFORMATEX *>(extra->GetFormat());

  HRESULT hr;
  if( FAILED( hr = m_pDS->CreateSoundBuffer( &dsbd, &sampleHandle, NULL ) ) )
```

```
    {
      return NULL;
    }

    // Add handle to the list
    IAudioBuffer *audioBuffer =
      (IAudioBuffer *)(new DirectSoundAudioBuffer(sampleHandle, resHandle));
     m_AllSamples.push_front(audioBuffer);

     return audioBuffer;
}
```

Notice the switch statement at the beginning of this code? It branches on the sound type, which signifies what kind of sound resource is about to play: WAV, MP3, OGG, or MIDI. In our simple example, we're only looking at WAV data or OGG data that has been decompressed, so if you want to extend this system to play other kinds of sound formats, you'll hook that new code in right there. For now, those other formats are short circuited and will force a failure.

The call to IDirectSound8::CreateSoundBuffer() is preceded by setting various values of a DSBUFFERDESC structure that informs DirectSound what kind of sound is being created. Take special note of the flags, since that member controls what can happen to the sound. An example is the DSBCAPS_CTRLVOLUME flag, which tells DirectSound that we want to be able to control the volume of this sound effect. Other examples include DSBCAPS_CTRL3D, which enables 3D sound, or DSBCAPS_CTRLPAN, which enables panning control. Take a look at the DirectSound docs to learn more about this important structure.

After we're sure we're talking about a sound data format we support, there are two things to do. First, the sound data is passed onto DirectSound's CreateSoundBuffer() method, which creates an IDirectSoundBuffer8 object. Next, the DirectSound sound buffer is handed to our C++ wrapper class, DirectSound AudioBuffer, and inserted into the master list of sound effects managed by Audio.

Releasing an audio buffer is pretty trivial:

```
void DirectSoundAudio::VReleaseAudioBuffer(IAudioBuffer *sampleHandle)
{
  sampleHandle->VStop();
  m_AllSamples.remove(sampleHandle);
}
```

The call to IAudioBuffer::VStop() stops the sound effect, and it is then removed from the list of active sounds.

The second piece of this platform-dependent puzzle is the implementation of the `DirectSoundAudioBuffer`, which picks up and defines the remaining unimplemented virtual functions from the `IAudioBuffer` interface.

```
class DirectSoundAudioBuffer : public AudioBuffer
{
protected:
  LPDIRECTSOUNDBUFFER m_Sample;
public:
  DirectSoundAudioBuffer(
    LPDIRECTSOUNDBUFFER sample,
    shared_ptr<ResHandle> resource);

  virtual void *VGet();
  virtual bool VRestore();

  virtual bool VPlay(int volume, bool looping);
  virtual bool VPause();
  virtual bool VStop();
  virtual bool VResume();

  virtual bool VTogglePause();
  virtual bool VIsPlaying();
  virtual void VSetVolume(int volume);

private:
  HRESULT FillBufferWithSound( );
  HRESULT RestoreBuffer( BOOL* pbWasRestored );
};
```

The methods in this class are pretty easy C++ wrappers around `IDirectSoundBuffer8`. The exceptions are `FillBufferWithSound()` and `RestoreBuffer()`.

```
DirectSoundAudioBuffer::DirectSoundAudioBuffer(
  LPDIRECTSOUNDBUFFER sample,
  shared_ptr<CSoundResource> resource)
 : AudioBuffer(resource)
{
  m_Sample = sample;
  FillBufferWithSound();
}

void *DirectSoundAudioBuffer::VGet()
{
   if (!VRestore())
    return NULL;
```

```
  return m_Sample;
}

bool DirectSoundAudioBuffer::VPlay(int volume, bool looping)
{
  if(!g_Audio->VActive())
    return false;

  VStop();
  m_Volume = volume;
  m_isLooping = looping;

  LPDIRECTSOUNDBUFFER pDSB = (LPDIRECTSOUNDBUFFER)VGet();
  if (!pDSB)
    return false;

  pDSB->SetVolume( volume );

  DWORD dwFlags = looping ? DSBPLAY_LOOPING : 0L;

  return (S_OK==pDSB->Play( 0, 0, dwFlags ) );
}

bool DirectSoundAudioBuffer::VStop()
{
  if(!g_Audio->VActive())
    return false;

  LPDIRECTSOUNDBUFFER pDSB = (LPDIRECTSOUNDBUFFER)VGet();
  if( pDSB  )
    return false;

  m_isPaused=true;
  pDSB->Stop();
  return true;
}

bool DirectSoundAudioBuffer::VResume()
{
  m_isPaused=false;
  return VPlay(VGetVolume(), VIsLooping());
}

bool DirectSoundAudioBuffer::VTogglePause()
{
  if(!g_Audio->VActive())
    return false;
```

```
  if(m_isPaused)
  {
    VResume();
  }
  else
  {
    VPause();
  }

  return true;
}

bool DirectSoundAudioBuffer::VIsPlaying()
{
  if(!g_Audio->VActive())
    return false;

  DWORD dwStatus = 0;
  LPDIRECTSOUNDBUFFER pDSB = (LPDIRECTSOUNDBUFFER)VGet();
  pDSB->GetStatus( &dwStatus );
  bool bIsPlaying = ( ( dwStatus & DSBSTATUS_PLAYING ) != 0 );

  return bIsPlaying;
}

void DirectSoundAudioBuffer::VSetVolume(int volume)

{
  const int gccDSBVolumeMin = DSBVOLUME_MIN;
  if(!g_Audio->VActive())
    return;

  LPDIRECTSOUNDBUFFER pDSB = (LPDIRECTSOUNDBUFFER)VGet();
  assert(volume>=0 && volume<=100 && "Volume must be between 0 and 100");

  // convert volume from 0-100 into range for DirectX
  // Don't forget to use a logarithmic scale!

  float coeff = (float)volume / 100.0f;
  float logarithmicProportion = coeff >0.1f  ? 1+log10(coeff)  : 0;
  float range = (DSBVOLUME_MAX - gccDSBVolumeMin );
  float fvolume = ( range * logarithmicProportion ) + gccDSBVolumeMin ;

  GCC_ASSERT(fvolume>=gccDSBVolumeMin && fvolume<=DSBVOLUME_MAX);
  HRESULT hr = pDSB->SetVolume( LONG(fvolume) );
  GCC_ASSERT(hr==S_OK);
}
```

Most of the previous code has a similar structure and is a lightweight wrapper around IDirectSoundBuffer8. The first few lines check to see if the audio system is running, the audio buffer has been initialized, and parameters have reasonable values. Take note of the VSetVolume method; it has to renormalize the volume value from 0–100 to a range compatible with DirectSound, and it does so with a logarithmic scale, since sound intensity is logarithmic in nature.

The last three methods in this class are a little trickier, so I'll give you a little more detail on them. The first, VRestore(), is called to restore sound buffers if they are ever lost. If that happens, you have to restore it with some DirectSound calls and then fill it with sound data again—it doesn't get restored with its data intact. The VRestore() method calls RestoreBuffer() to restore the sound buffer, and if that is successful, it calls FillBufferWithSound() to put the sound data back where it belongs.

```
bool DirectSoundAudioBuffer::VRestore()
{
  HRESULT hr;
  BOOL   bRestored;

   // Restore the buffer if it was lost
   if( FAILED( hr = RestoreBuffer( &bRestored ) ) )
     return NULL;

   if( bRestored )
   {
     // The buffer was restored, so we need to fill it with new data
     if( FAILED( hr = FillBufferWithSound( ) ) )
       return NULL;
   }

  return true;
}
```

This implementation of RestoreBuffer() is pretty much lifted from the DirectSound samples. Hey, at least I admit to it! If you're paying attention, you'll notice an unfortunate bug in the code—see if you can find it:

```
HRESULT DirectSoundAudioBuffer::RestoreBuffer( BOOL* pbWasRestored )
{
   HRESULT hr;

   if( m_Sample )
     return CO_E_NOTINITIALIZED;
   if( pbWasRestored )
     *pbWasRestored = FALSE;
```

```
    DWORD dwStatus;
    if( FAILED( hr = m_Sample->GetStatus( &dwStatus ) ) )
      return DXUT_ERR( L"GetStatus", hr );

    if( dwStatus & DSBSTATUS_BUFFERLOST )
    {
      // Since the app could have just been activated, then
      // DirectSound may not be giving us control yet, so
      // the restoring the buffer may fail.
      // If it does, sleep until DirectSound gives us control but fail if
      // if it goes on for more than 1 second
      int count = 0;
      do
      {
        hr = m_Sample->Restore();
        if( hr == DSERR_BUFFERLOST )
          Sleep( 10 );
      }
      while( ( hr = m_Sample->Restore() ) == DSERR_BUFFERLOST &&
              ++count < 100 );

      if( pbWasRestored != NULL )
        *pbWasRestored = TRUE;

      return S_OK;
    }
    else
    {
      return S_FALSE;
    }
}
```

The bug in the method is the termination condition of the do/while loop; it could try forever, assuming DirectSound was in some wacky state. This could hang your game and cause your players to curse your name and post all kinds of nasty things on the Internet. Making the code better depends on what you want to do when this kind of failure happens. You likely would throw up a dialog box and exit the game. It's totally up to you. The lesson here is that just because you grab something directly from a DirectX sample doesn't mean you should install it into your game unmodified!

The next method is FillBufferWithSound(). Its job is to copy the sound data from a sound resource into a prepared and locked sound buffer. There's also a bit of code to handle the special case where the sound resource has no data—in that case, the sound buffer gets filled with silence. Notice that "silence" isn't necessarily a buffer with all zeros.

```
HRESULT DirectSoundAudioBuffer::FillBufferWithSound( void )
{
  HRESULT hr;
  VOID   *pDSLockedBuffer = NULL;         // DirectSound buffer pointer
  DWORD  dwDSLockedBufferSize = 0;       // Size of DirectSound buffer
  DWORD  dwWavDataRead         = 0;     // Data to read from the wav file

  if( m_Sample )
    return CO_E_NOTINITIALIZED;

  // Make sure we have focus, and we didn't just switch in from
  // an app which had a DirectSound device
  if( FAILED( hr = RestoreBuffer( NULL ) ) )
    return DXUT_ERR( L"RestoreBuffer", hr );

  int pcmBufferSize = m_Resource->Size();
  shared_ptr<SoundResourceExtraData> extra =
   static_pointer_cast<SoundResourceExtraData>(m_Resource->GetExtra());

  // Lock the buffer down
  if( FAILED( hr = m_Sample->Lock( 0, pcmBufferSize,
                     &pDSLockedBuffer, &dwDSLockedBufferSize,
                     NULL, NULL, 0L ) ) )
    return DXUT_ERR( L"Lock", hr );

  if( pcmBufferSize == 0 )
  {
    // Wav is blank, so just fill with silence
    FillMemory( (BYTE*) pDSLockedBuffer,
      dwDSLockedBufferSize,
      (BYTE)(m_Resource->GetFormat()->wBitsPerSample == 8 ? 128 : 0 ) );
  }
  else
  {
    CopyMemory(pDSLockedBuffer,
            m_Resource->GetPCMBuffer(), pcmBufferSize);
    if( pcmBufferSize < (int)dwDSLockedBufferSize )
    {
      // If the buffer sizes are different fill in the rest with silence
      FillMemory( (BYTE*) pDSLockedBuffer + pcmBufferSize,
        dwDSLockedBufferSize - pcmBufferSize,
         (BYTE)(m_Resource->GetFormat()->wBitsPerSample == 8 ? 128 : 0 ) );
    }
  }
```

```
  // Unlock the buffer, we don't need it anymore.
  m_Sample->Unlock( pDSLockedBuffer, dwDSLockedBufferSize, NULL, 0 );

  return S_OK;
}
```

There's also some special case code that handles the case where the DirectSound buffer is longer than the sound data—any space left over is filled with silence.

There's one last method to implement in the `IAudioBuffer` interface, the `VGetProgress()` method:

```
float DirectSoundAudioBuffer::VGetProgress()
{
  LPDIRECTSOUNDBUFFER pDSB = (LPDIRECTSOUNDBUFFER)VGet();
  DWORD progress = 0;

  pDSB->GetCurrentPosition(&progress, NULL);
  float length = (float)m_Resource->Size();
  return (float)progress / length;
}
```

This useful little routine calculates the current progress of a sound buffer as it is being played. Sound plays at a constant rate, so things like music and speech will sound exactly as they were recorded. It's up to you, the skilled programmer, to get your game to display everything exactly in sync with the sound. You do this by polling the sound effect's progress when your game is about to start or change an animation.

Perhaps you have an animation of a window cracking and then shattering. You'd launch the sound effect and animation simultaneously, call `VGetProgress()` on your sound effect every frame, and set your animation progress accordingly. This is especially important because players can detect even tiny miscues between sound effects and animation.

## Sound Processes

All of the classes you've seen so far form the bare bones of an audio system for a computer game. What's missing is some way to launch and monitor a sound effect as it is playing, perhaps to coordinate it with an animation. If you paid some attention in Chapter 7, you'll remember the `Process` class. It turns out to be perfect for this job.

```
class SoundProcess : public Process
{
```

```
public:
  SoundProcess(
    shared_ptr<ResHandle> soundResource,
    int typeOfSound=PROC_SOUNDFX,
    int volume=100,
    bool looping=false);

  virtual ~SoundProcess();

  virtual void  VOnUpdate(const int deltaMilliseconds);
  virtual void  VOnInitialize();
  virtual void  VKill();

  virtual void  VTogglePause();

  void       Play(const int volume, const bool looping);
  void       Stop();

  void       SetVolume(int volume);
  int        GetVolume();
  int        GetLengthMilli();
  bool       IsSoundValid() { return m_SoundResource!=NULL; }
  bool       IsPlaying();
  bool       IsLooping() { return m_AudioBuffer->VIsLooping(); }
  float      GetProgress();

protected:
  SoundProcess();  //Disable Default Construction

  void  InitializeVolume();
  void  Replay() { m_bInitialUpdate = true; };

  shared_ptr<ResHandle> m_SoundResource;
  shared_ptr<IAudioBuffer> m_AudioBuffer;

  int       m_Volume;
  bool      m_isLooping;
};
```

This class provides a single object that manages individual sounds. Many of the methods are re-implementations of some `IAudioBuffer` methods, and while this isn't the best C++ design, it can make things a little easier in your code.

As you might expect, the parameters to initialize this object are a `ResHandle` and initial sound settings. One parameter needs a little explanation, `typeOfSound`. Every process has a type, and sound processes use this to distinguish themselves into sound categories such as sound effects, music, ambient background effects, or speech. This creates an easy way for a game to turn off or change the volume level of a particular type of sound, which most gamers will expect. If players want to turn down the music level so they can hear speech better, it's a good idea to let them.

```
SoundProcess::SoundProcess(
  shared_ptr<ResHandle> soundResource,
  int typeOfSound, int volume, bool looping)
  : CProcess(typeOfSound, 0),
   m_SoundResource(soundResource),
   m_Volume(volume),
   m_isLooping(looping)
{
  InitializeVolume();
}

SoundProcess::~SoundProcess()
{
  if (m_AudioBuffer)
  {
    g_Audio->VReleaseAudioBuffer(m_AudioBuffer.get());
  }
}
```

The meat of the code in `SoundProcess` is in the next few methods. One important concept to understand about sounds is that the code might create a sound process long before the sound should be played or even loaded. Since sound effects tend to require a lot of data, it's a good idea to be careful about when you instantiate sound effects. After all, you don't want your game to stutter or suffer wacky pauses. The code shown next assumes the simplest case, where you want the sound to begin playing immediately, but it's good to know that you don't have to do it this way.

```
void SoundProcess::VOnInitialize()
{
  if ( m_handle == NULL || m_handle->GetExtra() == NULL)
    return;

  //This sound will manage its own handle in the other thread
  IAudioBuffer *buffer = g_Audio->VInitAudioBuffer(m_handle);

  if (!buffer)
  {
    VKill();
    return;
  }
```

```
  m_AudioBuffer.reset(buffer);

  Play(m_Volume, m_isLooping);
}
```

The `VOnUpdate` method monitors the sound effect as it's being played. Once it is finished, it kills the process and releases the audio buffer. If the sound is looping, it will play until some external call kills the process. Again, you don't have to do it this way in your game. Perhaps you'd rather have the process hang out until you kill it explicitly:

```
void SoundProcess::VOnUpdate(const int deltaMilliseconds)
{
  // Call base
  Process::VOnUpdate(deltaMilliseconds);

  if ( IsDead() && IsLooping() )
  {
    Replay();
  }
}
```

This class overloads the `VKill()` method to coordinate with the audio system. If the process is going to die, so should the sound effect.

```
void SoundProcess::VKill()
{
  if ( IsPlaying() )
    Stop();
  Process::VKill();
}
```

Notice that the base class's `VKill()` is called at the end of the method, rather than the beginning. You can look at `VKill()` similar to a destructor, which means this calling order is a safer way to organize the code.

As advertised, the remaining methods do nothing more than pass calls into the `IAudioBuffer` object.

```
bool SoundProcess::IsPlaying()
{
  if ( ! m_handle || ! m_AudioBuffer )
    return false;

  return m_AudioBuffer->VIsPlaying();
}
```

```
int SoundProcess::GetLengthMilli()
{
  if ( m_handle && handle->GetExtra() )
  {
    shared_ptr<SoundResourceExtraData> extra =
      static_pointer_cast<SoundResourceExtraData>(m_handle->GetExtra());
   return extra->GetLengthMilli();
  }
  else
    return 0;
}

void SoundProcess::SetVolume(int volume)
{
  if(m_AudioBuffer==NULL)
    return;

  GCC_ASSERT(volume>=0 &&
       volume<=100 &&
       "Volume must be a number between 0 and 100");

  m_Volume = volume;
  m_AudioBuffer->VSetVolume(volume);
}

int SoundProcess::GetVolume()
{
  if(m_AudioBuffer==NULL)
    return 0;

  m_Volume = m_AudioBuffer->VGetVolume();
  return m_Volume;
}

void SoundProcess::TogglePause()
{
  if(m_AudioBuffer)
    m_AudioBuffer->VTogglePause();
}

void SoundProcess::Play(const int volume, const bool looping)
{
  GCC_ASSERT(volume>=0 &&
       volume<=100 &&
       "Volume must be a number between 0 and 100");
```

```
  if(!m_AudioBuffer)
    return;

  m_AudioBuffer->VPlay(volume, looping);
}

void SoundProcess::Stop()
{
  if(m_AudioBuffer)
    m_AudioBuffer->VStop();
}

float SoundProcess::GetProgress()
{
  if (m_AudioBuffer)
    return m_AudioBuffer->VGetProgress();

  return 0.0f;
}
```

## Launching Sound Effects

The only thing you need to see now is how to tie all this together to launch and monitor a sound effect in your game. It may seem a little anticlimactic, but here it is:

```
Resource resource("SpaceGod7-Level2.ogg");
shared_ptr<ResHandle> rh = g_pApp->m_ResCache->GetHandle(&resource);
shared_ptr<SoundProcess> sfx(new SoundProcess(srh, PROC_MUSIC, 100, true));
m_pProcessManager->Attach(sfx);
```

There's clearly an awful lot of work going on in the background, all of which you now know how to do. Launching a sound effect ties together much of the code you've seen in this book: a cooperative multitasker, the resource cache, and a bit of DirectX, which launches an extra thread to manage the problem of getting data to the sound card at exactly the right speed. Still, it's nice to know that all that functionality can be accessed with three lines of code.

If you want to launch three sound effects based on the same data, one playing as soon as the other is complete, here's how you do it. Each one plays at a lower volume level than the one before it.

```
Resource resource("blip.wav");
shared_ptr<SoundProcess> sfx1(new SoundProcess(srh, PROC_SOUNDFX, 100, false));
shared_ptr<SoundProcess> sfx2(new SoundProcess(srh, PROC_SOUNDFX, 60, false));
shared_ptr<SoundProcess> sfx3(new SoundProcess(srh, PROC_SOUNDFX, 40, false));
```

```
m_pView->m_pProcessManager->Attach(sfx1);
sfx1->SetNext(sfx2);
sfx2->SetNext(sfx3);
```

## Other Technical Hurdles

There are a few more wires to connect, in code and in your brain, before you're ready to install a working sound system in your game. Most sounds are tied directly to game objects or events. Even music is tied to the intensity of the game or, even better, the impending intensity of the game! Tying sounds to game objects and synchronization are critical problems in any game sound system. If you have multiple effects at one time, you'll also have to worry about mixing issues.

### Sounds and Game Objects

Imagine the following game situation: A wacky machine in a lab is active and makes some kind of "wub-wub-wub" sound tied to an animation. Your hero, armed with his favorite plasma grenade, tosses one over to the machine and stands back to watch the fun. The grenade explodes, taking the wacky machine and the "wub-wub-wub" noise with it. What's really going on in the background?

Your game has some grand data structure of game actors, one of which is the doomed machine. When the grenade goes off, there's likely a bit of code or script that searches the local area for actors that can be damaged. Each actor in the blast radius will get some damage, and the code that applies damage will notice the machine is a gonner.

What happens next is a core technical problem in computer games: When the machine is destroyed, related game actors or systems should be notified. This can include things like sound effects or animation processes. Most games solve this with the trigger/event system, and this is no exception.

For purposes of clarity, the audio system code presented in this chapter has no such hook, but the event system you read about in Chapter 11, "Game Event Management," is exactly what is needed to solve this problem. You'll see how these two systems are tied together in Chapter 21, "A Game of *Teapot Wars*."

### Timing and Synchronization

Imagine the following problem: You have a great explosion graphics effect that has a secondary and tertiary explosion after the initial blast. How could you synchronize the graphics to each explosion? The pacing of the sound is pretty much constant, so the graphics effect should monitor the progress of the sound and react accordingly. We can use the `Process` class to make this work:

```
class ExplosionProcess : public Process
{
public:
  ExplosionProcess() : Process(PROC_GAMESPECIFIC) { m_Stage=0; }

protected:
  int m_Stage;
  shared_ptr<SoundProcess> m_Sound;

  virtual void  VOnUpdate(unsigned long deltaMs);
  virtual void  VOnInit();
};

void ExplosionProcess::VOnInit()
{
  Process::VOnInit();
  Resource resource("explosion.wav");
  shared_ptr<ResHandle> srh = g_pApp->m_ResCache->GetHandle(&resource);
  m_Sound.reset(GCC_NEW SoundProcess(srh));
  // Imagine cool explosion graphics setup code here!!!!
  //
  //
  //
}

void ExplosionProcess::VOnUpdate(unsigned long deltaMs)
{
  float progress = m_Sound->GetProgress();

  switch (m_Stage)
  {
    case 0:
      if (progress>0.55f)
      {
        ++m_Stage;
        // Imagine secondary explosion effect launch right here!
      }
      break;

    case 1:
      if (progress>0.75f)
      {
        ++m_Stage;
        // Imagine tertiary explosion effect launch right here!
      }
      break;
```

```
    default:
      break;
  }
}
```

The `ExplosionProcess` owns a sound effect and drives the imaginary animation code. The sound effect is initialized during the `VOnInit()` call, and `VOnUpdate()` handles the rest as you've seen before. There's a trivial state machine that switches state as the sound progresses past some constant points, 55 percent and 75 percent of the way through.

Do you notice the hidden problem with this code? This is a common gotcha in computer game design. What happens if the audio designer decides to change the sound effect and bring the secondary explosion closer to the beginning of the sound? It's equally likely an artist will change the timing of an animated texture, which could have exactly the same effect. Either way, the explosion effect looks wrong, and it's anyone's guess who will get the bug: programmer, artist, or audio engineer.

**The Butterfly Effect**

Code, animations, and sound data are tightly coupled and mutually dependent entities. You can't easily change one without changing the others, and you can make your life hell by relating all three with hard-coded constants. There's no silver bullet for this problem, but there are preventative measures. It might seem like more work, but you could consider factoring the `ExplosionClass` into three distinct entities, each with its own animation and sound data. Either way, make sure that you have some asset tracking so you can tell when someone changes anything in your game: code, sounds, or animations. When something breaks unexpectedly, the first thing you check is changes to the files.

## Mixing Issues

Sound in your game will include sound effects, music, and speech. Depending on what's going on, you might have to change the volume of one or more of these elements to accentuate it. A good example of this is speech, and I'm not talking about the random barks of a drunken guard. Games will introduce clues and objectives with AI dialogue, and it's important that the player be able to hear it. If you played *Thief: Deadly Shadows*, there's a good example of this in the Seaside Mansion mission about halfway through the game. The thunder and lightning outside were so loud it was difficult to hear the AI dialogue.

That's one of the reasons there is this notion of `SoundType` in our audio system. It gives you a bit of data to hang on to if you want to globally change the volume of certain sounds. In the case of *Thief*, it would have been a good idea to cut the volume of the storm effects so the game clues in the AI dialogue would be crystal clear.

**Don't Depend on Dialogue**

Dialogue is great to immerse players in game fiction, but you can't depend on it 100 percent. If you give critical clues and objectives via dialogue, make sure that you have some secondary way to record and represent the objectives, such as a special screen where the player can read a synopsis. It's too easy for a player to miss something. If your game enables subtitles, you can provide a screen that shows the last conversation.

While we're talking about mixing, you've got to take some care when changing the levels of sound effects. Any discrete jump in volume is jarring. Solve this problem with a simple fade mechanism:

```
FadeProcess::FadeProcess(
  shared_ptr<SoundProcess> sound,
  int fadeTime,
  int endVolume)
: Process(PROC_INTERPOLATOR)
{
  m_Sound = sound;
  m_TotalFadeTime = fadeTime;
  m_StartVolume = sound->GetVolume();
  m_EndVolume = endVolume;
  m_ElapsedTime = 0;

  VOnUpdate(0);
}

void FadeProcess::VOnUpdate(unsigned long deltaMs)
{
  if (!m_bInitialUpdate)
    m_ElapsedTime += deltaMilliseconds;

  Process::VOnUpdate(deltaMilliseconds);

  if (m_Sound->IsDead())
    Succeed();

  float cooef = (float)m_ElapsedTime / m_TotalFadeTime;
  if (cooef>1.0f)
    cooef = 1.0f;
```

```
  if (cooef<0.0f)
    cooef = 0.0f;

  int newVolume = m_StartVolume +
    ( float(m_EndVolume - m_StartVolume) * cooef);

  if (m_ElapsedTime >= m_TotalFadeTime)
  {
    newVolume = m_EndVolume;
    Succeed();  }

  m_Sound->SetVolume(newVolume);
}
```

This class can change the volume of a sound effect over time, either up or down. It assumes the initial volume of the sound effect has already been set properly, and all the times are given in milliseconds.

Here's how you would create some background music and fade it in over 10 seconds:

```
Resource resource("SpaceGod7-Level2.ogg");
shared_ptr<ResHandle> rh = g_pApp->m_ResCache->GetHandle(&resource);
shared_ptr<SoundProcess> music(GCC_NEW SoundProcess(rh, PROC_MUSIC, 0, true));
m_pProcessManager->Attach(music);

shared_ptr<FadeProcess> fadeProc(new FadeProcess(music, 10000, 100));
m_pProcessManager->AttachProcess(fadeProc);
```

The fade process grabs a smart pointer reference to the sound it is modifying, and once the volume has been interpolated to the final value, the process kills itself. Note that the original sound is created with a zero volume, and the fade process brings it up to 100.

**Simlish**

Sims have their own language of gibberish called "Simlish," which is meant to sound like a real language. While there are a few words and phrases that come to have actual translations, it's mostly just designed to sound appropriate and go with the tone of the conversation. Even the music has to use this fake language, which presents an interesting challenge to the musicians who create the songs you can hear when your sim turns on its radio.

How was Simlish born? Well, there is no possible way to record all the speech and dialogue required for each interaction without it sounding completely stale after the first few times. By having Simlish, we are more easily able to create that illusion without shipping a terabyte of speech.

# Some Random Notes

In the last 50 pages or so, you've read about sound resources, audio buffers, audio systems, and sound processes. This is where most books would stop. Neither my editor nor my readers will find any surprise in me continuing on a bit about sound. Why? I haven't told you a thing about how to actually use sound in your game.

## Data-Driven Sound Settings

Sometimes I think this book is equally good at showing you how not to code game technology as it is at showing you how to code correctly. The observant programmer would notice that all my sound examples in the previous pages all had hard-coded constants for things like volume, fade-in times, or animation points.

From day one, most programmers learn that hard-coded constants are a bad thing, and they can become a complete nightmare in computer game programming. The reason that I use so many of them in this book is because they make the code easier to read and understand. Real computer games would load all of this data at runtime from a data file. If the data changes, you don't have to recompile. If the game can reload the data at runtime with a cheat key, you can test and tweak this kind of data and get instant feedback.

With this kind of data-driven solution, programmers don't even have to be in the building when the audio guys are making the sounds. Believe it or not, they actually work later than programmers. This leaves programmers doing what they do best—programming game technology! A bit of volume data can also be tweaked more easily than the original sound file can be releveled, so your audio engineer doesn't have to be in the building, either.

So who's left to set the level on new sound effects on a Saturday? It's so easy that even a producer could do it. For those of you outside the game industry, I could as well have said, "It's so easy, your boss could do it!"

**Record All Audio at Full Volume**

Every sound effect should be recorded at full volume, even if it is way too loud for the game. This gives the sound the highest degree of waveform accuracy before it is attenuated and mixed with the other sounds in the primary sound buffer.

## Background Ambient Sounds and Music

Most games have a music track and an ambient noise track along with the incident sounds you hear throughout the game. These additional tracks are usually long because they'll most likely loop back to their beginning until there's some environmental reason to change them.

An example of an ambient noise track could be the sounds of a factory, crowd noises, traffic, or some other noise. Sounds like these have the effect of placing the players in the environment and give the impression that there's a lot more going on than what they see. This technique was used brilliantly in *Thief: Deadly Shadows* in the city sections. You could clearly hear city dwellers, small animals, carts, and other such noise, and it made you feel as if you were in the middle of a medieval city. But be warned—if the background ambient has recognizable elements, such as someone saying, "Good morning," players will recognize the loop quickly and get annoyed. Keep any ambient background close to "noise" instead of easily discernible sounds.

Music adds to this environment by communicating gut-level intensity. It helps inform the player and add a final polish to the entire experience. Perhaps my favorite example of music used in a game is the original *Halo*. Instead of only reacting to the current events in the game, the music segues just before a huge battle, telling the player he'd better reload his shotgun and wipe the sweat off his controller.

**Live Music Rocks—from Professional Musicians**

On the *Microsoft Casino* project, I thought it would be a great idea to record live music. It would be classy and add a unique feel to the game. I'd never produced live music for a game, so I was a little nervous about it. The music was composed by an Austin composer, Paul Baker, who also conducted the band. I got to play the part of the big-time producer guy behind the glass in the recording studio. I thought it was really cool until I heard the band run through the music the first time. It was horrible! I thought I'd be fired and wondered quickly how I could salvage this disaster.

My problem was that I'd never seen how professional musicians work. They arrived that day having never seen the music before, and the first time they played it they were all sight-reading. After a break, they played it one more time, and it was nearly flawless. I thought I'd just heard a miracle, but that's just my own naiveté. There was one errant horn note, blurted a little off time, and they cleared everyone out of the room except for the one horn player. He said, "gimme two measures," and they ran the tape back. At exactly the right moment, he played the single note he screwed up, and it was mixed flawlessly into the recording. I was so impressed by the live performance that I'll never be afraid of doing it in other games.

The CPU budget for all this sound decompression is definitely a factor. The longish music and ambient noise tracks will certainly be streamed from a compressed source rather than loaded into memory in uncompressed PCM format. Different platforms and decompression algorithms will take different and sometimes surprising amounts of your CPU time, so you should keep track of this. Do some benchmarks on your own and set your budgets accordingly.

## Speech

In-game character speech is a great design technique to immerse the player and add dimension to the AI characters. Games use character speech to communicate story, provide clues, and show alert levels in patrolling guards. Players expect a great script, smooth integration of the speech effects with the graphics, and most importantly, the ability to ignore it if they want to.

### *Random Barks*

A *bark* is another way of saying "filler speech." It usually describes any bit of speech that is not part of a scripted sequence. Good examples of this are AI characters talking to themselves or reactions to game events like throwing a grenade around a corner.

Some of my favorite random barks came from the drunk guard in *Thief: Deadly Shadows*. It was perfect comic relief in what is normally a dark game with long stretches of tension. If you hid in a nearby shadow, you'd hear this inebriated and somewhat mentally challenged guard talk to himself for a really long time.

In the background, a piece of code selects a random speech file at random intervals. The code must keep track of the barks so it doesn't play the same thing three times in a row, and it should also make sure that the random barks don't overlap any scripted speech the AI character might have, either.

Something that works well is a queue for each AI character regarding speech. Here a high-priority scripted bark will wipe out any random barks in the queue, and you can keep already barked elements in the queue to record which ones have played in recent history.

#### Too Much of a Good Thing Is True

Back on *Microsoft Casino*, there was this "blue-haired old lady" character that was our first AI character installed in the game. She only had one random bark: "Have you even been to Hoover Dam?," she would say, waiting for her cards. We sent the build to Microsoft QA, and we waited patiently for the phone call, which came way too quickly for it to be news of acceptance. The lead QA on the phone told us that after just one hour of testing, no one in QA was "ever likely to ever visit the @%$#& Hoover Dam" and could we please remove the bark technology until more barks were recorded. The bark was so reviled, we had to remove it entirely from the game.

### *Game Fiction*

Characters talking among themselves or straight to the player are an excellent way to give objectives or clues. If you do this, you must beware of a few gotchas. First, you shouldn't force the player to listen to the speech again if he's heard it before. Second, you should record a summary of the clue or objective in a form that can be referenced later—it's too easy to miss something in a speech-only clue. The third gotcha involves localization.

One game that comes to mind that solved the first gotcha in an interesting way was *Munch's Odyssey*, an Xbox launch title. Throughout the game, this funny mystic character appears and tells you exactly what you need to do to beat the level. If you've heard the spiel before, you can hit a button on the controller and your character, Abe or Munch, will interrupt and say something like, "I've heard all this before," and the mystic guy will bark, "Whatever…" and disappear. Very effective.

The second gotcha is usually solved with some kind of in-game notebook or objectives page. It's too easy to miss something in scripted speech, especially when it tends to be more colorful and therefore a little easier to miss the point entirely. Almost every mission-based game has this design conceit—it keeps the players on track and keeps them from getting lost.

The last gotcha has to do with language translation. What if you record your speech in English and want to sell your game in Japan? Clearly, the solution involves some kind of subtitle to go along with the scripted speech. Re-recording the audio can be prohibitively expensive if you have a huge script and a small budget.

### *Lip Synching*

Synching the speech files to in-game character animations is challenging, from both a technology and tools standpoint. This is yet another one of those topics that could use an entire book, so let me at least convince you that the problem is a big one and not one to be taken lightly or without experience.

It turns out that human speech has a relatively small number of unique sounds and sound combinations. You can create convincing speech with only a few dozen sounds. Since each sound is made with a particular position of the mouth and tongue, it follows that an artist can create these positions in a character ahead of time.

While the speech is being played, a data stream is fed into the animation system that tells which phoneme to show on the character at each point in time. The animation system interpolates smoothly between each sound extreme, and you get the illusion that the character is actually talking.

**Cheap Hacks for Lip Synching**

There are ways of doing lip synching on the cheap, depending on your game. *Interstate 76* solved the lip synching problem by removing all the lips; none of their characters had mouths at all! Another clever solution is to have the characters animate to a particular phrase like "peas and carrots, peas and carrots." *Wing Commander II*, a game published by Origin Systems in the mid-1990s, had all its characters lip-synched to a single phrase: "Play more games like *Wing Commander II*."

### *Recording Speech*

Most games will use at most a few hundred sound effects. This relatively small number of sound files is trivial to manage compared to speech files in some games. *Thief: Deadly Shadows* had somewhere around 10,000 lines of speech. You can't just throw these files into a single directory. You've got to be organized.

The first thing you need is a script—one for each character. As part of the script, the character should be described in detail, even to the point of including a rendering of the character's face. Voice actors use the character description to get "into character" and create a great performance.

The recording session will most likely have the voice actor read the entire script from top to bottom, perhaps repeating a line or phrase a few times to get it right. It's critical to keep accurate records about which one of the lines you intend to keep and which you'll throw away. A few days later, you could find it difficult to remember.

You'll record to DAT tape or some other high-fidelity media and later split the session into individual, uncompressed files. Here's where your organization will come into key importance: You should have a database that links each file with exactly what is said. This will help foreign language translators record localized speech or create localized subtitles. It is, after all, quite likely that the actor may ad lib a bit and say something a little differently than the original script.

## The Last Dance

The one thing I hope you get from this chapter besides a bit of technology advice is that sound is a critically important part of your game. This book has certainly spent enough pages on it. Most programmers and designers tend to wait until the very end of the production cycle before bringing in the sound engineers and composers. By that time, it's usually too late to create a cohesive sound design in your game, and the whole thing will be horribly rushed. As much as sound designers have resigned themselves to this fate, it is still something you should try to avoid.

Get organized from the very beginning, and ask yourself whether each task in your game schedule needs an audio component. You'll be surprised how many objects need sound effects, how many levels need their own background ambient tracks, and how much speech you need to record. Basically, if it moves at all, it needs sound.

Sound technology will also stress more of your core game components than any other system, including resource cache, streaming, memory, main loop, and more. Once your sound system is working flawlessly, you can feel confident about your lower-level systems. That's another good reason to get sound in your game as early as possible.

Most importantly, don't forget that sound sets the emotional stage for players. They will get critical player direction, feel more immersed, and react more strongly to everything if you've done a good job with your sound system and the sounds that it makes possible.

# Chapter 14

*by Mike McShaffry*

## 3D Graphics Basics

I want to tell you up front that the next three chapters won't teach you everything you need to know about 3D graphics—actually, far from it. Walk the aisle of any decent computer bookstore, and you'll see racks of books devoted entirely to 3D graphics. I'm only including three 3D chapters in this book, so I can't compete with the classics on 3D graphics. What's lacking in volume, I'll try to make up in focus and content. My job in these three chapters is to open the door to 3D graphics, especially in the way that game programmers utilize 3D techniques within well-designed game architecture. Many samples and tutorials are so hard coded they don't even work well when you import them into a game that draws more than one object, or they simply fail to work when you make a simple change. My goal is to give you a fundamental understanding of 3D graphics concepts, show you an architecture that is a good place to experiment and learn, and thus give you just enough knowledge to have some fun.

In this chapter, I'll focus on the basics. First, you'll learn about the 3D rendering pipeline. Then you'll have a 3D math primer. Lastly, you'll learn about materials, textures, lights, and geometry. You'll need this knowledge before you can learn about vertex and pixel shaders in the next chapter. This will set the foundation so that you can start manipulating objects and creating scenes in Chapter 16, "3D Scenes."

Get caffeinated—this is going to be a fast trip through 3D graphics.

## 3D Graphics Pipeline

The word *pipeline* describes the process of getting a 3D scene up on a screen. It's a great word because it implies a beginning that accepts raw materials, a process that occurs along the way, and a conclusion from which the refined result pours. This is analogous to what happens inside 3D game engines. The raw materials or resources used in the pipeline include:

- **Geometry:** Everything you see on the screen starts with descriptions of their shape. Each shape is broken down into triangles, each of which is composed of three vertices, which is a basic drawable element in 3D engines. Some renderers support points, lines, and even curved surfaces, but the triangle is by far the most common. Meshes are collections of triangles.
- **Materials:** These elements describe appearance. You can imagine materials as paint that you apply to the geometry. Each material can describe colors, translucency, and how the material reflects light.
- **Textures:** These are images that can be applied to objects, just as you might have applied decals to plastic models or wallpaper to your kitchen.
- **Lights:** You must have light to see anything. Light can affect an entire scene or have a local effect that mimics a spotlight.
- **Camera:** Records the scene onto a render target, such as the screen. It even describes what kind of lens is used, such as a wide or narrow angle lens. You can have multiple cameras to split the screen for a multiplayer game or render a different view to create a rearview mirror.
- **Shader**: A shader is a bit of code that runs on the video card. It is able to consume all of the above and calculate exactly what pixels to paint to the screen in the right positions to faithfully render every triangle the camera can see. Shaders typically work on either vertex positions or individual pixels inside a triangle, but in truth they can be much more general than that.

Some of the processes applied to the raw materials include the following:

- **Transformations:** The same object can appear in the world in different orientations and locations. Objects are manipulated in 3D space via matrix multiplications.
- **Culling:** At the object level, visible objects are inserted into a list of objects that are in view of the camera; at the triangle level, individual triangles are removed if they don't meet certain criteria, such as facing the camera.

- **Lighting:** Each object in range of a light source is illuminated by calculating additional colors applied to each vertex.
- **Rasterization:** Polygons are drawn, sometimes in many passes, to handle additional effects such as lighting and shadows.

Graphics pipelines also come in two flavors: fixed-function and programmable. The fixed-function pipeline sets rendering states and then uses those states to draw elements with those exact states. A programmable pipeline is much more flexible—it allows programmers to have detailed control over every pixel on the screen. Many systems, like the Nintendo Wii, still use a fixed-function pipeline. Modern graphics cards running Direct3D 10 or above and consoles like the Xbox360 and the PS3 use a programmable pipeline.

Knowing both fixed-function and programmable pipelines can be a really useful thing, but there are only so many trees in the forest, and I think it is best that this chapter focus on a programmable pipeline, specifically Direct3D 11. For those of you who are still running on a system that can't use Direct3D 11, like a Windows XP machine, don't worry. All the code that accompanies this book contains code for Direct3D 9's fixed-function pipeline. The 3D graphics chapters in this book only describe Direct3D 11, but if you are interested in Direct3D 9, you can find more information about it in the third edition of this book or in comments in the source code.

Before you see Direct3D 11, I'm going to take a quick shortcut through two math classes you probably slept though in high school or college. I know that because I slept through the same classes—trigonometry and linear algebra.

## 3D Math 101

I'll try my best to make this topic interesting. I'll know I've succeeded if I get through writing it without losing consciousness. This stuff can make your eyes glaze over. Remember one thing: You must understand the math, or you'll be hopelessly confused if you attempt any 3D programming. Sure, you'll be able to compile a DirectX sample program, tweak some parameters, and make some pretty pictures. Once you leave "Sampleland" and start making changes to your 3D code, however, you won't have a clue why your screen is black and none of the pretty pictures show up. You'll attempt to fix the problem with random tweaks of various numbers in your code, mostly by adding and removing minus signs, and you'll end up with the same black screen and a mountain of frustration.

My advice is to start small. Make sure that you understand each component fully and then move to the next. Have patience, and you'll never tweak a negative sign in anger again.

**3D Code Can Look Correct and Still Be Wrong**

3D programming is easier to get wrong than right, and the difficult part is that a completely miscoded system can look and feel correct. There will be a point where things will begin to break down, but by that time you might have hundreds or thousands of lines of bogus code. If something is wrong, and you randomly apply a negative sign to something to fix it and don't understand why it fixed it, you should back up and review the math.

## Coordinates and Coordinate Systems

In a 2D graphics system, you express pixel coordinates with two numbers: (X,Y). These are screen coordinates to indicate that each integer number X and Y corresponds to a row and column of pixels, respectively. Taken together as a pair, they describe the screen location of exactly one pixel. If you want to describe a 2D coordinate system fully, you need a little more data, such as where (0,0) is on the screen, whether the X coordinate describes rows or columns, and in which direction the coordinates grow—to the left or right. Those choices are made somewhat arbitrarily. There's nothing that says you couldn't create a 2D graphics engine that uses the lower right-hand corner of the screen as your (0,0) point—your origin. There's nothing that would keep you from describing the X-axis as vertical and Y as horizontal, and both coordinates grow positive toward the upper left-hand side of the screen.

Nothing would keep you from doing this, except perhaps the risk of industry-wide embarrassment. I said that these choices of coordinate system are somewhat arbitrary, but they do have a basis in tradition or programming convenience. Here's an example. Since the display memory is organized in row order, it makes sense to locate the origin at the top left-hand side of the screen. Traditional Cartesian mathematics sets the horizontal as the X-axis and the vertical as the Y-axis, which means that programmers can relate to the graphics coordinates with ease. It doesn't hurt that the original designers of text-display systems read text from left to right, top to bottom. If these were reversed, programmers would be constantly slapping their foreheads and saying, "Oh yeah, those idiots made the X-axis vertical!"

### Which Way Is Up?

*Drawn to Life: The Next Chapter* is a Wii title I worked on that was technically a 3D game, but the camera was locked along a single plane, giving it the feel of a 2D platformer. One of my early tasks was getting a new enemy into the game and hooking up some basic AI. I went into the design tool and placed the spawn point for the monster. When I loaded up the game, the monster wasn't there. I couldn't find him anywhere. After banging my head against this problem for a while, one of the programmers came up and casually mentioned that they were using the Z-axis as the vertical axis, not Y. Y represented depth, so I was setting the position of the creature to somewhere behind the scenery instead of up in the air. This became a common bug throughout development, albeit an easy one to fix.

A 3D world requires a 3D coordinate system. Each coordinate is expressed as a triplet: (X,Y,Z). This describes a position in a three-dimensional universe. As you might expect, a location on any of the three axes is described with a floating-point number. The range that can be expressed in a 32-bit floating-point number in IEEE format is shown in Table 14.1.

The diameter of the known universe is on the order of $10^{26}$ meters. The smallest theoretical structures of the universe, *superstrings*, have an estimated length of $10^{-35}$ meters. You might believe that a 32-bit floating-point number is more than sufficient to create a 3D simulation of everything in our universe, but you'd be wrong. Even though the range is up to the task, the precision is not. Oddly enough, we may one day find out that the universe is best expressed in terms of 256-bit integers, which would give enough range and precision to represent a number from 0 to $\sim 10^{76}$, plenty to represent the known universe, ignoring irrational or transcendental numbers like $\pi$.

So where does that leave you and your 32-bit IEEE floating-point number with its decent range and lacking precision? The IEEE format stores an effective 24 bits of resolution in the mantissa. This gives you a range of $1.67 \times 10^7$. How much is that? As Table 14.2 indicates, you should set your smallest unit based on your game

**Table 14.1 Precision of Floating-Point Numbers**

| Single Precision, 32-bit | Double Precision, 64-bit |
|---|---|
| $\pm 2^{-126}$ to $(2-2^{-23}) \times 2^{127}$ | $\pm 2^{-1022}$ to $(2-2^{-52}) \times 2^{1023}$ |

**Table 14.2 Units of Measurement**

| Smallest Unit | Physical Description of Smallest Representable Object (as a Textured Polygon) | Upper Range in Meters | Physical Description of Area in the Upper Range |
|---|---|---|---|
| 100m | A group of redwood trees | $1.67 \times 10^9$ | Earth/Moon System |
| 1m | A human being | $1.67 \times 10^7$ | North and South America |
| 1cm | A coin | $1.67 \times 10^6$ | California |
| 1mm | A flea | $1.67 \times 10^5$ | San Francisco Bay Area |
| 100 µm | A grain of pollen | $1.67 \times 10^4$ | Downtown San Francisco |

design. Most games can safely use the 100 micrometer (µm) basis since your sandbox can be as big as downtown San Francisco. The human eye can barely detect objects 100µm across but can't discern any detail.

This is why most games set their basic unit of measurement as the meter, constrain the precision to 1mm, and set their maximum range to 100 kilometers. Most art packages like 3ds Max enable artists to set their basic unit of measurement. If you use such a package, you need to make sure they set it to the right value for your game.

**Agree with Your Artists on a Standard Unit of Measurement**

A common source of problems in computer game development is when artists and programmers can't seem to get their units of measurement correct. Game objects and game logic might use different units of measurement, such as feet instead of meters. One clue: If things in your game appear either three times too big or three times too small, someone screwed up the units of measurement.

Now that we've nailed the range and precision of the 3D coordinates, let's take a few moments to consider those arbitrary decisions about origin and axes directions. You've probably heard of 3D coordinate systems described as either left- or right-handed, and if you're like me, you tend to forget which is which, and the explanation with your fingers and thumbs was always just a little confusing because I couldn't remember how to hold my hands! Here's another way to visualize it. Imagine that you are standing at the origin of a classic 3D Cartesian coordinate system, and you are looking along the positive X-axis. The positive Y-axis points straight up. If the coordinate system is right-handed, the Z-axis will point to your right. A left-handed coordinate system will have a positive Z-axis pointed to the left.

Why is *handedness* important? For one thing, when you move objects around your world, you'll want to know where your positive Z-axis is and how it relates to the other two, or you might have things zig instead of zag. The tougher answer is that it affects the formulas for calculating important 3D equations, such as a cross product. I'm extremely glad I don't have to explain a 4D coordinate system. I don't think I have it in me.

**Converting Handedness**

Since some art packages have different handedness than 3D rendering engines, you have to know how to convert the handedness of objects from one coordinate system to another. If you don't do this, all of your objects will draw incorrectly, with the polygons facing the opposite way that they should, giving objects an "inside out" appearance. Here is how you do the conversion:

1. Reverse the order of the vertices on each triangle. If a triangle started with vertices v0, v1, and v2, they need to be flipped to v2, v1, and v0.
2. Multiply each Z coordinate in the model by –1.
   Here's an example:
   Original:
   V0 = (2.3, 5.6, 1.2) V1 = (1.0, 2.0, 3.0) V2 = (30.0, 20.0, 10.0)
   Becomes:
   V0 = (30.0, 20.0, –10.0) V1 = (1.0, 2.0, –3.0) V2 = (2.3, 5.6, –1.2)

## Vector Mathematics

Vector and matrix math was always the sleepiest part of linear algebra for me. Rather than just show you the guts of the dot product or cross product for the umpteenth time, I'll also tell you what they do. That's more important anyway. I'll also show you some safety rules regarding matrix mathematics, because they don't act like regular numbers.

Before we go any further, you need to know what a unit vector is because it is something you'll use all the time in 3D graphics programming. A unit vector is any vector that has a length of 1.0. If you have a vector of arbitrary length, you can create a unit vector that points in the same direction by dividing the vector by its length. This is also known as *normalizing* a vector:

```
Vec3 v(3, 4, 0);
float length = sqrt ( v.x * v.x + v.y * v.y + v.z * v.z);
```

```
Vec3 unit = v / length;
cout "Length=" << length << newline;
cout "Unit vector: (X,Y,Z)=(" << unit.x << "," << unit.y << "," << unit.z << ")"
<< newline;
```

The output generated would be:

```
Length=5.0
Unit vector (X,Y,Z): (0.6,0.8,0.0)
```

When we talk about dot-and-cross products, their inputs are almost always unit vectors (also called *normalized vectors*). The formulas certainly work on any arbitrary vector, but the results are relatively meaningless unless at least one of them is a unit vector. Take the same formulas and apply unit vectors to them, and you'll find some interesting results that you can use to calculate critical angles and directions in your 3D world.

A dot product of two vectors is a single floating-point number, sometimes called a *scalar*. The cross product of two vectors is another vector. Remember these two important facts, and you'll never get one confused with the other again. Another way to say this is dot products calculate angles and cross products calculate direction. The dot product is calculated with the following formula:

```
float dotProduct = ( v1.x * v2.x ) + ( v1.y * v2.y ) + (v1.z * v2.z);
```

Unit vectors never have any coordinate with an absolute value greater than 1.0. Given that, you'll notice that the results of plugging various numbers into the dot product formula have interesting effects. Assuming V1 and V2 are unit vectors:

- **V1 equals V2:** If you calculate the dot product of a vector with itself, the value of the dot product is always 1.0.
- **V1 is orthogonal to V2:** If the two vectors form a right angle to each other and they are the same length, the result of the dot product is always zero.
- **V1 points in the opposite direction to V2:** Two vectors of the same length pointing exactly away from each other have a dot product of −1.0.

If this relationship between vectors, right angles, and the range [-1.0, 1.0] is stirring some deep dark memory, you're correct. The dark memory is trigonometry, and the function you are remembering is the cosine. It turns out that you can use the dot product of two unit vectors to calculate the angle between two vectors. For two unit vectors *a* and *b*, the formula for calculating the angle between them is

$$\theta = \cos^{-1}\left(\frac{ab}{|a||b|}\right)$$

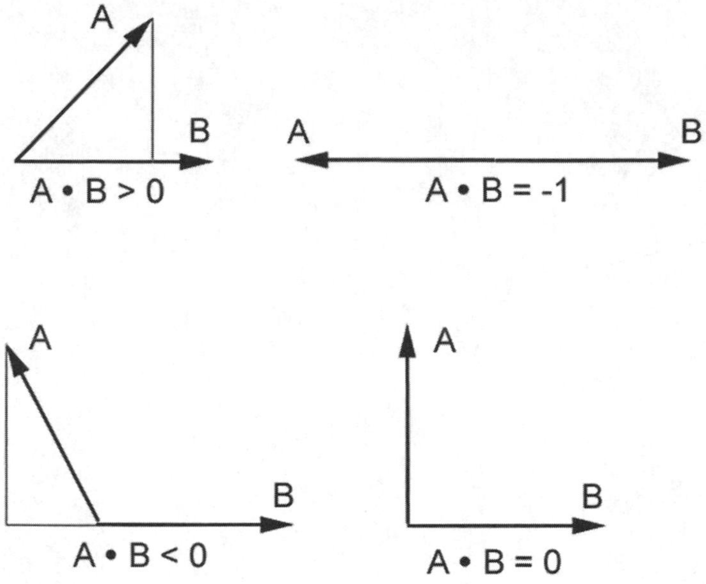


**Figure 14.1**
The dot product projects one vector onto another.

That is a complicated way of saying that if you divide the dot product of two vectors by their lengths multiplied together, you get the cosine of their angle. Take the arc-cosine of that number, and you have the angle! This is extremely useful in computer games, since you are always trying to figure out the angle between vectors.

Another way to visualize the dot product graphically is that *the dot product projects one vector onto the other and calculates the length of that vector*. This dot product relationship is shown in Figure 14.1, where the dot product equals the length of the projection of vector A onto B. As it turns out, this length is exactly the same as the projection of vector B onto vector A. Weird, huh?

The dot product can be useful by itself, since it can determine whether the angle between two vectors is acute, a right angle, or obtuse. The classic application of the dot product in 3D graphics is determining whether a polygon is facing toward or away from the camera (see Figure 14.2).

In Figure 14.2, the camera has a unit vector called the *look at vector*, and it points in the same direction as the camera. Each polygon has a normal vector that is orthogonal to the plane of the polygon. If the dot product between these two vectors is less than zero, the polygon is facing the camera and should be added to the draw list. In the case of Figure 14.2, the dot product for these two vectors is close to -1.0, so the polygon will be drawn.

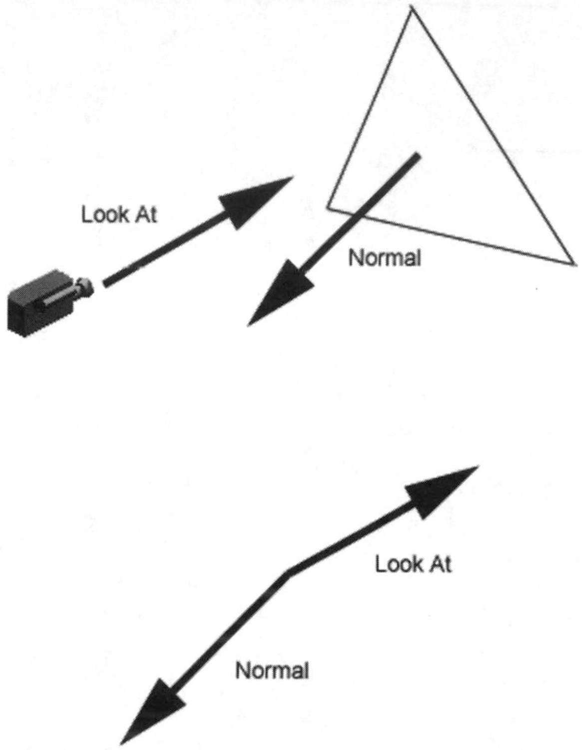


**Figure 14.2**
Dot products are used to see if a polygon is facing the camera—the dot product will be negative.

If you want the actual angle represented by the dot product, you must perform an arccosine operation. If you remember those hazy trig classes at all, you'll know that the arccosine isn't defined everywhere, only between values [−1.0, 1.0]. That's lucky, because dot products from unit vectors have exactly the same range. So where's the problem? The arccosine will always return positive numbers.

The dot product is directionless, giving you the same result no matter which vector you send in first: A dot B is the same as B dot A. Still not convinced this is a problem? Let's assume that you are using the dot product to determine the angle between your current direction and the direction vector that points to something you are targeting.

In Figure 14.3, the white arrow is the current direction, and the gray arrows are oriented 45 degrees away about the Y-axis. Notice that one of the gray arrows is pointing straight to our teapot target, but the other one is pointing in a completely wrong direction. Yet, the dot products between the white direction vector and both gray vectors are the same because the angles are the same!

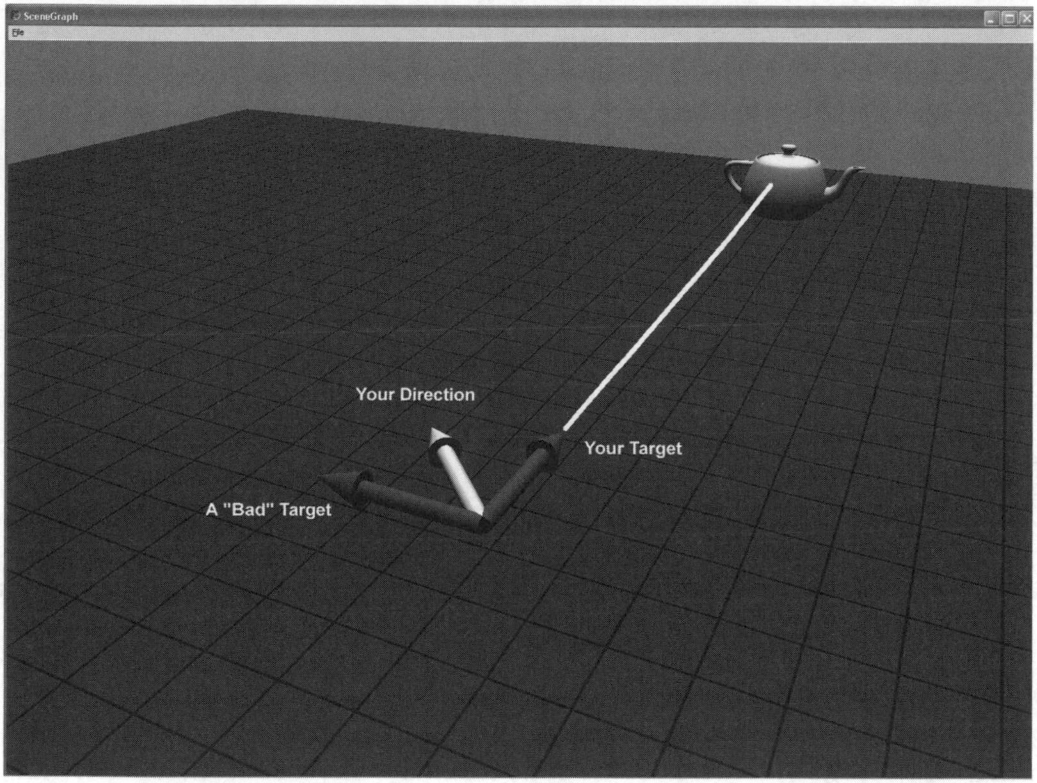


**Figure 14.3**
Dot products can't find targets.

Remember that the dot product measures angles and not direction. As you can see from the diagram, the dot product won't tell you which way to turn, only how much to turn. You need a cross product.

Graphically, the cross product returns a vector that is orthogonal to the plane formed by the two input vectors. The cross product vector should be normalized before you use it. Planes have two sides, and the resulting normal vector can only point in one direction. How does it know which way to point? It turns out that cross products are sensitive to the order of their input vectors. In other words, A cross B is not equal to B cross A. As you might expect, it is exactly negative. This is where the handedness of the coordinate system comes back into play. The cross product is always calculated with this formula:

```
cross.x = (A.y * B.z) – (B.y * A.z)
cross.y = (A.z * B.x) – (B.z * A.x)
cross.z = (A.x * B.y) – (B.x * A.y)
```

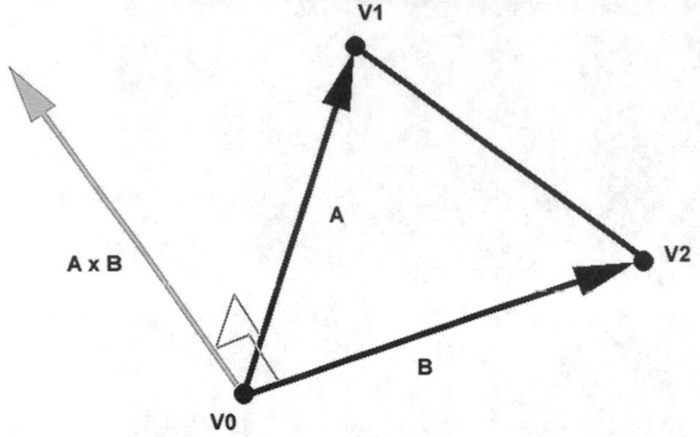


**Figure 14.4**
A cross product.

I'm going to borrow your right hand for a moment. Hold your right hand out in front of you, fingers together and totally flat. Make sure you are looking at your palm. Extend your thumb out, keeping your hand flat. Your thumb is vector A, and your forefinger is vector B. The result of the cross product, A cross B, is a vector pointing up out of your palm. If you did it backward, B cross A, the vector would be pointing away from you. This is the fundamental difference between left- and right-handed coordinate systems—determining which vectors get sent into the cross product in which order. It matters!

The classic use of the cross product is figuring out the normal vector of a polygon (see Figure 14.4). The normal vector is fundamental to calculating which polygons are facing the camera, and therefore, which polygons are drawn and which can be ignored. It is also good for calculating how much light reflects from the polygon back to the camera. By the way, if you take the cross product of two parallel vectors, the result will be a null vector—X, Y, and Z will all equal zero.

For any polygon that has three vertices, V0, V1, and V2, the normal vector is calculated using a cross product:

```
Vector A = V1 - V0;
Vector B = V2 - V0;
Vector Cross = CrossProduct(A, B);
```

In a right-handed coordinate system, the vertices are arranged in a counterclockwise order because they are seen when looking at the drawn side of the polygon.

Another use is figuring the direction. We have a dot product that tells us that we need to steer either left or right, but we can't figure out which. It turns out that the

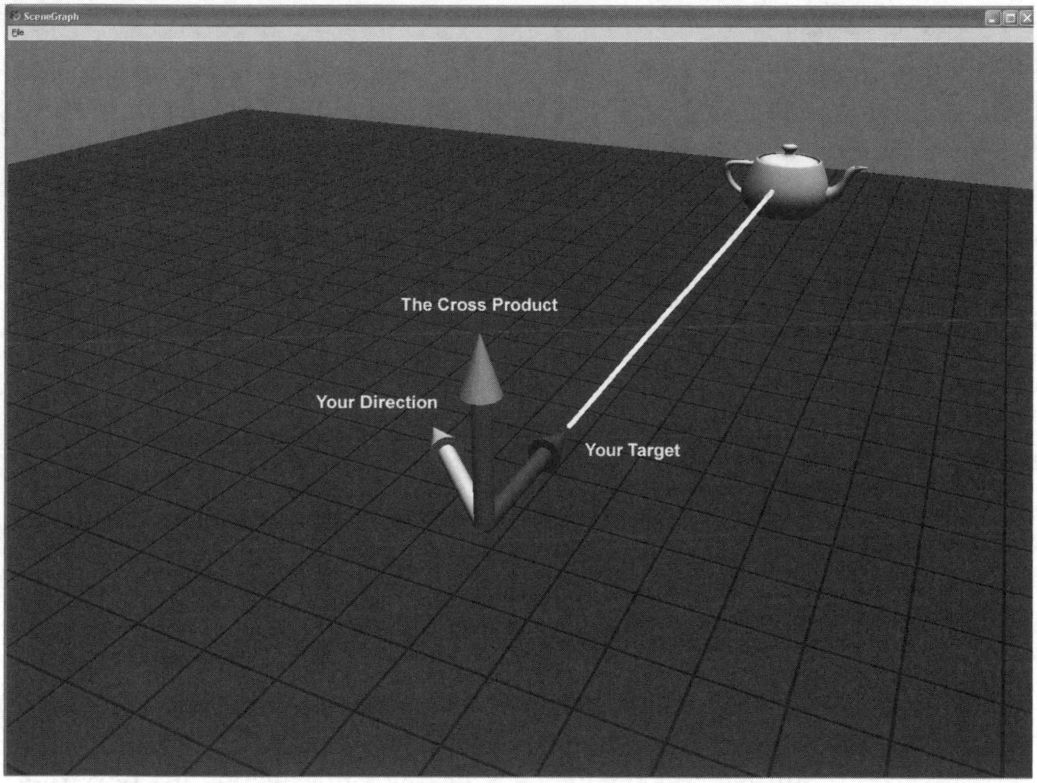


**Figure 14.5**
A cross product and a dot product together can find a target.

cross product between the direction vectors contains information about which way to steer.

The cross product between the target vector and your direction vector points up, indicating you should steer right (see Figure 14.5). If the cross product pointed down, the target would have been off to your left. The target example is somewhat contrived because you don't actually need the cross product at all. It makes a good example because it's a useful experiment to visualize the usefulness of the cross product.

**Find Targets with Just a Dot Product**

Through a little trickery, you can do it solely with the dot product, as long as you choose the correct vectors. If you use a vector that points to your right instead of straight ahead, your dot product will yield a positive number if you need to steer right, a negative number if you need to steer left, and something close to zero if your target is right in front of you. Even better, if your steering parameters range from –1.0 to steer hard left and 1.0 to lock it all the way to the right, you can send this dot product straight into your steering code. Cool, huh?

# C++ Math Classes

Before we get into the guts of a scene graph and how it works, we'll need some simple math classes for handling 3D and 4D vectors, matrices, and quaternions. Most programmers will create a math library with ultra-efficient implementations of these and other useful tidbits. For this book, I'm using DirectX D3DX math functions and structures as a base. Here are the reasons why I'm using this approach:

- The DirectX math functions are fairly well optimized for PC development and are a fair place to start for console development.
- The new XNA math libraries, which many of the Direct3D 11 samples and tutorials use, do not easily support encapsulation into classes meant to abstract their lineage, and they cannot be used by DirectX 9, which is still supported by the code in this book. D3DX based structures can be used in Direct3D 9, 10, and 11.
- By creating some platform-agnostic math classes for use in the scene graph code, you can replace them with any C++ implementation you like. Personally, I think the C++ versions are much easier to read, too. These classes are bare bones, really not much more than the very basics.

The classes you will use throughout the 3D code in this book include the following:

- `Vec3` & `Vec4`: Three- and four-dimensional vectors.
- `Quaternion`: A quaternion that describes orientation in 3D space.
- `Mat4 x 4`: A matrix that holds both orientation and translation.
- `Plane`: A flat surface that stretches to infinity; it has an "inside" and an "outside."
- `Frustum`: A shape like a pyramid with the point clipped off, usually used to describe the viewable area of a camera.

## Vector Classes

You should already be very familiar with the vector structures used by DirectX—`D3DXVECTOR3` and `D3DXVECTOR4`. Here's a very simple C++ wrapper for both of those structures:

```
class Vec3 : public D3DXVECTOR3
{
public:
  inline float Length()
```

```
    { return D3DXVec3Length(this); }
  inline Vec3 *Normalize()
    { return static_cast<Vec3 *>(D3DXVec3Normalize(this, this)); }
  inline float Dot(const Vec3 &b)
    { return D3DXVec3Dot(this, &b); }
  inline Vec3 Cross(const Vec3 &b) const
  {
    Vec3 out;
    D3DXVec3Cross(&out, this, &b);
    return out;
  }
  Vec3(D3DXVECTOR3 &v3)
    { x = v3.x; y = v3.y; z = v3.z; }
  Vec3() : D3DXVECTOR3() { }
  Vec3(const float _x, const float _y, const float _z)
    { x=_x; y=_y; z=_z; }
  inline Vec3(const class Vec4 &v4)
    { x = v4.x; y = v4.y; z = v4.z; }
};

class Vec4 : public D3DXVECTOR4
{
public:
  inline float Length()
    { return D3DXVec4Length(this); }
  inline Vec4 *Normalize()
    { return static_cast<Vec4 *>(D3DXVec4Normalize(this, this)); }
  inline float Dot(const Vec4 &b)
    { return D3DXVec4Dot(this, &b); }
  // If you want the cross product, use Vec3::Cross

  Vec4(D3DXVECTOR4 &v4)
    { x = v4.x; y = v4.y; z = v4.z; w = v4.w; }
  Vec4() : D3DXVECTOR4() { }
  Vec4(const float _x, const float _y, const float _z, const float _w)
    { x=_x; y=_y; z=_z; w=_w; }
  Vec4(const Vec3 &v3)
    { x = v3.x; y = v3.y; z = v3.z; w = 1.0f; }
};

typedef std::list<Vec3> Vec3List;
typedef std::list<Vec4> Vec4List;
```

The `Vec3` and `Vec4` classes wrap the DirectX `D3DXVECTOR3` and `D3DXVECTOR4` structures. The usefulness of the `Vec3` class is pretty obvious. As for `Vec4`, you need a four-dimensional vector to send in to a 4 × 4-transform matrix. If you remember your high school math, you can't multiply a 4 × 4 matrix and a three-dimensional vector. Only a four-dimensional vector will do.

The methods that are provided as a part of this class are

- `Length`: Finds the length of the vector.
- `Normalize`: Changes the vector to have the same direction but a length of 1.0f.
- `Dot`: Computes the dot product of the vector.
- `Cross`: Computes the cross product of the vector (only `Vec3` does this!).

## Matrix Mathematics

A 3D world is filled with objects that move around. It would seem like an impossible task to set each vertex and surface normal of every polygon each time an object moves. There's a shortcut, it turns out, and it concerns matrices. Vertices and surface normals for objects in your 3D world are stored in object space. As the object moves and rotates, the only thing that changes is the object's transform matrix. The original vertices and normals remain exactly the same. The object's transform matrix holds information about its position in the world and its rotation about the X-, Y-, and Z-axis.

Multiple instances of an object need not duplicate the geometry data. Each object instance only needs a different transform matrix and a reference to the original geometry. As each object moves, the only things that change are the values of each transform matrix. A transform matrix for a 3D engine is represented by a 4 × 4 array of floating-point numbers. This is enough information to store both the rotation and position of an object. If you only want to store the rotation and not the position, a 3 × 3 array is just fine. This is one of the reasons you see both matrices represented in DirectX and other renderers. I'll use the 4 × 4 `D3DXMATRIX` in this chapter for all of the examples because I want to use one data structure for rotation and translation. The matrix elements are set in specific ways to perform translations and different rotations. For each kind of matrix, I'll show you how to set the elements yourself or how to call a DirectX function to initialize it.

A translation matrix moves vectors linearly. Assuming that you have a displacement vector `t`, which describes the translation along each axis, you'll initialize the translation matrix with the values shown below.

```
// Create a DirectX matrix that will translate vectors
// +3 units along X and -2 units along Z
```

```
D3DXVECTOR3 t(3,0,-2);
D3DXMATRIX transMatrix;
D3DXMatrixTranslation(&transMatrix, t.x,t.y,t.z);
```

Here's how to do the same thing in DirectX:

```
D3DXVECTOR4 original(1, 1, 1, 1);
D3DXVECTOR4 result;
D3DXVec4Transform(&result, &original, &transMatrix);
```

The transform creates a new vector with values (4, 1, −1, 1). The DirectX function `D3DXVec4Transform` multiplies the input vector with the transform matrix. The result is a transformed vector.

$$\begin{bmatrix} 1 & 0 & 0 & 0 \\ 0 & 1 & 0 & 0 \\ 0 & 0 & 1 & 0 \\ T.x & T.y & T.z & 1 \end{bmatrix}$$

**Make Sure You Match 4 × 4 Matrices with a 4D Vector**

Did you notice my underhanded use of the `D3DXVECTOR4` structure without giving you a clue about its use? Matrix mathematics is very picky about the dimensions of vectors and matrices that you multiply. It turns out that you can only multiply matrices where the number of rows matches the number of columns. This is why a 4 × 4 matrix must be multiplied with a four-dimensional vector. Also, the last value of that 4D vector, W, should be set at 1.0, or you'll get odd results.

There are three kinds of rotation matrices, one for rotation about each axis. The most critical thing you must get through your math-addled brain is this: Rotations always happen around the origin. "What in the heck does that mean," you ask? You'll understand it better after you see an example. First, you need to get your bearings. Figure 14.6 shows an image of a teapot sitting at the origin. The squares are one unit across. We are looking at the origin from (X=6, Y=6, Z=6). The Y-axis points up. The X-axis points off to the lower left, and the Z-axis points to the lower right.

If you look along the axis of rotation, an object will appear to rotate counterclockwise if you rotate it in a positive angle. One way to remember this is by going back to the unit circle in trig, as shown in Figure 14.7.

*A special note to my high school geometry teacher, Mrs. Connally: You were right all along—I did have use for the unit circle after all.... I'm torturing other people with it!*

That means if you want to rotate the teapot so that the spout is pointing straight at us, you'll need to rotate it about the Y-axis. The Y-axis points up, so any rotation

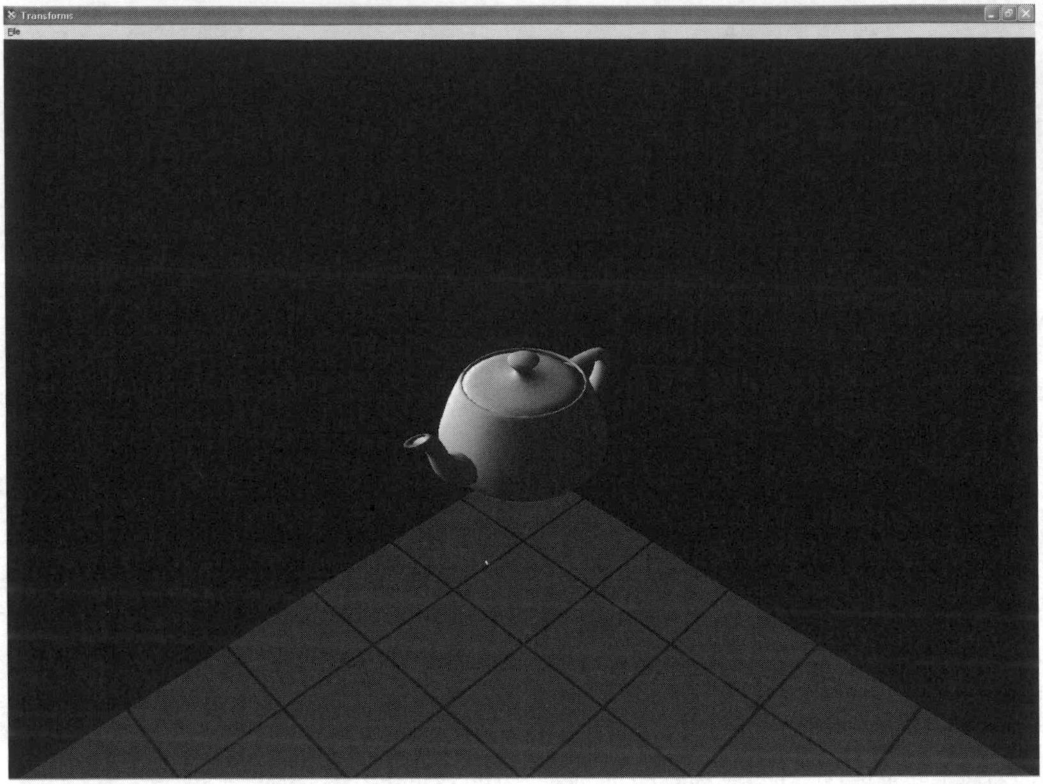

**Figure 14.6**
Displaying a teapot at the origin (0,0,0).

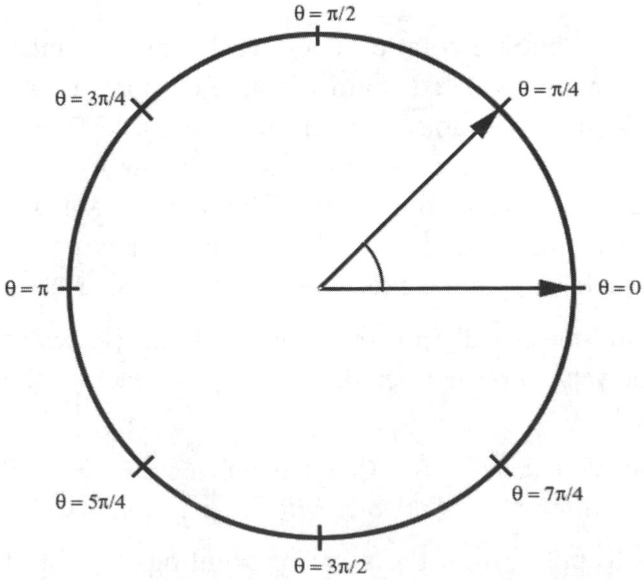


**Figure 14.7**
The ubiquitous unit circle.

about that axis will make the teapot appear as if it is sitting on a potter's wheel. How do you calculate the angle? Go back to your unit circle to figure it out. The angle you want is 45 degrees, or $\pi/4$. We also know that the angle should be negative. Here's why: If you were looking along the Y-axis, you'd be underneath the teapot looking straight up. The teapot's spout needs to twist clockwise to achieve the desired result, so the angle is negative.

A rotation matrix for the Y-axis looks like this:

$$\begin{bmatrix} \cos(\theta) & 0 & -\sin(\theta) & 0 \\ 0 & 1 & 0 & 0 \\ \sin(\theta) & 0 & \cos(\theta) & 0 \\ 0 & 0 & 0 & 1 \end{bmatrix}$$

Here's the code to create this matrix in DirectX:

```
float angle = -D3DX_PI / 4.0f;
D3DXMATRIX rotateY;
D3DXMatrixRotationY(&rotateY, angle);
```

Let's transform a vector with this matrix and see what happens. Since the teapot's spout is pointing down the X-axis, let's transform (x=1, y=0, z=0):

```
D3DXVECTOR4 original(1, 0, 0, 1);
D3DXVECTOR4 result(0,0,0,0);
D3DXVec4Transform(&result, &original, &rotateY);
```

Here's the result:

```
result   {...}   D3DXVECTOR4
   x   0.70710677   float
   y   0.00000000   float
   z   0.70710677   float
   w   1.0000000    float
```

Excellent, that's exactly what we want. The new vector is sitting on the X-Z plane, and both coordinates are in the positive. If we take that same transform, apply it to every vertex of the teapot, and then redraw it, we'll get the picture shown in Figure 14.8.

This matrix will create a rotation about the X-axis:

$$\begin{bmatrix} 1 & 0 & 0 & 0 \\ 0 & \cos(\theta) & \sin(\theta) & 0 \\ 0 & -\sin(\theta) & \cos(\theta) & 0 \\ 0 & 0 & 0 & 1 \end{bmatrix}$$

**Figure 14.8**
The teapotahedron rotated –π/4 radians around the Y-axis.

This matrix will create a rotation about the Z-axis:

$$\begin{bmatrix} \cos(\theta) & \sin(\theta) & 0 & 0 \\ -\sin(\theta) & \cos(\theta) & 0 & 0 \\ 0 & 0 & 1 & 0 \\ 0 & 0 & 0 & 1 \end{bmatrix}$$

The DirectX code to create those two rotations is exactly what you'd expect:

```
float angle = -D3DX_PI / 4.0f;
D3DXMATRIX rotateX, rotateZ;
D3DXMatrixRotationX( rotateX, angle);
D3DXMatrixRotationZ( rotateZ, angle);
```

With simple translation and rotation transforms firmly in your brain, you need to learn how to put multiple transforms into action. It turns out that you can multiply, or concatenate, matrices. The result encodes every operation into a single matrix. I know, it seems like magic. There's one important part of this wizardry: The concatenated matrix is sensitive to the order in which you did the original multiplication. Let's look at two examples, starting with two matrices you should be able to visualize:

```
D3DXMATRIX trans, rotateY;
D3DXMatrixTranslation(&trans, 3,0,0);
D3DXMatrixRotationY(&rotateY, -D3DX_PI / 4.0f);
```

The translation matrix will push your teapot down the X-axis, or to the lower left in your current view. The negative angle rotation about the Y-axis you've already seen.

In DirectX, you can multiply two matrices with a function call. I'm not going to bother showing you the actual formula for two reasons. First, you can find it for yourself on the Internet, and second, no one codes this from scratch. There's always an optimized version of a matrix multiply in any 3D engine you find, including DirectX:

```
D3DXMATRIX result;
D3DXMatrixMultiply(&result, &trans, &rotateY);
```

Note the order. This should create a transform matrix that will push the teapot down the X-axis and rotate it about the Y-axis, in that order. Figure 14.9 shows the results.

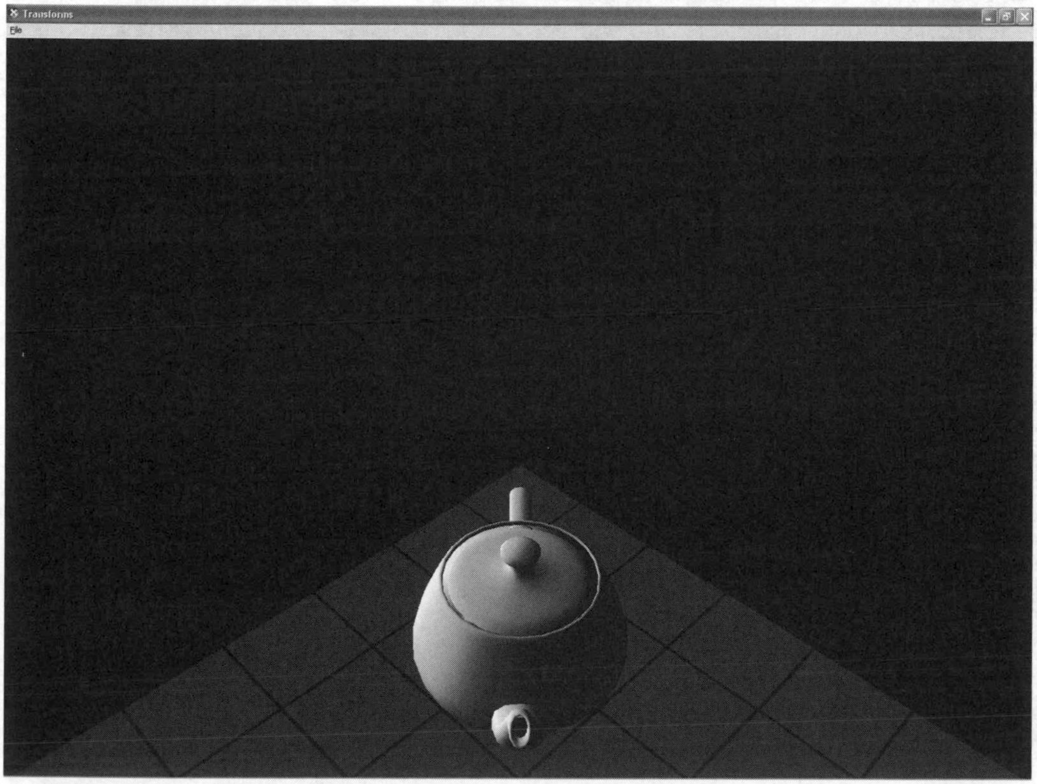

**Figure 14.9**
Translate down X-axis first and then rotate about the origin.

If you expected the teapot to be sitting on the X-axis, you must remember that any rotation happens about the origin, not the center of the object! This is a common mistake, and I've spent much of my 3D debugging time getting my matrices in the right order.

**Translations Always Come Last**

Always translate last. If you want to place an object in a 3D world, you always perform your rotations first, scale second, and translations third. Use "RST" as a helpful mnemonic, standing for rotate, scale, translate.

Let's follow my own best practice and see if you get a better result. First, you reverse the order of the parameters into the matrix multiplication API:

```
D3DXMATRIX result;
D3DXMatrixMultiply(&result, &rotateY, &trans );
```

Figure 14.10 shows the result.

**Figure 14.10**
Rotate about the origin first and then translate down the X-axis.

I'll show you one more, just to make sure you get it. The goal of this transformation is two rotations and one translation. I want the teapot to sit four units down the Z-axis, on its side with the top toward us, and the spout straight up in the air. Here's the code:

```
D3DXMATRIX rotateX, rotateZ, trans;
D3DXMatrixRotationZ(&rotateZ, -D3DX_PI / 2.0f);
D3DXMatrixRotationX(&rotateX, -D3DX_PI );
D3DXMatrixTranslation(&trans, 0,0,4);
D3DXMATRIX temp, result;
D3DXMatrixMultiply(&temp, &rotateZ, &rotateX);
D3DXMatrixMultiply(&result, &temp, &trans);
```

The first rotation about the Z-axis points our teapot's spout down the negative Y-axis, and the second rotation twists the whole thing around the X-axis to get the spout pointing straight up. The final translation moves it to its resting spot on the Z-axis (see Figure 14.11).

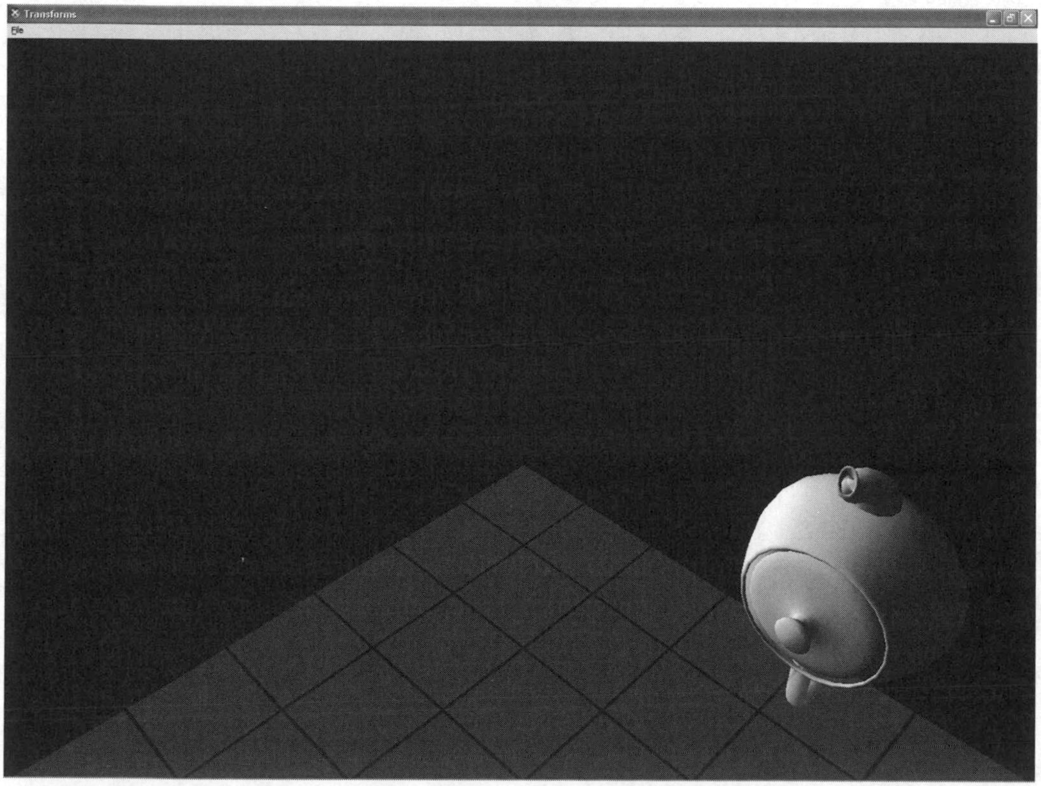


**Figure 14.11**
Rotate the teapot about the Z-axis, then the X-axis, and then translate down the Z-axis.

### *The `Mat4` × 4 Transform Matrix Class*

It can be convenient to wrap DirectX's `D3DXMATRIX` structure into a C++ class:

```
class Mat4x4 : public D3DXMATRIX
{
public:
  // Modifiers
  inline void SetPosition(Vec3 const &pos)
  {
    m[3][0] = pos.x;
    m[3][1] = pos.y;
    m[3][2] = pos.z;
    m[3][3] = 1.0f;
  }
   inline void SetPosition(Vec4 const &pos)
  {
    m[3][0] = pos.x;
    m[3][1] = pos.y;
    m[3][2] = pos.z;
    m[3][3] = pos.w;
  }

  // Accessors and Calculation Methods
  inline Vec3 GetPosition() const
  {
    return Vec3(m[3][0], m[3][1], m[3][2]);
  }

  inline Vec4 Xform(Vec4 &v) const
  {
    Vec4 temp;
    D3DXVec4Transform(&temp, &v, this);
    return temp;
  }

  inline Vec3 Xform(Vec3 &v) const
  {
    Vec4 temp(v), out;
    D3DXVec4Transform(&out, &temp, this);
    return Vec3(out.x, out.y, out.z);
  }

  inline Mat4x4 Inverse() const
  {
    Mat4x4 out;
```

```
    D3DXMatrixInverse(&out, NULL, this);
    return out;
  }

  // Initialization methods
  inline void BuildTranslation(const Vec3 &pos)
  {
    *this = Mat4x4::g_Identity;
    m[3][0] = pos.x;    m[3][1] = pos.y;    m[3][2] = pos.z;
  }
  inline void BuildTranslation(const float x, const float y, const float z )
  {
    *this = Mat4x4::g_Identity;
    m[3][0] = x;   m[3][1] = y;    m[3][2] = z;
  }
  inline void BuildRotationX(const float radians)
    { D3DXMatrixRotationX(this, radians); }
  inline void BuildRotationY(const float radians)
    { D3DXMatrixRotationY(this, radians); }
  inline void BuildRotationZ(const float radians)
    { D3DXMatrixRotationZ(this, radians); }
  inline void BuildYawPitchRoll(
    const float yawRadians, const float pitchRadians,
    const float rollRadians)
    { D3DXMatrixRotationYawPitchRoll(
      this, yawRadians, pitchRadians, rollRadians); }
  inline void BuildRotationQuat(const Quaternion &q)
    { D3DXMatrixRotationQuaternion(this, &q); }
   inline void BuildRotationLookAt(const Vec3 &eye, const Vec3 &at, const Vec3 &up) {
D3DXMatrixLookAtRH(this, &eye, &at, &up); }

  Mat4x4(D3DXMATRIX &mat) { memcpy(&m, &mat.m, sizeof(mat.m)); };
  Mat4x4() : D3DXMATRIX() { }

  static const Mat4x4 g_Identity;
};

const Mat4x4 Mat4x4::g_Identity(D3DXMATRIX(1,0,0,0,0,1,0,0,0,0,1,0,0,0,0,1));

inline Mat4x4 operator * (const Mat4x4 &a, const Mat4x4 &b)
{
  Mat4x4 out;
  D3DXMatrixMultiply(&out, &a, &b);
  return out;
}
```

There are three sections: the modifiers, the accessors and transforms, and finally the initializers. The modifiers simply set position; if you want to set rotations, there's another way I'll show you in a moment. The accessor `GetPosition()` returns the position component of the 4 × 4 matrix. The `Xform()` methods transform a `Vec3` or `Vec4` object into the space and position of the matrix. Don't worry yet because I'll show you an example of how to use this in a moment.

The initializer methods, those starting with `Build`, take various parameters you might have on hand to build a rotation or transform matrix. If you want one that encodes both rotation and transformation, just build two of them and multiply them. Multiplying matrices is the same thing as concatenating them.

There's also a static member, `g_Identity`, which forms a matrix that you use to set an object at the origin with no scaling or rotation.

Here's a quick example in C++ that does the following things:

- Builds two matrices, one for rotation and one for translation.
- Concatenates these matrices in one `Mat4` × `4` to encode both movements. Remember that rotation always comes first and then translation.
- Determines which direction in the 3D world is considered "forward" by the new orientation and position. This direction is sometimes referred to as a *frame* or *reference.*

```
Mat4x4 rot;
rot.BuildYawPitchRoll(D3DX_PI / 2.0f, -D3DX_PI / 4.0f, 0);

Mat4x4 trans;
trans.BuildTranslation(1.0f, 2.0f, 3.0f);

// don't mess up the order! Multiplying Mat4x4s isn't like ordinary numbers....
Mat4x4 result = rotOnly * trans;
Vec4 fwd(0.0f, 0.0f, 1.0f);          // forward is defined as positive Z
Vec4 fwdWorld = result.Xform(fwd);
```

There you have it. The `fwdWorld` vector points in the forward direction of the transform matrix. This is important because of two reasons. First, all of the code in this chapter will continue using these math classes, and this is exactly how you'd tell a missile what direction to move if you fired it from an object that was using the concatenated matrix.

I hope you've followed these bits about rotating things around an axis because it's a critical concept you need to understand before we talk about quaternions. If you think you might be hazy on the whole rotation thing, play with a Direct3D sample for a while, and you'll get it.

## Quaternion Mathematics

Orientation can be expressed as three angles: yaw, pitch, and roll. In our teapot example, yaw would be around the Y-axis, pitch would be around the Z-axis, and roll would be around the X-axis. By the way, this happens to be called the *Euler representation,* or *Euler angles* (you pronounce Euler like "oiler"). This method has a critical weakness. Imagine that you want to interpolate smoothly between two orientations. This would make sense if you had an object like an automated cannon that slowly tracked moving objects. It would know its current orientation and the target orientation, but getting from one to the other might be problematic with Euler angles.

There is a special mathematical construct known as a *quaternion,* and almost every 3D engine supports its use. A quaternion is a fourth-dimensional vector, and it can be visualized as a rotation about an arbitrary axis. Let's look at an example:

```
D3DXQUATERNION q;
D3DXQuaternionIdentity(&q);
D3DXVECTOR3 axis(0,1,0);
float angle = -D3DX_PI / 4.0;
D3DXQuaternionRotationAxis(&q, &axis, angle);
D3DXMATRIX result;
D3DXMatrixRotationQuaternion(&result, &q);
```

This code has exactly the same effect on our teapot as the first rotation example. The teapot rotates around the Y-axis $-\pi/4$ degrees. Notice that I'm not setting the values of the quaternion directly, I'm using a DirectX API. I do this because the actual values of the quaternion are not intuitive at all. Take a look at the resulting values from our simple twist around the Y-axis:

```
q  {...}   D3DXQUATERNION
   x   0.00000000   float
   y   -0.38268343   float
   z   0.00000000   float
   w   0.92387950   float
```

Not exactly the easiest thing to read, is it?

The quaternion is sent into another DirectX function to create a transformation matrix. This is done because vectors can't be transformed directly with quaternions—you still have to use a transform matrix.

**Figure 14.12**
Our teapot two-thirds of the way through a rotation—using quaternions.

If you think this seems like a whole lot of work with little gain, let's look at the interpolation problem. Let's assume that I want the teapot to turn so that the spout is pointing down the Z-axis, which would mean a rotation about the Y-axis with an angle of $-\pi/2$ degrees. Let's also assume that I want to know what the transformation matrix is at two-thirds of the way through the turn, as shown in Figure 14.12.

Here's the code:

```
D3DXQUATERNION start, middle, end;
D3DXQuaternionIdentity(&start);
D3DXQuaternionIdentity(&middle);
D3DXQuaternionIdentity(&end);

D3DXVECTOR3 axis(0,1,0);
float angle = -D3DX_PI / 2.0;
D3DXQuaternionRotationAxis(&start, &axis, 0);
D3DXQuaternionRotationAxis(&end, &axis, angle);
```

```
D3DXQuaternionSlerp(&middle, &end, &start, 0.66f);

D3DXMATRIX result;
D3DXMatrixRotationQuaternion(&result, &middle);
```

The two boundary quaternions, `start` and `end`, are initialized in the same way as you saw earlier. The target orientation quaternion, `middle`, is calculated with the DirectX method `D3DXQuaternionSlerp`. This creates a quaternion 66 percent of the way between our `start` and `end` quaternions.

I might not quite have convinced you yet, but only because I used a trivial rotation that was easy to display. Anyone can interpolate a rotation around a single axis. Quaternions can represent a rotation about a completely arbitrary axis, like (x=3.5, y=−2.1, z=0.04), and they can be much more useful than Euler angles.

**Compressing Quaternions? Don't Bother!**

When I was on *Thief: Deadly Shadows,* I was sharing an office with a friend of mine who was tasked with the job of compressing streams of quaternions. He was trying to save a few precious megabytes on our animations for the main character. His first few attempts were close, but some of the animations were completely wacko. The character's legs would lift up past his ears in a manner only suitable for a circus performer. The problem was a loss in precision in the quaternion stream, and when we thought about it and truly understood what a normalized quaternion was, it made perfect sense. A normalized quaternion is a fourth-dimensional vector whose origin sits at (0,0,0,0) and whose endpoint always sits on the surface of a fourth-dimensional hypersphere. Since a well-formed unit quaternion has a length of 1.0f, any loss of accuracy because of compression will trash the unit length and ruin the precision of the quaternion. So what did we do? We used Euler angles for storing and compression and converted them to quaternions during runtime. Euler angles can lose precision like crazy and still work just fine. Sometimes, the old-school solution is what you need.

### *The* `Quaternion` *Class*

The `D3DXQUATERNION` structure can be wrapped in a useful C++ wrapper class:

```
class Quaternion : public D3DXQUATERNION
{
public:
  // Modifiers
  void Normalize() { D3DXQuaternionNormalize(this, this); };
  void Slerp(const Quaternion &begin, const Quaternion &end, float cooef)
  {
     // performs spherical linear interpolation between begin & end
     // NOTE: set cooef between 0.0f-1.0f
     D3DXQuaternionSlerp(this, &begin, &end, cooef);
  }
```

```
    // Accessors
    void GetAxisAngle(Vec3 &axis, float &angle) const
    {
      D3DXQuaternionToAxisAngle(this, &axis, &angle);
    }

    // Initializers
    void BuildRotYawPitchRoll(
            const float yawRadians,
            const float pitchRadians,
            const float rollRadians)
    {
      D3DXQuaternionRotationYawPitchRoll(
        this, yawRadians, pitchRadians, rollRadians);
    }

    void BuildAxisAngle(const Vec3 &axis, const float radians)
    {
      D3DXQuaternionRotationAxis(this, &axis, radians);
    }

    void Build(const class Mat4x4 &mat)
    {
      D3DXQuaternionRotationMatrix(this, &mat);
    }

    Quaternion(D3DXQUATERNION &q) : D3DXQUATERNION(q) { }
    Quaternion() : D3DXQUATERNION() { }

    static const Quaternion g_Identity;
};

inline Quaternion operator * (const Quaternion &a, const Quaternion &b)
{
  // for rotations, this is exactly like concatenating
  // matrices - the new quat represents rot A followed by rot B.
  Quaternion out;
  D3DXQuaternionMultiply(&out, &a, &b);
  return out;
}

const Quaternion Quaternion::g_Identity(D3DXQUATERNION(0,0,0,1));
```

The quaternion is useful for orienting objects in a three-dimensional space. The `Quaternion` class just presented gives you the three most used methods for initializing it: from yaw-pitch-roll angles, an axis and rotation around that axis, and a $4 \times 4$

matrix. The class also has an operator * to multiply two quaternions, which performs a similar mathematical operation as concatenating matrices. The modifiers let you normalize a quaternion and perform a spherical linear interpolation on them. You saw the interpolation in the previous pages when I showed you how to orient the teapot in between two different rotations. `Slerp()` does the same thing.

The identity quaternion is also provided as a global static so you can get to it quickly, especially for initializing a quaternion. This is something I like to do instead of forcing a default initialization all the time. You can use it if you want and start with the identity, or you can use one of the builder methods.

### *The* `Plane` *Class*

The plane is an extremely useful mathematical device for 3D games. Here's a simple wrapper around the DirectX plane structure, `D3DXPLANE`:

```
class Plane : public D3DXPLANE
{
public:
  inline void Normalize();

  // normal faces away from you if you send in verts
  // in counter clockwise order....
  inline void Init(const Vec3 &p0, const Vec3 &p1, const Vec3 &p2);
  bool Inside(const Vec3 &point, const float radius) const;
  bool Inside(const Vec3 &point) const;
};

inline void Plane::Normalize()
{
  float mag;
  mag = sqrt(a * a + b * b + c * c);
  a = a / mag;
  b = b / mag;
  c = c / mag;
  d = d / mag;
}

inline void Plane::Init(const Vec3 &p0, const Vec3 &p1, const Vec3 &p2)
{
  D3DXPlaneFromPoints(this, &p0, &p1, &p2);
  Normalize();
}

bool Plane::Inside(const Vec3 &point) const
```

```
{
  // Inside the plane is defined as the direction the normal is facing
  float result = D3DXPlaneDotCoord(this, &point);
  return (result >= 0.0f);
}

bool Plane::Inside(const Vec3 &point, const float radius) const
{
  float fDistance;   // calculate our distances to each of the planes

  // find the distance to this plane
  fDistance = D3DXPlaneDotCoord(this, &point);

  // if this distance is < -radius, we are outside
  return (fDistance >= -radius);
}
```

Basically, if you know three points on the surface of the plane, you'll have enough information to create it mathematically. You can also create planes in other ways, and you're perfectly free to extend this bare-bones class to create more constructors, but this simple version goes a surprisingly long way.

Once the plane is initialized, you can ask whether a point or a sphere (defined by a point and a radius) is on the inside or outside of the plane. Inside is defined as being on the same side as the plane normal. The plane normal is defined by the coefficients `a`, `b`, and `c` inside the `D3DXPLANE` structure and is calculated for you when the `Plane` class is constructed.

The `Plane` is rarely used by itself. It is usually used to create things like BSP trees, portals, and a camera view frustum, which you'll see how to create next.

### *The* `Frustum` *Class*

Imagine sitting in front of a computer screen and seeing four lines coming from your eyeball and intersecting with the corners of the screen. For the sake of simplicity, I'll assume you have only one eyeball in the center of your head. These lines continue into the 3D world of your favorite game. You have a pyramid shape with the point at your eyeball and its base somewhere out in infinity. Clip the pointy end of the pyramid with the plane of your computer screen and form a base of your pyramid at some arbitrary place in the distance. This odd clipped pyramid shape is called the *viewing frustum*, as shown in Figure 14.13. The shape is actually a cuboid, since it is topologically equivalent to a cube, although pushed out of shape. This shape is what defines the total viewing area of a camera in a 3D game. Any object completely

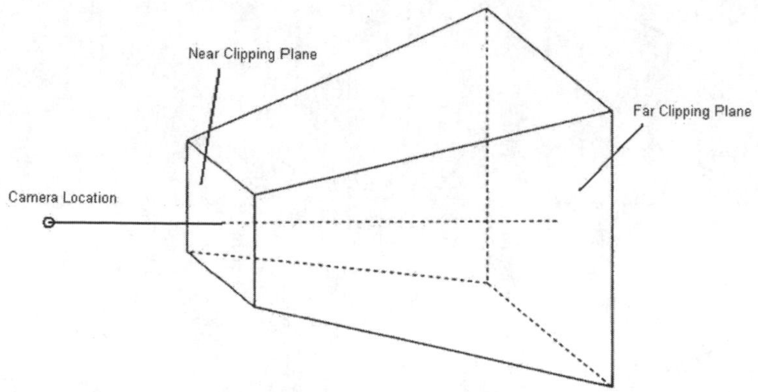


**Figure 14.13**
The view frustum with near and far clipping planes.

outside the frustum doesn't need to be drawn, so it is an indispensible member of any 3D graphics engine.

The camera is at the tip of the pyramid, looking at the frustum through the near clipping plane. Any object that is totally outside the six planes that describe the frustum are outside the viewing area, which means they can be skipped during the rendering passes. The six planes include the near and far clipping planes and the four other planes that make up the top, left, right, and bottom of the frustum. It turns out to be really efficient to test a point or a sphere against a frustum, and that is exactly how this frustum will be used to cull objects in the scene graph. If you didn't do this, you'd be sending every triangle in your scene into the renderer, even if it wouldn't be seen by the player. That means your scenes would have to be a lot less complicated, or shall I say boring, to keep up a fast frame rate.

A frustum is defined with four parameters: the field of view, the aspect ratio, the distance to the near clipping plane, and the distance to the far clipping plane. The field of view, or FOV, is the full angle made by the tip of the pyramid at the camera location (see Figure 14.14). The aspect ratio is the width of the near clipping plane divided by the height of the near clipping plane. For a 640 × 480 pixel screen, the aspect ratio would be 640.f/480.f or 1.33333334. The distance to the near and far clipping planes should be given in whatever units your game uses to measure distance—feet, meters, cubits, whatever. With these parameters safely in hand, the six `Plane` objects can be built.

Here's the code for defining the `Frustum` class:

```
class Frustum
{
```

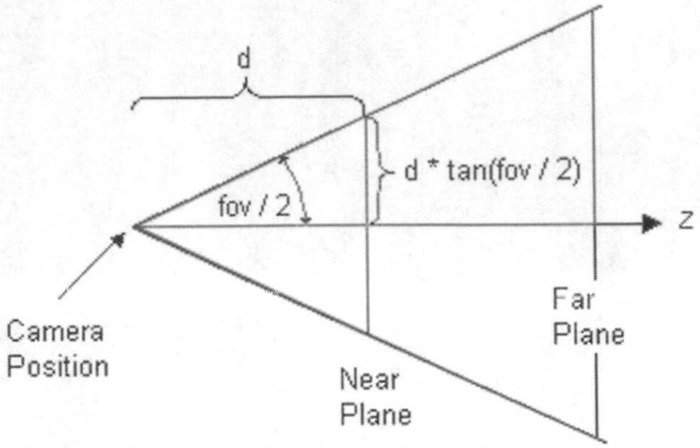


**Figure 14.14**
Calculating the points of the view frustum.

```
public:
  enum Side { Near, Far, Top, Right, Bottom, Left, NumPlanes };

  Plane m_Planes[NumPlanes]; // planes of the frusum in camera space
  Vec3 m_NearClip[4];         // verts of the near clip plane in camera space
  Vec3 m_FarClip[4];          // verts of the far clip plane in camera space

  float m_Fov;                // field of view in radians
  float m_Aspect;             // aspect ratio - width divided by height
  float m_Near;               // near clipping distance
  float m_Far;                // far clipping distance

public:
  Frustum();

  bool Inside(const Vec3 &point) const;
  bool Inside(const Vec3 &point, const float radius) const;
  const Plane &Get(Side side) { return m_Planes[side]; }
  void SetFOV(float fov) { m_Fov=fov; Init(m_Fov, m_Aspect, m_Near, m_Far); }
  void SetAspect(float aspect)
    { m_Aspect=aspect; Init(m_Fov, m_Aspect, m_Near, m_Far); }
  void SetNear(float nearClip)
    { m_Near=nearClip; Init(m_Fov, m_Aspect, m_Near, m_Far); }
  void SetFar(float farClip)
    { m_Far=farClip; Init(m_Fov, m_Aspect, m_Near, m_Far); }
  void Init(const float fov, const float aspect,
    const float near, const float far);

  void Render();
};
```

```
Frustum::Frustum()
{
  m_Fov = D3DX_PI/4.0f;  // default field of view is 90 degrees
  m_Aspect = 1.0f;       // default aspect ratio is 1:1
  m_Near = 1.0f;         // default near plane is 1m away from the camera
  m_Far = 1000.0f;       // default near plane is 1000m away from the camera
}

bool Frustum::Inside(const Vec3 &point) const
{
  for (int i=0; i<NumPlanes; ++i)
  {
    if (!m_Planes[i].Inside(point))
      return false;
  }

  return true;
}

bool Frustum::Inside(const Vec3 &point, const float radius) const
{
  for(int i = 0; i < NumPlanes; ++i)
  {
    if (!m_Planes[i].Inside(point, radius))
      return false;
  }

  // otherwise we are fully in view
  return true;
}
```

The next method, `Init()`, is a little heavy on the math. The algorithm is to find the eight points in space made by corners of the view frustum and use those points to define the six planes. If you remember your high school geometry, you'll remember that the tangent of an angle is equal to the length of the opposite side divided by the adjacent side. Since we know the length D from the camera to the near clipping plane, we can find the length between the center point of the near clipping plane to the right edge and also the top using the aspect ratio. The same operation is repeated for the far clipping plane, and that gives us the 3D location of the corner points:

```
void Frustum::Init(const float fov, const float aspect, const float nearClip, const
float farClip)
{
  m_Fov = fov;
  m_Aspect = aspect;
```

```
    m_Near = nearClip;
    m_Far = farClip;

    double tanFovOver2 = tan(m_Fov/2.0f);
    Vec3 nearRight = (m_Near * tanFovOver2) * m_Aspect * g_Right;
    Vec3 farRight = (m_Far * tanFovOver2) * m_Aspect * g_Right;
    Vec3 nearUp = (m_Near * tanFovOver2 ) * g_Up;
    Vec3 farUp = (m_Far * tanFovOver2)  * g_Up;

    // points start in the upper right and go around clockwise
    m_NearClip[0] = (m_Near * g_Forward) - nearRight + nearUp;
    m_NearClip[1] = (m_Near * g_Forward) + nearRight + nearUp;
    m_NearClip[2] = (m_Near * g_Forward) + nearRight - nearUp;
    m_NearClip[3] = (m_Near * g_Forward) - nearRight - nearUp;

    m_FarClip[0] = (m_Far * g_Forward) - farRight + farUp;
    m_FarClip[1] = (m_Far * g_Forward) + farRight + farUp;
    m_FarClip[2] = (m_Far * g_Forward) + farRight - farUp;
    m_FarClip[3] = (m_Far * g_Forward) - farRight - farUp;

    // now we have all eight points. Time to construct six planes.
    // the normals point away from you if you use counter clockwise verts.

    Vec3 origin(0.0f, 0.0f, 0.0f);
    m_Planes[Near].Init(m_NearClip[2], m_NearClip[1], m_NearClip[0]);
    m_Planes[Far].Init(m_FarClip[0], m_FarClip[1], m_FarClip[2]);
    m_Planes[Right].Init(m_FarClip[2], m_FarClip[1], origin);
    m_Planes[Top].Init(m_FarClip[1], m_FarClip[0], origin);
    m_Planes[Left].Init(m_FarClip[0], m_FarClip[3], origin);
    m_Planes[Bottom].Init(m_FarClip[3], m_FarClip[2], origin);
}
```

With the location of the corner points correctly nabbed, the planes of the view frustum can be created with three known points for each one. Don't forget that the order in which the points are sent into the plane equation is important. The order determines the direction of the plane's normal and therefore which side of the plane is the inside versus the outside.

## Transformations

One of the processes in a 3D graphics pipeline transforms arbitrary points in the 3D game universe into 2D points on a display. There are three things to consider: an object's position and orientation in the 3D world, the position and orientation of the camera or viewpoint, and the physical dimensions of the display and field of view. Each one requires the definition of a transform, which is stored in a `Mat4 x 4` object. The three transforms are called the *world transform*, the *view transform*, and the *projection transform*.

### World Transform

When objects are created by a programmer plotting out 3D points on graph paper or an artist models something in 3ds Max, they exist in object space. As the object moves around the 3D world, it is much easier to modify a single `Mat4` × 4 object than to change each individual point that describes the shape of the object. That `Mat4 x 4` matrix describes the world transform, and it can be used to move and reorient any object, just as you saw with the teapotahedron on the previous pages.

### View Transform

If you are going to render the scene, you need to have a camera. That camera must have an orientation and a position just like any other object in the world. Similar to any other object, the camera needs a transform matrix that converts world space vertices to camera space.

Calculating the transform matrix for a camera can be tricky. In many cases, you want the camera to look at something, like a teapot. If you have a desired camera position and a target to look at, you don't quite have enough information to place the camera. The missing data is a definition of the *up* direction for your world. This last bit of data gives the camera a hint about how to orient itself. The `BuildRotationLookAt` method of the `Mat4 x 4` class wraps `D3DXMatrixLookAtLH`, which takes these inputs and constructs the view transform:

```
Mat4x4 matView;
Vec3 vFromPt   = Vec3( 6.0f, 6.0f, 6.0f );
Vec3 vLookatPt = Vec3( 0.0f, 0.0f, 0.0f );
Vec3 vUpVec    = Vec3( 0.0f, 1.0f, 0.0f );
matView.BuildRotationLookAt( &vFromPt, &vLookatPt, &vUpVec );
```

By the way, the `LH` at the end of the DirectX function's name is a hint that this function assumes a left-handed coordinate system. There is a right-handed version of this and most other matrix functions, as well.

The `vFromPt` is out along the positive values of X, Y, and Z, and the `vLookatPt` point is right back at the origin. The last parameter defines the up direction. If you think about a camera as having an orientation constraint similar to a camera boom like you see on ESPN, it can move anywhere, pan around to see its surroundings, and pitch up or down. It doesn't tilt, at least not normally. This is important, because if tilting were allowed in constructing a valid view transform, there could be many different orientations that would satisfy your input data.

**Straight Up and Straight Down Are Tricky!**

This system isn't completely perfect because there are two degenerate orientations. Given the definition of up as (X=0, Y=1, Z=0) in world space, the two places you can't easily look are straight up and straight down. You can construct the view transform for this degenerate case quite easily by creating a view transform looking straight forward in the normal way and then using a 90-degree rotation about the Y-axis to transform the matrix to look straight up.

Remember that the camera's view transform is a matrix, just like any other. You don't have to use the look-at function to calculate it, but it tends to be the most effective camera positioning function there is.

### *Projection Transform*

Using the world transform and the view transform, vertices from object space can be transformed into vertices from world space and then transformed into camera space. Now we need to take all those 3D vertices sitting in camera space and figure out where they belong on your computer screen and which objects sit in front of other objects. The view frustum will help determine what gets drawn and what gets culled.

Every object inside the view frustum will be drawn on your screen. The projection transform takes the camera space (X,Y,Z) of every vertex and transforms it into a new vector that holds the screen pixel (X,Y) location and a measure of the vertices' distance into the scene.

Here's the code to create the projection transform using the settings of the viewing frustum and the screen dimensions:

```
Mat4x4 matProj;
m_Frustum.SetAspect(DXUTGetWindowWidth() / (FLOAT) DXUTGetWindowHeight());
D3DXMatrixPerspectiveFovLH( &m_Projection, m_Frustum.m_Fov, m_Frustum.m_Aspect,
m_Frustum.m_Near, m_Frustum.m_Far );
```

The DirectX function that helps you calculate a projection matrix—something you don't want to do by yourself—accepts four parameters after the address of the matrix:

- **Field of view:** Expressed in radians, this is the width of the view angle. $\pi/4$ is a pretty standard angle. Wider angles such as $3\pi/4$ make for some weird results. Try it and see what happens.
- **Aspect ratio:** This is the aspect ratio of your screen. If this ratio were 1.0, the projection transform would assume you had a square screen. A 1280 × 960 screen has a 1.333 aspect ratio.

- **Near clipping plane:** This is the distance between your eye and the near view plane. Any object closer will get clipped. The units are usually meters, but feel free to set them to whatever standard makes sense for your game.
- **Far clipping plane:** The distance between your eye and the far clipping plane. Anything farther away will be clipped.

**Set Far Clipping Plane Distance to Something Far, but Not Too Far**

Don't set your far clipping plane to some arbitrarily large number in the hopes that nothing in your huge 3D world will get clipped. The trade-off is that the huge distance between your near and far clipping plane will create sorting problems in objects very close or very far from the camera—depending on your renderer. These weird sorting problems manifest themselves as if two polygons were run through a paper shredder, since the individual pixels on two coincident polygons will sort incorrectly. This problem is caused by numerical inaccuracy, and the polygons will sort into exactly the depth in 3D space. If you see this problem, first check the art to make sure the artists actually placed the polygons correctly and then check your far clipping plane distance. This problem is sometimes called "Z fighting."

Also, don't set your near clipping plane to zero, with the hope that you'll be able to see things very close to the camera. There's a relationship between the near clipping plane and the field of view. If you arbitrarily move the near clipping plane closer to the camera without changing the field of view, weird things begin to happen. My suggestion is to write a little code and see for yourself.

## Geometry

Did you know that everything from teapots to cars to volleyball-playing beach bunnies can be made out of triangles? We all know that a geometric triangle is made up of three points. In a 3D world, a triangle is composed of three vertices. A vertex holds important information the shader will use to draw the triangle, and as you might expect, there can be a lot more than its location in a 3D space.

Different renderers will support different kinds of triangles and therefore different kinds of vertices that create those triangles. Once you get your feet wet with one rendering technology, such as DirectX 11, you'll quickly find analogs in any other rendering technology, such as OpenGL. In our example, our vertex will contain a position in 3D space, a normal vector, and a texture coordinate.

```
struct D3D11Vertex_UnlitTextured
{
  D3DXVECTOR3 Pos;
  D3DXVECTOR3 Normal;
  D3DXVECTOR2 Uv;
};
```

As you might expect, a position in 3D space is a 3D vector. A normal vector is also a 3D vector, and a texture coordinate is a 2D vector. Three of those define the three points required to render one triangle on the screen. Next let's dig in to how lighting and texturing work.

## Lighting, Normals, and Color

In DirectX 11 and many other rendering technologies, you can assign colors to vertices yourself, or you can instruct the renderer to calculate those colors by looking at vertex data and the lights that illuminate the vertex. You can even do both. Everyone has seen games that show subtle light pools shining on walls and floors—a nice and efficient effect but completely static and unmoving. Other illumination is calculated in real time, such as when your character shines a flashlight around a scene. Multiple lights can affect individual vertices, each light adding a color component to the vertex color calculation.

One of the simplest kinds of lighting is *diffuse* lighting, which simply adds a bit of the light color to the native color of the triangle, depending on how it is oriented to the light. To understand how this works, you need to know about *normal* vectors, which are an important part of the vertex definition that enables lighting calculations.

When light hits an object, the color of light is added to the object's defined color. Perform a little experiment to see this in action. Take a playing card, like the ace of spades, and place it flat on a table lit by a ceiling lamp. The card takes on a color component that reflects the color of that lamp. If your lamp is a fluorescent light, the card will appear white with a slight greenish tint. If your lamp is incandescent, the card will take on a slightly yellowish color.

If you take the card in your hand and slowly turn it over, the brightness and color of the card face with the spade changes. As the card approaches an edge-on orientation to the lamp, the effects of the lighting diminish to their minimum. The light has its maximum effect when the card is facing perpendicular to the light and its minimum effect when the card is edge-on to the light. This happens because when light hits a surface at a low angle it spreads out and has to cover a larger area with the same number of photons. This gives you a dimming effect.

Diffuse lighting attempts to simulate this effect. With the card sitting flat on the table again, take a pencil and put the eraser end in the middle of the card and point the tip of the pencil straight up in the air, toward your ceiling lamp. You've just created a normal vector. Turn the card as before, but hold the pencil and turn it as well, as if it were glued to the card. Notice that the light has a maximum effect when the angle between the pencil and the light is 180 degrees, minimum effect when the angle between the light and the pencil is 90 degrees, and no effect when the card faces away from the light.

Each vertex gets its own normal vector. This might seem like a waste of memory, but consider this: If each vertex has its own normal, you can change the direction of the normal vectors to "fool" the lighting system. You can make the 3D object take on a smoother shading effect. This is a common technique to blend the edges of coincident triangles. The illusion you create allows artists to create 3D models with fewer polygons.

The normals on the teapot model are calculated to create the illusion of a smooth shape, as shown in Figure 14.15.

Now that you know what a normal vector is, you need to know how to calculate one. If you want to find the normal vector for a triangle, you'll need to use a cross product as shown here:

```
Vec3 triangle[3];
triangle[0] = Vec3(0,0,0);
triangle[1] = Vec3(5,0,0);
triangle[2] = Vec3(5,5,0);
```

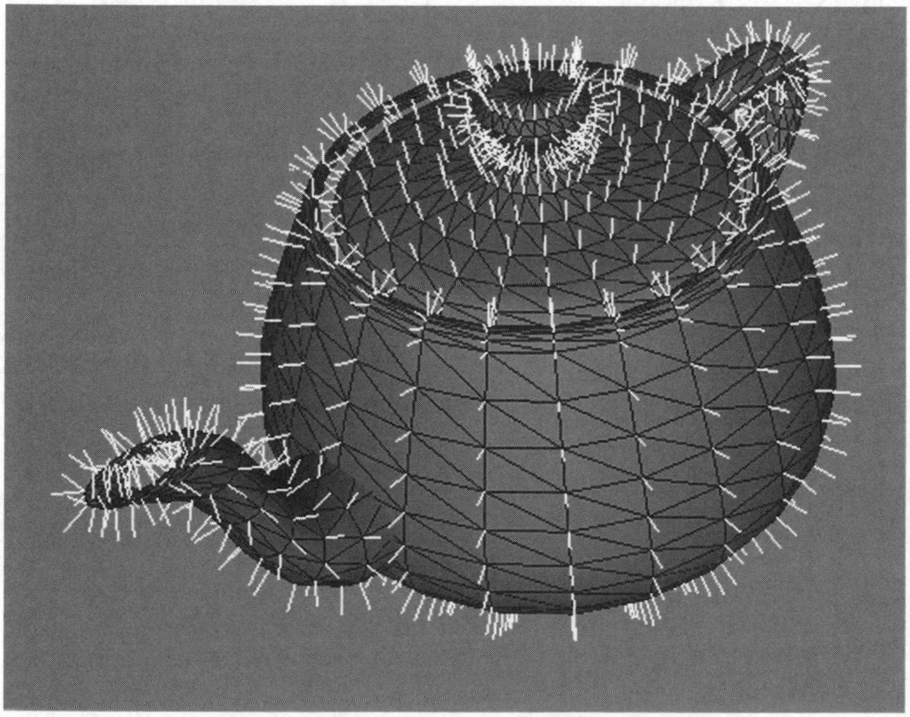

**Figure 14.15**
Vertex normals on a teapotahedron.

```
Vec3 edge1 = triangle[1]-triangle[0];
Vec3 edge2 = triangle[2]-triangle[0];

Vec3 normal = edge1.Cross(edge2);
normal.Normalize();
```

Our polygon is defined with three positions in 3D space. These positions are used to construct two edge vectors, both pointing away from the same vertex. The two edges are sent into the cross product function, which returns a vector that is pointing in the right direction but is the wrong size. All normal vectors must be exactly one unit in length to be useful in other calculations, such as the dot product. The `Vec3::Normalize()` function calculates the unit vector by dividing the temp vector by its length. The result is a normal vector you can apply to a vertex.

If you take a closer look at the teapot figure, you'll notice that the normal vectors are really the normals of multiple triangles, not just a single triangle. You calculate this by averaging the normals of each triangle that shares your vertex. Calculate the average of multiple vectors by adding them together and dividing by the number of vectors, exactly as you would calculate the average of any other number.

**Calculate Your Normals Ahead of Time**

Calculating a normal is a somewhat expensive operation. Each triangle will require two subtractions, a cross product, a square root, and three divisions. If you create 3D meshes at runtime, try to calculate your normals once, store them in object space, and use transforms to reorient them.

You might be wondering why I didn't mention ambient lighting—a color value that is universally applied to every vertex in the scene. This has the effect of making an object glow like a light bulb, and it isn't very realistic. Ambient lighting values are a necessary evil in today's 3D games because they simulate low-light levels on the back or underside of objects due to light reflecting all about the scene. In the next few years, I expect this light hack to be discarded completely in favor of more advanced techniques with pixel shaders using environment-based lighting effects.

## Materials

When light hits something, the light color is added to the color of the object. This color is typically defined by a material—basically a fancy way of describing how an object reflects light. DirectX 9 defined this with a structure still useful in Direct3D 11: `D3DMATERIAL9`.

```
typedef struct _D3DMATERIAL9 {
   D3DCOLORVALUE Diffuse;
   D3DCOLORVALUE Ambient;
   D3DCOLORVALUE Specular;
   D3DCOLORVALUE Emissive;
   float Power;
} D3DMATERIAL9;
```

**Black Objects Everywhere? Set Your Material!**

A common mistake with almost any renderer is not to set a material for your object. Most shaders use multiplication to combine the lights affecting the object with the object's color. If that color is not defined, it will typically be zeroed out to black, and as everyone knows, zero times anything is still zero. If your game has a black background, objects without a material defined will completely disappear from your scene!

Other than the critical information about needing a default material and texture, the DirectX SDK documentation does a pretty fair job of showing you what happens when you play with the specular and power settings. They can turn a plastic ping-pong ball into a ball bearing, highlights and everything.

The material defines how light reflects off the polygons. In Direct3D, this includes different colors for ambient, diffuse, specular, and emissive light. It is convenient to wrap the D3DMATERIAL9 structure in a class, which will be used in the next chapter to control how objects look, or even if they are transparent. Here is the source code for the class:

```
#define fOPAQUE (1.0f)
#define fTRANSPARENT (0.0f)

typedef D3DXCOLOR Color;

Color g_White( 1.0f, 1.0f, 1.0f, fOPAQUE );
Color g_Black( 0.0f, 0.0f, 0.0f, fOPAQUE );
Color g_Cyan( 0.0f, 1.0f, 1.0f, fOPAQUE );
Color g_Red( 1.0f, 0.0f, 0.0f, fOPAQUE );
Color g_Green( 0.0f, 1.0f, 0.0f, fOPAQUE );
Color g_Blue( 0.0f, 0.0f, 1.0f, fOPAQUE );
Color g_Yellow( 1.0f, 1.0f, 0.0f, fOPAQUE );
Color g_Gray40( 0.4f, 0.4f, 0.4f, fOPAQUE );
Color g_Gray25( 0.25f, 0.25f, 0.25f, fOPAQUE );
Color g_Gray65( 0.65f, 0.65f, 0.65f, fOPAQUE );
Color g_Transparent (1.0f, 0.0f, 1.0f, fTRANSPARENT );
```

```
class Material
{
  D3DMATERIAL9 m_D3DMaterial;
public:
  Material()
  {
    ZeroMemory( &m_D3DMaterial, sizeof( D3DMATERIAL9 ) );
    m_D3DMaterial.Diffuse = g_White;
    m_D3DMaterial.Ambient = Color(0.10f, 0.10f, 0.10f, 1.0f);
    m_D3DMaterial.Specular = g_White;
    m_D3DMaterial.Emissive = g_Black;
  }

  void SetAmbient(const Color &color)
    {  m_D3DMaterial.Ambient = color;  }
  const Color GetAmbient() { return m_D3DMaterial.Ambient; }

  void SetDiffuse(const Color &color)
    {  m_D3DMaterial.Diffuse = color;   }
  const Color GetDiffuse() { return m_D3DMaterial.Diffuse; }

  void SetSpecular(const Color &color, const float power)
  {
    m_D3DMaterial.Specular = color;  m_D3DMaterial.Power = power;
  }
  void GetSpecular(Color &_color, float &_power)
   { _color = m_D3DMaterial.Specular; _power = m_D3DMaterial.Power; }

  void SetEmissive(const Color &color)
    { m_D3DMaterial.Emissive = color;   }
  const Color GetEmissive() { return m_D3DMaterial.Emissive; }

  void SetAlpha(const float alpha)
    {  m_D3DMaterial.Diffuse.a = alpha;   }
  bool HasAlpha() const { return GetAlpha() != fOPAQUE; }
  float GetAlpha() const { return m_D3DMaterial.Diffuse.a; }
};
```

The material has four different color components. Generally, you'll set the ambient and diffuse color to the same thing, but you might get a black object by mistake. If you set an object's diffuse and ambient material to 100% blue, and you put that object in an environment with 100% red light, it will appear black. That's because a 100% blue object doesn't reflect any red light. Fix this by putting a little red in either the diffuse or ambient color. The specular color is usually set to white or gray and defines the color of the shininess the object takes on. Lastly, the emissive component allows an object to light itself. This is a good idea for things like explosions or light bulbs—anything that emits light. The alpha setting uses the diffuse alpha component; it is read and used by the simple pixel shader you'll see in the next chapter.

The last property is used to classify how the scene node is drawn, opaque or transparent.

## Textured Vertices

A texture is a piece of two-dimensional art that is applied to a model. Each vertex gets a texture coordinate. Texture coordinates are conventionally defined as (U,V) coordinates, where U is the horizontal component and V is the vertical component. These coordinates are described as floating-point numbers, where (0.0f,0.0f) signifies the top left of the texture and grows to the left and down for DirectX—in OpenGL it describes the bottom left of the texture. The coordinate (0.5f, 0.5f) would signify the exact center of the texture. Each vertex gets a texture coordinate for every texture.

Numbers greater than 1.0 can tile the texture, mirror it, or clamp it, depending on the addressing mode of the renderer. If you wanted a texture to tile three times in the horizontal direction and four times in the vertical direction on the surface of a single polygon, the texture (U,V) coordinate that would accomplish that task would be (3.0f, 4.0f). Numbers less than 0.0f are also supported. They have the effect of mirroring the texture.

## Texturing

Creating a texture is as easy as popping into Photoshop, Paint.NET, or any bitmap-editing tool. That leaves out tools like Macromedia Flash or Illustrator because they are vector tools and are no good for bitmaps.

Go into one of these tools and create an image 128 × 128 pixels in size, and save it out as a JPG. Figure 14.16 shows my version.

**Figure 14.16**
A sample texture.

If you are working in Photoshop, you'll want to save the PSD file for future editing, but our next step can't read PSDs. While you can use the DirectX Texture tool to save your texture in DirectX's DDS format, DirectX can load BMP, DIB, HDR, JPG, PFM, PNG, PPM, and TGA files, too. Choosing which of these formats to use has something to do with what tools are generating the textures, but also how you want them compressed. There's a good discussion of that in Chapter 8, "Loading and Caching Game Data."

In Direct3D 11, a texture is loaded from a file or, as you'll see below, from our resource cache. Once in memory, it is stored in an `ID3D11ShaderResourceView` structure, which is sent to a pixel shader. The pixel shader also needs information about how the texture is to be sampled—or put another way, if the pixel shader knows exactly where in the texture to sample, the sampling method will determine what color will be returned by that sample.

## Subsampling

If you've ever seen old 3D games or perhaps just really bad 3D games, you'll probably recall an odd effect that happens to textured objects as you back away from them. This effect, called *scintillation*, is especially noticeable on textures with a regular pattern, such as a black-and-white checkerboard pattern. As the textured objects recede in the distance, you begin to notice that the texture seems to jump around in weird patterns. This is due to an effect called *subsampling*.

Assume for the moment that a texture appears on a polygon very close to its original size. If the texture is 128 × 128 pixels, the polygon on the screen will look almost exactly like the texture. If this polygon were reduced to half of this size, 64 × 64 pixels, the renderer must choose which pixels from the original texture must be applied to the polygon. So what happens if the original texture looks like the one shown in Figure 14.17?

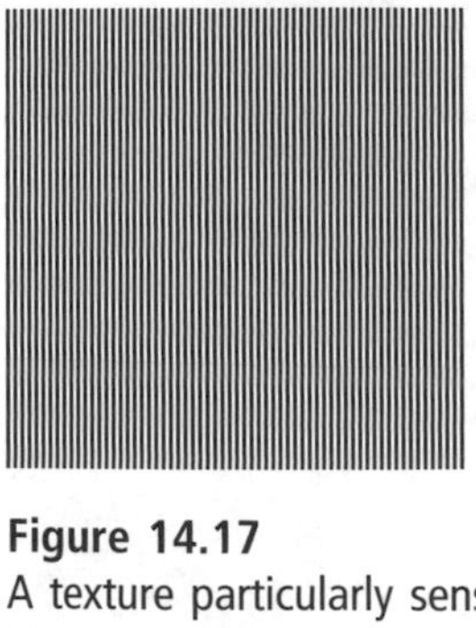

**Figure 14.17**
A texture particularly sensitive to subsampling.

This texture is 128 × 128 pixels, with alternating vertical lines exactly one pixel in width. If you reduced this texture in a simple paint program, you might get nothing but a 64 × 64 texture that is completely black. What's going on here?

When the texture is reduced to half its size, the naive approach would select every other pixel in the grid, which in this case happens to be every black pixel on the texture. The original texture has a certain amount of information, or frequency, in its data stream. The frequency of the above texture is the number of alternating lines. Each pair of black-and-white lines is considered one wave in a waveform that makes up the entire texture. The frequency of this texture is 64, since it takes 64 waves of black-and-white lines to make up the texture.

Subsampling is what occurs if any waveform is sampled at less than twice its frequency. In the previous case, any sample taken at 128 samples or fewer will drop critical information from the original data stream.

It might seem weird to think of textures having a frequency, but they do. A high frequency implies a high degree of information content. In the case of a texture, it has to do with the number of undulations in the waveform that make up the data stream. If the texture were nothing more than a black square, it would have a minimal frequency and therefore carry only the smallest amount of information. A texture that is a solid black square, no matter how large, can be sampled at any rate whatsoever. No information is lost because there isn't that much information to begin with.

In case you are wondering whether or not this subject of subsampling can apply to audio waveforms, it can. Let's assume that you have a high-frequency sound, say a tone at 11KHz. If you attempt to sample this tone in a WAV file at 11KHz, exactly the frequency of the tone, you won't be happy with the results. You'll get a subsampled version of the original sound. Just as the texture turned completely black, your subsampled sound would be a completely flat line, erasing the sound altogether.

It turns out there is a solution for this problem, and it involves processing and filtering the original data stream to preserve as much of the original waveform as possible. For sounds and textures, the new sample isn't just grabbed from an original piece of data in the waveform. The data closest to the sample is used to figure out what is happening to the waveform, instead of one value of the waveform at a discrete point in time.

In the case of our lined texture used previously, the waveform is alternating from black to white as you sample horizontally across the texture, so naturally if the texture diminishes in size, the eye should begin to perceive a 50 percent gray surface. It's no surprise that if you combine black and white in equal amounts you get 50 percent gray.

For textures, each sample involves the surrounding neighborhood of pixels—a process known as *bilinear filtering*. The process is a linear combination of the pixel values on all sides sampled pixel—nine values in all. These nine values are weighted and combined to create the new sample. The same approach can be used with sounds as well, as you might have expected.

Bilinear filtering is done right on the video card and is very fast, but processing textures at runtime to avoid subsampling is a different story, since the system would have to create a set of smaller textures from a source texture. This processing can be expensive, so most game engines do this processing as textures are imported into the game, and they store these reduced images for each texture as a part of the game assets. This master texture is known as a *mip-map*.

## Mip-Mapping

Mip-mapping is a set of textures that has been preprocessed to contain one or more levels of size reduction. In practice, the size reduction is in halves, all the way down to one pixel that represents the dominant color of the entire texture. You might think that this is a waste of memory, but it's actually more efficient than you'd think. A mip-map uses only one-third more memory than the original texture, and considering the vast improvement in the quality of the rendered result, you should provide mip-maps for any texture that has a relatively high frequency of information. It is especially useful for textures with regular patterns, such as our black-and-white line texture.

The DirectX Texture Tool can generate mip-maps for you. To do this, you just load your texture and select Format, Generate Mip Maps. You can then see the resulting reduced textures by pressing PageUp and PageDn.

**Really Long Polygons Can Be Trouble**

One last thing about mip-maps: As you might expect, the renderer will choose which mip-map to display based on the screen size of the polygon. This means that it's not a good idea to create huge polygons on your geometry that can recede into the distance. The renderer might not be able to make a good choice that will satisfy the look of the polygon edge, both closest to the camera and the one farthest away. Some older video cards might select one mip-map for the entire polygon and would therefore look strange. You can't always count on every player to have modern hardware. If you have to support these older cards, you should consider breaking up longer polygons into ones that are more square.

Also, while we're on the subject, many other things can go wrong with huge polygons in world space, such as lighting and collision. It's always a good idea to tessellate, or break up, larger surfaces into smaller polygons that will provide the renderer with a good balance between polygon size and vertex count.

You might have heard of something called *trilinear filtering*. If the renderer switches between one mip-map level on the same polygon, it's likely that you'll notice the switch. Most renderers can sample the texels from more than one mip-map and blend their color in real time. This creates a smooth transition from one mip-map level to another, a much more realistic effect. As you approach something like a newspaper, the mip-maps are sampled in such a way that eventually the blurry image of the headline can resolve into something you can read and react to.

## Introducing `ID3D11Device` and `ID3D11DeviceContext`

In the following pages you'll see some code that uses two DXUT11 functions: `DXUTGetD3D11Device()` and `DXUTGetD3D11DeviceContext()`. `DXUTGetD3D11Device()` returns a `ID3D11Device *` and represents a virtual adapter. You use it to create resources used in rendering, everything from textures to geometry. `DXUTGetD3D11DeviceContext()` returns `ID3D11DeviceContext *`, and it represents the current state of the virtual adapter. You'll use this to set which resources are being used by all subsequent calls, such as setting the graphics system to use a specific texture. Of course, this is a gross oversimplification of these two interfaces, the full description of which is much better done by a dedicated Direct3D 11 book, but at least you'll have some inkling of what they do by looking at what kinds of methods each of these interfaces supports.

## Loading Textures in D3D11

You are finally ready to see how to load textures for Direct3D 11, and you can do so right from the resource cache described in Chapter 8. Textures need to be processed into two interfaces for Direct3D 11. First, the `ID3DShaderResourceView` interface defines data that can be used by the shader, in this case our texture data. Second, the `ID3DSamplerState` defines how the data is to be sampled, most especially to avoid the problems of subsampling you just learned.

First, we define a class that implements `IResourceExtraData` interface so that textures managed by the `ResCache` class from Chapter 8 can be loaded:

```
class D3DTextureResourceExtraData11 : public IResourceExtraData
{
  friend class TextureResourceLoader;
```

```
public:
  D3DTextureResourceExtraData11();
  virtual ~D3DTextureResourceExtraData11()
    { SAFE_RELEASE(m_pTexture); SAFE_RELEASE(m_pSamplerLinear); }
  virtual std::string VToString() { return "D3DTextureResourceExtraData11"; }

  ID3D11ShaderResourceView * const *GetTexture() { return &m_pTexture; }
  ID3D11SamplerState * const *GetSampler() { return &m_pSamplerLinear; }

protected:
  ID3D11ShaderResourceView *m_pTexture;
  ID3D11SamplerState* m_pSamplerLinear;
};
```

This class simply encapsulates the two interfaces Direct3D 11 needs to access textures. Next, we define a loader class for textures:

```
class TextureResourceLoader : public IResourceLoader
{
public:
  virtual bool VUseRawFile() { return false; }
  virtual bool VDiscardRawBufferAfterLoad() { return true; }
  virtual unsigned int VGetLoadedResourceSize(char *rawBuffer,
    unsigned int rawSize)
    { return 0; }
  virtual bool VLoadResource(char *rawBuffer, unsigned int rawSize,
    shared_ptr<ResHandle> handle);
};
```

The class helps the resource cache know how to process the raw texture bits. First, `VUseRawFile()` tells the resource cache to expect some processing after the raw bits are available in memory. The method `VDiscardRawBufferAfterLoad()` tells the resource cache that once the raw bits have been processed they are no longer needed and don't have to be counted as taking up space in the resource cache, which also describes why `VGetLoadedResourceSize()` returns zero. For textures, Direct3D 11 manages texture memory, and while we probably could create a more complicated relationship between our resource cache and Direct3D 11, for now we'll stick to something simpler. The last method is what does the processing of the raw texture bits into something Direct3D 11 can consume. If you weren't using a resource cache at all, this method is all you really would need after the texture file is read into memory:

```
bool TextureResourceLoader::VLoadResource(char *rawBuffer,
  unsigned int rawSize, shared_ptr<ResHandle> handle)
```

```
{
  shared_ptr<D3DTextureResourceExtraData11> extra =
    shared_ptr<D3DTextureResourceExtraData11>(
    GCC_NEW D3DTextureResourceExtraData11());

  // Load the Texture
  if ( FAILED ( D3DX11CreateShaderResourceViewFromMemory(
    DXUTGetD3D11Device(), rawBuffer, rawSize, NULL, NULL,
    &extra->m_pTexture, NULL ) ) )
    return false;

  // Create the sample state
  D3D11_SAMPLER_DESC sampDesc;
  ZeroMemory( &sampDesc, sizeof(sampDesc) );
  sampDesc.Filter = D3D11_FILTER_MIN_MAG_MIP_LINEAR;
  sampDesc.AddressU = D3D11_TEXTURE_ADDRESS_WRAP;
  sampDesc.AddressV = D3D11_TEXTURE_ADDRESS_WRAP;
  sampDesc.AddressW = D3D11_TEXTURE_ADDRESS_WRAP;
  sampDesc.ComparisonFunc = D3D11_COMPARISON_NEVER;
  sampDesc.MinLOD = 0;
  sampDesc.MaxLOD = D3D11_FLOAT32_MAX;
  if( FAILED( DXUTGetD3D11Device()->CreateSamplerState( &sampDesc,
    &extra->m_pSamplerLinear ) ) )
    return false;

  handle->SetExtra(shared_ptr<D3DTextureResourceExtraData11>(extra));
  return true;
}
```

This method makes two calls to Direct3D 11 utility functions. The first, `D3DX11CreateShaderResourceViewFromMemory`, fills the shader resource view interface with the texture data. Next, the sampler state is created by filling a `D3D11_SAMPLER_DESC` structure with a description of the kind of sampler needed and calling `ID3D11Device::CreateSamplerState()`. The filter parameter, `D3D11_FILTER_MIN_MAG_MIP_LINEAR`, requests a sampler that will use linear interpolation for minimization, magnification, and mip-level sampling; this is a good choice to avoid subsampling issues. Minimization is what happens when the texture is rendered so far away as to only take up a single pixel. Magnification is what happens when the texture is so close that a single texel fills the entire screen. There are almost two dozen other filter types in Direct3D 11, so it makes for a great experiment to change this value and see what results. Some of the filters have the ability to use multiple sampling methods, compare the results, and then choose one over the other; that is why you would choose to set the `ComparisonFunc` member of the structure. For this simple filter, we'll leave it at the default setting.

The texture address setting determines what happens when the texture coordinates are close to the border of the texture or are outside of the [0.0, 1.0] range. The choice made above is for the texture to wrap, so that if a texture coordinate were set to (4.0, 3.0), the texture would repeat four times in the horizontal dimension and three times in the vertical. You can also choose other settings to mirror the texture, clamp it, set a specific border color, or even mirror the texture once. These are all defined in the `D3D11_TEXTURE_ADDRESS` enum and found in the Direct 3D 11 documentation.

The `MinLOD` and `MaxLOD` members define which mip-maps, if they are defined, are available to the sampler. Typically, you would leave these at the default settings and have them all available.

Once the loader is defined, you can then access and set the texture with this code:

```
Resource resource(m_textureResource);
shared_ptr<ResHandle> texture = g_pApp->m_ResCache->GetHandle(&resource);
if (texture)
{
  shared_ptr<D3DTextureResourceExtraData11> extra =
    static_pointer_cast<D3DTextureResourceExtraData11>(texture->GetExtra());
  DXUTGetD3D11DeviceContext()->PSSetShaderResources( 0, 1,
    extra->GetTexture());
  DXUTGetD3D11DeviceContext()->PSSetSamplers( 0, 1, extra->GetSampler() );
}
```

Note that the first two parameters to the pixel shader methods define the start slot (defined above to be zero), and the number of shader resources to set (defined above as one). This is very specific to how the shader is written; if the shader expected five textures instead of one, you would load the other four textures and make extra calls to `PSSetShaderResources()`. I know, I haven't said a word yet about what a shader looks like from the inside, but for now just take my word for it that in addition to sending texture resources, you'll send all the other data we've been talking about, including triangle mesh data, which is coming up next.

## Triangle Meshes

We've been talking so far about individual vertices. It's time to take that knowledge and create some triangle meshes. You might define a mesh as a long list of vertices, with each group of three vertices (or *verts*, as programmers say) defining one triangle. If you look at the teapot mesh in Figure 14.15 again, you'll quickly discover that you'll be duplicating a lot of data.

Instead of sending only vertex data to the shader, you can send an index along with it. This index is an array of numbers that define the verts of each triangle, allowing you to avoid serious vertex duplication and save tons of memory. Here's the code that created the grid verts and indices in the teapot example:

```
// Create the vertex buffer - we'll need enough verts
// to populate the grid. If we want a 2x2 grid, we'll
// need 3x3 set of verts.
m_numVerts = (m_squares+1)*(m_squares+1);    // Create vertex buffer

// Fill the vertex buffer. We are setting the tu and tv texture
// coordinates, which range from 0.0 to 1.0
D3D11Vertex_UnlitTextured *pVerts =
  GCC_NEW D3D11Vertex_UnlitTextured[m_numVerts];
GCC_ASSERT(pVerts && "Out of memory");

for( int j=0; j<(m_squares+1); j++ )
{
  for (int i=0; i<(m_squares+1); i++)
  {
    // Which vertex are we setting?
    int index = i + (j * (m_squares+1) );
    D3D11Vertex_UnlitTextured *vert = &pVerts[index];

    // Default position of the grid is centered on the origin, flat on
    // the XZ plane.
    float x = (float)i - (m_squares/2.0f);
    float y = (float)j - (m_squares/2.0f);
    vert->Pos = Vec3(x,0.f,y);
    vert->Normal = Vec3(0.0f, 1.0f, 0.0f);

    // The texture coordinates are set to x,y to make the
    // texture tile along with units - 1.0, 2.0, 3.0, etc.
    vert->Uv.x     = x;
    vert->Uv.y     = y;
  }
}

D3D11_BUFFER_DESC bd;
ZeroMemory( &bd, sizeof(bd) );
bd.Usage = D3D11_USAGE_DEFAULT;
bd.ByteWidth = sizeof( D3D11Vertex_UnlitTextured ) * m_numVerts;
bd.BindFlags = D3D11_BIND_VERTEX_BUFFER;
bd.CPUAccessFlags = 0;
D3D11_SUBRESOURCE_DATA InitData;
ZeroMemory( &InitData, sizeof(InitData) );
InitData.pSysMem = pVerts;
```

```
hr = DXUTGetD3D11Device()->CreateBuffer( &bd, &InitData, &m_pVertexBuffer );
if( FAILED( hr ) )
  return hr;

// The number of indices equals the number of polygons times 3
// since there are 3 indices per polygon. Each grid square contains
// two polygons. The indices are 16 bit, since our grids won't
// be that big!

m_numPolys = m_squares * m_squares * 2;
WORD *pIndices = GCC_NEW WORD[m_numPolys * 3];
GCC_ASSERT(pIndices && "Out of memory!");

// Loop through the grid squares and calc the values
// of each index. Each grid square has two triangles:
//
//      A - B
//      | / |
//      C - D
WORD *current = pIndices;
for( int j=0; j<m_squares; j++ )
{
  for (int i=0; i<m_squares; i++)
  {
    // Triangle #1  ACB
    *(current) = WORD(i + (j*(m_squares+1)));
    *(current+1) = WORD(i + ((j+1)*(m_squares+1)));
    *(current+2) = WORD((i+1) + (j*(m_squares+1)));

    // Triangle #2  BCD
    *(current+3) = WORD((i+1) + (j*(m_squares+1)));
    *(current+4) = WORD(i + ((j+1)*(m_squares+1)));
    *(current+5) = WORD((i+1) + ((j+1)*(m_squares+1)));
    current+=6;
  }
}
```

I've commented the code pretty heavily to help you understand what's going on. When the code is executed, `pVerts` holds the list of vertices, and `pIndices` holds the indexes into that list that defines the triangles of the grid mesh. Take a few minutes to stare at the code that assigns the index numbers—it's the last nested `for` loop. If you have trouble figuring it out, trace the code with a 2 × 2 grid, and you'll get it.

Once these two data structures are defined, you have to create the vertex buffer and index buffer that can be consumed by Direct3D 11. Here's the code to do that:

```
HRESULT hr;

D3D11_BUFFER_DESC bd;
ZeroMemory( &bd, sizeof(bd) );
bd.Usage = D3D11_USAGE_DEFAULT;
bd.ByteWidth = sizeof( D3D11Vertex_UnlitTextured ) * m_numVerts;
bd.BindFlags = D3D11_BIND_VERTEX_BUFFER;
bd.CPUAccessFlags = 0;
D3D11_SUBRESOURCE_DATA InitData;
ZeroMemory( &InitData, sizeof(InitData) );
InitData.pSysMem = pVerts;
hr = DXUTGetD3D11Device()->CreateBuffer( &bd, &InitData, &m_pVertexBuffer );
if( SUCCEEDED ( hr ) )
{
  bd.Usage = D3D11_USAGE_DEFAULT;
  bd.ByteWidth = sizeof( WORD ) * m_numPolys * 3;
  bd.BindFlags = D3D11_BIND_INDEX_BUFFER;
  bd.CPUAccessFlags = 0;
  InitData.pSysMem = pIndices;
  hr = DXUTGetD3D11Device()->CreateBuffer( &bd, &InitData, &m_pIndexBuffer );
}

SAFE_DELETE_ARRAY(pVerts);
SAFE_DELETE_ARRAY(pIndices);
return hr;
```

In the creation of both the vertex buffer and the index buffer, a `D3D11_BUFFER_DESC` structure is used to describe what kind of buffer we are creating. `ByteWidth` is set to the number of bytes in the entire buffer. `BindFlags` is set to either `D3D11_BIND_VERTEX_BUFFER` or `D3D11_BIND_INDEX_BUFFER`. In both cases, a `D3D11_SUBRESOURCE_DATA` structure is initialized with a pointer to the data. A successful result will create an `ID3D11Buffer`, which you'll use during rendering.

## Still with Me?

This chapter skimmed the surface of 3D basics like a rock skipping on a pond. 3D math, transforms, frustums, lighting, textures, and geometry—all in just a few pages. I know it isn't nearly enough information, and there is a lot more depth to all those subjects. I encourage you to go find out more about them, but know you'll at least have a little more knowledge and experience, and maybe you won't feel quite so lost. You'll also recognize a lot more code in the Direct3D 11 samples and tutorials.

Next, you'll learn how all of the resources you learned about in this chapter get sent into vertex and pixel shaders. Get ready for another run across the pond.

# Chapter 15

*by Mike McShaffry*

## 3D Vertex and Pixel Shaders

Shaders are rapidly dominating 3D graphics architecture. There are a few platforms out there that don't support shaders, such as the Nintendo Wii, which still uses fixed-function pipelines. But when even smart phones start to use shaders, it is high time to dig in and figure them out. Much of my own learning about them was pretty frustrating. It seemed there was no middle ground between drawing a very lame triangle and drawing fur. I hope the following introduction will help you see a path to getting started with shaders.

A shader is a program that can affect the position of a vertex, the color of a pixel, or both. Shaders can create interesting effects by manipulating geometry, as is frequently done for water surfaces, or changing the appearance of something as mundane as a teapotahedron (see Figure 15.1).

Shaders can be written in assembly or high-level languages. Microsoft developed HLSL, which stands for High Level Shader Language, for use within DirectX. There is a standard for OpenGL called GLSL and Nivida's Cg, or C for Graphics, which are similar to HLSL. All look and feel a lot like C, but don't be fooled. They aren't C.

Just like any high-level language, shaders compile to assembler language. The shader compiler lives in your graphics drivers, and depending on your graphics card, the compiler can do some pretty interesting things with the resulting assembly. One example is loops, which are generally unrolled instead of actually looping in the way you are used to. Different shader versions have drastically different support for numbers of texture coordinates or even the size of the shader.

**Figure 15.1**
Different effects created by pixel and vertex shaders.

You can compile shaders ahead of time for all the different shader versions and test them against your video cards, and this is definitely recommended for a commercial environment. Compiling at runtime is how most programmers develop shaders. In the example you are about to see, the shader will be loaded and compiled at runtime.

**Compiling Shaders == Lunchtime**

I worked at Slipgate on an unannounced MMO. This was a triple-A game with *tons* of shaders in it. It took close to an hour to recompile every single shader for all platforms. Fortunately, this was a very rare occurrence; usually shaders were modified in small batches, so it wasn't too bad. There were a few times during development, however, where we were forced to do this massive recompile. When that happened, productivity ground to a complete halt. We just went to lunch.

This chapter will present you with an example of a vertex shader written in HLSL, the C++ code you need to access it within your game, and the same for a pixel shader. There are other types of shaders, such as geometry shaders and compute shaders, but those are beyond the scope of this book. Worry not, there's a set of further reading at the end of this chapter.

## The Vertex Shader and Shader Syntax

A vertex shader is just a program—in fact, very similar to a C program. Its job is to take vertices from the game, process them, and send them along to the pixel shader. By process, the thing you see most often in a vertex shader is transformation and lighting. But you can do much more; any operation supported by the shader syntax is fair game, even moving the vertices around before you transform them. Vertex shaders do their work and then send the output on to the pixel shader, which you'll see next.

The shader below is relatively simple and doesn't look completely different from a C program. Variables, data structures, and functions have a familiar look—but as you would expect, there are differences. Many of these differences come from the fact that the shader runs on the GPU in a video card, and that hardware expects data to be presented in very specific ways. Second, the syntax helps "hook up" the shader with data sent to it from C++. This chapter will present the shader first and then the C++ code to send it the data it needs to do its work.

The simple vertex shader presented below does the following three things:

- Transforms the position of a vertex from object space into screen space.
- Transforms the normal vector from object space to world space.
- Passes the texture coordinate through as-is.

```
//--------------------------------------------------------------------------------------
// File: GameCode4_VSMain_VS.hlsl
// The vertex shader file for the GameCode4.
//--------------------------------------------------------------------------------------
// Globals
//--------------------------------------------------------------------------------------
cbuffer cbMatrices : register( b0 )
{
  matrix   g_mWorldViewProjection  : packoffset( c0 );
  matrix   g_mWorld                : packoffset( c4 );
};

cbuffer cbLights : register( b1 )
{
  float4  g_LightDiffuse[8];
  float4  g_LightDir[8];
```

```
  float4   g_fAmbient;
  int      g_nNumLights;
};

cbuffer cbObjectColors : register( b2 )
{
  float4  g_vDiffuseObjectColor   : packoffset( c0 );
  float4  g_vAmbientObjectColor   : packoffset( c1 );
  bool    g_bHasTexture : packoffset( c2.x );
};


// Input / Output structures
//-----------------------------------------------------------------------------
struct VS_INPUT
{
  float4 vPosition   : POSITION;
  float3 vNormal     : NORMAL;
  float2 vTexcoord   : TEXCOORD0;
};

struct VS_OUTPUT
{
  float4 vDiffuse    : COLOR0;
  float2 vTexcoord   : TEXCOORD0;
  float4 vPosition   : SV_POSITION;
};

// Vertex Shader
//-----------------------------------------------------------------------------
VS_OUTPUT GameCode4_VSMain( VS_INPUT Input )
{
  VS_OUTPUT Output;

  float3 vNormalWorldSpace;
  float dotProduct;
  float4 dottedLightColor;

  Output.vPosition = mul( Input.vPosition, g_mWorldViewProjection );
  vNormalWorldSpace = mul( Input.vNormal, (float3x3)g_mWorld );
  Output.vTexcoord = Input.vTexcoord;

  // Compute simple directional lighting equation
  float4 vTotalLightDiffuse = float4(0,0,0,0);
  for(int i=0; i<g_nNumLights; i++ )
  {
```

```
        dotProduct = dot(vNormalWorldSpace, g_LightDir[i]);
        dotProduct = max(0, dotProduct);
        dottedLightColor = g_LightDiffuse[i] * dotProduct;
        vTotalLightDiffuse += dottedLightColor;
    }

    Output.vDiffuse.rgb = g_vDiffuseObjectColor * vTotalLightDiffuse +
                          g_vAmbientObjectColor * g_fAmbient;

    Output.vDiffuse.a = 1.0f;
    return Output;
}
```

The first thing you notice is a comment, using the familiar syntax of the "//" to begin one. As always, it is a good idea to comment well. This is especially true in shaders, where very simple-looking operations can have interesting results.

The next block of code defines a `cbuffer`, which is very similar to a `struct` in C, except that you can define where the data will be stored and how it is packed. In earlier shader models, each parameter needed by the shader had to be sent individually, which lowered performance greatly. Starting with shader model 4.0, constant buffers could group parameters together so they could be submitted to the video card at once. The maximum size of a constant buffer is 4,096 vectors, each vector containing up to four 32-bit values. You are limited to 14 constant buffers per pipeline stage.

It's a good idea to group data that changes at the same rate into the same constant buffer. For example, if you have data that changes only once per frame, such as a transformation matrix or lighting, store those separately from data that changes more frequently. A great example of this would be a texture or material, which could change for each object in your scene.

Packing and storing the `cbuffer` is done with the `register` and `packoffset` keyword. The `register (b0)` tells the shader to put the constant buffer into slot zero. This isn't truly necessary in this simple shader, but if you had more than one constant buffer, this is a clear way to define which slot it occupies and which you'll need to know for your C++ code that sends data to the shader. Packing tells the shader compiler how you want data stored, especially if you have simple integers or Booleans you want to send to the shader.

The `cbuffer cbMatrices` structure defined at the top of the shader stores two 4 × 4 matrices. The first, `g_mWorldViewProjection`, stores the transformation needed to get from object space to screen space. Each position member of each vertex is transformed using this matrix to resolve a 3D position in object space to a pixel in screen space—a 2D X,Y coordinate and a depth measured into the screen. The second matrix, `g_mWorld`, will be used to transform a normal vector into world space, which will be used by the pixel shader to calculate lighting on a per-pixel basis.

In addition to transforming vertex positions into screen space, the vertex shader also combines the defined object color or a piece of its texture with as many as eight lights defined in the environment. To help with this, the vertex shader defines two more constant buffers, `cbObjectColors` and `cbLights`. `cbObjectColors` stores a diffuse and ambient color and whether there is a valid texture, which will be used later in the pixel shader. `cbLights` stores the color and direction of up to eight directional lights, an ambient light color, and the number of valid lights.

Notice the difference in `register` values for both `cbuffer` objects. `cbObjectColors` is set to slot one, and `cbLights` is set to slot two. This isn't mandatory, as the shader compiler would automatically set them to those values because of their order of definition, but it's good to have this example. `cbObjectColors` has a `bool` that is specifically put into `c2.x`, which is the first 32-bit member of the third vector in the structure. The `cbLights` constant buffer has a similar issue with the `g_nNumLights` member not being a full 4 vector, but the `packoffset` definitions have been left off, so the shader compiler could set them as it wants.

Just as you might pack a structure in C++ to save space or create code that will access it with more specificity than the defaults, you can use `packoffset` to override the shader compiler to create a very tightly defined structure. It's completely up to you and your needs. These shaders could have all forgone both `register` and `packoffset` keywords and used the defaults, since there isn't anything really special about them.

The next block of code defines the `VS_INPUT` structure. It stores a position, a normal, and a texture coordinate and maps to the `D3DVertex_UnlitTextured` `struct` used in the previous chapter to create geometry. Here it is again:

```
struct D3D11Vertex_UnlitTextured
{
  Vec3 Pos;
  Vec3 Normal;
  Vec2 Uv;
};
```

One syntax different from C is after the colon for each member: `POSITION`, `NORMAL`, and `TEXCOORD0`. These are called *semantics*, and they provide a way to identify each member so that each member can be linked to the data you define in C++.

The VS_OUTPUT structure is defined similarly, except there is a special semantic, SV_POSITION. This is a system value semantic, and it tells the shader compiler that this value will be interpreted as a pixel location on the display. The entire VS_OUTPUT structure will be sent to the pixel shader.

The next block of code defines a function, GameCode4_VS_Main. This function accepts VS_INPUT and returns VS_OUTPUT. The syntax is similar to C, and just like C there are over 100 intrinsic functions you can call upon. The one you see first, mul, multiplies or concatenates two matrices. Other intrinsic functions perform data type conversions, vector operations like a dot product, trigonometric functions like cosine, and even functions to compute high-precision partial derivatives. For now, we'll stick to the simple stuff.

The vertex shader function uses mul to transform the vPosition member in VS_INPUT from object space to screen space, and to transform the vNormal member from object space to world space. The vTexcoord member is just sent along as is. With all the members of VS_OUTPUT assigned, it is returned, and the shader function exits.

If there are lights to worry about, the shader enters a loop. Another shader-intrinsic function, dot, calculates the dot product between the light's direction vector and the normal vector sent in from the vertex shader. The dot product calculates an angle if you recall, and if that angle is 90 degrees, the dot product is 0.0f. The max intrinsic function makes sure that the dot product doesn't contribute a negative value to the light calculation. The light's diffuse color is multiplied by the dot product to scale the light's contribution down to zero if the normal is at right angles to the light direction. The light's contribution, stored in dottedLightColor, is accumulated in the combined contributions of all the lights, vTotalLightDiffuse.

After the lights are accumulated, the final result is combined with the object's material and stored in Output.vDiffuse. This is one of the simplest lighting models, where the lights are accumulated for each vertex and combined with the object's material, which results in a color for each vertex. The pixel shader, which you will see shortly, interpolates this color value for each pixel and, if it exists, combines that with a value sampled from the texture.

## Compiling the Vertex Shader

The shader is typically stored in an HLSL text file. To use it, it must be loaded and compiled. It is possible to precompile shaders, saving some loading time, but it can be useful to compile them at runtime so that different levels of shaders on the target machine can be supported.

Compiling a shader file is done with this helper function: `CompileShader()`:

```
HRESULT CompileShader(
  LPCSTR pSrcData,
  SIZE_T SrcDataLen,
  LPCSTR pFileName,
  LPCSTR szEntryPoint,
  LPCSTR szShaderModel,
  ID3DBlob** ppBlobOut )
{
  HRESULT hr = S_OK;

  DWORD dwShaderFlags = D3DCOMPILE_ENABLE_STRICTNESS;
#if defined( DEBUG ) || defined( _DEBUG )
  // Set the D3DCOMPILE_DEBUG flag to embed debug information in the shaders.
  // Setting this flag improves the shader debugging experience, but still
  // allows the shaders to be optimized and to run exactly the way they will
  // run in the release configuration of this program.
  dwShaderFlags |= D3DCOMPILE_DEBUG;
#endif

  ID3DBlob* pErrorBlob;
  hr = D3DX11CompileFromMemory( pSrcData, SrcDataLen,
    pFileName, NULL, NULL, szEntryPoint, szShaderModel,
    dwShaderFlags, 0, NULL, ppBlobOut, &pErrorBlob, NULL );
  if( FAILED(hr) )
  {
    if( pErrorBlob != NULL )
      OutputDebugStringA( (char*)pErrorBlob->GetBufferPointer() );
    if( pErrorBlob ) pErrorBlob->Release();
    return hr;
  }
  if( pErrorBlob )
    pErrorBlob->Release();

  return S_OK;
}
```

This helper function was lifted almost verbatim from the Direct3D11 samples, with one important modification. Instead of loading the shader straight from a file, this code loads it from the resource cache. This means that the resource cache is responsible for loading the shader file into memory, and from there you need to send it to

D3DX11CompileFromMemory() to let Direct3D11 compile the shader. The parameters you need to send into this function are

- pSrcData: A pointer to the shader in memory
- SrcDataLen: The size of the shader in bytes
- pFileName: The name of the shader file, which will help with debugging
- pDefines: Shader defines, which we have set to NULL
- pInclude: Shader includes, which we have set to NULL
- pFunctionName: The name of the entry point function
- pProfile: A string that defines the shader model
- Flags1: Shader compile flags, which are set at the beginning of the function
- Flags2: Effect compile flags, which we have set to zero
- pPump: A pointer to a thread pump interface, which is NULL
- ppShader: Where the compiled shader will be stored
- ppErrorMsgs: Where error messages will be stored
- pHResult: A pointer to store a return value if pPump is defined

For our simple shaders, most of the advanced parameters can be set to NULL. One that deserves a little more attention, however, is pProfile. Just as in releases of software, each major revision of HLSL brought new capabilities. When you write a shader, you write to a specific model, and you tell the shader compiler which model it needs to run on. If you specify vertex shader model 4.0 with vs_4_0 as the pProfile parameter, and you've used anything in the shader that requires shader model 5, the compile will fail.

Moreover, if you want to specify a version of Direct3D, such as 9.1 or 10.0, you can append this to the pProfile string. For example, if you want to set the shader compiler to compile a vertex shader for model 4.0 with a Direct3D level of 9.1, you would set the pProfile string to vs_4_0_level_9_1.

## C++ Helper Class for the Vertex Shader

Having a compiled shader isn't much good if you can't get data to it from your game, so it makes some sense to design a helper class for the shader. Here's the helper class for the vertex shader you saw earlier:

```
class GameCode4_Hlsl_VertexShader
{
```

```
public:
  GameCode4_Hlsl_VertexShader();
  ~GameCode4_Hlsl_VertexShader();

  HRESULT OnRestore(Scene *pScene);
  HRESULT SetupRender(Scene *pScene, const SceneNode *pNode);

protected:
  ID3D11VertexShader*        m_pVertexShader;
  ID3D11InputLayout*         m_pVertexLayout11;
  ID3D11Buffer*              m_pcbVSMatrices;
  ID3D11Buffer*              m_pcbVSMaterial;
  ID3D11Buffer*              m_pcbVSLighting;
  bool                       m_enableLights;
};
```

The vertex shader needs some data to do its work: the constant buffer with the two transform matrices, a constant buffer holding the lights affecting the vertices, the object's material, and a triangle mesh that describes the geometry the shader will process. Look at the protected members of this class. The first defines a pointer to an object that implements the `ID3D11VertexShader` interface—basically, this is just a pointer to the loaded shader. The next member, `m_pVertexLayout11`, defines the layout of the vertices the shader expects, essentially what will become `VS_INPUT`. The next member, `m_pcbVSMatrices`, defines a pointer to an `ID3D11Buffer` that will hold the two transformation matrices the vertex shader needs, which will present itself in the shader as `cbuffer cbMatrices`. The next member, `m_pcbVSMaterial`, holds information about the diffuse and ambient colors of the object and whether the object is textured. The last member, `m_pcbVSLighting`, holds the color and direction of up to eight directional lights.

The constructor and destructor for this class are relatively trivial:

```
GameCode4_Hlsl_VertexShader::GameCode4_Hlsl_VertexShader()
{
  m_pVertexLayout11 = NULL;
  m_pVertexShader = NULL;
  m_pcbVSMatrices = NULL;
  m_pcbVSMaterial = NULL;
  m_pcbVSLighting = NULL;
  m_enableLights = true;
}

GameCode4_Hlsl_VertexShader::~GameCode4_Hlsl_VertexShader()
{
  SAFE_RELEASE(m_pVertexLayout11);
```

```
  SAFE_RELEASE(m_pVertexShader);
  SAFE_RELEASE(m_pcbVSMatrices);
  SAFE_RELEASE(m_pcbVSMaterial);
  SAFE_RELEASE(m_pcbVSLighting );
}
```

If you don't call SAFE_RELEASE for those Direct3D objects, you are sure to get one of those dreaded warning messages at the exit of your game! The two meaty methods of this class are OnRestore(), which initializes this class, and SetupRender(), which is called any time the shader is used to render graphics to the screen. Here is OnRestore():

```
HRESULT GameCode4_Hlsl_VertexShader::OnRestore()
{
  HRESULT hr;

  SAFE_RELEASE(m_pVertexLayout11);
  SAFE_RELEASE(m_pVertexShader);
  SAFE_RELEASE(m_pcbVSMatrices);
  SAFE_RELEASE(m_pcbVSMaterial);
  SAFE_RELEASE(m_pcbVSLighting );

  //==========================================================================
  // Load and compile the vertex shader. Using the lowest
  //  possible profile for broadest feature level support
  ID3DBlob* pVertexShaderBuffer = NULL;
  std::string hlslFileName = "Effects\\GameCode4_VS.hlsl";
  Resource resource(hlslFileName.c_str());
  shared_ptr<ResHandle> pResourceHandle =
    g_pApp->m_ResCache->GetHandle(&resource);   if ( FAILED
(CompileShader(pResourceHandle->Buffer(), pResourceHandle->Size(),
hlslFileName.c_str(), "GameCode4_VSMain", "vs_4_0_level_9_1",
&pVertexShaderBuffer ) ) )
  {
    SAFE_RELEASE ( pVertexShaderBuffer );
    return hr;
  }

  if ( FAILED  ( DXUTGetD3D11Device()->CreateVertexShader(
    pVertexShaderBuffer->GetBufferPointer(),
    pVertexShaderBuffer->GetBufferSize(), NULL, &m_pVertexShader ) ) )
  {
    SAFE_RELEASE ( pVertexShaderBuffer );
    return hr;
  }
```

```
    //=======================================================================
    // Create the vertex input layout and release the pVertexShaderBuffer object
    if ( SUCCEEDED ( DXUTGetD3D11Device()->CreateInputLayout(
      D3D11VertexLayout_UnlitTextured,
      ARRAYSIZE( D3D11VertexLayout_UnlitTextured ),
      pVertexShaderBuffer->GetBufferPointer(),
      pVertexShaderBuffer->GetBufferSize(), &m_pVertexLayout11 ) );
    {

      //=====================================================================
      // Setup the constant buffer for the two transformation matrices
      D3D11_BUFFER_DESC Desc;
      Desc.Usage = D3D11_USAGE_DYNAMIC;
      Desc.BindFlags = D3D11_BIND_CONSTANT_BUFFER;
      Desc.CPUAccessFlags = D3D11_CPU_ACCESS_WRITE;
      Desc.MiscFlags = 0;
      Desc.ByteWidth = sizeof( ConstantBuffer_Matrices );
      V_RETURN( DXUTGetD3D11Device()->CreateBuffer( &Desc, NULL,
                                            &m_pcbVSMatrices ) );

      Desc.ByteWidth = sizeof( ConstantBuffer_Material );
      V_RETURN( DXUTGetD3D11Device()->CreateBuffer( &Desc, NULL,
                                            &m_pcbVSMaterial ) );

      Desc.ByteWidth = sizeof( ConstantBuffer_Lighting );
      V_RETURN( DXUTGetD3D11Device()->CreateBuffer( &Desc, NULL,
                                            &m_pcbVSLighting ) );
    }
    SAFE_RELEASE ( pVertexShaderBuffer );

    return S_OK;
}
```

The first few lines simply release the D3D11 objects, if they happen to contain anything. This might happen if the D3D11 device were lost, which could happen if the player switched to another application or dragged the game from one monitor to another.

The next section of code, defined by the comment headers, loads the shader from the resource cache. The free function, `CompileShader()`, you've seen in the previous section. The entry point of our shader is set to `GameCode4_VSMain`. The string parameter for the shader model is set to `vs_4_0_level_9_1`, which tells the shader compiler to support vertex shaders model 4.0, compatible with Direct3D 9.1. The compiled shader is stored in `pVertexShaderBuffer`. If the compile fails for any reason, you'll know about it here. The vertex shader is then created with a call to ID3D11Device::CreateVertexShader().

Next, the vertex input layout is defined and set for the shader. Recall the definition for VS_INPUT in the vertex shader? That input structure needs a layout definition, which is defined as follows:

```
// Create our vertex input layout
const D3D11_INPUT_ELEMENT_DESC D3D11VertexLayout_UnlitTextured[] =
{
  { "POSITION", 0, DXGI_FORMAT_R32G32B32_FLOAT, 0, 0,
   D3D11_INPUT_PER_VERTEX_DATA, 0 },
  { "NORMAL",   0, DXGI_FORMAT_R32G32B32_FLOAT, 0, 12,
   D3D11_INPUT_PER_VERTEX_DATA, 0 },
  { "TEXCOORD", 0, DXGI_FORMAT_R32G32_FLOAT,    0, 24,
   D3D11_INPUT_PER_VERTEX_DATA, 0 },
};
```

This is the data structure sent into ID3D11Device::CreateInputLayout (), and is an array of D3D11_INPUT_ELEMENT_DESC structures. For each member, it defines a single element of each vertex. The first member of the D3D11_INPUT_ ELEMENT_ DESC structure is the SemanticName, which the vertex shader will use to access the data. The next member, SemanticIndex, enables you to send in more than one value with the same SemanticName, as you might do if there were multiple texture coordinates for each vertex. The next member, Format, is a value from the DXGI_ FORMAT enum defined in Direct3D, which has 115 different members. The values chosen for our vertex format define 3D, 32-bit floating-point vectors for the position and normal data, and a 2D 32-bit floating-point vector for the texture data. The fourth member defines the input slot, which for this simple example with only one vertex buffer is set to zero. If your shader accepted more than one vertex buffer, you'd set the input slot to match which vertex buffer the shader should read from. The fifth member defines the AlignedByteOffset, which you always set to the byte offset of the data member. The last two members, set to their defaults for this simple example, are used when a vertex shader can draw instances of the same object in multiple positions by using additional transformation matrices.

With the input layout defined, it is sent into the ID3D11Device::CreateInput-Layout() method, which results in the initialization of the m_pVertexLayout11 member of our class. With all that homework complete, the pVertexShaderBuffer is no longer needed, so it is released.

The next block of code in this shader setup routine creates the data structure that maps to the cbuffer cbPerObject structure in the vertex shader that holds the two transformation matrices for processing vertex positions into screen space and vertex normals from object space into world space. Defining a constant buffer for Direct3D 11 is done by filling in the D3D11_BUFFER_DESC structure and sending the result into ID3D11Device::CreateBuffer(). This is simply creating a data buffer with a size sufficient for the data we're going to copy into it during rendering. As you might expect, the definition for the ConstantBuffer_Matrices is just the two transform matrices the vertex shader needs:

```
struct ConstantBuffer_Matrices
{
   Mat4x4 m_WorldViewProj;
   Mat4x4 m_World;
};
```

The results are stored in the m_pcbVSMatrices member of the class. The two C++ structures referenced in the D3D11_BUFFER_DESC for material and lighting are defined as follows:

```
struct ConstantBuffer_Material
{
  Vec4 m_vDiffuseObjectColor;
  Vec4 m_vAmbientObjectColor;
  BOOL m_bHasTexture;
  Vec3 m_vUnused;
};
struct ConstantBuffer_Lighting
{
  Vec4 m_vLightDiffuse[MAXIMUM_LIGHTS_SUPPORTED];
  Vec4 m_vLightDir[MAXIMUM_LIGHTS_SUPPORTED];
  Vec4 m_vLightAmbient;
  UINT m_nNumLights;
  Vec3 m_vUnused;
};
```

There is a notable difference in these structures from the ConstantBuffer_Matrices structure. At the end of each one, there is a Vec3 m_vUnused member. The reason for this is that in each case, the previous member occupies only one byte of the structure, leaving it at a size that can't be properly aligned. GPU hardware is notoriously picky about the size of structures, and if you don't send data to them aligned on 16-byte boundaries, you'll get an E_INVALIDARG error coming back from the call to CreateBuffer().

So here's a quick review. The shader source code was loaded, compiled, and created ready to use for rendering. The vertex layout was defined. The constant buffers for the transform matrices, lighting, and materials were defined. This process only needs to be done once, as long as the ID3D11Device remains valid.

The next method is run in each frame and initializes all the data for the shader:

```
HRESULT GameCode4_Hlsl_VertexShader::SetupRender(Scene *pScene, const SceneNode
*pNode)
{
  HRESULT hr;

  // Set the vertex shader and the vertex layout
  DXUTGetD3D11DeviceContext()->VSSetShader( m_pVertexShader, NULL, 0 );
  DXUTGetD3D11DeviceContext()->IASetInputLayout( m_pVertexLayout11 );

  // Get the projection & view matrix from the camera class
  Mat4x4 mWorldViewProjection =
    pScene->GetCamera()->GetWorldViewProjection(pScene);
  Mat4x4 mWorld = pScene->GetTopMatrix();
  D3D11_MAPPED_SUBRESOURCE MappedResource;

  // ----- Transform Matrices -----
   V( DXUTGetD3D11DeviceContext()->Map(
    m_pcbVSMatrices, 0, D3D11_MAP_WRITE_DISCARD, 0, &MappedResource ) );
  ConstantBuffer_Matrices* pVSMatrices =
    ( ConstantBuffer_Matrices* )MappedResource.pData;
  D3DXMatrixTranspose( &pVSMatrices->m_WorldViewProj, &mWorldViewProjection );
  D3DXMatrixTranspose( &pVSMatrices->m_World, &mWorld );
  DXUTGetD3D11DeviceContext()->Unmap( m_pcbVSMatrices, 0 );

  // ----- Lighting -----
  V( DXUTGetD3D11DeviceContext()->Map( m_pcbVSLighting, 0,
    D3D11_MAP_WRITE_DISCARD, 0, &MappedResource ) );
    D3D11_MAP_WRITE_DISCARD, 0, &MappedResource ) );
  ConstantBuffer_Lighting* pLighting =
    ( ConstantBuffer_Lighting* )MappedResource.pData;

  if (m_enableLights)
    pScene->GetLightManager()->CalcLighting(pLighting, pNode);
  else
  {
    pLighting->m_nNumLights = 0;
    pLighting->m_vLightAmbient = Vec4(1.0f, 1.0f, 1.0f, 1.0f);
  }

  DXUTGetD3D11DeviceContext()->Unmap( m_pcbVSLighting, 0 );
```

```
  // ----- Material -----
  V( DXUTGetD3D11DeviceContext()->Map( m_pcbVSMaterial, 0,
     D3D11_MAP_WRITE_DISCARD, 0, &MappedResource ) );
  ConstantBuffer_Material* pPSMaterial =
    ( ConstantBuffer_Material* )MappedResource.pData;

  Color color = pNode->VGet()->GetMaterial().GetDiffuse();
  pPSMaterial->m_vDiffuseObjectColor =
    Vec4(color.r, color.g, color.b, color.a);
  color = (m_enableLights) ?
    pNode->VGet()->GetMaterial().GetAmbient() :
    Color(1.0f, 1.0f, 1.0f, 1.0f);
  pPSMaterial->m_vAmbientObjectColor =
    Vec4(color.r, color.g, color.b, color.a);
  pPSMaterial->m_bHasTexture = false;

  DXUTGetD3D11DeviceContext()->VSSetConstantBuffers( 0, 1, &m_pcbVSMatrices );
  DXUTGetD3D11DeviceContext()->VSSetConstantBuffers( 1, 1, &m_pcbVSLighting );
  DXUTGetD3D11DeviceContext()->VSSetConstantBuffers( 2, 1, &m_pcbVSMaterial );

  return S_OK;
}
```

This code looks a little more complicated than it is. Each time the vertices are rendered, the `ID3D11DeviceContext` is informed of the shader being used and the vertex layout it expects. The nearly dozen lines of code following grab the two transform matrices we need from a class you will be introduced to in the next chapter, the `Scene` class. The matrices are transposed, an operation that flips the rows into columns and columns into rows. This is because the native format used by the `DXUT` matrix structure isn't what is expected by the video card hardware. The `D3D11_MAPPED_SUBRESOURCE` structure is what is defined and sent into the `ID3D11DeviceContext::Map()` method to create a buffer space the transposed matrices can be sent to.

I admit, I'm cheating a bit by giving you a peek at some objects you'll see in the next chapter. I'm talking about the `Scene` object stored in `pScene`. For now, just know that this defines a scene in your game, and a part of that scene includes lights. The `SceneNode` object stored in `pNode` stores a renderable object in that scene—in fact, the very object that the pixel shader is about to render. A part of the `SceneNode` class defines the material applied to the object. The call to `pScene->GetLightManager()->CalcLighting()` is what fills the lighting structure with all the information about what lights are currently affecting the vertices sent to the shader.

Take a closer look at the calls to `ID3D11DeviceContext::VSSetConstantBuffers()` at the end. I purposely moved them together to make a point: When there are more multiple constant buffers in a shader, you must use the first parameter, `StartSlot`, to identify which constant buffer you are setting. Since the `cbMatrices` structure in the vertex shader is defined as being in register zero, the slot number in `VSSetConstantBuffers()` is set to zero. For the lights, it is set to slot one, and the materials are set to slot two. If the `register` directive weren't used, the slots you would specify would simply be in the order in which the constant buffers were declared in the shader.

## The Pixel Shader

A pixel shader is responsible for painting pixels, or *rasterization*. Every pixel on the screen is a combination of an object's color, the texture color if one exists, and lighting. The pixel shader below is an example of one that calculates all of these values on a per-pixel basis.

```
//--------------------------------------------------------------------------------------
// File: GameCode4_PS.hlsl
// The pixel shader file for GameCode4
//--------------------------------------------------------------------------------------

//--------------------------------------------------------------------------------------
// Globals
//--------------------------------------------------------------------------------------
cbuffer cbObjectColors : register( b0 )
{
  float4  g_vDiffuseObjectColor   : packoffset( c0 );
  float4  g_vAmbientObjectColor   : packoffset( c1 );
  bool    g_bHasTexture: packoffset( c2.x );
};

// Textures and Samplers
//--------------------------------------------------------------------------------------
Texture2D   g_txDiffuse : register( t0 );
SamplerState g_samLinear : register( s0 );

// Input structure
//--------------------------------------------------------------------------------------
struct PS_INPUT
{
  float4 vDiffuse : COLOR0;
  float2 vTexcoord   : TEXCOORD0;
};
```

```
// Pixel Shader
//-----------------------------------------------------------------------------
float4 GameCode4_PSMain( PS_INPUT Input ) : SV_TARGET
{
  float4 vOutputColor;

  if (g_bHasTexture)
    vOutputColor =
      g_txDiffuse.Sample( g_samLinear, Input.vTexcoord ) * Input.vDiffuse;
  else
    vOutputColor = Input.vDiffuse;
    return vOutputColor;
}
```

The pixel shader is much simpler than the vertex shader, since all it has to do is mix a texture sample with the diffuse color sent in from the vertex shader.

Since this pixel can process a texture, there are globals that store a `Texture2D` structure and a `SamplerState`, which map to the `ID3D11ShaderResourceView` and `ID3D11SamplerState` resources you learned about in the texturing section earlier.

The `VS_INPUT` structure defines the data that is output from the vertex shader, which will be the diffuse color calculated by the vertex shader and the texture coordinate at the pixel location. The call to `Sample` grabs the texel from the texture, based on the value of `Input.vTexcoord`. This value is multiplied by `Input.vDiffuse` to blend the light, object color, and texture together. If no texture is defined, `vOutputColor` is simply set to the `Input.vDiffuse` value.

## C++ Helper Class for the Pixel Shader

Just as you saw with the vertex shader, there is a C++ class designed to set up the pixel shader and communicate data to it.

```
class GameCode4_Hlsl_PixelShader
{
public:
  GameCode4_Hlsl_PixelShader(std::string textureResource);
  ~GameCode4_Hlsl_PixelShader();

  HRESULT OnRestore(Scene *pScene);
  HRESULT SetupRender(Scene *pScene, const SceneNode *pNode);
  HRESULT SetTexture(std::string textureName);
  HRESULT SetTexture(ID3D11ShaderResourceView* const *pDiffuseRV,
                     ID3D11SamplerState * const *ppSamplers);
  void EnableLights(bool enableLights) { m_enableLights = enableLights; }
```

```
protected:
  ID3D11PixelShader*  m_pPixelShader;
  ID3D11Buffer*       m_pcbPSMaterial;
  std::string         m_textureResource;
};
```

The class definition is somewhat similar to the one you saw for the vertex shader, just simpler. The differences include an additional `ID3D11Buffer *` member, since this shader accepts two constant buffers: one for the material definition and the other for lighting. It also defines the string used to grab the texture from the resource cache and a Boolean that controls whether the lights are active. The constructor and destructor are fairly trivial and similar to the vertex shader class:

```
GameCode4_Hlsl_PixelShader::GameCode4_Hlsl_PixelShader(
  std::string textureResource)
{
  m_textureResource = textureResource;
  m_pPixelShader = NULL;
  m_pcbPSMaterial = NULL;
}

GameCode4_Hlsl_PixelShader::~GameCode4_Hlsl_PixelShader()
{
  SAFE_RELEASE(m_pPixelShader);
  SAFE_RELEASE(m_pcbPSMaterial);
}
```

As before, the shader is set up and is very similar to the vertex shader, with the one difference that there are two constant buffers to create:

```
HRESULT GameCode4_Hlsl_PixelShader::OnRestore(Scene *pScene)
{
   HRESULT hr;
   SAFE_RELEASE(m_pPixelShader);
   SAFE_RELEASE(m_pcbPSMaterial);

  //===============================================================
  // Set up the pixel shader and related constant buffers
  ID3DBlob* pPixelShaderBuffer = NULL;

  std::string hlslFileName = "Effects\\GameCode4_PS.hlsl";
  Resource resource(hlslFileName.c_str());
  shared_ptr<ResHandle> pResourceHandle =

    g_pApp->m_ResCache->GetHandle(&resource);
  if ( FAILED (CompileShader(pResourceHandle->Buffer(),
```

```
                pResourceHandle->Size(),
                hlslFileName.c_str(), "GameCode4_PSMain",
                "ps_4_0_level_9_1", &pPixelShaderBuffer ) ) )
  {
    SAFE_RELEASE (pPixelShaderBuffer);
    return hr;
  }

  if ( SUCCEEDED ( DXUTGetD3D11Device()->CreatePixelShader(
    pPixelShaderBuffer->GetBufferPointer(),
    pPixelShaderBuffer->GetBufferSize(), NULL, &m_pPixelShader ) ) )
  {
    // Setup constant buffer
    D3D11_BUFFER_DESC Desc;
    Desc.Usage = D3D11_USAGE_DYNAMIC;
    Desc.BindFlags = D3D11_BIND_CONSTANT_BUFFER;
    Desc.CPUAccessFlags = D3D11_CPU_ACCESS_WRITE;
    Desc.MiscFlags = 0;
    Desc.ByteWidth = sizeof( ConstantBuffer_Material );
    hr = DXUTGetD3D11Device()->
      CreateBuffer( &Desc, NULL, &m_pcbPSMaterial );
  }
  SAFE_RELEASE( pPixelShaderBuffer );
  return hr;
}
```

This is very similar to the vertex shader, except that the shader model string is set to `ps_4_0_level_9_1`. This lets the shader compiler know it is compiling to pixel shader model 4.0, compatible with Direct3D 9.1. And of course, instead of calling `CreateVertexShader()`, `CreatePixelShader()` is called. The code for setting up the constant buffer for the object's material is exactly the same as you saw in the vertex shader.

Just before rendering, the following method is called to set up the data for the pixel shader—very similar to the vertex shader's helper, only simpler since there is only one constant buffer to set up:

```
HRESULT GameCode4_Hlsl_PixelShader::SetupRender(Scene *pScene, const SceneNode
*pNode)
{
  HRESULT hr;
  DXUTGetD3D11DeviceContext()->PSSetShader( m_pPixelShader, NULL, 0 );

  D3D11_MAPPED_SUBRESOURCE MappedResource;
  V( DXUTGetD3D11DeviceContext()->Map(
```

```
    m_pcbPSMaterial, 0, D3D11_MAP_WRITE_DISCARD, 0, &MappedResource ) );
  ConstantBuffer_Material* pPSMaterial =
    ( ConstantBuffer_Material* )MappedResource.pData;

  Color color = pNode->VGet()->GetMaterial().GetDiffuse();
  pPSMaterial->m_vDiffuseObjectColor = Vec4(color.r, color.g,
                                             color.b, color.a);

  if (m_textureResource.length() > 0)
    pPSMaterial->m_bHasTexture = true;
  else
    pPSMaterial->m_bHasTexture = false;

  DXUTGetD3D11DeviceContext()->Unmap( m_pcbPSMaterial, 0 );
  DXUTGetD3D11DeviceContext()->PSSetConstantBuffers(
     0, 1, &m_pcbPSMaterial );
  // Set up the texture
  SetTexture(m_textureResource);
  return S_OK;
}
```

The last methods are utility methods for setting the texture, either from a texture name that must be loaded from the resource cache, or a texture that is already loaded:

```
HRESULT GameCode4_Hlsl_PixelShader::SetTexture(std::string textureName)
{
  m_textureResource = textureName;
  if (m_textureResource.length() > 0 )
  {
    Resource resource(m_textureResource);
    shared_ptr<ResHandle> texture = g_pApp->m_ResCache->GetHandle(&resource);
    if (texture)
    {
      shared_ptr<D3DTextureResourceExtraData11> extra =
static_pointer_cast<D3DTextureResourceExtraData11>(texture->GetExtra());
      SetTexture(extra->GetTexture(), extra->GetSampler());
    }
  }
  return S_OK;
}

HRESULT GameCode4_Hlsl_PixelShader::SetTexture(
  ID3D11ShaderResourceView* const *pDiffuseRV,
  ID3D11SamplerState * const *ppSamplers)
{
```

```
    DXUTGetD3D11DeviceContext()->PSSetShaderResources( 0, 1, pDiffuseRV );
    DXUTGetD3D11DeviceContext()->PSSetSamplers( 0, 1, ppSamplers );
    return S_OK;
}
```

The first method uses the resource cache and the texture loader to grab the raw bits of the texture and create a D3DTextureResourceExtraData11 object, as you saw in the texture section in this chapter. That class defines both the ID3DShaderResourceView and the ID3D11SamplerState the pixel shader will use to sample the texture and set the right color for any textured pixel it draws.

## Rendering with the Shader Helper Classes

So far all you've done is set up everything, but nothing in the code you've seen in this or the previous chapter has rendered a single pixel yet. There's one bit of code you need to actually engage both shaders and make pretty things appear on your screen.

From the last chapter, you learned how to define a vertex buffer and an index buffer that holds your geometry. You'll use those now. You'll also use an instantiated GameCode4_Hlsl_VertexShader object and a GameCode4_Hlsl_PixelShader object—each of which has already had the OnRestore() method called to initialize it. With those four objects, you render to the screen with this code:

```
m_VertexShader.SetupRender(pScene, pNode);
m_PixelShader.SetupRender(pScene, pNode);

// Set vertex buffer
UINT stride = sizeof( D3D11Vertex_UnlitTextured );
UINT offset = 0;
DXUTGetD3D11DeviceContext()->
    IASetVertexBuffers( 0, 1, &m_pVertexBuffer, &stride, &offset );

// Set index buffer
DXUTGetD3D11DeviceContext()->
    IASetIndexBuffer( m_pIndexBuffer, DXGI_FORMAT_R16_UINT, 0 );

// Set primitive topology
DXUTGetD3D11DeviceContext()->
    IASetPrimitiveTopology( D3D11_PRIMITIVE_TOPOLOGY_TRIANGLELIST );

DXUTGetD3D11DeviceContext()->DrawIndexed( m_numPolys * 3, 0, 0 );
```

Here's the cast of characters:

- m_VertexShader is an instantiation of the GameCode4_Hlsl_VertexShader class.

- `m_PixelShader` is an instantiation of the `GameCode4_Hlsl_VertexShader` class.
- `m_pVertexBuffer` and `m_pIndexBuffer` are `ID3D11Buffer` objects initialized as you saw in the last chapter.
- `pScene` and `pNode` are cameos from the next chapter, and they describe the scene your game is drawing and the particular object being rendered by the shader.

The vertex and index buffer are set, and then the primitive topology is set. The topology in this example is a triangle list, but many others are also supported. The topology defines how the indexes refer into your vertex buffer, and if you are clever, you can use this to optimize the size of your index buffer or draw different primitives like lines instead of triangles. Definitely look further into books written specifically for Direct3D 11 or into the samples to learn more.

## Shaders—It's Just the Beginning

You've seen enough to be really dangerous in Direct3D 11 and perhaps even be dangerous in any other renderer you choose, such as OpenGL. The concepts I presented are the same. The only things different are the function calls, the coordinate systems, the texturing support, how they expect your geometry, and so on. This chapter's goal was pretty aggressive, but even so I've only scratched the surface.

I suggest that you go play around a bit in Direct3D 11's sample projects and get your bearings. With what you learned, you'll probably be more at ease with them, and maybe you won't get as lost as I did when I first learned Direct3D 11. Even while writing this book, I spent plenty of hours cursing at `E_INVALIDARG` errors and black screens. With any luck, you've got just enough knowledge in your head to perform some of your own twisting and cursing, but hopefully a little less that I did.

## Further Reading

- *Programming Vertex and Pixel Shaders,* Wolfgang Engel
- *Practical Rendering and Computation with Direct3D 11,* Jason Zink, Matt Pettineo, Jack Hoxley

# Chapter 16

*by Mike McShaffry*

# 3D Scenes

In the previous pages, you learned something about how to draw 3D geometry, but there's much more to a 3D game than drawing a few triangles. Even a relatively boring 3D game has characters, interesting environments, dynamic objects, and a few special effects here and there. Your first attempt at a 3D engine might be to just draw everything. You might think that your blazing-fast Nvidia video card can handle anything you throw at it, but you'd be wrong. It turns out to be pretty tricky to get 3D scenes to look right and draw quickly.

This chapter exposes you to one solution for architecting a 3D engine—something that can organize all the visible components of your game world and hopefully draw them fast. Commercial 3D engines are highly optimized and pretty complicated, but there are basic architectural ideas that ring true. With any luck, you'll end this chapter with a healthy respect for the programmers who build 3D engines and have a little knowledge you can use to play with your very own.

## Scene Graph Basics

A *scene graph* is a dynamic data structure, similar to a multiway tree. Each node represents an object in a 3D world or perhaps an instruction to the renderer. Every node can have zero or more children nodes. The scene graph is traversed every frame to draw the visible world. Many commercial renderers use a scene graph as their basic data structure. Before you get too excited, what you are about to see is a basic introduction to the concepts and code behind a scene graph—think of this as a scene graph with training wheels.

## ISceneNode Interface Class

The base class for all nodes in the scene graph is the interface class ISceneNode. Everything else inherits from that class and extends the class to create every part of your 3D world, including the simple geometry, meshes, a camera, and so on. Here's the ISceneNode class:

```
class ISceneNode
{
public:
  virtual const SceneNodeProperties * const VGet() const=0;

  virtual void VSetTransform(const Mat4x4 *toWorld,
                             const Mat4x4 *fromWorld=NULL)=0;

  virtual HRESULT VOnUpdate(Scene *pScene, DWORD const elapsedMs)=0;
  virtual HRESULT VOnRestore(Scene *pScene)=0;

  virtual HRESULT VPreRender(Scene *pScene)=0;
  virtual bool VIsVisible(Scene *pScene) const=0;
  virtual HRESULT VRender(Scene *pScene)=0;
  virtual HRESULT VRenderChildren(Scene *pScene)=0;
  virtual HRESULT VPostRender(Scene *pScene)=0;

  virtual bool VAddChild(shared_ptr<ISceneNode> kid)=0;
  virtual bool VRemoveChild(ActorId id)=0;

  virtual HRESULT VOnLostDevice(Scene *pScene)=0;

  virtual ~ISceneNode() { };
};
```

Each node has certain properties that affect how the node will draw, such as its material, its geometric extents, what game actor it represents, and so on. We'll cover the details of the SceneNodeProperties structure in the next section.

As you learned previously, every object in a 3D universe needs a transform matrix. The matrix encodes the orientation and position of the object in the environment. In a scene graph, this idea is extended to a hierarchy of objects. For example, imagine a boat with people on it, and those people have guns in their hands. When the boat moves, all the people on the boat move with it. Their position and orientation stay the same relative to the boat. When the people aim their weapons, the bones of their arms move and the guns move with them.

This effect is done by concatenating matrices. Every node in the hierarchy has a matrix that describes position and orientation relative to its parent node. As the scene graph is traversed, the matrices are multiplied to form a single matrix that perfectly describes the position and orientation of the node in the 3D world—even if it is a gun attached to a hand attached to a forearm attached to a shoulder attached to a guy standing on a boat.

Take notice that the `VSetTransform()` method takes two `Mat4x4` objects, not just one. It turns out to be really convenient to store two matrices for each scene node—the first one we just discussed about transforming object space to the space of its parent (usually world space if there's no complicated hierarchy involved). This is the `toWorld` parameter in the `SetTransform()` and `GetTransform()` APIs. The second one does the opposite: It transforms 3D world back into object space. This is great if you want to know where a bullet strikes an object. The bullet's trajectory is usually in world space, and the `fromWorld` transform matrix will tell you where that trajectory is in object space.

This can be a little confusing, so if your brain is swimming a bit, don't worry. Mine did too when I first read it. You can imagine this by thinking about your hand as a self-contained hierarchical object. The root would be your palm, and attached to it are five children—the first segment of each of your five fingers. Each of those finger segments has one child, the segment without a fingernail. Finally, the segment with the fingernail attaches, making the palm its great-grandfather. If the transform matrix for one of those finger segments is rotated around the right axis, the finger should bend, carrying all the child segments with it. If I change the translation or rotation of the palm (the root object), everything moves. That is the basic notion of a hierarchical animation system.

**That's Gotta Hurt!**

It's common for artists to create human figures with the hips, or should I say, groin, as the root node. It's convenient because it is close to the center of the human body and has three children: the torso and two legs. One fine day the *Ultima VIII* team went to the park for lunch and played a little Ultimate Frisbee. As happens frequently in that game, two players went to catch the Frisbee at the same time and collided, injuring one of the players. He was curled up on the ground writhing in pain, and when I asked what happened I was told that he took a blow to the root of his hierarchy.

The call to `VSetTransform()` will calculate the inverse transform matrix for you if you don't send it in. Yes, it's somewhat expensive. If you've ever seen the formula for calculating the determinant of a 4 × 4 matrix, you know what I'm talking about. If you've never seen it, just imagine an entire case of alphabet soup laid out on a recursive grid. It's gross.

The two methods, `VOnRestore()` and `VOnUpdate()`, simply traverse their children nodes and recursively call the same methods. When you inherit from `SceneNode` and create a new object, don't forget to call the base class's `VOnRestore()` or `VOnUpdate()` if you happen to overload them. If you fail to do this, your children nodes won't get these calls. The `VOnRestore()` method is meant to re-create any programmatically created data after it has been lost. This is a similar concept to the section on lost 2D DirectDraw surfaces.

The `VOnUpdate()` method is meant to handle animations or anything else that is meant to be decoupled from the rendering traversal. That's why it is called with the elapsed time, measured in milliseconds. You can use the elapsed time to make sure animations or other movements happen at a consistent speed, regardless of computer processing power. A faster CPU should always create a smoother animation, not necessarily a faster one!

The `VPreRender()` method is meant to perform any task that must occur before the render, such as setting render states. The `VIsVisible()` method performs a visibility test. The `VRender()` method does exactly what it advertises: it renders the object. A recursive call to `VRenderChildren()` is made to traverse the scene graph, performing all these actions for every node. The `VPostRender()` method is meant to perform a postrendering action, such as restoring a render state to its original value.

The `VAddChild()` method adds a child node. You'll see different implementations of this interface class add children in different ways. No, you shouldn't attach a node to itself; you'll run out of stack space in your infinitely recursive scene graph before you know what happened.

## SceneNodeProperties and RenderPass

When I first designed the `ISceneNode` class and the implementation class you'll see in a few pages, `SceneNode`, the first attempt, loaded the class full of virtual accessor methods: `VGetThis()`, `VGetThat()`, and `VGetTheOtherDamnThing()`. What I really wanted was a structure of these properties and a single virtual accessor that would give me read-only access to the data in that structure. The structure, `SceneNodeProperties`, is defined as follows:

```
typedef unsigned int ActorId;

class SceneNodeProperties
```

```
{
  friend class SceneNode;

protected:
  ActorId          m_ActorId;
  std::string      m_Name;
  Mat4x4           m_ToWorld, m_FromWorld;
  float            m_Radius;
  RenderPass       m_RenderPass;
  Material         m_Material;
  AlphaType        m_AlphaType;

  void SetAlpha(const float alpha)
    { m_AlphaType=AlphaMaterial; m_Material.SetAlpha(alpha); }

public:
  const ActorId &ActorId() const { return m_ActorId; }
  Mat4x4 const &ToWorld() const { return m_ToWorld; }
  Mat4x4 const &FromWorld() const { return m_FromWorld; }
  void Transform(Mat4x4 *toWorld, Mat4x4 *fromWorld) const;

  const char * Name() const { return m_Name.c_str(); }

  bool HasAlpha() const { return m_Material.HasAlpha(); }
  virtual float Alpha() const { return m_Material.GetAlpha(); }

  RenderPass RenderPass() const { return m_RenderPass; }
  float Radius() const { return m_Radius; }

  Material const &GetMaterial() const { return m_Material; }
};

void SceneNodeProperties::Transform(Mat4x4 *toWorld, Mat4x4 *fromWorld) const
{
  if (toWorld)
    *toWorld = m_ToWorld;

  if (fromWorld)
    *fromWorld = m_FromWorld;
}
```

All of the accessors to this class are `const`, which gives the read-only access I wanted. The implementation of `SceneNode` will perform all of the modifying, which is important since modifying some of these values can have repercussions throughout the scene graph.

The first two data members, `m_ActorId` and `m_Name`, help to relate the scene node to an object in your game logic and identify the scene node or the scene node type. Just as you learned in Chapter 6, "Game Actors and Component Architecture," game engines typically assign unique identifiers to objects in the game.

The `Mat4x4` data members, `m_ToWorld` and `m_FromWorld`, define the transform matrices. `Transform()` copies the member variables into memory you pass in. Generally, you don't want to just allow direct access to the transform matrices because changing them directly might break something. Various inherited classes of `SceneNode` or `ISceneNode` might filter or otherwise set the transforms themselves.

The next data member, `m_Radius`, defines the radius of a sphere that includes the visible geometry of a scene node. Spheres are really efficient for various tests, such as visibility tests or ray-intersection tests. The only problem with spheres is that they don't closely match most geometry, so you can't use them alone. Some commercial games actually do this, though, and you can tell when you play. An easy way to tell is if gunshots seem to hit, even though you aimed too far to the left or right. Better games will use the sphere as a first pass test, since it is so fast, and go to other more expensive tests if needed.

**Instead of Bounding Spheres, Use Axis-Aligned Bounding Boxes**

A great optimization to this simple idea would be to replace the sphere with something called an *axis-aligned bounding box*, or AABB. This is a shape that is a rectangular solid, but its faces are always aligned parallel to the X-, Y-, and Z-axes. As objects move and rotate, the dimensions of the AABB change to make sure the visible geometry is always inside the smallest possible AABB. They aren't hard to code, but they do take a little more work than a simple sphere. I'll leave that to you as an exercise.

When a scene graph is traversed, like most tree-like data structures, it is traversed in a particular order. This order, when combined with various render state settings, creates different effects or enables an efficient rendering of the entire scene. Every node of your scene graph belongs to one of a few different possible render passes—one for static objects, one for dynamic objects, one for the sky, and perhaps others.

The reason you want to do this is mainly for efficiency. The goal is to minimize redrawing pixels on the screen each frame. It makes sense to draw your scenery, objects, and sky in whatever order approaches this goal, hoping to draw things mostly from front to back to get all your closest objects drawn first. With any luck, by the time you get to your sky, you won't have to render hardly any pixels from it at all. After everything, you run through your transparent objects from back to front to make sure they look right. The `m_RenderPass` data member keeps track of which render pass your scene node belongs to and should hold one value from the following enumeration:

```
enum RenderPass
{
  RenderPass_0,                        // A constant to define the starting pass
  RenderPass_Static = RenderPass_0,    // environments and level geometry
  RenderPass_Actor,                    // objects and things that can move
  RenderPass_Sky,                      // the background 'behind' everything
  RenderPass_NotRendered,              // objects that don't render but exist
  RenderPass_Last                      // not used - a counter for for loops
};
```

Notice the member `RenderPass_NotRendered`? You might wonder why that is in there at all, but there is a reason. Some objects in your scene graph need to be there so they can be included in the scene, but they aren't actually processed in any specific render pass. A good example of these kinds of objects might be those that only show up in your game editor, like trigger areas or spawn points.

## SceneNode—It All Starts Here

That's it for the basics. You've seen the design for the `ISceneNode` interface and what each scene node is supposed to implement. You've also seen `SceneNodeProperties` and how it stores data that affects how the scene node draws. You've also seen how the `RenderPass` setting groups renderable objects into broad categories of renderability and render order.

Here's the base implementation of `SceneNode` that inherits from the `ISceneNode` interface class:

```
typedef std::vector<shared_ptr<ISceneNode> > SceneNodeList;

class SceneNode : public ISceneNode
{
  friend class Scene;

protected:
  SceneNodeList          m_Children;
  SceneNode             *m_pParent;
  SceneNodeProperties    m_Props;

public:
  SceneNode(ActorId actorId,
        std::string name,
        RenderPass renderPass,
```

```
        const Color &diffuseColor,
        const Mat4x4 *to,
        const Mat4x4 *from=NULL)
  {
    m_pParent= NULL;
    m_Props.m_ActorId = actorId;
    m_Props.m_Name = name;
    m_Props.m_RenderPass = renderPass;
    m_Props.m_AlphaType = AlphaOpaque;
    VSetTransform(to, from);
    SetRadius(0);
    m_Props.m_Material.SetDiffuse(diffuseColor);
  }

  virtual ~SceneNode();
  virtual const SceneNodeProperties * const VGet() const { return &m_Props; }
  virtual void VSetTransform(
    const Mat4x4 *toWorld, const Mat4x4 *fromWorld=NULL);

  virtual HRESULT VOnRestore(Scene *pScene);
  virtual HRESULT VOnUpdate(Scene *, DWORD const elapsedMs);
  virtual HRESULT VPreRender(Scene *pScene);
  virtual bool VIsVisible(Scene *pScene) const;
  virtual HRESULT VRender(Scene *pScene) { return S_OK; }
  virtual HRESULT VRenderChildren(Scene *pScene);
  virtual HRESULT VPostRender(Scene *pScene);

  virtual bool VAddChild(shared_ptr<ISceneNode> kid);
  virtual bool VRemoveChild(ActorId id);

  void SetAlpha(float alpha) { m_Props.SetAlpha(alpha); }
  float GetAlpha() const { return m_Props.Alpha(); }

  Vec3 GetPosition() const { return m_Props.m_ToWorld.GetPosition(); }
  void SetPosition(const Vec3 &pos) { m_Props.m_ToWorld.SetPosition(pos); }

  Vec3 GetDirection(const Vec3 &pos) const
    { return m_Props.m_ToWorld.GetDirection (pos); }

  void SetRadius(const float radius) { m_Props.m_Radius = radius; }
  void SetMaterial(const Material &mat) { m_Props.m_Material = mat; }
};
```

Every scene node has an STL `vector<>` of scene nodes attached to it. These child nodes, child nodes of child nodes, and so on create the scene graph hierarchy. Most of the scene graph will be pretty flat, but some objects, such as articulated vehicles and characters, have a deep hierarchy of connected parts.

You might wonder why I chose an STL `vector<>` instead of a `list<>`. It's an easy choice because all scene nodes tend to keep a similar number of children. Even if the number of children changes, say when a car loses a wheel in a crash, it's easy enough to make the node invisible. Lists are much better for structures that need fast insertion and deletion, and vectors are fastest for iteration and random access, which makes them a better candidate to store child nodes. There's nothing stopping you, of course, from creating a special scene node that uses STL `list<>` to store its children.

Here's how the `SceneNode` class implements the `VSetTransform` method:

```
void SceneNode::VSetTransform(const Mat4x4 *toWorld, const Mat4x4 *fromWorld)
{
  m_Props.m_ToWorld = *toWorld;
  if (!fromWorld)
    m_Props.m_FromWorld = m_Props.m_ToWorld.Inverse();
  else
    m_Props.m_FromWorld = *fromWorld;
}
```

If the calling routine already has the `fromWorld` transform, it doesn't have to be calculated with a call to the expensive `D3DXMatrixInverse` function. The `fromWorld` transformation is extremely useful for things like *picking*, which is finding the exact intersection of a ray with a polygon on a scene node. You might decide that some objects in your scene don't need this, but in this "training wheels" scene graph, it is convenient for every node to have it.

This kind of picking is similar to the ray cast provided by most physics systems, but this one is for visible geometry, not physical geometry. Most games actually consolidate the calls to both, giving the caller the opportunity to grab the right target based on what it looks like or how it is physically represented in the game world. These are usually very different, since the visible geometry is often finely detailed, and the physical geometry is a simplified version of that.

The `VOnRestore()` and `VOnUpdate()` implementations iterate through `m_Children` and call the same method; child classes will usually do something useful, such as create geometry, load textures, or handle animations and call these methods of `SceneNode` to make sure the entire scene graph is handled:

```
HRESULT SceneNode::VOnRestore(Scene *pScene)
{
```

```
  SceneNodeList::iterator i = m_Children.begin();
  SceneNodeList::iterator end = m_Children.end();
  while (i != end)
  {
    (*i)->VOnRestore(pScene);
    ++i;
  }
  return S_OK;
}

HRESULT SceneNode::VOnUpdate(Scene *pScene, DWORD const elapsedMs)
{
  SceneNodeList::iterator i = m_Children.begin();
  SceneNodeList::iterator end = m_Children.end();
  while (i != end)
  {
    (*i)->VOnUpdate(pScene, elapsedMs);
    ++i;
  }
  return S_OK;
}
```

The next two methods, `VPreRender()` and `VPostRender()`, call some of the scene graph's matrix management methods. They deal with setting the world transform matrix before the render and then restoring it to its original value afterward. You'll see how this is done in detail when I talk about the `Scene` class in the next section.

```
HRESULT SceneNode::VPreRender(Scene *pScene)
{
  pScene->PushAndSetMatrix(m_Props.m_ToWorld);
  return S_OK;
}

HRESULT SceneNode::VPostRender(Scene *pScene)
{
  pScene->PopMatrix();
  return S_OK;
}
```

`VIsVisible()` is responsible for visibility culling. In real commercial games, this is usually a very complicated and involved process, much more than you'll see here. You have to start somewhere, though, and you can find a staggering amount of material on the Internet that will teach you how to test for object visibility in a 3D rendered scene. What's really important is that you know that you can't ignore it, no matter how simple your engine is. Here is `VIsVisible()`:

```
bool SceneNode::VIsVisible(Scene *pScene) const
{
  // transform the location of this node into the camera space
  // of the camera attached to the scene

  Mat4x4 toWorld, fromWorld;
  pScene->GetCamera()->VGet()->Transform(&toWorld, &fromWorld);
  Vec3 pos = VGet()->ToWorld().GetPosition();

  pos = fromWorld.Xform(pos);

  Frustum const &frustum = pScene->GetCamera()->GetFrustum();
  return frustum.Inside(pos, VGet()->Radius());
}
```

If you recall the `Frustum` class, you'll realize that this object was in camera space, with the camera at the origin and looking down the positive Z-axis. This means we can't just send the object location into the `Frustum::Inside()` routine; we have to transform it into camera space first. The first lines of code in `VIsVisible()` do exactly that. The location of the scene node is transformed into camera space and sent into the frustum for testing. If the object passes the visibility test, it can be rendered.

Any class that inherits from `SceneNode` will overload `VRender()` and do something useful like communicate with a shader. I'll get to that when I talk about different child classes of `SceneNode`, such as `CameraNode` or `SkyNode`.

`VRenderChildren()` is responsible for iterating the other scene nodes stored in `m_Children` and calling the main rendering methods:

```
HRESULT SceneNode::VRenderChildren(Scene *pScene)
{
  // Iterate through the children....
  SceneNodeList::iterator i = m_Children.begin();
  SceneNodeList::iterator end = m_Children.end();
  while (i != end)
  {
    if ((*i)->VPreRender(pScene)==S_OK)
    {
      // You could short-circuit rendering
      // if an object returns E_FAIL from
      // VPreRender()

      // Don't render this node if you can't see it
      if ((*i)->VIsVisible(pScene))
      {
```

```
            float alpha = (*i)->VGet()->m_Material.GetAlpha();
            if (alpha==fOPAQUE)
            {
              (*i)->VRender(pScene);
            }
            else if (alpha!=fTRANSPARENT)
            {
              // The object isn't totally transparent...
              AlphaSceneNode *asn = GCC_NEW AlphaSceneNode;
              assert(asn);
              asn->m_pNode = *i;
              asn->m_Concat = *pScene->GetTopMatrix();

              Vec4 worldPos(asn->m_Concat.GetPosition());
              Mat4x4 fromWorld = pScene->GetCamera()->VGet()->FromWorld();
              Vec4 screenPos = fromWorld.Xform(worldPos);
              asn->m_ScreenZ = screenPos.z;

              pScene->AddAlphaSceneNode(asn);
            }
          }

          (*i)->VRenderChildren(pScene);
        }
        (*i)->VPostRender(pScene);
        ++i;
      }

      return S_OK;
    }
```

Every child scene node in the m_Children vector gets the same processing. First, VPreRender() is called, which at a minimum pushes the local transform matrix onto the matrix stack. Since code called in VPreRender() might alter an object's visibility, it is called before the visibility check, which is made with VIsVisible(). If this method returns false, the scene node isn't visible and doesn't need to be drawn. If it is visible, the scene node is checked if it is in any way transparent, because the renderer draws them after everything else. If the scene node is 100 percent opaque, VRender() is called to draw the object. Then, regardless of opacity, VRenderChildren() is called to render child nodes, followed by VPostRender().

Transparent objects need to draw after everything else in a special render pass. If they drew in the regular order, they wouldn't look right, since some of the background objects might actually draw after the transparent objects. What needs to happen is this: All transparent objects get stuck in a special list, and after the scene graph has been completely traversed, the scene nodes in the alpha list get drawn. But wait, there's more. You can't just stick a pointer to the scene node in a list. You have to remember a few more things, like the value of the top of the matrix stack. When the list gets traversed, it won't have the benefit of the entire scene graph and all the calls to `VPreRender()` and `VPostRender()` to keep track of it. To make things easy, there's a little structure that can help remember this data:

```
struct AlphaSceneNode
{
  shared_ptr<ISceneNode> m_pNode;
  Mat4x4 m_Concat;
  float m_ScreenZ;

  // For the STL sort...
  bool const operator < (AlphaSceneNode const &other)
    { return m_ScreenZ < other.m_ScreenZ; }
};

typedef std::list<AlphaSceneNode *> AlphaSceneNodes;
```

The `m_ScreenZ` member stores the depth of the object in the scene. Larger values are farther away from the camera and are therefore farther away. When you draw transparent objects together, such as a forest of trees with transparent textures on them, you have to draw them from back to front or they won't look right. The list of alpha objects is stored in the `Scene` class, which you'll see in the next section.

You might wonder why the `RenderPass` enumeration doesn't just have a special pass for transparent objects. The reason is that objects can dynamically change from opaque to transparent at runtime, such as when a creature you just killed fades away from sight. If there were some objects that were guaranteed to have translucency, never to change, then a fair optimization to this design could make use of a special render pass for those objects.

There's only `VAddChild()` left, and besides adding a new scene node to the `m_Children` member, it also sets a new radius for the parent. If the child node extends geometry beyond the parent's radius, the parent's radius should be extended to include the children:

```
bool SceneNode::VAddChild(shared_ptr<ISceneNode> kid)
{
  m_Children.push_back(kid);

  // The radius of the sphere should be fixed right here
  Vec3 kidPos = kid->VGet()->ToWorld().GetPosition();
  Vec3 dir = kidPos - m_Props.ToWorld().GetPosition();
```

```
  float newRadius = dir.Length() + kid->VGet()->Radius();
  if (newRadius > m_Props.m_Radius)
    m_Props.m_Radius = newRadius;
  return true;
}
```

Don't forget that SceneNode is just a base class. You'll need to inherit from it to get anything useful to draw on the screen. I'll show you the Scene class, which manages the entire scene graph, and then move on to some interesting types of scene nodes.

## The Scene Class

The top-level management of the entire scene node hierarchy rests in the capable hands of the Scene class. It serves as the top-level entry point for updating, rendering, and adding new SceneNode objects to the scene hierarchy. It also keeps track of which scene nodes are visible components of dynamic actors in your game.

Here is the definition of the Scene, a container for SceneNode objects of all shapes and sizes:

```
typedef std::map<ActorId, shared_ptr<ISceneNode> > SceneActorMap;

class CameraNode;
class SkyNode;
class LightNode;
class LightManager;

class Scene
{
protected:
  shared_ptr<SceneNode>    m_Root;
  shared_ptr<CameraNode>   m_Camera;
  shared_ptr<IRenderer>    m_Renderer;

ID3DXMatrixStack          *m_MatrixStack;
  AlphaSceneNodes          m_AlphaSceneNodes;
  SceneActorMap            m_ActorMap;

  LightManager            *m_LightManager;

  void RenderAlphaPass();

public:

  Scene();
  virtual ~Scene();
```

```
HRESULT OnRender();
HRESULT OnRestore();
HRESULT OnLostDevice();
HRESULT OnUpdate(const int deltaMilliseconds);

shared_ptr<ISceneNode> FindActor(ActorId id);
bool AddChild(ActorId id, shared_ptr<ISceneNode> kid)
{
  if (id.valid())
  {
    // This allows us to search for this later based on actor id
    m_ActorMap[*id] = kid;
  }
  shared_ptr<LightNode> pLight = dynamic_pointer_cast<LightNode>(kid);
  if (pLight != NULL &&
     m_LightManager->m_Lights.size()+1 < MAXIMUM_LIGHTS_SUPPORTED)
  {
    m_LightManager->m_Lights.push_back(pLight);
  }
  return m_Root->VAddChild(kid);
}

bool RemoveChild(ActorId id)
{
  if (id == INVALID_ACTOR_ID)
    return false;

  shared_ptr<ISceneNode> kid = FindActor(id);
  shared_ptr<LightNode> pLight = dynamic_pointer_cast<LightNode>(kid);
  if (pLight != NULL)
    m_LightManager->m_Lights.remove(pLight);

  m_ActorMap.erase(id);
  return m_Root->VRemoveChild(id);
}

// Camera accessor / modifier
void SetCamera(shared_ptr<CameraNode> camera) { m_Camera = camera; }
const shared_ptr<CameraNode> GetCamera() const { return m_Camera; }

void PushAndSetMatrix(const Mat4x4 &toWorld);
void PopMatrix()
const Mat4x4 *GetTopMatrix() ;

LightManager *GetLightManager() { return m_LightManager; }
```

```
    void AddAlphaSceneNode(AlphaSceneNode *asn)
      { m_AlphaSceneNodes.push_back(asn); }
};
```

The Scene class has seven data members:

- m_Root: The root scene node of the entire visible world. It has no parents, and everything that is drawn is attached either as a child or to a descendant scene node.
- m_Camera: The active camera. In this simple scene graph, there is only one camera, but there's nothing that says you can't have a list of these objects.
- m_MatrixStack: A nifty DirectX object that manages a stack of transform matrices, this data structure holds the current world transform matrix as the scene graph is traversed and drawn.
- m_AlphaSceneNodes: A list of structures that holds the information necessary to draw transparent scene nodes in a final render pass.
- m_ActorMap: An STL map that lets the scene graph find a scene node matched to a particular ActorId.
- m_LightManager: A helper class to manage multiple directional lights in the scene.

The root node, m_Root, is the top-level scene node in the entire scene graph. There is some special code associated with the root node, which I'll show you shortly. For now, you can consider the root node as the same kind of object that all tree-like data structures have.

The camera node is a little special. It could be attached anywhere in the scene graph, especially if it is a first- or third-person camera that targets a particular object. All the same, the scene graph needs quick access to the camera node, because just before rendering the scene, the scene graph uses the camera location and orientation to set the view transform you learned about in Chapter 14, "3D Graphics Basics." I'll show you how that is done when I talk about the CameraNode class, in "A Simple Camera" later on in this chapter.

The interesting bit that you might not have seen before is a Direct3D matrix stack. You've already seen that matrix concatenation is a common task in 3D graphics. Any number of matrices could be multiplied, or concatenated, to create any bizarre and twisted set of rotation and translation operations. In the case of a hierarchical model like a human figure, these matrix concatenations can get tedious unless you can push them onto and pop them from a stack. The ID3DXMatrixStack helps us do exactly that as the scene graph is being traversed.

The next data member is the actor map. This is an STL map that relates unique actor IDs (really just a plain old unsigned integer) with a particular scene node. This is necessary when the scene graph needs to change a scene node based on an ActorId. A good example of this is when the physics system bounces something around. Since the physics system doesn't know or care anything about a pointer to a scene node, it will inform game subsystems of the bouncing via an event with an ActorId. When the scene graph hears about it, it uses the ActorId to find the right scene node to manipulate.

The final data member is for a light manager to manage a list of lights that illuminate the scene. These lights inherit from SceneNode to add information about how the light illuminates objects. You'll learn about the LightNode class a little later in the "Putting Lights in Your Scene" section of this chapter.

Here's the implementation of the Scene class:

```
Scene::Scene()
{
  m_Root.reset(GCC_NEW RootNode());
  m_LightManager = GCC_NEW LightManager;
  D3DXCreateMatrixStack(0, &m_MatrixStack);
}

Scene::~Scene()
{
  SAFE_RELEASE(m_MatrixStack);
  SAFE_DELETE(m_LightManager);
}
```

The constructor and destructor are simple enough. They simply manage the creation and release of the root node, the DirectX matrix stack object, and the LightManager. The other data structures have default constructors and are managed by smart pointers, so there is a little more happening here behind the scene. Yes, that was a terrible pun, but I'm not sorry.

Let's now look at OnRender(), OnRestore(), and OnUpdate():

```
HRESULT Scene::OnRender()
{
  if (m_Root && m_Camera)
  {
    // The scene root could be anything, but it
```

```
    // is usually a SceneNode with the identity
    // matrix

    m_Camera->SetViewTransform(this);
    m_LightManager->CalcLighting(this);

    if (m_Root->VPreRender(this)==S_OK)
    {
      m_Root->VRender(this);
      m_Root->VRenderChildren(this);
      m_Root->VPostRender(this);
    }
  }

  RenderAlphaPass();

  return S_OK;
}

HRESULT Scene::OnRestore()
{
  if (!m_Root)
    return S_OK;

  return m_Root->VOnRestore(this);
}

HRESULT Scene::OnUpdate(const int deltaMilliseconds)
{
  if (!m_Root)
    return S_OK;

  static DWORD lastTime = timeGetTime();
  DWORD elapsedTime = 0;
  DWORD now = timeGetTime();

  elapsedTime = now - lastTime;
  lastTime = now;

  return m_Root->VOnUpdate(this, elapsedTime);
}
```

These methods clearly use the root node for all the heavy lifting. (I'll bet you thought there was going to be a little more meat to these methods!)

You'll notice that `OnRender()` must first check for the existence of a root node and a camera. Without either of these, there's not much more that can be done. If everything checks out fine, the camera's SetViewTransform() method is called to send the camera position and orientation into the rendering device. The LightManager::CalcLighting() method runs through the list of lights and calculates data that will be sent to shaders during this frame. Then the rendering methods of the root node are called, which in turn propagate throughout the entire scene graph. Finally, the scene graph calls the RenderAlphaPass() method to handle any scene nodes that were found to have some translucency during this render.

The OnRestore() method is so trivial I think I can trust you to figure it out. There is one trick, though. The camera node must clearly be attached to the scene graph as a child of a scene node, in addition to having it as a member of the scene graph. If it isn't, it would never have its critical virtual functions called properly.

Lastly, OnUpdate() is what separates rendering from updating. Updating is generally called as fast as possible, where the render pass might be delayed to keep a particular frame rate. Rendering is usually much more expensive than updating, too. You'll also notice that the update pass is called with a delta time in milliseconds, where the render is called with no parameters. That in itself is telling since there shouldn't be any time-variant code running inside the render pass, such as animations. Keep that stuff inside the update pass, and you'll find your entire graphics system will be flexible enough to run on pokey hardware and still have the chops to blaze on the fast machines.

```
void Scene::PushAndSetMatrix(const Mat4x4 &toWorld)
{
  m_MatrixStack->Push();
  m_MatrixStack->MultMatrixLocal(&toWorld);
  DXUTGetD3DDevice()->SetTransform(D3DTS_WORLD, m_MatrixStack->GetTop());
}

void Scene::PopMatrix()
{
  m_MatrixStack->Pop();
  DXUTGetD3DDevice()->SetTransform(D3DTS_WORLD, m_MatrixStack->GetTop());
}

const Mat4x4 *Scene::GetTopMatrix()
{
  return static_cast<const Mat4x4 *>(m_MatrixStack->GetTop());
}
```

Remember matrix concatenation? I don't think I've gone two paragraphs without mentioning it. There's a useful thing in both Direct3D and OpenGL called a *matrix stack*, and it is used to keep track of matrices in a hierarchy. The call to VPreRender()

pushes a new matrix on the matrix stack and then concatenates it with what was already there, creating a new matrix. Once that is done, the new matrix is used to draw anything sent into the render pipeline.

This is a little confusing, and I won't ask you to visualize it because when I tried I got a pounding headache—but here's the gist of it. The matrix that exists at the top of the stack is either the identity matrix or the result of all the concatenated matrices from the hierarchy in your scene nodes in the scene graph. Before you traverse child nodes, the parent's current matrix is pushed on the stack. Each child concatenates its matrix with the parent on the top of the stack. When all the children are done, the stack is popped, and the parent's matrix is restored.

As you can see, this is quite efficient and extremely flexible for implementing hierarchical objects. The push/pop methods are called by the `SceneNode::VPreRender()` and `SceneNode::VPostRender()`, respectively. The `GetTopMatrix()` method gives you read-only access to the top matrix, which is useful for storing off the world matrix of a scene node during the render pass.

Here's how the `Scene` class implements `FindActor()`:

```
shared_ptr<ISceneNode> Scene::FindActor(ActorId id)
{
  SceneActorMap::iterator i = m_ActorMap.find(id);
  if (i==m_ActorMap.end())
  {
    return shared_ptr<ISceneNode>();
  }

  return (*i).second;
}
```

This is pretty standard STL `<map>` usage, and since we have defined the `ActorId` to be unique, we don't have to worry about finding multiple actors for a particular scene node.

The last method of the `Scene` class is `RenderAlphaPass`. This method is called after the normal rendering is done, so all the transparent scene nodes will draw on top of everything else. Here's basically what happens in this method:

- The current world transform is saved off.
- Z-sorting is disabled.
- Alpha blending is turned on.
- The alpha nodes in the alpha list are sorted.

- Each node in the alpha list is rendered and then removed from the list.
- The old render states are restored to their old values.

```
void Scene::RenderAlphaPass()
{
  D3DRendererAlphaPass11 alphaPass;

  m_AlphaSceneNodes.sort();
  while (!m_AlphaSceneNodes.empty())
  {
    AlphaSceneNodes::reverse_iterator i = m_AlphaSceneNodes.rbegin();
    DXUTGetD3DDevice()->SetTransform(D3DTS_WORLD, &((*i)->m_Concat));
    (*i)->m_pNode->VRender(this);
    delete (*i);
    m_AlphaSceneNodes.pop_back();
  }
}
```

There is a special class, `D3DRendererAlphaPass11`, that manages setting the `ID3D11DeviceContext` for alpha blending. Upon construction the device settings are set, and upon destruction the device is returned to the state it was previously in.

When you want to do an alpha pass in Direct3D 11, or actually any other kind of blending, you define it with the `D3D11_BLEND_DESC` structure, create the blend state by calling `ID3D11Device::CreateBlendState()`, and set the blend state with a call to `ID3D11DeviceContext::OMSetBlendState()`. You can tell just by looking at the blend state structure that blending is a large subject, one that is best covered by a dedicated 3D graphics book. The parameters sent into the blend state used here involve a simple alpha blend, using the source pixel's alpha value.

```
class D3DRendererAlphaPass11
{
protected:
  ID3D11BlendState* m_pOldBlendState;
  FLOAT m_OldBlendFactor[ 4 ];
  UINT m_OldSampleMask;

  ID3D11BlendState* m_pCurrentBlendState;

public:
  D3DRendererAlphaPass11();
  ~D3DRendererAlphaPass11();
};

D3DRendererAlphaPass11::D3DRendererAlphaPass11()
{
```

```
  DXUTGetD3D11DeviceContext()->OMGetBlendState(&m_pOldBlendState,
                              m_OldBlendFactor, &m_OldSampleMask);
  m_pCurrentBlendState = NULL;

  D3D11_BLEND_DESC BlendState;
  ZeroMemory(&BlendState, sizeof(D3D11_BLEND_DESC));

  BlendState.AlphaToCoverageEnable = false;
  BlendState.IndependentBlendEnable = false;
  BlendState.RenderTarget[0].BlendEnable = TRUE;
  BlendState.RenderTarget[0].SrcBlend = D3D11_BLEND_SRC_ALPHA;
  BlendState.RenderTarget[0].DestBlend = D3D11_BLEND_INV_SRC_ALPHA;
  BlendState.RenderTarget[0].BlendOp = D3D11_BLEND_OP_ADD;
  BlendState.RenderTarget[0].SrcBlendAlpha = D3D11_BLEND_ZERO;
  BlendState.RenderTarget[0].DestBlendAlpha = D3D11_BLEND_ZERO;
  BlendState.RenderTarget[0].BlendOpAlpha = D3D11_BLEND_OP_ADD;
  BlendState.RenderTarget[0].RenderTargetWriteMask =
    D3D11_COLOR_WRITE_ENABLE_ALL;

  DXUTGetD3D11Device()->CreateBlendState(&BlendState, &m_pCurrentBlendState);
  DXUTGetD3D11DeviceContext()->OMSetBlendState(m_pCurrentBlendState, 0,
                                               0xffffffff);
}
```

If you set a material color to 75% red, 50% translucency, you set the values of the Color structure to (0.75f, 0.0f, 0.0f, 0.5f). That's 75% red, 0% for blue and green, and 50% for alpha. This value makes its way into the pixel shader where it is blended with lights, as you saw in the previous chapter. If the `ID3D11DeviceContext` has a blending state set, then the pixel just calculated by the pixel shader is blended with the pixel value already on in the display buffer. The types and methods of blending are pretty mind boggling, actually, so when you learn about them, have some patience. When the alpha pass is done, the destructor of the class simple restores the previous blending state:

```
D3DRendererAlphaPass11::~D3DRendererAlphaPass11()
{
  DXUTGetD3D11DeviceContext()->OMSetBlendState(m_pOldBlendState,
                              m_OldBlendFactor, m_OldSampleMask);
  SAFE_RELEASE(m_pCurrentBlendState);
  SAFE_RELEASE(m_pOldBlendState);
}
```

You will see this technique again for setting and restoring device context states for the skybox, which comes a little later.

## Special Scene Graph Nodes

The SceneNode class doesn't draw anything at all. It just performs a lot of Direct3D11 and scene graph homework. We need some classes that inherit from SceneNode to construct an interesting scene. Here are the ones I'll show you:

- class RootNode: Manages children as separate render passes for different kinds of scene nodes.
- class CameraNode: Manages the camera and view frustum culling.
- class LightNode: Creates a directional diffuse light in your scene.
- class SkyNode: Creates a sky that appears to be infinitely far away.
- class D3DShaderMeshNode11: Wraps a Direct3D SDKMESH file.

### Implementing Separate Render Passes

Different render passes help optimize rendering or create interesting full-screen effects. Drawing things in the right order can do wonders for performance. Fill rate performance, or the lack of it, means that the more times you completely overdraw a pixel, the more valuable time you've wasted. Figuring out when you can safely ignore a pixel, or all the pixels in a polygon, or all the polygons in a mesh can get pretty complicated. One obvious way to do this is not to draw any pixels that are completely behind other pixels by using a depth test and generally drawing big foreground stuff first and small background stuff later. Draw the sky last, but draw it before your transparent objects, since it could cover the entire screen. One way to do this is by creating a special scene node that manages all this, and that scene node happens to be the root node of the entire scene graph:

```
class RootNode : public SceneNode
{
public:
  RootNode();
  virtual bool VAddChild(shared_ptr<ISceneNode> kid);
  virtual HRESULT VRenderChildren(Scene *pScene);
  virtual bool VIsVisible(Scene *pScene) const { return true; }
};

RootNode::RootNode()
: SceneNode(optional_empty(), "Root", RenderPass_0, &Mat4x4::g_Identity)
{
  m_Children.reserve(RenderPass_Last);

  shared_ptr<SceneNode> staticGroup(
```

```
    new SceneNode(INVALID_ACTOR_ID,
      "StaticGroup", RenderPass_Static, g_White, &Mat4x4::g_Identity));
  m_Children.push_back(staticGroup);    // RenderPass_Static = 0

  shared_ptr<SceneNode> actorGroup(
    new SceneNode(INVALID_ACTOR_ID,
      "ActorGroup", RenderPass_Actor,   g_White, &Mat4x4::g_Identity));
  m_Children.push_back(actorGroup);     // RenderPass_Actor = 1

  shared_ptr<SceneNode> skyGroup(
    new SceneNode(INVALID_ACTOR_ID,
      "SkyGroup", RenderPass_Sky,       g_White, &Mat4x4::g_Identity));
  m_Children.push_back(skyGroup);       // RenderPass_Sky = 2

  shared_ptr<SceneNode> invisibleGroup(
    GCC_NEW SceneNode(INVALID_ACTOR_ID,
      "InvisibleGroup", RenderPass_NotRendered, g_White,
      &Mat4x4::g_Identity));
  m_Children.push_back(invisibleGroup);    // RenderPass_NotRendered = 3
}
```

The root node has child nodes that are added directly as a part of the constructor—one child for each render pass you define. In the previous case, there are three render passes: one for static actors, one for dynamic actors, and one for the sky. When other scene nodes are added to the scene graph, the root node actually adds them to one of these children, based on the new scene node's `m_RenderPass` member variable:

```
bool RootNode::VAddChild(shared_ptr<ISceneNode> kid)
{
  // Children that divide the scene graph into render passes.
  // Scene nodes will get added to these children based on the value of the
  // render pass member variable.

  RenderPass pass = kid->VGet()->RenderPass();
  if ((unsigned)pass >= m_Children.size() || !m_Children[pass])
  {
    GCC_ASSERT(0 && _T("There is no such render pass"));
    return false;
  }

  return m_Children[pass]->VAddChild(kid);
}
```

This lets the root node have a very fine control over when each pass gets rendered and even what special render states get set for each one:

```
HRESULT RootNode::VRenderChildren(Scene *pScene)
{
  for (int pass = RenderPass_0; pass < RenderPass_Last; ++pass)
  {
    switch(pass)
    {
      case RenderPass_Static:
      case RenderPass_Actor:
        m_Children[pass]->VRenderChildren(pScene);
        break;

      case RenderPass_Sky:
      {
        D3DRendererSkyBoxPass11 skyBoxPass;
        m_Children[pass]->VRenderChildren(pScene);
        break;
      }
    }
  }

  return S_OK;
}
```

For static and dynamic actors, the root node doesn't do anything special other than draw them. The sky node needs a little extra attention since it is something that looks infinitely far away, even though if you were to see it the way it actually existed in the 3D world, it would look like it was a box worn over the viewer's head. That requires a little Direct3D trickery.

The trickery involves changing the normal operation of the depth stencil, which is also called a *Z-buffer*. When pixels are transformed into screen space, the X and Y values map directly to the X and Y coordinates of the display. The Z value is set to something that determines its depth into the scene as compared to the front and rear clipping planes of the view frustum. Any pixel "deeper" in the scene will get covered by one in the same location, but shallower. This gives the viewer the impression that a 3D world really exists, even though it is projected onto a 2D screen, since every pixel of every object sorts just the way it should.

The skybox is actually something that is geometrically small, like a box hovering around the camera. But because it resets the depth stencil, it always looks like it is behind every other object. Here's the helper class that sets the `ID3DDeviceContext` for rendering a skybox:

```
D3DRendererSkyBoxPass11::D3DRendererSkyBoxPass11()
{
  // Depth stencil state
  D3D11_DEPTH_STENCIL_DESC DSDesc;
  ZeroMemory( &DSDesc, sizeof( D3D11_DEPTH_STENCIL_DESC ) );
  DSDesc.DepthEnable = TRUE;
  DSDesc.DepthWriteMask = D3D11_DEPTH_WRITE_MASK_ZERO;
  DSDesc.DepthFunc = D3D11_COMPARISON_LESS;
  DSDesc.StencilEnable = FALSE;
  DXUTGetD3D11Device()->CreateDepthStencilState(&DSDesc,
                                                   &m_pSkyboxDepthStencilState );
  DXUT_SetDebugName( m_pSkyboxDepthStencilState, "SkyboxDepthStencil" );

  UINT StencilRef;
  DXUTGetD3D11DeviceContext()->OMGetDepthStencilState(
    &m_pOldDepthStencilState, &StencilRef );
  DXUTGetD3D11DeviceContext()->OMSetDepthStencilState(
    m_pSkyboxDepthStencilState, 0 );
}

D3DRendererSkyBoxPass11::~D3DRendererSkyBoxPass11()
{
  DXUTGetD3D11DeviceContext()->OMSetDepthStencilState(
    m_pOldDepthStencilState, 0 );
  SAFE_RELEASE(m_pOldDepthStencilState);
  SAFE_RELEASE(m_pSkyboxDepthStencilState);
}
```

The goal for the skybox is to simulate drawing in the far background, without actually being in the far background. This little trick requires changing the depth stencil settings to draw the polygons of the sky without affecting the current Z values of the display buffer. Depth stencil state, just like blending states, has a wide range of cool effects you can create, this being but one very simple one.

## A Simple Camera

You'll need a camera if you want to take pictures, right? The camera in a 3D scene inherits from `SceneNode` just like everything else and adds some data members to keep track of its viewable area, the projection matrix, and perhaps a target scene node that it will follow around:

```
class CameraNode : public SceneNode
{
```

```
public:
  CameraNode(Mat4x4 const *t, Frustum const &frustum)
   : SceneNode(INVALID_ACTOR_ID, "Camera", RenderPass_0, g_Black, t),
     m_Frustum(frustum),
     m_bActive(true),
     m_DebugCamera(false),
     m_pTarget(shared_ptr<SceneNode>()),
     m_CamOffsetVector( 0.0f, 1.0f, -10.0f, 0.0f )
  {
  }

  virtual HRESULT VRender(Scene *pScene);
  virtual HRESULT VOnRestore(Scene *pScene);
  virtual bool VIsVisible(Scene *pScene) const { return m_bActive; }

  virtual HRESULT SetViewTransform(Scene *pScene);

  const Frustum &GetFrustum() { return m_Frustum; }
  void SetTarget(shared_ptr<SceneNode> pTarget)
  {
    m_pTarget = pTarget;
  }
  void ClearTarget() { m_pTarget = shared_ptr<SceneNode>(); }
  shared_ptr<SceneNode> GetTarget() { return m_pTarget; }

  Mat4x4 GetWorldViewProjection(Scene *pScene);
  HRESULT SetViewTransform(Scene *pScene);

  Mat4x4 GetProjection() { return m_Projection; }
  Mat4x4 GetView() { return m_View; }

  void SetCameraOffset( const Vec4 & cameraOffset )
  {
    m_CamOffsetVector = cameraOffset;
  }

protected:
  Frustum      m_Frustum;
  Mat4x4       m_Projection;
  Mat4x4       m_View;
  bool         m_bActive;
  bool         m_DebugCamera;
  shared_ptr<SceneNode> m_pTarget;
  Vec4         m_CamOffsetVector;
};
```

The VRender() method calls the Frustum::Render() method to draw the camera's viewable area, but only if the debug camera is enabled:

```
HRESULT CameraNode::VRender(Scene *pScene)
{
  if (m_DebugCamera)
  {
    m_Frustum.Render();
  }

  return S_OK;
}
```

**Create a Special Camera for Debugging**

When I was working on *Thief: Deadly Shadows*, it was really useful to have a special "debug" camera that moved about the scene without affecting the code that was being checked against the "real" camera. The process worked like this: I would key in a special debug command, and the debug camera would be enabled. I could free-fly it around the scene, and the "normal" camera was visible because the view frustum of the normal camera would draw, and I could visually debug problems like third-person movement issues, scene culling issues, and so on. It was kind of like having a backstage pass to the internals of the game!

The VOnRestore() chain can be called when the player resizes the game screen to a different resolution. If this happens, the camera view frustum shape will probably change, and so will the projection matrix, which is really a Mat4x4 structure that describes the shape of the view frustum in a transform matrix. Notice the D3DXMatrixPerspectiveFovLH call—the LH stands for "left-handed."

```
virtual HRESULT CameraNode::VOnRestore(Scene *pScene)
{
  m_Frustum.SetAspect(DXUTGetWindowWidth() / (FLOAT) DXUTGetWindowHeight());
  D3DXMatrixPerspectiveFovLH( &m_Projection, m_Frustum.m_Fov,
    m_Frustum.m_Aspect, m_Frustum.m_Near, m_Frustum.m_Far );
  return S_OK;
}
```

The camera's SetView() method is called just before rendering the scene. It reads the "from world" transform stored in the scene node and sends that into the rendering device:

```
HRESULT CameraNode::SetView(Scene *pScene)
{
  //If there is a target, make sure the camera is
  //rigidly attached right behind the target
```

```
  if(m_pTarget.valid())
  {
    Mat4x4 mat = (*m_pTarget)->VGet()->ToWorld();
    Vec4 at = m_CamOffsetVector;
    Vec4 atWorld = mat.Xform(at);
    Vec3 pos = mat.GetPosition() + Vec3(atWorld);
    mat.SetPosition(pos);
    VSetTransform(&mat);
  }
  return S_OK;
}
```

The simple example above also implements a bare-bones third-person follow camera—the camera's position and orientation are sucked from the target scene node and moved based on the `m_CamOffsetVector`. This is the classic "pole cam" technique, which actually works fairly well considering it involves only the complexity of a single vector offset. Of course, a real third-person camera would detect environment geometry and have all kinds of interpolators to make sure the camera movement was smooth and pleasing to the player. I'll leave that happy work as an exercise for you, but if you are smart you'll reserve a few months for it! It's much more complicated than you think.

## Putting Lights in Your Scene

Lighting has been described previously, but not in the context of being an object that sits in the scene graph. In the "men on boats" example at the beginning of this chapter, you could imagine that those men carried torches. As the boat slid by objects on the shore, you would expect those torches to affect those objects, making them more visible as the boat approached and fading into darkness as it continued. This task is easily accomplished by making a light part of the scene graph, so that whenever it moves or its parent node moves or reorients, it will affect objects in the way that you would expect.

Since the base class, `SceneNode`, already defines a material color as a part of `SceneNodeProperties`, the `LightNode` class only needs to define lighting specific properties, which are stored in the `LightProperties` structure:

```
struct LightProperties
{
  float m_Attenuation[3];  /* Attenuation coefficients */
  float m_Range;
  float m_Falloff;
  float m_Theta;
```

```
  float m_Phi;
};
```

These parameters can be set and sent into vertex and pixel shaders by the `LightManager` class, which you'll see shortly. Here is the definition of the `LightNode` class:

```
class LightNode : public SceneNode
{
protected:
  LightProperties m_LightProps;

public:
   LightNode(const ActorId actorId, std::string name, const LightProperties &props,
const Color &diffuseColor, const Mat4x4 *t)
         const LightProperties &props, const Color &diffuseColor,
         const Mat4x4 *t)
    : SceneNode(actorId, name, RenderPass_NotRendered, diffuseColor, t)
   {
     m_LightProps = props;
   }
};
```

The heavy lifting of the `LightNode` class is really done by `SceneNode`, since it already contains the material that defines the light's color and the transformations that describe the location and orientation of the light in the 3D world.

Getting lighting information into shaders is done by the `LightManager` class.

```
typedef std::list<shared_ptr<LightNode> > Lights;

class LightManager
{
  friend class Scene;
protected:
  Lights   m_Lights;
  Vec4     m_vLightDir[MAXIMUM_LIGHTS_SUPPORTED];
  Color    m_vLightDiffuse[MAXIMUM_LIGHTS_SUPPORTED];
  Vec4     m_vLightAmbient;
public:
  int GetLightCount(const SceneNode *node) { return m_Lights.size(); }
  const Vec4 *GetLightAmbient(const SceneNode *node)
    { return &m_vLightAmbient; }
  const Vec4 *GetLightDirection(const SceneNode *node) { return m_vLightDir; }
  const Color *GetLightDiffuse(const SceneNode *node)
    { return m_vLightDiffuse; }
```

```
    void CalcLighting(Scene *pScene);
    void CalcLighting(ConstantBuffer_Lighting* pLighting, SceneNode *pNode);
};
```

The `LightManager` exists to pull relevant lighting information out of all the lights in the scene and send just the lighting data affecting an individual object into the shaders. In this simple example, the class assumes that all lights affect all objects. But the architecture supports something more complicated—all that needs to be done is to write code in the `Get` methods to return just the lighting information for the `SceneNode` in question.

In each frame, the `LightManager` iterates over all the lights in the scene and reads their color, position, and orientation information. It can also pull additional information, such as what is contained in the `LightProperties` structure for a more complicated lighting model. The method that accomplishes this task is `CalcLighting()`:

```
void LightManager::CalcLighting(Scene *pScene)
{
  pScene->GetRenderer()->VCalcLighting(&m_Lights, MAXIMUM_LIGHTS_SUPPORTED);

  int count = 0;
  GCC_ASSERT(m_Lights.size() < MAXIMUM_LIGHTS_SUPPORTED);
  for(Lights::iterator i=m_Lights.begin();
     i!=m_Lights.end();
     ++i, ++count)
  {
    shared_ptr<LightNode> light = *i;

    if (count==0)
    {
      // Light 0 is the only one we use for ambient lighting. The rest are
      // ignored in the simple shaders used for GameCode4.
      Color ambient = light->VGet()->GetMaterial().GetAmbient();
      m_vLightAmbient = Vec4(ambient.r, ambient.g, ambient.b, 1.0f);
    }

    Vec3 lightDir = light->GetDirection();
    m_vLightDir[count] = D3DXVECTOR4(lightDir.x, lightDir.y, lightDir.z,
                                     1.0f);
    m_vLightDiffuse[count] = light->VGet()->GetMaterial().GetDiffuse();
  }
}
```

The next method is called to initialize the constant buffer used in the pixel shader introduced in the previous chapter. This method is called from `GameCode4_Hlsl_-PixelShader::SetupRender()` for each `SceneNode`:

```
void LightManager::CalcLighting(ConstantBuffer_Lighting* pLighting,
                                SceneNode *pNode)
{
  int count = GetLightCount(pNode);
  if (count)
  {
    pLighting->m_vLightAmbient = *GetLightAmbient(pNode);
    memcpy(pLighting->m_vLightDir, GetLightDirection(pNode),
        sizeof( Vec4 ) * count );
    memcpy(pLighting->m_vLightDiffuse, GetLightDiffuse(pNode),
        sizeof( Vec4 ) * count);
    pLighting->m_nNumLights = count;
  }
}
```

All this method does is copy precalculated values into a structure that will be sent into the shader. This simple lighting model is vertex based but calculated per pixel because of the code in the pixel shader. Many more interesting models are possible, especially those that operate as a separate render pass after the objects have been drawn. With this basic introduction into how lights can be added into scenes, how they can be managed with a light manager class, and how they communicate with shaders, you can now explore some great lighting experiments.

## Rendering the Sky

The sky in computer games is usually a very simple object, such as a cube or faceted dome. The trick to making the sky look like it is infinitely far away is to keep its position coordinated with the camera. The following class implements a cube-shaped sky. The textures that are placed on the cube are created to give the players the illusion they are looking at a dome-shaped object. You've already seen how the depth stencil gets set to make the effect work, but that's not the whole job.

As you look out the window of a moving car, it seems that the sky isn't moving relative to anything else. It is moving, of course, but it moves so slowly that you can't perceive it. In computer games, this effect is simulated by having the sky literally move as the camera moves but still keep its orientation. Here's the class to make that work.

```
class D3DSkyNode11 : public SceneNode
{
```

```
protected:
  DWORD                       m_numVerts;
  DWORD                       m_sides;
  const char *                m_textureBaseName;
  shared_ptr<CameraNode>      m_camera;
  bool                        m_bActive;

  ID3D11Buffer*               m_pIndexBuffer;
  ID3D11Buffer*               m_pVertexBuffer;

  GameCode4_Hlsl_VertexShader m_VertexShader;
  GameCode4_Hlsl_PixelShader  m_PixelShader;

public:
  D3DSkyNode11(const char *textureFile, shared_ptr<CameraNode> camera);
  virtual ~ D3DSkyNode11 ();
  HRESULT VOnRestore(Scene *pScene);
  HRESULT VRender(Scene *pScene);
  HRESULT VPreRender(Scene *pScene);
  bool VIsVisible(Scene *pScene) const { return m_bActive; }
};
```

This class makes use of the vertex and pixel shader classes you learned about in the previous chapter. The constructor and destructor are fairly simple. Note that the text string sent into the pixel shader constructor is empty—that's because the sky node is going to do something a little special.

```
D3DSkyNode11::D3DSkyNode11 (const char *pTextureBaseName,
                            shared_ptr<CameraNode> camera)
: SceneNode(INVALID_ACTOR_ID "Sky", RenderPass_Sky, g_White,
            &Mat4x4::g_Identity)
, m_camera(camera)
, m_bActive(true)
, m_PixelShader("")
{
  m_textureBaseName = pTextureBaseName;
  m_pVertexBuffer = NULL;
  m_pIndexBuffer = NULL;
  m_PixelShader.EnableLights(false);
}

D3DSkyNode11::~D3DSkyNode11 ()
{
  SAFE_RELEASE(m_pVertexBuffer);
  SAFE_RELEASE(m_pIndexBuffer);
}
```

This sky node needs five textures: one each for the north, east, south, west, and top sides of the box. The texture base name sent into the constructor lets a programmer set a base name, like "Daytime" or "Nighttime," and the textures that are actually read append side name suffixes to the actual texture filename. You'll see how this is used in the `VRender()` method. `VOnRestore()` creates the vertex and index buffers for the skybox. To do this, two triangles are created from four vertices, and then they are transformed to make the four other sides. First, a 90-degree rotation around the vertical makes the east, south, and west sides of the box. Then a 90-degree rotation around the horizontal creates the top side.

```
HRESULT SkyNode::VOnRestore(Scene *pScene)
{
  HRESULT hr;
  V_RETURN (SceneNode::VOnRestore(pScene) );

  SAFE_RELEASE(m_pVertexBuffer);
  SAFE_RELEASE(m_pIndexBuffer);

  V_RETURN (m_VertexShader.OnRestore(pScene) );
  V_RETURN (m_PixelShader.OnRestore(pScene) );

  m_numVerts = 20;

  // Fill the vertex buffer. We are setting the tu and tv texture
  // coordinates, which range from 0.0 to 1.0
  D3D11Vertex_UnlitTextured *pVertices =
    GCC_NEW D3D11Vertex_UnlitTextured[m_numVerts];
  GCC_ASSERT(pVertices && "Out of memory in D3DSkyNode11::VOnRestore()");
  if (!pVertices)
    return E_FAIL;

  D3D11Vertex_UnlitTextured skyVerts[4];
  D3DCOLOR skyVertColor = 0xffffffff;
  float dim = 50.0f;

  skyVerts[0].Pos = Vec3( dim, dim, dim ); skyVerts[0].Uv = Vec2 (1.0f, 0.0f);
  skyVerts[1].Pos = Vec3(-dim, dim, dim ); skyVerts[1].Uv = Vec2 (0.0f, 0.0f);
  skyVerts[2].Pos = Vec3( dim,-dim, dim ); skyVerts[2].Uv = Vec2 (1.0f, 1.0f);
  skyVerts[3].Pos = Vec3(-dim,-dim, dim ); skyVerts[3].Uv = Vec2(0.0f, 1.0f);

  Vec3 triangle[3];
  triangle[0] = Vec3(0.f,0.f,0.f);
  triangle[1] = Vec3(5.f,0.f,0.f);
  triangle[2] = Vec3(5.f,5.f,0.f);
```

```
Vec3 edge1 = triangle[1]-triangle[0];
Vec3 edge2 = triangle[2]-triangle[0];

Vec3 normal;
normal = edge1.Cross(edge2);
normal.Normalize();

Mat4x4 rotY;
rotY.BuildRotationY(D3DX_PI/2.0f);
Mat4x4 rotX;
rotX.BuildRotationX(-D3DX_PI/2.0f);

m_sides = 5;

for (DWORD side = 0; side < m_sides; side++)
{
  for (DWORD v = 0; v < 4; v++)
  {
    Vec4 temp;
    if (side < m_sides-1)
    {
      temp = rotY.Xform(Vec3(skyVerts[v].Pos));
    }
   else
    {
      skyVerts[0].Uv = Vec2(1.0f, 1.0f);
      skyVerts[1].Uv = Vec2 (1.0f, 1.0f);
      skyVerts[2].Uv = Vec2 (1.0f, 1.0f);
      skyVerts[3].Uv = Vec2 (1.0f, 1.0f);
      temp = rotX.Xform(Vec3(skyVerts[v].Pos));
    }
    skyVerts[v].Pos = Vec3(temp.x, temp.y, temp.z);
  }
  memcpy(&pVertices[side*4], skyVerts, sizeof(skyVerts));
}

D3D11_BUFFER_DESC bd;
ZeroMemory( &bd, sizeof(bd) );
bd.Usage = D3D11_USAGE_DEFAULT;
bd.ByteWidth = sizeof( D3D11Vertex_UnlitTextured ) * m_numVerts;
bd.BindFlags = D3D11_BIND_VERTEX_BUFFER;
bd.CPUAccessFlags = 0;
D3D11_SUBRESOURCE_DATA InitData;
ZeroMemory( &InitData, sizeof(InitData) );
InitData.pSysMem = pVertices;
```

```
  hr = DXUTGetD3D11Device()->CreateBuffer( &bd, &InitData, &m_pVertexBuffer );
  SAFE_DELETE(pVertices);

  if( FAILED( hr ) )
    return hr;

  // Loop through the grid squares and calc the values
  // of each index. Each grid square has two triangles:
  //
  //      A - B
  //      | / |
  //      C - D

  WORD *pIndices = GCC_NEW WORD[m_sides * 2 * 3];
  WORD *current = pIndices;
  for (DWORD i=0; i<m_sides; ++i)
  {
    // Triangle #1  ACB
    *(current) = WORD(i*4);
    *(current+1) = WORD(i*4 + 2);
    *(current+2) = WORD(i*4 + 1);

    // Triangle #2  BCD
    *(current+3) = WORD(i*4 + 1);
    *(current+4) = WORD(i*4 + 2);
    *(current+5) = WORD(i*4 + 3);
    current+=6;
  }

  bd.Usage = D3D11_USAGE_DEFAULT;
  bd.ByteWidth = sizeof(WORD) * m_sides * 2 * 3;  //// each side has 2 triangles
  bd.BindFlags = D3D11_BIND_INDEX_BUFFER;
  bd.CPUAccessFlags = 0;
  InitData.pSysMem = pIndices;
  hr = DXUTGetD3D11Device()->CreateBuffer( &bd, &InitData, &m_pIndexBuffer );
  SAFE_DELETE_ARRAY(pIndices);

  if( FAILED( hr ) )
    return hr;

  return S_OK;
}
```

The vertex buffer is created first using the rotation transformations; then the index buffer is created. This code is actually very similar to what you saw in Chapter 14 to create the index buffer for the grid object. If you have trouble visualizing it, it might be a good idea to get out the graph paper. To be honest, that's how I created this code in the first place!

The real trick to making the sky node special is the code inside `VPreRender()`:

```
HRESULT SkyNode::VPreRender(Scene *pScene)
{
  Vec3 cameraPos = m_camera->VGet()->ToWorld().GetPosition();
  Mat4x4 mat = m_Props.ToWorld();
  mat.SetPosition(cameraPos);
  VSetTransform(&mat);

  return SceneNode::VPreRender(pScene);
}
```

This code grabs the camera position and moves the sky node exactly as the camera moves. This gives a completely convincing illusion that the objects like sun, moon, mountains, and other backgrounds rendered into the sky textures are extremely far away, since they don't appear to move as the player moves.

The code to render the sky should look a little familiar, since you saw snippets of it at the end of the previous chapter:

```
HRESULT D3DSkyNode11::VRender(Scene *pScene)
{
  HRESULT hr;
  V_RETURN (m_VertexShader.SetupRender(pScene) );
  V_RETURN (m_PixelShader.SetupRender(pScene, this) );

  // Set vertex buffer
  UINT stride = sizeof( D3D11Vertex_UnlitTextured );
  UINT offset = 0;
  DXUTGetD3D11DeviceContext()->
    IASetVertexBuffers( 0, 1, &m_pVertexBuffer, &stride, &offset );

  // Set index buffer
  DXUTGetD3D11DeviceContext()->
    IASetIndexBuffer( m_pIndexBuffer, DXGI_FORMAT_R16_UINT, 0 );

  // Set primitive topology
  DXUTGetD3D11DeviceContext()->
    IASetPrimitiveTopology( D3D11_PRIMITIVE_TOPOLOGY_TRIANGLELIST );

  for (DWORD side = 0; side < m_sides; side++)
  {
    const char *suffix[] =
      { "_n.jpg", "_e.jpg", "_s.jpg", "_w.jpg", "_u.jpg" };
```

```
    std::string name = m_textureBaseName;
    name += suffix[side];

    m_PixelShader.SetTexture(name);
    DXUTGetD3D11DeviceContext()->DrawIndexed( 6, side * 6, 0 );
  }
  return S_OK;
}
```

First, the vertex and pixel shaders have their `SetupRender()` methods called. This is what sets up the transformation matrices in the vertex shader and the lighting and material constant buffers in the pixel shader. Then the vertex and index buffers are sent into the `ID3D11DeviceContext`, and the primitive topology is set to a triangle list, which is how we've set up the indices into the vertex buffer. Then a loop begins that sets the pixel shader's texture, and a call to `DrawIndexed()` is made to draw one side of the skybox.

If you read this and said to yourself, "What a fool—McShaffry is setting a different texture for each face of the sky and that's too expensive!" you'd be absolutely right. There is a better way to do this, although it does require some advanced shader code and a different kind of texture, called a *cube map*. A cube map is basically a large texture with all faces present, so there's only one texture to manage. As an exercise, try writing the shaders to use a cube map, create the C++ helper classes to interface with the shaders, and convert this sky node class to use it. That will utilize almost every 3D graphics topic you've learned so far.

## Using Meshes in Your Scene

A 3D game would be pretty boring with nothing but grids and sky. If you want interesting shapes, you'll need to create them in a modeling tool like 3ds Max, Maya, or ZBrush. Modeling tools are precise tools for creating shapes for your game levels or dynamic objects. Direct3D can't read files from these modeling tools directly, but it can read SDKMESH files, which are used in the Direct3D samples and tutorials.

This file format isn't meant for commercial games, but it can be used to get used to the idea of how to read them, create a `SceneNode` around them, and put them into a 3D world. The first task is to load the mesh, and like many other things you've seen, it is convenient to be able to load meshes from the resource cache. The raw bits of the SDKMESH file can't be used directly by Direct3D 11. It is loaded into a Direct3D utility class, `CDXUTSDKMesh`. That means we have to define a resource loader class that will help the resource cache load the raw bits into an object directly usable by Direct3D 11.

```
class D3DSdkMeshResourceExtraData11 : public IResourceExtraData
{
  friend class SdkMeshResourceLoader;

public:
  D3DSdkMeshResourceExtraData11() { };
  virtual ~D3DSdkMeshResourceExtraData11() { }
  virtual std::string VToString() { return "D3DSdkMeshResourceExtraData11"; }
  CDXUTSDKMesh m_Mesh11;
};

class SdkMeshResourceLoader : public IResourceLoader
{
public:
  virtual bool VUseRawFile() { return false; }
  virtual bool VDiscardRawBufferAfterLoad() { return false; }
  virtual unsigned int VGetLoadedResourceSize(char *rawBuffer, unsigned int
                                               unsigned int rawSize)
    { return rawSize; }
  virtual bool VLoadResource(char *rawBuffer, unsigned int rawSize,
                             shared_ptr<ResHandle> handle);
  virtual std::string VGetPattern() { return "*.sdkmesh"; }
};

bool SdkMeshResourceLoader::VLoadResource(char *rawBuffer,
                                          unsigned int rawSize,
                                          shared_ptr<ResHandle> handle)
{
  shared_ptr<D3DSdkMeshResourceExtraData11> extra =
    shared_ptr<D3DSdkMeshResourceExtraData11>(
      GCC_NEW D3DSdkMeshResourceExtraData11());

  // Load the Mesh
  if (SUCCEEDED ( extra->m_Mesh11.Create( DXUTGetD3D11Device(),
    (BYTE *)rawBuffer, (UINT)rawSize, true ) ) )
  {
    handle->SetExtra(shared_ptr<D3DSdkMeshResourceExtraData11>(extra));
  }
  return true;
}
```

This loader is trivial. All it really does is call the `Create()` method of the `CDXUTSDKMesh` class with the raw bits of the SDKMESH file as inputs.

There's one subtle thing about the resource loaded code above that you haven't seen before. This is the first time that VDiscardRawBufferAfterLoad() has returned false. Here's why: the CDXUTSDKMesh class refers to the raw bits in the mesh, so if they were discarded after the resource was loaded, the mesh would have invalid data in it. It just goes to show that not every DXUT class or any SDK class from any vendor out there operates similarly to others in the same library!

Meet the D3DShaderMeshNode11 class:

```
class D3DShaderMeshNode11 : public SceneNode
{
public:
  D3DShaderMeshNode11(const ActorId actorId,
    std::string name,
    std::string sdkMeshFileName,
    RenderPass renderPass,
    const Color &color,
    const Mat4x4 *t)
  : SceneNode(actorId, name, renderPass, diffuseColor, t),
    m_PixelShader("")
  {
    m_sdkMeshFileName = sdkMeshFileName;
  }

  virtual ~D3DShaderMeshNode11();
  virtual HRESULT VOnRestore(Scene *pScene);
  virtual HRESULT VOnLostDevice(Scene *pScene) { return S_OK; }
  virtual HRESULT VRender(Scene *pScene);
protected:
  std::string m_sdkMeshFileName;

  GameCode4_Hlsl_VertexShader   m_VertexShader;
  GameCode4_Hlsl_PixelShader   m_PixelShader;
};
```

This class looks somewhat similar to the SkyNode class—it has the two C++ shader helper classes you've come to know and love, but there is no vertex or index buffer defined. That's because the CDXUTSDKMesh class already has them. Note also that the constructor doesn't have a specific texture to send in to the pixel shader.

The VOnRestore() method is very simple—all it does is call the VOnRestore() methods of the SceneNode parent class and the two shaders before making a call to the resource cache to reload the SDKMESH file.

```
HRESULT D3DShaderMeshNode11::VOnRestore(Scene *pScene)
{
```

```
  HRESULT hr;

  V_RETURN(SceneNode::VOnRestore(pScene) );

  V_RETURN (m_VertexShader.OnRestore(pScene) );
  V_RETURN (m_PixelShader.OnRestore(pScene) );

  // Force the Mesh to reload
  Resource resource(m_sdkMeshFileName);
  shared_ptr<ResHandle> pResourceHandle =
    g_pApp->m_ResCache->GetHandle(&resource);
  shared_ptr<D3DSdkMeshResourceExtraData11> extra =
    static_pointer_cast<D3DSdkMeshResourceExtraData11>(
      pResourceHandle->GetExtra());
  return S_OK;
}
```

The really interesting bit happens in `VRender()`. After the calls to the shader `SetupRender()` methods, notice how the vertex and index buffers get set:

```
HRESULT D3DShaderMeshNode11::VRender(Scene *pScene)
{
  HRESULT hr;

  V_RETURN (m_VertexShader.SetupRender(pScene) );
  V_RETURN (m_PixelShader.SetupRender(pScene, this) );

  //Get the Mesh
  Resource resource(m_sdkMeshFileName);
  shared_ptr<ResHandle> pResourceHandle =
    g_pApp->m_ResCache->GetHandle(&resource);
    shared_ptr<D3DSdkMeshResourceExtraData11> extra =
    static_pointer_cast<D3DSdkMeshResourceExtraData11>(
      pResourceHandle->GetExtra());

  //IA setup
  UINT Strides[1];
  UINT Offsets[1];
  ID3D11Buffer* pVB[1];
  pVB[0] = extra->m_Mesh11.GetVB11( 0, 0 );
  Strides[0] = ( UINT )extra->m_Mesh11.GetVertexStride( 0, 0 );
  Offsets[0] = 0;
  DXUTGetD3D11DeviceContext()->IASetVertexBuffers( 0, 1, pVB, Strides,
                                                   Offsets );
  DXUTGetD3D11DeviceContext()->IASetIndexBuffer(extra->m_Mesh11.GetIB11(0),
    extra->m_Mesh11.GetIBFormat11( 0 ), 0 );
```

```
  //Render
  D3D11_PRIMITIVE_TOPOLOGY PrimType;
  for( UINT subset = 0; subset < extra->m_Mesh11.GetNumSubsets(0); ++subset )
  {
    // Get the subset
    SDKMESH_SUBSET *pSubset = extra->m_Mesh11.GetSubset( 0, subset );
    PrimType = CDXUTSDKMesh::GetPrimitiveType11(
      ( SDKMESH_PRIMITIVE_TYPE )pSubset->PrimitiveType );
    DXUTGetD3D11DeviceContext()->IASetPrimitiveTopology( PrimType );

    ID3D11ShaderResourceView* pDiffuseRV = extra->m_Mesh11.GetMaterial(
      pSubset->MaterialID )->pDiffuseRV11;
    DXUTGetD3D11DeviceContext()->PSSetShaderResources( 0, 1, &pDiffuseRV );

    DXUTGetD3D11DeviceContext()->DrawIndexed( ( UINT )pSubset->IndexCount, 0,
                                              ( UINT )pSubset->VertexStart );
  }
  return S_OK;
}
```

Rendering geometry requires setting the vertex and index buffers, defining a primitive topology, setting texture resources, and finishing with a draw call. In the case of a mesh, you may have many different types of geometry using multiple textures. That's why there's a loop, similar to what you saw earlier with the skybox, except all the skybox did was reset the texture. This shows that in the case of a mesh, you can even reset the primitive topology. That implies something really important: A single vertex buffer and a single index buffer can contain multiple primitive topologies! Triangle lists, strips, line lists, strips, and others can all be represented in a single vertex and index buffer pair.

**Watch Those Long Load Times**

Balancing load times and runtime frame rate is one of the trickiest problems in game development. Load times tend to be slow because the files are intentionally stripped down to the bare bones and compressed to pack as many game assets on the digital media as possible. Frame rate suffers if the game assets have to be tweaked every frame or if they simply aren't formatted for the fastest rendering on the player's hardware. Here's a good rule of thumb: Don't make the player wait more than 60 seconds for a load for every 30 minutes of gameplay. And whatever you do, make sure you have a nice screen animation during the load so players don't confuse your long load times with a game crash!

## What's Missing?

That is all you need to create a simple scene graph. It may seem like an extremely simplistic architecture, but it's more flexible than you'd think. Each node you design can add functionality and special effects to all its children nodes. Here are some examples:

- **Billboard node:** Sets the transform matrix of all the child nodes such that they always face the camera. Use this for trees or light glare.
- **Level of detail node:** A node that chooses one node in its child list for rendering based on the node's distance from the camera.
- **BSP node:** A node that sets its visibility based on which side of the BSP plane the camera is and where it is facing.
- **Material node:** Sets the default material for all children nodes.
- **World sector node:** Defines a 3D volume that completely contains all of its children nodes. You use it to determine if any children need to be drawn based on camera direction or interposed opaque world sectors.
- **Mirror node:** Defines a portal through which the scene is re-rendered from a different point of view and stenciled onto a texture.
- **Lots more shader effects!**

I'm sure you can come up with other cool stuff.

## Still Hungry?

When the last three chapters were first outlined, I knew that I was going to leave plenty of questions completely unanswered. The chapters covered too much in too few pages. My publisher being willing, I could have spent more pages on 3D graphics, shaders, and architecture, but even if I doubled or tripled my coverage of these subjects I would still only scratch the surface. As with other chapters in this book, my goal is to give you just enough knowledge to be dangerous and point you to the next steps.

## Further Reading

- *3D Game Engine Design,* David H. Heberly
- *3D Game Engine Architecture,* David H. Heberly

# Chapter 17

*by Mike McShaffry*

# Collision and Simple Physics

Even the simplest 2D game needs collision. After all, if the objects in a game can't interact, how fun could the game possibly be? *Breakout* is a great example of a simple game. A ball bounces off walls, bricks, and the paddle. If you look at it this way, the core of the game experience is created by the 2D collision algorithm. It's almost impossible to design a game without at least some rudimentary collision. Perhaps a text adventure like *Zork* is one example, but hey, it hasn't exactly been flying off the shelves lately. If you are familiar with *Zork*, that's great because you know your game history. If you've actually played *Zork*, well, then you are probably as "mature" as I am.

Collision is a purely mathematical calculation to determine the spatial relationship between objects such as points, lines, planes, or polygonal models. I'll point you to some great resources outside of this book that provide good solutions. I'm not going to pretend I can offer something better.

Physics, on the other hand, is a much more complicated beast altogether. A physics simulation in your game will make it possible to stack objects on top of each other, fall down slopes and stairs accurately, and interact with other dynamic objects in a visually realistic fashion. It can also create motion under force such as you'd see with motors and springs. It can constrain the movements of objects similar to a door on hinges or a pendulum swinging in a grandfather clock.

In the spring of 2004, I worked on *Thief: Deadly Shadows*. This game used the Havok physics engine on every movable object, including rag dolls for characters. *Thief* might not use physics as its core game experience, but it certainly creates a convincing illusion of a complete world in which the player can interact with objects in a meaningful way and affect the events of the game. Here's an example: You could knock a barrel down a flight of stairs, and each impact reported by the collision system would trigger a sound effect that you heard through the speakers. The actions would also trigger sound events in the AI subsystem. This would bring curious guards around to investigate the noise.

You might think for a moment that you could have a similar game experience without a complicated physics simulation, and you are right. The aforementioned barrel could have simply shattered into bits when you knocked into it, and the same guard could have investigated it. The fundamental difference is one of realism and how far the player has to go to imagine what happens versus seeing it in front of his eyes.

Many games don't have super-accurate physics simulations, something you've probably suspected, but perhaps you've wondered why the designers and programmers stopped short of doing. A truly accurate physics simulation for every game object is an expensive proposition, CPU-wise. Every game will make reasonable optimizations to make things faster. For example, most physics simulations assume that buildings and other architecture are essentially infinite weight and impossible to break. Load any racing game, like *Project Gotham 4,* and try running into a barricade with a Ferrari at over 200 mph and tell me that a real barricade would survive that impact without being horribly mangled. It won't, and therefore that simulation isn't completely accurate.

But it is quite a bit of fun to rebound off barricades in games like *Project Gotham* at high speed to get around corners faster, isn't it? The point I'm trying to make is that you have to understand your game before you decide that a physics simulation will actually add to the fun. A game like *Thief* benefited from accurate physics, but *Project Gotham* would have been remiss to create something perfectly accurate in every way, even if it could have afforded the CPU budget.

Think about this for a moment: Is it better to have the pendulum in a grandfather clock act under a completely realistic physics simulation or a simple scripted animation? The answer is completely dependent on your game, and by the end of this chapter, hopefully you'll be able to answer that question for yourself.

Since I only have one chapter to talk about collision and physics, I only have time to show you how to use an existing system (specifically the open source library, Bullet) in your game. We'll cover the basics and get right into how you can best use these complicated pieces of technology.

# Mathematics for Physics Refresher

I don't know about you, but every time I read anything that has anything to do with math, I somehow feel all of the intelligence leak right out of my skull. I think it has something to do with the presentation. I hope to do better here because if you can't get past understanding these concepts, you'll be pretty lost when you get around to debugging physics and collision code.

## Meters, Feet, Cubits, or Kellicams?

What you are about to read is true (even though you might not believe it), so read it over and over until you have no doubt:

*Units of measure don't matter in any physics calculation. All the formulas will work, as long as you are consistent.*

I'm sure you remember the unfortunate story about the Mars Lander that crashed because two different units of measurement were used? One team used meters, and the other team used feet. This error is frighteningly simple to make, so don't laugh too hard. It's not just the programmers who need to agree on the units of measure for a game project. Artists use units of measurement, too, and they can cause all kinds of trouble by choosing the wrong ones.

A unitless measure of distance can therefore be anything you like: meters, feet, inches, and so on. There are two other properties that can also be unitless: mass and time. You'll generally use kilograms or pounds for mass, and I'll go out on a limb here and suggest you use seconds for time. Whatever you use, just be consistent. All other measurements, such as velocity and force, are derived from various combinations of distance, mass, and time.

By the way, if you are wondering how I knew how to spell Kellicams (the unit of measure used by the Klingon Empire), I did what any author would do: I searched Google and chose the spelling that gave me the most returns.

## Distance, Velocity, and Acceleration

When you need to work with objects moving through space, you'll be interested in their position, velocity, and acceleration. Each one of these is represented by a 3D vector:

```
Vec3 m_Pos;
Vec3 m_Vel;
Vec3 m_Accel;
```

Velocity is the change in position over time, and likewise acceleration is the change in velocity over time. You calculate them like this:

```
Vec3 CalcVel(const Vec3 &pos0, const Vec3 &pos1, const float time)
{
  return (pos1 - pos0) / time;
}

Vec3 CalcAccel(const Vec3 &vel0, const Vec3 &vel1, const float time)
{
  return (vel1 - vel0) / time;
}
```

This is fairly pedantic stuff, and you should remember this from the math you learned in high school. In computer games, you frequently need to go backward. You'll have the acceleration as a vector, but you'll want to know what happens to the position of an object during your main loop. Here's how to do that:

```
inline Vec3 HandleAccel(Vec3 &pos, Vec3 &vel, const Vec3 &accel, float time)
{
  vel += accel * time;
  pos += vel * time;
  return pos;
}
```

Notice that when the acceleration is handled, both the velocity and the position change. Both are sent into `HandleAccel()` as references that will hold the new values.

Now that you've seen the code, take a quick look Table 17.1, which contains mathematical formulas for calculating positions and velocities. Hopefully, you won't pass out.

You probably recognize these formulas. When you first learned these formulas, you were using scalar numbers representing simple one-dimensional measurements like

**Table 17.1 Formulas for Calculating Positions and Velocities**

| Formula | Description |
|---|---|
| $p = p_0 + vt$ | Find a new position (p) from your current position ($p_0$), velocity (v), and time (t) |
| $v = v_0 + at$ | Find a new velocity (v) from your current velocity ($v_0$), acceleration (a), and time (t) |
| $p = p_0 + v_0t + (at^2)/2$ | Find a new position (p) from your current position ($p_0$), velocity ($v_0$), acceleration (a), and time (t) |

distance in feet or meters. In a 3D world, we're going to use the same formulas, but the inputs are going to be 3D vectors to represent position, speed, and acceleration in 3D space. Luckily, these vectors work exactly the same as scalar numbers in these equations, because they are only added together or multiplied by time, a scalar number itself.

## Mass, Acceleration, and Force

Whenever I have a particularly nasty crash when mountain biking, some joker in my mountain biking group quips, "F=ma, dood. You okay?" This formula is Newton's Second Law of Motion and says that force is calculated by multiplying the mass of the object in question with its acceleration. In the case of an unfortunate mountain biker taking an unexpected exit from the bike, the acceleration is the change in the biker's velocity over time, or deceleration actually, multiplied by the biker's weight. Crashing at the same speed, the heavier biker gets hurt more. If the same biker crashes while riding downhill, the slightly faster speed does quite a bit more damage because acceleration has a time squared component and is therefore much more serious than a change in mass.

Force is typically measured in Newtons. One Newton, symbolized by the letter N, is defined as the force required to accelerate a mass of one kilogram at a rate of one meter per second squared.

$$N = (\mathrm{kg})\mathrm{m/s}^2$$

Try not to confuse acceleration and force. Gravity is a force, and when it is applied to an object, it causes acceleration. Galileo discovered an interesting property about this acceleration by dropping things from the Leaning Tower of Pisa: It doesn't matter how much something weighs because they all fall at the same rate, excepting any large differences in air resistance. This is extremely unintuitive until you remember that even though more massive objects exert a greater gravitational force, this force is used to accelerate the larger mass, and therefore the acceleration remains the same. The only way you get higher acceleration is with stronger gravitational fields. Feel free to find a black hole and experiment—I'll watch from a few light years away.

### Who Wins, a Tissue or the Planet?

While it might not feel this way to you, gravitation is an incredibly weak force compared to something like electricity. You can prove it to yourself by placing an object, like your cell phone, on a piece of tissue paper. Grab both sides of the tissue paper and lift it, suspending your cell phone over the ground. The force that keeps the cell phone from tearing through the tissue paper is the electrical force binding the material of the tissue paper together. So the electrical bonds present in that tiny piece of tissue paper are sufficient to withstand the gravitational force exerted on the cell phone *by the entire planet Earth.*

---

Heavier things exert a larger force in a gravitational field, such as when you place a weight on your chest. At sea level, Earth's gravity causes an acceleration of exactly 9.80665 meters/s$^2$ on every object. Thus, a one kilogram object exerts a force of 9.80665N. To get an idea of how big that force is, lie down and set this book on your chest. It turns out to be around 1.5 kilograms, give or take Chapter 5, so you will experience a force of about 1.5N. So one Newton is not all that big, really, if you are the size of a human being and the force is somewhat distributed over a book-sized area. Balance this book on a fork, tines downward, and you'll see how that distribution will change your perception of one Newton. Area, as it seems, makes a huge difference.

Let's look at the code that would apply a constant acceleration, like gravity, to an object. We'll also look at code that applies an instantaneous force. Forces are vectors and are therefore additive, so multiple forces ($f_0$, $f_1$, $f_2$, …) on one object are added together to get an overall force ($f$):

$$f_0 + f_1 + f_2 + \cdots$$

or in shorthand, we write

$$F = \sum_{x=0}^{n} f_x$$

Just so you know, the C++ version of that math formula is a simple `for` loop:

```
Vec3 AddVectors(const Vec3 *f, int n)
{
  Vec3 F = Vec3(0,0,0);
  for (int x = 0; x < n; x++)
    F += f[x];

  return F;
}
```

A constant force over time equates to some acceleration over time, depending on the object's mass. An impulse is instantaneous, so it only changes the acceleration once. Think of it like the difference between the force of a rocket motor and the force of hitting something with a golf club: One happens over time, and the other is instantaneous. Take a look at a simple game object class:

```
typedef std::list<Vec3> Vec3List;
```

```
class GameObject
{
    Vec3 m_Pos;
    Vec3 m_Vel;
    Vec3 m_Accel;
    Vec3List m_Forces;
    Vec3List m_Impulses;
    float m_Mass;

    void AddForce(const Vec3 &force) { m_Forces.push_back(force); }
    void AddImpulse(const Vec3 &impulse) { m_Impulses.push_back(impulse); }
    void OnUpdate(const float time);
};
```

This class contains 3D vectors for position, velocity, and acceleration. It also has two lists: one for constant forces and the other for impulses, each of which is modified by accessor methods that push the force or impulse onto the appropriate list. The real action happens in the `OnUpdate()` call.

```
void GameObject::OnUpdate(const float time)
{
  if (m_Mass == 0.0f)
    return;

  // Add constant forces...
  Vec3 F(0,0,0);
  Vec3List::iterator it;
  for (it=m_Forces.begin(); it!=m_Forces.end(); it++)
  {
    F += *it;
  }

  // Also add all the impulses, and then clear the list
  for (it=m_Impulses.begin(); it!=m_Impulses.end(); it++)
  {
    F += *it;
  }
  m_Impulses.clear();

  // calculate new acceleration
  m_Accel = F / m_Mass;
  m_Vel += m_Accel * time;
  m_Pos += m_Vel * time;
}
```

The two loops add all the forces being applied to the game object. The first loop just iterates through and accumulates a result. The second loop is different, because as it accumulates the result, the list is emptied. This is because the forces are impulses, and thus they only happen once. The resulting acceleration is calculated by dividing the accumulated force (F) by the object's mass. Once that is done, you can update the object's velocity and position. I'll leave the implementation of `RemoveForce()` up to you.

**Physics Engines Are Very Time Sensitive**

You must be extremely careful with the value of time. If you send in a value either too big or too small, you'll get some unpredictable results. Very small values of time can accentuate numerical imprecision in floating-point math, and since time is essentially squared in the position calculation, you can run into precision problems there, too. If your physics system is acting strangely, check how often it is being called first.

## Rotational Inertia, Angular Velocity, and Torque

When an object moves through space, its location always references the center of mass. Intuitively, you know what the center of mass is, but it is interesting to note some special properties about it. For one thing, when the object rotates freely, it always rotates about the center of mass. If the object is sitting on the ground, you can tip it, and it will only fall when the center of mass is pushed past the base of the object. That's why it's easier to knock over a cardboard tube standing on its end than a pyramid sitting on its base.

Different objects rotate very differently, depending on their shape and how their weight is distributed around the volume of the shape. A Frisbee spins easily when I throw it, but it doesn't spin as well end-over-end, like when my youngest nephew throws it! Mathematically, this property of physical objects is called the *inertia tensor*. It has a very cool name, and you can impress your friends by working it into conversations.

The inertia tensor is something that is calculated ahead of time and stored in the physical properties of the object. It's pretty expensive to create at runtime. It is a $3 \times 3$ matrix, describing how difficult it is to rotate an object on any possible axis. An object's shape, density, and mass are all used to compute the inertia tensor; it is usually done when you create an object. It's much more preferable to precompute the inertia tensor and store it. This calculation isn't trivial. As you might expect, the inertia tensor is to orientation as mass is to position; it is a property of the object that will affect how the object rotates.

Angular velocity is a property of physics objects that describes the axis of spin and the speed at the same time in one 3D vector. The magnitude of the vector is the spin in whatever units per second, and the direction of the vector shows the rotational axis.

Angular force is called *torque* and is measured by a force applied about a spin radius. Think of a wrench. As you push on it to get a bolt loose, you apply a certain force to the end of a wrench of some length. A particularly stubborn bolt might come loose if you put a long pipe over the end of your wrench, but the wise mechanic knows that you have a pretty good chance to break the end right off that nice wrench. This is a good reason to buy Craftsman.

*Torque* is measured by force, specified in Newton-meters for the metric system or foot-pounds for the medieval system. As you might expect, 5 Newton-meters is a 5 Newton force applied about a 1 meter length.

## Distance Calculations and Intersections

The best resource I've found for calculating distances is a website, and it would be crazy of me to simply regurgitate the content they have. Just visit www.realtimerendering.com/intersections.html. This resource is so great because it has collected the best of the best in finding these collisions and intersections and listed them all in a big matrix. This took a lot of research, and I'd be completely remiss if I didn't point you to it.

As of this printing, this website is a great resource for finding collisions/intersections between any of the following objects:

- Ray
- Plane
- Sphere
- Cylinder
- Cone
- Triangle
- Axis-Aligned Bounding Box (AABB)
- Oriented Bounding Box (OBB)
- Viewing Frustum
- Convex Polyhedron

If you want to perform collision detection on arbitrary static and dynamic meshes, such as a teapot against a stairway, you'll need more firepower. For that, I'd suggest going straight to a real physics SDK.

## Choosing a Physics SDK

There are a lot of options these days for programmers who don't want to write their own collision system or a system to handle dynamics. Some of these systems have really interesting components for handling nonrigid bodies like bowls of Jell-o or vehicles.

Whether you choose to grab one off-the-shelf or write your own, it should have the following minimum set of features:

- Allow user data to relate physics objects with your game objects.
- Optimize collisions for static actors or geometry.
- Trap and report collision events.
- Provide a fast raycaster.
- Draw debug information visually.
- Output errors in a rational way.
- Allow custom memory allocators.
- Add and remove objects, or regions of objects, from the physics simulation for optimal CPU usage.
- Save and load its own state.

As the physics system simulates the movements of physical objects in a game, it will need some way to associate objects in its data structures to actual objects in your game. This is especially true since the physics object will usually have a simpler geometry than the visible object—a good reason to keep them separate. When physics objects are created, look for a way to provide a reference, or special user data, to these objects so you can figure out which physics and game object pairs match.

Most physics systems allow static, or unmovable, actors by setting their mass to zero. These objects would be the geometry that makes the walls, floors, terrain, and the rest of the environment, as well as any really heavy object that will never be moved, like a tree. Most physics systems take advantage of static actors to speed dynamics calculations.

Besides moving objects around, you'll want to know if and when they collide. You'll also want to know all kinds of things about the collision, such as the force of the collision, the collision normal, and the two objects that collided. All these things are great for playing back sounds, spawning particle effects, or imparting damage and destruction to the objects concerned.

Any game is going to need a good raycaster. A raycaster is something that returns one or more objects that intersect with a probe ray. It is an extremely useful routine for finding out whether objects are in the line of sight of an AI process, determining where to put bullet holes, and probing the surrounding geometry for moving cameras, objects, or characters. If possible, you should also be able to do something called a *shapecast*, which takes an entire object, like a sphere, and casts it instead of a simple ray. This kind of thing is invaluable for creating good third-person cameras. Depending on your physics system, raycasts or shapecasts can be expensive.

Most physics SDKs can send lots of debug information into your rendering pipeline so that things like collision shapes, acceleration vectors, and contact points are drawn so you can actually see their magnitudes and directions. Watching physics data structures visually is the only way to debug physics. You simply can't just look at the data structures and diagnose problems easily. Consider this example: Two objects seem to react in unexpected ways when they collide. When you look at the collision mesh data, you find that they look correct in the debugger's watch window. When you turn the physics debug renderer on, you might notice that one of the collision hulls is simply the wrong shape and needs to be fixed. You'd never figure this out looking at a long list of points in 3D space.

Most physics errors come from bad data or misuse of the API. For this reason, any decent physics SDK should have a good way to report errors back to you in the debug build. DirectX does this by sending error or informational messages to the debugger's output window. A good physics system should do the same thing. If your artists have created a collision mesh the physics system can't handle, it's nice to know right away rather than after you've spent all night debugging the problem.

Memory allocation is always a concern in computer games. They simply don't use memory in the manner that best suits the standard C-runtime memory allocator, and for that reason, most games write their own memory allocation scheme. A physics system can be just as hard on memory as a graphics subsystem, and thus it needs to use the same optimized memory system as the rest of your game. Look for hooks in the SDK that let you circumvent the default memory allocator with your own.

Physics is expensive enough that you only want to simulate areas of the game the player can actually see or be affected by. For this reason, most good physics systems have easy ways for groups of objects to be enabled or disabled as a group, which allows you to turn on and off areas to make the very best use of your CPU budget.

A physics system should be able to stream so that you can save and load its state. Even if your game doesn't have a load/save feature, it is likely that your game editor has a save feature; otherwise, it wouldn't be much of a game editor. In many game editors, physics objects are placed in the level and simulated until they find a stable position. Usually, you'd do this for candles sitting on tables and other props, but you could do it for something as complicated as a stone bridge. It might be fun to blow up something like that in your game! Either way, you can't count on designers to place the objects with such accuracy, so it's best to let the physics system simulate it until it stabilizes and then save the state.

Now that you've acquired a physics SDK with everything on your checklist, let's talk a little about how to actually use it.

## Object Properties

Physical objects have properties that affect their movement and interactions with other objects. We've already talked about mass, position, velocity, force, the inertia tensor, angular velocity, and torque. These properties describe object motion under force in free space. When objects bump into each other or into infinitely heavy objects, their reactions are dependent on three more properties: restitution, static friction, and dynamic friction.

*Restitution* is the amount of bounce that an object has when it hits something and is usually expressed in a positive floating-point number. A good way to think of this is how high a ball will bounce when you drop it. If the restitution is 0.0f, you've got a piece of playdough, and when it hits it will simply stick to the ground. If you've got something like 0.99f, you've got a nice superball that will bounce around for a long time. It's a bad idea to assign restitutions of greater than 1.0f, since the object will simply continue to gain energy forever.

*Static friction* and *dynamic friction* describe how much energy is lost when two materials are in contact and at rest or are in relative motion. Oddly enough, friction changes drastically in these two conditions. This is why it's so hard to regain control of a car once it's in a skid—the dynamic friction is lower than the static friction. You experience this same issue when pushing heavy objects; it's easier to keep them moving than it is to get them moving initially. Note that most physics implementations support only a single coefficient of friction and don't accommodate both types.

The coefficient of friction, usually represented by $\mu$, is a number that is calculated by the ratio of the force (F) required to move an object over the normal force (N), which on a flat surface is simply the mass of the object multiplied by the acceleration due to gravity:

$$F = \mu N$$
$$\mu = F/N$$

So if it took a 700N force to move an object that weighed 100Kg (thus exerting a 980N force on whatever surface it was sitting on), the coefficient of static friction would be about 0.714f. Once the object was moving, if all you had to apply was 490N to keep it moving at a steady speed, the coefficient of dynamic friction (or sliding friction) would be 0.5f.

Intuitively, the friction between two objects has everything to do with what those objects are made of. Many physics systems let you specify this coefficient on a material-by-material basis, which isn't exactly accurate. If you look on the Web, you'll find that these numbers are presented in tables that match two materials together, such as steel on steel or brass on oak or steel on ice. In other words, you'll likely need to tweak values for your objects until they seem right. A good safety tip is to make this a data file somewhere that you can tweak at runtime. Trust me, you will need to do this.

Here are some of the examples of this used in the GameCode4 code base, defined in *Dev/Assets/Config/physics.xml*:

```
<PhysicsMaterials>
  <PlayDough friction="0.9" restitution="0.05"/>
  <Normal friction="0.5" restitution="0.25"/>
  <Bouncy friction="0.5" restitution="0.95"/>
  <Slippery friction="0.0" restitution="0.25"/>
 </PhysicsMaterials>
```

This XML file is eventually read in by the physics engine into this structure:

```
struct MaterialData
{
  float m_restitution;
  float m_friction;

 MaterialData(float restitution, float friction)
 {
   m_restitution = restitution;
   m_friction = friction;
 }
};
```

One final note on the properties of restitution and friction: You'd better have a physics SDK that can assign these materials to specific triangles of a mesh. While this isn't that critical for dynamic objects, it is surely needed for your environment mesh, or you might have to decide to make your entire world out of plastic!

The next material property is density, a measure of an object's mass per unit of volume. This is typically represented by a floating-point number, with 1.0 representing the density of pure water. This value is usually called *specific gravity*. These figures can easily be saved in an XML file, allowing your game objects to be described with something other than a number:

```
<DensityTable>
  <!-- specific gravity -->
  <air>0.0013</air>
  <water>1.000</water>

  <!-- Synthetics -->
  <styrofoam>0.0100</styrofoam>

  <!-- Woods -->
  <balsa>0.0170</balsa>
  <bamboo>0.3500</bamboo>
  <pine>0.5000</pine>

  <!-- Biologic -->
  <blood>1.060</blood>
  <bone>1.800</bone>

  <!-- Metals and Stone -->
  <silicon>2.400</silicon>
  <aluminum>2.650</aluminum>

  <!-- Many more can follow! -->
</DensityTable>
```

## Collision Hulls

Your physics objects will require representations in the physical world, and these might be very different from their visible geometry. For example, a perfect sphere is a mathematical construct in a physical world and has only a location and a radius, whereas a visible representation might need quite a few polygons to look good. You should use mathematical representations in the physical world where and when you can, and you'll save memory and CPU time.

The trade-off is whether things will act like they appear. In the case of the sphere object representing a bowling ball in your game, you'll be quite happy. If the same sphere were representing a box or a crate, I think you'd be a lot less happy. That example is pretty trivial to make a point, but there are tougher problems. Before we cover some of those, let's talk about how collision geometry is built. You'll need to know this if you want to use a mesh editor such as Blender or 3ds Max.

## Requirements of Good Collision Geometry

A collision mesh has to have a few properties to make the math in the physics SDK efficient, or even possible. First, the mesh has to be convex. Good examples of convex meshes are those that represent any regular solid such as a sphere, cube, or even dodecahedron. Concave meshes, on the other hand, have valleys and holes.

The classic teapot is a good example of a concave mesh (see Figure 17.1). If I had the actual teapot in front of me, and I had a piece of string, it would be trivial for me to place the string on two parts of the object and observe the string cross empty space. On a convex mesh, this can't be done anywhere on the object's surface. An easier way to remember is by using the name *concave* because, simply put, it has caves.

Another requirement of a collision hull is that it be *manifold,* a mathematical term that describes how the triangles fit together and form edges. A manifold edge has exactly two triangles on either side. A manifold mesh has no holes or dangling

**Figure 17.1**
The classic teapot is concave.

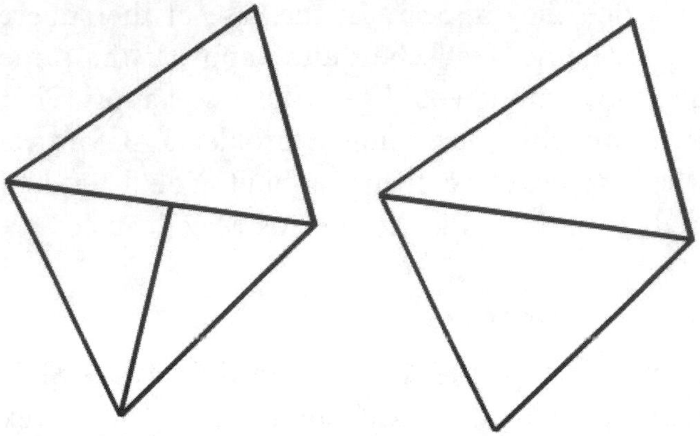

**Figure 17.2**
The left-hand triangles are non-manifold—the right-hand triangles are okay.

polygons. It represents a completely solid object. It also has no T-joints on any triangle edge. This usually isn't a problem for artists because they know it screws up the object's lighting anyway.

This might be hard to visualize, so I've dusted off my Photoshop skills and made a drawing for you (see Figure 17.2). The left-hand triangles are clearly non-manifold because of the T-joint. The triangles on the right satisfy the requirement that each edge must border exactly two triangles. The remaining requirement is that the mesh be completely closed and have no holes in it.

If you're worried that it might be tough to make meshes that always satisfy the requirements of your physics system, you're right. It's sometimes easy for artists to forget what the requirements are, especially when the heat is on and they're trying to get a ton of work done. The best thing is to make sure that your artists double-check their work, hopefully by actually importing their work into the game and seeing for themselves if anything is awry.

## Visible Geometry Versus Collision Geometry

It's a good thing to note that while the position and orientation of a physics object are related to the visual position and orientation, they aren't necessarily the same. They are probably the same for symmetrical objects like a sphere or a cube, but not much else. The position of an object in the physical world is always the center of mass, and that might not be the anchor point of the visible geometry. When you set the location for a 3D object, it is the anchor point on that object that will be positioned precisely at the new location. Likewise, the default orientation of an object in the physics simulation is usually an inertia tensor, such that it aligns with the X-, Y-, and Z-axes.

Maybe you can visualize this, but I certainly can't, and it won't necessarily match a reasonable orientation for the object for programmers and artists, such as orienting a gun with the barrel pointed straight down one of the X-, Y-, or Z-axes. Therefore, you'll probably need to apply a transformation to get from the orientation and position of your physics object to find the correct position and orientation for your visible geometry.

**Asymmetric Objects Are Great for Testing**

One test object you should definitely create is a completely asymmetric object. A good example is a cube with three corner vertices pulled or pushed around, as long as the shape is still convex. This will help you if you think your physical and visible coordinate systems are out of whack. If they are, the wireframe for the physical geometry won't match the visible geometry. If you integrate a new physics SDK with your game engine, and you use only balls or cubes as test objects, there's almost no way to tell if your transforms are correct. Use a crazy, convex object, and you'll notice problems right away.

If the collision and visible geometry are different, and they usually are, there are a couple of things you'll want to keep in mind:

- If you can simplify the physical geometry without sacrificing too much in the way of geometrical accuracy, go for it.
- Lean on the side of making physical geometry a little smaller than the visible geometry for objects and static environment meshes. This will create some graphical errors, but the objects that move won't get stuck so much or appear to hit something that isn't there.

## Collision Hulls for Human Characters

You might think that you'd want to represent a human character by a rag doll. If the character is unconscious or dead and is therefore under complete control of the physics system, that is probably okay. However, while the character is under kinematic control, in other words under control of the animation system, you may want something a lot simpler, trading accuracy in the simulation for some CPU cycles. The same thing goes for the player character as human AIs. Take a look at Figure 17.3, which is a simple capsule shape.

This simple shape has some great advantages and just a few disadvantages. First, the rounded hemisphere at the top keeps most objects from stacking on top of a character. The rounded hemisphere at the bottom allows for fairly natural looking ascent or descent of stairs and curbs. The cylinder that makes up the torso creates a convenient

**Figure 17.3**
A collision hull for a human character.

shape for sliding around objects or having objects slide around the character. Of course, anytime the collision geometry doesn't match the visible geometry, you'll see some anomalies. One of these is when a character's arm or leg pokes out of the capsule—this will show up in the game as characters sinking into walls and doors. If the capsule is too large, the character might not fit through doorways or be able to slip past other characters.

**Crowded Games Require Smaller Collision Hulls**

If you've played Valve's *Left 4 Dead*, you probably recognize that the collision hulls for the player characters and the zombies don't interact with each other that much, or at least not so that you can tell. That's because there are so many human characters running around that large collision hull circumferences would cause you to get stuck behind your fellow AIs and cause all manner of frustration. Also, if you notice the game environments, there are not a lot of vertical objects like pipes or beams to get stuck on. Make sure you take your game design into careful consideration when designing the collision hulls, and that will influence the design of your game environment.

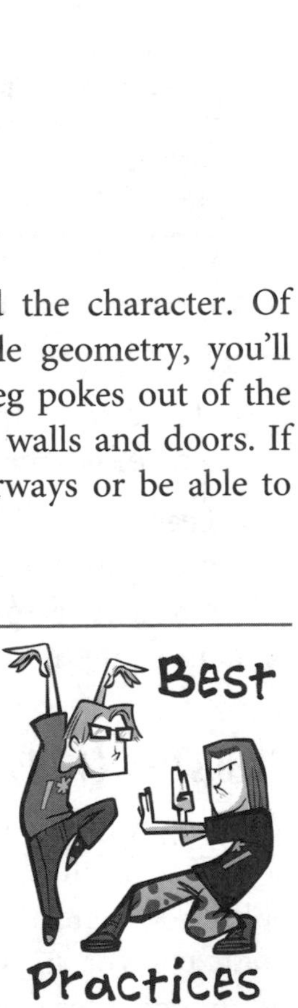


Just in case I wasn't clear, the character hull isn't under physics control. It is a shape that you move around yourself and check the physics system for collisions only when you move it. How you move the hull is completely dependent on your game. You could choose to allow the animation data to help you and minimize foot sliding. Or you could find some flexibility by having a totally analog movement system tied right to the controller and have the animation system queue off the distance you actually moved. You'll still get some feet sliding, but you'll also have some freedom to move exactly how you want. The choice is yours.

I could probably write a whole chapter just on character movement. It's a big subject, and it's not one to be tackled lightly. One bit of advice, if you are just starting out: Don't worry about sliding feet, and certainly don't worry about hovering feet above stairs and ramps, at least at first. Some games solve this problem, but they also tend to have huge budgets. The important bit is to make your game fun first. You can spend any amount of money on cool ankle blending on your main character, but no one will give a damn if your game isn't fun to start with.

**The Movement Gym**

As part of this tuning process, you should create a special map level in your game that looks like an obstacle course. Create every kind of environment and object your character can navigate: stairs, ladders, slopes, ledges, doorways, and windows of every width, a forest of trees or columns, crawlspaces, and anything else you can think of. Every time you make a change to any code or data, including the shape of the character hull, run through the obstacle course and make sure that everything still works. You'll be surprised how easy it is to tweak something and completely break your entire character movement system.

## Special Objects: Stairs, Doorways, and Trees

Some objects need special collision hulls because they interact with characters or objects in ways that don't necessarily have a direct correlation to their visible shape. Good examples of these objects are stairs, doorways, and trees.

Stairs are tough because you really want two completely different collision shapes, depending on the dynamic object interacting with them. Most objects like crates and barrels would use a pretty similar, although simplified, version of the visible geometry. When they fall or roll down stairs, they'll react to the edges and corners and bounce around exactly as you'd expect. Characters, on the other hand, are usually a different story.

When you watch a character ascend or descend a staircase, the head doesn't follow a sharp square wave. Instead, it bobs smoothly with each step, but not too much. This bobbing is even less when the character is moving quickly, such as running. If you put a naive solution in your character/physics model, your character would probably follow the exact shape of the stairway, causing a very unnatural and jerky movement. The easiest solution to this problem is to make two collision hulls for stairs—one for characters and one for every other kind of object. The collision hull for characters should be a simple ramp, which will create a nice movement when characters move up and down stairs. The second collision hull for the stairway will look like stairs, although perhaps a very low polygon version of them for efficiency. Using this second collision hull, normal objects will roll and bounce, instead of sliding. Using two hulls for stairways is a good economical trick to make your game look good for characters and objects.

**Get Character Movement Done Early**

Your character movement really is at the heart of your game, if you think about it. You should therefore make sure that your character movement system is scheduled extremely early in development before the level geometry is built. Then designers will be able to test everything against a completely final character movement system. Wait too long, and the designers will have to guess how high your character can jump or what slopes it can climb. Believe me, you don't want them to guess on stuff like that.

I like running through doorways in games, which is probably why I get fragged a lot. Your artists probably don't know this, but it's easy to create a door that's hard to walk through by making it too small or by having odd door jamb geometry. Doors should be a little bigger than you experience every day. This helps the player have some leeway on either side when walking through. If the character is running all the time, you'll want even more slop in the door size, or the collision hull will get caught on the sides too easily. Rebounding is a possible solution, but if the door is too small, you'll just hit the other side and come to a complete halt.

Vegetation, especially trees, should have collision geometry for the big woody parts like the trunk, but be sure to leave it completely off the foliage. These objects are usually part of the physics simulation as static objects, and as such, they won't move even if they are hit by a huge force. This includes landing a 1969 Buick in the canopy of something as wispy as an ornamental pear tree. Basically, any object stuck in a tree in your game will likely look a little stupid or be annoying.

## Using a Collision System

Any collision system worth its salt should be able to do a few basic things: report collision events, perform raycasts and shapecasts, and handle phantom objects. Collision events have more than just a location and two objects, and this extra information will help you spawn some important game logic changes or game view changes. Raycasting and shapecasting are important for a number of reasons, some of which will become apparent shortly. Phantom volumes that can detect entry and exit events, sometimes called *triggers*, are usually simple enough to be handled with your own code, unless they aren't simple shapes. Finally, a good collision system should support collision groups because not every object needs to be able to collide with every other object.

A collision event should give you at a very minimum the following data: the two objects that collided (or separated), the sum normal of the collision, and the force of the collision. While it might not have occurred to you yet, objects separating are equally as important in computer games as objects colliding. If two objects collide, the game might impart damage to them or cause a sound effect to play. The force of the collision might alter these events. You might want to run some kind of particle-effect animation for forceful collisions, for example.

Some collision systems will give you more data, such as a list of contact points and the collision normal for each of those points. This might be useful for spreading out the particle effect or determining whether one object had sufficient force at one point to penetrate the other object or cause some kind of special damage. I admit that last example is a bit of a reach. I can't think of any game that really goes that far just yet, but someone might figure out a good use for this data.

Raycasting is both a savior and a curse. It stabs a ray from a start location in your game world to any other point and gives you the collision information for anything it intersects along the way. This is really useful for detecting line of sight from an AI creature to your player's character, or perhaps it can be used to probe the surrounding geometry to figure out where to place a third-person camera. The problem with raycasting is that it's only accurate to a point.

I know that was a horrible pun, but I'm actually serious. The ray is infinitely thin, and it can therefore slip through the smallest cracks in your geometry. If you want to know something about the general shape of the local geometry, such as if your character is standing next to an open window, you can make a few stabs with these rays, but they might miss something important, such as bars over the windows. Your raycasts could instruct your character animation system to allow your player to climb right through those bars.

I'll give you one more example. Let's say you want to make a single raycast to determine if an AI creature can see your player. You could easily hide behind the thinnest pole, if you were lucky enough to stand in exactly the right place. The ray could intersect the pole, causing it to believe there was a solid object in the way. A simple hack uses more raycasts from the center of the creature's forehead to various parts of the player's body, like an arm or a foot. Then it's very difficult to hide, but those raycasts are more performance intensive. Everything is a trade-off.

This can get expensive fast, though. Raycasts can be pretty expensive, especially if you want a list of objects sorted by distance, rather than a simple yes or no answer to the "did my ray hit anything" question. Back to the line-of-sight question—a good trick is to cache the results of multiple raycasts over many game loops. If you cast one ray per loop from an AI character, and your game is running at 30Hz, that's 30 rays per second you can cast! Since human beings can only perceive delays lasting longer than about 100ms, or 1/10$^{th}$ of a second—a good general rule—you can even spread these raycasts out farther to once every other frame or perhaps more. This is a game tuning thing, and you'll just have to play with it.

Another option is the shapecast. Think of this as pushing a geometrical shape from a start location in your game world along a straight line to somewhere else. This is more expensive than a single raycast, but it can be much more accurate if you are moving an object in your game and want it to follow geometry closely. A good example of this is a wall-following scheme, where your character closely follows the geometry of a wall, including beams and wall sconces. Once you've validated the move direction, move the character away from the wall a bit and shape cast it back into the wall. If something like a beam or sconce is in the way, the new position of your character will accommodate the annoying geometry. This is exactly how the wall-flattening algorithm worked in *Thief: Deadly Shadows.*

Phantom objects, or triggers, are usually pretty simple to code without a physics or collision system. They are usually simple proximity alarms that fire when some dynamic object gets within range or leaves the active area. You use these things to open automatic doors, or perhaps fire poison darts, or something like that. If you have a physics system, however, you can make these areas into any arbitrary shape, as long as it is convex. This can be really useful for tuning triggers into tight areas in your level. If all your trigger shapes have to be spheres or cubes, you'd have to make enough room for them to stay out of other rooms or hallways nearby.

The idea behind a collision group is simple: It optimizes the entire collision system. As you might expect, a collision system's algorithmic complexity grows with the complexity of the geometry in question. Remove some of this geometry, and you speed up your simulation. This is done by sorting objects into collision groups, essentially lists of objects that can collide with one another and those that can't. For example, objects like a bunch of crates on the first floor can't collide with another group of crates on the second floor if they are physically separated by something like an elevator. Set those objects into different collision groups, and your physics system will thank you for it by running a few milliseconds faster.

## Integrating a Physics SDK

Most programmers aren't going to write their own physics system. They'll most likely grab a physics SDK off the shelf and integrate it into their game. Since I'm probably describing most of the readers of this book, let's discuss this important integration task.

Note that the code presented in this section is only a tiny part of integrating a physics SDK into a complete game. The functionality here won't get you much past bouncing balls on a ground plane, so don't expect more than that. The goal is to show you how a third-party physics system fits into the game architecture presented in this book. It's up to you to extend this class for additional functionality or use a different SDK than the one I chose.

It helps to discuss an interface class for a simple physics system. The interface shown here creates a few objects and manages their movements. If you want to abstract an entire physics system, you'd extend this class quite a lot. Actually, you'd extend this interface and probably create a few new ones. We'll keep it simple for now, just to get you started. After the interface discussion, we'll implement it using the Bullet Physics SDK available from www.bulletphysics.com, which is available for free under the Zlib license.

```
class IGamePhysics
{
public:
  // Initialization and Maintenance of the Physics World
  virtual bool VInitialize()=0;
  virtual void VOnUpdate( float deltaSeconds ) = 0;

  virtual void VSyncVisibleScene() = 0;

  // Initialization of Physics Objects
  virtual void VAddSphere(float radius,
    WeakActorPtr actor, const Mat4x4& initialTransform,
    const std::string& densityStr, const std::string& physicsMaterial)=0;
  virtual void VAddBox(const Vec3& dimensions,
    WeakActorPtr gameActor, const Mat4x4& initialTransform,
    const std::string& densityStr, const std::string& physicsMaterial) = 0;
  virtual void VRemoveActor(ActorId id)=0;

  // Debugging
  virtual void VRenderDiagnostics() = 0;

  // Physics world modifiers
  virtual void VCreateTrigger(WeakActorPtr gameActor, const Vec3 &pos,
    const float dim)=0;
  virtual void VApplyForce(const Vec3 &dir, float newtons, ActorId aid)=0;
  virtual void VApplyTorque(const Vec3 &dir, float newtons, ActorId aid)=0;
  virtual bool VKinematicMove(const Mat4x4 &mat, ActorId aid)=0;
}
```

The first method, `VInitialize()`, initializes the physics system. `VOnUpdate()` starts the physics simulation, which recalculates new positions and orientations for moving objects and queues physics event callbacks like collision or trigger events. The next method, `VSyncVisibleScene()`, is responsible for iterating through all of the physics objects and updating the visible geometry with new locations and orientations.

The methods responsible for adding objects to the physics simulation come next. Each takes parameters that describe the geometry of the object, a weak pointer to the actor, the actor's initial position, and of what density and material the object is made.

The `VRenderDiagnostics()` method is a special routine that draws physics debug data to the renderer. It is a critical tool for you to debug physics problems. The remaining interface methods create different physics objects and attach them to the simulation, such as a sphere. It is through methods like `VCreateSphere()` that you add physical presence to your game objects so they can move just like they would in the real world.

Here's the implementation of that interface using the Bullet Physics SDK. You'll see the term *rigid body* in the code, which is how Bullet refers to solid objects in the physics simulation.

```
class BulletPhysics : public IGamePhysics, GCC_noncopyable
{
  // these are all of the objects that Bullet uses to do its work.
  //  see BulletPhysics::VInitialize() for some more info.
  btDynamicsWorld*                   m_dynamicsWorld;
  btBroadphaseInterface*             m_broadphase;
  btCollisionDispatcher*             m_dispatcher;
  btConstraintSolver*                m_solver;
  btDefaultCollisionConfiguration* m_collisionConfiguration;
  BulletDebugDrawer*                 m_debugDrawer;

  // tables read from the XML
  typedef std::map<std::string, float> DensityTable;
  typedef std::map<std::string, MaterialData> MaterialTable;
  DensityTable m_densityTable;
  MaterialTable m_materialTable;
  void LoadXml();
  float LookupSpecificGravity(const std::string& densityStr);
  MaterialData LookupMaterialData(const std::string& materialStr);

  // keep track of the existing rigid bodies: To check them for updates
  //  to the actors' positions, and to remove them when their lives are over.
```

```
  typedef std::map<ActorId, btRigidBody*> ActorIDToBulletRigidBodyMap;
  ActorIDToBulletRigidBodyMap m_actorIdToRigidBody;
  btRigidBody * FindBulletRigidBody( ActorId id ) const;

  // also keep a map to get the actor id from the btRigidBody*
  typedef std::map<btRigidBody const *, ActorId>BulletRigidBodyToActorIDMap;
  BulletRigidBodyToActorIDMap m_rigidBodyToActorId;
  ActorId FindActorID( btRigidBody const * ) const;

  // Data used to store which collision pair (bodies that are touching) need
  //  Collision events sent.  When a new pair of touching bodies are
  //  detected, they are added to m_previousTickCollisionPairs and an event
  //  is sent. When the pair is no longer detected, they are removed
  //  and another event is sent.
  typedef std::pair< btRigidBody const *, btRigidBody const * > CollisionPair;
  typedef std::set< CollisionPair > CollisionPairs;
  CollisionPairs m_previousTickCollisionPairs;

  // helpers for sending events relating to collision pairs
  void SendCollisionPairAddEvent( btPersistentManifold const * manifold,
     btRigidBody const * body0, btRigidBody const * body1 );
  void SendCollisionPairRemoveEvent( btRigidBody const * body0,
    btRigidBody const * body1 );

  // common functionality used by VAddSphere, VAddBox, etc
  void AddShape(StrongActorPtr pGameActor, btCollisionShape* shape,
    float mass, const std::string& physicsMaterial);

  // helper for cleaning up objects
  void RemoveCollisionObject( btCollisionObject * removeMe );

  // callback from bullet for each physics time step.  set in VInitialize
  static void BulletInternalTickCallback(
    btDynamicsWorld * const world, btScalar const timeStep );

public:
  BulletPhysics() { };
  virtual ~BulletPhysics();

  // Initialization and Maintenance of the Physics World
  virtual bool VInitialize() override;
  virtual void VSyncVisibleScene() override;
  virtual void VOnUpdate( float deltaSeconds ) override;

  // Initialization of Physics Objects
  virtual void VAddSphere(float radius, WeakActorPtr pGameActor,
```

```
    const std::string& densityStr,
    const std::string& physicsMaterial) override;
  virtual void VAddBox(const Vec3& dimensions, WeakActorPtr pGameActor,
    const std::string& densityStr,
    const std::string& physicsMaterial) override;
  virtual void VRemoveActor(ActorId id) override;

  // Debugging
  virtual void VRenderDiagnostics()override;

  // Physics world modifiers
  virtual void VCreateTrigger(WeakActorPtr gameActor, const Vec3 &pos,
    const float dim) override;
  virtual void VApplyForce(const Vec3 &dir, float newtons,
    ActorId aid) override;
  virtual void VApplyTorque(const Vec3 &dir, float newtons,
    ActorId aid) override;
  virtual bool VKinematicMove(const Mat4x4 &mat, ActorId aid) override;
};
```

You'll notice our new class wraps the Bullet data structures for the SDK and a set of components, including a world, a collision dispatcher, a constraint solver, and other components of the Bullet physics system. They are created separately, so the user (that's you!) can easily customize the various behaviors of Bullet.

For our example, we'll use the most common default components that Bullet provides: `btBroadphaseInterface`, `btCollisionDispatcher`, `btConstraintSolver`, and `btDefaultCollisionConfiguration`. I'll describe these components in more detail in a second.

You'll also notice when you look at the code that our physics system uses a physics system-specific vector class, `btvec`, and a transform matrix, `btTransform`. It is quite common for a physics system to have its own data structures or classes for common fundamental mathematics: vectors, matrices, and so on. This can be somewhat annoying, but it is a small price to pay for not having to write your own physics system from scratch.

The next data structures hold the density and materials tables, which are read in from XML during initialization. This is a great way to let your physics materials be data driven. These data structures are accompanied by some helper functions, `LookupSpecificGravity()` and `LookupMaterialData()`, which return data for matching a name with the floating-point density or the restitution and friction, respectively.

Two `std::map` structures come next. The game engine refers to actors by their ID, which needs to be mapped to the core Bullet representation of an actor, the btRigidBody. As these objects are manipulated internally by the physics system, the second map provides an easy way to map events like collisions back on to the actors.

## Components of the Bullet SDK

The most important component managed by Bullet is the btDynamicsWorld object. This is the parent object that manages the other components and provides the main interface point to Bullet's internal physics system. When btDynamicsWorld's constructor is called, we pass in pointers to the other components in order to specify our desired behavior.

One of those components is a subclass of btBroadphaseInterface. This class manages the "broad phase" of collision detection, which is the first test. This phase is fast but inaccurate, using simple axis-aligned bounding boxes as placeholders for actual collision geometry. This implementation uses Bullet's btDbvtBroadphase, which has good default behavior. Once a possible collision has passed this test, it is sent to the "narrow phase," managed by btCollisionDispatcher.

The btCollisionDispatcher handles very precise collision detection between objects in the system. Detecting collisions this way can be very slow, however, so it only tests collisions that have passed the broad phase. Once collisions are detected, this object also dispatches the collision pairs to the world to be handled, hence the name.

Next, let's look at the subclass of btConstraintSolver. In Bullet, a "constraint" is a spring, hinge, or motor—basically anything that restricts an object's freedom of motion. You can have hinge constraints on a door, slider constraints like a piston, or basically anything you can think of. The btSequentialImpulseConstraintSolver manages these. Unfortunately, the scope of our physics system is too narrow to really demonstrate constraints, but trust me, they're cool.

The final initialization component is btDefaultCollisionConfiguration. This object manages some aspects of memory usage for the physics system. We're using the default configuration because we don't want to do anything fancy with memory allocation. A good exercise for you would be to implement your own pooled memory manager and have Bullet use it. If you have a free weekend, of course.

The last object created here is BulletDebugDrawer, which actually handles debugging tasks for your game engine. After all, a physics system can't draw a line with a renderer it knows nothing about, so you get to help it along. The same goes with error reporting. Your game should be able to define how it wants to handle physics system errors or informational messages.

For more information about any of these classes, consult the Bullet documentation or, better yet, read the Bullet source code and examples. Open source is great that way!

## Initialization

Let's take a look at the implementation of the `IGamePhysics` interface, `BulletPhysics`. The `init` function for this implementation class runs through the following tasks:

- Initializes the `btDynamicsWorld` and components' members.
- Creates the internal tick callback, which is used to send collision events.
- Sets debug rendering parameters.

```
bool BulletPhysics::VInitialize()
{
  LoadXml();

  // this controls how Bullet does internal memory management
  m_collisionConfiguration = GCC_NEW( btDefaultCollisionConfiguration();

  // manages how Bullet detects precise collisions between objects
  m_dispatcher =
    GCC_NEW btCollisionDispatcher( m_collisionConfiguration.get() );

  // Bullet uses this to quickly (imprecisely) detect collisions between
  // objects. Once a possible collision passes the broad phase, it will be
  // passed to the slower but more precise narrow-phase collision detection
  // (btCollisionDispatcher).
  m_broadphase = GCC_NEW btDbvtBroadphase();

  // Manages constraints which apply forces to the physics simulation.
  // Used for e.g. springs, motors. We don't use any constraints right
  // now.
  m_solver = GCC_NEW btSequentialImpulseConstraintSolver;

  // This is the main Bullet interface point. Pass in all these components
  //  to customize its behavior.
  m_dynamicsWorld = GCC_NEW
    btDiscreteDynamicsWorld( m_dispatcher, m_broadphase, m_solver,
                             m_collisionConfiguration );

  // also set up the functionality for debug drawing
  m_debugDrawer = GCC_NEW BulletDebugDrawer;

  if(!m_collisionConfiguration || !m_dispatcher || !m_broadphase ||
    !m_solver || !m_dynamicsWorld || !m_debugDrawer)
```

```
  {
    GCC_ERROR("BulletPhysics::VInitialize failed!");
    return false;
  }

  m_dynamicsWorld->setDebugDrawer( m_debugDrawer );

  // and set the internal tick callback to our own method
  //  "BulletInternalTickCallback"
  m_dynamicsWorld->setInternalTickCallback( BulletInternalTickCallback );
  m_dynamicsWorld->setWorldUserInfo( this );

  return true;
}
```

This method looks more complicated than it is. This function loads the XML file holding the materials and density tables, and then it creates the components of the physics system and passes them into the constructor of the physics world. Bullet has a wide array of initialization parameters, as you might expect, so all this code is setting up what components Bullet will use.

One important piece of code in the initialize function turns on a few rendering diagnostics by setting up the `BulletDebugDrawer`, which has the capability of visibly rendering collision shapes, contact points, and contact normals. Depending on what your problem is, you might want other things, but this is a good basic set. If you were really smart, you'd create a little command line debug console in your game and be able to turn on/off different physics debug information at a whim. That's exactly what we had for *Thief: Deadly Shadows*, and it saved our butts on more than one occasion. You don't want to draw them all because there's too much information. In fact, you might even want to filter the information for particular objects, which is something you can do in the debug renderer class you write yourself.

## Shutdown

Shutting down the physics system is pretty easy. Clean up all of the `btRigidBody` objects that you've allocated and added to the physics system and then delete the physics system components.

```
BulletPhysics::~BulletPhysics()
{
  // delete any physics objects which are still in the world

  // iterate backwards because removing the last object doesn't affect the
  //  other objects stored in a vector-type array
```

```
    for ( int i=m_dynamicsWorld->getNumCollisionObjects()-1; i>=0; --i )
    {
      btCollisionObject * const obj
        = m_dynamicsWorld->getCollisionObjectArray()[i];

      RemoveCollisionObject( obj );
    }
    m_actorBodies.clear();

    SAFE_DELETE(m_debugDrawer);
    SAFE_DELETE(m_dynamicsWorld);
    SAFE_DELETE(m_solver);
    SAFE_DELETE(m_broadphase);
    SAFE_DELETE(m_dispatcher);
    SAFE_DELETE(m_collisionConfiguration);
}
```

## Updating the Physics System

Inside `BaseGameLogic::VOnUpdate()`, you'll call two methods of this physics class to update the physics simulation and sync the visible scene to the results of any movement under the control of the physics system.

```
if (m_pPhysics)
{
  m_pPhysics->VOnUpdate(deltaMilliseconds);
  m_pPhysics->VSyncVisibleScene();
}
```

Let's look at the guts of these methods:

```
void BulletPhysics::VOnUpdate( float const deltaSeconds )
{
   // Bullet uses an internal fixed timestep (default 1/60th of a second)
   //  We pass in 4 as a max number of sub steps. Bullet will run the
   //  simulation in increments of the fixed timestep until "deltaSeconds"
   //  amount of time has passed, but will only run a maximum of 4 steps
   //  this way.
   m_dynamicsWorld->stepSimulation( deltaSeconds, 4 );
}
```

Simple, eh? The important thing to know here is that Bullet's `stepSimulation()` function makes sure that even if your game is running slower than 60Hz, the physics system is always ticked at a maximum time delay of 1/60th of a second. This is important because a large time delay can create instability in the simulation. Physics systems generally don't deal well with deep interpenetrations of objects, which happens a lot when objects move a large distance in between simulation steps.

### The Incredible Bouncing Camera

Physics systems are horribly sensitive to frame rate. When I was working on *Thief: Deadly Shadows*, I had to program a simple spring attached to the camera system, which created a smooth movement of the camera under lots of game situations, for example, when the main character jumped off a wall. On my first attempt, I noticed that the camera could easily bounce out of control, as if the spring were getting more and more energy until the camera system crashed. After a little debugging, I noticed the system crashed more easily in areas with a low frame rate. The problem was that my spring system wasn't being ticked at a high enough frame rate, say 60Hz, and the spring calculation would accumulate energy. The solution was pretty easy. I just called the spring calculation in a tight loop, with a delay of no more than 1/60th of a second, and everything was fine.

The trade-off is that ticking your physics simulation multiple times in one game loop is expensive, so try your best to keep enough CPU budget around for everything: rendering, AI, sound decompression, resource streaming, and physics.

Another important note is that Bullet automatically calls an "internal callback" once every internal time step. This callback is specified by the user. For our purposes, let's set it as `BulletInternalTickCallback`. This function handles dispatching collision events.

After the physics system has updated itself, you can grab the results and send them to your game's data structures. Any decent physics system lets you set a user data member of its internal physics objects. Doing this step is critical to getting the new position and orientation data to your game. First, take a look at a small helper class called `ActorMotionState`:

```
struct ActorMotionState : public btMotionState
{
  Mat4x4 m_worldToPositionTransform;

  ActorMotionState( Mat4x4 const & startingTransform )
    : m_worldToPositionTransform( startingTransform ) { }

  // btMotionState interface: Bullet calls these
  virtual void getWorldTransform( btTransform& worldTrans ) const
    { worldTrans = Mat4x4_to_btTransform( m_worldToPositionTransform ); }

  virtual void setWorldTransform( const btTransform& worldTrans )
    { m_worldToPositionTransform = btTransform_to_Mat4x4( worldTrans ); }
};
```

This class makes it easy to convert the transform matrices returned from Bullet to the one used in the game engine, Mat4x4. The conversion functions themselves aren't all that exciting, so you can look them up in the GameCode4 source code. Now you can take a look at how VSyncVisibleScene() works:

```
void BulletPhysics::VSyncVisibleScene()
{
  // check all the existing actor's bodies for changes.
  // If there is a change, send the appropriate event for the game system.
  for ( ActorIDToBulletRigidBodyMap::const_iterator it =
      m_actorBodies.begin();
      it != m_actorBodies.end();
      ++it )
  {
    ActorId const id = it->first;

    // Get the ActorMotionState.  This object is updated by Bullet.
    // It's safe to cast the btMotionState to ActorMotionState,
    //  because all the bodies in m_actorBodies were created through
    //  AddShape()
    ActorMotionState const * const actorMotionState =
      static_cast<ActorMotionState*>
       (it->second->getMotionState());
    GCC_ASSERT( actorMotionState );

    StrongActorPtr pGameActor =
      MakeStrongPtr(g_pApp->m_pGame->VGetActor(id));
    if (pGameActor && actorMotionState)
    {
      shared_ptr<TransformComponent> pTransformComponent =
        MakeStrongPtr(pGameActor->GetComponent<TransformComponent>
        (TransformComponent::g_Name));
      if (pTransformComponent)
      {
        if (pTransformComponent->GetTransform() !=
          actorMotionState->m_worldToPositionTransform)
        {
          // Bullet has moved the actor's physics object.
          // Sync the transform and inform the game an actor has moved
          pTransformComponent->SetTransform(
            actorMotionState->m_worldToPositionTransform);
          IEventManager::Get()->VQueueEvent(
            GCC_NEW EvtData_Move_Actor(id,
              actorMotionState->m_worldToPositionTransform) );
```

```
            }
        }
      }
    }
  }
```

In Bullet, each physics actor has a `btMotionState` that manages how the physics system communicates with the game engine. As Bullet processes the physics world, it updates the position and orientation stored in each `btMotionState` for each actor. The class `ActorMotionState` converts the Bullet's transform matrices to `Mat4x4`.

So once you get to `VSyncVisibleScene`, you loop through all the motion states. Each actor with a motion state should also have a `TransformComponent`, which stores just one data member, a `Mat4x4`, representing an actor's position and orientation. For each motion state that has different data from the `TransformComponent`, the physics system overwrites the actor's transform and sends an event to any game system that cares about the object moving.

You might wonder if this breaks the game view and game logic architecture. It does not, and here's why. When you hand an object over to the physics system, it becomes the de facto authority on the movements of that actor. Other subsystems like the renderer simply need to know that the actor has moved.

## Creating a Simple Physics Object

Bullet represents all nondynamic physical bodies with the `btRigidBody` class. Let's take a look at how you'd create a sphere object, given a radius and a related game actor:

```
void BulletPhysics::VAddSphere(float const radius, WeakActorPtr pGameActor,
 const std::string& densityStr, const std::string& physicsMaterial)
{
  StrongActorPtr pStrongActor = MakeStrongPtr(pGameActor);
  if (!pStrongActor)
    return;

  // create the collision body, which specifies the shape of the object
  btSphereShape * const collisionShape = new btSphereShape( radius );

  // calculate absolute mass from specificGravity
  float specificGravity = LookupSpecificGravity(densityStr);
  const float volume = (4.f / 3.f) * GCC_PI * radius * radius * radius;
  const btScalar mass = volume * specificGravity;

  AddShape(pStrongActor, collisionShape, mass, physicsMaterial);
}
```

```
void BulletPhysics::AddShape(StrongActorPtr pGameActor,
  btCollisionShape* shape, float mass, const std::string& physicsMaterial)
{
  GCC_ASSERT(pGameActor);

  ActorId actorID = pGameActor->GetId();
  GCC_ASSERT(m_actorIdToRigidBody.find( actorID ) ==
    m_actorIdToRigidBody.end() && "Actor with more than one physics body?");

  // lookup the material
  MaterialData material(LookupMaterialData(physicsMaterial));

  // localInertia defines how the object's mass is distributed
  btVector3 localInertia( 0.f, 0.f, 0.f );
  if ( mass > 0.f )
    shape->calculateLocalInertia( mass, localInertia );

  Mat4x4 transform = Mat4x4::g_Identity;
  shared_ptr<TransformComponent> pTransformComponent =
    MakeStrongPtr(pGameActor->GetComponent<TransformComponent>
    (TransformComponent::g_Name));
  GCC_ASSERT(pTransformComponent);
  if (!pTransformComponent)
    // Physics can't work on an actor that doesn't have a TransformComponent!
    return;

  transform = pTransformComponent->GetTransform();

  // set the initial transform of the body from the actor
  ActorMotionState * const myMotionState =
    GCC_NEW ActorMotionState(transform);

  btRigidBody::btRigidBodyConstructionInfo rbInfo(
    mass, myMotionState, shape, localInertia );

  // set up the material properties
  rbInfo.m_restitution = material.m_restitution;
  rbInfo.m_friction    = material.m_friction;

  btRigidBody * const body = new btRigidBody(rbInfo);
  m_dynamicsWorld->addRigidBody( body );

  // add it to the collection to be checked for changes in VSyncVisibleScene
  m_actorIdToRigidBody[actorID] = body;
  m_rigidBodyToActorId[body] = actorID;
}
```

Most physics systems have easy ways to create basic shapes like spheres, boxes, and capsules. In Bullet, spheres are represented by the `btSphereShape` class. Creating an object in the physics system is as simple as creating the object's shape and then passing that shape to a new `btRigidBody`.

You'll notice that we've separated out the creation of the shape in `VAddSphere()` and the creation of the body in `AddShape()`. This is good practice because you can then reuse the code in `AddShape()` when you create other types of objects.

Although we don't do it in this example, physics actors can be described with multiple base shapes, which is a great feature. You could describe a hammer quite accurately with two bodies, each with different sizes, shapes, and properties. In this case, we only have the one sphere shape. The mass is calculated based on the volume and density of the material, so the user can customize whether he wants an object that is dense like iron or light like styrofoam.

Next comes the position, which is sucked right out of the actor's `TransformComponent`. You pass this in to a new `ActorMotionState`, which tracks any actor being moved by the physics engine. You pass this motion state along with other configuration info into the constructor for the new `btRigidBody` and add the `btRigidBody` object to the physics system.

## Creating a Convex Mesh

Spheres are nice, but they aren't all that interesting. You'll probably want to create an object that has a more interesting shape, and one way to do that is to use a convex mesh. This is an object that has an arbitrary shape, with one restriction: it can't have any holes or empty space in between parts of the same object. So a potato is a convex mesh, but a donut is not.

Creating them in Bullet is pretty easy:

```
void BulletPhysics::VAddPointCloud(Vec3 *verts,
                                   int numPoints,
                                   WeakActorPtr *pGameActor,
                                   const std::string densityStr,
                                   const std::string physicsMaterial)
{
  StrongActorPtr pStrongActor = MakeStrongPtr(pGameActor);
  if (!pStrongActor)
    return;

  btConvexHullShape * const shape = new btConvexHullShape();
```

```
  // add the points to the shape one at a time
  for ( int ii=0; ii<numPoints; ++ii )
    shape->addPoint( Vec3_to_btVector3( verts[ii] ) );

  // approximate absolute mass using bounding box
  btVector3 aabbMin(0,0,0), aabbMax(0,0,0);
  shape->getAabb( btTransform::getIdentity(), aabbMin, aabbMax );

  const btVector3 aabbExtents = aabbMax - aabbMin;

  const float volume = aabbExtents.x() * aabbExtents.y() * aabbExtents.z();
  const btScalar mass = volume * specificGravity;

  AddShape( pStrongActor, shape, mass, physicsMaterial );
}
```

Notice we're using our friend `AddShape()` to avoid duplicating work.

What this does is add the vertices of the convex mesh one by one, and Bullet will create a shrink-wrap of polygons that represents the minimum volume object that contains all the points. It will even reorder the polygons from your rendering representation, so it might turn out more efficient for the collision system's algorithms. That's cool!

The `aabbMin` and `aabbMax` are the extents of the shape's axis-aligned bounding box. It isn't a great measure of actual volume by any stretch, but it's better than nothing, and it's a good thing to know how to get these values from Bullet if you need them.

## Creating a Trigger

Another useful object is the trigger. A trigger is something that gives you a callback if objects enter or leave it, which can be very useful for many things. For example, you can spawn some AIs when the player moves through a certain doorway.

Bullet triggers are the same as other objects, except they have no mass, and they don't collide with anything. Not colliding means that objects will move straight through them as if they're not even there. The only thing they need to do is generate an event for the game system when something touches them.

```
void BulletPhysics::VCreateTrigger(WeakActorPtr pGameActor,
  const Vec3 &pos, const float dim)
{
  StrongActorPtr pStrongActor = MakeStrongPtr(pGameActor);
  if (!pStrongActor)
    return;
```

```
    // create the collision body, which specifies the shape of the object
    btBoxShape * const boxShape
      = new btBoxShape( Vec3_to_btVector3( Vec3(dim,dim,dim) ) );

    // triggers are immovable.  0 mass signals this to Bullet.
    btScalar const mass = 0;

    // set the initial position of the body from the actor
    Mat4x4 triggerTrans = Mat4x4::g_Identity;
    triggerTrans.SetPosition( pos );
    ActorMotionState * const myMotionState
      = GCC_NEW ActorMotionState( triggerTrans );

    btRigidBody::btRigidBodyConstructionInfo
      rbInfo( mass, myMotionState, boxShape, btVector3(0,0,0) );
    btRigidBody * const body = new btRigidBody(rbInfo);

    m_dynamicsWorld->addRigidBody( body );

    // a trigger is just a box that doesn't collide with anything.  That's
    //   what "CF_NO_CONTACT_RESPONSE" indicates.
    body->setCollisionFlags(
      body->getCollisionFlags() | btRigidBody::CF_NO_CONTACT_RESPONSE );

    m_actorIdToRigidBody[pStrongActor->GetId()] = body;
    m_rigidBodyToActorId[body] = pStrongActor->GetId();
}
```

Of course, as long as the mesh components are convex, you can create a complicated trigger zone on virtually any shape at all. Zones like that can be quite useful if you want something to fire the trigger when it is in exactly the right place and yet not intruding on other spaces, perhaps behind walls.

## Applying Force and Torque

So far, the only force that would be represented in the physics simulation is gravity, which Bullet sets for you automatically to Earth-gravity, $9.8 m/s^2$, in the direction of negative Y, which is exactly how our game world is set up. Getting anything to move requires the application of a linear force, or a torque. Here are the two methods for doing that:

```
void BulletPhysics::VApplyForce(const Vec3 &dir, float newtons, ActorId aid)
{
  btRigidBody * pRigidBody = FindBulletRigidBody(actorId);
  GCC_ASSERT(pRigidBody);
```

```
  if (!pRidigBody)
    return;
  btVector3 const force( dir.x * newtons,
                         dir.y * newtons,
                         dir.z * newtons );
  body->applyCentralImpulse( force );
}

void BulletPhysics::VApplyTorque(const Vec3 &dir, float magnitude, ActorId aid)
{
  btRigidBody * pRigidBody = FindBulletRigidBody(actorId);
  GCC_ASSERT(pRigidBody);
  if (!pRidigBody)
    return;

  btVector3 const torque( dir.x * magnitude,
                          dir.y * magnitude,
                          dir.z * magnitude );
  body->applyTorqueImpulse( torque );
}
```

These are both applied as instantaneous force impulses, essentially like smacking something with a golf club or hitting a wrench with a hammer. Sometimes you also might like to tell Bullet to stop an actor or move it with a specific velocity.

```
void BulletPhysics::VStopActor(ActorId actorId)
{
  VSetVelocity(actorId, Vec3(0.f, 0.f, 0.f));
}

void BulletPhysics::VSetVelocity(ActorId actorId, const Vec3& vel)
{
  btRigidBody * pRigidBody = FindBulletRigidBody(actorId);
  GCC_ASSERT(pRigidBody);
  if (!pRidigBody)
    return;
  btVector3 btVel = Vec3_to_btVector3(vel);
  pRigidBody->setLinearVelocity(btVel);
}
```

## The Physics Debug Renderer

One other important method of the `IPhysics` interface is `VRenderDiagnostics`:

```
void BulletPhysics::VRenderDiagnostics()
{
```

```
  m_dynamicsWorld->debugDrawWorld();
}
```

This method obviously doesn't do any of the rendering. Part of the `BaseGamePhysics` class is a member that does the heavy lifting. Bullet lets you inherit from one of their base classes and implement your own draw routines.

A physics system can't know or care how you render your visible geometry. It could be a text display, and it wouldn't know any different except for all the extra CPU time it would get! You simply can't debug physics problems looking at raw data, so the easiest debugging technique for physics problems is to draw physics data as visible geometry. Collision hulls show up as wireframes around your objects. Contact points and normals are drawn as lines, and forces can be drawn as lines of different lengths in the direction of the force. Bullet provides an easy way for you to do this. You simply inherit from the `btIDebugDraw` class, overload a few methods, and you'll see everything you need to debug physics:

```
class BulletDebugDrawer : public btIDebugDraw
{
public:
  // btIDebugDraw interface
  virtual void   drawLine(const btVector3& from,
                          const btVector3& to,
                          const btVector3& color);
  virtual void   drawContactPoint(const btVector3& PointOnB,
                                  const btVector3& normalOnB,
                                  btScalar distance,
                                  int lifeTime,
                                  const btVector3& color);
  virtual void   reportErrorWarning(const char* warningString);
  virtual void   draw3dText(const btVector3& location,
                            const char* textString);
  virtual void   setDebugMode(int debugMode);
  virtual int    getDebugMode() const;
};
```

Pretty simple. You just overload the provided methods to render on-screen, and there's your debug info! There's an incredible amount of useful stuff you can do with this data, including histories, averages, and statistics of all sorts. But for this example, you just draw on-screen in the simplest manner possible.

The code for `drawLine()` is in the GameCode4 source code in *Dev\Source\GCC4\Physics\PhysicsDebugDrawer.cpp*.

**Don't Count Memory Used Only for Debugging**

This tip might be a little off the subject, but the last paragraph reminded me of it, so here goes. Whenever you have memory allocated for diagnostic or debugging purposes, make sure that you don't count it in your game's memory budget! You can send the testers into a panic if they see the memory budget skyrocket, and the only reason it did so was that you allocated a couple of megabytes for some debugging routine.

Another simple yet interesting method is `reportErrorWarning`:

```
void BulletDebugDrawer::reportErrorWarning(const char* warningString)
{
  OutputDebugString( warningString );
}
```

The reason you want to send errors and warnings to the debug window is pretty simple; there is a wealth of information that can help you diagnose problems sitting in the error stream. You must trap it yourself and send it somewhere useful, such as the output window in the debugger, a log file, or preferably both. While writing this chapter, I used this very code to figure out that I was sending in incorrect data while trying to create a collision hull for a test object. If that's not good advertising, I don't know what is.

This version merely forwards the error message to the debug output stream. It's a good start, but there's a whole world of things you can do with this information, including popping up a dialog box, recording the data in a database, emailing a message to your physics programmer, and so on.

## Receiving Collision Events

Moving objects around realistically provides a great visual look to your game, but when objects collide and interact, your game gets really interesting. A collision event can be defined as when two objects change their contacts either by colliding or separating. In Bullet, generating these events is a little tricky, but you can do it by using the internal tick callback. This callback is set up in `VInitialize()`, and Bullet calls it once every internal time step. It's a great place to put any work that needs to happen continuously within the physics system.

```
void BulletPhysics::BulletInternalTickCallback(
  btDynamicsWorld * const world, btScalar const timeStep )
{
  GCC_ASSERT( world );
```

```
GCC_ASSERT( world->getWorldUserInfo() );
BulletPhysics * const bulletPhysics =
  static_cast<BulletPhysics*>( world->getWorldUserInfo() );

CollisionPairs currentTickCollisionPairs;

// look at all existing contacts
btDispatcher * const dispatcher = world->getDispatcher();
for ( int manifoldIdx=0;
    manifoldIdx<dispatcher->getNumManifolds(); ++manifoldIdx )
{
  // get the "manifold", or data corresponding to a contact point
  //   between two physics objects
  btPersistentManifold const * const manifold =
    dispatcher->getManifoldByIndexInternal( manifoldIdx );
  GCC_ASSERT( manifold );
  if (!manifold)
    continue;

  // Get the two bodies used in the manifold.  Bullet stores them as void*,
  //   so we must cast them back to btRigidBody*s.  Manipulating void*
  //   pointers is usually a bad idea, but we know this
  //   is safe because we only ever add btRigidBodys to the simulation
  btRigidBody const * const body0 =
    static_cast<btRigidBody const *>(manifold->getBody0());
  btRigidBody const * const body1 =
    static_cast<btRigidBody const *>(manifold->getBody1());

  // always create the pair in a predictable order
  const bool swapped = body0 > body1;

  btRigidBody const * const sortedBodyA = swapped ? body1 : body0;
  btRigidBody const * const sortedBodyB = swapped ? body0 : body1;

  CollisionPair const thisPair =
    std::make_pair( sortedBodyA, sortedBodyB );
  currentTickCollisionPairs.insert( thisPair );

  if ( bulletPhysics->m_previousTickCollisionPairs.find( thisPair ) ==
     bulletPhysics->m_previousTickCollisionPairs.end() )
  {
    // this is a new contact, which wasn't in our list before.
    // send an event to the game.
    bulletPhysics->SendCollisionPairAddEvent( manifold, body0, body1 );
  }
}
```

```
  CollisionPairs removedCollisionPairs;

  // Use the STL set difference function to find collision pairs that
  //  existed during the previous tick but not any more
  std::set_difference( bulletPhysics->m_previousTickCollisionPairs.begin(),
    bulletPhysics->m_previousTickCollisionPairs.end(),
    currentTickCollisionPairs.begin(), currentTickCollisionPairs.end(),
    std::inserter( removedCollisionPairs, removedCollisionPairs.begin() ) );

  for ( CollisionPairs::const_iterator it = removedCollisionPairs.begin(),
      end = removedCollisionPairs.end(); it != end; ++it )
  {
    btRigidBody const * const body0 = it->first;
    btRigidBody const * const body1 = it->second;

    bulletPhysics->SendCollisionPairRemoveEvent( body0, body1 );
  }

  bulletPhysics->m_previousTickCollisionPairs = currentTickCollisionPairs;
}
```

This code does three things: First it collects all of the collision pairs from the physics system. A *collision pair* is any two objects whose physics shapes overlap in the physics world. So a box sitting on the floor is a collision pair, just like an arrow passing through a tent is a collision pair. The code finds all the pairs of objects that are touching each other during this tick.

Next, it compares the collision pairs with the previous tick's collision pairs. If there are any new ones, then an event is sent indicating that the two objects came into contact with one another. If there are any pairs that existed in the previous tick but no longer exist, an event is sent to tell the game system that the objects separated from each other. Both of these events are quite useful in a game.

The great thing about using an event system for handling collision and separation is that the physics system doesn't have to interpret the event and figure out what to do with it. That should be up to the other game subsystems. The sound system, for example, might listen for collisions and play sounds based on the force and type of object. You might have a damage manager that controls things like hit point reduction or spawning a destruction event. Either way, the physics system doesn't have to know or care about all these other things in your game.

The final thing that this internal tick callback does is store the list of collision pairs. This saves them for you so you can compare them during the *next* tick.

## A Final Word on Integrating Physics SDKs

Throughout this chapter, I've described physics in general and one SDK in particular from Bullet (www.bulletphysics.com). There are certainly others:

- **Havok (www.havok.com)** An extremely fully featured commercially licensable physics engine, but expensive and likely out of reach for small game companies or individuals.
- **PhysX (http://www.geforce.com/Hardware/Technologies/physx)** A commercial grade physics engine owned by NVidia and optimized for use with GPU-based physics. A software driver is also available.
- **Newton Game Dynamics (http://physicsengine.com)** A commercially licensable game engine within reach of budget games.
- **Open Dynamics Engine (www.ode.org)** An open source engine that anyone can use for free.
- **Tokamak Physics Engine (www.tokamakphysics.com)** Older versions are free, and newer versions are commercially licensable and within reach of budget games.

The SDKs are developed so rapidly that an exhaustive review of each of them in this book would quickly become stale. I suggest you go to their websites, check out the developer forums and licensing terms, and do a little surfing for others. New ones come out all the time.

Whatever you do, don't think for a minute that you can plug in one of these physics systems in a day or two and completely change the feel of your game. Integrating this technology is much more than making it link and getting collision events sent around. You have to write a lot of code to have your game react to what the physics system does to your dynamic objects and the events it detects. That, my young Feynman, is an amazing amount of work, and you shouldn't underestimate it.

### Super Bouncy Barrels

I think I mentioned before that *Thief: Deadly Shadows* used the Havok Physics SDK. *Thief's* version of Unreal, Warfare 2.5, didn't really have a good dynamics simulation, and Havok seemed to be pretty cool. For the longest time, the correct impulses created by kinematic animation, such as characters bumping into things, were drastically exaggerated. These huge impulses would send huge barrels and crates spinning across the map just by touching them, and while it was funny at first, after a few weeks everyone just wanted things to work. The problem was that the two physics programmers were so busy wiring everything else that they postponed this issue to focus on bigger problems. Until, of course, an Eidos executive saw a barrel launch into orbit during a demo and simply demanded this horrible problem be fixed immediately. There was just too much work and too few people doing it.

## But Wait, There's So Much More

I have to admit to you right now that I changed my major in college from computer science, science option to the business option because I failed a physics test. Granted, I had totally forgotten that the test was going to happen, and had I studied for it, I probably would have stuck with it.

I suggest you have a little more patience than I do. This stuff is devilishly difficult and is probably one of the most challenging areas of game programming. It tricks you by making a 20-minute task to get a sphere bouncing around on a checkerboard floor seem easy and then forces you into six months of solid hell getting elevators to lift objects properly.

Either way, collision, physics, and dynamics are in our games to stay. The challenge is making a great physics simulation in your game translate directly to the fun factor. That's not as easy as you think, but I have faith, and I can't wait to see where this goes.

# Chapter 18

*by David "Rez" Graham*

# An Introduction to Game AI

Artificial intelligence (or simply "AI") is our attempt to make computers think. While we've gotten rather good at mimicking certain behaviors, especially in game development where players are willing to suspend disbelief, we have yet to come anywhere close to truly emulating the human brain. I have no doubt that we will one day achieve this feat and very much hope that I'm alive to see it. I often wonder what will become of these artificial creations of ours and how they will be treated. Think about it—an artificial brain with the capability to think and reason as we do. Will it also be able to feel? Dream? Love? Hate? If so, what does that say about our own consciousness?

Artificial intelligence is a very broad subject that covers a number of real-world applications. Many of them are unrelated to games. A patient may call into a hospital and speak with an automated representative controlled by complex speech recognition software and ask about test results. These tests may have been performed by an expert system written and trained to deal with her particular illness. The fuel she puts into her car on the way to pick up her prescription is a mixture that's refined and processed by complex analysis software. The opponent she curses under her breath in the video game she plays on her handheld in the waiting room is really just a set of simple control states with transitional branches between those states, but it still manages to outmaneuver her troops.

Game AI is in a class all its own. AI programmers have a unique set of problems because they have to make the game "fun" while not overtaxing the CPU. When I go to the AI roundtables at the Game Developer's Conference, I'm continually intrigued by the dichotomy between experienced video game AI developers and developers coming from academia or other fields of AI. Academics tend to want to create as intelligent an agent as possible, whereas game developers often just want the player to have fun. Game AI is not about trying to make something smart; it's about making something *look* smart while still being able to be beaten, though not too easily. That's what makes the game fun, and the key to game AI is fun through illusion, not true intelligence. If you have a military shooter game, who cares whether or not the enemies really work together as a team as long as the player believes they do? As AI programmers, we're the ultimate illusionists. And we have to do it all within a tiny fraction of CPU time.

## AI Techniques

AI programming is one part science and two parts art. I've spent most of my career working on AI for games. Most of the time in AI development is spent trying to balance everything elegantly so it all behaves in a cohesive fashion. For example, at what point does a sim get hungry? When should sims start looking for food? What if they really have to go to the bathroom, or they're about to pass out? Should food take priority, and if so, how hungry does a sim have to be before it will get food and risk passing out? RPGs, shooters, strategy games, and any other game with a significant AI presence will need to balance factors appropriate to that title.

AI often works best when you can exploit emergent behavior. In the *Sims* example, there are a number of competing systems all weighing against each other to make the final decision. There's no `if` statement saying that if hunger is less than 20, start finding food. Instead, the sim weighs its desire for food against its desire for everything else and chooses an action based on all of these things. This gives us the emergent behavior of sim prioritizing food over other things. In the game *F.E.A.R.*, it often appears that the soldiers are working together, but there is absolutely no code to do this directly. It's mostly just the clever use of assets and the emergent behavior of the group from the combined behaviors of the individuals. We'll talk more about these concepts later in this chapter.

### Hard-Coded AI

In the early days of game programming, AI was often completely hard coded. Let's look at a trivial example: that of a light timer. Suppose you want to build a vacation timer for your lights so that they come on at a specified time and turn off at another time. The implementation might look something like this:

```
// Assume this global function sends the status message to actually turn the
// lights on and off.
void SetLightStatus(bool status);

class LightTimer
{
  float m_startLightsOn, m_endLightsOn;  // a float representing the hour
                                           // e.g., 13.5 == 1:30pm
  bool m_lightsOn;

public:
  explicit LightTimer(float startTime, float endTime) :
    m_startLightsOn(startTime),
    m_endLightsOn(endTime),
    m_lightsOn(false)
  {
  }

  // assume this is called periodically
  void UpdateLights(float currentTime)
  {
    // the end time doesn't wrap to the beginning of the day
    if (m_endLightsOn >= m_startLightsOn)
    {
      if (currentTime >= m_startLightsOn && currentTime < m_endLightsOn)
        TurnOnLights();
      else
        TurnOffLights();
    }
    else  // end time wraps to beginning; e.g., start at 7pm and end at 4am
    {
      if (currentTime >= m_startLightsOn || currentTime < m_endLightsOn)
        TurnOnLights();
      else
        TurnOffLights();
    }
  }

private:
  void TurnOnLights(void)
  {
    if (!m_lightsOn)
    {
      SetLightStatus(true);
      m_lightsOn = true;
```

```
    }
  }

  void TurnOffLights(void)
  {
    if (m_lightsOn)
    {
      SetLightStatus(false);
      m_lightsOn = false;
    }
  }

};
```

This class is pretty simple. The update function checks to see if the time passed is within the start and end times and turns on the lights if necessary. It also turns them off when outside of that time zone. Since time is cyclical, the function takes into account whether or not the end time has wrapped around back to the beginning.

This is a good example of hard-coded AI logic. The algorithm is 100% deterministic and will do its job exactly as asked, but is it optimal? Probably not. If your house is worth breaking into, the thief may case the place. If he notices that your lights are always coming on and turning off at exactly the same times over the course of a couple of days, he can be reasonably sure that it's just a timer program. How can we make an AI that outsmarts the thief?

## Randomization

The next step is randomization. The easiest implementation would be to instantiate the `LightTimer` class with random start times and end times and then do it again every 24 hours or so. This would certainly solve the problem of being deterministic, but it falls on the exact opposite side of the spectrum. A thief casing your house will realize something is very odd since most people do have a schedule when they are home.

A better solution is to create a random deviation from the start and end times. This is pretty trivial to implement and gives us what we want: a reasonable pattern without the appearance of being run by a program.

To implement this, two new variables are added: `m_desiredStartTime` and `m_desiredEndTime`. The constructor, `TurnOnLights()`, and `TurnOffLights()` functions all need to change:

```
explicit LightTimer(float startTime, float endTime) :
  m_desiredStartTime(startTime),
  m_desiredEndTime(endTime),
  m_startLightsOn(GetDeviatedTime(m_desiredStartTime)),
  m_endLightsOn(GetDeviatedTime(m_desiredEndTime)),
  m_lightsOn(false)
{
}

void TurnOnLights(void)
{
  if (!m_lightsOn)
  {
    SetLightStatus(true);
    m_lightsOn = true;
    m_startLightsOn = GetDeviatedTime(m_desiredStartTime);
  }
}

void TurnOffLights(void)
{
  if (m_lightsOn)
  {
    SetLightStatus(false);
    m_lightsOn = false;
    m_endLightsOn = GetDeviatedTime(m_desiredEndTime);
  }
}
```

As you can see, m_startLightsOn and m_endLightsOn are set to a deviation from the desired start and end times. The GetDeviatedTime() function is very simple:

```
float GetDeviatedTime(float desiredTime)
{
  float normalizedRand = (float)rand() / (float)RAND_MAX;
  float deviatedTime = desiredTime + (normalizedRand * 2) - 1;

  // wrap deviatedTime if it goes below 0 or above 24
  if (deviatedTime < 0.0f)
    deviatedTime = 24.f - fmod(fabs(deviatedTime), 24.f));
  else if (deviatedTime >= 24.0f)
    deviatedTime = fmod(deviatedTime, 24.0f);
  return deviatedTime;
}
```

This function will return a new time that is within one hour in either direction of the desired time. If you set your start time for 6 p.m. (18.0), then your lights will come on sometime between 5 p.m. and 7 p.m. This is definitely much better, but it's still not perfect. Most people don't arrive home at a random time like this, but rather they tend toward a specific time. We could certainly set a smaller deviation, but a better solution would be to apply a nonlinear curve to the deviation, such as a normal distribution (also known as a *Gaussian distribution,* which generates a bell curve). That would make values closer to the desired number more probable than the ones farther away. This will make the times the light comes on or turns off a bit more believable.

### Weighted Randoms

*Weighted randoms* are a close cousin to the distribution curve. While a distribution curve is essentially an analog device, weighted randoms are more "digital." The idea is that for some number of possible decisions, each of those decisions is given a weight. The weights are all added up, and a random number is generated from zero up to the sum of all weights. This determines which action is chosen. For example, let's say I have a creature that can attack, cast a fire spell, or run away. I decide that 60% of the time I want this creature to attack, 30% of the time it should cast the fire spell, and 10% of the time it should run away. I can decide what to do by generating a single number from 0–99. If the number is less than 60, the creature attacks. If it's greater than or equal to 60 and less than 90, the creature casts the fire spell. Otherwise, the creature runs. This is a very easy way to create potentially complex decisions.

Games have been using this technique with great success for years. In fact, the original *Dragon Warrior* for the NES used this exact method for deciding what its opponents would do. Each monster had a table with a number of behaviors, and a number was generated to choose a slot randomly. Since multiple slots could contain the same entry, this gave the weighted random.

## Finite State Machines

A finite state machine is a construct that can exist in any number of finite states. For example, in the previous *Dragon Warrior* example, each action could actually be thought of as a state within a state machine. The creature's state machine has some number of states that it can possibly exist in, with each state determining a specific behavior. A video game itself is often managed as a state machine, where the title screen is one state, playing the game is another state, the options menu may be a third state, and so on.

### Lua to the Rescue

This type of system is a perfect place for a scripting language like Lua. Features like tables and dynamic typing will save a huge amount of work when compared to attempting the same implementation in C++. Most of the examples you'll see in this chapter are written in Lua using the systems described in Chapter 12, "Scripting with Lua." If you need a refresher, now would be a good time.

Let's take a look at a basic state machine implementation:

```
TeapotStateMachine = class(nil,
{
  _teapot = nil,
  _currentState = nil,
  _brain = nil,
});

function TeapotStateMachine:Destroy()
  self._currentState = nil;
  self._brain = nil;
end

function TeapotStateMachine:SetState(newState)
  if (self._currentState == nil or
     not self._currentState:IsInstance(newState)) then
    self:_InternalSetState(newState);
  end
end

function TeapotStateMachine:ChooseBestState()
  if (self._brain) then
    local newState = self._brain:Think();
    self:SetState(newState);
  end
end

function TeapotStateMachine:Update(deltaMs)
  if (self._currentState) then
    self._currentState:Update(deltaMs);
  end
end

function TeapotStateMachine:_InternalSetState(newState)
  self._currentState = newState:Create({_teapot = self._teapot});
  self._currentState:Init();
end
```

This class is a bit of a spoiler. I wrote the AI system for the *Teapot Wars* sample game you'll see in Chapter 21, "A Game of *Teapot Wars*," while writing this chapter, so it made sense to use it here as an example of a working state machine. The enemies are all teapots, hence the reference to teapots in the code.

Every teapot is given a state machine instance, which contains a back-reference to the teapot itself (the Lua script component), a current state, and a brain. The current state is the state the teapot is in right now. The brain is an object containing a `Think()` function that returns the best state for the teapot.

The `Destroy()` function is self explanatory. The `SetState()` function checks to see if the current state is `nil` or if the new state is not the same as the current state. If either condition is true, it sets the new state. We need to check to make sure the states are different because choosing the same state really means choosing to continue doing what the teapot is doing.

`ChooseBestState()` tells the state machine to find the best state for the given situation. This is the AI update function and is called periodically by a script process. If the teapot has a brain, it calls the `Think()` function on that brain to find the best state and attempts to set it. The `Update()` function runs the current state and is called every frame by another script process. The `_InternalSetState()` function instantiates the state object and calls its `Init()` function.

States are typically self contained with rules defining how the state machine transitions from one state to another. One of the big advantages of state machines is that states can often be reused among many different creatures. The chances are good that you'll get a lot of use out of a patrol or attack state, and with a bit of parameterization you can reuse these states across many different types of creatures.

Let's say we want to make a guard that patrols an area until the player gets within a certain radius and then attacks. If the player gets too far away, he resumes his patrol. If his health gets too low during the fight, he runs away. To do this with a state machine, you need three states: one that defines the pacing behavior, one for the attack behavior, and the third for the running away behavior. These states are connected by transitional logic, as shown in Figure 18.1.

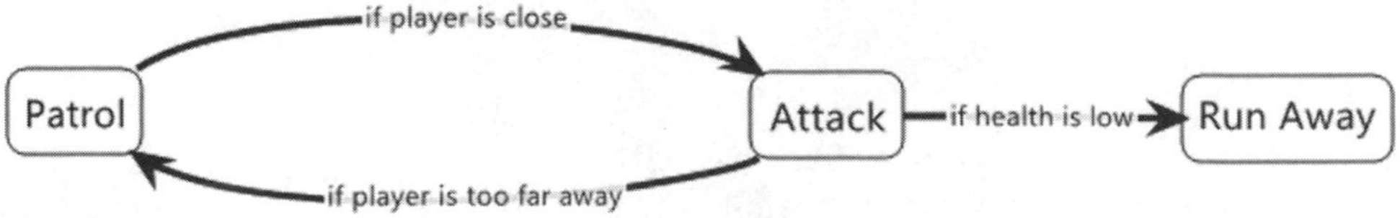


**Figure 18.1**
Guard's state machine.

States can have any number of implementations but are typically implemented with an abstract base class that defines an update function. Each state implements this update function to provide the appropriate behavior for that state. Here's the base state class for teapots:

```
TeapotState = class(nil,
{
  _teapot = nil,
  _teapotMoveSpeed = 7,
});

function TeapotState:Init()
  if (self._teapot == nil) then
    print("Invalid teapot in TeapotState");
    return false;
  end

  return true;
end

function TeapotState:Update(deltaMs)
  error("Calling unimplemented TeapotState.Update() function");
end
```

This defines the interface for all states. The `Init()` function is called in the state machine class when the state is set as the current state, and the `Update()` function is called every frame. Notice how the `Update()` function just throws an error. This is a way of defining a pure virtual function. All subclasses must implement this function, or this error will get thrown. If we didn't define this error, a generic "attempting to call a nil value" error would be thrown instead. At least this error gives us specific information.

**Too Many Script Processes**

You might have noticed that the states above look an awful lot like the `ScriptProcess` interface. It's true that these states could all be made into script processes with their own update tick, but this doesn't scale very well. Remember, crossing the Lua/C++ boundary is expensive, especially if you're doing it every frame. Having 100 script processes all running is much more expensive than having a single script process that loops through 100 states.

The basic logical state machine in Figure 18.1 has been fully implemented for the teapots. I'm not going to go through the implementation for each state because it's more trigonometry than AI, but if you're curious, they all exist in the Game Coding Complete source code at *Dev\Assets\Scripts\TeapotStates.lua*.

The transitional logic is all encapsulated in the teapot brain, which is owned by the state machine. The interface for the teapot brain is as follows:

```
TeapotBrain = class(nil,
{
  _teapot = nil,
});

function TeapotBrain:Init()
  return true;
end

function TeapotBrain:Think()
  error("Calling unimplemented base class version of TeapotBrain.Think()");
end
```

This interface is extremely simple because it just defines an `Init()` function and a `Think()` function. `Init()` gives the brain a chance to do some initialization. `Think()` is called when a new decision needs to be made. It goes through whatever decision-making processes it uses and returns the most appropriate state. Here's a hard-coded brain that implements the transitional logic in Figure 18.1:

```
HardCodedBrain = class(TeapotBrain,
{
  --
});

function HardCodedBrain:Think()
  local playerPos = Vec3:Create(g_actorMgr:GetPlayer():GetPos());
  local pos = Vec3:Create(self._teapot:GetPos());
  local diff = playerPos - pos;

  -- player close
  if (diff:Length() < 20) then
    -- hit points low, run
    if (self._teapot.hitPoints <= 1) then
       return RunAwayState;
    -- hit points not low, attack
    else
      return AttackState;
    end

  -- player not close, resume patrol
```

```
  else
    return PatrolState;
  end
end
```

This function subtracts the player's position from the teapot's position. If the length of that vector is less than 20, the player is considered "close." The teapot then checks its hit points. If it only has one hit point, it runs away; otherwise, it attacks. If the player is not close, the teapot patrols.

We can take this a step further by making the transitional logic generic as well. Let's say we have a land mine that sits idle until the player gets close and then explodes. We can define these states, as shown in Figure 18.2.

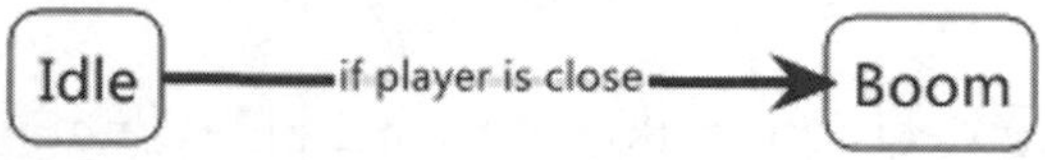


**Figure 18.2**
Mine's state machine.

Notice how the logical condition to switch states is the same here; both the patrol state of the guard and this idle state check to see if the player is close. The definition of "close" is likely different in each case, but the logic is the same.

Each of these pieces of transitional logic can be encapsulated into generic functions, and each state can have a list of one or more of these functions paired with a target state. Each tick, the state iterates through the list of transitions, and if any transition returns `true`, the state it is paired with becomes the new state. Each transition can be parameterized with whatever is appropriate for that transition. For example, the distance check for the mine's idle and the guard's patrol states can each be set to separate distances. You can even create "and" and "or" transitions that are parameterized with two other transitions, allowing you to set up rather complex logical chains. This is exactly what I built for *Drawn to Life: The Next Chapter.*

The basic concept of state machines is rather simple, but they can grow to be extremely complex. The typical monster in *Drawn to Life* had around 15–20 states, each with 2–3 transitions. Most of these states were shared with other enemies, with one or perhaps two unique states that helped define that particular creature. The iteration time on the enemies was very quick, and most states had fewer than 100 lines of code. Once the core system was in place, I could crank out the initial implementation of an enemy in about a day.

While the states in a state machine are meant to implement specific behaviors, the bulk of decision making tends to come from the transitional logic between states.

An AI controlled character will be in a particular state and need to decide between some number of target states he can switch to. Simple AI characters are purely reactionary; for example, they stay in a state until some specific condition is met such as the player getting too close. Platformer games tend to use reactive AI. The previous examples were reactive AI as well. Other AIs are active, meaning they will constantly seek the best possible action to maximize their happiness. A sim from *The Sims* or an AI opponent in an RTS are examples of active AIs.

There are many different techniques available when deciding which state to transition to or which action to run. The hard-coded approach you saw in the previous section is perfectly fine for simple and somewhat deterministic games. Let's briefly look at a few other techniques for decision making.

## Decision Trees

A decision tree is a simple way of representing decision making. Each nonleaf node in the tree is called a *decision node,* and it represents a single decision with a binary yes/no answer. Each leaf node is called an *action node,* and it represents an action. In our case, this action is a new state.

Decision nodes have a `true` node and a `false` node, which can be either another decision node or an action node. A decision is made by starting at the root node and recursively walking down the tree until an action node is reached. Figure 18.3 shows

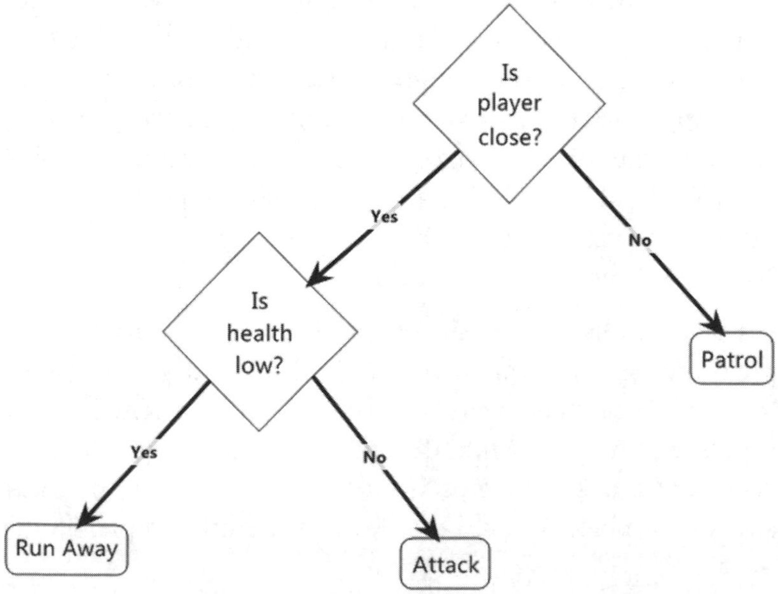


**Figure 18.3**
Decision tree for guard.

an example of a decision tree that could be used to replace the transitional logic for the patrolling guard above.

The diamonds represent decision nodes, while the rounded rectangles represent action nodes. This simple decision tree can be applied each time a decision needs to be made by the guard. Decision trees can easily be shared, and individual nodes can be shared across different trees. Decision trees are often built from XML data definitions, which are in turn are generated from visual tools over which designers have control. The programmer writes different decision nodes and action nodes, while the designer uses them to build the desired behavior.

Writing a simple decision tree system is relatively simple. Let's start with a definition of decision nodes:

```
DecisionNode = class(nil,
{
  _brain = nil,
  _trueNode = nil,
  _falseNode = nil,
});

function DecisionNode:Decide()
  error("Calling unimplemented function DecisionNode.Decide()");
  return nil;
end

function DecisionNode:SetTrueNode(node)
  self._trueNode = node;
end

function DecisionNode:SetFalseNode(node)
  self._falseNode = node;
end
```

A decision node has a back reference to the brain, the `true` node, and the `false` node. Since this is an abstract base class, the `Decide()` function is defined with the same error pattern as above. It will eventually return the action to perform, which it does by recursively calling the appropriate child. This class also defines functions for adding a `true` node and `false` node.

Here is the action node definition:

```
ActionNode = class(DecisionNode,
{
  _action = nil;
});
```

```
function ActionNode:Decide()
  return self._action;
end

function ActionNode:SetTrueNode(node)
  error("Action nodes cannot have children");
end

function ActionNode:SetFalseNode(node)
  error("Action nodes cannot have children");
end
```

This class inherits from `DecisionNode` and implements the `Decide()` function to simply return the action. This ends the recursive chain and causes the action to be sent all the way back up to the initial `Decide()` call. Note that `SetTrueNode()` and `SetFalseNode()` are redefined to kick out errors. Action nodes are leaf nodes by definition, so attempting to add a child is an error.

Let's take a look at a couple of decision node implementations so you can get a feel for how these nodes interact:

```
IsObjectCloseNode = class(DecisionNode,
{
  _testObjId = nil,
  _closeDistance = 25,  -- default definition for what "close" means
});

function IsObjectCloseNode:Decide()
  if (self._testObjId) then
    local actor = g_actorMgr:GetActorById(self._testObjId);
    if (actor) then
      local actorPos = Vec3:Create(actor:GetPos());
      local teapotPos = Vec3:Create(self._teapot:GetPos());
      local diff = actorPos - teapotPos;
      if (diff:Length() <= self._closeDistance) then
        return self._trueNode:Decide();
      end
    end
  end

  return self._falseNode:Decide();
end

IsHealthLowNode = class(DecisionNode,
{
  _lowValuePercentage = 0.34,  - - default definition of what "low" means
});
```

```
function IsHealthLowNode:Decide()
  local hitPointPercentageLeft =
    self._teapot.hitPoints / self._teapot.maxHitPoints;
  if (hitPointPercentageLeft <= self._lowValuePercentage) then
    return self._trueNode:Decide();
  else
    return self._falseNode:Decide();
  end
end
```

The first node is the `IsObjectCloseNode` class, and it checks to see if the object ID stored in `_testObjId` is "close," defined by the `_closeDistance` variable. This replaces the hard-coded check to see if the player is close with a more generic version. This is a great example of how you can parameterize nodes to make them more reusable. For example, this node could be used to detect how close a health pack is with no modifications.

The `Decide()` function is pretty straightforward and very similar to the hard-coded block you saw earlier. If the object is valid and is found to be within the appropriate distance, the `true` node's `Decide()` function is called. Otherwise, the `false` node's `Decide()` function is called. This steps down a level in the tree and starts the process again. `IsHealthLowNode` works in the same way. The only difference is the actual logic.

**Use Percentages Instead of Absolutes**

Notice the usage of the `_lowValuePercentage` variable. You might be wondering why I'm using a percentage here instead of an absolute value. Using a percentage allows the max hit points for the teapot to change without having to update this logic at all. It will always consider anything less than 34% of the max hit points to be "low." If I used an absolute value, I'd have to update it whenever the max hit points of the teapot changed.

The only thing left is the brain itself:

```
DecisionTreeBrain = class(TeapotBrain,
{
  _root = nil,
});

function DecisionTreeBrain:Init()
  self:_BuildDecisionTree();
  return true;
end
```

```
function DecisionTreeBrain:Think()
  return self._root:Decide();
end
```

This class implements the TeapotBrain class. The Init() function calls a private _BuildDecisionTree() function. My version of this function (which you can see in the GameCode4 source code at *Dev\Assets\Scripts\DecisionTreeBain.lua*) manually creates the tree you saw in Figure 18.3. In a real game, this would load an XML resource and build the tree from that. You've seen XML used quite a bit in this book, and there are plenty of examples all over the place in the actor system and the game editor you'll see in Chapter 22, "A Simple Game Editor in C#." I leave this as an exercise for you.

The Think() function of DecisionTreeBrain simply calls the root nodes Decide() function and returns the results. This function starts the chain of recursion to find the appropriate state to be in.

Decision trees are extremely useful. The example here is trivial, but it could easily be expanded into dozens or even hundreds of nodes. The tree is still relatively efficient, since whole chunks of the decision-making process are culled with each decision. Assuming a perfectly balanced tree, each decision will cut the possible decisions in half.

Even if you're processing hundreds of nodes, the nature of the tree structure means you can easily make the decision across multiple frames. At each step, you check to see how much time has passed. If the decision is taking too long, you simply save the current node and return. The next time, the decision-making process can be picked up at the last node. Just be careful with this; the decisions already made may no longer be valid. As long as the decision doesn't take more than a couple of frames, this is rarely a problem. You just have to validate the final result at the end. Attempting to grab a pickup may not be the right decision if the pickup is no longer there.

The decision tree shown here is a binary decision tree where each decision node results in a yes or no answer that determines where to go next. It's perfectly valid to have nonbinary decision trees. You could have a node with multiple children based on a range of values. For example, the IsHealthLowNode class could be changed into a ProcessHealthNode class that has three different children. If their health were low, the AI could find health or run away. If their health were especially high, they could be much more aggressive. If their health were in the middle somewhere, they could act normally.

## Fuzzy Logic

This system works fairly well, but it's not exactly realistic. The value of "close" is an absolute value, and humans don't think in absolutes like that. For example, let's say I see Mike on the GDC showroom floor and want to say hello. If I say hello from too far away, he won't hear me through the hustle and bustle of the conference, so I need to walk up to him until I am reasonably "close" before saying anything. What is "close"? In this case, let's say it's about 30 feet. In the system above, I would walk up to exactly 30 feet away and say hello. If multiple people were all trying to say hello to Mike, we would all form a perfect 30-foot radius circle around him, which would look a bit creepy. What we really need is a way to model approximate values, or *fuzzy values*.

The basic idea of fuzzy logic is that objects can belong to multiple fuzzy sets by different amounts. For example, let's say the player is behind some cover. My enemy AI needs to know how to behave in this situation. If the player is fully behind cover, the enemy will flush him out with a grenade. If the player is not behind cover at all, the enemy will fire with his assault rifle. What happens if the player is partly behind cover? What we really have here are two possible sets the player can belong to—one where he is behind cover and one where he is not behind cover. The player is able to belong to both sets by some degree. The amount of belonging is typically represented by a number between zero and one. In this example, the player might be behind cover by 0.6 and exposed by 0.4.

Likewise, when I'm walking up to Mike, I am becoming more a part of the close set and less a part of the far set. When I get to 30 feet away, I might belong to the close set by 0.5 and the far set by 0.5. Notice how the degrees of membership are adding up to 1. It's common in fuzzy logic to have degrees of membership for mutually exclusive sets add up to 1.

In order to assign degrees of membership within fuzzy sets, some translation needs to occur. If I am exactly 35.2 feet away from Mike, what is my degree of membership in the close and far fuzzy sets? In order to find this out, we need to translate my absolute position into these degrees of membership. This is called *fuzzification*. In order to process the data to make a decision, we need to go in reverse, which is called *defuzzification*.

The simplest way to fuzzify these types of values is to provide a simple cutoff. Let's use 20 feet and 40 feet for our cutoff values. If I am less than 20 feet away, I completely belong to the close set. If I'm more than 40 feet away, I belong completely to the far set. In the case of anything in between, I will belong to both sets by a degree of membership equal to a linearly interpolated value between those cutoffs. This value can be expressed as follows:

```
degree of membership = (inputValue - lowCutoff) / (highCutoff - lowCutoff)
```

This formula will give you the degree of membership in the close set. Subtract this number from 1 to get the degree of membership in the far set.

There are other fuzzification methods, of course. You could apply a logarithmic curve or Gaussian curve (aka bell curve). Nothing says that your degree of membership values need to add up to 1, although it is typically best that they do. It makes the math a bit easier, as you'll see below.

Defuzzification is a bit trickier. There is rarely a direct mapping from the degree of membership to a useful value. For example, if the player is behind cover by 0.6 and exposed by 0.4, what is the correct behavior? We could just generate a random number and choose to throw the grenade 60% of the time. This works for extremely small fuzzy sets, but what happens when we're trying to take into account multiple sets? For example, let's say we're using fuzzy logic to model the personality. The AI belongs to the aggressive set by 0.4 and the cautious set by 0.6. If the AI is cautious and the player is behind cover, toss a grenade. Is this AI cautious? Do we just randomly decide if this AI is cautious for this particular decision?

One way of solving this problem is to use the highest degree of membership. In this cause, the AI would be considered cautious because he belongs to that set more than the opposing aggressive set. He would also consider the player to be within cover. This is certainly simple, but it just masks the same problems we had in the first place with the AI being too predictable.

If the result you're looking for is a number, a blended approach becomes very useful. How long the AI will take aim can be directly determined by its degree of membership in the cautious set as well as its degree of membership in the behind cover set. You could blend these two together, normalize the results, and then apply that as a multiplier to the maximum time an AI will take to aim. This approach allows the AI to easily take into account both its own cautious nature and how deep within cover the player is.

For Boolean results, a cutoff is typically determined. If you belong to a set by more than the cutoff value, the Boolean value is `true`. Otherwise, it is `false`.

The real power of fuzzy logic comes from being able to write logical sentences. You use logical sentences every day, such as this one:

```
if (distance < 20 and health > 1) then Attack() end
```

This is a simple logical sentence with an AND. You could also make OR or even NOT one of the values. You can apply these same logical operators to fuzzy logic systems:

```
IF player is close AND I am healthy THEN Attack END
```

It works exactly the same way, but how do you apply this logic to fuzzy sets? The magic comes from the attack action, which in itself is a fuzzy set. The AI can belong to this action set as well as others.

```
AttackSet = player is close AND I am healthy
RunSet = player is close AND I am hurt
```

So what are the degrees of membership for the attack set and run set? As it turns out, you need to redefine AND, OR, and NOT for fuzzy sets.

Given the following sentence:

```
R = A AND B
```

The traditional logical AND is defined by the truth table shown in Table 18.1.

**Table 18.1 Truth Table for AND**

| A | B | A AND B |
|---|---|---|
| 0 | 0 | 0 |
| 0 | 1 | 0 |
| 1 | 0 | 0 |
| 1 | 1 | 1 |

You need to maintain this truth table for fuzzy sets as well. The most common definition of AND for fuzzy sets turns out to be:

```
R = min(A, B)
```

In this case, A and B are the degrees of membership in those sets. Assuming that the degree of membership in both bases is absolute (for example, 1 or 0), then this truth table still holds true. With mixed values, the truth of the statement A AND B is essentially equal to the least true member.

The reverse can be said about OR, which has the truth table shown in Table 18.2.

**Table 18.2 Truth Table for OR**

| A | B | A OR B |
|---|---|---|
| 0 | 0 | 0 |
| 0 | 1 | 1 |
| 1 | 0 | 1 |
| 1 | 1 | 1 |

In this case, the degree of truthfulness of the statement `A OR B` is equal to the most true member. Thus, we can define `OR` as follows:

```
R = max(A, B)
```

This same exercise can be continued to define results for `NOT`, `XOR`, and other logical operator you want.

Let's take a step back and reconsider the attack and run fuzzy sets. Let's say the player belongs to the close set by 0.6 and the far set by 0.4. Let's also say that the AI guard belongs to the healthy set by 0.3 and the hurt set by 0.7. In this case, the attack set will be 0.3, and the run set will be 0.6. This could be translated into a behavior by mixing the results:

```
attackPercentage = 0.3 / (0.3 + 0.6)
runPercentage = 0.6 / (0.3 + 0.6)
```

You could use these percentages to find the chance that the AI will run versus staying and fighting, but a much cooler use of this would be to set up his behavior so that he spends about 66.7% of the time running and the other 33.3% of the time shooting at the player. In other words, he does *both* behaviors at the same time, just in different degrees. The overall behavior you'd see is that as the player approached and wounded the enemy, he would fall back and continue firing. Eventually, his health would drop low enough that he wouldn't belong to the healthy fuzzy set at all, and he would just run without attacking.

Hopefully, this example shows you a little bit of the power of fuzzy logic. You can take these techniques further by applying fuzzy action sets to all sorts of things to create extremely complex behavior with just a handful of actions.

## Utility Theory

Stuart Russell and Peter Norvig provide an excellent definition for utility theory in their book *Artificial Intelligence: A Modern Approach*: "Utility theory says that every state has a degree of usefulness, or utility, to an agent and that the agent will prefer states with higher utility."

With this definition, you can see that every possible state has a utility value assigned to it, which is calculated every time a decision needs to be made and is based on how much happier the agent will be in the new state compared to its current state. Calculating the utility value is done by taking the current world state and seeing what the anticipated world state is after performing some action. The delta in happiness between those two states is the utility of that action. The action with the highest utility is then chosen.

Determining how useful a particular state is or how happy the agent will be in that state depends on the game. In *The Sims,* the ideal state is calculated using motives like hunger, energy, fun, social, and so on. In games like *Chess,* an analysis of the board is performed, which could include material, pawn structure, piece positioning, king safety, and so on. A strategy game might take any number of things into account, like the safety of the workers, troop strength, and research. Coming up with a strong utility function is one of the most important steps.

**My Favorite Topic**

I must admit that the utility theory is one of my favorite topics in AI. That's probably why I work on *Sims* games these days. Whenever I go to the Game Developer's Conference and meet up with colleagues, there are certain architectural cliques that people form. Some people love decision trees and refuse to believe that anything else is better. Others, like me, believe that utility theory is the way to go. The reality is that none of these sides are wrong; it's just a matter of preference.

The basic algorithm for determining an action is as follows (in pseudocode):

```
function GetBestAction()
  bestUtility = 0
  bestAction = none
  for action in currentWorldState.GetPossibleActions()
    tempWorldState = currentWorldState
    tempWorldState.ApplyAction(action)
    utility = tempWorldState.Utility()
    if utility > bestUtility
      bestAction = action
      bestUtility = utility
  return bestAction
```

This algorithm loops through all possible actions given the current world state. The world state is then copied and an action applied to it. The utility of the new state is then compared to the best utility value found so far. The action that produces the highest amount of utility is chosen.

Updating a model of the world may seem like overkill, but it's actually an important step. For example, an action to make and eat dinner in *The Sims* could take an hour or so in sim time. During that time, the sim's other motives are decaying, so the sim needs to take that into account. Furthermore, the sim could choose between two different meals, one that takes longer but tastes better than the other. Utility is often calculated by utility-over-time.

The world model doesn't have to be (and really shouldn't be) a complete one. For *The Sims,* a sim typically only cares what an action will do for that sim and not what effect it may have on others. This means that the utility is defined as a function of the delta between the sim's current state and the sim's state after the action is performed. Every game determines this state differently.

As an example, let's consider a turn-based RPG, similar to *Final Fantasy* or the old *Dragon Warrior* games. These were fairly popular on the NES and SNES. The player chooses an action to attack, run away, or heal. This has an effect, followed by the monster being able to do the same. Attacking does some random amount of damage, healing heals a random amount of damage and costs a magic point, while running away gives you a 50% chance to flee. In this model, you might have the following function to decide what to do:

```
function Teapot:Decide(opponent)
  local bestUtility = 0;
  local bestAction = nil;

  for i, action in ipairs(self._actions) do
    -- build the world state
    local tempWorldState = WorldState:Create();
    tempWorldState:Build(self, opponent);

    -- apply the action
    tempWorldState:ApplyAction(action, self, opponent);

    -- grab the utility
    local utility = tempWorldState:GetUtility();
    if (utility > bestUtility) then
      bestUtility = utility;
      bestAction = action;
    end
```

```
  end

  return bestAction;
end
```

In this case, the world state is built every loop. This is not entirely uncommon in situations where the world state is small and keeping track of it isn't necessary. The `Build()` function's job is to grab what it needs from the world (in this case, the teapot and the opponent) so the AI function can do its thing. Here's a possible `Build()` function:

```
function WorldState:Build(teapot, opponent)
  self.opponentHp = opponent:GetHp();
  self.opponentMp = opponent:GetMp();
  self.survivalChance =
    self:_CalculateSurvivalChance(teapot:GetHp(), opponent);
  self.killChance =
    1 - self:_CalculateSurvivalChance(opponent:GetHp(), teapot);
end

function WorldState:_CalculateSurvivalChance(defenderHp, attacker)
  if (defenderHp > attacker:GetMaxDamage()) then
    return 1;
  elseif (defenderHp <= attacker:GetMinDamage()) then
    return 0;
  else
    local range = attacker:GetMaxDamage() - attacker:GetMinDamage();
    local chance = (defenderHp - attacker:GetMinDamage()) / range;
    return chance;
  end
end
```

The `Build()` function retrieves the hit points of the two combatants. It also calculates the survival chance of the teapot and the kill chance for the opponent (player). The survival chance is the chance that the character can survive another round. The kill chance is the reverse of that.

Finally, with the world state built, you can apply an action and get the utility from it. Applying an action causes the AI to apply the average effect; in other words, the AI considers that it will be healed the average amount of hit points or will inflict the average amount of damage. A state in which the teapot attempts to run away gives the agent a 50% survival chance, which makes it look pretty good as a last resort when the hit points are low. Here's a sample utility function applied to a given world state:

```
function WorldState:GetUtility()
  local lifeScore = 100 * self.survivalChance;
  local attackScore = 100 - self.opponentHp;
  attackScore = attackScore + (attackScore * self.killChance);
  return lifeScore + attackScore;
end
```

The first line of this function considers the agent's chance for life. It multiplies 100 (the max hit points) by the survival chance of the agent. The attack score considers the agent's desire to kill the player. It is equal to the amount of damage done (max hit points minus current hit points). The attack score is further modified by the kill chance. The kill chance is the percentage chance that another attack on the following turn will result in the player's death. If there is no chance, it has no effect on the score. If there is a 100% chance, it will double the attack score. Anything in between is possible. Finally, the life score and attack score are added together and returned. Each line of code in this utility function directly affects the behavior and personality of this agent.

- The agent prefers states in which it is alive and has a good chance at remaining so.
- The agent prefers states in which the player is more injured.
- The agent greatly prefers states in which the player is near death.

This is by far the simplest utility-based system I've ever written, but it does a great job showing how all the pieces fit together. In order to test this out during the writing of this chapter, I created a mini combat RPG game. It's not part of the *Teapot Wars* code like everything else in this chapter has been; it's a stand-alone console program that runs a single Lua file. I've included it with the GameCode4 source code in case you want to play around with it. You can find it at *\Dev\Extra\UtilityDemo*. The *utility.lua* file contains all the code. Just run the *UtilityDemo.exe* program to play the game.

**Agents Can Complain About Work Just Like Us**

*Rat Race* used a system called *UtilEcon*, which stood for *Utility Economy*. The system was designed to be a goal-oriented system where agents would wander around the world and trade utility with each other through speech. We had a speech system tied into this, so there were different types of utility for different types of conversations. That way you'd tend to hear the gossipy people in the office say the gossip lines, while the workaholics would say the work lines. The system worked really well and added quite a bit to the atmosphere. "Oh look, there's Joy complaining again."

## Goal-Oriented Action Planning

Utility theory is a great technique for deciding what an agent wants to do, but it's not as good for deciding how an agent should perform this action. Goal-Oriented Action Planning, or GOAP, is a popular methodology that helps solve this particular problem. It centers on the idea of goals, which are desirable world states that the agent wants to achieve. It achieves these states through actions, much like you saw previously. An example of a goal might be to kill the player. An action that satisfies this goal could be attacking the player. An agent often has multiple goals, although only one is typically active at any given time. The AI update is then split into two stages: The first selects the most relevant goal, and the second attempts to solve that goal by choosing an action or sequence of actions.

This first step of choosing a goal can be elegantly solved by applying utility theory, decision trees, or any other method you've seen thus far in this chapter. The second part is often a bit trickier. For example, let's say you've decided that the goal you want to solve is eating a meal. Unfortunately, you don't have any food, so you need to formulate a plan, or a series of actions, that will get you to the goal state of eating food. This could involve finding your car keys, driving to the store, purchasing food, and then returning to cook said food.

The idea behind GOAP is that each action has a set of conditions it can satisfy, as well as a set of preconditions that must be true in order to be satisfied. For example, eating food will satisfy my goal of eating, but it has the precondition of requiring cooked food. The action of cooking food satisfies this goal, but it has the precondition of having a raw food object. When a final action is chosen, the algorithm walks backward from the goal action through the preconditions, searching for actions that will solve each one. Finally, at the end of the search, you're left with an action sequence that can be executed to achieve the original goal. GOAP is extremely flexible. As long as a sequence of actions exists to solve a goal, the agent will find a way.

One problem with GOAP (and most forms of advanced AI) is world representation. This is very much the same problem we had when talking about utility theory. How can you represent the world in a compact manner? Goals are often expressed as desirable world states. I desire a world state in which my hunger level is fully satisfied. The teapot agent desires a world state in which the player is dead. This world state then needs to be generated, complete with preconditions and effects.

The other problem is how to search through the action space to find the desirable world state. Fortunately, there are a number of search algorithms that can help you. The best one I've heard was Jeff Orkin's talk at the Game Developer's Conference in 2006, where he proposed using the A* algorithm, a common search algorithm used in pathfinding, to search through the action space for the sequence of actions that would satisfy the world state. Considering that we're literally looking for a "path" through a graph of actions, this one makes total sense.

A full implementation of GOAP is beyond the scope of this book, but there are a number of texts written on the subject. The best I've read is in *AI Game Programming Wisdom 2*. The article is called "Applying Goal-Oriented Action Planning to Games," written by Jeff Orkin. I highly recommend you check it out.

## PathFinding

I get a lot of questions about pathfinding with regards to AI. I find this a little strange since I honestly don't consider pathfinding to be an AI problem. Pathfinding is really just an optimized search algorithm across a data structure, typically a graph. The same algorithm can apply to many classifications of problems, including generating an action plan from a GOAP model. On *The Sims*, pathfinding is handled by a completely different team called MoTech (Motion Technology; they handle things like animation programming), while the sim behavior AI is handled by me on the gameplay team. This is fairly common in most companies where I've worked: A systems engineer handles a lot of the pathing, while someone on the gameplay team handles the behaviors.

The problem of finding a valid path through terrain is one of simplification. The world itself is simplified into a graph of nodes (or a mesh with edges; either way, the principle is the same) that is then traversed with a search algorithm to find a good path between two nodes in that graph. This graph or mesh represents the walkable terrain. This is the technique we used at Super-Ego Games in *Rat Race* (see Figure 18.4).

So how do you go about creating such a system? Let's start with the nodes. A node describes a point in space that the agent must reach. Nodes are connected by arcs, which are essentially straight lines. For most pathing graphs, an agent may freely move between any two nodes directly connected by an arc. Thus, in order to move from one node to its neighboring node, all you need to do is rotate to face the correct direction and move in a straight line as described earlier in this chapter.

There's a slight problem with this method. Since the nodes are all connected by straight lines, it's possible that the agent's motion will look a bit robotic, especially if the graph is laid out like a grid. If the agent wanted to move onto a perpendicular arc, it would walk to the node, make a 90-degree turn, and then walk to the next point. This doesn't look natural at all. There are two things you can do to combat this problem. The first is to ensure that the nodes are not placed in an obvious

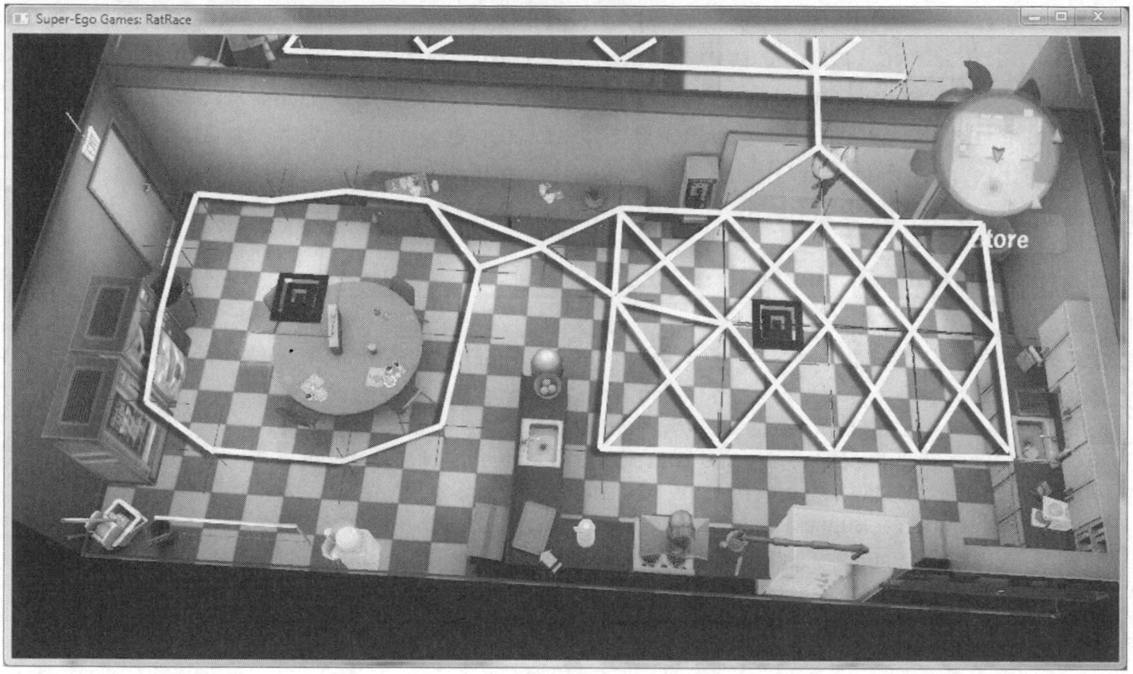


**Figure 18.4**
Pathing graph for *Rat Race.*

grid-like fashion. Place a few nodes around a turn to create a curve instead of simply placing the corner node with two perpendicular arcs. I like to make a little Y-shaped triangle of nodes and arcs near such corners.

The second thing you can do is allow each node to have a tolerance that describes how close the agent has to be to the node in order to be considered to have hit it. Using these two techniques together, you can get a much smoother path. If you really want to go for broke, you can do a little prediction and figure out when to start turning and how sharply you need to turn. This will give your agents a very smooth curve, though perhaps it will be too smooth in some instances. For example, when someone is near a wall and turns a corner, there is very little curve. Another alternative would be to add that information into the node classes, but this may be a bit much to ask of designers (who typically create and tweak these graphs). I've found that you can get pretty decent results with the first two methods.

Now you need to describe the arc that connects these nodes. You could make arcs unidirectional, bidirectional, or both. You could give each arc a weight that gives a rough description of the difficulty for traversing that area. You could even allow multiple arcs to connect the same nodes but have different weights on those arcs for different types of agents. For example, you could have one arc used by ground-based agents and another used by flying agents. That way, you could easily have it so the ground agents tend to stick to the roads, while the flying agents don't really care. The weights can even be dynamic. Let's say you're making a real-time strategy game, and you want the flying units to avoid the guard towers the player sets up. One way of solving this problem would be to have the guard towers themselves increase the weight of nearby arcs. The flying units would tend to avoid them.

**Rude NPC Behavior Should Be Corrected**

When I was working at Super-Ego Games, I worked on an adventure game for the PlayStation 3 called *Rat Race*, which was set in an office. Being an adventure game, one of the major things you did was talk to the NPCs. Unfortunately, other NPCs would plow right through the middle of these conversations. We ended up creating conversation pathing objects that would spawn in the middle of conversations, which would significantly raise the weight of any arcs within a radius around that point. We also forced NPCs with affected arcs in their path to replan. This caused NPCs to do the polite thing and walk around the conversation.

## A* (A-Star)

There are many different searching algorithms to choose from, but A* (pronounced *A-Star*) happens to be one of the most common used for this purpose. When most people think of pathfinding, they think of A*. As I mentioned, A* is really just a general-purpose search algorithm that happens to fit the problem of pathfinding really well. It will find a path with a relatively small cost and do it fairly quickly. There are many different implementations of A*, but they all come from the same basic algorithm. A* was first described in 1968 by Peter Hart, Nils Nilsson, and Bertram Raphael.

The A* algorithm works by analyzing each node and assigning it three values. The first is the total cost to this node by the current path so far. This value is usually referred to as $g$, or *goal*. The second value is an estimated cost from this node to the goal. It's often referred to as $h$, or *heuristic*. The third value is an estimated cost from the start of the path through this node to the goal, which is really just $g + h$. This value is often called $f$, or *fitness*.

The point of these three values is to keep track of your progress so you know how well you're doing. The value of $g$ is something you know for sure since it's a calculated value (the sum of the costs of every node in the path so far), but how do you find out how to calculate $h$ and, by extension, $f$? The only rule for calculating $h$ is that it can't be greater than the actual cost between this node and the goal node. Of course, the more accurate the guess, the faster you can find a path. In this case, a simple distance check will suffice:

```
diff = pathingNodePosition - goalNodePosition
heuristic = diff.Length()
```

This allows us to easily calculate *f*.

The algorithm also maintains a priority queue called the *open set*. The open set is a list of nodes that are being considered, and the node with the lowest fitness score is at the front of the queue. The process starts with the node nearest the starting location. During each iteration of the algorithm, the front node is popped off the queue. The neighbors of this node are evaluated (potentially updating their magic values) and added to the open set. This process continues until the node removed from the queue is the goal node. Note that it's quite possible to see the goal node from a particular neighbor and ignore it if its *f* score is not low enough. This simply means that you haven't found the best path yet. Once you have processed a node, you mark it as closed. This allows you to ignore neighbors you've already processed. If the open set ever becomes empty before finding the goal node, it means you're done, and no path could be found.

### You Can't Always Get There from Here

No matter how solid you think the data is, there are times when you won't be able to find a path. Make sure that you have a graceful recovery plan.

### Agents Can Be Stubborn

While working on *Rat Race* for Super-Ego Games, our solution to failing to find a path was to re-run the higher decision-making logic. Unfortunately, the decision was almost always to try and do the exact same thing. Since AI was only updating once a second, the NPC would take a half step, stop, play a confused-looking idle animation (many of our idle animations were confused looking; it was a comedy game after all), and then repeat the process. Our solution was to have them abandon that particular decision, which meant that they couldn't choose it the second time around.

I've written a complete (albeit simple) pathfinding system that's included with the source code for this book. It's a bit lengthy to reprint here, but you can check it out yourself. The code is highly commented, and if you have any questions, you can always ask me. I frequent the Game Coding Complete forums quite often. The code lives in *pathing.h* and *pathing.cpp* in the *Dev\Source\GCC4\AI* directory.

Keep in mind that this is by no means the only way to navigate through the world. Remember, the key to successful navigation is to simplify the agents' view of the world so you can cut down on how much you have to process. A few hundred or even a few thousand pathing nodes are *much* faster to process than trying to deal with world geometry at runtime.

Another very common technique is something called a *navigation mesh,* which is a simple mesh that can be built by the artists or designers and represents the walkable terrain. The concept is really no different than the graph above. The center of each triangle is a node, and the edges that connect to other triangles are the arcs. There will probably have to be a bit more smoothing involved or else the paths may not look good, but if your meshes are dense enough with decent tolerances, it may not be much of an issue. *Game Programming Gems* has an article called "Simplified 3D Movement and Pathfinding Using Navigation Meshes" that serves as a great introduction to using navigation meshes if you find yourself interested in learning more.

## Dynamic Avoidance

Most of the time, you'll probably want to have multiple agents all navigating through the world at once. What happens if two or more agents are trying to hit the same node at the same time? What about two agents coming toward each other along the same arc? Figure 18.5 shows exactly what could happen.

The simplest solution to both of these issues is to turn off the node or arc in question. As soon as an agent starts traveling down an arc, give it exclusive access to that arc. If another agent happens to reach a point in its path where it has to travel down that same arc in the opposite direction, force it to replan from its current node to its target node, ignoring that particular arc.

The above scenario works well for relatively open areas, but what happens when your agents are in a confined space such as an office building? When I worked on *Rat Race*, we had this exact problem. There were over a dozen agents in a small office building, all pathing around the world. It was okay most of the time, but there were several choke points where it all just broke down, like the stairwell. The solution to this problem was to implement a dynamic avoidance algorithm. Each agent was given a personal comfort radius around it. If another agent entered that radius and they were both moving, they would calculate how much they had to turn to avoid

**Figure 18.5**
Multiple agents trying to reach a single node.

each other's comfort zones. This ended up working really well and solved most of our issues concerning people running into each other.

Having multiple agents all moving around using complex pathing graphs can be very taxing on the system. In larger game worlds, a common practice is to allow the A* algorithm to stop at any time so that a single path can be built across multiple frames. This is easy enough to implement with the system you've built. All you need to do is to store the `AStar` object for each path being built and have an event sent when the path is done. This sounds like a perfect job for a `Process` object. In Chapter 20, "Introduction to Multiprogramming," you'll learn an even better solution using threads.

## Further Reading

Here is a short list of books I've found very helpful in becoming a better AI programmer:

- *Artificial Intelligence for Games,* Ian Millington, published by The Morgan Kaufmann Series in Interactive 3D Technology

- *Artificial Intelligence: A Modern Approach,* Stuart Russell and Peter Norvig, published by Prentice-Hall, Inc.
- The *AI Game Programming Wisdom* series, Charles River Media
- The *Game Programming Gems* series, Charles River Media

# Chapter 19

*by Mike McShaffry*

# Network Programming for Multiplayer Games

I remember the very moment the Internet became relevant to my job, and it completely changed the way I worked. A colleague of mine walked into my office and showed me a website for the very first time. He'd made it himself, and although it was very simple, I knew right away that the Internet was going to change the world. Well, maybe it wasn't quite that clear. I missed out on the Netscape IPO, but it was certainly clear after that.

At the time, computer games could be played via modem or over a LAN, but they were quite the bear to program. Once gamers started playing online game, companies started using the Internet, and the communications protocols it uses, for hooking up fragfests. Now, whether you're playing with a buddy in the next office or a friend from overseas, or just checking out the latest game on Facebook, pretty much all network games use Internet protocols to communicate.

As it turns out, getting two computers to talk to each other is pretty easy. The trouble happens when you try to make some sense of the bits coming in from the other side: keeping track of them and their memory buffers, changing the raw data stream into useful game data, and trying to create a plug-in architecture that doesn't care if you are playing locally or from afar.

This chapter covers moving bits across the network, how you come up with the bits to send, and how you transform that raw data back into something your game can use just as if there were no network at all. First, we'll start with a little primer on the

Internet and its two most common Internet protocols: the transport control protocol (TCP) and the user datagram protocol (UDP).

## How the Internet Works

You probably have some familiarity with TCP and UDP. You might have heard that UDP is what all good network games use, and TCP is for chat windows. The truth, as usual, is a little more complicated than that. TCP is a guaranteed, full-duplex protocol. It looks and feels just as if there were no remote connection at all. You can write code that simply pulls bits out just as they were sent in, in the right order, with nothing missing and no duplications. It is easier to program because you don't have to worry so much about wacky Internet problems that can happen during packet transmission: packet loss, packet splitting, or even corruption. The best analogy is a pipe—what goes in will come out the other side, or you'll receive an error telling you something bad happened to the connection. The possibility of problems exists, and you should watch out for socket exceptions. Unlike files or UNIX-style pipes, you won't get an "end of file" marker.

UDP is a little more like sending messages by using those crazy bicycle messengers you see in downtown areas. You don't know when or even if your package will get to its destination. You also won't be informed if the package (your data) was split into multiple pieces during the transmission. I guarantee you that if you required a bicycle messenger to carry a 10,000-page document, that person would get friends to help, and it would be up to the receiver to make some sense of it when it all arrived.

By design, UDP is fairly lightweight, but the messages aren't guaranteed to arrive at their destination in any order, to arrive in one piece, or to arrive at all. TCP, the guaranteed delivery service, doesn't give its guarantees of a pipe-like connection lightly. It does its work by having the receiver acknowledge the reception of a complete, uncorrupted packet of data by sending a message back, essentially saying, "OK, I got packet #34, and it checks out, thanks." If the sender doesn't receive an acknowledgement, or an *ACK*, it will resend the missing or otherwise corrupted packet.

Of course, you don't have to wait to receive the ACK before sending another message; you can set your TCP connection to allow you to stuff data in as fast as you want. It will send the data as quickly as possible and worry about keeping track of the ACKs internally. This kind of socket is called a *nonblocking* socket because it operates asynchronously. A blocking socket can be useful if you want to enforce a rigid exchange between two computers, something like talking over a two-way radio. One computer sends data, and it blocks until the data is received by the other side. When I say "blocks," I mean exactly that—the socket function that sends data will not return until the data actually gets to the other side. You can see that this kind of thing would be bad for servers or clients; you generally want to send and receive data without waiting for the other side to get it and answer. This is the same, regardless of whether you use TCP or UDP.

## Winsock or Berkeley?

You may have heard about Berkeley sockets, or the Berkeley implementation of the sockets API. It's called that because it was developed for the Berkeley UNIX operating system, and it is a commonly used implementation of the TCP/UDP protocols. Of course, Microsoft developed an implementation of TCP/UDP as well, called *WinSock*. You might wonder which one is better and debate endlessly about it, but I'll leave it to the experts and Internet forums. I like to use Berkeley sockets for multiplayer games, even under Windows. There's a caveat to that, and I'll clue you in on it later.

Here is why I like to use Berkeley. When there's a more standard API out there that works, I tend to gravitate toward it. Forgive me for an example that will show my age—but it's really a little like why Sony VHS won over Betamax. It had more to do with the fact that more people were using VHS and nothing at all to do with the fact that Betamax was a superior format. Actually, the people who were using VHS represented the porn industry, and some say that's why it succeeded so quickly! But I digress.

You are free to use Berkley-style sockets on a Windows machine, as I have done throughout this chapter. Since space is such a premium—God knows this book is heavy enough to give you cramps if you hold it too long—I'll show you how to use TCP to get your game running as a multiplayer game. You can investigate UDP once you've mastered TCP. First, you have to know something about the Internet. After all, you can't send data to another computer on the Internet until you connect to the computer, and you can't connect to it until you can identify it uniquely from every other computer on the Net.

You are free to use WinSock or Berkeley sockets to connect to other computers, regardless of their choice of sockets implementation. As long as you send and receive data formatted as both sides expect, you can set up network communications with any other computer on the Internet. You can use your program to connect to Web servers, FTP sites, whatever you want. You just have to know what IP address to connect to, how to format the bytes you send, and how to parse the bytes you receive.

## Internet Addresses

Every computer that has TCP/IP installed has an IP address to identify the computer on the network. I say "the network" and not "the Internet" very specifically because not every network is visible to the Internet. Some, like the one in my house and the network where I work, are hidden from the Internet at large. They act like their very own mini-Internets. The computers on these mini-Internets only need a unique IP address for their network. Other computers, like the one that hosts my website, are attached directly. These computers need a unique IP address for the Internet at large.

Right now there are two common Internet protocols, IPv4 and IPv6. IPv4 has been around since the early 1980s and is most commonly used throughout the world. But that is beginning to change because the address space of IPv4 is quickly running out. IPv6 increases the address size from 32 bits to 128 bits, basically giving every person on the planet Earth approximately $4.8 \times 10^{28}$ addresses for his personal use. There are many other improvements and differences, which after you read this chapter you'll have enough knowledge to absorb. Since IPv6 is still fairly new and not everyone can use it, this chapter will focus on IPv4.

The IPv4 address is a 4-byte number, something you can store in an unsigned int. Here's the address for the computer that hosts my website, for example: 3486000987, or expressed in hexadecimal: 0xCFC8275B. People usually write Internet addresses in dotted decimal format to make them easier to remember. The above address would be expressed like this: 207.200.39.91. This may be easier to remember than 3486000987, but it's still no cakewalk.

This address has two parts: the network ID number and the host ID number. The host ID is the individual computer. Different networks have different sizes, and the designers of the Internet were wise to realize this. If they had simply chosen to use two bytes to represent the network ID and the host ID, the Internet would be limited to 65,536 networks and 65,536 computers on each network. While that might have seemed fine back in 1969 when the first four computers inaugurated ARPANET, as it was called, it would hardly seem sufficient now. The solution was to separate the network into address classes, as shown in Table 19.1.

Table 19.1 provides a summary of the IP address classes that are used to create IP addresses. The total size of the Internet, if you have a calculator handy, is about 3.7 billion computers on 2.1 million networks of various sizes, most of them very small.

**Table 19.1 IP Address Classes**

| Class | Network ID Bytes | Hosts on Network | Networks on Internet |
|---|---|---|---|
| A | 1 | 16,777,216 | 127 |
| B | 2 | 65,536 | 16,384 |
| C | 3 | 254 | 2,097,152 |

Here's a quick example of some of the holders of Class A address blocks on the Internet:

- General Electric Company
- Level 3 Communications
- Army Information Systems Center
- IBM Corporation
- DoD Intel Information Systems, Defense Intelligence Agency
- AT&T
- Xerox Palo Alto Research Center
- Hewlett-Packard Company
- Apple Computer, Inc.
- Massachusetts Institute of Technology
- Ford Motor Company
- Computer Sciences Corporation
- U.S. Defense Information Systems Agency
- UK Ministry of Defense
- Halliburton

Interesting list of organizations, isn't it? It's a virtual who's who of the military industrial complex.

As you might have guessed, there's a central authority for handing out unique network ID numbers to those who want to get on the Net. This authority is called the Internet Corporation for Assigned Names and Numbers (ICANN). Once the network ID is assigned, it's up to the local network administrator to hand out unique host IDs. In the case of the network in my house, the unique host IDs are handed out by a device I have hooked up to my network. Whenever one of my computers boots, it is assigned a host ID automatically. The device that hands out the addresses is called a Dynamic Host Configuration Protocol (DHCP) server and is exactly what you find on most wireless routers. If I didn't have one of these devices, I'd have to assign each of my computers a unique IP address. What a hassle.

There are some special IP addresses you should know about, as well as some special network IDs (see Table 19.2).

**Table 19.2 Special IP Addresses and Network IDs**

| Address | Description |
|---|---|
| 127.0.0.1 | Called the loopback address and always refers to your computer. It is also called the localhost. |
| 127.x.x.x | Loopback subnet; this network ID is used for diagnostics. |
| 255.255.255.255 | This IP address refers to all hosts on the local network. |
| 10.x.x.x<br>172.(16-31).x.x<br>192.168.x.x | Private networks; any address with these network IDs is considered on the local network, and not on the Internet at large. Use these addresses for your home or local company network if they don't need to be visible on the Internet. |

## The Domain Name System

When you browse the Web, your Web browser program attaches to another computer on the Internet, downloads a Web page and anything attached to it, and renders the Web page so you can see it. But when you browse the Web, you don't go to http://207.46.131.43, do you? If you put this specific address in your browser, you'll be rewarded with Microsoft's Web page.

Luckily for us, there's an easier way to find computers on the Internet. Clearly, www.microsoft.com is easier to read and remember than 207.46.131.43. The designers of the Internet designed a distributed database called the Domain Name System, or DNS.

This system is structured like a hierarchical tree. The first level of the tree consists of the top-level domains (TLD), some of which are listed in Table 19.3.

TLDs are also available for foreign countries to use, although they are generally used in as free and open a manner as the rest of the Internet. For example, .uk is used for

**Table 19.3 Top-Level Domains**

| TLD | Description |
| --- | --- |
| .edu | Educational institutions, mainly in the U.S. (reserved) |
| .gov | United States government (reserved) |
| .int | International organizations (reserved) |
| .mil | United States military (reserved) |
| .com | Commercial (open for general use) |
| .net | Networks (open for general use) |
| .org | Organizations (open for general use) |

the United Kingdom, and .cn is used for mainland China. Funny, the Pacific island of Tuvalu that sits midway between Hawaii and Australia got lucky and pulled .tv as its TLD. The television industry has made excellent use of these addresses.

As you can tell from Table 19.3, some of these TLDs are restricted and either managed by ICANN or somehow sponsored by an authority agreed upon to manage assigning unique names within their domain. The open, general-use TLDs like .com, .net, and .org are managed by ICANN.

Domain names within these top-level domains are issued by ICANN or another sponsoring authority. When you register for a domain name, you have to provide all kinds of information, but the really important piece of information is the primary name server. The primary name server is the IP address of the computer that retains the authoritative version of your domain name. It propagates this information to other name servers all over the Internet. Name servers generally update themselves every few hours. Any new or changed domain name takes a few days to register with enough name servers to be resolved quickly by anyone on the Internet.

I'll show you how to use the sockets API to find Internet addresses in just a bit.

## Useful Programs and Files

There are a few useful programs you'll find installed on virtually any computer, UNIX or Windows. You'll use them for checking Internet connectivity and other useful things. They are listed in Table 19.4.

**Table 19.4 Useful Programs and Files for Internet Work**

| Name | Description |
|---|---|
| ping | This little program attempts to send information to another computer and tells you the time in milliseconds it took for the packets to arrive. The other computer must be set up to answer, which might not be the case if the computer is behind a firewall. |
| netstat | This program can show you the state of current sockets on your computer. It can tell you if they are listening for connections, connected, or about to be closed. |
| tracert | This program tells you what Internet hops your packets have to make before they are received by the host computer. |
| Telnet | This program attaches to a host computer and sends/receives text messages. It can be great for debugging network code if your debug code can send/receive in text mode. |
| hosts | This is a file that holds locally overridden DNS information. If you want to force a DNS name like goober.mcfly.com to be any legal IP address, you can do it in this file. On Windows machines, look for it in the *system32\drivers\etc* directory. Windows machines also have a file `lmhosts`, which stands for LanManHosts, which is used by the Windows peer networking protocol, or SMB protocol. UNIX machines running the free Samba server may also have an *lmhosts* file. |

## Sockets API

Well, I've now given you enough knowledge to be dangerous. All you need is some source code. The sockets API is divided into a few different useful areas of code.

- Utility functions
- Domain Name Service (DNS) functions
- Initialization and shutdown
- Creating sockets and setting socket options
- Connecting client sockets to a server
- Server functions
- Reading and writing from sockets

## Sockets Utility Functions

There are some useful conversion functions that help you deal with Internet addresses and data that has been sent by another computer. The first two functions, `inet_addr()` and `inet_ntoa()`, perform conversions from a text string dotted decimal IP address and the four-byte unsigned integer. You'll notice the input parameter for `inet_ntoa()` is a structure called `in_addr`:

| | |
|---|---|
| `unsigned long inet_addr( const char* cp );` | Takes a string value like `127.0.0.1` and converts it to an unsigned integer you can use as an IP address. |
| `char* FAR inet_ntoa( struct in_addr in );` | Takes an `in_addr` structure and converts it to a string. Note: Copy the string from the return pointer; don't assume it will be there for long. It points to a static `char` buffer and may be overwritten the next time a socket's function is called. |

The `in_addr` structure is something that helps you break up IP addresses into their component parts. It's not just a normal unsigned integer, because the values of the bytes are in a specific order. This might seem confusing until you recall that different machines store integers in Big-endian or Little-endian order. In a Big-endian system, the most significant value in the sequence is stored at the lowest storage address (for example, "big end first"). In a Little-endian system, the least significant value in the sequence is stored first. Take a look at how the two systems store the 4-byte integer 0x80402010:

```
Big-endian       80 40 20 10
Little-endian    10 20 40 80
```

They are exactly backward from each other. Intel processors use Little-endian, and Motorola processors use Big-endian. The Internet standard is Big-endian. Some processors such as ARM and PowerPC are actually bi-endian and have the ability to switch between the two, typically on startup. This means that you have to be really careful with the data you get from strange computers because it might be in the wrong order. For certain sockets data structures, you are also expected to put things in network order. Luckily, there are some helper functions for that.

**The Rules Are There for a Reason**

It's a good idea to always use the converter functions, even if you know you'll never have an Internet application that has to talk to something with a different *endian-ness*. After all, there were a lot of programmers in the 1960s that never thought they'd need more than two digits to store the year, right?

The helper functions convert 4-byte and 2-byte values to and from network order:

| | |
|---|---|
| `u_long htonl( u_long hostlong );` | Converts a 4-byte value from host-byte order to network-byte order. |
| `u_long ntohl( u_long hostlong );` | Converts a 4-byte value from network-byte order to host-byte order. |
| `u_short htons( u_short hostshort );` | Converts a 2-byte value from host-byte order to network-byte order. |
| `u_short ntohs( u_short hostshort );` | Converts a 2-byte value from network-byte order to host-byte order. |

Here's a short bit of code that uses the utility/conversion functions:

```
unsigned long ipAddress = inet_addr("128.64.16.2");

struct in_addr addr;
addr.S_un.S_addr = htonl(0x88482818);

char ipAddressString[16];
strcpy(ipAddressString, inet_ntoa(addr));

printf("0x%08x 0x%08x %s\n:", ipAddress, addr.S_un.S_addr, ipAddressString);
```

The output, on my decidedly Little-endian Intel-powered Dell laptop, is this:

```
0x02104080 0x18284888 136.72.40.24
```

The first value, 0x02104080, is the unsigned long that is the converted IP address for 128.64.16.2. This is already in network order, so you can use it in socket functions without converting it. The next value, 0x18288488, shows you what happens when you send 0x88482818 through the `htonl()` function on my Dell. Your mileage may vary if you happen to use a non-Intel–based machine! The last string on the output line is 136.72.40.24, which is the dotted decimal format for the IP address given by `htonl(0x88482818)`.

This can be devilishly confusing, so choose a nice calm day to start playing with network programming.

## Domain Name Service (DNS) Functions

The next set of functions helps you make use of DNS:

| | |
|---|---|
| `struct hostent* FAR gethostbyname( const char* name );` | Retrieves host information, such as IP address, from a dotted-decimal format string, such as "www.yahoo.com." If the host doesn't exist, you'll get back NULL. |
| `struct hostent* FAR gethostbyaddr( const char* addr, int len, int type );` | Retrieves host information, such as IP address, from an `in_addr` structure for IPv4 or `in6_addr` structure for IPv6. If the host doesn't exist, you'll get back NULL. |

Both of these functions look up host information based on an address, either a text string in dotted-decimal notation or an IP address in network order. Don't let the `const char *` fool you in `gethostbyaddr()` because it doesn't want a text string. Here's a quick example of using both of these:

```
const char *host = "ftp.microsoft.com";
struct hostent *pHostEnt = gethostbyname(host);

if (pHostEnt == NULL)
  fprintf(stderr, "No such host");
else
{
  struct sockaddr_in addr;
  memcpy(&addr.sin_addr,pHostEnt->h_addr,pHostEnt->h_length);
  printf("Address of %s is 0x%08x\n", host, ntohl(addr.sin_addr.s_addr));
}
```

Both functions return a pointer to a data structure, hostent. The data structure stores information about the host, such as its name, IP address, and more. The structure is allocated and managed by the sockets system, so don't do anything other than read it. Notice the liberal sprinkling of network-to-host conversion functions.

The output of the code is this line:

```
Address of ftp.microsoft.com is 0xcf2e858c
```

Instead of using the gethostbyname() function, I could have used these lines and used gethostbyaddr():

```
unsigned int netip = inet_addr("207.46.133.140");
pHostEnt = gethostbyaddr((const char *)&netip, 4, PF_INET);
```

The DNS lookup functions make it easy for you to specify IP addresses in a human-readable form, which is important for setting up a server IP address in an options file or in a dialog box without getting out the calculator.

**DNS Functions Failing?**

You can call the conversion functions anytime you want, but the DNS lookup functions will fail if you try to call them before you've initialized the sockets API.

## Sockets Initialization and Shutdown

Even if you are programming Berkeley-style sockets on a Windows machine, you'll call the Windows Sockets API to initialize the sockets system and shut it down:

| | |
|---|---|
| `int WSAStartup( WORD wVersionRequested, LPWSADATA lpWSAData );` | Initializes the Sockets API; you must call it before calling any other sockets function. |
| `int WSACleanup(void);` | Call this to deregister the application from using sockets, usually in your application cleanup code. |

In the first function, WSAStartup(), you send in the version number of the sockets implementation you want. At this writing, the most recent version of sockets is version 2.2, and it has been that way for years. Notice that you want to send in the minor version number in the high order byte and the major version in the low order byte. If for some reason you wanted to initialize Windows Sockets version 2.0, you'd send 0x0002 into the `WSAStartup()` function. As you can see below, you can also use the `MAKEWORD` macro to set the version number properly.

```
WORD wVersionRequested = MAKEWORD( 0, 2 );      // set to 2.0
WSADATA wsaData;
int err = WSAStartup( wVersionRequested, &wsaData );
```

`WSAStartup()` also takes a pointer to the `WSADATA` structure. This structure is filled with data that describes the socket implementation and its current status, but that's about it.

`WSACleanup()` is called when you are ready to shut down your application.

## Creating Sockets and Setting Socket Options

The embodiment of a socket is the socket handle. You should already be familiar with using handles from working with resources in the resource cache. The difference comes in the multistep manner in which you create a connected socket. The easiest connection style is a client-side connection. Doing this requires three steps. First, you ask the sockets API to create a socket handle of a particular type. You have the option of changing socket options, which tells the sockets API more information about how you want the socket to act. After that, you can connect the socket with another computer. It is a little more involved than opening a file, but sockets are a little more complicated.

### socket()

The following is the API to create a socket, interestingly enough:

```
SOCKET socket (int address_family, int socket_type, int protocol );
```

***Parameters:***

- **Address Family:** Will always be `PF_INET` for communicating over the Internet using IPv4. Other address families include `PF_IPX`, `PF_DECnet`, `PF_APPLE-TALK`, `PF_ATM`, and `PF_INET6`.
- **Socket Type:** Use `SOCK_STREAM` for connected byte streams. `SOCK_DGRAM` is for connectionless network communication, and `SOCK_RAW` is for raw sockets, which lets you write socket programs at a lower level than TCP or UDP. You will generally use `SOCK_STREAM`.
- **Protocol:** Use `IPPROTO_TCP` for TCP and `IPPROTO_UDP` for UDP sockets.

*Return Value*

The socket() function returns a valid handle for a socket if one was created or INVALID_SOCKET if there was some kind of error.

Here's an example of how to create a TCP socket handle:

```
SOCKET sock = socket(PF_INET, SOCK_STREAM, IPPROTO_TCP);
if ((sock == INVALID_SOCKET)
{
  // handle error!
}
```

### setsockopt()

Now that you have a socket handle, you can decide how you'd like the socket to act when it is open. You do this by setting the socket options through a function called setsockopt(). There is a wide variety of options, and I'm happy to show you some common ones, specifically the ones used in the client/server code in this chapter. Make sure you look at the complete sockets documentation for socket options. I'm only scratching the surface here.

```
int setsockopt (
  SOCKET socket,
  int level,
  int optionName,
  const char* optionValue,
  int optLen );
```

***Parameters***:

- **Socket:** A valid socket handle.
- **Level:** Either SOL_SOCKET or IPPROTO_TCP, depending on the option chosen.
- **Option Name:** The identifier of the socket option you want to set.
- **Option Value:** The address of the new value for the option. For Boolean values, you should send in a 4-byte integer set to either 1 or 0.
- **Option Length:** The length in bytes of the option value.

*Return Value:*

Returns zero if the option was set or SOCKET_ERROR if there was an error.

Here are some examples of setting socket options:

```
int value = 1;
setsockopt(sock, IPPROTO_TCP, TCP_NODELAY, (char *)&value, sizeof(value));
```

```
setsockopt(sock, SOL_SOCKET, SO_DONTLINGER, (char *)&value, sizeof(value));
setsockopt(sock, SOL_SOCKET, SO_KEEPALIVE, (char *)&value, sizeof(value));
```

The first option, `TCP_NODELAY`, disables an internal buffering mechanism in an attempt to sacrifice some network bandwidth for a speedier sending of packets. It is especially important when you want to send a high number of small packets, as is common in many multiplayer computer games.

The next option, `SO_DONTLINGER`, ensures a speedy return from a call to close the socket. The socket will be closed gracefully, but the call will essentially happen in the background. This is a clear win for any application that has to support a high number of connections, but it is still good for a computer game, no matter how many connections you have.

The last one of interest is `SO_KEEPALIVE`. It sends a packet of data at regular intervals if no other data has been sent. The default interval is two hours, but on some systems it can be configurable. This is probably only useful for a server system that supports a high number of connections. In a multiperson shooter, it will be pretty obvious if someone's remote connection goes dark.

### ioctlsocket()

Another useful socket control function is `ioctlsocket()`, which has a few uses, but the most important one to you, the fledgling multiplayer game programmer, is to set whether a socket is a blocking socket or a nonblocking socket:

```
int ioctlsocket( SOCKET s, long command, u_long* argumentPointer );
```

***Parameters:***

- **Socket:** A valid socket handle.
- **Command:** `FIONBIO` controls blocking. `FIONREAD` will return the number of bytes ready in the socket's input buffer, and `SIOCATMARK` will tell you if there is any out-of-band (OOB) data to be read. OOB data is only available for sockets that have the `SO_OOBINLINE` socket options set.
- **Argument Pointer:** A pointer to a `u_long` that holds the argument to the command or stores the result of the command.

***Return Value:***

Returns zero if the option was set or `SOCKET_ERROR` if there was an error.

A blocking socket is one that will wait to send or receive data. A nonblocking socket performs these tasks asynchronously. When you call the socket's function to receive data on a blocking socket, it won't return until there is actually data to receive.

Blocking sockets are easier to program, but they aren't nearly as useful in game programming. Imagine using a blocking socket on a multiplayer game. Each client would be completely stopped, frozen in place, until some data was received. A nonblocking socket is the only way a game can continue processing anything in the same thread, which is why it is used overwhelmingly over the blocking sort.

Here's how you call the `ioctlsocket()` function to set your socket to nonblocking:

```
unsigned long val = 1;  // 1=non blocking, 0=blocking
ioctlsocket(m_sock, FIONBIO, &val);
```

There's one thing you should watch out for, however. You can only call this function on a "live" socket, meaning that it is a client socket that has been connected to a server or a server socket that is listening for clients.

### *Connecting Sockets to a Server and Understanding Ports*

Once you have a socket handle and set the options with `ioctlsocket()`, the socket will be ready to connect to another computer. For a socket to connect, the computer accepting the connection must be listening for it. This differentiates server-side sockets from client-side sockets, even though they all use the same `SOCKET` handle structure and they all use the same functions to send and receive data.

For now, imagine you are simply creating a socket to attach to something like an FTP server, such as ftp.microsoft.com. Here you are, over a dozen pages into a networking chapter, and I haven't even mentioned ports yet. Well, I can't put it off any longer.

The designers of the Internet realized that computers on the Internet might have multiple connections to other computers simultaneously. They facilitated this by adding ports to the IP protocol. In addition to specifying an IP address of a computer, you must specify a port as well. Ports can be numbered from 1 to 65535, where 0 is reserved. Various client/server applications like FTP and Telnet use well-known port assignments, which is simply an agreement that certain server applications will use certain ports. Most popular server applications like Telnet and FTP use ports in the 0–1024 range, but new server applications, like those for common chat programs and multiplayer games, use higher port numbers. For example, *Doom* used port 666—quite appropriate! The choice of port is fairly arbitrary. The only real limitation is that you can't have two different applications on the same server listening on the same port number.

If you are creating a server, it's up to you to choose a good port that isn't already dominated by something else that everyone uses. There are plenty to go around, and some quick searches on the Internet will give you plenty of current information about which applications are using which port.

The port and IP address make a unique connection identifier. A server that listens on a particular port, like 21 for FTP, can accept many hundreds, if not thousands, of connections. A client can even make multiple connections to the same server on the same port. The IP protocol distinguishes actual connections internally, so they don't get confused, although I'd hate to be a programmer trying to debug an application like that!

### connect()

Enough already. Here's the API for actually connecting a socket to a server that is listening for connections:

```
int connect( SOCKET s, const struct sockaddr* name, int namelen);
```

***Parameters:***

- **Socket:** A valid socket handle.
- **Name:** A structure that holds the address family, port, and address of the server.
- **NameLen:** Always `sizeof(struct sockaddr)`.

***Return Value:***

Returns zero if the function succeeded or `SOCKET_ERROR` if there was an error.

Here's an example of how you connect a socket:

```
struct sockaddr_in sa;
sa.sin_family = AF_INET;
sa.sin_addr.s_addr = htonl(ip);
sa.sin_port = htons(port);

if (connect(m_sock, (struct sockaddr *)&sa, sizeof(sa)))
{
  // HANDLE ERROR HERE
}
```

The address family is set to `AF_INET` since we're using the Internet. The IP address and port are set, and the structure is sent into the `connect()` function along with the socket handle. If this didn't work for some reason, there are two things to try to help figure out what the problem is.

- First, try connecting with Telnet, one of the utility programs you can access from the command line. If it doesn't work, there's something wrong with the address or port, or perhaps your network can't see the remote computer.
- If Telnet works, try reversing the byte order of the port or IP address. This is easy to screw up.

## Server Functions

You've seen how to create sockets on the client side, so now you're ready to create a server-side socket. You create the socket handle with the same `socket()` function you saw earlier, and you are free to also call the `setsockopt()` function to set the options you want. Instead of calling `connect()`, though, you call two other functions: `bind()` and `listen()`.

### bind()

A server has to bind a socket to a particular IP address and port within the system before it can accept connections. After it is bound to an address and a port, you call `listen()` to open the server side for client connections:

```
int bind( SOCKET s, const struct sockaddr* name, int namelen);
```

***Parameters:***

- **Socket:** A valid socket handle.
- **Name:** A structure that holds the address family, port, and address of the server.
- **NameLen:** Always `sizeof(struct sockaddr)`.

***Return Value:***

Returns zero if the function succeeded or `SOCKET_ERROR` if there was an error.

Here's an example of how you bind a socket to a particular port using the local IP address of the server. The port is specified in the `struct sockaddr` in network byte order. The address family is `AF_INET` for Internet addresses, and since we want the socket to be bound to the local IP address, the address member is set to `ADDR_ANY`.

```
struct sockaddr_in sa;
sa.sin_family = AF_INET;
sa.sin_addr = ADDR_ANY;
sa.sin_port = htons(portnum);

if (bind(m_sock, (struct sockaddr *)&sa, sizeof(sa)))
{
  // HANDLE ERROR HERE
}
```

### listen()

After you've bound a socket to a particular port, you can open it up to accept connections with the `listen()` function:

```
int listen( SOCKET s, int backlog);
```

***Parameters:***

- **Socket:** A valid socket handle.
- **Backlog:** The maximum length of the queue of incoming connections. Set it to `SOMAXCONN` if you want the underlying service provider to use its default value. If a client attempts to connect and the backlog is full, the connection will be refused.

***Return Value:***

Returns zero if the function succeeded or `SOCKET_ERROR` if there was an error.

Here's an example of using `listen()` to set the backlog to 256:

```
if (listen(m_sock, 256) == SOCKET_ERROR)
{
  // HANDLE ERROR HERE
}
```

**`accept()`**

When a remote client attaches to the listen socket with `connect()`, the server side will detect input on the listen socket. Exactly how this happens you'll see in a moment with the `select()` function. Once input is detected on a listen socket, you call `accept()` to establish the connection.

```
SOCKET accept( SOCKET listenSock, const struct sockaddr* name, int namelen);
```

***Parameters:***

- **Listen Socket:** A valid socket handle to a listen socket.
- **Name:** A structure that receives the address of the connecting client.
- **NameLen:** Always `sizeof(struct sockaddr)`.

***Return Value:***

Returns zero if the function succeeded or `INVALID_SOCKET` if there was an error.

There are a few things to be aware of when using `accept()`. First and foremost, it will block if there are no client connections ready and the listen socket is set to blocking. If the listen socket is set to nonblocking and there are no client connections ready, it will return an error and could put the listen socket in an unusable state. Basically, don't call `accept()` until you have input on the listen socket connection and you can be sure you have at least one client ready to start talking. You can check for this by calling the `select()` function, which is up next.

**select()**

The last server-side method is `select()`. This function lets you poll the state of all your open sockets. You create three arrays of socket pointers that will be polled. The first set will be polled for input, the second set for output, and the third set for exceptions. Here's the `fd_set` structure definition and the definition for `select()`.

```
typedef struct fd_set {
 u_int fd_count;
 SOCKET fd_array[FD_SETSIZE];
} fd_set;

int select(
  int nfds,
  fd_set* readfds,
  fd_set* writefds,
  fd_set* exceptfds,
  const struct timeval* timeout );
```

***Parameters:***

- **nfds:** Ignored in WinSock; only included for compatibility with Berkeley sockets.
- **readfds, writefds, exceptfds:** The arrays of pointers to sockets to be polled for input, output, and exceptions.
- **timeout:** A pointer to a `timeout` structure. Set it to NULL if you want `select()` to block until something happens on one of the sockets, or set it to a valid `timeout` structure with all zeros to make a quick poll.

***Return Value:***

Returns zero if the function timed out, `SOCKET_ERROR` if there was an error, or the number of sockets contained within the structures that are ready to process.

This function is a real boon for the server-side programmer. It helps with servers that have tons of client connections and you don't want to block on any of them, whether they are set to blocking or nonblocking. This function can tell your program which sockets are ready to read from, write to, or have suffered an exception of some kind.

**Maximum Client Connections Is 64 by Default**

By default, the `fd_set` structure can hold 64 sockets. That size is defined as `FD_SETSIZE` in the WINSOCK2.H header file. In C++, you can define your own `FD_SETSIZE`, as long as it's defined before the WINSOCK2 header file is included. You can set this compiler `#define` in the command line or project properties. If it is defined anywhere after `#include WinSock2.h`, it will break horribly.

## Socket Reading and Writing

The two most common functions used for sending and receiving data are `send()` and `recv()`. They each take similar parameter lists, with the exception that they use different flags, and one of them will clearly stomp all over the buffer you send in.

```
int send( SOCKET s, const char* buffer, int length, int flags);
int recv( SOCKET s, char* buffer,       int length, int flags);
```

***Parameters:***

- **Socket:** A valid socket handle.
- **Buffer:** Either the source data buffer for sending or the destination buffer for receiving.
- **Length:** The size of the buffer in bytes.
- **Flags:**
    - **For `send`:** `MSG_DONTROUTE` informs sockets you don't want the data routed, which can be ignored on WinSock. `MSG_OOB` tells sockets to send this packet as out-of-band data.
    - **For `recv`:** `MSG_PEEK` peeks at the data but doesn't remove it from the input buffer, and `MSG_OOB` processes out-of-band data.

***Return Value:***

Returns the number of bytes actually sent or received or `SOCKET_ERROR` if there was an error. The `recv()` function will return 0 if the socket was gracefully closed.

There are a few points to clarify. If you have a 10-byte receive buffer, and there are 20 bytes ready to read, the remaining 10 bytes will be there when you call `recv()` a second time. Conversely, if you have a 10-byte buffer, and there are only 5 bytes ready to read, the function will dutifully return 5, and the first 5 bytes of your buffer will have new data.

That's certainly a whirlwind tour of the most used socket functions. There are certainly more of them to learn, but what you just read will give you an excellent start. What you are about to see next is one way to organize these C functions into a usable set of classes designed to make your single-player game a multiplayer game.

# Making a Multiplayer Game with Sockets

If you've followed the advice in this book, you've organized your game into three major components: the application layer, the game logic layer, and the game view layer. The game logic and game view can call directly into the application layer for performing tasks like opening files and allocating memory. The game view and game logic talk to each other through an event system, as described in Chapter 11, "Game Event Management."

If you guessed that the socket classes belong in the application layer, you'd be exactly right. They are similar to files, really, in that they provide a stream of data your game can use. Sockets also tend to be slightly different on Windows and UNIX platforms, which is another good reason to stick them in the application layer.

I provided an important diagram in Chapter 2, "What's in a Game?," to describe how the logic/view architecture could easily support a networked game. Figure 19.1 shows this diagram again so that you don't have to go all the way back to Chapter 2.

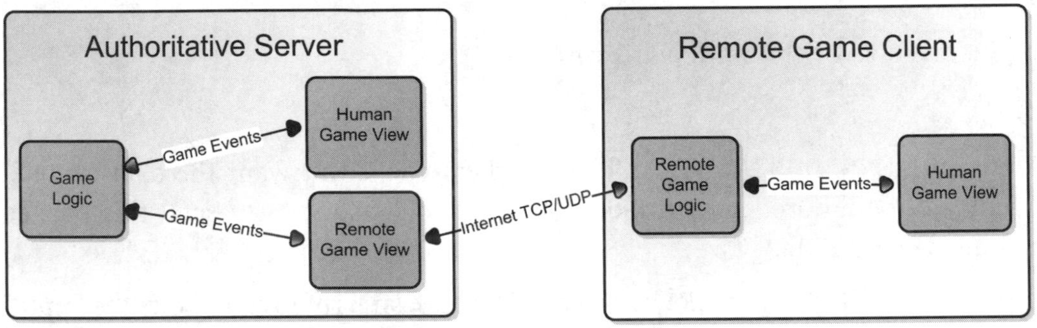


**Figure 19.1**
A remote game client attaching to a server.

Recall that this game architecture supports game logic and multiple views of that logic. These might include a human player view, an AI player view, and a remote player view. The events that are being generated by the authoritative machine acting as the game server can be serialized, sent over the Internet, and reconstructed as the same events on the remote machine. The remote machine can also send events in the form of game commands, like "fire my 105mm cannon at the n00b," back to the server.

While this high-level explanation seems easy, the reality is, as always, a bit more complicated. I'll take you through the whole thing, step-by-step. I'm going to break this job into four pieces so your brains don't explode.

- **Packet Classes:** Create objects to handle packets of data that will be sent and received through socket connections.
- **Core Socket Classes:** Create base objects to handle client connections.
- **Core Server Classes:** Create base objects to handle server connections.
- **Wire Socket Classes into the Event System:** Create an event forwarder that listens to events locally and sends them on to a remote computer.

One thing you should know right away—all the code samples in this chapter assume a single-threaded environment. There are plenty of network programming examples out there that use one thread per connection and blocking calls to every socket. This may be an easy way to implement network communications, but it isn't the most efficient way.

## Packet Classes

Data that is sent or received via sockets has a format, just like any file you read from beginning to end. The format of the data will usually come in chunks, or packets, of discrete units, each of which is essentially a stand-alone piece of data. The format and interpretation of these packets is totally up to you. Just as you define the structure of your data files, you can define the structure of your packet stream. These packets might carry username and password data, data for events like "Change Game State" or "Move Actor," or game commands like "Set Throttle to 100%."

As your program reads data from a socket, it needs to have some way of determining what kind of packet is coming in and how many bytes to expect. When the correct number of bytes is ready, the packet is read from the socket as an atomic unit, encapsulated with a C++ packet object, and then handled by your game.

The exact opposite happens when you want to send a packet. The block of bytes that makes up the packet is assembled, or streamed, into a memory buffer. The size of the buffer is sent along with the packet as well

Most multiplayer games send binary data over network connections. This is because the information in the packets contains things like game events, movement deltas, and game commands that can be encoded very efficiently in a binary format. If this data were sent in clear text, it would be much larger. Think of it as the same thing as storing your data in a database or XML. XML might be easier to read, but it takes more space.

This packet class is for binary formatted packets. It allocates its own buffer of bytes and stores the size of the buffer in the first four bytes, but note that it stores them in network order. This is generally a good idea, even though I know I might never be using this system on anything other than my Dell.

```
class BinaryPacket
{
protected:
  char *m_Data;

public:
  inline BinaryPacket(char const * const data, u_long size);
  inline BinaryPacket(u_long size);
```

```
  virtual ~BinaryPacket() { SAFE_DELETE(m_Data); }
  virtual char const * const VGetData() const { return m_Data; }
  virtual u_long VGetSize() const { return ntohl(*(u_long *)m_Data); }
  inline void MemCpy(char const *const data, size_t size, int destOffset);
};
```

Here I've defined two different constructors, both of which take the size of the buffer as an expected parameter. The first one takes a pointer to a data buffer that the `BinaryPacket` object will copy into its own buffer. The second expects the API programmer, that's you, to make repeated calls to `MemCpy()` to fill the buffer.

Here's the implementation of the constructors and `MemCpy()`:

```
inline BinaryPacket::BinaryPacket(char const * const data, u_long size)
{
  m_Data = GCC_NEW char[size + sizeof(u_long)];
  assert(m_Data);
  *(u_long *)m_Data = htonl(size+sizeof(u_long));
  memcpy(m_Data+sizeof(u_long), data, size);
}

inline BinaryPacket::BinaryPacket(u_long size)
{
  m_Data = GCC_NEW char[size + sizeof(u_long)];
  assert(m_Data);
  *(u_long *)m_Data = htonl(size+sizeof(u_long));
}

inline void BinaryPacket::MemCpy(char const *const data, size_t size, int destOffset)
{
  assert(size+destOffset <= VGetSize()-sizeof(u_long));
  memcpy(m_Data + destOffset + sizeof(u_long), data, size);
}
```

## Core Socket Classes

As you might expect, I've written a class to encapsulate a socket handle. It has four virtual functions that can be overridden by implementers of child classes, or the class can even be used as-is.

```
#define MAX_PACKET_SIZE (256)
#define RECV_BUFFER_SIZE (MAX_PACKET_SIZE * 512)

class NetSocket
{
  friend class BaseSocketManager;
  typedef std::list< shared_ptr <IPacket> > PacketList;
```

```
public:
  NetSocket(SOCKET new_sock, unsigned int hostIP);
  virtual ~NetSocket();

  bool Connect(unsigned int ip, unsigned int port, bool forceCoalesce = 0);
  void SetBlocking(bool blocking);
  void Send(shared_ptr<IPacket> pkt, bool clearTimeOut=1);

  virtual int  VHasOutput() { return !m_OutList.empty(); }
  virtual void VHandleOutput();
  virtual void VHandleInput();
  virtual void VTimeOut() { m_timeOut=0; }
  void HandleException() { m_deleteFlag |= 1; }
  void SetTimeOut(unsigned int ms=45*1000) { m_timeOut = timeGetTime() + ms; }
  int GetIpAddress() { return m_ipaddr; }

protected:
  SOCKET m_sock;      // the socket handle
  int m_id;           // a unique ID given by the socket manager

  // note: if deleteFlag has bit 2 set, exceptions only close the
  //   socket and set to INVALID_SOCKET, and do not delete the NetSocket
  int m_deleteFlag;

  PacketList m_OutList;            // packets to send
  PacketList m_InList;             // packets just received

  char m_recvBuf[RECV_BUFFER_SIZE];     // receive buffer
  unsigned int m_recvOfs, m_recvBegin;  // tracking the read head of
                                        // the buffer

  int m_sendOfs;                 // tracking the output buffer
  unsigned int m_timeOut;        // when will the socket time out
  unsigned int m_ipaddr;         // the ipaddress of the remote connection

  int m_internal;              // is the remote IP internal or external?
  int m_timeCreated;           // when the socket was created
};
```

The class is relatively self-documenting, but there are a couple of things worthy of discussion. The `m_deleteFlag` member helps handle reconnections if the remote side drops out for a little while. Next, the input and output lists are ordered lists of packets to be sent and received, and they are implemented as STL lists. There is no output buffer, since it can use the already allocated memory of the packets in the output list. There is an input buffer, since you'll use it to compose packets as they stream in from the remote computer.

Also, note the maximum packet size and the size of the receive buffer defined just before the class. These sizes are totally up to you and what you expect to receive in the way of packets from the remote computers. Your mileage may vary with different choices, especially in terms of server memory. If you expect to have a few hundred clients attached, this memory buffer can get pretty big indeed.

Here are the constructors and destructor:

```
NetSocket::NetSocket()
{
  m_sock = INVALID_SOCKET;
  m_deleteFlag = 0;
  m_sendOfs = 0;
  m_timeOut = 0;
  m_recvOfs = m_recvBegin = 0;
  m_internal = 0;
  m_bBinaryProtocol = 1;
}

NetSocket::NetSocket(SOCKET new_sock, unsigned int hostIP)
{
  // set everything to zero
  m_deleteFlag = 0;
  m_sendOfs = 0;
  m_timeOut = 0;
  m_recvOfs = m_recvBegin = 0;
  m_internal = 0;

  // check the time
  m_timeCreated = timeGetTime();

  m_sock = new_sock;
  m_ipaddr = hostIP;

  // ask the socket manager if the socket is on our internal network
  m_internal = g_pSocketManager->IsInternal(m_ipaddr);

  setsockopt (m_sock, SOL_SOCKET, SO_DONTLINGER, NULL, 0);
}

NetSocket::~NetSocket()
{
  if (m_sock != INVALID_SOCKET)
  {
    closesocket(m_sock);
```

```
    m_sock = INVALID_SOCKET;
  }
}
```

The two different constructors handle two different cases when creating network connections. The default constructor handles the case where a client wishes to connect to a server. The second constructor, using an already initialized socket handle, handles the server side.

The next method is called when you want to connect a new `NetSocket` to a server listening for connections.

```
bool NetSocket::Connect(unsigned int ip, unsigned int port, bool forceCoalesce)
{
  struct sockaddr_in sa;
  int x = 1;

  // create the socket handle
  if ((m_sock = socket(AF_INET, SOCK_STREAM, 0)) == INVALID_SOCKET)
    return false;

  // set socket options - in this case turn off Nagle algorithm if desired
  if (!forceCoalesce)
    setsockopt(m_sock, IPPROTO_TCP, TCP_NODELAY, (char *)&x, sizeof(x));

  // last step - set the IP address and port of the server, and call connect()
  sa.sin_family = AF_INET;
  sa.sin_addr.s_addr = htonl(ip);
  sa.sin_port = htons(port);

  if (connect(m_sock, (struct sockaddr *)&sa, sizeof(sa)))
  {
    closesocket(m_sock);
    m_sock = INVALID_SOCKET;
    return false;
  }
  return true;
}
```

Just as described in the socket primer earlier in this chapter, the process for connecting a socket to a server has three steps. First, you create the socket handle. Second, you call the socket options. In this case, `NetSocket` supports disabling the packet-grouping algorithm by default. This increases network traffic, but it can improve performance if you send/receive tons of tiny packets, like games tend to do. Finally, you connect the socket to the remote server.

Right after the socket is connected, you probably want to set it to nonblocking. Here's a method that does exactly that, and it is exactly like you saw in the primer:

```
void NetSocket::SetBlocking(bool blocking)
{
  unsigned long val = blocking ? 0 : 1;
  ioctlsocket(m_sock, FIONBIO, &val);
}
```

It's now time to learn how this class sends packets to the remote computer. Whenever you have a packet you want to send, the `Send()` method simply adds it to the end of the list of packets to send. It doesn't send the packets right away. This is done once per update loop by the `Send()` method:

```
void NetSocket::Send(shared_ptr<IPacket> pkt, bool clearTimeOut)
{
  if (clearTimeOut)
    m_timeOut = 0;
  m_OutList.push_back(pkt);
}
```

The `VHandleOutput()` method's job is to iterate the list of packets in the output list and call the socket's `send()` API until all the data is gone or there is some kind of error.

```
void NetSocket::VHandleOutput()
{
  int fSent = 0;
  do
  {
    GCC_ASSERT(!m_OutList.empty());
    PacketList::iterator i = m_OutList.begin();

    shared_ptr<IPacket> pkt = *i;
    const char *buf = pkt->VGetData();
    int len = static_cast<int>(pkt->VGetSize());

    int rc = send(m_sock, buf+m_sendOfs, len-m_sendOfs, 0);
    if (rc > 0)
    {
      g_pSocketManager->AddToOutbound(rc);
      m_sendOfs += rc;
      fSent = 1;
    }
    else if (WSAGetLastError() != WSAEWOULDBLOCK)
```

```
    {
      HandleException();
      fSent = 0;
    }
    else
    {
      fSent = 0;
    }

    if (m_sendOfs == pkt->VGetSize())
    {
      m_OutList.pop_front();
      m_sendOfs = 0;
    }

  } while ( fSent && !m_OutList.empty() );
}
```

The idea behind reading the socket for input is similar, but there's some buffer management to worry about. For efficiency's sake, there's a single monolithic buffer for each `NetSocket` object. Depending on how the remote sends data, you might get your packet in chunks. TCP is guaranteed to send things in the right order, and it won't split them up, but you might attempt to send something large, like a movie file. In any case, you want to collect bytes in the read buffer until you have a valid packet and then copy those bytes into a dynamic data structure like `BinaryPacket` so your game can process it.

Since you might receive multiple packets in a single read, the read buffer operates in a round-robin fashion. The read/write heads continually advance until they get too close to the end of the buffer, and then they copy any partial packets to the beginning of the buffer and start the whole process over.

```
void NetSocket::VHandleInput()
{
  bool bPktReceived = false;
  u_long packetSize = 0;
  int rc = recv(m_sock,
                m_recvBuf+m_recvBegin+m_recvOfs,
                RECV_BUFFER_SIZE-(m_recvBegin+m_recvOfs), 0);
  if (rc==0)
    return;

  if (rc == SOCKET_ERROR)
  {
    m_deleteFlag = 1;
```

```
    return;
  }

  const int hdrSize = sizeof(u_long);
  unsigned int newData = m_recvOfs + rc;
  int processedData = 0;

  while (newData > hdrSize)
  {
    packetSize = *(reinterpret_cast<u_long*>(m_recvBuf+m_recvBegin));
    packetSize = ntohl(packetSize);

    // we don't have enough new data to grab the next packet
    if (newData < packetSize)
      break;

    if (packetSize > MAX_PACKET_SIZE)
    {
      // prevent nasty buffer overruns!
      HandleException();
      return;
    }

    if (newData >= packetSize)
    {
      // we know how big the packet is...and we have the whole thing
      shared_ptr<BinaryPacket> pkt(
        GCC_NEW BinaryPacket(
          &m_recvBuf[m_recvBegin+hdrSize], packetSize-hdrSize));
      m_InList.push_back(pkt);
      bPktRecieved = true;
      processedData += packetSize;
      newData -= packetSize;
      m_recvBegin += packetSize;
    }
  }

  g_pSocketManager->AddToInbound(rc);
  m_recvOfs = newData;

  if (bPktRecieved)
  {
    if (m_recvOfs == 0)
    {

      m_recvBegin = 0;
```

```
    }
    else if (m_recvBegin + m_recvOfs + MAX_PACKET_SIZE > RECV_BUFFER_SIZE)
    {
      // we don't want to overrun the buffer - so we copy the leftover bits
      // to the beginning of the receive buffer and start over
      int leftover = m_recvOfs;
      memcpy(m_recvBuf, &m_recvBuf[m_recvBegin], m_recvOfs);
      m_recvBegin = 0;
    }
  }
}
```

**Easy to Read or Super Efficient? Do Both!**

When you define your packet definitions and protocols, make sure you can easily switch between a tight, efficient packet definition and an easy-to-read definition such as clear text. You'll use one for production, but the other is invaluable for debugging.

## A Socket Class for Listening

A listen socket is an easy extension of the `NetSocket` class. It adds the capability to listen for client connections and accept them, adding new sockets to the global socket manager:

```
class NetListenSocket: public NetSocket
{
public:
  NetListenSocket() { };
  NetListenSocket(int portnum) { port = 0; Init(portnum); }

  void Init(int portnum);
  SOCKET AcceptConnection(unsigned int *pAddr);

  unsigned short port;
};
```

There are five steps to create a listen socket: You create a socket handle, set the socket options, bind the socket to a listen port, set it to nonblocking, and finally call `listen()`.

```
void NetListenSocket::Init(int portnum)
{
  struct sockaddr_in sa;
  int value = 1;
```

```
  // create socket handle
  if ((m_sock = socket(AF_INET, SOCK_STREAM, 0)) == INVALID_SOCKET)
  {
    GCC_ERROR("NetListenSocket Error: Init failed to create socket handle");
  }

  // set socket options to reuse server socket addresses even if they are
  // busy - this is important if your server restarts and you don't want
  // to wait for your sockets to time out.

  if (setsockopt(m_sock, SOL_SOCKET, SO_REUSEADDR,
     (char *)&value, sizeof(value))== SOCKET_ERROR)
  {
    closesocket(m_sock);
    m_sock = INVALID_SOCKET;
    GCC_ERROR("NetListenSocket Error: Init failed to set socket options");
  }

  memset(&sa, 0, sizeof(sa));
  sa.sin_family = AF_INET;
  sa.sin_addr.s_addr = ADDR_ANY;
  sa.sin_port = htons(portnum);

  // bind to port
  if (bind(m_sock, (struct sockaddr *)&sa, sizeof(sa)) == SOCKET_ERROR)
  {
    closesocket(m_sock);
    m_sock = INVALID_SOCKET;
    GCC_ERROR("NetListenSocket Error: Init failed to bind");
  }

  // set nonblocking - accept() blocks under some odd circumstances otherwise
  SetBlocking(false);

  // start listening
  if (listen(m_sock, 256) == SOCKET_ERROR)
  {
    closesocket(m_sock);
    m_sock = INVALID_SOCKET;
    GCC_ERROR("NetListenSocket Error: Init failed to listen");
  }

  port = portnum;
}
```

If the listen socket gets any input, it means there's a client ready to attach. The method that handles the attachment and creates a new socket handle is `AcceptConnection()`.

```
SOCKET NetListenSocket::AcceptConnection(unsigned int *pAddr)
{
  SOCKET new_sock;
  struct sockaddr_in sock;
  int size = sizeof(sock);

  if ((new_sock = accept(m_sock, (struct sockaddr *)&sock, &size))==
      INVALID_SOCKET)
    return INVALID_SOCKET;

  if (getpeername(new_sock, (struct sockaddr *)&sock, &size) == SOCKET_ERROR)
  {
    closesocket(new_sock);
    return INVALID_SOCKET;
  }
  *pAddr = ntohl(sock.sin_addr.s_addr);
  return new_sock;
}
```

This method is a simple wrapper around `accept()`, which does all the heavy lifting. There's a utility function, `getpeername()`, which basically grabs the IP address of the new client and returns it in an output parameter.

You should be asking two questions right now. First, why don't I simply create a `NetSocket()` object right here and return that? Second, who or what actually calls this `AcceptConnect()` method? The answer to the first question is: I don't return a `NetSocket` object because I assume you'll want to create your own child class that inherits from `NetSocket` but overloads the `VHandleInput()` and `VHandleOutput()` methods. You'll see a class that does exactly that when I show you some more server-side code. Here's the answer to the second question: The server-side code itself! You'll see that in a few pages.

## A Socket Manager Class

Sockets need a socket manager, whether they are on a client or on a server. A socket manager organizes multiple sockets into a manageable group, takes care of handling the initialization and shutdown of the sockets system, and provides some useful utility functions. It also provides a useful base class for more specialized socket managers for servers and clients.

```
class BaseSocketManager
{
public:
  BaseSocketManager();
  virtual ~BaseSocketManager() { Shutdown(); }
```

```
  bool Init();
  void Shutdown();

  int AddSocket(NetSocket *socket);
  void RemoveSocket(NetSocket *socket);

  bool Send(int sockId, shared_ptr<IPacket> packet);
  void DoSelect(int pauseMicroSecs, int handleInput = 1);

  void SetSubnet(unsigned int subnet, unsigned int subnetMask)
  {
    m_Subnet = subnet;
    m_SubnetMask = subnetMask;
  }
  bool IsInternal(unsigned int ipaddr);

  unsigned int GetHostByName(std::string hostName);
  const char *GetHostByAddr(unsigned int ip);

  void AddToOutbound(int rc) { m_Outbound += rc; }
  void AddToInbound(int rc) { m_Inbound += rc; }

protected:
  WSADATA m_WsaData;        // describes sockets system implementation

  typedef std::list<NetSocket *> SocketList;
  typedef std::map<int, NetSocket *> SocketIdMap;

  SocketList m_SockList;     // a list of sockets
  SocketIdMap m_SockMap;     // a map from integer IDs to socket handles

  int m_NextSocketId;       // a ticker for the next socket ID

  unsigned int m_Inbound;           // statistics gathering - inbound data
  unsigned int m_Outbound;          // statistics gathering - outbound data
  unsigned int m_MaxOpenSockets;  // statistics gathering - max open sockets

  unsigned int m_SubnetMask;  // the subnet mask of the internal network
  unsigned int m_Subnet;      // the subnet of the internal network

  NetSocket *FindSocket(int sockId);
};
```

One of the core features of the socket manager is the notion that each socket has a companion identifier. In this implementation of the manager, a counter is used to guarantee a unique ID for each socket in the system. This is different than a handle because this ID could be something much more significant, such as a player ID number or an account ID number or whatever. On *Ultima Online*, this ID was a unique player ID number that was assigned to it by the account login system when new accounts were created. You can use whatever you want, but it is a good thing to associate an unchanging ID number with each socket, since socket handles can change if the socket is dropped and reconnected.

Another thing that the socket manager tracks is statistics for socket traffic and the maximum number of sockets the manager has managed at one time. This can be useful if you decide to track that sort of thing in production or even after release. As an example, *Ultima Online* tracked all manner of statistics about player activity, network activity, and so on.

If you set the subnet members, the socket manager can tell if a socket is coming from an internal IP address. For example, it can ensure that an IP address is on the local network and deny access from an IP address coming from the Internet. This feature proved to be pretty useful to mask off special functions, like the "God" commands in *Ultima Online*, from anyone outside of the development team.

Like other members of the application layer, the socket manager is a singleton object. It can manage both client and listen sockets, although the implementations in this chapter favor a straight client or straight server paradigm.

```
BaseSocketManager *g_pSocketManager = NULL;

BaseSocketManager::BaseSocketManager()
{
  m_Inbound = 0;
  m_Outbound = 0;
  m_MaxOpenSockets = 0;
  m_SubnetMask = 0;
  m_Subnet = 0xffffffff;

  g_pSocketManager = this;
  ZeroMemory(&m_WsaData, sizeof(WSADATA));
}

bool BaseSocketManager::Init()
{
  if (WSAStartup(0x0202, &m_WsaData)==0)
    return true;
  else
  {
    GCC_ERROR("WSAStartup failure!");
    return false;
  }
```

```
}

void BaseSocketManager::Shutdown()
{
  // Get rid of all those pesky kids...
  while (!m_SockList.empty())
  {
    delete *m_SockList.begin();
    m_SockList.pop_front();
  }

  WSACleanup();
}
```

You've seen before that performing any task that can fail in a constructor is generally a bad idea. Therefore, the socket manager class uses an initialization method that can return a Boolean value. It also uses a `Shutdown()` method apart from the destructor so you can have more control over the life and death of sockets in your application.

Once a `NetSocket` object exists, it is added to the socket manager with the `AddSocket()` method. It adds the socket to the socket list, updates the map of socket IDs to socket handles, and updates the maximum number of sockets opened. The `RemoveSocket()` method removes the socket from the list and the map, and then it frees the socket.

```
int BaseSocketManager::AddSocket(NetSocket *socket)
{
  socket->m_id = m_NextSocketId;
  m_SockMap[m_NextSocketId] = socket;
  ++m_NextSocketId;
  m_SockList.push_front(socket);
  if (m_SockList.size()) > m_MaxOpenSockets)
    ++m_MaxOpenSockets;

  return socket->m_id;
}

void BaseSocketManager::RemoveSocket(NetSocket *socket)
{
  m_SockList.remove(socket);
  m_SockMap.erase(socket->m_id);
  SAFE_DELETE(socket);
}
```

Your game needs a high-level function to send a packet to a particular socket ID. High-level game systems certainly won't care to have a direct reference to a socket handle, so they use the socket ID to figure out which socket is going to get the packet. In the case of a server system with hundreds of attached clients, this function makes short work of finding a socket handle that corresponds to a generic socket ID.

```
NetSocket *BaseSocketManager::FindSocket(int sockId)
{
  SocketIdMap::iterator i = m_SockMap.find(sockId);
  if (i==m_SockMap.end())
    return NULL;

  return (*i).second;
}

bool BaseSocketManager::Send(int sockId, shared_ptr<IPacket> packet)
{
  NetSocket *sock = FindSocket(sockId);
  if (!sock)
    return false;
  sock->Send(packet);
  return true;
}
```

The real meat of the socket manager class is `DoSelect()`. There are four stages of this method:

- Set up which sockets are going to be polled for activity.
- Call the `select()` API.
- Handle processing of any socket with input, output, or exceptions.
- Close any sockets that need closing.

```
void BaseSocketManager::DoSelect(int pauseMicroSecs, int handleInput)
{
  timeval tv;
  tv.tv_sec = 0;
  // 100 microseconds is 0.1 milliseconds or .0001 seconds
  tv.tv_usec = pauseMicroSecs;

  fd_set inp_set, out_set, exc_set;
  int maxdesc;

  FD_ZERO(&inp_set);
  FD_ZERO(&out_set);
  FD_ZERO(&exc_set);

  maxdesc = 0;
```

```
// set everything up for the select
for (SocketList::iterator i = m_SockList.begin();
    i != m_SockList.end(); ++i)
{
  NetSocket *pSock = *i;
  if ((pSock->m_deleteFlag&1) || pSock->m_sock == INVALID_SOCKET)
    continue;

  if (handleInput)
    FD_SET(pSock >m_sock, &inp_set);

  FD_SET(pSock->m_sock, &exc_set);

  if (pSock->VHasOutput())
    FD_SET(pSock->m_sock, &out_set);

  if ((int)pSock->m_sock > maxdesc)
    maxdesc = (int)pSock->m_sock;
 }

int selRet = 0;
// do the select (duration passed in as tv, NULL to block until event)
selRet = select(maxdesc+1, &inp_set, &out_set, &exc_set, &tv) ;
if (selRet == SOCKET_ERROR)
{
  GCC_ERROR("Error in DoSelect!");
  return;
}

// handle input, output, and exceptions
if (selRet)
{
  for (SocketList::iterator i = m_SockList.begin();
    i != m_SockList.end(); ++i)
  {
    NetSocket *pSock = *i;

    if ((pSock->m_deleteFlag&1) || pSock->m_sock == INVALID_SOCKET)
      continue;

    if (FD_ISSET(pSock->m_sock, &exc_set))
      pSock->HandleException();

    if (!(pSock->m_deleteFlag&1) && FD_ISSET(pSock->m_sock, &out_set))
      pSock->VHandleOutput();
```

```
      if (  handleInput
        && !(pSock->m_deleteFlag&1) && FD_ISSET(pSock->m_sock, &inp_set))
      {
        pSock->VHandleInput();
      }
    }
  }

  unsigned int timeNow = timeGetTime();

  // handle deleting any sockets
  SocketList::iterator i = m_SockList.begin();
  while (i != m_SockList.end())
  {
    pSock = *i;
    if (pSock->m_timeOut && pSock->m_timeOut < timeNow)
      pSock->VTimeOut();

    if (pSock->m_deleteFlag&1)
    {
      switch (pSock->m_deleteFlag)
      {
       case 1:
         g_pSocketManager->RemoveSocket(pSock);
         i = m_SockList.begin();
         break;

       case 3:
         pSock->m_deleteFlag = 2;
         if (pSock->m_sock != INVALID_SOCKET)
         {
            closesocket(pSock->m_sock);
            pSock->m_sock = INVALID_SOCKET;
         }
         break;
      }
    }
    i++;
  }
}
```

Notice the liberal use of `FD_ZERO`, `FD_SET`, and `FD_ISSET`. These are accessors to the `fd_set` structures that are sent into the `select()` method and store the results. This method's job is to poll all the sockets you send into it for input, output, and exceptions. The socket list is iterated three times in this method, which may seem inefficient. The truth is if you use `select()`, which polls sockets, the real inefficiency is inside the select statement itself. The other code doesn't really take that much more time. Sockets could also have their delete flags set inside calls to `VHandleInput()` or `VHandleOutput()`, so it makes sense to iterate through them after those methods are finished.

The code at the end of the method has two kinds of socket shutdown. The first, if the delete flag is set to 1, removes the socket entirely from the socket manager. This would occur if the socket were shut down elegantly from both sides, perhaps by trading an "L8R" packet or something. The second case allows the `NetSocket` object to exist, but the socket handle will be shut down. This allows for a potential reconnection of a socket if a player drops off the game for a moment but then comes back. If that happened, the unsent packets still in the `NetSocket` object would still be ready to send to the newly reconnected player.

The `DoSelect()` method is the only thing you need to call in your main loop to make the entire sockets system work. You'll want to call this method after you tick the Event Manager but before updating the game, assuming you are using the socket system to send events across the network:

```
  // allow event queue to process for up to 20 ms
  IEventManager::Get()->VUpdate(20);

  if (g_pApp->m_pBaseSocketManager)
    g_pApp->m_pBaseSocketManager->DoSelect(0);  // pause 0 microseconds

  g_pApp->m_pGame->VOnUpdate(fTime, fElapsedTime);
```

The last three methods in the socket manager class are some utility methods. The first one uses the subnet and subnet mask members to figure out if a particular IP address is coming from the internal network or from somewhere outside.

```
bool BaseSocketManager::IsInternal(unsigned int ipaddr)
{
  if (!m_SubnetMask)
    return false;

  if ((ipaddr & m_SubnetMask) == m_Subnet)
    return false;

  return true;
}
```

The next two methods wrap the DNS functions you already know how to use: `gethostbyname()` and `gethostbyaddr()`.

```
unsigned int BaseSocketManager::GetHostByName(const std::string &hostName)
{
  struct hostent *pHostEnt = gethostbyname(hostName.c_str());
  struct sockaddr_in tmpSockAddr; //placeholder for the ip address

  if(pHostEnt == NULL)
  {
    GCC_ERROR("Error occurred");
    return 0;
  }

  memcpy(&tmpSockAddr.sin_addr,pHostEnt->h_addr,pHostEnt->h_length);
  return ntohl(tmpSockAddr.sin_addr.s_addr);
}
const char *BaseSocketManager::GetHostByAddr(unsigned int ip)
{
  static char host[32];

  int netip = htonl(ip);
  struct hostent *lpHostEnt = gethostbyaddr((const char *)&netip, 4, PF_INET);

  if (lpHostEnt)
  {
    strcpy(host, lpHostEnt->h_name);
    return host;
  }

  return NULL;
}
```

The BaseSocketManager class is about 99 percent of what you need to create a client-side socket manager or a server-side socket manager. Classes that inherit from it can make it easy to create connections between clients and servers.

## Core Client-Side Classes

An easy example of an extension of the BaseSocketManager class is a class to manage the client side of a game. Its job is to create a single socket that attaches to a known server.

```
class ClientSocketManager : public BaseSocketManager
{
  std::string m_HostName;
  unsigned int m_Port;

public:
  ClientSocketManager(const std::string &hostName, unsigned int port)
```

```
    {
      m_HostName = hostName;
      m_Port = port;
    }
    bool Connect();
};

bool ClientSocketManager::Connect()
{
  if (!BaseSocketManager::Init())
    return false;

  RemoteEventSocket *pSocket = GCC_NEW RemoteEventSocket;

  if (!pSocket->Connect(GetHostByName(m_HostName), m_Port) )
  {
    SAFE_DELETE(pSocket);
    return false;
  }
  AddSocket(pSocket);
  return true;
}
```

I haven't shown you the `RemoteEventSocket` class yet, so hang tight because you'll see it shortly. All you need to know for now is that `RemoteEventSocket` is an extension of the `NetSocket` class, and it handles all the input and output for the local game client. In practice, you define whatever socket you want to handle all your client packets and initialize it in your version of the `ClientSocketManager` class.

Here's an example of how you might use this class to create a client connection to a server at shooter.fragfest.com, listening on port 3709:

```
ClientSocketManager *pClient =
  GCC_NEW ClientSocketManager("shooter.fragfest.com", 3709);
if (!pClient->Connect())
{
  GCC_ERROR("Couldn't attach to game server.");
}
```

## Core Server-Side Classes

The server side is a little trickier, but not terribly so. The complexity comes from how sockets work on the server side. Let's review what happens on the server side once the sockets system is running and the server has a listen socket open.

- Initialize the server socket manager and attach a listen socket.
- Call DoSelect() on the server socket manager.
- If there's input on the listen socket, create a new socket and attach it to the socket manager.
- Handle input/output exceptions on all other sockets.

What we need is a class that extends NetListenSocket by overloading VHandleInput() to create new clients. The clients are encapsulated by the RemoteEventSocket, which is the final piece to this puzzle. Its job is to send game events generated on the server to a remote client and fool the client into thinking that the events were actually generated locally.

```
class GameServerListenSocket: public NetListenSocket
{
public:
  GameServerListenSocket(int portnum) { Init(portnum); }
  void VHandleInput();
};

void GameServerListenSocket::VHandleInput()
{
  unsigned int theipaddr;
  SOCKET new_sock = AcceptConnection(&theipaddr);

  int value = 1;
  setsockopt(new_sock, SOL_SOCKET, SO_DONTLINGER,
    (char *)&value, sizeof(value));

  if (new_sock != INVALID_SOCKET)
  {
    RemoteEventSocket * sock =
      GCC_NEW RemoteEventSocket(new_sock, theipaddr);
    int sockId = g_pSocketManager->AddSocket(sock);
    int ipAddress = g_pSocketManager->GetIpAddress(sockdId);
    shared_ptr<EvtData_Remote_Client> pEvent (
      GCC_NEW EvtData_Remote_Client( sockId, ipAddress ) );
    IEventManager::Get()->VQueueEvent(pEvent);
  }
}
```

Notice another cameo from Chapter 11? Here, the method calls the Event Manager's VQueueEvent() with a new event: EvtData_Remote_Client. The event takes the socket ID and the IP address and passes them onto any game subsystem that is listening. This is how the game attaches new players. It relates the socket ID to an object or actor in the game and a new kind of game view that fools the server into thinking that the client is actually a human player playing on the same system.

You are now ready to see the final piece of this puzzle—how the sockets system ties into the event system and the game views.

## Wiring Sockets into the Event System

Let's take inventory. What have you learned so far in this chapter?

- `NetSocket()` and `ClientSocketManager()` work together to create the generic client side of the network communications.
- `NetListenSocket()` and `BaseSocketManager()` work together to create the generic server side of the network communications.
- `GameServerListenSocket()` is a custom server-side class that creates special sockets that can take network data and translate them into events that game systems can listen to, just like you saw in Chapter 10, "User Interface Programming."

So what's left? A few things, actually. You need a socket that can translate network data into events, and you also need a class that can take events and create network packets to be sent along to remote computers—client or server. Both the client and the server will do this because they both generate and listen for events coming from the other side.

Translating C++ objects of any kind requires streaming. There are tons of useful implementations of streams out there, and in my great practice of doing something rather stupid to make a point, I'm going to show you how to use STL `istrstream` and `ostrstream` templates.

Even though I'm an old-school C hound and still use `printf()` everywhere, I'm sure many of you have seen streams like this:

```
char nameBuffer[64];
cout << "Hello World! What is your name?";
cin >> nameBuffer;
```

The `istrstream` and `ostrstream` work very similarly. Think of them as a string-based memory stream that you can read from and write to very easily. At some point in this book, I mentioned how useful it was to use streams to initialize C++ objects and use them to save them out to disk for saved games. Well, here's an example of what this looks like with a simple C++ object:

```
class EvtData_Remote_Client : public BaseEventData
{
  int m_socketId;
  int m_ipAddress;

public:
  static const EventType sk_EventType;

  // Note - only VSerialize and VDeserialze are included here to save trees!
  virtual void VSerialize(std::ostrstream &out) const
  {
    out << m_socketId << " ";
    out << m_ipAddress;
  }

  virtual void VDeserialize( std::istrstream &in )
  {
    in >> m_socketId;
    in >> m_ipAddress;
  }
};
```

This is a portion of the `EvtData_Remote_Client` object: It stores the socket ID and the IP address of the remote client. Notice two virtual functions for serializing the object, either in or out, with streams. My choice for the stream class being string based and not binary makes my network packets completely enormous, but they are easy on my eyes and easy to debug. The best thing is, once the basic system is running, I can even replace these text stream objects with something better, such as a class that compresses binary streams on the fly. Look on the Internet, and you'll find neat stream technology out there.

Back to the task at hand, you've seen a quick introduction into using streams to turn C++ objects into raw bits that can be sent to a disk or across the Internet. Now you're ready to see the `RemoteEventSocket` class, which converts the network socket data into events that can be sent on to the local event system. There are only two methods in this class: One overloads to `VHandleInput()`, and the other takes the incoming packets and turns them into events.

```
class RemoteEventSocket: public NetSocket
{
public:
  enum
  {
    NetMsg_Event,
```

```
    NetMsg_PlayerLoginOk,
  };

  // server accepting a client
  RemoteEventSocket(SOCKET new_sock, unsigned int hostIP)
  : NetSocket(new_sock, hostIP) {  }

  // client attach to server
  RemoteEventSocket() { };
  virtual void VHandleInput();

protected:
  void CreateEvent(std::istrstream &in);
};

void RemoteEventSocket::VHandleInput()
{
  NetSocket::VHandleInput();

  // traverse the list of m_InList packets and do something useful with them
  while (!m_InList.empty())
  {
    shared_ptr<IPacket> packet = *m_InList.begin();
    m_InList.pop_front();
    const char *buf = packet->VGetData();
    int size = static_cast<int>(packet->VGetSize());

    std::istrstream in(buf+sizeof(u_long), (size-sizeof(u_long)));

    int type;
    in >> type;
    switch(type)
    {
      case NetMsg_Event:
        CreateEvent(in);
        break;

      case NetMsg_PlayerLoginOk:
      {
        int serverSockId, actorId;
        in >> serverSockId;
        in >> actorId;
        shared_ptr<EvtData_Network_Player_Actor_Assignment> pEvent
          (GCC_NEW EvtData_Network_Player_Actor_Assignment(actorId,
           serverSockId));
        IEventManager::Get()->VQueueEvent(pEvent);
```

```
        break;
      }
      default:
        GCC_ERROR("Unknown message type.");
    }
  }
}
```

You'll see that I've created a little handshaking. There are two types of messages in this simple design. The first is a normal event, in which case the packet is sent on to `CreateEvent()`. The second is a special case message from the server that tells the local client what its socket ID is. This is how different clients, all playing the same multiplayer game, tell each other apart, because their server socket IDs must all be unique. If they didn't do this, it would be difficult for the server to know which actor is controlled by which remote player, or which player's score to tally when there is a successful kill.

The `CreateEvent()` method looks in the stream for an event type, which is sent in string format. The event type is used to create a new event object, which then uses the stream to initialize itself.

```
void RemoteEventSocket::CreateEvent(std::istrstream &in)
{
  EventType eventType;
  in >> eventType;
  IEventDataPtr pEvent(CREATE_EVENT(eventType));
  if (pEvent)
  {
    pEvent->VDeserialize(in);
    IEventManager::Get()->VQueueEvent(pEvent);
  }
  else
  {
    GCC_ERROR("ERROR Unknown event type from remote: 0x" +
           ToStr(eventType, 16));
  }
}
```

This event was generated on a remote machine, sent over the network, re-created from the bit stream, and put back together again just like Dr. McCoy in a transporter beam. Recipients of the event really have no idea it was generated from afar and sent across the Internet. You'll notice some nice trickery with a call to `CREATE_EVENT`. This method uses a very useful template class, `GenericObjectFactory`. Its purpose is to take some kind of unique identifier and call the constructor of a class that matches that identifier. The source code for this class is in the companion source code to this book, in *Dev\Source\GCC4\Utilities\templates.h*, and it isn't too hard to follow. This kind of construction can be used for any class and makes it much easier to add new C++ classes that will be streamed, whether by the Internet or perhaps a save game file.

One last thing—you need to see how local events are sent into the network. If you think I'm going to use streams again, you are right. The class holds a socket ID, which will be used when sending the event to the network classes. The `ForwardEvent()` implementation creates a stream that has the event message identifier first, followed by the event type (which is really the name of the event), followed finally by the event itself. This stream object now contains the serialized event and enough data to be reconstructed on the remote computer.

```
class NetworkEventForwarder
{
public:
  NetworkEventForwarder(int sockId) { m_sockId = sockId; }
  void ForwardEvent( IEventDataPtr pEventData );
protected:
  int m_sockId;
};

void NetworkEventForwarder::ForwardEvent( IEventDataPtr pEventData )
{
  std::ostrstream out;

  out << static_cast<int>(RemoteEventSocket::NetMsg_Event) << " ";
  out << pEventData->VGetEventType() << " ";
  pEventData.VSerialize(out);
  out << "\r\n";

  shared_ptr<BinaryPacket> eventMsg(
    GCC_NEW BinaryPacket(out.rdbuf()->str(), out.pcount()));

  g_pSocketManager->Send(m_sockId, eventMsg);
}
```

**You Can't Serialize Pointers**

You have to be really careful when designing any C++ objects that are going to be serialized. For one thing, they can't contain pointers. If a local C++ object had a direct pointer to another game data structure like an actor or a sound, once it got to the remote computer the pointer would surely point to garbage. This is why you see so many handles, ID numbers, and other stuff that refers to objects indirectly through a manager of some sort. An actor ID should be guaranteed to be unique on the server, and thus it will be unique on all the clients, too.

There's one last class you need to know about—the NetworkGameView. This is a "fake" view that fools the authoritative game server into thinking someone is sitting right there playing the game, instead of a few hundred milliseconds by photon away. As you can see, it's not much more than a pretty face.

```
class NetworkGameView : public IGameView
{
public:
  // IGameView Implementation - everything is stubbed out.
  virtual HRESULT VOnRestore() { return S_OK; }
  virtual void VOnRender(double fTime, float fElapsedTime) { }
  virtual void VOnLostDevice() { }
  virtual GameViewType VGetType() { return GameView_Remote; }
  virtual GameViewId VGetId() const { return m_ViewId; }
  virtual void VOnAttach(GameViewId vid, ActorId aid)
    { m_ViewId = vid; m_PlayerActorId = aid; }
  virtual LRESULT CALLBACK VOnMsgProc( AppMsg msg ) { return 0; }
  virtual void VOnUpdate( int deltaMilliseconds ) { };

  void SetPlayerActorId(ActorId actorId) { m_ActorId = actorId; }
  void AttachRemotePlayer(int sockID);
  int HasRemotePlayerAttached() { return m_SockId != -1; }

  NetworkGameView(int sockId)

protected:
  GameViewId m_ViewId;
  ActorId m_ActorId;
  int m_SockId;
};

NetworkGameView::NetworkGameView()
{
  m_SockId = -1;
  m_ActorId = INVALID_ACTOR_ID;
  IEventManager::Get()->VAddListener(
    MakeDelegate(this, &NetworkGameView::NewActorDelegate),
      EvtData_New_Actor::sk_EventType);
}
```

The constructor registers to listen for a single event when new actors are created. For the game-specific events, you'll create a NetworkEventForwarder class both on the server side and on the client side to listen for events and forward them to the other computer across the Internet.

There's really only one method, AttachRemotePlayer(), which is called by the game logic when new remote views are added. This is where the NetMsg_PlayerLoginOk message is generated by the server, which contains the unique socket ID number down to the client so all the players of a multiplayer game don't get confused.

```
void NetworkGameView::AttachRemotePlayer(int sockID)
{
  m_SockId = sockID;
  std::ostrstream out;
  out << static_cast<int>(RemoteEventSocket::NetMsg_PlayerLoginOk) << " ";
  out << m_SockId << " ";
  out << m_ActorId << " ";
  out << "\r\n";

  shared_ptr<BinaryPacket> gvidMsg(GCC_NEW BinaryPacket(out.rdbuf()->str(),
     (u_long)out.pcount()));
  g_pSocketManager->Send(m_SockId, gvidMsg);
}
```

## Gosh, if It's That Easy

There is much more to network programming than I've had the pages to teach you here. First, remote games need to be very smart about handling slow Internet connectivity by predicting moves and handing things elegantly when those predictions are wrong. For enterprise games like *World of Warcraft,* you have to take the simple architecture in this book and extend it into a hierarchy of server computers. You also have to create technology that prevents cheating and hacking. These tasks could, and do, fill volumes on the subject.

Still, I hope you feel that what you've seen in this chapter is an excellent start. Certainly, if you want to learn network programming without starting from scratch, the code in this chapter and on the book's website will give you something you can play with. You can experiment with it, break it, and put it back in good order. That's the best way to learn.

That is, of course, how I started, only I believe the little record player I ruined when I was a kid never did work again. Sorry, Mom!

# Chapter 20

*by Mike McShaffry*

# Introduction to Multiprogramming

The general term for creating software that can figuratively or actually run in multiple, independent pieces simultaneously is *multiprogramming.*

There are few subjects in programming as tricky as this. It turns out to be amazingly simple to get multiple threads chewing on something interesting, like calculating π to 1,000,000 digits. The difficulty comes in getting each of these jobs to play nicely with each other's memory and getting them to send information to each other so that the results of their work can be put to good use.

The code you will learn in this chapter will work on single or multiprocessor Windows systems, but it is easy enough to port to others. The concepts you will learn are also portable to any system that has threading built into the operating system.

The first question you should ask is why should we bother with multithreading at all? Isn't one thread on one CPU enough?

## What Multiprogramming Does

A CPU is amazingly fast, and many desktop CPUs are now sitting solidly in the 2–3GHz range, and some systems on the market are peaking over 5GHz. If you happen to have a really nice lab and can get your transistors down to near absolute zero, you can get it to switch at 500GHz like IBM and Georgia Tech did back in 2006. But what does that really mean?

Gigahertz, as it is applied to CPUs, measure the clock speed of the CPU. The clock speed is the basic measure of how fast things happen—anything from loading a bit of memory into a register to doing a mathematical operation like addition. Different instructions take different cycles, or ticks, of the clock. Different types of processors, such as GPUs, are highly optimized for certain kinds of operations, such as floating-point division, and can perform multiple operations in a single tick of the system clock.

In the Georgia Tech experiment, they were able to get a transistor to switch at 500GHz, but that does not mean you could pile those transistors onto a super-cooled chip and have a CPU run at that speed. Sorry to throw cold water on the party, but the transistors in a chip have to carefully coordinated. Think of it like this—just because I can create a vehicle capable of rocketing across a dry lake bed faster than the speed of sound doesn't mean I can take millions of those same vehicles and try to do the same on a regular-surface street.

Many processors are capable of executing instructions in parallel in a single core if they use different parts of the processor. With the advent of multicore processors, it is even possible to perform more than one instruction in a single cycle. Most new computers now have two or even four cores. Some processors are even capable of out-of-order execution, where the processor executes instructions in an order governed by availability of input data rather than the order set by the programmer or compiler.

As fast as CPUs are and the tricks they pull to keep busy, they spend most of their time waiting around. Take a look at Figure 20.1, a snapshot of the CPU load running *Teapot Wars,* which you'll see in Chapter 21, "A Game of *Teapot Wars.*"

The figure shows a few spikes, but there's still plenty of headroom. So what's going on? Is *Teapot Wars* written so efficiently? Hardly. The CPU, or CPUs in this case, spends most of its time waiting for the video hardware to draw the scene. This is a pretty common thing in computer game software, since preparing the scene and communicating to the video card take so much time.

It turns out there is a solution for this problem, and it involves multithreading. Instead of creating a monolithic program that runs one instruction after another, the programmer splits the program into multiple, independent pieces. Each piece is launched independently and can run on its own. If one piece, or *thread,* becomes stuck waiting for something, like the optical media drive to spin up so a file can be read, the processor can switch over to another thread and process whatever instructions it has.

If you think this is similar to what happens when you run 50 different applications on your desktop machine, you are very close to being right. Each application exists

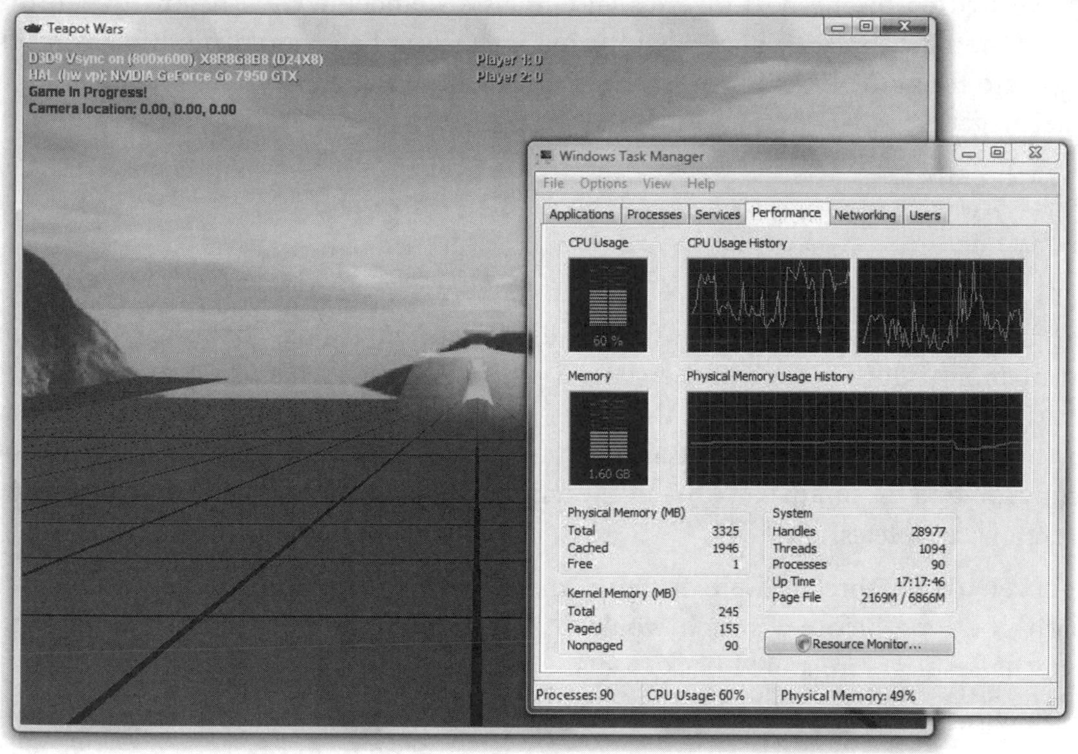


**Figure 20.1**
CPU load running *Teapot Wars.*

independently of other applications and can access devices like your hard drive or your network without any problems at all, at least until you run out of memory or simply bog your system down.

Under Windows and most operating systems, applications run as separate processes, and the operating system has very special rules for switching between processes since they run in their own memory space. This switching is relatively expensive, since a lot of work has to happen so that each application believes it has the complete and full attention of the CPU.

The good news is that under Windows and other operating systems each process can have multiple threads of execution, and switching between them is relatively cheap. Each thread has its own stack space and full access to the same memory as the other threads created by the process. Being able to share memory is extremely useful, but it does have its problems.

The operating system can switch from one thread to another at any time. When a switch happens, the values of the current thread's CPU registers are saved. They are then overwritten by the next thread's CPU registers, and the CPU begins to run the code for the new thread. This leads to some interesting behaviors if multiple threads manipulate the same bit of memory. Take a look at the assembly for incrementing a global integer:

```
++g_ProtectedTotal;
006D2765 mov         eax,dword ptr [g_ProtectedTotal (9B6E48h)]
006D276A add         eax,1
006D276D mov         dword ptr [g_ProtectedTotal (9B6E48h)],eax
```

There are three instructions. The first loads the current value of the variable from main memory into eax, one of the general purpose registers. The second increments the register, and the third stores the new value back into memory. Remember that each thread has full access to the memory pointed to by g_ProtectedTotal, but its copy of eax is unique. A thread switch can happen after each assembler level instruction completes.

If a dozen or so threads were running these three instructions simultaneously, it wouldn't be long before a switch would happen right after the add instruction but before the results were stored back to main memory.

In my own experiments, the results were pretty sobering: 20 threads each incrementing the variable 100,000 times created an end result of 902,149. This means 1,097,851 additions were completely missed. I ran this experiment on a Windows 64-bit system equipped with an Intel Core i7-2600 CPU.

Lucky for you and everyone else out there wanting to take full advantage of their CPUs, there are ways to solve this problem. But first, you should know how you create the thread in the first place.

## Creating Threads

Under Windows, you use the CreateThread() API. For you programmers who desire a more portable solution, you can also choose the _beginthread() call or the threading calls in the Boost C++ library.

```
DWORD g_maxLoops = 20;            // shouldn't be on a stack!
DWORD g_UnprotectedTotal = 0;     // the variable we want to increment

DWORD WINAPI ThreadProc( LPVOID lpParam )
{
  DWORD maxLoops = *static_cast<DWORD *>(lpParam);
  DWORD dwCount = 0;
  while( dwCount < maxLoops )
  {
```

```
    ++dwCount;
    ++g_UnprotectedTotal;
  }
  return TRUE;
}

void CreateThreads()
{
  for (int i=0; i<20; i++)
  {
    CreateThread(
        NULL,     // default security attributes
        0,        // default stack size
        (LPTHREAD_START_ROUTINE) ThreadProc,
        &g_maxLoops, // thread parameter is how many loops
        0,        // default creation flags
        NULL);    // receive thread identifier
  }
}
```

To create a thread, you call the `CreateThread()` API with a pointer to a function that will run as the thread procedure. The thread will cease to exist when the thread procedure exits or something external stops the thread, such as a call to `TerminateThread()`. The thread procedure, `ThreadProc`, takes one variable, a void pointer that you may use to send any bit of data your thread procedure needs. In the previous example, a `DWORD` was set to the number of loops and used as the thread parameter. The thread can be started in a suspended state if you set the default creation flags to `CREATE_SUSPENDED`, in which case you'll need to call `ResumeThread(m_hThread)` to get it started.

Take special note of where the parameter to the thread process is stored, because it is a global. Had it been local to the `CreateThreads()` function, it would have been stored on the stack. The address of this would have been passed to the thread procedures, and goodness knows what it would have in it at any given moment. This is a great example of how something seemingly trivial can have a huge effect on how your threads run.

### The Stack Can Be a Dangerous Place

Be careful about where you store data that will be accessed by thread procedures. The stack is right out, since it will be constantly changing. Allocate specific memory for your thread procedures or store them globally.

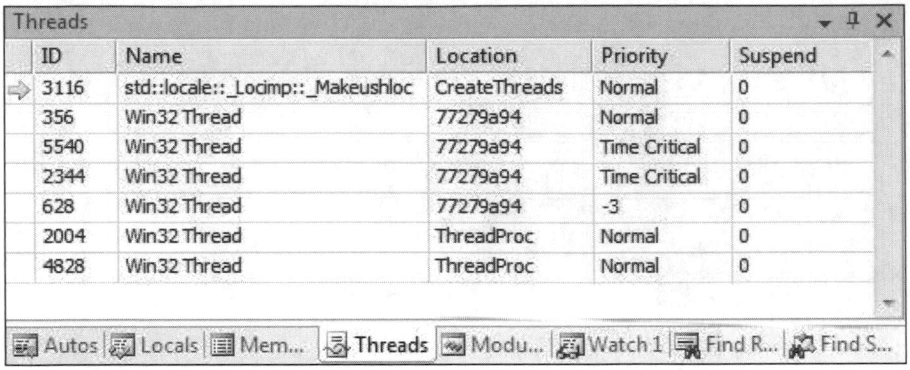
Threads
ID
Name
Location
Priority
Suspend
3116
std::locale::_Locimp::_Makeushloc
CreateThreads
Normal
0
356
Win32 Thread
77279a94
Normal
0
5540
Win32 Thread
77279a94
Time Critical
0
2344
Win32 Thread
77279a94
Time Critical
0
628
Win32 Thread
77279a94
-3
0
2004
Win32 Thread
ThreadProc
Normal
0
4828
Win32 Thread
ThreadProc
Normal
0
Autos
Locals
Mem...
Threads
Modu...
Watch 1
Find R...
Find S...

**Figure 20.2**
The Threads window in Visual Studio.

When you have multiple threads running in your game, you can debug each of them, to a point. In Visual Studio, you can show the Threads window by selecting Debug→Window→Threads from the main menu (see Figure 20.2).

When you hit a breakpoint, all threads stop execution. If you double-click on a row in the Threads window, you will see where execution has stopped in that thread. You can easily set breakpoints in the thread procedure, but if you run multiple threads using the same procedure, you can never tell which thread will hit the breakpoint first! It can become a little confusing.

Creating a thread is pretty trivial, as you have seen. Getting these threads to work together and not wipe out the results of other threads working on the same memory is a little harder.

## Process Synchronization

There's really no use in having threads without having some way to manage their access to memory. In the early days of computing, programmers tried to solve this with algorithms and logic. When I was in college, one of my favorite instructors, Dr. Rusinkiewicz, had a ridiculous story he told to show us how these engineers tried to create a heuristic to handle this problem.

Imagine two railways that share a tunnel in the Andes Mountains in South America. One railway runs in Bolivia, and the other runs in neighboring Peru. The tunnel was filled with curves, and it was impossible for either engineer to see an oncoming train in time to stop. But both governments agreed that the trains were never in the tunnel long enough for there to be any real risk, so they allowed the trains to run. For a few months, nothing bad happened, but one day the trains crashed head-on in the tunnel. The governments of the two countries agreed that what they were doing wasn't safe, and something must be done.

A bowl was placed at the beginning of the shared section of track. When an engineer arrived, he would check the bowl. If it was empty, he would put a rock in it and drive into the tunnel. He would then walk back, remove the rock, and continue on his trip. This worked for a few days, and then the Peruvians noticed that their train never arrived. Fearing the worst, a search team was sent out to find the train. It was waiting at the junction, and as the search team watched, the Bolivian train roared by, not even stopping. The Bolivian engineer ignored the rules, just put a rock in the bowl, and never intended to take it out. He was fired and another, more honest, Bolivian engineer replaced him.

For years nothing bad happened, but one day neither train arrived. A team was sent to investigate, and they found that the trains had crashed, and two rocks were in the bowl. Somehow both engineers must have passed each other in the dark tunnel while placing their rocks. The two countries decided that the current system wasn't working, and something must be done to fix the problem. They decided that the bowls were being used the wrong way. The Bolivian engineer would put a rock in the bowl when he was driving across, and the Peruvian engineer would always wait until the bowl was empty before driving across.

This didn't even work for a single day. The Peruvian train had until this time run twice per day, and the Bolivian train once per day. The new system prevented crashes, but now each train could only run once per day since it relied on trading permission to run through the pass. Again, the governments put their best minds at work to solve the problem.

They bought another bowl.

Now, two bowls were used at the pass. Each engineer had his own bowl. When he arrived, he would drop a rock into his bowl, walk to the other engineer's bowl, and check it. If there was a rock there, he would go back to his bowl, remove the rock, and take a siesta. This seemed to work for many years, until both trains were so late a search team was sent out to find out what happened.

Luckily, both trains were there, and both engineers were simultaneously dropping rocks into their bowls, checking the other, finding a rock, and then taking a siesta. Finally, the two governments decided that bowls and rocks were not going to solve this problem.

What they needed was a semaphore.

## Test and Set, the Semaphore, and the Mutex

The computer software version of a semaphore relies on a low-level hardware instruction called a test-and-set instruction. It checks the value of a bit, and if it is zero, it sets the bit to one, all in one operation that cannot be interrupted by the CPU switching from one thread to another.

Traditionally, a semaphore is set to an integer value that denotes the number of resources that are free. When a process wishes to gain access to a resource, it decrements the semaphore in an atomic operation, using a test-and-set. When it is done with the resource, it increments the semaphore in the same atomic operation. If a process finds the semaphore equal to zero, it must wait.

A mutex is a binary semaphore, and it is generally used to give a process exclusive access to a resource. All others must wait.

Windows has many different ways to handle process synchronization. A mutex can be created with `CreateMutex()`, and a semaphore can be created with `CreateSemaphore()`. But since these synchronization objects can be shared between Windows applications, they are fairly heavyweight and shouldn't be used for high performance thread safety in a single application, like our game. Windows programmers should use the critical section.

## The Windows Critical Section

The critical section under Windows is a less expensive way to manage synchronization among the threads of a single process. Here's how to put it to use:

```
DWORD g_ProtectedTotal = 0;
DWORD g_maxLoops = 20;
CRITICAL_SECTION g_criticalSection;

DWORD WINAPI ThreadProc( LPVOID lpParam )
{
  DWORD maxLoops = *static_cast<DWORD *>(lpParam);
  DWORD dwCount = 0;
   while( dwCount < maxLoops )
   {
    ++dwCount;

    EnterCriticalSection(&g_criticalSection);
    ++g_ProtectedTotal;
    LeaveCriticalSection(&g_criticalSection);
  }
  return TRUE;
}

void CreateThreads()
{
```

```
  InitializeCriticalSection(&g_criticalSection);

  for (int i=0; i<20; i++)
  {
    HANDLE m_hThread = CreateThread(
          NULL,           // default security attributes
          0,              // default stack size
          (LPTHREAD_START_ROUTINE) ThreadProc,
          &g_maxLoops, // thread parameter is how many loops
          0,              // default creation flags
          NULL);          // receive thread identifier
  }
}
```

The call to InitializeCriticalSection() does exactly what it advertises—it initializes the critical section object, declared globally as CRITICAL_SECTION g_criticalSection. You should treat the critical section object as opaque and not copy it or attempt to modify it. The thread procedure makes calls to EnterCriticalSection() and LeaveCriticalSection() around the access to the shared global variable, g_ProtectedTotal.

If another thread is already in the critical section, the call to EnterCriticalSection() will block and wait until the other thread leaves the critical section. Windows does not guarantee any order in which the threads will get access, but it will be fair to all threads. Notice that the critical section is made as small as possible—not even the increment to the dwCount member variable is inside. This is to illustrate an important point about critical sections: In order to achieve the maximum throughput, you should minimize the time spent in critical sections as much as possible.

If you want to check the critical section and only enter it if it is not locked, you can call TryEnterCriticalSection(). This function will return true only if the critical section is validly entered by the calling thread.

There are two useful C++ classes that help manage the creation and use of critical sections, CriticalSection and ScopedCriticalSection.

```
class CriticalSection : public GCC_noncopyable
{
public:
  CriticalSection() { InitializeCriticalSection( &m_cs ); }
  ~CriticalSection(){ DeleteCriticalSection( &m_cs ); }
  void Lock()       { EnterCriticalSection( &m_cs ); }
  void Unlock()     { LeaveCriticalSection( &m_cs ); }
protected:
```

```
  mutable CRITICAL_SECTION m_cs;
};

class ScopedCriticalSection : public GCC_noncopyable
{
public:
  ScopedCriticalSection( CriticalSection & csResource)
    : m_csResource( csResource)
    { m_csResource.Lock(); }
  ~ScopedCriticalSection() { m_csResource.Unlock(); }
private:
  CriticalSection & m_csResource;
};
```

If you had a bit of code that needed to be thread safe, you would first declare a `CriticalSection` object and use the `ScopedCriticalSection` object in your threads to block until the critical section was free.

```
CriticalSection g_Cs;

void ThreadSafeFunction()
{
  ScopedCriticalSection(&g_Cs);
  // do dangerous things here!
}
```

Because the `ScopedCriticalSection` object locks the critical section in the constructor and unlocks it in the destructor, the code in the same scope of this object is now thread safe and easy to read at the same time. You'll see this class used in a better example shortly.

## Interesting Threading Problems

There are a number of interesting threading problems you should be aware of: racing, starvation, and deadlock.

*Racing* is a condition where two or more threads are reading or writing shared data, and the final result requires the threads to run in a precise order, which can never be guaranteed. The classic problem is the writer-reader problem, where a writer thread fills a buffer, and a reader thread processes the buffer. If the two threads aren't synchronized properly, the reader will overtake the writer and read garbage.

The solution to this problem is easy with a shared count of bytes in the buffer, changed only by the writer thread using a critical section.

**Figure 20.3**
The dining philosophers.

Starvation and deadlock is a condition where one or more threads gains access to a shared resource and continually blocks access to the starving thread. The classic illustration of this problem is called the *dining philosophers' problem,* first imagined by Tony Hoare, a British computer scientist best known for creating the Quicksort algorithm. It goes like this. Five philosophers sit around a circular table, and they are doing one of two things: eating or thinking. When they are eating, they are not thinking, and when they are thinking, they are not eating. The table has five chopsticks, one sitting between each philosopher. In order to eat, each person must grab two chopsticks, and he must do this without speaking to anyone else.

You can see that if every philosopher grabbed the chopstick on his left and held onto it, none of them could ever grab a second chopstick, and they would all starve. This is analogous to a deadlock.

If they were eating and thinking at different times, one philosopher could simply get unlucky and never get the chance to get both chopsticks. He would starve, even though the others could eat. That is similar to process starvation.

The solution to the dining philosophers problem might sound familiar since I mentioned something about it in Chapter 5, "Game Initialization and Shutdown." If you want to avoid deadlock in any shared resource situation, always ask for resources in a particular order and release them in the reverse order.

With the dining philosophers, things are a little more complicated because of their arrangement and how the resources are used. The solution involves numbering the philosophers. Even-numbered philosophers should attempt to pick up their left chopstick first, and odd-numbered philosophers must pick up their right chopstick first. If they can't acquire both chopsticks, they must relinquish the one they have and try again later. This solution, and those to other interesting problems of this sort, can be found in Andrew Tannenbaum's book, *Modern Operating Systems.*

If you find yourself at a table with four other people and only five chopsticks between you, simply agree to pick up the left chopstick first and the right chopstick second. When you are ready to stop eating and start thinking, put them down in reverse order. Believe it or not, no deadlock will happen, and no one will starve.

There are a number of these interesting problems, which you should look up and try to solve on your own:

- Cigarette smokers' problem
- Sleeping barbers' problem
- Dining cryptographers' protocol

## Thread Safety

As you might imagine, there are often more things you *shouldn't* do in a thread than you should. For one thing, most STL and ANSI C calls are not thread safe. In other words, you can't manipulate the same `std::list` or make calls to `fread()` from multiple threads without something bad happening to your program. If you need to do these things in multiple concurrent threads, either you need to use the thread safe equivalent of these calls or you need to manage the calls with critical sections. A good example of this is included in the GameCode4 source code, which manages any `std::basic_ostream< char_type, traits_type>` and allows you to safely write to it from multiple threads. Look in the *Multicore\SafeStream.h* file for the template class and an example of how it can be used.

## Multithreading Classes in GameCode4

You are ready to see how these concepts are put to work in the GameCode4 architecture. There are two systems that make this easy: the Process Manager and the Event Manager. If you recall from Chapter 7, "Controlling the Main Loop," the `ProcessManager` is a container for cooperative processes that inherit from the `Process` class. It is simple to extend the `Process` class to create a real-time version of it, and while the operating system manages the thread portion of the class, the data and existence of it are still managed by the `ProcessManager` class. This turns out to be really useful, since initialization and process dependencies are still possible, even between normal and real-time processes.

Communication between real-time processes and the rest of the game happens exactly where you might expect—in the Event Manager. A little bit of code has to be written to manage the problem of events being sent to or from real-time processes, but you'll be surprised how little. Passing messages is a great way to synchronize processes running in different threads, and it also avoids problems that arise with shared data.

After the basic classes are written, you'll see how you can write a background real-time process to handle decompression of part of a Zip file.

## The `RealtimeProcess` Class

The goal with the `RealtimeProcess` class is to make it really easy to create real-time processes. Here's the class definition:

```
class RealtimeProcess : public Process
{
protected:
  HANDLE m_hThread;
  DWORD m_ThreadID;
  int m_ThreadPriority;
public:
  // Other prioities can be:
  // THREAD_PRIORITY_ABOVE_NORMAL
  // THREAD_PRIORITY_BELOW_NORMAL
  // THREAD_PRIORITY_HIGHEST
  // THREAD_PRIORITY_TIME_CRITICAL
  // THREAD_PRIORITY_LOWEST
  // THREAD_PRIORITY_IDLE
  //
  RealtimeProcess( int priority = THREAD_PRIORITY_NORMAL )
  : Process(PROC_REALTIME)
  {
    m_ThreadID = 0;
    m_ThreadPriority = priority;
  }
  virtual  ~RealtimeProcess() { CloseHandle(m_hThread); }
  static DWORD WINAPI ThreadProc ( LPVOID lpParam );
protected:
  virtual void VOnInit();
  virtual void VOnUpdate(unsigned long deltaMs) { }
  virtual void VThreadProc(void) = 0;
};
```

The members of this class include a Windows HANDLE to the thread, the thread ID, and the current thread priority. This is set to THREAD_PRIORITY_NORMAL, but depending on what the process needs to do, you might increase or decrease the priority. Note that if you set it to THREAD_PRIORITY_TIME_CRITICAL, you'll likely notice a serious sluggishness of the user interface, particularly the mouse pointer. It's a good idea to play nice and leave it at the default or even put it at a lower priority.

**Thread Priority Shuffle**

While working on *Barbie*, one of the engineers built a multithreaded loader that would load the data needed for the game in the background while the intro movie played. Unfortunately, on single-core machines, the intro movie got really choppy and would cut in and out. We considered delaying the start of the background loading until after the movie, although that would defeat the purpose. On a whim, one engineer tried lowering the priority of the loader thread. It worked perfectly, and the choppiness was completely gone.

The thread process is defined by ThreadProc, which is called by the operating system when the thread is created. That, in turn, will call VThreadProc, which will be defined by an inherited class. The RealtimeProcess class is meant to be a base class. Child classes will write their own thread process and send a pointer to it in the constructor.

Notice that the class does implement a VOnUpdate() method, but it is just a stub. All of the real processing in this class will be done by a thread function pointed to by m_lpRoutine.

VOnInit() is where the call to CreateThread() happens:

```
void RealtimeProcess::VOnInit(void)
{
  Process::VOnInit();
  m_hThread = CreateThread(
           NULL,          // default security attributes
           0,             // default stack size
           ThreadProc,    // thread process
           this,          // thread parameter is a pointer to the process
           0,             // default creation flags
           &m_ThreadID); // receive thread identifier

  if( m_hThread == NULL )
  {
```

```
        GCC_ERROR("Could not create thread!");
        Fail();
        return;
    }

    SetThreadPriority(m_hThread, m_ThreadPriority);
}

DWORD WINAPI RealtimeProcess::ThreadProc( LPVOID lpParam )
{
    RealtimeProcess *proc = static_cast<RealtimeProcess *>(lpParam);
    proc->VThreadProc();
    return TRUE;
}
```

Note the thread parameter in the call to `CreateThread()`? It is a pointer to the static `ThreadProc` method, which casts the thread parameter back to a pointer to the process instance. All the base classes must do is define the `VThreadProc` member function.

The only new call you haven't seen yet is the call to `SetThreadPriority()`, where you tell Windows how much processor time to allocate to this thread.

Here's how you would create a real-time process to increment a global integer, just like you saw earlier:

```
class ProtectedProcess : public RealtimeProcess
{
public:
    static DWORD g_ProtectedTotal;
    static CRITICAL_SECTION g_criticalSection;
    DWORD m_MaxLoops;
    ProtectedProcess(DWORD maxLoops)
        : RealtimeProcess(ThreadProc)
        { m_MaxLoops = maxLoops; }
    virtual void VThreadProc(void);
};

DWORD ProtectedProcess::g_ProtectedTotal = 0;
CriticalSection ProtectedProcess::g_criticalSection;

void ProtectedProcess::VThreadProc(void)
{
    DWORD dwCount = 0;

    while( dwCount < m_MaxLoops )
```

```
    {
      ++dwCount;

      {
        // Request ownership of critical section.
        ScopedCriticalSection locker(g_criticalSection);
        ++g_ProtectedTotal;
      }
    }
  Succeed();
}
```

The thread process is defined by `VThreadProc()`. Two static members of this class are the variable the process is going to increment and the critical section that will be shared between multiple instances of the real-time process. Just before the thread process returns, `Succeed()` is called to tell the Process Manager to clean up the process and launch any dependent processes.

As it turns out, you instantiate a real-time process in exactly the same way you do a cooperative process:

```
for( i=0; i < 20; i++ )
{
  shared_ptr<Process> proc(GCC_NEW ProtectedProcess(100000));
  procMgr->AttachProcess(proc);
}
```

The above example instantiates 20 processes that will each increment the global variable 100,000 times. The use of the critical sections ensures that when all the processes are complete, the global variable will be set to exactly 2,000,000.

## Sending Events from Real-Time Processes

There's probably no system in the GameCode4 architecture that uses STL containers more than the `EventManager` class. Given that STL containers aren't thread safe by themselves, there's one of two things that can be done.

We could make all the containers in the Event Manager thread safe. This includes two `std::map` objects, three `std::pair` objects, and two `std::list` objects. This would be a horrible idea, since the vast majority of the event system is accessed only by the main process and doesn't need to be thread safe. A better idea would be to create a single, thread-safe container that could accept events that were sent by real-time processes. When the event system runs its `VUpdate()` method, it can empty this queue in a thread-safe manner and handle the events sent by real-time processes along with the rest.

A thread-safe queue was posted by Anthony Williams on www.justsoftwaresolutions.co.uk.

```
template<typename Data>
class concurrent_queue
{
private:
  std::queue<Data> the_queue;
  CriticalSection m_cs;
  HANDLE m_dataPushed;
public:
  concurrent_queue() { m_dataPushed = CreateEvent(NULL, TRUE, FALSE, NULL);
  void push(Data const& data)
  {
    {
      ScopedCriticalSection locker(m_cs);
      the_queue.push(data);
    }
    PulseEvent(m_dataPushed);
  }

  bool empty() const
  {
    ScopedCriticalSection locker(m_cs);
    return the_queue.empty();
  }

  bool try_pop(Data& popped_value)
  {
    ScopedCriticalSection locker(m_cs);
    if(the_queue.empty())
    {
      return false;
    }
      popped_value=the_queue.front();
    the_queue.pop();
    return true;
  }

  void wait_and_pop(Data& popped_value)
  {
    ScopedCriticalSection locker(m_cs);
    while(the_queue.empty())
    {
      WaitForSingleObject(m_dataPushed);
```

```
    }

    popped_value=the_queue.front();
    the_queue.pop();
  }
};
```

The m_dataPushed handle is a mechanism that allows one thread to notify another thread that a particular condition has become true. Without it, a reader thread manipulating the queue would have to lock the mutex, check the queue, find that it was empty, release the lock, and then find a way to wait for a while before checking it all over again. When WaitForSingleObject() is called, the thread blocks until there is something to read. The call to PulseEvent signals there is something there. This increases concurrency immensely.

Here's how the EventManager class you saw in Chapter 11, "Game Event Management," needs to change to be able to receive events from real-time processes:

```
typedef concurrent_queue<IEventDataPtr> ThreadSafeEventQueue;

class EventManager : public IEventManager
{
  // Add a new method and a new member:
public:
  virtual bool VThreadSafeQueueEvent ( const IEventDataPtr &pEvent );

private:
  ThreadSafeEventQueue m_RealtimeEventQueue;
}

bool EventManager::VThreadSafeQueueEvent ( const IEventDataPtr &pEvent )
{
  m_RealtimeEventQueue.push(inEvent);
  return true;
}
```

The concurrent queue template is used to create a thread-safe queue for IEventDataPtr objects, which are the mainstay of the event system. The method VThreadSafeQueueEvent() can be called by any process in any thread at any time. All that remains is to add the code to EventManager::VTick() to read the events out of the queue:

```
bool EventManager::VUpdate ( unsigned long maxMillis )
{
  unsigned long curMs = GetTickCount();
  unsigned long maxMs =
```

```
    maxMillis == IEventManager::kINFINITE
    ? IEventManager::kINFINITE
    : (curMs + maxMillis );

  EventListenerMap::const_iterator itWC = m_registry.find( 0 );

  // This section added to handle events from other threads
  //-------------------------------------------------------------
  IEventDataPtr pRealtimeEvent;
  while (m_RealtimeEventQueue.try_pop(pRealtimeEvent))
  {
    VQueueEvent(pRealtimeEvent);

    curMs = GetTickCount();
    if ( maxMillis != IEventManager::kINFINITE )
    {
      if ( curMs >= maxMs )
      {
        GCC_ERROR("A realtime process is spamming the event manager!");
      }
    }
  }
  // -------------------------------------------------------------

  // swap active queues, make sure new queue is empty after the
  // swap ...
  // THE REST OF VUpdate() IS UNCHANGED!!!!
```

There is a new section of code at the top of the method to handle events from real-time processes. The call to `try_pop()` grabs an event out of the real-time queue if it exists, but if the queue is empty, it returns immediately. Since real-time processes can run at a higher priority, it is possible they could spam the Event Manager faster than the Event Manager could consume them, so a check is made to compare the current tick count against the maximum amount of time the Event Manager is supposed to run before exiting.

## Receiving Events in Real-Time Processes

Real-time processes should also be able to receive events from other game subsystems. This requires the same strategy as before, using a thread-safe queue. Here's the definition of a real-time process that can listen for events:

```
class EventReaderProcess : public RealtimeProcess
{
public:
```

```
  EventReaderProcess() : RealtimeProcess(ThreadProc)
  {
    IEventManager::Get()->VAddListener(
      MakeDelegate(this, &EventReaderProcess::UpdateTickDelegate),
        EvtData_Update_Tick::sk_EventType);
  }
  void UpdateTickDelegate(IEventDataPtr pEventData);
  virtual void VThreadProc(void);
protected:
  static ThreadSafeEventQueue m_RealtimeEventQueue;
};

void EventReaderProcess::UpdateTickDelegate(IEventDataPtr pEventData)
{
  IEventDataPtr pEventClone = pEventData->VCopy();
  m_RealtimeEventQueue.push(pEventClone);
}

DWORD g_EventsRead = 0;

void EventReaderProcess::VThreadProc(void)
{
  // wait for all threads to end
  while (m_EventsRead < 100000)
  {
    IEventDataPtr e;
    if (m_RealtimeEventQueue.try_pop(e))
      ++m_EventsRead;
  }
  Succeed();
}
```

Note that this process has its own thread-safe event queue, to make this example much simpler. The Event Manager has a real-time event queue of its own to receive events from real-time processes, but it doesn't have one to manage sending events to real-time processes. It would be a great assignment to refactor this system so that the Event Manager could manage the reception and sending of all events, real-time or otherwise. This trivial example simply waits until 100,000 `EvtData_Update_Tick` events are seen in the thread-safe event queue. One thing you should notice is that when the event is received by the delegate, it is copied before being sent in to the real-time event queue. That is because `shared_ptr<>` objects are not thread safe, so the event is cloned to avoid any problems.

With those tools, you have everything you need to write your own real-time processes, including having them send and receive events from other threads and game subsystems.

## Background Decompression of a Zip File

One classic problem in game software is how to decompress a stream without halting the game. The stream could be anything from a portion of a music file to a movie to level data. The following class and code show how you can set up a background process to receive requests from the game to decompress something in the background and send an event when the decompression is complete.

```
class DecompressionProcess : public RealtimeProcess
{
public:
  EventListenerPtr m_pListener;
  static void Callback(int progress, bool &cancel);
  DecompressionProcess() : RealtimeProcess(ThreadProc)
  {
    IEventManager::Get()->VAddListener(
      MakeDelegate(this, &DecompressionProcess::DecompressRequestDelegate),
       EvtData_Decompress_Request::sk_EventType);
  }
  virtual ~DecompressionProcess()
  {
    IEventManager::Get()->VRemoveListener(
      MakeDelegate(this, &DecompressionProcess::DecompressRequestDelegate),
       EvtData_Decompress_Request::sk_EventType);
  }
  virtual void VThreadProc(void);

  ThreadSafeEventQueue m_RealtimeEventQueue;

  // event delegates
  void DecompressRequestDelegate(IEventDataPtr pEventData)
  {
    IEventDataPtr pEventClone = pEventData->VCopy();
    m_RealtimeEventQueue.push(pEventClone);
  }
};
```

The DecompressionProcess class is a real-time process that registers to listen for an event, the EvtData_Decompress_Request event, which simply stores the name of the Zip file and the name of the resource in the Zip file to decompress. It is declared exactly the same as other events you've seen.

Here's `VThreadProc()`:

```
void DecompressionProcess::VThreadProc(void)
{
  while (1)
  {
    // check the queue for events we should consume
    IEventDataPtr e;
    if (m_RealtimeEventQueue.try_pop(e))
    {
      // there's an event! Something to do….
      if (EvtData_Decompress_Request::sk_EventType == e->VGetEventType())
      {
        shared_ptr<EvtData_Decompress_Request> decomp =
           static_pointer_cast<EvtData_Decompress_Request>(e);

        ZipFile zipFile;
        bool success = FALSE;

        if (zipFile.Init(decomp->m_zipFileName.c_str()))
        {
          int size = 0;
          int resourceNum = zipFile.Find(decomp->m_fileName.c_str());
          if (resourceNum >= 0)
          {
            char *buffer = GCC_NEW char[size];
            zipFile.ReadFile(resourceNum, buffer);

            // send decompression result event
            IEventDataPtr e(
              GCC_NEW EvtData_Decompression_Progress (
                100, decomp->m_zipFileName,
                decomp->m_fileName, buffer) );
            IEventManager::Get()->VThreadSafeQueueEvent(e);
          }
        }
      }
    }
    else
    {
      Sleep(10);
```

```
    }
  }
  Succeed();
}
```

This process is meant to loop forever in the background, ready for new decompression requests to come in from the Event Manager. Once the decompression request comes in, the method initializes a `ZipFile` class, exactly as you saw in Chapter 8, "Loading and Caching Game Data."

After the resource has been decompressed, an event is constructed that contains the progress (100%), the Zip file name, the resource name, and the buffer. It is sent to the Event Manager with `VThreadSafeQueueEvent()` method.

The event can be handled by any delegate in the usual way.

```
const EvtData_Decompression_Progress & castEvent =
  static_cast< const EvtData_Decompression_Progress & >( event );
if (castEvent.m_buffer != NULL)
{
  const void *buffer = castEvent.m_buffer;
  // do something with the buffer!!!!
}
```

Note that I'm bending one of my own rules here by allowing a pointer to sit in an event. The only reason that I can sleep at night is that I know that this particular event won't ever be serialized, so the pointer will always be good. I also know that this process doesn't have an exit condition and will happily sit in the `while (1)` as long as the game is running. If this keeps you up at night, you could implement a new event that would shut down the process cleanly.

## Further Work

One improvement you could make to the real-time event processor is to double-buffer the events, just as the regular event queue does. This would help protect the real-time event queue from being spammed by a misbehaving event sender.

Decompressing a data stream is a good example, but there are plenty of other tasks you could use this system for if you had a spare weekend. These include rendering, physics, AI tasks such as pathfinding, and others.

Rendering is probably the most common subsystem besides audio that is run in a separate thread. It is already highly compartmentalized, especially if you use the architecture in this book. Much of the rendering pipeline prepares data that is sent to the video hardware, and this preparation can be quite CPU intensive. As long as you protect any shared data with the game logic, such as the location and orientation of objects, you should achieve a good performance boost by doing this.

AI is a great choice to put in a background process. Whether you are programming a chess game or calculating an A* solution in a particularly dense path network, doing this in its own thread might buy you some great results. The magic length of time a human can easily perceive is 1/10th of one second, or 100 milliseconds. A game running at 60 frames per second has exactly 16 milliseconds to do all the work needed to present the next frame, and believe me, rendering and physics are going to take most of that. This leaves AI with a paltry 2–3 milliseconds to work. Usually, this isn't nearly enough time to do anything interesting.

So, running a thread in the background, you can still take those 2–3 milliseconds per frame, spread them across 10 or so frames, and all the player will perceive is just a noticeable delay between the AI changing a tactic or responding to something new. This gives your AI system much more time to work, and the player just notices a better game.

Running physics in a separate thread is a truly interesting problem. On one hand, it seems like a fantastic idea, but the moment you dig into it, you realize there are significant process synchronization issues to solve. Remember that physics is a member of the game logic, which runs the rules of your game universe. Physics is tied very closely with the game logic, and having to synchronize the game logic and the physics systems in two separate threads seems like an enormous process synchronization problem, and it is.

Currently, the physics system sends movement events when actors move under physics control. Under a multithreaded system, more concurrent queues would have to buffer these movement events, and since they would happen quite a bit, it might drop the system's efficiency greatly.

One solution to this would be to tightly couple the physics system to the game logic and have the game logic send movement messages to other game subsystems, like AI views or human views. Then it might be possible to detach the entire game logic into its own thread, running separately from the `HumanView`. With a little effort, it may even be possible to efficiently separate each view into its own thread. I'll leave that exercise to a sufficiently motivated reader with a high tolerance for frustrating bugs.

## About the Hardware

Games have had multiple processors since the early 1990s, but the processors were very dedicated things. They were a part of audio hardware first, and then in the mid to late 1990s, the advent of dedicated floating-point (FPU) and video processors revolutionized the speed and look of our games. Both were difficult for programmers to deal with, and in many ways, most game programmers, except for perhaps John Miles, the author of the Miles Sound System, were happily coding in a completely single-threaded environment. They let the compiler handle anything for the FPU and pawned tough threading tasks off to gurus who were comfortable with the reader/writer problems so common with sound systems.

The demands of the gaming public combined with truly incredible hardware from Intel, IBM, and others has firmly put those days behind us. Mostly, anyway. The Nintendo Wii is the only holdout of the bunch, sporting a single-core PowerPC CPU built especially for the Wii by IBM.

The other consoles have much more interesting and capable hardware. The PS3 has a Cell processor jointly designed by IBM, Sony Computer Entertainment, and Toshiba. The main processor, the Power Processing Element, or PPE, is a general purpose 64-bit processor and handles most of the workload on the PS3. In addition, there are eight other special-purpose processors called *Synergistic Processing Elements*, or SPEs. Each has 256KB of local memory that may be used to store instructions and data. Each SPE runs at 3.2GHz, which is quite amazing since there are *eight* of them.

To get the best performance out of the PS3, a programmer would have to create very small threads on each one to handle one step of a complicated task. That last sentence, I assure you, was about 1,000,000 times easier for me to write than it would be to actually accomplish on a game.

The Xbox360 from Microsoft has a high-performance processor, also designed by IBM, based on a slightly modified version of the Cell PPE. It has three cores on one die, runs at 3.2GHz each, and has six possible total hardware threads available to the happy engineer writing the next Xbox360 blockbuster.

While it doesn't take a math genius to see that the PS3 Cell processor seems to have the upper hand on the Xbox360 Xenon, from a programming perspective, the Xenon is a much friendlier programming environment, capable of handling general purpose threads that don't need to fit in a tiny 256KB space.

## About the Future

Looking at the past, it is easy to see a trend. Smaller sizes and higher speeds are getting exponentially more difficult for companies like IBM to achieve on new processor designs. It seems the most cost-effective solution for consumers is to simply give the box more CPUs, albeit extremely capable ones. The ITRS, or *International Technology Roadmap for Semiconductors*, predicts that by 2020 we could see CPUs with 1,000 cores. The truth is that programmers who haven't played in the somewhat frightening but challenging multiprogramming arena are going to be left behind. It takes an order of magnitude of more planning and sincere care and dedication to avoid seriously difficult bugs in this kind of environment.

At some point, we can all hope that compilers will become smart enough or will develop languages specifically for the purpose of handling tricky multiprogramming problems. There have been attempts, such as Modula and concurrent Pascal, but nothing so far seems to be winning out over us monkeys smashing our femur bones on the monolith of C++. C# is certainly a rising star in my opinion, but even it doesn't seem to have any syntax or structures to make multiprogramming a brain-dead proposition. Perhaps in a future release of NET, we'll see something.

Perhaps a reader of this book will think about that problem and realize we don't need new techniques, but simply a new language to describe new techniques.

Either way, multiprogramming is in your future whether you like it or not. So go, play carefully, and learn.

## Further Reading

*Modern Operating Systems,* Andrew Tannenbaum

# Chapter 21

*by David "Rez" Graham*

## A Game of Teapot Wars!

You've seen a lot of source code in this book, including everything from resource management to rendering to network code. All of this code has come directly from, or has been adapted from, a computer game that actually saw real players and some time in the sun. The one thing you haven't seen yet is how to put it all together into a cohesive engine and how to actually build a game. Seeing how everything fits together is extremely important to understanding the motives behind all these systems and abstractions we've been drilling into your head for this entire book.

The game we've created is called *Teapot Wars,* which you can see in Figure 21.1.

*Teapot Wars* is a game where teapots battle each other to the death utilizing their fearsome spout cannon. This game features the use of advanced physics, networked multiplayer, AI, and everything else you've learned. This is a simple game, but in this simplicity is hidden nearly all of the code you've seen in this book. It ties together the architecture we've been pushing; it uses the application layer, the game logic, and game views as a basis for the game and ties them together with the event system. It uses Lua for most of the gameplay code and AI and XML for data-driven actors. The game even works as a multiplayer game over the Internet.

The teapot has an interesting history. You might wonder why you see it virtually everywhere in computer graphics. DirectX even has a built-in function to create one. I did a little research on the Internet and found this explanation:

> "Aside from that, people have pointed out that it is a useful object to test with. It's instantly recognizable, it has complex topology, it self-shadows, there are hidden

surface issues, it has both convex and concave surfaces, as well as 'saddle points.' It doesn't take much storage space—it's rumored that some of the early pioneers of computer graphics could type in the teapot from memory," quoted directly from http://www.sjbaker.org/wiki/index.php?title=The_History_of_The_Teapot.

**Figure 21.1**
*Teapot Wars*—the next AAA game on the Xbox360!

Some 3D graphics professionals have even given this shape a special name—the "teapotahedron." It turns out that the original teapot that has come to be the official symbol of SIGGRAPH now lies in the Ephemera Collection of the Computer History Museum in Mountain View, California. These lovely teapots, in a way, are the founding shapes of the 3D graphics industry and therefore the computer game industry. It's quite fitting that we make them the heroes of our game.

## Making a Game

The first step in making a game from the GameCode4 engine is to create the game project. This project should be separate from the engine and under no circumstances should any code from the engine include any files from your game project. In the *Dev/Source* directory, you'll find the *TeapotWars* folder. This folder contains all of

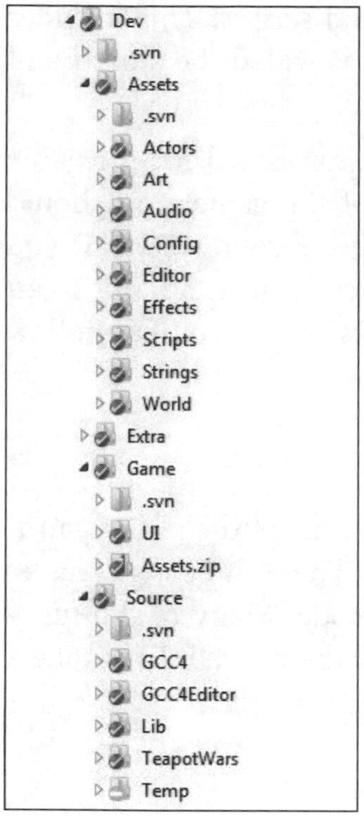


**Figure 21.2**
*Teapot Wars* directory structure.

the game-specific C++ code for the entire game. Notice how there aren't many files here. Most of the game's complexity comes from the engine itself and the Lua gameplay code. You'll find the solution file in *Dev/Source/TeapotWars/Msvc*. The directory structure of *Teapot Wars* (see Figure 21.2) should look very familiar; it's the exact same directory structure Mike showed you in Chapter 4, "Building Your Game."

Once you have the game project set up, it's time to create the core classes used to manage the game. These classes are extensions of the application, logic, and view classes you saw in previous chapters, and they manage your game-specific C++ code and override any virtual functions that need overriding.

The next major components to the game project are the event system and process system. You are likely to have many game-specific events and processes that will need to be written. They should all go here as well.

The majority of your gameplay systems should be written (or at least prototyped) in Lua. You will need to decide how these systems will be structured and distributed. You may need to write some game-specific Lua glue functions, although much of the communication can and should happen through the event system.

Finally, you'll need to decide how to handle your resources and scripts. This includes deciding on the directory structure, level structure, and how it will all be stored and loaded.

In this chapter, you'll see how each of these challenges was approached for the game of *Teapot Wars*. Before we start digging into the internals of the game, you should take the time to download the code base and get it running on your system if you haven't already. I won't be able to cover every single line of code in detail, but I can offer a guided tour of how this game came together. It works best if you can follow along in the code.

## Creating the Core Classes

In the GameCode4 engine, there are several core classes that control the entire game. They are `GameCodeApp`, `BaseGameLogic`, and `HumanView`. These three core classes are meant to be used as base classes for your game-specific code. Many of the functions defined in the base classes are meant to be overridden here as well. Let's take a look at the *Teapot Wars* classes and see how they're defined.

### The *Teapot Wars* Application Layer

The application layer is the place that holds all the operating system-dependent code like initialization, strings, the resource cache, and so on. *Teapot Wars* creates the `TeapotWarsApp` class, which extends the `GameCodeApp` class you saw in Chapter 5, "Game Initialization and Shutdown." Here's the definition of `TeapotWarsApp`:

```
class TeapotWarsApp : public GameCodeApp
{
protected:
  virtual BaseGameLogic *VCreateGameAndView();

public:
  virtual TCHAR *VGetGameTitle() { return _T("Teapot Wars"); }
  virtual TCHAR *VGetGameAppDirectory()
  {
    return _T("Game Coding Complete 4\\Teapot Wars\\4.0");
  }
  virtual HICON VGetIcon();

protected:
  virtual void VRegisterGameEvents(void);
  virtual void VCreateNetworkEventForwarder(void);
  virtual void VDestroyNetworkEventForwarder(void);
};
```

As you can see, there's really not a lot to this class. In fact, its entire purpose is to override various virtual functions from the base class. It acts as a configuration class of sorts. The `BaseGameApp` class calls these functions (some of which have no meaningful base class implementation) and expects that they will do the appropriate thing. For example, `VRegisterGameEvents()` is defined like this in `BaseGameApp`:

```
virtual void VRegisterGameEvents(void) {}
```

This function is called in `BaseGameApp::InitInstance()`, and its purpose is to allow the game-specific subclass to register all of its game events in the appropriate place during game initialization. This is a very common design pattern called the *Template Method Pattern* (not to be confused with C++ templates).

The `VCreateGameAndView()` function is responsible for creating the concrete, game-specific logic and human view objects. This is one of the functions you absolutely must override in your subclass since it's defined as pure virtual in the base class. The other three are `VGetGameTitle()`, `VGetGameAppDirectory()`, and `VGetIcon()`. You can see these functions in *TeapotWars.h* and *TeapotWars.cpp*.

That's all there is to the *Teapot Wars* application layer. The base class `GameCodeApp` does almost all the work for you.

## The Game Logic

The game logic is where all of the C++ game logic resides, and it is where most of your gameplay events will get handled and where a lot of the game management will take place. In *Teapot Wars*, this class is called `TeapotWarsLogic`, and it is derived from `BaseGameLogic`. As you learned in Chapter 2, "What's in a Game?", the game logic represents the game itself, separated from the operating system and rendering.

Before we dig into the internals of the game logic, let's take a look at how the *Teapot Wars* game itself is organized. Every game of *Teapot Wars* starts with the main menu, which you can see in Figure 21.3.

The player is presented with two main options: He can create a new game, or he can join an existing game. If you create a new game, you choose the level XML file you want to load, the number of AI teapots, and the number of players involved. If you choose to join a game, all you need to do is fill out the port number and host name. When everything is set, you click on the Start Game button at the bottom. This will take you right into the game.

In reality, there's a lot more going on under the hood when you click on Start Game. First, the game environment is loaded. If this is a network game, the host tells each attached client which level XML file to load, but all loading happens from your local

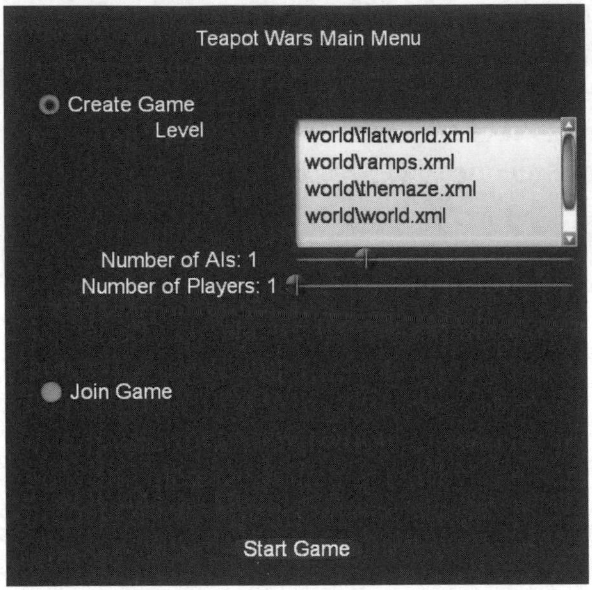


**Figure 21.3**
*Teapot Wars* main menu.

machine. Telling the clients to load a single level file is much better than spamming a bunch of "new actor" events across the network.

Once the level has been loaded, the game needs to wait for all the expected clients to connect. After that, all the teapots are created by the server and distributed to each client. Then the game waits for all players to spawn into their level and gain control of their teapots. Then the game starts running, and it's every teapot for itself!

Each of these stages is separated into different states for processing by the game logic. The states are represented by the `BaseGameState enum`:

```
enum BaseGameState
{
  BGS_Invalid,
  BGS_Initializing,
  BGS_MainMenu,
  BGS_WaitingForPlayers,
  BGS_LoadingGameEnvironment,
  BGS_WaitingForPlayersToLoadEnvironment,
  BGS_SpawningPlayersActors,
  BGS_Running
};
```

Each of these values corresponds to a different state the game can be in. All of these states are managed by the game logic classes. Most of the processing happens in

BaseGameLogic, and any game-specific processing that needs to occur is put in the TeapotWarsLogic class. Let's take a look at the TeapotWarsLogic class:

```
class TeapotWarsLogic : public BaseGameLogic
{
protected:
  std::list<NetworkEventForwarder*> m_networkEventForwarders;

public:
  TeapotWarsLogic();
  virtual ~TeapotWarsLogic();

  // Update
  virtual void VSetProxy();
  virtual void VMoveActor(const ActorId id, Mat4x4 const &mat);

  // Overloads
  virtual void VChangeState(BaseGameState newState);
  virtual void VAddView(shared_ptr<IGameView> pView,
                        ActorId actorId=INVALID_ACTOR_ID);
  virtual shared_ptr<IGamePhysics> VGetGamePhysics(void) {return m_pPhysics;}

  // set/clear render diagnostics
  void ToggleRenderDiagnostics() {m_RenderDiagnostics = !m_RenderDiagnostics;}

  // event delegates
  void RequestStartGameDelegate(IEventDataPtr pEventData);
  void GameStateDelegate(IEventDataPtr pEventData);
  void RemoteClientDelegate(IEventDataPtr pEventData);
  void NetworkPlayerActorAssignmentDelegate(IEventDataPtr pEventData);
  void NewGameDelegate(IEventDataPtr pEventData);

protected:
  virtual bool VLoadGameDelegate(TiXmlElement* pLevelData);

private:
  void RegisterAllDelegates(void);
  void RemoveAllDelegates(void);
  void CreateNetworkEventForwarder(const int socketId);
  void DestroyAllNetworkEventForwarders(void);
};
```

Much like TeapotWarsApp, this class mostly overrides virtual functions to change or augment the behavior of the game logic. One big difference between this class and the application layer is that TeapotWarsLogic defines a number of delegate functions. These are the listener functions for various game events that it needs to process. If you have game-specific logic systems in C++, this is how you would communicate with them.

The game states are handled by two functions: `VOnUpdate()` and `VChangeState()`. `VOnUpdate()` is the heart of the game logic. This function is responsible for processing the game state, updating all objects, and performing any per-frame operations the game logic needs to perform. Here is the `VOnUpdate()` function defined in `BaseGameLogic`:

```
void BaseGameLogic::VOnUpdate(float time, float elapsedTime)
{
  int deltaMilliseconds = int(elapsedTime * 1000.0f);
  m_Lifetime += elapsedTime;

  switch(m_State)
  {
   case BGS_Initializing:
    // If we get to here we're ready to attach players
    VChangeState(BGS_MainMenu);
    break;

   case BGS_MainMenu:
    break;

   case BGS_LoadingGameEnvironment:
    if (!g_pApp->VLoadGame())
    {
     GCC_ERROR("The game failed to load.");
     g_pApp->AbortGame();
    }
    break;

   case BGS_WaitingForPlayersToLoadEnvironment:
    if (m_ExpectedPlayers + m_ExpectedRemotePlayers <= m_HumanGamesLoaded)
    {
     VChangeState(BGS_SpawningPlayersActors);
     break;
    }

   case BGS_SpawningPlayersActors:
    VChangeState(BGS_Running);
    break;

   case BGS_WaitingForPlayers:
    if (m_ExpectedPlayers + m_ExpectedRemotePlayers ==
       m_HumanPlayersAttached )
```

```
      {
        VChangeState(BGS_LoadingGameEnvironment);
      }
      break;

    case BGS_Running:
      m_pProcessManager->UpdateProcesses(deltaMilliseconds);

      // update the physics
      if(m_pPhysics && !m_bProxy)
      {
        m_pPhysics->VOnUpdate(elapsedTime);
        m_pPhysics->VSyncVisibleScene();
      }

      break;

    default:
      GCC_ERROR("Unrecognized state.");
  }

  // update all game views
  for (GameViewList::iterator it = m_gameViews.begin();
       it != m_gameViews.end(); ++it)
  {
    (*it)->VOnUpdate(deltaMilliseconds);
  }

  // update game actors
  for (ActorMap::const_iterator it = m_actors.begin();
       it != m_actors.end(); ++it)
  {
    it->second->Update(deltaMilliseconds);
  }
}
```

The function begins by updating the lifetime of the object. Then it processes the game state in a big `switch` statement. Any logic that needs to happen every frame while in a specific state can happen here. For example, the Process Manager and physics system are only updated during the `BGS_Running` state. After that, the views are all updated, followed by all the actors. The views and actors must all be updated regardless of what state the game is in.

State processing often needs to occur when one state transitions to a new state. This logic is placed into the `VChangeState()` function.

```
void BaseGameLogic::VChangeState(BaseGameState newState)
{
  if (newState==BGS_WaitingForPlayers)
  {
    // Get rid of the Main Menu...
    m_gameViews.pop_front();

    // Note: Split screen support would require this to change!
    m_ExpectedPlayers = 1;
    m_ExpectedRemotePlayers = g_pApp->m_Options.m_expectedPlayers - 1;
    m_ExpectedAI = g_pApp->m_Options.m_numAIs;

    if (!g_pApp->m_Options.m_gameHost.empty())
    {
      VSetProxy();
      m_ExpectedAI = 0;         // the server will create these
      m_ExpectedRemotePlayers = 0;  // the server will create these

      if (!g_pApp->AttachAsClient())
      {
        // Throw up a main menu
        VChangeState(BGS_MainMenu);
        return;
      }
    }
    else if (m_ExpectedRemotePlayers > 0)
    {
      BaseSocketManager *pServer = GCC_NEW BaseSocketManager();
      if (!pServer->Init())
      {
        // Throw up a main menu
        VChangeState(BGS_MainMenu);
        return;
      }

      pServer->AddSocket(
        new GameServerListenSocket(g_pApp->m_Options.m_listenPort));
      g_pApp->m_pBaseSocketManager = pServer;
    }
  }

  m_State = newState;
}
```

`VChangeState()` is called whenever the game state needs to be changed. For `BaseGameLogic`, all it really cares about is detecting when the game begins waiting for players. It starts by popping the front game view, which is assumed to be the main menu since the main menu is the only thing that can transition to this state. Then it reads the options from the application layer to find out how many objects it can expect.

The main menu code itself is relatively straightforward, and it can be found in *Dev/Source/TeapotWars/TeapotWarsView.h* and *TeapotWars.cpp*.

The next block takes care of networking. The game logic really has two modes: It can either be a full game logic, or it can be a proxy that pretends to be a game logic. If you're playing a multiplayer game, only the server gets a true game logic object; all the other players get proxies. This proxy is responsible for serializing events coming in from the local game views and forwarding them to the server. When the server game logic sends events, these are caught by the proxy game logics and forwarded to the appropriate places. There's a flag on `BaseGameLogic` that is set to `true` if this game logic is just a proxy.

The first part checks to see if the application layer has a listed game host. Some methods, such as a menu interface or simple game options file, will set the game host before the `BGS_WaitingForPlayers` state is entered. If the game is a remote client, the logic is set to a proxy logic by calling `VSetProxy()`, which sets the `m_bProxy` member of the `BaseGameLogic` class to `true`. After that point, most of the game logic is short-circuited, and the game events will simply come in from the remote server.

If the game is an authoritative server expecting remote players, a new socket manager is created and initialized. This class was covered in Chapter 19, "Network Programming for Multiplayer Games."

If either case fails, the game goes back to the main menu. If this is neither a client nor a server, it is considered to be a single-player game.

The game-specific logic class will often need to handle processing states and state changes. The `VOnUpdate()` and `VChangeState()` functions can be overridden for just that purpose. In *Teapot Wars,* only the `VChangeState()` function needs to be overridden to handle actor spawning.

```
void TeapotWarsLogic::VChangeState(BaseGameState newState)
{
  BaseGameLogic::VChangeState(newState);

  switch(newState)
  {
    case BGS_WaitingForPlayers:
    {
```

```
    // spawn all local players (should only be one, though we might
    // support more in the future)
    GCC_ASSERT(m_ExpectedPlayers == 1);
    for (int i = 0; i < m_ExpectedPlayers; ++i)
    {
      shared_ptr<IGameView> playersView(
        GCC_NEW TeapotWarsHumanView(g_pApp->m_Renderer));
      VAddView(playersView);

      if (m_bProxy)
      {
        // if we are a remote player, all we have to do is spawn
        // our view - the server will do the rest.
        return;
      }
    }

    // spawn all remote players' views on the game
    for (int i = 0; i < m_ExpectedRemotePlayers; ++i)
    {
      shared_ptr<IGameView> remoteGameView(GCC_NEW NetworkGameView);
      VAddView(remoteGameView);
    }

    // spawn all AI's views on the game
    for (int i = 0; i < m_ExpectedAI; ++i)
    {
      shared_ptr<IGameView> aiView(
        GCC_NEW AITeapotView(m_pPathingGraph));
      VAddView(aiView);
    }
    break;
  }

  case BGS_SpawningPlayersActors:
  {
    if (m_bProxy)
    {
      // only the server needs to do this.
      return;
    }

    for (auto it = m_gameViews.begin(); it != m_gameViews.end(); ++it)
    {
```

```
    shared_ptr<IGameView> pView = *it;
    if (pView->VGetType() == GameView_Human)
    {
      StrongActorPtr pActor =
        VCreateActor("actors\\player_teapot.xml", NULL);
      if (pActor)
      {
        shared_ptr<EvtData_New_Actor> pNewActorEvent(
          GCC_NEW EvtData_New_Actor(
          pActor->GetId(), pView->VGetId()));
        IEventManager::Get()->VTriggerEvent(pNewActorEvent);
      }
    }
    else if (pView->VGetType() == GameView_Remote)
    {
      shared_ptr<NetworkGameView> pNetworkGameView =
        static_pointer_cast<NetworkGameView, IGameView>(pView);
      StrongActorPtr pActor =
        VCreateActor("actors\\remote_teapot.xml", NULL);
      if (pActor)
      {
        shared_ptr<EvtData_New_Actor> pNewActorEvent(
          GCC_NEW EvtData_New_Actor(pActor->GetId(),
                                    pNetworkGameView->VGetId()));
        IEventManager::Get()->VQueueEvent(pNewActorEvent);
      }
    }
    else if (pView->VGetType() == GameView_AI)
    {
      shared_ptr<AITeapotView> pAiView =
        static_pointer_cast<AITeapotView, IGameView>(pView);
      StrongActorPtr pActor =
        VCreateActor("actors\\ai_teapot.xml", NULL);
      if (pActor)
      {
        shared_ptr<EvtData_New_Actor> pNewActorEvent(
          GCC_NEW EvtData_New_Actor(
          pActor->GetId(), pAiView->VGetId()));
        IEventManager::Get()->VQueueEvent(pNewActorEvent);
      }
    }
  }

  break;
```

```
      }
    }
  }
```

The first thing this function does is to call the base class version. This is extremely important because there is a lot of important processing that happens there.

If the BGS_WaitingForPlayers state is the state being transitioned to, the code spawns all the local players, unless this is a proxy. If this is a proxy, there is very little to do except attach a view. Otherwise, the appropriate type of view is created for that type of player and added to the list of views the game logic maintains. These views are often game-specific views tied directly to that game.

The BGS_SpawningPlayersActors state signals that it's time to spawn all the actors into the world. It loops through all the game views and creates the appropriate type of actor. It also sends the EvtData_New_Actor event to let other systems know that an actor has been created.

Let's take a look at a few examples of how the engine handles some of the events sent from the game layer. In the Scene class (which you saw in Chapter 16, "3D Scenes"), there are two delegates that respond to the creation and destruction of actors. Here's the one for new actors:

```
void Scene::NewRenderComponentDelegate(IEventDataPtr pEventData)
{
  shared_ptr<EvtData_New_Render_Component> pCastEventData =
    static_pointer_cast<EvtData_New_Render_Component>(pEventData);

  ActorId actorId = pCastEventData->GetActorId();
  shared_ptr<SceneNode> pSceneNode(pCastEventData->GetSceneNode());

  //TODO: Add real error handling here.
  if (FAILED(pSceneNode->VOnRestore(this)))
  {
    GCC_ERROR("Failed to add scene node to the scene for actorid " +
              ToStr(actorId));
    return;
  }

  AddChild(actorId, pSceneNode);
}
```

This delegate is registered to receive the EvtData_New_Render_Component event, which is sent from the render component. Any actor that has a render component will trigger this event, which includes the actor ID and the scene node for the actor.

This delegate calls VOnRestore() on the scene node to get it into a renderable state and adds it as a child to the scene.

When an actor is destroyed, the EvtData_Destroy_Actor event is sent. The scene must also catch this event to properly remove the child:

```
void Scene::DestroyActorDelegate(IEventDataPtr pEventData)
{
  shared_ptr<EvtData_Destroy_Actor> pCastEventData =
    static_pointer_cast<EvtData_Destroy_Actor>(pEventData);
  RemoveChild(pCastEventData->GetId());
}
```

## The Game View for a Human Player

The game view's job is to present the game, accept input, and translate that input into commands for the game logic. There are three kinds of views that can attach to *Teapot Wars*: a view for a local human player, a view for an AI player, and a view that represents a player on a remote machine. The last one, NetworkGameView, was presented at the end of Chapter 19.

The view for the human player is responsible for the 3D graphics, audio, and user interface of the game. There are two classes that make this system work. The first is TeapotWarsHumanView, which inherits from the HumanView class presented in Chapter 10, "User Interface Programming." This class hooks into the Windows application layer message pump for user interface processing and organizes user interface objects, like buttons and text strings on top of a 3D scene background. The second class is TeapotController, which reads input from the keyboard and mouse and translates input into commands that are sent to the game logic.

The code for the TeapotWarsHumanView is quite a bit longer. It has a lot of work to do, keeping track of the 3D scene, audio, graphical object creation, and presenting the user interface.

```
class TeapotWarsHumanView : public HumanView
{
protected:
  bool m_bShowUI;               // If true, it renders the UI control text
  std::wstring m_gameplayText;  // text being displayed at the top-center

  shared_ptr<TeapotController> m_pTeapotController;
  shared_ptr<MovementController> m_pFreeCameraController;
  shared_ptr<SceneNode> m_pTeapot;
  shared_ptr<StandardHUD> m_StandardHUD;
```

```
public:
  TeapotWarsHumanView(shared_ptr<IRenderer> renderer);
  virtual ~TeapotWarsHumanView();

  virtual LRESULT CALLBACK VOnMsgProc( AppMsg msg );
  virtual void VRenderText();
  virtual void VOnUpdate(unsigned long deltaMs);
  virtual void VOnAttach(GameViewId vid, ActorId aid);

  virtual void VSetControlledActor(ActorId actorId);
  virtual bool VLoadGameDelegate(TiXmlElement* pLevelData) override;

  // event delegates
  void GameplayUiUpdateDelegate(IEventDataPtr pEventData);
  void SetControlledActorDelegate(IEventDataPtr pEventData);

private:
  void RegisterAllDelegates(void);
  void RemoveAllDelegates(void);
};
```

This class manages a number of view objects and relies on the `HumanView` class to handle most of the heavy lifting It has a reference to the `TeapotController` for handling player input, a `MovementController` that implements the debug free-fly camera, a teapot scene node, which represents the currently controlled teapot, and a `StandardHUD` object for UI rendering.

Like the application layer and game logic, most of the functions defined in this class are either overridden virtual functions or event handler delegates. The delegates handle events coming from the Lua code. You'll see those later in this chapter. The other functions are implementations of techniques you've learned on how to render text and manage a scene in Direct3D. The `TeapotWarsHumanView` class can be found at *Dev/Source/TeapotWars/TeapotWarsView.h* and *TeapotWarsView.cpp*.

A game view that presents the game to a human needs a way for that human to affect the game. It's a common practice to factor control systems that have a particular interface, like the keyboard WASD controls, into a class that can be attached and detached as necessary. This controller class isn't exactly WASD, since the A and D keys control steering rather than strafing, but I'm sure you'll forgive the departure.

```
class TeapotController : public IPointerHandler, public IKeyboardHandler
{
protected:
  bool                    m_bKey[256];      // Which keys are up and down
  shared_ptr<SceneNode>   m_object;
```

```
public:
  TeapotController(shared_ptr<SceneNode> object);
  void OnUpdate(const DWORD elapsedMs);

public:
  virtual bool VOnPointerMove(const CPoint &mousePos, const int radius)
  {
    return true;
  }
  virtual bool VOnPointerButtonDown(const CPoint &mousePos, const int radius,
                                    const std::string &buttonName);
  virtual bool VOnPointerButtonUp(const CPoint &mousePos, const int radius,
                                  const std::string &buttonName)
  {
    return (buttonName == "PointerLeft");
  }

  bool VOnKeyDown(const BYTE c) { m_bKey[c] = true; return true; }
  bool VOnKeyUp(const BYTE c) { m_bKey[c] = false; return true; }
};

TeapotController::TeapotController(shared_ptr<SceneNode> object)
: m_object(object)
{
  memset(m_bKey, 0x00, sizeof(m_bKey));
}
```

As you can see from the class definition, really the only methods that have any meat to them are the response to the left mouse button and OnUpdate(). Keyboard events are recorded as they happen, which are used in OnUpdate().

Here's what happens when the player presses the left mouse button:

```
bool TeapotController::VOnPointerButtonDown(const CPoint &mousePos,
  const int radius, const std::string &buttonName)
{
  if (buttonName != "PointerLeft")
    return false;
  ActorId actorId = m_object->VGet()->ActorId();
  GCC_ASSERT(actorId != INVALID_ACTOR_ID &&
    "The teapot controller isn't attached to a valid actor!");
  shared_ptr<EvtData_Fire_Weapon> pFireEvent(
   GCC_NEW EvtData_Fire_Weapon(actorId));
  IEventManager::Get()->VQueueEvent(pFireEvent);
  return true;
}
```

The code queues a "Fire Weapon" event. Note that in a commercial game, this wouldn't be hard-coded to the left mouse button necessarily. Instead, there would be an intermediate layer that translated specific user interface events into mappable game events, which enables the user to set up his keyboard and mouse the way he likes it.

**Hard-Coded WASD**

The first game I worked on as an engineer was *Barbie Diaries: High School Mystery*. The input system used a hard-coded WASD key configuring. We were an adventure game company, so key configuration wasn't a huge issue for us. Unfortunately, the next project ended up being on the PlayStation 3, so I was assigned the task of rewriting that system. It was pretty grueling, but I learned a huge amount about designing an input system API. Sometimes the painful tasks are the ones you learn the most from.

Here's the `OnUpdate()` method of the controller:

```
void TeapotController::OnUpdate(DWORD const deltaMilliseconds)
{
  if (m_bKey['W'] || m_bKey['S'])
  {
    const ActorId actorID = m_object->VGet()->ActorId();
    shared_ptr<EvtData_Thrust> pEvent(
      GCC_NEW EvtData_Thrust(actorID, m_bKey['W']? 1.0f : -1.0f));
    IEventManager::Get()->VQueueEvent(pEvent);
  }
  if (m_bKey['A'] || m_bKey['D'])
  {
    const ActorId actorID = m_object->VGet()->ActorId();
    shared_ptr<EvtData_Steer> pEvent(
      GCC_NEW EvtData_Steer(actorID, m_bKey['A']? -1.0f : 1.0f ));
    IEventManager::Get()->VQueueEvent(pEvent);
  }
}
```

The controller keeps a record of what keys are down on the keyboard, and it responds to the mouse-down event as well. Since the controller implements the `IMouseHandler` and `IKeyboardHandler` interfaces, it wires in nicely to the base `HumanView` class. The interface events are translated into the two gameplay events that are handled in Lua: "Thrust" and "Steer." You'll see their definitions later on in this chapter.

## Game Events

You've already seen most of the events that will be fired during a highly addictive session of *Teapot Wars*. When objects collide, for example, the physics system sends a collision event just like the one you saw in Chapter 17, "Collision and Simple Physics." There are five new events that are specific to *Teapot Wars*: `EvtData_Fire_Weapon`, `EvtData_Thrust`, `EvtData_Steer`, `EvtData_Gameplay_UI_Update`, and `EvtData_SetControlledActor`. Each of these events inherits from `ScriptEvent` and is exposed to Lua using the techniques you learned in Chapter 12, "Scripting with Lua."

You've already seen how the "Fire Weapon," "Thrust," and "Steer" events are triggered from the `TeapotController` event previously in this chapter. The other two events are triggered from script and handled by the `TeapotWarsHumanView` class. The "Set Controlled Actor" event is sent during initialization to tell the view which actor is the controlled actor. The "Gameplay UI Update" event is sent whenever the gameplay code needs to update the text at the top of the screen.

There's nothing new or special about these events; they work exactly like all the other events you've seen. You can find them in *Dev/Source/TeapotWars/TeapotEvents.h*.

## Gameplay

The vast majority of the gameplay in *Teapot Wars* is defined in Lua. You can find these Lua scripts in *Dev/Assets/Scripts*. If you are using Decoda, there's even a Decoda project file there for you to use. Before digging too deeply into the gameplay implementation, I'd like to talk a bit about the design.

The level is a simple grid where you and one of enemies face off in a battle to the death. Multiple teapots enter, but only one will survive. If any teapot falls off the grid, that teapot dies. Each teapot can take three hits before being destroyed, although everyone is periodically healed.

AI teapots in the world are controlled by the decision tree you saw in Chapter 18, "An Introduction to Game AI." Teapots will patrol two points on the grid until one of their foes approaches; then they attack! If the AI teapot drops to one hit point, it will run until it gets healed.

Now that you have a little context, load up the game and play around with it for a bit. Come back when you're ready, and I'll show you how the level is loaded.

### Loading the Level

When the game starts up, a level XML file is loaded to determine which actors to create and where to create them. It also determines which script files to load. For

*Teapot Wars,* the level files exist are created in the *Dev/Assets/World* directory. Here's an example of a level file:

```
<World>
  <!-- A list of static actors to load.  Static actors have no
  game view attached.  This is for stuff like level geometry.-->
  <StaticActors>
    <Actor resource="actors\grid.xml" />
    <Actor resource="actors\light.xml" />
    <Actor resource="actors\afternoon_sky.xml" />
    <Actor resource="actors\music.xml" />
  </StaticActors>

 <Script preLoad="scripts\LevelInit.lua" postLoad="scripts\LevelPostInit.lua"/>
</World>
```

The first block defines all of the static actors, which have no game view. The grid geometry, lights, the skybox, and even the background music are all stored as static entities. The second block is the script configuration. This element defines a preload script and a postload script. The preload script is executed as the very first thing during a level load. The postload script happens at the very end. This is useful to get the dependency order correct. These two scripts are the only scripts the level automatically executes. Let's take a look at the preload script:

```
require("scripts\\ActorManager.lua");

g_actorMgr = ActorManager:Create();

function AddPlayer(scriptObject)
  g_actorMgr:AddPlayer(scriptObject);
end

function RemovePlayer(scriptObject)
  g_actorMgr:RemovePlayer(scriptObject);
end

function AddEnemy(scriptObject)
  g_actorMgr:AddEnemy(scriptObject);
end

function RemoveEnemy(scriptObject)
  g_actorMgr:RemoveEnemy(scriptObject);
end
```

```
function AddSphere(scriptObject)
  g_actorMgr:AddSphere(scriptObject);
end

function RemoveSphere(scriptObject)
  g_actorMgr:RemoveSphere(scriptObject);
end
```

The first line calls `require()`, which executes the `ActorManager.lua` script if it hasn't already been executed. This is similar to C++ `#include` statements. The next line instantiates a global `ActorManager` class. The rest of the file defines a number of add and remove functions for various types of actors. These are called from the XML-defined constructor and destructor for various game actors, as described at the end of Chapter 12. It allows actors to be automatically added to and removed from the Lua actor manager when they are created and destroyed.

## The Actor Manager

Most of the action takes place in the actor manager. Here's the class definition:

```
ActorManager = class(nil,
{
  _player = nil,  -- this will be filled automatically when
                  -- player_teapot.xml is loaded
  _enemies = {},  -- a map of enemy teapots; key = actor id
  _spheres = {},  -- a map of spheres; key = actor id

  -- processes
  _enemyProcesses = nil;

  _enemyHealer = nil,  -- process that periodically heals all enemies
  _enemyThinker = nil,  -- process that causes enemies to make a new decision
  _enemyUpdater = nil,  -- process that updates all enemy states
});
```

The first three variables track the different types of actors in the world. The remaining four handle special script processes that apply various gameplay effects, as described in the comments next to each one.

When an AI teapot is created, the script component calls the constructor function, which in turn calls `ActorManager:AddEnemy()`.

```
function ActorManager:AddEnemy(scriptObject)
  -- add the enemy to the list of enemies
  local actorId = scriptObject:GetActorId();
  if (self._enemies[actorId] ~= nil) then
```

```
    print("Overwriting enemy actor; id = " .. actorId);
  end
  self._enemies[actorId] = scriptObject;

  -- set up some sample game data
  scriptObject.maxHitPoints = 3;
  scriptObject.hitPoints = scriptObject.maxHitPoints;

  -- create the teapot brain
  local brain = nil;
  if (TEAPOT_BRAIN) then
    brain = TEAPOT_BRAIN:Create({_teapot = scriptObject});
    if (not brain:Init()) then
      print("Failed to initialize brain");
      brain = nil;
    end
  end

  -- set up the state machine
  scriptObject.stateMachine =
    TeapotStateMachine:Create({_teapot = scriptObject, _brain = brain});

  -- set the initial state
  scriptObject.stateMachine:SetState(PatrolState);

  -- increment the enemy count and create the enemy processes if necessary
  if (self._enemyProcesses == nil) then
    self:_CreateEnemyProcesses();
  end

  -- make sure the UI is up to date
  self:UpdateUi();
end
```

The `scriptObject` parameter is a table that contains an `__object` pointer back to the C++ `BaseScriptComponent` object (see Chapter 12 for details).

The first block checks to see if the enemy has already been added to the map. If it has, the code simply overwrites it. The next block sets up some variables on the enemy object. Keep in mind that this only sets the variables on the Lua table wrapping the C++ object, so these variables won't be available in C++.

The next block of code creates the brain for the teapot. It looks at the global `TEAPOT_BRAIN` constant and instantiates an object of that type, passing in the script object to the constructor. `TEAPOT_BRAIN` is defined at the top of this file:

```
TEAPOT_BRAIN = DecisionTreeBrain;
```

This was done so you could easily experiment with the other brains you saw in Chapter 18. You can also create your own brain if you feel so inclined.

All teapots are controlled by a state machine where their current state defines their behavior. The next two lines create that state machine and set the initial state to `PatrolState`.

Next, there's a check to see if the enemy processes have been created for periodically healing, running AI, and allowing the state to run its update logic. If these processes have been created, they are created here. Finally, the UI is updated since a new teapot has just arrived.

## Sending and Receiving Events

Events and processes are extremely important in Lua. Events are your main method of communication to and from the C++ code. Without events, your scripts are deaf, blind, and mute. Nothing special was added to make events work with *Teapot Wars*; it uses the same mechanisms you saw in Chapter 11, "Game Event Management," and Chapter 12. Let's take a look at all works in *Teapot Wars* by examining the `UpdateUi()` function you saw at the bottom of `AddEnemy()`. This function provides a good example of sending an event from the gameplay code out to C++.

```
function ActorManager:UpdateUi()
  -- Build up the UI text string for the human view
  local uiText = "";
  if (self._enemies ~= nil) then
    for id, teapot in pairs(self._enemies) do
      uiText = uiText .. "Teapot " .. id .. " HP: " ..
        teapot.hitPoints .. "\n";
    end
  end

  QueueEvent(EventType.EvtData_Gameplay_UI_Update, uiText);
end
```

This function loops through all enemies and builds a string that lists the actor's ID along with its current hit points. After that, it calls the exported C++ `QueueEvent()` function to send it out. This event will be caught by the `TeapotWarsHumanView` class in C++. Here's the delegate registered to listen for this event:

```
void TeapotWarsHumanView::GameplayUiUpdateDelegate(IEventDataPtr pEventData)
{
  shared_ptr<EvtData_Gameplay_UI_Update> pCastEventData =
    static_pointer_cast<EvtData_Gameplay_UI_Update>(pEventData);
```

```
  if (!pCastEventData->GetUiString().empty())
    m_gameplayText = s2ws(pCastEventData->GetUiString());
  else
    m_gameplayText.clear();
}
```

This event delegate is pretty simple: It just casts the event to the proper type and reads it from the event. The `s2ws()` function converts the ASCII string into a `std::wstring`, which is then stored in a member variable. During the next render pass, this string is rendered to the top-middle portion of the screen.

This is great for sending events, but what about receiving them? It is often useful to have all of the event listeners in one place since most event listeners just call into another system. *Teapot Wars* has an *Events.lua* file for just that purpose:

```
function OnPhysicsCollision(eventData)
  g_actorMgr:OnPhysicsCollision(eventData);
end

function OnFireWeapon(eventData)
  g_actorMgr:OnFireWeapon(eventData);
end

function RegisterListeners()
  if (EventType.EvtData_PhysCollision ~= nil) then
    RegisterEventListener(EventType.EvtData_PhysCollision,
                          OnPhysicsCollision);
  end

  if (EventType.EvtData_Fire_Weapon ~= nil) then
    RegisterEventListener(EventType.EvtData_Fire_Weapon, OnFireWeapon);
  end
end
```

This file declares three functions. The first two are event listener delegates, and the third is called to register those listeners. Let's say a collision is registered by the physics system in C++. This will trigger the `EvtData_PhysCollision` event, which will be handled by `OnPhysicsCollision()`. That function calls into the actor manager.

```
function ActorManager:OnPhysicsCollision(eventData)
  local actorA = self:GetActorById(eventData.actorA);
  local actorB = self:GetActorById(eventData.actorB);

  -- one of the actors isn't in the script manager
  if (actorA == nil or actorB == nil) then
```

```
    return;
  end

  local teapot = nil;
  local sphere = nil;

  if (actorA.actorType == "Teapot" and actorB.actorType == "Sphere") then
    teapot = actorA;
    sphere = actorB;
  elseif (actorA.actorType == "Sphere" and actorB.actorType == "Teapot") then
    teapot = actorB;
    sphere = actorA;
  end

  -- needs to be a teapot and sphere collision for us to care
  if (teapot == nil or sphere == nil) then
    return;
  end

  -- If we get here, there was a collision between a teapot and a
  -- sphere.  Damage the teapot.
  self:_DamageTeapot(teapot);

  -- destroy the sphere
  self:RemoveSphere(sphere);
  QueueEvent(EventType.EvtData_Request_Destroy_Actor, sphere:GetActorId());

  -- play the hit sound
  QueueEvent(EventType.EvtData_PlaySound, "audio\\computerbeep3.wav");
end
```

This function checks the types of the actors (defined in the actor XML), and if one is a teapot and the other is a sphere, it causes the teapot to take damage. The sphere is destroyed by sending an event out to the engine. A sound is also played by sending an event.

As you can see, events are the key to interacting with the C++ code.

## Processes

Processes are what give your scripts a heartbeat. Without processes, your script would be lifeless. Like the event system, nothing special was done to the process system for *Teapot Wars*—it uses the same system described in Chapter 7, "Controlling the Main Loop" and the `ScriptProcess` you saw in Chapter 12.

A great example of where a process is needed is in the AI update for the teapots. Teapots need a way to periodically update their states and make decisions. This all starts with the `_CreateEnemyProcesses()` function you saw in `AddEnemy()`.

```
function ActorManager:_CreateEnemyProcesses()
  self._enemyProcesses = {};

  -- Create all enemy processes.  Each process is appended to the end of
  -- the _enemyProcesses list.
  self._enemyProcesses[#self._enemyProcesses+1] =
    EnemyUpdater:Create({_enemies = self._enemies});
  self._enemyProcesses[#self._enemyProcesses+1] =
    EnemyHealer:Create({_enemies = self._enemies, frequency = 15013});
  self._enemyProcesses[#self._enemyProcesses+1] =
    EnemyThinker:Create({_enemies = self._enemies, frequency = 3499});

  -- attach all the processes
  for i, proc in ipairs(self._enemyProcesses) do
    AttachProcess(proc);
  end
end
```

This function is responsible for creating the three processes used by the actor manager, which are stored in the `_enemyProcesses` table. Once the processes have been created, the function loops through the list and calls the exported C++ function `AttachProcess()` to attach it to the game logics Process Manager.

**Use Prime Numbers**

In the `_CreateEnemyProcesses()` function, you may note the use of some odd frequency values. Why would I use 3499 instead of 3500? Those frequencies are all being set to prime numbers that are close to the value I want. This makes the processes tend to update on separate frames. It's not perfect, but without a process scheduling system, it works well enough.

The processes themselves are rather simple. Here's the `EnemyThinker` process, used to run an AI update:

```
EnemyThinker = class(ActorManagerProcess,
{
  --
});
```

```
function EnemyThinker:OnUpdate(deltaMs)
  print("Running AI update for enemies");
  for id, actor in pairs(self._enemies) do
    actor.stateMachine:ChooseBestState();
  end
end
```

This class only has the `OnUpdate()` function, which loops through all the actors and calls `ChooseBestState()` on their state machine, just like you saw in Chapter 19.

**Don't Cross the Streams**

One alternative to the design above would be to make every AI state into a `ScriptProcess` object. This would certainly work, but it would cause a lot more traffic across the C++/Lua boundary. It's much better to have only a few `ScriptProcess` objects that do more work than to have a bunch of `ScriptProcess` objects that do very little work.

## An Exercise Left to the Reader

It may not look like it, but *Teapot Wars* is an excellent example of how to make a game. I've worked on a lot of projects in my career, and they all looked very much like *Teapot Wars* in the early days. The excellence isn't in the game itself, it's in the potential. If you took this game and spent six months to a year on it, you could easily have something to compete in the Independent Games Festival.

I get emails from budding game developers all the time asking me what they can do to make a game. The answer to this question is simple: Make a game. You can read every book in the world on game development, go to a school specializing in game programming, play every game under the sun, post on every message board, and talk to everyone about game development. None of it takes the place of actually sitting down and making something. Conversely, don't bite off more than you can chew. Games take a *long time* to make, even simple ones. Start really simply (like *Teapot Wars*) and build from that.

To use a video game analogy, making games is a lot like leveling up in *Ultima VII*. In *Ultima VII*, you would gain experience by killing monsters, which would cause you to level up. Leveling up didn't do anything except give you training points; you'd have to find a trainer to spend those training points and make your character better. Visiting a trainer is useless without the experience to back it up, and gaining experience isn't productive without the benefits of a trainer.

This book is like the trainer from *Ultima VII*, and making games is like killing monsters. This book is a great guide to help temper your own experience, but it's doesn't do much good until you really sit down and build a game from start to finish.

It is my sincere hope that *Teapot Wars* gives you a starting point. Knowing where and how to start is often the hardest part. Once you have a leg up, you can gain momentum and tear through huge amounts of code. You can build system after system and add level after level. When you finally look up, you'll notice that the sun is coming up and wonder if you should possibly get to bed. It's an amazing feeling to be in the zone like that.

So, as one final exercise from me to you, I challenge you to make *Teapot Wars* better. Add some more gameplay elements, expand the level, improve the AI, and add some models and animation. Take it as far as you can and then post the results here:

http://www.mcshaffry.com/GameCode/

I can't wait to see what you come up with.

# Chapter 22

*by Mike McShaffry*

# A Simple Game Editor in C#

Assembling the thousands of assets needed for a game is not a job for Visual Studio. Instead, the 3D models, shaders, textures, scripts, audio files, and other data are typically assembled in a *game editor*. Sometimes called a *level editor,* this tool manages the assets, creates a great environment for game designers to practice their craft, and ultimately packages everything into a form that the game engine can consume.

One of the most popular game editors, the Unreal Editor, allows its users to have control over things like lighting, scripted camera control, shader creation, and basic geometry placement. Let's not forget about saving and loading the levels, which is also pretty important. Some editors allow you to view animations on characters, while other engines break things like that into separate tools. For our purposes, we want to make sure that our editor handles the most essential task for a level editor —adding objects to our level, adjusting its properties, and saving the level to a file.

You'll see things you've learned over the previous chapters, while adding a new wrinkle. The application layer, view, and logic will be written in C++, but the editor application itself will be written in C#.

## Why C#?

Why would anyone want to write an editor in C#? C# is arguably slower than C++, but it is improving all the time. However, C# enables you to develop complicated

Windows applications very quickly, and as a very wise programmer once said, "Engineers are expensive, upgrading your CPU is cheap." C# has great GUI integration, database support, and tons of example code and open source classes for you to play with. C# code also looks much cleaner than writing Windows Forms using C++. So for tools programming, C# is hard to beat.

But, you say, the game engine is written in C++, how can that work? It turns out that this isn't much of a problem at all.

## How the Editor Is Put Together

I'm going to let you in on a personal bias—no matter what language the editor is written in, it should always be an extension of the game engine. I've probably spent more time in my programming career creating tools, including game editors, and this philosophy has worked for me every time. The reason I like this idea so much is that if the game editor is using all the technology in the game to do its work, then the game technology ends up being pretty well tested and stable.

Of course, there is a dark side to this problem, too, which is where other toolsmiths decide to write the game editor as a parallel technology. You see, if the core of the game editor is under rapid development, it can become a very unstable tool and create quite dangerous situations for the editor programmer. Designers can be, well, energetic in their ability to explain to you the details of how many hours of work they just lost in the latest editor crash.

There are three steps to creating a game editor. First, the editor architecture is created in C++, including the application layer, the logic layer, and the view layer. Next, a C++ DLL is created that wraps key editor classes and methods with C free functions that create an easy interface into the DLL. Finally, a C# application is created that can load the DLL and use these free functions to access the editor DLL and create game worlds.

## The Editor Architecture

Just like you've seen in the game architecture, you need to create the application, logic, and view layers for the editor. They'll be written in C++, since they create a performance-critical interface to the rest of the game engine. There's some trickiness involved in getting C# to talk to C++, but we'll handle that further down the line.

**The Editor Is an Extension of the Game**

As you review the code for the application, logic, and view layers, you'll notice that their classes look very similar to their *Teapot Wars* counterparts. When writing a real editor, you'll want your level editor to use the same engine that runs your game. In our case, the classes look like simplified versions of their *Teapot Wars* counterparts to make it easier to explain how the level editor works.

## The Application Layer

The level editor's application layer is a very simple extension of the `GameCodeApp` class.

```
class EditorApp : public GameCodeApp
{
public:
  EditorApp() : GameCodeApp() { m_bIsEditorRunning = true; }
  TCHAR *VGetGameTitle()      { return _T("GameCode4 Editor"); }
  TCHAR *VGetGameAppDirectory()
    { return _T("Game Coding Complete 4\\Editor\\1.0"); }
  HICON VGetIcon()
    { return LoadIcon(GetInstance(), MAKEINTRESOURCE(IDI_ICON1));

protected:
  BaseGameLogic *VCreateGameAndView();
};

BaseGameLogic* EditorApp::VCreateGameAndView()
{
  BaseGameLogic *game = GCC_NEW EditorLogic();
  game->VInit();

  shared_ptr<IGameView> gameView(GCC_NEW EditorHumanView(g_pApp->m_Renderer));
  game->VAddView(gameView);

  return game;
}
```

This should be pretty familiar, because you looked at code like this in Chapter 5, "Game Initialization and Shutdown." This code creates an instance of the game logic class, `EditorLogic`, which will inherit from `BaseGameLogic`. It also creates a view class, `EditorHumanView`.

## The Editor's Logic Class

The editor logic is pretty simple. Since this is a basic level editor, it doesn't need physics. In a level editor for a commercial game, a running physics system will ensure legal placement of objects and make sure they settle properly. In the example below, there is a physics system, but it is completely empty of code—a NULL physics system. I'll leave implementing a real physics system in the editor to you as an exercise. Any calls to the physics system will just end in stubs and not do anything at all.

The `EditorLogic` class will look familiar to you if you've looked over the `TeapotWarsBaseLogic` class in the previous chapter:

```
class EditorLogic : public BaseGameLogic
{
public:
  EditorLogic();
  ~EditorLogic() { }

  virtual bool VLoadGame(const char* levelName);
  const std::string &GetProjectDirectory(void) { return m_ProjectDirectory; }

  // We need to expose this information so that the C# app can
  // know how big of an array to allocate to hold the list of
  // actors
  int GetNumActors() { return (int)m_actors.size(); }

  // Exposes the actor map so that the global functions
  // can retrieve actor information
  const ActorMap& GetActorMap() { return m_actors; }

  shared_ptr<EditorHumanView> GetHumanView();

protected:
  std::string m_ProjectDirectory;
};
```

As you can see, most of the `EditorLogic` class is defined right in the constructor. `EditorLogic` is a thin wrapper around `BaseGameLogic`, since all it has to do is provide some accessor methods to the actor lists and manage a view. Here's the constructor:

```
EditorLogic::EditorLogic()
: BaseGameLogic()
{
  m_ProjectDirectory = getcwd(NULL, 0);
  int slashGamePos = m_ProjectDirectory.rfind("\\Game");
  m_ProjectDirectory = m_ProjectDirectory.substr(0, slashGamePos);
```

```
  m_pPhysics.reset(CreateNullPhysics());
}
```

The constructor initializes the m_ProjectDirectory member with the assumption that the current working directory is where the final game asset files are built. This is pretty common even among commercial editors. Assuming a little bit about a valid directory structure can actually save a ton of headaches down the road, especially considering where your raw game assets are stored. The physics system is initialized with a NULL physics stub. The NULL physics class implements all of the pure virtual functions of the IGamePhysics interface with empty stubs.

```
bool EditorLogic::VLoadGame(const char* levelName)
{
  while (m_actors.size() > 0)
  {
    ActorId id = m_actors.begin()->first;
    VDestroyActor(id);
  }

  if (!BaseGameLogic::VLoadGame(levelName))
  {
    return false;
  }
  VChangeState(BGS_Running);
  return true;
}

shared_ptr<EditorHumanView> EditorLogic::GetHumanView()
{
  GCC_ASSERT(m_gameViews.size()==1);
  shared_ptr<IGameView> pGameView = *m_gameViews.begin();
  shared_ptr<EditorHumanView> editorHumanView =
    static_pointer_cast<EditorHumanView>( pGameView );
  return editorHumanView;
}
```

VLoadGame() simply destroys all the existing actors before calling the overloaded method of BaseGameLogic. GetHumanView() returns a pointer to the view that creates a rendered image of the contents of the game universe. Since we don't have any AIs or extra players, we'll only have one view for the editor, which simplifies things greatly.

## The Editor View

The classes for the editor view are very similar to their *Teapot Wars* counterparts.

In a normal game, the human view is responsible for the sound manager, drawing the world, and grabbing user input. The editor view is simpler in one way, not needing a sound system, but more complicated since it receives input from the C# side of things. The following code is in *Source\Editor\EditorGameView.cpp*:

```
EditorHumanView::EditorHumanView(shared_ptr<IRenderer> renderer)
  : HumanView(renderer)
{ }

void EditorHumanView::VOnUpdate( unsigned long deltaMilliseconds )
{
  // Much like TeapotWarsView::VOnUpdate, except
  // we only have one controller in the editor

  HumanView::VOnUpdate( deltaMilliseconds );

  if (m_pFreeCameraController)
  {
    m_pFreeCameraController->OnUpdate(deltaMilliseconds);
  }
}
```

This is similar to, but simpler than, the parallel functions in the `TeapotWarsHumanView` class. Both call into the `HumanView` class, which creates the 3D scene, attaches a camera, and registers delegates for events. The only real difference between the two is `TeapotWarsHumanView` attaches a main menu for choosing the level and setting up other game parameters. `VOnUpdate()` is also very simple, only calling `HumanView::OnUpdate()` and ticking the camera controller.

Here's what the view does when a new level is loaded:

```
bool EditorHumanView::VLoadGameDelegate(TiXmlElement* pLevelData)
{
  if (!HumanView::VLoadGameDelegate(pLevelData))
    return false;

  // The MovementController is hooked up to the keyboard and mouse
  // handlers, since this is our primary method for moving the camera around.
  m_pFreeCameraController.reset(
    GCC_NEW MovementController(m_pCamera, 90, 0, true));
  m_pCamera->ClearTarget();

  m_KeyboardHandler = m_pFreeCameraController;
  m_PointerHandler = m_pFreeCameraController;
```

```
  m_pScene->VOnRestore();
  return true;
}
```

The only task here is to hook up the keyboard and mouse handlers and then restore the scene to make sure all the resources are loaded and ready to draw when the first frame is rendered. If you don't do that here, you might see a black window in the game view area before the editor is fully initialized.

As you learned in Chapter 21, "A Game of *Teapot Wars*," the `Scene` class registers delegates to listen for events, such as when a new actor is created. Actors like AI spawn points or trigger zones are invisible in the game but should most certainly be visible in the editor. Render components are a great example of how some components may be "editor only" and get stripped out when the game files are built. In this simple editor, there are no editor only components, but that would be a great extension to the component system.

## Functions to Access the Game Engine

While it is possible to instantiate objects in C++ and pass their pointers to C#, doing so requires a lot of preparation work, and it makes this sample editor a lot more complicated. Instead of creating an instance of the editor application layer and passing that pointer to the C# editor app, I'll use C-style functions that will access the global instance of the application layer and communicate data between the two with simple data structures like XML. This not only simplifies the code and my explanation of it, but it also makes the editor extensible without modifying much, if any, C# code.

These C++ functions are all going to be exported and exposed in a DLL that the C# application will load and call into. These free functions fall into a few general categories of functionality: the editor framework, accessing actor data, and modifying actors. I'll start with the editor framework.

### *Editor Framework Functions*

One of the functions that definitely needs to be exposed is the entry point to the application, which you read about back in Chapter 5. It is very similar to the original `GameCode4()` function, but it has a different beginning and ending.

```
int EditorMain(int *instancePtrAddress,
  int *hPrevInstancePtrAddress,
  int *hWndPtrAddress,
  int nCmdShow,
  int screenWidth, int screenHeight)
{
  // C# passes HINSTANCE and HWND values to C++ DLL as (int *)
```

```
    HINSTANCE hInstance = (HINSTANCE)instancePtrAddress;
    HINSTANCE hPrevInstance = (HINSTANCE) hPrevInstancePtrAddress;
    HWND hWnd = (HWND)hWndPtrAddress;
    WCHAR *lpCmdLine = L"";

    // Note - you can and should put your _CrtSetDebugFlag() calls right here
    // to track any memory corruptions or leaks...

    Logger::Init("logging.xml");
    g_pApp >m_Options.Init("FditorOptions.xml", lpCmdLine);

    DXUTSetCallbackMsgProc( GameCodeApp::MsgProc );
    DXUTSetCallbackFrameMove( GameCodeApp::OnUpdateGame );
    DXUTSetCallbackDeviceChanging( GameCodeApp::ModifyDeviceSettings );

    DXUTSetCallbackD3D11DeviceAcceptable(GameCodeApp::IsD3D11DeviceAcceptable);
    DXUTSetCallbackD3D11DeviceCreated( GameCodeApp::OnD3D11CreateDevice );
    DXUTSetCallbackD3D11SwapChainResized(GameCodeApp::OnD3D11ResizedSwapChain);
    DXUTSetCallbackD3D11SwapChainReleasing(
      GameCodeApp::OnD3D11ReleasingSwapChain );
    DXUTSetCallbackD3D11DeviceDestroyed( GameCodeApp::OnD3D11DestroyDevice );
    DXUTSetCallbackD3D11FrameRender( GameCodeApp::OnD3D11FrameRender );

    // Show the cursor and clip it when in full screen
    DXUTSetCursorSettings( true, true );

    // Perform application initialization
    if (!g_pApp->InitInstance (hInstance, lpCmdLine, hWnd,
                               screenWidth, screenHeight))
      return FALSE;

    // This is where the game would normally call the main loop, but the
    // C# application will control this, so we don't need to call
    // DXUTMainLoop() here.

    return true;
}
```

The first few lines of `EditorMain()` cast some integer pointers into Windows handles for the application instance and window. C# pointers are very different beasts because the Common Language Runtime (CLR) uses managed memory. The C# application will pass the correct values into this function as integers.

At the very end of the function, instead of starting the main loop with `DXUTMainLoop()`, the function simply exits. The C# editor will handle its own main loop, calling the DXUT functions to render and update the game. If you called

DXUTMainLoop() here, the C# editor wouldn't get any control until DXUTMainLoop() returned.

If the C# editor application's main loop is going to be responsible for handling messages, the editor needs to expose a few other functions as C free functions.

```
void WndProc(int *hWndPtrAddress, int msg, int wParam, int lParam)
{
  HWND hWnd = (HWND)hWndPtrAddress;
  DXUTStaticWndProc( hWnd, msg, WPARAM(wParam), LPARAM(lParam) );
}

void RenderFrame()
{
  DXUTRender3DEnvironment();
}

int Shutdown()
{
  DXUTShutdown();
  return g_pApp->GetExitCode();
}
```

RenderFrame() exposes the rendering call, DXUTRender3DEnvironment(), to the C# application so it can render a frame if the editor isn't handling any other messages. WndProc() exposes the C++ side message handling function so that the editor can forward any appropriate messages to be handled by the editor game engine, such as user input to move the camera position around. Finally, Shutdown() shuts down the DirectX device and exits the editor.

The next method opens an existing level file, but before you see that, you need to know a little more about how to pass strings between C# and C++, since they store strings differently. One method is to use a type common to both, the BSTR type, which is also used by COM. BSTR strings are converted easily to std::wstring objects, which the game engine can convert to a std::string with ws2s.

```
std::string ws2s(const std::wstring& s)
{
   int slength = (int)s.length() + 1;
   int len = WideCharToMultiByte(CP_ACP, 0, s.c_str(), slength, 0, 0, 0, 0)-1;
   std::string r(len, '\0');
   WideCharToMultiByte(CP_ACP, 0, s.c_str(), slength, &r[0], len, 0, 0);
   return r;
}
```

Its companion function does the opposite and converts a `std::string` back to a `std::wstring`.

```
std::wstring s2ws(const std::string &s)
{
  int slength = (int)s.length() + 1;
    int len = MultiByteToWideChar(CP_ACP, 0, s.c_str(), slength, 0, 0)-1;
  std::wstring r(len, '\0');
    MultiByteToWideChar(CP_ACP, 0, s.c_str(), slength, &r[0], len);
  return r;
}
```

Now you can take a look at the `OpenLevel()` function, which converts the filename sent by C# to something the `EditorLogic` class can load.

```
void OpenLevel( BSTR fullPathLevelFile )
{
  std::string levelFile = ws2s(std::wstring(fullPathLevelFile,
                              SysStringLen(fullPathLevelFile)));
  EditorLogic* pEditorLogic = (EditorLogic*)g_pApp->m_pGame;
  if (pEditorLogic)
  {
    std::string assetsDir = "\\Assets\\";
    int projDirLength = pEditorLogic->GetProjectDirectory().length()
                        + assetsDir.length();
    g_pApp->m_Options.m_Level =
      levelFile.substr(projDirLength, levelFile.length()-projDirLength);
    pEditorLogic->VChangeState(BGS_LoadingGameEnvironment);
  }
}
```

Note again the assumption of a specific directory structure. I've taken a cue from other commercial editors that assume where all their game assets are stored, and in truth, it makes sense to store them all under a commonly structured directory hierarchy. Once the filename has been constructed from the input parameter, it is copied into the game option's object, and the editor logic's current state is set to `BGS_LoadingGameEnvironment`. This will start the loading process.

### *Actor Accessor Functions*

There are five functions the editor uses to access actor data so that it can be presented in the editors user interface: The first two retrieve the number of actors in the actor list and an array of their IDs.

```
int GetNumActors()
{
  EditorGame* pGame = (EditorGame*)g_pApp->m_pGame;
  return ( pGame ) ? pGame->GetNumActors() : 0;
}

void GetActorList( int *ptr, int numActors )
{
  EditorGame* pGame = (EditorGame*)g_pApp->m_pGame;
  if ( pGame )
  {
    ActorMap::const_iterator itr;
    int actorArrayIndex;
    for ( itr = pGame->GetActorMap().begin(), actorArrayIndex = 0;
      itr != pGame->GetActorMap().end() && actorArrayIndex < numActors;
      ++itr,
      ++actorArrayIndex )
    {
      ActorId actorId = itr->first;
      ptr[actorArrayIndex] = actorId;
    }
  }
}
```

`GetNumActors()` is pretty simple. It uses the global application layer pointer to get to the game logic. Once it has a pointer to the game logic, it gets the number of actors in the level and returns that. The reason why you need the number of actors is that the C# editor application will be allocating space for an array of integers. The editor will use the number of actors to determine how large of an array to allocate. `GetActorList()` fills that array with the actors in this level by iterating through the actor data structure stored in the editor logic.

The next two functions get XML information from a specific actor.

```
int GetActorXmlSize ( ActorId actorId )
{
  StrongActorPtr pActor = MakeStrongPtr(g_pApp->m_pGame->VGetActor(actorId));
  if ( !pActor )
  {
    return 0;
  }
  std::string xml = pActor->ToXML();
  return xml.length();
}
```

```
void GetActorXml ( int *actorXMLAddress, ActorId actorId )
{
  StrongActorPtr pActor = MakeStrongPtr(g_pApp->m_pGame->VGetActor(actorId));
  if ( !pActor )
  {
    return;
  }
  std::string xml = pActor->ToXML();

  strncpy_s(reinterpret_cast<char *>(actorXMLAddress),
      xml.length()+1, xml.c_str(), xml.length());
}
```

Both methods get a strong pointer to the actor, and they call `Actor::ToXML()`. C# needs to be able to know how much memory to allocate before retrieving the XML data, which is why there are two functions. The address to the memory allocated by C# is sent in as a pointer to an integer, which is a common method for sending an unknown amount of data across the C++/C# barrier.

The `ToXML()` method uses TinyXML to run through all the components attached to an actor to create the complete definition of an actor that will, at some point, be saved to a level file.

```
std::string Actor::ToXML()
{
  TiXmlDocument outDoc;

  // Actor element
  TiXmlElement* pActorElement = GCC_NEW TiXmlElement("Actor");
  pActorElement->SetAttribute("type", m_type.c_str());

  // components
  for (auto it = m_components.begin(); it != m_components.end(); ++it)
  {
    StrongActorComponentPtr pComponent = it->second;
    TiXmlElement* pComponentElement = pComponent->VGenerateXml();
    pActorElement->LinkEndChild(pComponentElement);
  }

  outDoc.LinkEndChild(pActorElement);
  TiXmlPrinter printer;
  outDoc.Accept(&printer);

  return printer.CStr();
}
```

Each component has its own definition of VGenerateXML(), but for the sake of completeness, here's the definition for the TransformComponent, which stores the position and orientation of an actor:

```
TiXmlElement* TransformComponent::VGenerateXml(void)
{
  TiXmlElement* pBaseElement = GCC_NEW TiXmlElement(VGetName());

  TiXmlElement* pPosition = GCC_NEW TiXmlElement("Position");
  Vec3 pos(m_transform.GetPosition());
  pPosition->SetAttribute("x", ToStr(pos.x).c_str());
  pPosition->SetAttribute("y", ToStr(pos.y).c_str());
  pPosition->SetAttribute("z", ToStr(pos.z).c_str());
  pBaseElement->LinkEndChild(pPosition);

  TiXmlElement* pDirection = GCC_NEW TiXmlElement("YawPitchRoll");
  Vec3 orient(m_transform.GetYawPitchRoll());
  orient.x = RADIANS_TO_DEGREES(orient.x);
  orient.y = RADIANS_TO_DEGREES(orient.y);
  orient.z = RADIANS_TO_DEGREES(orient.z);
  pDirection->SetAttribute("x", ToStr(orient.x).c_str());
  pDirection->SetAttribute("y", ToStr(orient.y).c_str());
  pDirection->SetAttribute("z", ToStr(orient.z).c_str());
  pBaseElement->LinkEndChild(pDirection);
}
```

The resulting XML for a particular actor might look like this:

```
<Actor type="Grid">
  <TransformComponent>
    <Position x="0" y="0" z="0"/>
    <YawPitchRoll x="0" y="0" z="0"/>
  </TransformComponent>
  <PhysicsComponent>
    <Shape>Box</Shape>
    <Density>Infinite</Density>
    <PhysicsMaterial>Normal</PhysicsMaterial>
    <RigidBodyTransform>
      <Scale x="50" y="0.01" z="50" />
   </RigidBodyTransform>
  </PhysicsComponent>
  <GridRenderComponent>
    <Color r="0.4" g="0.4" b="0.4" a="1.0"/>
    <Texture>art\grid.dds</Texture>
    <Division>100</Division>
```

```
  </GridRenderComponent>
</Actor>
```

This particular actor is a Grid, the type that forms the floor and walls of the *Teapot Wars* game. It has three components: a `TransformComponent` that stores its location and orientation, a `PhysicsComponent` that tells the physics engine how it behaves in the game world, and a `GridRenderComponent` that tells the rendering engine how it appears.

Throughout the rest of this chapter, I'll be referring to components, their definitions, and how the editor interacts with them to do its work.

Every game editor needs a method to select an actor from the visual display. To do this requires a special bit of technology called a *raycaster*, which mathematically calculates which objects in the game world are intersected by a ray given two endpoints. `PickActor()` is a function that does exactly this.

```
int PickActor(int *hWndPtrAddress)
{
  HWND hWnd = (HWND)hWndPtrAddress;
  CPoint ptCursor;
  GetCursorPos( &ptCursor );

  // Convert the screen coordinates of the mouse cursor into
  // coordinates relative to the client window
  ScreenToClient( hWnd, &ptCursor );
  RayCast rayCast(ptCursor);
  EditorGame* pGame = (EditorGame*)g_pApp->m_pGame;
  if (!pGame)
    return INVALID_ACTOR_ID;

  shared_ptr<EditorGameView> gameView = pGame->GetHumanView();
  if (!pView)
    return INVALID_ACTOR_ID;

  // Cast a ray through the scene. The RayCast object contains an array of
  // Intersection objects.
  pView->GetScene()->Pick(&rayCast);
  rayCast.Sort();

  // If there are any intersections, get information from the first
  // intersection.
  if (!rayCast.m_NumIntersections)
  {
    return INVALID_ACTOR_ID;
  }
```

```
  Intersection firstIntersection = rayCast.m_IntersectionArray[0];
  return firstIntersection.m_actorId;
}
```

PickActor() will take the current cursor position and convert the position into coordinates relative to the editor window. If you remember the Frustum class from Chapter 14, "3D Graphics Basics," the ray will go from the camera location through the near clipping plane at exactly the mouse position.

The RayCast class is designed with this purpose in mind, and it is a part of the GameCode4 source code. RayCast::Pick() will fill member variables, indicating the number of intersections and the actor information of all actors intersected by the ray, sorted by their distance from the camera. The code grabs the first actor ID in the list of intersection and returns the actor ID. This will allow users to click on objects in the world and then find out information about them.

### *Actor Modification Functions*

A game editor wouldn't be much of an editor without the ability to create, modify, and remove actors from the game world. Here are those functions:

```
void CreateActor( BSTR bstrActorXMLFile )
{
  std::string actorResource = ws2s(std::wstring(bstrActorXMLFile,
                                    SysStringLen(bstrActorXMLFile)));
  StrongActorPtr pActor = g_pApp->m_pGame->VCreateActor(actorResource, NULL);
  if (!pActor)
    return INVALID_ACTOR_ID;

  // fire an event letting everyone else know that we created a new actor
  shared_ptr<EvtData_New_Actor> pNewActorEvent(
    GCC_NEW EvtData_New_Actor(pActor->GetId()));
  IEventManager::Get()->VQueueEvent(pNewActorEvent);
  return pActor->GetId();
}
```

The CreateActor() function creates actors just as you saw in the previous chapter. The call to VCreateActor() is made with the name of the actor resource sent from the editor, and it uses NULL for the override options, which you'll see more about later. Once the actor is created, an event is sent to inform all other game systems, especially the Scene class in the editor's view, that a new actor is ready. The actor ID is returned to the editor.

Next up is ModifyActor(), which the editor calls any time the properties of an actor are changed.

```
void ModifyActor ( BSTR bstrActorModificationXML )
{
  std::string actorModificationXML =
    ws2s(std::wstring(bstrActorModificationXML,
    SysStringLen(bstrActorModificationXML)));

  TiXmlDocument doc;
  doc.Parse(actorModificationXML.c_str());
  TiXmlElement* pRoot = doc.RootElement();
  if (!pRoot)
     return;

  g_pApp->m_pGame->VModifyActor(atoi(pRoot->Attribute("id")), pRoot);
}
```

The BSTR parameter sent from the editor is a bit of XML data the editor creates to tell the game engine exactly how the actor is changing. Basically, the XML contains a snippet of the component XML you saw previously, but only the part that has changed. For example, if the editor changed the orientation of a Grid actor to rotate 90 degrees around the Y-axis, the XML sent from the editor would look like this:

```
<Actor type="Grid">
  <TransformComponent>
    <YawPitchRoll x="0" y="90" z="0"/>
  </TransformComponent>
</Actor>
```

The BaseGameLogic::VModifyActor() method finds the actor and calls a member of the ActorFactory class you've never seen before, which is very similar to the ActorFactory::VCreateComponent() method that initializes a new actor. It runs through the XML above, either creates or finds the components, and initializes them.

```
void ActorFactory::ModifyActor(StrongActorPtr pActor, TiXmlElement* overrides)
{
  // Loop through each child element and load the component
  for (TiXmlElement* pNode = overrides->FirstChildElement();
     pNode; pNode = pNode->NextSiblingElement())
  {
    ComponentId componentId = ActorComponent::GetIdFromName(pNode->Value());
    StrongActorComponentPtr pComponent =
      MakeStrongPtr(pActor->GetComponent<ActorComponent>(componentId));
    if (pComponent)
    {
      pComponent->VInit(pNode);
    }
```

```
    else
    {
      pComponent = VCreateComponent(pNode);
      if (pComponent)
      {
        pActor->AddComponent(pComponent);
        pComponent->SetOwner(pActor);
      }
    }
  }
}
```

The trick here is that a component doesn't need a complete XML description to be initialized—just the members that are either different from the default values defined in the C++ component class or those members that have been recently modified.

For the previous XML snippet, the code would find the `TranformComponent` of the Grid actor and call `VInit()`, which would save the new orientation of the actor.

The last function that modifies actors is simply one that destroys an actor given its ID.

```
void DestroyActor( ActorId actorId )
{
  g_pApp->m_pGame->VDestroyActor(actorId);
}
```

With all the accessor functions defined, it is time to create the DLL.

## Creating the DLL

When you create a DLL, you usually want to expose functions to any consumer of that DLL. This is done with the `_declspec` keyword in a C++ header file. Here's how this looks:

```
#include "Editor.h"

#define DllExport _declspec(DLLexport)

// Editor Framework Functions
extern "C" DllExport int EditorMain(
  int *instancePtrAddress,
  int *hPrevInstancePtrAddress,
  int *hWndPtrAddress,
```

```
  int nCmdShow, int screenWidth, int screenHeight);
extern "C" DllExport void RenderFrame();
extern "C" DllExport int Shutdown();
extern "C" DllExport void OpenLevel( BSTR lFileName );

// Actor accessor functions
extern "C" DllExport int GetNumActors();
extern "C" DllExport void GetActorList(int *actorIdArrayPtr, int size);
extern "C" DllExport int PickActor(int *hWndPtrAddress);
extern "C" DllExport int GetActorXmlSize ( ActorId actorId );
extern "C" DllExport void GetActorXml ( int *actorXmlPtrAddress,
  ActorId actorId );

// Actor XML functions
extern "C" DllExport void RemoveActor( ActorId actorId );
extern "C" DllExport void CreateActor( BSTR bstrActorResource );
extern "C" DllExport void ModifyActor ( BSTR bstrActorModificationXML );
```

Each exported function must have `extern "C" _declspec(DLLexport)` before the declaration. The macro at the top of the last code segment helps keep the code looking cleaner. As you read the remainder of this chapter, more C functions will be added to this list as the C# editor side is explored.

The editor project settings are exactly the same as those set for the project that created *Teapot Wars*, with one exception. Under Configuration Properties->General, the Configuration Type should be set to "Dynamic Library (.dll)" instead of "Application (.exe)."

## Wrapping Up the Editor Architecture

The editor application, logic, and view classes are thin extensions of the base classes you've seen in earlier chapters. They can add actors to a scene, render them, and receive events on how to modify the actors, either by moving them around or deleting them. The editor doesn't need too much more than that, at least from the game engine itself. It does, however, need a fairly complicated user interface, a way to load and save levels, create and modify actor properties, and package everything to be used by the game engine. For that, we need to wrap the C++ editor implementation with C#.

Getting that to work means the C# application needs to send information to and retrieve information from the C++ code. This gets a little tricky, and for context, we need to go over differences between managed and unmanaged code.

**Fast Iteration Makes Games More Fun**

In a commercial game editor, rather than using a stripped-down version of the game, many editors completely surround and extend the game. This enables content developers like level designers and artists to run the game inside the editor so they can test their work. Editors that don't work this way force content developers to change something in the editor, save the level, load the game, find the spot they changed, see the change in the game, and decide whether they like what they did. If they don't like it, and I guarantee they won't, they exit the game, load the editor, find the spot they changed again, and start the whole process over.

**`tuning.reload`**

On *The Sims*, we have a magic console command called `tuning.reload`, which allows us to make a change in the tuning editor, save out the data files, and run this command to reload the tuning files while the game is running. A common path when iterating on a gameplay feature is to make a tuning change, reload the tuning, and test the feature. This process is repeated until the feature is working as expected without having to reload the game. There are similar console commands to reload parts of the world and other data. We even have one to reload any scripts that were changed.

Being able to modify the game while it is running is a huge benefit to the gameplay engineers and designers. It means that they can theoretically work on their feature without ever having to spend time waiting for the game to load, and it makes developing features extremely fast.

## The C# Editor Application

When the editor is complete, it should look like Figure 22.1.

Many commercial game editors look fairly similar to this design. The window on the left side is what you created at the beginning of this chapter, a panel that forms the surface for DirectX to render the game world. The panel on the right side has an upper and a lower part. The upper part is a tabbed view, showing either all the assets in the editor's Assets folder or a list of all the actors in the scene. The lower panel displays all of the components of any selected actor. This particular design was inspired somewhat by the Unity 3 editor, which is rapidly increasing in popularity, even among professional game developers.

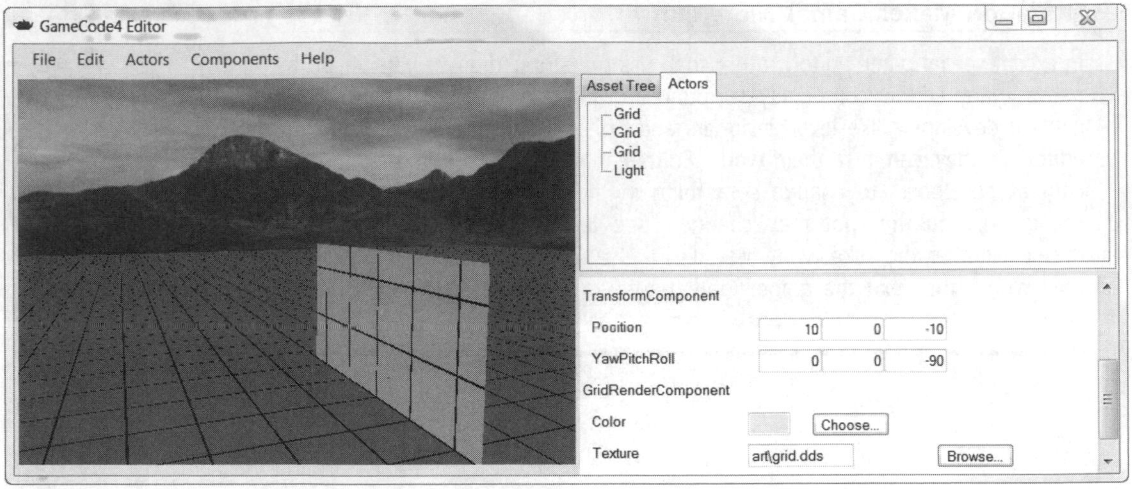


**Figure 22.1**
The final product—a C# editor using a C++ DLL.

### One Window Isn't Enough

Most commercial game editors have multiple windows rendering simultaneously. One of these windows looks like the rendered window in Figure 21.2 and looks pretty much as you would expect the game to look. Other windows show the world in wireframe, usually directly along the X-, Y-, and Z-axes. This can really help content creators see exactly where an object is placed in the world. In many of these editors, each window is completely configurable, too, allowing the user to set up his display panels in exactly the right way to help him work quickly and correctly.

### Fewer Clicks Make Happier Game Developers

In any software development, from websites to tool development, it makes sense to do everything you can to minimize the number of mouse clicks it takes to do anything. This is especially true with the most commonly used features. Put buttons for them right on the main menu and provide hot keys.

## Differences Between Managed Code and Unmanaged Code

With .NET, managed code is not actually compiled into machine code but is instead written into an intermediary format. The .NET common language runtime (CLR) compiles the intermediary code into machine code at the time of execution. Unmanaged code is compiled directly into machine code similar to a C++ compiler. Some of the benefits from managed code are that it is portable to any machine that has the .NET CLR installed, and the CLR can even detect the state of the machine to maximize performance. This managed environment comes at some cost of performance. In addition, C# uses a garbage-collecting memory manager, meaning that programs are not responsible for cleaning up memory after themselves, although there are exceptions.

C# cannot load static libraries, only dynamically linked libraries. Any unmanaged code that you call from C# will have to live inside a DLL. Before you see the guts of some C# Windows Forms, you need to see how C# gains access to the C++ DLL.

## NativeMethods Class

The NativeMethods class declares hooks into the DLL so they can be called from C#. There are a few ways to go about this, but one of the easiest is to declare a C# static class and then declare all the C free functions in a manner that C# can call them.

```
static class NativeMethods
{
  const string editorDllName = "GCC4EditorDLL_2010.dll";

  // Editor Framework - initializing, message processing, rendering, shutdown
  [DllImport(editorDllName, CallingConvention = CallingConvention.Cdecl)]
  public unsafe static extern int EditorMain(
    IntPtr instancePtrAddress, IntPtr hPrevInstancePtrAddress,
    IntPtr hWndPtrAddress, int nCmdShow, int screenWidth, int screenHeight);

  [DllImport(editorDllName, CallingConvention = CallingConvention.Cdecl)]
  public unsafe static extern void WndProc(
    IntPtr hWndPtrAddress, int msg, int wParam, int lParam);

   [DllImport(editorDllName, CallingConvention = CallingConvention.Cdecl)]
  public static extern void RenderFrame();

  [DllImport(editorDllName, CallingConvention = CallingConvention.Cdecl)]
  public static extern int Shutdown();

  [DllImport(editorDllName, CallingConvention = CallingConvention.Cdecl)]
  public static extern void OpenLevel([MarshalAs(UnmanagedType.BStr)]
    string lFileName);

  // Actor accessor functions
  [DllImport(editorDllName, CallingConvention = CallingConvention.Cdecl)]
```

```
    public static extern int GetNumActors();
    [DllImport(editorDllName, CallingConvention = CallingConvention.Cdecl)]
    public unsafe static extern void GetActorList(IntPtr actorIdArrayPtrAddress,
                                                  int size);

    [DllImport(editorDllName, CallingConvention = CallingConvention.Cdecl)]
    public unsafe static extern int GetActorXmlSize(uint actorId);
    [DllImport(editorDllName, CallingConvention = CallingConvention.Cdecl)]
    public unsafe static extern void GetActorXml(IntPtr actorXMLPtrAddress,
                                                 uint actorId);
    [DllImport(editorDllName, CallingConvention = CallingConvention.Cdecl)]
    public unsafe static extern int PickActor(IntPtr hWndPtrAddress);

    // Actor modification functions
    [DllImport(editorDllName, CallingConvention = CallingConvention.Cdecl)]
    public static extern int CreateActor([MarshalAs(UnmanagedType.BStr)]
      string lactorResource);
    [DllImport(editorDllName, CallingConvention = CallingConvention.Cdecl)]
    public static extern void ModifyActor([MarshalAs(UnmanagedType.BStr)]
      string lactorModXML);
    [DllImport(editorDllName, CallingConvention = CallingConvention.Cdecl)]
    public unsafe static extern void DestroyActor(uint actorId);
}
```

There are a few things you should notice. First, the DLL to be loaded is explicitly declared. Next, `[DllImport(editorDllName, CallingConvention = CallingConvention.Cdecl)]` is declared prior to the function. The `DllImport` attribute imports the function from the DLL, and it matches the export declarations in the C++ code you saw previously. This is part of the Platform Invocation Services, or PInvoke. Next, all of these functions are declared `unsafe`. The C++ game engine runs in unmanaged code, which basically means there is no memory tracking, garbage collection, and other safety systems built into the CLR. That's why this code is declared unsafe.

## Program Class

The `Program` class is the entry point of the C# application.

```
using System;
using System.Collections.Generic;
using System.Windows.Forms;

namespace EditorApp
{
  static class Program
```

```
  {
    /// <summary>
    /// The main entry point for the application.
    /// </summary>
    [STAThread]
    static void Main()
    {
      Application.EnableVisualStyles();
      Application.SetCompatibleTextRenderingDefault(false);

      EditorForm form = new EditorForm();

      MessageHandler messageHandler = form.GetMessageHandler();
      Application.AddMessageFilter(messageHandler);
      Application.Idle +=
        new EventHandler(messageHandler.Application_Idle);

      Application.Run(form);
    }
  }
}
```

The first two lines are typical of C# Windows Forms applications, and they ensure that the window, buttons, menus, and other visual components draw as you would expect them to. The next line creates the `EditorForm`, which contains all of the user interface elements of the editor.

The next three lines are critical to shepherding Windows messages, like `WM_MOUSE`, from the C# application to the C++ side of things. Lastly, the call to `Application.Run(form)` gets everything running.

## `MessageHandler` Class

To get Windows messages from the C# application to C++, you need to set up a special helper class. If a mouse button is clicked on the rendered image of the game, the message shouldn't go to the placeholder panel on the C# Windows Form, but rather it should be trapped and sent to the C++ game engine. Luckily, there's an interface class for exactly that, the `IMessageFilter` interface. As messages are trapped, they are converted to Windows messages that the C++ game engine can consume, and they are sent in to the `WndProc()` free function defined in the DLL. It is called by using the `NativeMethods` class, which imports all of the exposed DLL functions.

```
using System;
using System.Collections.Generic;
```

```
using System.Text;
using System.Windows.Forms;

namespace EditorApp
{
  public class MessageHandler : IMessageFilter
  {
    const int WM_LBUTTONDOWN = 0x0201;
    const int WM_LBUTTONUP = 0x0202;
    const int WM_LBUTTONDBLCLK = 0x0203;
    const int WM_RBUTTONDOWN = 0x0204;
    const int WM_RBUTTONUP = 0x0205;
    const int WM_RBUTTONDBLCLK = 0x0206;
    const int WM_MBUTTONDOWN = 0x0207;
    const int WM_MBUTTONUP = 0x0208;
    const int WM_MBUTTONDBLCLK = 0x0209;

    const int WM_KEYDOWN = 0x0100;
    const int WM_KEYUP = 0x0101;
    const int WM_SYSKEYDOWN = 0x0104;
    const int WM_SYSKEYUP = 0x0105;
    const int WM_CLOSE = 0x0010;

    IntPtr m_formHandle;
    IntPtr m_displayPanelHandle;
    EditorForm m_parent;

    // We take both the EditorForm's handle and its
    // displayPanel handle, since messages will sometimes be for the
    // form or the display panel.

    public MessageHandler( IntPtr formHandle,
      IntPtr displayPanelHandle, EditorForm parent )
    {
      m_formHandle = formHandle;
      m_displayPanelHandle = displayPanelHandle;
      m_parent = parent;
    }

    public bool PreFilterMessage(ref Message m)
    {
      // Intercept messages only if they occur for the EditorForm
      // or its display panel.
      if (m.HWnd == m_displayPanelHandle || m.HWnd == m_formHandle)
      {
```

```
        switch (m.Msg)
        {
          case WM_LBUTTONDOWN:
          case WM_LBUTTONUP:
          case WM_LBUTTONDBLCLK:
          case WM_RBUTTONDOWN:
          case WM_RBUTTONUP:
          case WM_RBUTTONDBLCLK:
          case WM_MBUTTONDOWN:
          case WM_MBUTTONUP:
          case WM_MBUTTONDBLCLK:
          case WM_KEYDOWN:
          case WM_KEYUP:
          case WM_SYSKEYDOWN:
          case WM_SYSKEYUP:
          case WM_CLOSE:
          {
            NativeMethods.WndProc(m_displayPanelHandle,
              m.Msg, m.WParam.ToInt32(), m.LParam.ToInt32());
            // If the left mouse button is up, try doing a
            // raycast to see if it intersects with an actor
            if (m.Msg == WM_LBUTTONUP)
            {
              m_parent.SelectActor();
            }
            return true;
          }
        }
      }
    return false;
  }
```

This class determines if the window handle for these messages matches either the handle for the `EngineDisplayForm`, which contains the entire editor interface, or the `DisplayPanel`, which is a placeholder for the graphics display rendered by the `EditorHumanView`. If this were a message that occurred on another part of the editor, such as the game assets tree or the component editor, `PreFilterMessage()` would simply ignore the message.

One message that the C# editor application needs to trap is `WM_LBUTTONUP`. This will call `EngineDisplayForm::SelectActor()` so that you can click directly on the actor you are interested in and have its properties show up in the `ActorPropertiesForm`.

Similar to the main loop in C++, when the editor application isn't processing messages, it is idle and can do other jobs like render the 3D world.

```
public void Application_Idle(object sender, EventArgs e)
  {
    try
    {
      // Render the scene if we are idle
      NativeMethods.RenderFrame();
    }
    catch (Exception ex)
    {
      MessageBox.Show(ex.Message);
    }
    m_parent.Invalidate();
  }
}
```

`Application_Idle()` calls into `NativeMethods.RenderFrame()`. This function is called when the application is idle. At the end of the `Application_Idle()`, `m_parent.Invalidate()` invalidates the entire surface of the editor, so it will be redrawn and display any changes to actor lists or actor components.

## The C# Editor User Interface

You've been looking at a lot of code that wraps a C++ game engine with a C# Windows Form application. As interesting as that might have been, all of this work is just setting up the basics of a very extendable and data-driven editor.

**Go Learn C# Windows Forms!**

If you haven't done any programming in C# or especially Windows Forms, the following sections are going to be fairly confusing. They assume you know how to create a Windows Form and add methods to handle events, such as when control data changes or when a control has been clicked on, and much more.

### The `EditorForm` Class

The `EditorForm` class holds all of the controls of the game editor. It handles the following tasks:

- Reserving a space for the game engine to draw the game world and accept input, such as mouse clicks or drags to move the view or modify actors.
- Displaying and managing a complete list of all available game assets, such as textures, audio files, Lua scripts, and so on.
- Reading actor information from the game engine and sending any changes to actor components back to the game engine.
- Displaying a complete list of all the actors in the current scene and allowing them to be selected for modification.
- Displaying the components of the currently selected actor so it can be modified.
- Displaying a menu for opening levels, creating new components on selected actors, and so on.

I'll cover each of these areas in the next few sections.

```
public partial class EditorForm : Form
{
  private string m_ProjectDirectory;
  private string m_AssetsDirectory;
  private string m_CurrentLevelFile;

  private List<XmlNode> m_ActorsXmlNodes = new List<XmlNode>();
  private int m_SelectedActorId = 0;

  private MessageHandler m_messageFilter;
  private ActorComponentEditor m_ActorComponentEditor;

  public EditorForm()
  {
    var currentDirectory = Directory.GetCurrentDirectory();
    var parentDirectory = Directory.GetParent(currentDirectory);
    m_ProjectDirectory = parentDirectory.FullName;
    m_AssetsDirectory = m_ProjectDirectory + "\\Assets";

    InitializeComponent();
    try
    {
      // This is how we get the instance handle for our C# app.
      System.IntPtr hInstance = Marshal.GetHINSTANCE(this.GetType().Module);

      // This is how we get the window handle for
      // the panel we'll be rendering into.
      IntPtr hwnd = this.DisplayPanel.Handle;
```

```
            // Call into our Dll main function, which will set up an
            // instance of the EditorApp project.
            NativeMethods.EditorMain(
              hInstance, IntPtr.Zero, hwnd, 1,
              this.DisplayPanel.Width, this.DisplayPanel.Height);

            InitializeAssetTree();

            m_messageFilter = new MessageHandler(
              this.Handle, this.DisplayPanel.Handle, this);

            m_ActorComponentEditor = new ActorComponentEditor(
              Panel_ActorComponents, m_ProjectDirectory);
          }
          catch(Exception e)
          {
            MessageBox.Show("Error: " + e.ToString());
          }
        }
      }
```

The first lines initialize the `m_ProjectsDirectory` and `m_AssetsDirectory` members, which are constructed assuming the editor application is running in the directory where the game assets will eventually be saved. The member `m_CurrentLevelFile` is set only after a level file has been loaded.

The call to `InitializeComponent()` is what C# Windows Forms use to create and attach all the menus, panels, or other user interface objects. This function is generated code by Visual Studio anytime you add or remove these components within the Forms Designer.

The call to `GetHINSTANCE()` grabs the instance handle for this application, and the next line gets the window handle for the panel that will become the main rendering area on the C# form. These handles are converted into integer values and then passed into the `EditorMain` function in the unmanaged C++ DLL.

The next line calls `InitializeAssetTree()`, reads the project directory, and populates a tree view with all the filenames. A tree view of every game asset is convenient for anyone using the editor to easily browse and edit the files that can be used to create the game.

The next two lines initialize some helper classes for the `EditorForm`. The first of these initializes the `MessageHandler` object, which you read about in the previous section. The next object, `ActorComponentEditor`, you'll read about in the next section.

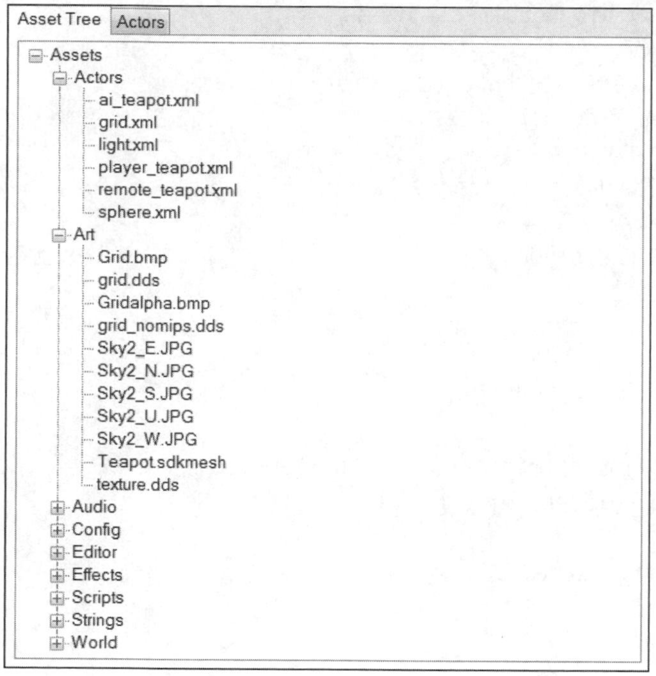


**Figure 22.2**
The asset tree for *Teapot Wars.*

### *The Asset Tree*

The asset tree is the complete list of every file in the *Assets* directory (see Figure 22.2). The editor will eventually package all of these files into a Zip file that will be loaded by the game's resource cache.

One of the components on the `EditorForm` is a `TreeView`, named `TreeView_Assets`. The editor walks the entire directory, and for each file or directory, it adds a `TreeNode`. The code to do this is called when the editor is initialized.

```
private void InitializeAssetTree()
{
  TreeView_Assets.Nodes.Clear();

  var stack = new Stack<TreeNode>();
  var rootDirectory = new DirectoryInfo(m_AssetsDirectory);
  var node = new TreeNode(rootDirectory.Name) { Tag = rootDirectory };

  stack.Push(node);
  while (stack.Count > 0)
  {
    var currentNode = stack.Pop();
    var directoryInfo = (DirectoryInfo)currentNode.Tag;
```

```
    foreach (var directory in directoryInfo.GetDirectories())
    {
      FileAttributes attributes = File.GetAttributes(directory.FullName);
      if ((attributes & FileAttributes.Hidden) == 0 )
      {
        var childDirectoryNode = new TreeNode(directory.Name);
        childDirectoryNode.Tag = directory;
        currentNode.Nodes.Add(childDirectoryNode);
        stack.Push(childDirectoryNode);
      }
    }
    foreach (var file in directoryInfo.GetFiles())
    {
      FileAttributes attributes = File.GetAttributes(file.FullName);
      if ((attributes & FileAttributes.Hidden) == 0 )
      {
        var childNode = new TreeNode(file.Name);
        childNode.Tag = file.FullName;
        currentNode.Nodes.Add(childNode);
      }
    }
  }
  TreeView_Assets.Nodes.Add(node);
}
```

First, notice that the method uses an iterative algorithm rather than a recursive one, which isn't absolutely required when walking a directory tree but is typically a safer way to initialize a tree structure. A recursive algorithm uses stack space to store data and therefore opens the possibility of overflowing the stack. Iterative algorithms can do the same work in less memory, although they are a little harder to read. Second, if hidden files are found in the directory structure, they aren't added to the tree. Ignoring hidden files can be really useful if you use a source code repository like SVN, which stores additional information in hidden *.svn* directories. Finally, for convenience, the `TreeNode.Tag` member is initialized to the full file path of the filename.

Notice the `var` keyword used to declare variables? That is C#'s equivalent of C++'s `auto` keyword, which can be a real convenience without losing strong typing.

A game editor should always make it convenient to open an asset file, which can be managed easily with the following code:

```
private void TreeView_Assets_MouseDoubleClick(object sender, MouseEventArgs e)
{
```

```
    TreeNode node = TreeView_Assets.SelectedNode;
    if (node != null && node.Nodes.Count == 0)
    {
      string file = node.Tag.ToString();
      if(File.Exists(file))
      {
        Process.Start(file);
      }
    }
}
```

This code is hooked up to the TreeView's `MouseDoubleClick` event handler. The full file name associated with the TreeNode is sent into `Process.Start()`, which launches any application associated with the file.

### *Actors List*

After the editor loads a level, it needs to initialize a data member that stores the XML representation of each actor. This member is a C# `List` of `XmlNode` objects. At the same time, a `TreeView` will also receive information about each actor so that actors can be selected by name. For a very simple level with three Grid objects and a Light, the actor TreeView would look like Figure 22.3.

Right away, you'll notice a problem, I bet. The three Grid actors look exactly the same in the actor list, even though they are different actors. In a commercial game, there might be hundreds or even thousands of objects all deriving from the same actor archetype. That's why most commercial editors allow objects to get custom name attributes, not only to make working on the game easier for game designers, but you could also use this custom name to search the actor list in the game. That might make a good weekend project!

The editor code must initialize the `TreeView` and the `List<XmlNode>` data member, `m_ActorsXmlNodes`, by getting data from the game engine. First, an array of

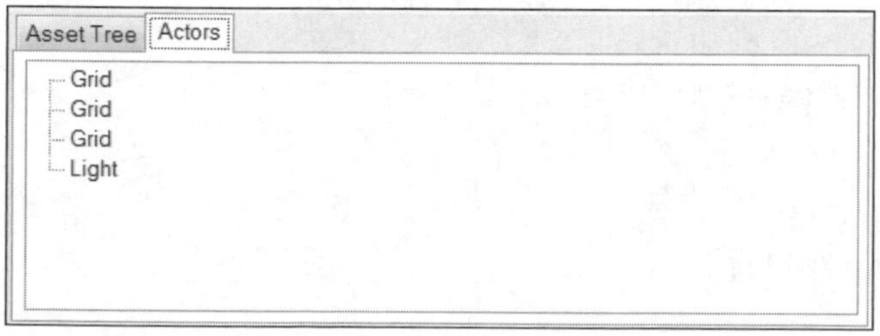


**Figure 22.3**
The actor list for a very simple level.

valid ActorID objects is accessed, and for each actor ID, the editor asks the game engine for its XML definition. The actor ID list is accessed with the following code:

```
private int[] GetActorList()
{
  // We need to know how many actors there are,
  // in order to find out how much memory to allocate
  int numActors = NativeMethods.GetNumActors();

  IntPtr tempArray = Marshal.AllocCoTaskMem(numActors * sizeof(uint));
  NativeMethods.GetActorList(tempArray, numActors);

  // Copy the memory into an array of ints and dispose of our
  // our memory.
  int[] actorList = new int[numActors];
  Marshal.Copy(tempArray, actorList, 0, numActors);
  Marshal.FreeCoTaskMem(tempArray);

  return actorList;
}
```

The editor uses the NativeMethods class to make calls to the game engine, first to find out how many actors there are and then to fill the array with their actor IDs. The memory buffer used for this purpose is allocated from the COM task memory allocator, which is a good way to pass data from an unmanaged C++ DLL to a managed C# application. When the data has been read into managed memory, the tempArray buffer is freed.

Retrieving the XML definition from an actor is done in a similar way.

```
private XmlElement GetActorXml(uint actorId)
{
  int xmlSize = NativeMethods.GetActorXmlSize(actorId);
  if (xmlSize == 0)
    return null;

  IntPtr tempArray = Marshal.AllocCoTaskMem((xmlSize + 1) * sizeof(char));
  NativeMethods.GetActorXml(tempArray, actorId);
  string actorXml = Marshal.PtrToStringAnsi(tempArray);
  Marshal.FreeCoTaskMem(tempArray);

  XmlDocument actorDoc = new XmlDocument();
  actorDoc.Load(new StringReader(actorXml));
  return actorDoc.DocumentElement;
}
```

It follows a similar pattern as before: When obtaining data from unmanaged C++, the code asks for the size of memory needed with `GetActorXmlSize()`. Then a temporary unmanaged memory buffer of that size is allocated, the data is copied into that buffer with a call to the C++ DLL, and finally the results are processed into managed memory.

The processing includes a call to `Marshal.PtrToStringAnsi()`, which can convert an unmanaged ANSI string into a managed C# string. Once that is done, the string is converted into an `XmlElement`, which is a very useful class to read and write XML. You'll be seeing much more of `XmlElement` shortly because it is the backbone data structure for the editor.

The next method uses `GetActorList()` and `GetActorXml()` to initialize the actor TreeView and the `List<XmlNode>`.

```
private void InitializeActors()
{
  TreeView_Actors.Nodes.Clear();
  int[] actorList = GetActorList();

  // Game starts actors at Id=1, so we'll make a space for a null actor here.
  m_ActorsXmlNodes.Add(null);

  // Add each actor as its own node in the treeview.
  for (int i = 0; i < actorList.GetLength(0); i++)
  {
    uint actorId = Convert.ToUInt32(actorList[i]);

    TreeNode node = new TreeNode();

    XmlElement actorXml = GetActorXml(actorId);
    if (actorXml != null)
    {
      node.Name = actorList[i].ToString();
      m_ActorsXmlNodes.Add((XmlNode)actorXml);
      node.Text = actorXml.GetAttribute("type");
    }
    else
    {
      node.Text = "<undefined actor - no xml>";
    }
    TreeView_Actors.Nodes.Add(node);
  }
}
```

When an actor in the actor list is clicked, the editor needs to show its properties and allow them to be changed. That is the job of the class you'll see next, the `ActorComponentEditor`. It is informed of the selected actor with a method that is hooked into the AfterSelect event of the actor TreeView.

```
private void TreeView_Actors_AfterSelect(object sender, TreeViewEventArgs e)
{
  TreeNode node = TreeView_Actors.SelectedNode;
  if (node != null)
  {
    m_SelectedActorId = node.Index + 1;    // Game starts Actor Ids at 1
    m_ActorComponentEditor.ShowActorComponents(
      m_SelectedActorId, GetActorXml(m_SelectedActorId));
  }
}
```

### *The Menu Bar*

The `EditorForm` has a menu bar attached, which is used for all manner of editor functions. Making these functions work is a matter of hooking up a method to each menu item through the C# Windows Forms Designer. Double-clicking on any menu item automatically jumps to the handler code or adds it if it doesn't exist. Not every method of the editor's menu bar will be discussed here, as many of them are extremely simple. Three worth mentioning are for opening a level, saving a level, and building the project.

```
private void openLevelToolStripMenuItem_Click(object sender, EventArgs e)
{
  OpenFileDialog dialog = new OpenFileDialog();

  dialog.InitialDirectory = m_AssetsDirectory + "\\World";
  dialog.Filter = "XML files (*.xml)|*.xml";
  dialog.FilterIndex = 1;
  dialog.RestoreDirectory = true;

  if (dialog.ShowDialog() == DialogResult.OK)
  {
    string fileName = dialog.FileName;
    NativeMethods.OpenLevel(fileName);
    InitializeActors();
  }
}
```

Opening a level is actually done by the C++ DLL. Once the level load is complete, `InitializeActors()` will reinitialize the actor list.

Saving a level requires creating and writing an XML file like this:

```
private void saveLevelToolStripMenuItem_Click(object sender, EventArgs e)
{
  XmlDocument levelXml = new XmlDocument();
  XmlElement world = levelXml.CreateElement("World");
  levelXml.AppendChild(world);
  XmlElement staticActors = levelXml.CreateElement("StaticActors");
  world.AppendChild(staticActors);

  int[] actorList = GetActorList();

  for (int i = 0; i < actorList.GetLength(0); i++)
  {
    uint actorId = Convert.ToUInt32(actorList[i]);
    XmlElement actorXml = GetActorXml(actorId);
    if (actorXml != null)
    {
      staticActors.AppendChild(
        staticActors.OwnerDocument.ImportNode(actorXml, true));
    }
  }

  // Save the document to a file and auto-indent the output.
  XmlTextWriter writer = new XmlTextWriter(m_CurrentLevelFile, null);
  writer.Formatting = Formatting.Indented;
  levelXml.Save(writer);
}
```

The level file format is basically a list of actors and their components.

```
<World>
 <StaticActors>
  <Actor type="Grid">
   …component XML definitions go here
  </Actor>
  <Actor type="Light">
   …component XML definitions go here
  </Actor>
 </StaticActors>
</World>
```

The root level element, `World`, contains the actor list defined by the `StaticActors` element. A good extension for this format might add level specific information, such as a definition for background music or where the level chains to after it is completed. In this simple example, just the actor list is shown.

The XmlDocument is responsible for creating new elements by calling CreateElement(), and each element can have multiple children, which are attached with the AppendChild() method. Notice the call to ImportNode() inside the loop? This call is required to create a copy of an XmlElement created in a different XmlDocument object.

Once the entire XmlDocument object is ready, it is saved by creating an XmlTextWriter. The formatting is set so that it makes for easier human reading and editing.

The last menu action is for building the Zip file that contains the entire *Assets* directory. For that, a helper class, ZipFileUtility, is needed.

```
private void buildProjectToolStripMenuItem_Click(object sender, EventArgs e)
{
  ZipFileUtility.Create(m_AssetsDirectory,
    m_ProjectDirectory + "\\Assets.zip");
}
```

System.IO.Packaging has a convenient class called ZipPackaging, which can create or read Zip files, and will form the basis of the ZipFileUtility class.

```
class ZipFileUtility
{
  public static void Create(string rootDirectoryName, string zipFileName)
  {
    DirectoryInfo rootDirectory = new DirectoryInfo(rootDirectoryName);
    int rootDirLen = rootDirectory.FullName.Length;

    using (Package package = ZipPackage.Open(zipFileName, FileMode.Create))
    {
      var stack = new Stack<string>();
      stack.Push(rootDirectory.FullName);

      while (stack.Count > 0)
      {
        var currentNode = stack.Pop();
        var directoryInfo = new DirectoryInfo(currentNode);
        foreach (var directory in directoryInfo.GetDirectories())
        {
          FileAttributes attributes =
            File.GetAttributes(directory.FullName);
          if ((attributes & FileAttributes.Hidden) == 0 &&
              directory.Name != "Editor")
          {
            stack.Push(directory.FullName);
          }
```

```
        }
        foreach (var file in directoryInfo.GetFiles())
        {
          FileAttributes attributes = File.GetAttributes(file.FullName);
          if ((attributes & FileAttributes.Hidden) == 0)
          {
            string relativeFromRoot =
              file.FullName.Substring(rootDirLen);
            Uri relUri = GetRelativeUri(relativeFromRoot);

            PackagePart packagePart = package.CreatePart(
              relUri, System.Net.Mime.MediaTypeNames.Application.Octet,
              CompressionOption.Maximum);
            using (FileStream fileStream = new FileStream(file.FullName,
              FileMode.Open, FileAccess.Read))
            {
              CopyStream(fileStream, packagePart.GetStream());
            }
          }
        }
      }
    }
  }
```

The `Create()` method uses an iterative algorithm to walk the entire directory tree. Any directories it finds, except for those named *Editor,* are processed. Ignoring anything named *Editor* allows editor-specific data to be stored in the *Assets* directory but excluded from the final Zip file that the game will read with its resource cache. As you saw previously with the assets tree, hidden files are also excluded.

For each included file, a `PackagePart` object is created and written to the Zip file. There are three helper methods that are a part of the `ZipFileUtility` class, and all are called from the `Create` method. The first is `CopyStream`, which reads a target stream and copies it in chunks to a target stream—it can be extremely useful for large files.

```
private static void CopyStream(Stream source, Stream target)
{
  const int bufSize = 16384;
  byte[] buf = new byte[bufSize];
  int bytesRead = 0;
  while ((bytesRead = source.Read(buf, 0, bufSize)) > 0)
    target.Write(buf, 0, bytesRead);
}
```

The second helper method is `GetRelativeUri()`, which constructs a properly formatted filename to be included into the Zip file. It requires the filename to be relative to the root of the Zip file and not contain any illegal characters.

```
private static Uri GetRelativeUri(string currentFile)
{
  string pastBackslashes = currentFile.Substring(currentFile.IndexOf('\\'));
  string nukeDoubleBackslash = pastBackslashes.Replace('\\', '/');
  string nukeSpaces = nukeDoubleBackslash.Replace(" ', '_');

  return new Uri(RemoveAccents(relPath), UriKind.Relative);
}

private static string RemoveAccents(string input)
{
  string normalized = input.Normalize(NormalizationForm.FormKD);
  Encoding removal = Encoding.GetEncoding(Encoding.ASCII.CodePage,
    new EncoderReplacementFallback(""),
    new DecoderReplacementFallback(""));
  byte[] bytes = removal.GetBytes(normalized);
  return Encoding.ASCII.GetString(bytes);
}
```

**Always Use Relative Path Names**

Learning from someone else's mistakes is vastly better than learning from your own. Did you notice the code in the `GetRelativeUri()` previous code example? Not only is this important for making well-formed Zip files, but it also enables your entire project to be stored in a way that a game developer likes. Not everyone stores his development projects on his C:\ drive, and it can be extremely inconvenient to assume a specific location for the project root directory. Store your filenames as relative to the project root, and everyone will be much happier.

## The `ActorComponentEditor` Class

So far you've seen the basic framework of the C# editor, but nothing yet has actually been able to view or modify all of the properties of an actor, such as its color, position, or texture filename. This is the job of the `ActorComponentEditor` class, shown in Figure 22.4.

Before jumping in to the code, it makes some sense to explain the idea behind the design. If you remember from Chapter 6, "Game Actors and Component Architecture," actors are containers for components. These components are represented by

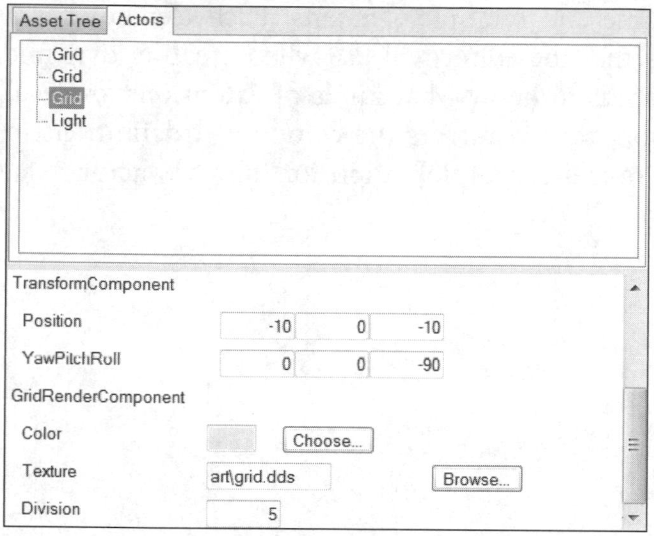


**Figure 22.4**
The `ActorComponentsEditor` showing two components.

C++ classes, such as the `TransformComponent`, which stores position and orientation, or the `GridRenderComponent`, which stores the color, texture filename, and size of a grid scene node. Each of these components has member data that should be exposed to the editor. Exposing these data members to the editor would mean creating controls like a text box to edit a filename or a combo box to make a selection from a list.

One method might be to simply write some C# code that mirrors each C++ component. It does create a weakness in the editor, however. If the C++ component changes by adding or removing data members, the editor must be changed, recompiled, and redistributed to anyone using it. Wouldn't a better solution be data driven?

Imagine an XML file that defined components from the editor's point of view:

```
<Components>
  <Component name="TransformComponent">
    <Element name="Position" type="Vec3" fieldNames="x,y,z" />
    <Element name="YawPitchRoll" type="Vec3" fieldNames="x,y,z" />
  </Component>
  <Component name="GridRenderComponent">
    <Element name="Color" type="RGBA" />
    <Element name="Texture" type="File"
      extensions="Image Files(*.JPG;*.GIF;*.DDS)□*.JPG;*.GIF;*.DDS" />
    <Element name="Division" type="int" />
  </Component>
</Components>
```

Each component definition has a name and multiple elements. Each element has a name, a type, and optional attributes that the editor will use when creating dynamic controls. For example, the file type needs to know what kinds of extensions are legal for the file. Each component definition exactly mirrors the component definitions in the actor XML files. For example, here is a partial definition for the Grid actor:

```
<Actor type="Grid">
  <TransformComponent>
    <Position x="0" y="0" z="0"/>
    <YawPitchRoll x="0" y="0" z="0"/>
  </TransformComponent>
  <GridRenderComponent>
    <Color r="0.4" g="0.4" b="0.4" a="1.0"/>
    <Texture>art\grid.dds</Texture>
    <Division>100</Division>
  </GridRenderComponent>
  <!--other components follow! -->
</Actor>
```

The ActorComponentsEditor could then read each component's definition and know exactly what controls to create so each component could be edited. Then the only time the editor must be changed is when a new data type is introduced.

**Keep the Game and Editor in Sync**

You can try very hard to limit dependencies between the game and the editor, but there will inevitably be a few. Even though the components and elements are defined as XML data for the editor to read, there are still dependencies on the existence of the components in C++, how their XML is structured, and more. When this type of dependency is inevitable, it makes good sense to put comments in the C++ and C# code specifying exactly how to keep the editor and the game in perfect harmony.

### *Data Members and Initialization*

The ActorComponentEditor has data members that keep track of the component's definition, the selected actor, and the C# Windows Form, a Panel, that will contain the dynamically created controls.

```
class ActorComponentEditor
{
  Dictionary<string, XmlNode> m_ComponentsByName;
  XmlDocument m_SelectedActorComponents;
  int m_SelectedActorId;
```

```
    XmlNode m_ActorXml;
    string m_AssetsDirectory;

    const int g_LabelColumnWidth = 160;
    int m_LineSpacing;
    Panel m_Panel;

    public ActorComponentEditor(Panel panel, string projectDirectory)
    {
      m_ComponentsByName = new Dictionary<string, XmlNode>();
      m_Panel = panel;
      m_LineSpacing = m_Panel.Font.Height * 2;

      m_AssetsDirectory = projectDirectory + "\\Assets";

      XmlDocument componentsXML = new XmlDocument();
      componentsXML.Load(m_AssetsDirectory + "\\Editor\\components.xml");

      XmlElement root = componentsXML.DocumentElement;
      XmlNodeList components = root.SelectNodes("child::*");
      foreach (XmlNode component in components)
      {
        m_ComponentsByName[component.Attributes["name"].Value] = component;
      }
    }
```

Take a look at the use of the `XmlElement` method, `SelectNodes()`. The parameter passed in to this method is an XPath, which is commonly used to specify or search for elements or attributes of an XML document.

### *A Quick XPath Tutorial*

The `ActorComponentEditor` makes heavy use of XPath because the same XPath definition can be used to match elements in the actor XML and the editor components' XML.

For example, the `Division` element of the `GridRenderComponent` in the Grid actor could be defined as "/Actor/GridRenderComponent/Division." XPath also allows searching elements by their number. Since this same element is the third element of the second child of the root node, the XPath would be `"/*[1]/*[3]/*[4]"`.

Since `XmlElements` can be traversed, it is a simple matter to write a utility class to create XPath descriptions.

```
class XPathUtility
{
```

```
static int GetNodePosition(XmlNode child)
{
  int count = 1;
  for (int i = 0; i < child.ParentNode.ChildNodes.Count; i++)
  {
    if (child.ParentNode.ChildNodes[i] == child)
    {
      // XPath starts counting at 1, not 0
      return count;
    }
    if (child.ParentNode.ChildNodes[i].Name == child.Name)
    {
      ++count;
    }
  }
    // child node not found in its parent's ChildNodes property.
    throw new InvalidOperationException();
}

public static string GetXPathToNode(XmlNode node)
{
  if (node.NodeType == XmlNodeType.Attribute)
  {
    // attributes have an OwnerElement, not a ParentNode; also they have
    // to be matched by name, not found by position
    return String.Format(
      "{0}/@{1}",
      GetXPathToNode(((XmlAttribute)node).OwnerElement),
      "*" //node.Name
    );
  }

  if (node.ParentNode == null)
  {
    // the only node with no parent is the root node, which has no path
    return "";
  }
  // the path to a node is the path to its parent, plus "/*[n]", where
  // n is its position among its siblings.
  return String.Format(
    "{0}/{1}[{2}]",
    GetXPathToNode(node.ParentNode),
    "*",
    GetNodePosition(node)
```

```
    );
  }
}
```

`GetNodePosition()` traverses siblings until it finds the matching `XmlElement`. If it isn't found, then it throws an exception, probably just a result of some late-night programming. `GetXPathToNode()` uses a recursive implementation, calling itself to create the XPath for parent nodes.

### *Showing Actor Components*

When an actor is selected, the actor components are read to create all the controls needed to edit their values.

```
public unsafe void ShowActorComponents(int selectedActorId, XmlNode actorXml)
{
  m_SelectedActorId = selectedActorId;
  m_ActorXml = actorXml;

  m_SelectedActorComponents = new XmlDocument();
  XmlNode editorComponents = m_SelectedActorComponents.CreateElement("Actor");
  m_SelectedActorComponents.AppendChild(editorComponents);

  m_Panel.Controls.Clear();

  XmlNodeList actorValueComponents = m_ActorXml.SelectNodes("child::*");
  int lineNum = 0;
  foreach (XmlNode actorValueComponent in actorValueComponents)
  {
    XmlNode sourceEditorComponent =
      m_ComponentsByName[actorValueComponent.Name];
    XmlDocument ownerDoc = editorComponents.OwnerDocument;
    XmlNode editorComponent = ownerDoc.ImportNode(sourceEditorComponent,true);
    editorComponents.AppendChild(editorComponent);
    lineNum = AddComponentUI(actorValueComponent, editorComponent, lineNum);
  }
}
```

The `m_ActorXml` member holds the actor XML values that are read in from the game and stored in the level XML file. The `m_SelectedActorComponents` member is initialized to hold a parallel XML structure that mirrors the actor XML, but instead of storing actor values, it stores the component names, element names, and element types of each component. For each component, the `AddComponentUI()` method is called to create all the controls.

```
public int AddComponentUI(XmlNode actorComponentValues,
                          XmlNode editorComponentValues, int lineNum)
{
  string componentName = actorComponentValues.Name.ToString();
  string componentXpath = XPathUtility.GetXPathToNode(actorComponentValues);
  try
  {
    AddElementLabel(componentName, lineNum);
    ++lineNum;
    int elementNum = 0;

    foreach (XmlNode inputField in editorComponentValues)
    {
      string xpath = XPathUtility.GetXPathToNode(inputField);
      string elementName = inputField.Attributes["name"].Value;
      string elementType = inputField.Attributes["type"].Value;

      XmlNode actorValues = actorComponentValues.ChildNodes[elementNum];

      AddElementLabel("   " + elementName, lineNum);

      switch (elementType)
      {
        case "Vec3":
          AddVec3(actorValues, xpath, lineNum);
          ++lineNum;
          break;

        case "RGBA":
          AddRGBA(actorValues, xpath, lineNum);
          ++lineNum;
          break;

        case "File":
          AddFileElement(actorValues, xpath, lineNum);
          ++lineNum;
          break;

        // Imagine more code here to initialize more types!

        default:
         AddElementLabel("   " + elementName + ": "
                         + elementType + " (unknown!)", lineNum);
          ++lineNum;
          break;
      }
```

```
      ++elementNum;
    }
  }
  catch (Exception e)
  {
    MessageBox.Show("Error in ComponentName " + componentName + "\n") ;
  }

  return lineNum;
}
```

The idea behind adding a dynamic control and attaching it to code that runs when it changes is pretty similar, no matter what type of data you are editing. Let's take a look at the code needed to select a file:

```
public void AddFileElement(XmlNode actorValues, string xpath, int lineNum)
{
  const int boxWidth = 160;
  const int horizSpacing = 20;

  TextBox textBox = new TextBox();
  Drawing.Point location = new Drawing.Point(
    g_LabelColumnWidth, lineNum * m_LineSpacing);
  textBox.Name = xpath;
  textBox.Location = location;
  textBox.Text = actorValues.FirstChild.Value;
  textBox.TextChanged += new EventHandler(FileElementChanged);
  m_Panel.Controls.Add(textBox);

  Button button = new Button();
  location = new Drawing.Point(
    g_LabelColumnWidth + boxWidth + horizSpacing, lineNum * m_LineSpacing);
  button.Name = xpath + "Button";
  button.Text = "Browse...";
  button.Location = location;
  button.MouseClick += new MouseEventHandler(SelectFile);
  m_Panel.Controls.Add(button);
}
```

A text box is created with the value set to the value stored in `actorValues.FirstChild.Value`. Since file elements are defined in XML like this, `<Texture>art\grid.dds</Texture>`, the first child is the text "art.grid.dds." The name of the text box is the XPath of the element in the XML. Because there may be multiple text boxes created, this is a convenient way to distinguish which control goes with which XML element. Even better, the XPath can be used to find both the actor values and the editor's component definition. An event handler is also attached that will run anytime the value of the text box is changed.

A button is also created next to the text box that will bring up the typical open file dialog box. Its name is set to the XPath of the actor element as well, but with "Button" attached to the end. This will not only uniquely identify the button in case there are multiple file elements in the actor, but it will enable us to find the exact text box control the button is associated with.

### *Editing Actor Components*

The C# Windows Form holds the controls for editing different element types, but there needs to be a way to actually change these values and have them reflect in visual display. Some controls can be edited directly, such as those for position. Others, like a choice of color or a filename, can make good use of helper dialog boxes. Here is `SelectFile()`, the code that will run when the Browse button is pressed:

```
private void SelectFile(object sender, MouseEventArgs e)
{
  OpenFileDialog openFile = new OpenFileDialog();
  Button button = (Button)sender;
  string buttonDesc = "Button";
  string textBoxElementName =
    button.Name.Substring(0, button.Name.Length - buttonDesc.Length);

  XmlNode fileElement = FindEditorElementFromXPath(textBoxElementName);

  openFile.Filter = fileElement.Attributes["extensions"].Value;
  openFile.ShowDialog();
  if (openFile.FileNames.Length > 0)
  {
    try
    {
      string fileName = openFile.FileNames[0];
      if (fileName.StartsWith(m_AssetsDirectory))
      {
        TextBox textBox = (TextBox)m_Panel.Controls[textBoxElementName];
        textBox.Text = fileName.Substring(m_AssetsDirectory.Length + 1);
      }
      else
      {
```

```
        MessageBox.Show("Error - This file isn't a part of this " +
          "project (it must be in " + m_AssetsDirectory + ").");
      }
    }
    catch
    {
      MessageBox.Show("ElementName is incorrect in SelectFile");
    }
  }
}
```

This code would get run anytime a button associated with a file element is pressed. The first order of business is to find the actual name of the text box control. Since the button has the same name as its companion text box control, with "Button" added to the end, a call to `Substring()` quickly finds the text box name. Later on, this string will be used to find the actual control by accessing `m_Panel.Controls` with the name of the text box. Since this is a file element, it is important to find the allowed extensions for the file. In the case of a texture file, extensions might be DDS, JPG, BMP, and so on. A helper function, `FindEditorElementFromXPath()`, uses the XPath name of the control to find the `XmlElement` the editor uses to get hints about how the element needs to be edited.

```
private XmlNode FindEditorElementFromXPath(string xpath)
{
  XmlNode root = m_SelectedActorComponents.FirstChild;
  XmlNodeList nodeList = root.SelectNodes(xpath);
  return nodeList[0];
}
```

Recall that the `m_SelectedActorComponents` member was initialized when the actor was selected, and for each component defined in the actor, this `XmlElement` received a child node from the editor's components definition. The XPath names of the controls map each control to the value stored in the actor and the hints to the editor on how it is edited.

The last method in this trio is `FileElementChanged()`, which is called anytime the value in the text box changes. Its job is to construct an XML string that will be sent to the C++ `EditorLogic` class.

```
private void FileElementChanged(object sender, EventArgs e)
{
  TextBox textBox = (TextBox)sender;
  string xPath = textBox.Name;
  string newValue = textBox.Text;
```

```
  XmlDocument xmlDoc = new XmlDocument();
  XmlElement xmlActor = xmlDoc.CreateElement("Actor");
  xmlDoc.AppendChild(xmlActor);

  XmlAttribute xmlActorId = xmlDoc.CreateAttribute("id");
  xmlActorId.InnerText = m_SelectedActorId.ToString();
  xmlActor.Attributes.Append(xmlActorId);

  XmlNode elementNode = FindActorElementFromXPath(xPath);
  XmlNode componentNode = elementNode.ParentNode;

  string componentName = componentNode.Name;
  string elementName = elementNode.Name;

  XmlElement xmlComponent = xmlDoc.CreateElement(componentName);
  xmlActor.AppendChild(xmlComponent);

  XmlElement xmlElementName = xmlDoc.CreateElement(elementName);
  xmlComponent.AppendChild(xmlElementName);

  xmlElementName.InnerText = newValue;

  NativeMethods.ModifyActor(xmlDoc.InnerXml);
}
private XmlNode FindActorElementFromXPath(string xpath)
{
  XmlNodeList nodeList = m_ActorXml.SelectNodes(xpath);
  return nodeList[0];
}
```

This code grabs the text box control and creates a snippet of XML. Assume for the sake of argument that the component being modified is the `<Texture>` element of the `GridRenderComponent`. Also assume that the actor ID is 1, and the new texture name is *art\sky.jpg*. Here is the XML that would be created:

```
<Actor id="1">
  <GridRenderComponent>
    <Texture>art\sky.jpg</Texture>
  </GridRenderComponent>
</Actor>
```

Once the XML is created, it is sent into `NativeMethods.ModifyActor()`. If you recall from the earlier section "Actor Modification Functions," this will cause the `GridRenderComponent` of the actor to be reinitialized, but since the only part of the XML that is defined is the texture name, only that element will be modified. All the other values currently in the actor remain the same.

**Editors Need Robust Error Checking**

One thing that is missing is checks on the data types. This occurred because the author was focusing most of his time on getting C# and C++ to play nice and trying to stamp out linker errors! However, you should make sure that data being passed to the editor game engine is all legitimate. You don't want to send any data that isn't appropriate to the unmanaged DLL. At best, nothing happens. At worst, the entire application crashes, taking with it several hours of work! There is nothing more dangerous to a programmer's well being than a person whose finest work has been lost by an editor bug.

## Future Work

The editor framework presented in this chapter is a great beginning, but there are plenty of projects ahead for the would-be tools programmer. Remember that a game editor's purpose is to enable rapid development and iteration. It should also be able to optimize the level files so that the game's data is always as small as possible. Here are a few projects you can work on that will push this simple editor toward that goal:

- Create mouse controls for moving and positioning actors in the game world. Follow the lead of many commercial editors and create a tool bar that can set the display panel to move objects instead of the camera.
- Allow object picking with the mouse—this requires some additional cooperation between the display panel, the `EditorHumanView`, and the C# application.
- Allow multiple visual displays with a wireframe mode to let game designers have a fine degree of accuracy when placing actors.
- Create level properties that can be added into the level file for adding background music or level chaining.
- Create new actor components.
- Add the physics system so objects will already be stable when the game begins running, and the editor can be sure not to place objects interpenetrating each other.
- Create the ability for actor components themselves to be instanced so that if actors only use the default values of the XML definitions in the *Assets\Actors*.xml* files, it doesn't take up more memory in the game or the save game file.

- Most importantly, allow the game to be running in the background while the editor is changing or viewing actor property values. Being able to launch the game and run from any position in a level file can really speed development.

That list should keep you, and me, plenty busy.

## Further Reading

- **http://msdn.microsoft.com/:** A lot of the reference material in MSDN is hair-rippingly frustrating, but they've got some good examples on how to set up C# projects.
- **http://blogs.msdn.com/csharpfaq/default.aspx/:** And while we're talking about C#, this FAQ is a helpful guide to some common questions.
- **http://www.swig.org/:** It was sometimes frustrating getting the code to run in a managed environment. As you can see, I eventually went with exporting C-style functions, but ideally you'd want to be able to export entire classes. SWIG will take your C++ classes and wrap them in a manner that is usable from C#. Not only that, but it will wrap your classes for other languages as well!
- **http://www.unity3d.com/:** This is currently one of my favorite game development environments, and it's no surprise the simple editor built in this chapter was inspired from Unity's design.

## Chapter 23

*by David "Rez" Graham*

# Debugging and Profiling Your Game

By the end of any game development project, the programmers and their teammates spend all of their time fixing bugs and tweaking performance. As important as debugging is (especially in game development), techniques in debugging are rarely taught. They tend to just come from experience or are traded around the programming team. Since I'm communicating to you through a book, we can't trade much, but since you bought the book, I think we can call it even.

Games are complicated pieces of software, and they push every piece of hardware in the system. Bugs are usually pilot error, but there are plenty of cases where bugs trace their roots to the compiler, operating system, drivers, and even specific pieces of hardware. Bugs also happen as a result of unexpected interactions in code written by different programmers; each module functions perfectly in a unit test, but failures are seen after they are integrated. Programmers spend lots of time hunting down issues in code they didn't write.

If you are going to have any chance at all of fixing broken code, whether you wrote it or not, you should have a few ideas and techniques in your toolbox. It's not uncommon to spend more time debugging than writing new code, especially toward the end of a project.

I need to warn you up front that you're going to see some assembly code and other heavy metal in this chapter. You simply can't perform the task of debugging without a basic working knowledge of assembly code and how the CPU really works. This is not a gentle chapter because we're not discussing a gentle problem. However, it's not brutally hard to learn assembly, and you have an excellent teacher—your debugger.

Most C++ debuggers, Visual Studio included, let you look at your source code at the same time as the assembly code. Take some time to learn how each C++ statement is broken down into its assembly instructions, and you'll end up being a much better programmer for it. Fear not—I'm with you in spirit, and I wasn't born with a full knowledge of assembly.

**Atari 2600 Games for Fun and Profit**

I first learned x86 assembly language in college on an old 8088 processor. We created little assembly language programs that would write to the serial port and control different circuits we built on breadboards. It was a huge amount of fun! In an attempt to teach myself another form of assembly (6502 in this case), I started working on a small game for the Atari 2600. Using assembly language for fun little projects like these is a great way to teach yourself this useful tool.

## The Art of Handling Failure

If you are looking for some wisdom about handling personal failure, stop reading and call a shrink. My focus here is to discuss application failure, the situation where some defensive code has found an anomaly and needs to handle it. There's a great conversation you can start with a group of programmers about how to handle errors or failures in games. The subject has more gray area than you'd think, and therefore it doesn't have a single best strategy. The debate starts when you ask if games should ignore failures or if they should stop execution immediately.

I'm talking about the release build, of course. The debug build should always report any oddity so that programmers can catch more bugs in the act. The release build strips asserts, so there's a good question about what should happen if the assert condition would have been satisfied in the release build. Does the game continue, or should it halt? As with many things, there's no right answer. Here's an example of two functions that handle the same error in two different ways:

```
void DetectFixAndContinue(int variable)
{
  if (variable < VARIABLE_MINIMUM)
  {
    variable = VARIABLE_MINIMUM;
    GCC_ERROR("Parameter is invalid");

  }
  // More code follows...
}
void DetectAndBail(int variable)
```

```
{
  if (variable < VARIABLE_MINIMUM)
  {
    throw ("Parameter is invalid");

  }
  // More code follows...
}
```

The first function resets the errant variable and calls the GCC_ERROR() macro to alert a programmer that something has gone wrong. The execution continues, since the variable now has a legal value. The second function throws an exception, clearly not allowing the execution to continue.

The debate most programmers have goes something like this: If you ever reach code where an assert condition in debug mode evaluates to false, then something has gone horribly wrong. Since you can't predict the nature of the failure, you must assume a worst-case scenario and exit the program as elegantly as possible. After all, the failure could be bad enough to corrupt data, save game files, or worse.

The other side of the argument takes a kinder, gentler approach. Failures can and will happen, even in the shipping product. If the program can fix a bogus parameter or ignore corrupt data and continue running, it is in the best interests of the player to do so. After all, he might get a chance to save his game and reload it later without a problem. Since we're working on computer games, we have the freedom to fudge things a little; there are no human lives at stake, and there is no property at risk due to a program failure. Both arguments are valid. I tend to favor the second argument because computer games are frequently pushed into testing before they are ready and released way before testing is completed. Bugs will remain in the software, and if the game can recover from them it should.

**Some Bugs Are Acceptable, Aren't They?**

Never forget that your game's purpose is entertainment. You aren't keeping an airplane from getting lost, and you aren't reporting someone's heartbeat. Remember that games can get away with lots of things that other software can't. If you are relatively sure that you can make a choice to allow the game to continue instead of crash, I suggest you do it.

Of course, this is true unless you work on a massive multiplayer title, and you are working on anything server side. Bugs here affect everyone on the server, and they can result in actual lost value for players and, in turn, the company. In that case, you get to code and test every bit as carefully as the programmer down the street working on banking software.

That's not to say that games can't find themselves in an unrecoverable situation. If a game runs out of memory, you're hosed. You have no choice but to bring up a dialog and say, "Sorry dude. You're hosed," and start throwing exceptions. If you're lucky, your exit code might be able to save the game into a temporary file, much like Microsoft Word sometimes does when it crashes. When the game reloads, it can read the temporary file and attempt to begin again just before everything went down the toilet. If this fails, you can exit again and lose the temporary file. All hope is lost. If it succeeds, your players will worship the ground you walk on. Trust me, as many times as Microsoft Word has recovered pieces of this book after my laptop's batteries ran out of electrons, I can appreciate a little data recovery.

**Use `@err,hr` in Your Watch Window**

If a Windows function fails, you must usually call `GetLastError()` to determine the exact nature of the error. Instead, simply put `@err,hr` in your debugger's watch window. This will show you a string-formatted version of the error.

## Debugging Basics

Before you learn some debugging tricks, you should know a little about how the debugger works and how to use it. Almost every computer has special assembly language instructions or CPU features that enable debugging. The Intel platform is no exception. A debugger works by stopping execution of a target program and associating memory locations and values with variable names. This association is possible through symbolic information that is generated by the compiler. One human readable form of this information is a MAP file. Here's an example of a MAP file generated by the linker in Visual Studio:

```
Sample
 Timestamp is 3c0020f3 (Sat Nov 24 16:36:35 2001)
 Preferred load address is 00400000

 Start         Length    Name                   Class
 0001:00000000 000ab634H .text                  CODE
 0001:000ab640 00008b5fH .text$AFX_AUX          CODE
 0001:000b41a0 0000eec3H .text$AFX_CMNCTL       CODE
 0002:00000000 000130caH .rdata                 DATA
 0002:000130d0 00006971H .rdata$r               DATA
 0002:000275d0 00000000H .edata                 DATA
 0003:00000000 00000104H .CRT$XCA               DATA
 0003:00000104 00000109H .CRT$XCC               DATA
 0003:00001120 00026e6aH .data                  DATA
 0003:00027f90 00011390H .bss                   DATA
```

```
0004:00000000 00000168H .idata$2                DATA
0004:00000168 00000014H .idata$3                DATA
0005:00000000 00000370H .rsrc$01                DATA

 Address          Publics by Value              Rva+Base     Lib:Object

0001:00000b80     ??0GameApp@@QAE@XZ            00401b80 f   GameApp.obj
0001:00000ca0     ??_EGameApp@@UAEPAXI@Z        00401ca0 f i GameApp.obj
0001:00000ca0     ??_GGameApp@@UAEPAXI@Z        00401ca0 f i GameApp.obj
0001:00000d10     ??1GameApp@@UAE@XZ            00401d10 f   GameApp.obj
0001:00000e20     ?OnClose@GameApp@@UAEXXZ      00401e20 f   GameApp.obj
0001:00000ec0     ?OnRun@GameApp@@UAE_NXZ       00401ec0 f   GameApp.obj
0001:00001a10     ??0CFileStatus@@QAE@XZ        00402a10 f i GameApp.obj
0001:00001d00     ?OnIdle@GameApp@@UAEHJ@Z      00402d00 f   GameApp.obj
0001:00001e30     ?Update@GameApp@@UAEXK@Z      00402e30 f   GameApp.obj
```

The file maps the entire contents of the process as it is loaded into memory. The first section describes global data. The second section, which is much more interesting and useful, describes the memory addresses of methods and functions in your game.

Notice first that the symbol names are "munged." These are the actual names of the methods after the C++ symbol manager incorporates the class names and variable types into the names. The number that appears right after the name is the actual memory address of the entry point of the code. For example, the last function in the MAP file is `?Update@GameApp@@UAEXK@Z` and is loaded into memory address 0 × 00402e30. You can use that information to track down crashes.

Have you ever seen a crash that reports the register contents? Usually you'll see the entire set of registers: EAX, EBX, and so on. You'll also see EIP, the extended instruction pointer. You may have thought that this dialog box was nothing more than an annoyance—a slap in the face that your program is flawed. Used with the MAP file, you can at least find the name of the function that caused the crash. Here's how to do it:

1. Assume the crash dialog reported an EIP of 0x00402d20.
2. Looking at the MAP file above, you'll see that `GameApp::OnIdle` has an entry point of 0 × 00402d00 and `GameApp::Update` has an entry point of 0 × 00402e30.
3. The crash thus happened somewhere inside `GameApp::OnIdle`, since it is located in between those two entry points.

A debugger uses a much more complete symbol table. For example, Visual Studio stores these symbols in a PDB file, or program database file. That's one of the reasons it's so huge—because it stores symbolic information of every identifier in your program. The debugger can use this information to figure out how to display the contents of local and global variables and figure out what source code to display as you step through the code. This doesn't explain how the debugger stops the debugged application cold in its tracks, however. That trick requires a little help from the CPU and a special interrupt instruction. If you use Visual Studio and you are running on an Intel processor, you can try this little program:

```
void main()
{
  __asm int 3
}
```

You may have never seen a line of code that looks like this. The `__asm` keyword tells the compiler that the rest of the line should be treated as an assembly language instruction. Alternatively, you can follow the `__asm` keyword with curly braces. Everything inside these curly braces is parsed as assembly. The `int 3` assembly statement evokes the breakpoint interrupt. Without dragging you through all the gory details of interrupt tables, it suffices to say that a program with sufficient privileges can "trap" interrupts so that when they are evoked, a special function is called. This is almost exactly like registering a callback function, but it happens at a hardware level. DOS-based games used to grab interrupts all the time to redirect functions such as the mouse or display system to their own evil ends. Debuggers trap the breakpoint interrupt, and whenever you set a breakpoint, the debugger overwrites the opcodes, or the machine level instructions, at the breakpoint location with those that correspond to `int 3`. When the breakpoint is hit, control is passed to the debugger, and it puts the original instructions back. If you press the "Step into" or "Step over" command, the debugger finds the right locations for a new breakpoint and simply puts it there without you ever being the wiser.

**Hard-Coded Breakpoints Are Cool**

I've found it useful to add hard-coded breakpoints, like the one in the earlier code example, to functions in the game. It can be convenient to set one to make sure that if control ever passes through that section of code, the debugger will always trap it. Be careful, though! If a debugger is not present, the program may crash. There's also a Windows function called `SetDebugBreak()` that does the same thing but is processor independent.

So now you have the most basic understanding of how a debugger does its work. It has a mechanism to stop a running program in its tracks, and it uses a compiler and linker-generated data file to present symbolic information to programmers.

## Using the Debugger

When you debug your code, you usually set a few breakpoints and watch the contents of variables. You have a pretty good idea of what should happen, and you'll find bugs when you figure out why the effect of your logic isn't what you planned. This assumes a few things. First, you know where to set the breakpoints, and second, you can interpret the effect the logic has on the state of your game. These two things are by no means trivial in all cases. This problem is made difficult by the size and complexity of the logic.

### Where Is That Bug Anyway?

A screwed-up sound effect may have nothing at all to do with the sound system. It could be a problem with the code that loads the sound from the game data files, or it could be random memory corruption that changed the sound effect after it was loaded. The problem might also be a bad sound driver, or it might even be a bogus sound effect file from the original recording. Knowing where to look first has more to do with gut feeling than anything else, but good debugger skills can certainly speed up the process of traversing the fault tree—a catch phrase NASA uses to describe all possible permutations of a possible systems failure.

Debuggers like the one in Visual Studio can present an amazing amount of information, as shown in Figure 23.1.

The debugger provides some important windows beyond the normal source code window you will use all of the time.

- **Call stack:** From bottom to top, this window shows the functions and parameters that were used to call them. The function at the top of the list is the one you are currently running. It's extremely useful to double-click on any row of the call stack window; the location of the function call will be reflected in the source code window. This helps you understand how control passes from the caller to the called.
- **Watch/Locals/etc:** These windows let you examine the contents of variables. Visual Studio has some convenient debug windows like "Locals" and "Autos" that keep track of specific variables so you don't have to type them in yourself.
- **Breakpoints:** This window shows the list of breakpoints. Sometimes you want to enable/disable every breakpoint in your game at once or perform other bits of homework.
- **Threads:** Most games run multiple threads to manage the sound system, resource caching, or perhaps the AI. If the debugger hits a breakpoint or is

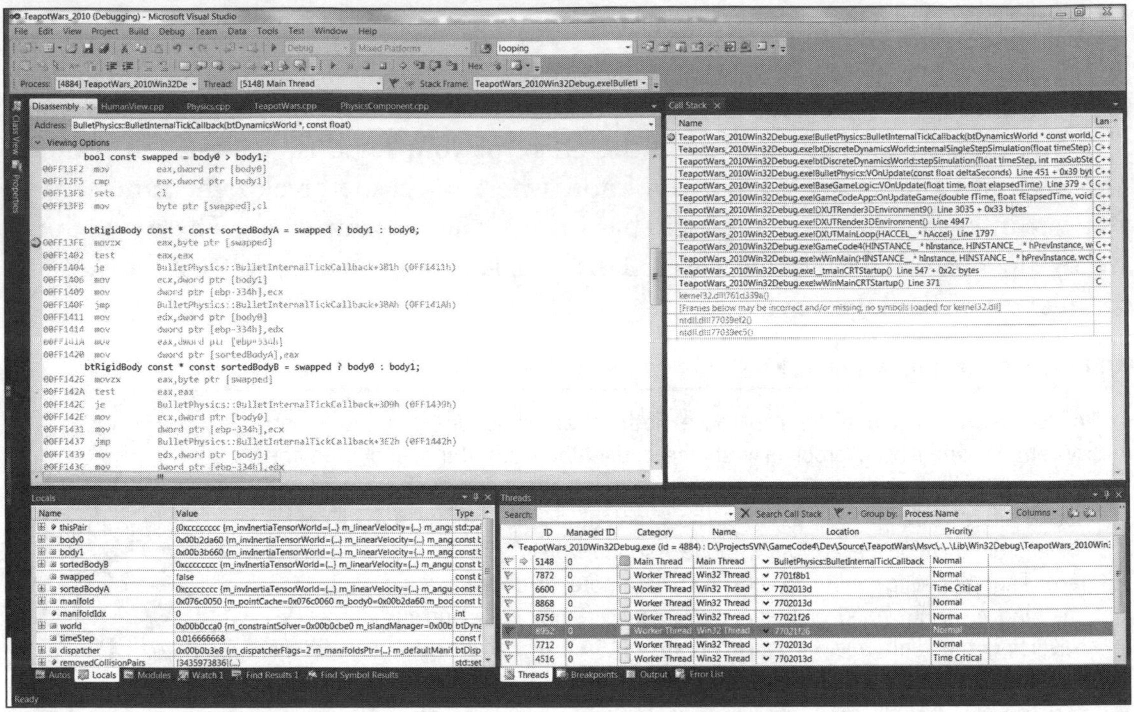


**Figure 23.1**
Using the Visual Studio debugger.

stopped, this window will show you what thread is running. It's the only way to distinguish between different threads of execution, and it is critical to debugging multithreaded applications. If you double-click on any line in this window, the source window will change to show the current execution position of that thread.

- **Disassembly:** This is a window that shows the assembly code for the current function. Sometimes you need to break a C++ statement down into its components to debug it or perhaps skip over a portion of the statement. I'll have more to say about these techniques later.

Beyond the windows, there are some actions that you'll need to know how to perform:

- **Set/clear breakpoints:** A basic debugging skill.
- **Stepping the instruction pointer:** These are usually controlled by hot keys because they are so frequently used. Debuggers will let you execute code one line at a time and either trace into functions or skip over them (F11 and F10,

respectively). There's also a really useful command that will let you step out of a current function (Shift-F11) without having to watch each line execute.

- **Setting the instruction pointer:** This takes a little care to use properly, since you can mess up the stack. I like to use it to skip over function calls or skip back to a previous line of code so that I can watch it execute again.

As we run through some debugging techniques I'll refer to these windows and actions. If you don't know how to do them in your debugger, now is a good time to read the docs and figure it out.

## Installing Windows Symbol Files

If you've ever had a program crash deep in some Windows API call, your call stack might look like this:

```
ntdll.dll!77f60b6f()
ntdll.dll!77fb4dbd()
ntdll.dll!77f79b78()
ntdll.dll!77fb4dbd()
```

Useless, right? Yes, that call stack is useless, but only because you didn't install the Windows symbol files. Even though I write letters to Bill Gates every day, Microsoft still hasn't published the source code for pretty much anything they ever wrote. Yet they have, in their infinite wisdom, graciously supplied the next best thing.

You can install the debug symbols for your operating system, and that indecipherable call stack will turn into something you and I can read. Here's the same debug stack after the debug symbols have been installed:

```
ntdll.dll!_RtlDispatchException@8() + 0x6
ntdll.dll!_KiUserExceptionDispatcher@8() + 0xe
00031328()
ntdll.dll!ExecuteHandler@20() + 0x24
ntdll.dll!_KiUserExceptionDispatcher@8() + 0xe
000316f4()
ntdll.dll!ExecuteHandler@20() + 0x24
ntdll.dll!_KiUserExceptionDispatcher@8() + 0xe
00031ac0()
```

You might not know exactly what that call stack represents, but now you have a function name to help you, so you can search the Web or MSDN for help, whereas before you installed the debug symbols, you had nothing but a number.

There are a few ways to install debug symbols. You can install them from the Visual Studio CD-ROM, or you can download them from MSDN. Search for "System Debug Symbols," and you're sure to find them. Once you have the right symbols installed for your OS, the debugger will happily report the loaded symbols when you begin a debug session:

```
'TeapotWars.exe': Loaded 'C:\WINDOWS\system32\ntdll.dll', Symbols loaded.
'TeapotWars.exe': Loaded 'C:\WINDOWS\system32\kernel32.dll', Symbols loaded.
'TeapotWars.exe': Loaded 'C:\WINDOWS\system32\gdi32.dll', Symbols loaded.
```

Etc., etc.

The problem with this solution is that the symbols you install will eventually become stale since they won't reflect any changes in your operating system as you update it with service packs. You can find out why symbols aren't loading for any EXE or DLL with the help of `DUMPBIN.EXE`, a utility included with Visual Studio. Use the `/PDBPATH:VERBOSE` switch as shown here:

```
Microsoft (R) COFF/PE Dumper Version 7.00.9466
Copyright (C) Microsoft Corporation. All rights reserved.

Dump of file c:\windows\system32\user32.dll

File Type: DLL
 PDB file 'c:\windows\system32\user32.pdb' checked. (File not found)
 PDB file 'user32.pdb' checked. (File not found)
 PDB file 'C:\WINDOWS\symbols\dll\user32.pdb' checked. (PDB signature mismatch)
 PDB file 'C:\WINDOWS\dll\user32.pdb' checked. (File not found)
 PDB file 'C:\WINDOWS\user32.pdb' checked. (File not found)

 Summary
     2000 .data
     4000 .reloc
    2B000 .rsrc
    54000 .text
```

Do you see the "PDB signature mismatch" line about halfway down this output? That's what happens when the *user32.pdb* file is out of sync with the *user32.dll* image on your computer. It turns out this is easy to fix, mainly because Microsoft engineers had this problem multiplied by about 100,000. They have thousands of applications out there with sometimes hundreds of different builds. How could they ever hope to get the debug symbols straight for all these things? They came up with a neat solution called the *Microsoft Symbol Server*. It turns out you can use this server, too. Here's how to do it.

First, install the Microsoft Debugging Tools, which can be found at www.microsoft.com/ddk/debugging. Use the SYMCHK utility to pull the latest symbol information from Microsoft that matches a single EXE or DLL, or all of the ones in your Windows directory. Don't grab them all, though, if you can help it because you'll be checking and downloading hundreds of files. Here's how to grab an individual file:

```
C:\Program Files\Debugging Tools for Windows>symchk
c:\windows\system32\user32.dll /s
SRV*c:\windows\symbols*http://msdl.microsoft.com/download/symbols

SYMCHK: FAILED files = 0
SYMCHK: PASSED + IGNORED files = 1
```

This crazy utility doesn't actually put the new *USER32.DLL* where you asked. On my system, it actually stuck it in *C:\WINDOWS\Symbols\user32.pdb\3DB6D4ED1*, which Visual Studio will never find. The reason it does this is to keep all the *USER32.PDB* files from different operating systems or different service packs apart. If you installed the Windows symbols from MSDN into the default location, you'll want to copy it back into *C:\Windows\Symbols\dll*, where Visual Studio will find it.

You can also set up your own symbol server and even include symbols for your own applications. To find out how to do this, go up to http://msdn.microsoft.com and search for "Microsoft Symbol Server."

## Debugging Full-Screen Games

Back when Mike wrote the first edition of this book, multiple monitor setups were rare. Now I walk around my workplace, and that's all I see. If you can afford it, a multiple monitor setup is the easiest way to debug full-screen applications, and it is the only way to develop console applications.

As much work as the Microsoft DirectX team has put into its efforts to help you debug full-screen games, this still doesn't work very well if you have a single monitor setup. This has nothing to do with the folks at DirectX; it has more to do with Visual Studio not overriding exclusive mode of the display. One manifestation of the problem occurs when your game hits a breakpoint while it's in full-screen mode. The game stops cold, but the computer doesn't switch focus to the debugger. Basically, the only thing you can do at this point is to tap the F5 button to resume execution of the game.

If your game runs exclusively in full-screen mode, your only solution is a multimonitor setup. Every programmer should have two monitors: one for displaying the game screen and the other for displaying the debugger. DirectX will use the primary display for full-screen mode by default. It is possible to write code that enumerates the display devices so your game can choose the best display. This is a good idea because you can't count on players to set up their display properties in the way that benefits your game. If your game runs in windowed mode as well as full-screen mode, you have a few more options, even in a single monitor setup.

**Deal with DirectX Lost Devices and Resources**

Most of the bugs in full-screen mode happen as a result of switching from full-screen to windowed mode or vice versa. This happens because DirectX features are lost and need to be restored after the switch, something that is easily forgotten by coders. Another problem that happens as a result of the switch is that surfaces can have the wrong pixel format. There's no guarantee that the full-screen pixel depth and format are identical to that of windowed mode. When the switch happens, lost or invalid surfaces refuse to draw and return errors. Your program might handle these errors by exiting or attempting to restore all the surfaces again. Of course, since the surface in question won't get restored in the first place, your game might get caught in a weird obsessive and repetitive attempt to fix something that can't be fixed.

It would be nice if you could simulate this problem entirely in windowed mode. To a large extent, you can. If you've followed the advice of the DirectX SDK, you always should check your display surfaces to see if they have been lost before you perform any action on them. It turns out that if you change your display settings while your game is running in windowed mode, you will essentially simulate the event of switching between windowed mode and full-screen mode. There are a few windows messages your game should handle to make this a little easier. You can see how to do this in the *GameCode4* source code. Just look for `WM_` and you'll see how all these messages are handled. You'll need to handle `WM_DISPLAYCHANGE`, the message that is sent when the display changes, and `WM_ACTIVATE`, the message that signifies gain and loss of focus.

**Got Full-Screen Display Bugs?**

About 90 percent of all full-screen display bugs can be found and solved with a single monitor setup using windowed mode. Just start your game, change the bit depth, and see what happens. The other 10 percent can only be solved with a multimonitor setup or via remote debugging. It's much easier to debug these problems on a multimonitor rig, so make sure that at least one programmer has two monitors.

## Remote Debugging

One solution for debugging full-screen-only games is remote debugging. The game runs on one computer and communicates to your development box via your network. One interesting thing about this setup is that it is as close to a pristine runtime environment as you can get. (Another way of saying it's very close to the environment people have when actually playing the game.) I don't know about you, but people like my Mom don't have a copy of Visual Studio lying around. The presence of a debugger can subtly change the runtime environment, something that can make the hardest, nastiest bugs very difficult to find.

Remote debugging is a pain, not because it's hard to set up but because you have to make sure that the most recent version of your game executable is easily available for the remote machine. Most debuggers have a mechanism for remote debugging, and Visual Studio is no exception.

**To Copy or to Share, That Is the Question**

Any wired or even a wireless network can allow you to share a directory on your development machine and have the remote machine read your game's executable and data files right where you develop. If your network is really slow or your game image is huge, it's going to be faster to copy the entire image of your game over to the test machine and run it from there. The only problem with this solution is that you have to constantly copy files from your development box over to the test machine, and it's easy to get confused regarding which files have been copied where. On a fast network, you can also eliminate file copying by sharing your development directory so the remote machine can directly access the most recent build.

On the remote system, you will run a little utility that serves as a communications conduit for your debugger. This utility for Visual Studio is called *MSVSMON.EXE*. Run a search for this file where you installed Visual Studio and copy the contents of the entire directory to a shared folder on your primary development machine. The utility runs on the remote machine, and a convenient way to get it there is to place it in a shared spot on your development machine. *MSVSMON.EXE* requires some of the DLLs in that directory, and it's small enough to just copy the whole thing to the remote machine.

Since the methods for running the remote debugger change with updates to Visual Studio, the best way to learn how to do this is to go up to MSDN and search for "Set Up Remote Debugging." There are a few steps you need to follow. First, you share or copy your application to the remote machine. Next, run *MSVSMON.EXE* on the remote machine to start the remote debugging monitor (see Figure 23.2). Back on your development machine, set your debugging properties to launch a remote debugger and the remote debugging properties to find your remote machine. Make sure that you have the right permissions or an administrator account on the remote machine, or you won't be able to connect. You'll also need to open ports in your firewall.

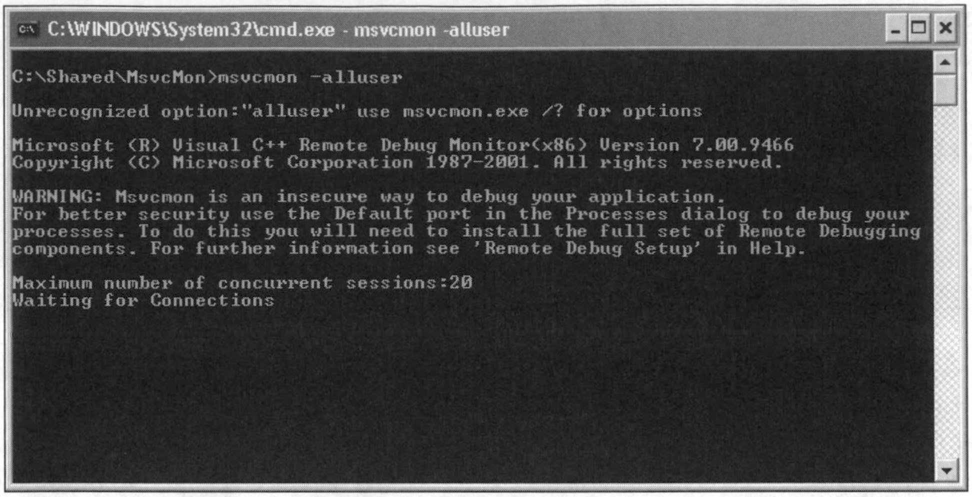


**Figure 23.2**
Running *MSVSMON* with the `/noauth` switch.

Once you get the connection madness out of the way, the remote machine is ready to start your game. Start the debugging session on your development machine (F5 in Visual Studio), and you'll see your game initialize on the remote machine. When you find a bug and rebuild your application, make sure that the remote machine has access to the most recent bits.

## Debugging Minidumps

UNIX programmers have had a special advantage over Windows programmers since the beginning of time because when a UNIX program crashes, the operating system copies the entire memory image of the crashed program to disk. This is called a *core dump*.

Needless to say, the core dump is usually quite large. UNIX debuggers can read the core dump and allow a programmer to look at the state of the process at the moment the crash occurred. Assuming the symbol files for the executable in question are available, they can see the entire call stack and even find the contents of local variables. This doesn't always expose the bug entirely, as some crashes can happen as a result of a bug's misbehavior in a completely separate part of the program, but this information is much better than a tester just telling you the game crashed.

Windows dump files have been debuggable by a little-known Windows debugger called WinDBG since the Windows NT days. These dump files were just as huge as the UNIX core dumps. It didn't matter very much, since most Windows developers didn't even know that WinDBG even existed—they always used the debugger in Visual Studio.

Since Windows XP, applications don't just crash and burn. A little dialog box appears, asking you if you want to send the crash information to Microsoft. One button click and a few short seconds later, and the dialog thanks you for your cooperation. What in the heck is going on here? Windows is sending a minidump of the crashed application to Microsoft. A minidump, as the name implies, is a tiny version of the UNIX-style core dump. You can generate one yourself by going into the Debug menu under Visual Studio and selecting Save Dump As when your application is sitting at a breakpoint. This tiny file stores enough information to give you some clues about the crash.

For Windows geeks, it's time to let you in on a little secret: Visual Studio can debug these very same minidump files. Here's how to reload it, because it isn't exactly obvious. Double-click on the minidump file in Windows Explorer, and it will launch a surprisingly blank-looking Visual Studio. The trick is to execute the minidump by pressing F5. Visual Studio will prompt you to save a solution file. Go ahead and save it alongside the minidump. Once you save, the last state of your debugged process will appear before your very eyes.

**Keep Your Source Tree and PDBs Forever**

The minidump is really convenient, but there are a few gotchas to using minidumps. First, you must ensure that the minidump file matches exactly with the source code and symbol tables that were used to build the executable that crashed. This means that for any version of the executable that goes into your test department, you must save a complete build tree with source code and PDB files or the minidump will be useless. Second, the minidump's SLN file might need a hint about where to find the symbols. If the source window shows up with nothing but an assembler, it's likely that your source code tree can't be located. Open the properties page, and you'll see only one item under the Configuration tree: Debugging. Set the Symbol Path to the directory containing your PDB files, and you'll see the source tree.

The only thing left out of this discussion is how to save your game-generated minidump files when bad goes to worse. You'll need to call the `MiniDumpWriteDump()` in your general exception handler, which is one of the functions exported from *DBGHELP.DLL*. This call will generate a DMP file. You can add more information to the DMP file if you define a callback function that can insert more information into the dump file, such as some specific game state information that might give a programmer a leg up on investigating the crash.

**Minidumps Rock**

On *The Sims Medieval*, we ran multiple soak tests every night. This is where one or more people ran the game and just let it simulate all night. If the game crashed or threw an exception, a minidump file was automatically generated. These files were all posted to a particular shared drive (along with the PDB files) so that the tech director and lead engineer could sift through them. We found and fixed a huge number of very difficult bugs this way.

Another trick we used was that whenever the build machine created a new build, it would save all the PDB files with it. If QA ever hit a nasty crash, they could give us the dump file and tell us the build number. This allowed us to pull the appropriate build (complete with PDBs) and load up the dump to see exactly where they crashed.

There's a simple and extremely useful class in the GameCode4 codebase called `MiniDumper` that you can use to generate minidumps. You can find it in the *Dev\Source\GCC4\Debugging* folder.

## Graphics and Shader Debugging

DirectX, OpenGL, and consoles are all moving away from the fixed-function pipeline and into the world of shaders. Shaders can be extremely complex and are a complete nightmare to debug if you don't have the proper tools. Fortunately, you have several to choose from, depending on your particular hardware setup. Personally, I'm partial to nVidia's PerfHUD, and if you have an nVidia card, I suggest checking it out. If you use DirectX, you can take a look at PIX, which comes with the DirectX SDK.

Since this book uses DirectX, let's take a look at PIX. You can find it in the DirectX SDK folder. When you start up the program, you see an uninteresting blank screen. Go to File → New Experiment, and you will be presented with a number of options. One of the more useful options is "A single-frame capture of Direct3D whenever F12 is pressed." When you select this option and run your game through PIX, every time you press F12, the data for that rendering call will be saved. Once you exit the program, PIX will show you all the frames you captured, and you can walk through the entire graphics pipeline call-by-call and watch the scene being built before your eyes. You can examine the various D3D objects, inspect the shaders, and even see the shader assembly code that your HLSL code produced.

This is only the beginning. In the Render tab, you can right-click anywhere and select "Debug this pixel" to watch exactly how that single pixel color was built. You can see every vertex shader, pixel shader, and Direct3D call that had any effect on that pixel and see them applied in order. You can even debug the HLSL shader code directly!

Just click the "Debug Pixel (x, y)" link, and you'll be inside the shader debugger. You can single-step through the shader and watch exactly how it executed.

PIX is an extremely powerful tool. I strongly suggest you check out a few tutorials and get acquainted with it if you plan to do any graphics programming at all.

## Debugging Techniques

I think I could write an entire book about debugging. Certainly many people have, and for good reason. You can't be a good programmer unless you have at least passable debugging skills. Imagine for a moment that you are a programmer who never writes buggy code. Hey, stop laughing. I also want you to close your eyes and imagine that you have absolutely no skill at debugging. Why would you? Your code is always perfect! But the moment you are assigned to a team of programmers, your days are numbered. If you can't solve logic problems caused by another programmer's code, you are useless to a team.

If you have good debugging skills, you'll have much more fun programming. I've always looked at really tough bugs as a puzzle. Computers are deterministic, and they execute instructions without interpretation. That truth paves your way to solve every bug if you devote enough patience and skill to the problem.

### Debugging Is an Experiment

When you begin a bug hunt, one implication is that you know how to recognize a properly running program. For any piece of code, you should be able to predict its behavior just by carefully reading each line. Debugging a program requires that you figure out why the behavior of the program is different than what you expect. Certainly the computer's CPU isn't surprised. It executes exactly what you instructed. This delta is the cornerstone of debugging. As each instruction executes, the programmer tests the new state of the process against the predicted state by looking at memory and the contents of variables. The moment the prediction is different than the observed, the programmer has found the bug.

Clearly, you have to be able to predict the behavior of the system given certain stimuli, such as user input or a set of game data files. You should be able to repeat the steps to watch the behavior on your machine or anyone else's machine. When the bug manifests itself as a divergence from nominal operation, you should be able to use what you observed to locate the problem or at least narrow the source of the problem. Repeat these steps enough times, and you'll find the bug. What I've just described is the method any scientist uses to perform experiments.

It might seem odd to perform experiments on software, certainly odd when you wrote the software in question. Scientists perform experiments on complicated phenomena that they don't understand in the hopes that they will achieve knowledge. Why then must programmers perform experiments on systems that spawned from their own minds? The problem is that even the simplest, most deterministic systems can behave unpredictably given particular initial states. If you've never read Stephen Wolfram's book, *A New Kind of Science*, take a few months off and try to get through it. This book makes some surprising observations about complex behavior of simple systems. I'll warn you that once you read it, you may begin to wonder about the determinism of any system, no matter how simple!

**Hypothesis, Experimentation, and Analysis**

Debugging is a serious scientific endeavor. If you approach each debugging task as an experiment, just like you were taught in high school, you'll find that debugging is more fun and less frustrating.

Complex and unpredicted behavior in computer programs requires setting up good debugging experiments. If you fell asleep during the lecture in high school on the scientific method, now's a good time to refresh your memory. The examples listed in Table 23.1 show you how to run a successful experiment, but there's a lot more to good debugging than blindly running through the experimental method.

The first step seems easy: Observe the behavior of the system. Unfortunately, this is not so easy. The most experienced software testers I know do their very best to accurately observe the behavior of a game as it breaks. They record what keys they pressed, what options they turned off, and as best they can exactly what they did. In many cases, they leave out something innocuous. One of the first things I do when I don't observe the same problem a tester observed is go down to the test lab and watch them reproduce the bug myself. Sometimes, I'll notice a little wiggle of the mouse or the fact that they're running in full-screen mode and have a "Eureka" moment.

**Bugs in Games Are Extremely Tricky to Find**

Unlike most software systems, games rely not only on random numbers but also change vast amounts of data extremely quickly in seemingly unpredictable ways. The difficulty in finding game bugs lies in the simple fact that games run so much code so quickly that it's easy for a bug to appear to come from any of the many subsystems that manipulate the game state.

**Table 23.1 How to Run a Successful Debugging Experiment**

| Scientific Method as It Applies to Software Systems | Example #1 | Example #2 |
|---|---|---|
| Step 1: Observe the behavior of a computer game. | Observation: A call to `OpenFile()` always fails. | Observation: The game crashes on the low-end machine when it tries to initialize. |
| Step 2: Attempt to explain the behavior that is consistent with your observations and your knowledge of the system. | Hypothesis: The input parameters to `OpenFile()` are incorrect, specifically the filename. | Hypothesis: The game is crashing because it is running out of video memory. |
| Step 3: Use your explanation to make predictions. | Predictions: If the proper filename is used, `OpenFile()` will execute successfully. | Predictions: If the amount of video memory were increased, the game would initialize properly. The game will crash when the original amount of video memory is restored. |
| Step 4: Test your predictions by performing experiments or making additional observations. Modify the hypothesis and predictions based on the results. | Experiment: Send the fully qualified path name of the file and try `OpenFile()` again. | Experiment: Switch the current video card with others that have more memory. |
| Step 5: Repeat steps three and four until there is no discrepancy between your explanations and the observations. | Results: `OpenFile()` executed successfully with a fully qualified path name. | Results: The game properly initializes with a better video card installed. |
| Step 6: Explain the results. | Explanation: The current working directory is different than the location of the file in question. The path name must be fully qualified. | Explanation: Video memory requirements have grown beyond expectations. |

The second step, attempt to explain the behavior, can be pretty hard if you don't know the software like the back of your hand. It's probably safe to say that you should know the software, the operating system, the CPU, video hardware, and audio hardware pretty well, too. Sound tough? It is. It also helps to have a few years of game programming under your belt so that you've been exposed to the wacky behavior of broken games. This is probably one of the most frustrating aspects of programming in general: A lack of understanding and experience can leave you shaking your head in dismay when you see your game blow up in your face. Everybody gets through it, though, usually with the help of, dare I say, more experienced programmers.

Steps three through five represent the classic experimental phase of debugging. Your explanation will usually inspire some sort of test, input modification, or code change that should have predictable results. There's an important trick to this rinse and repeat cycle: Take detailed notes of everything you do. Inevitably, your notes will come in handy as you realize that you're chasing a dead-end hypothesis. Your notes should send you back to the point where your predictions were accurate. This will put you back on track.

**Change One Thing at a Time—and Don't Rewrite Anything—Yet**

Another critical aspect to the experiment-driven debugging process is that you should try to limit your changes to one small thing at a time. If you change too much during one experiment cycle, you won't be able to point to the exact change that fixed the problem. Change for change's sake is a horrible motivation to modify buggy code. Resist that temptation. Sometimes there is a desire to rip a subsystem out altogether and replace it without truly understanding the nature of the problem. This impulse is especially strong when the subsystem in question was written by a programmer who has less than, shall we say, stellar design and coding skills. The effect of this midnight remodeling is usually negative because it isn't guaranteed to fix the bug, and you'll demoralize your teammate at the same time.

Assuming that you follow Table 23.1, you'll eventually arrive at the source of the problem. If you're lucky, the bug can be fixed with a simple tweak of the code. Perhaps a loop exited too soon or a special case wasn't handled properly. You make your mod, rebuild the game, and perform your experiments one last time. Congratulations, your bug is fixed. Not every programmer is so lucky, and certainly I haven't been. Some bugs, once exposed in their full glory, tell you things about your game that you don't want to hear. I've seen bugs that told us we had to completely redesign the graphics system we were using. Other bugs enjoy conveying the message that some version of Windows can't be supported without sweeping modifications. Others make you wonder how the game ever worked in the first place.

If this ever happens to you, and I'm sure it will, I feel your pain. Grab some caffeine and your sleeping bag; it's going to be a long week.

## Reproducing the Bug

A prerequisite of observing the behavior of a broken game is reproducing the bug. I've seen bug reports that say things like, "I was doing so-and-so, and the game crashed. I couldn't get it to happen again." In light of an overwhelming number of reports of this kind, you might be able to figure out what's going on. Alone, these reports are nearly useless. *You cannot fix what you cannot observe.* After all, if you can't observe the broken system with certainty, how can you be sure you fixed the problem? You can't.

Most bugs can be reproduced easily by following a specific set of steps, usually observed and recorded by a tester. It's important that each step, however minor, is recorded from the moment the game is initialized. Anything missing might be important. Also, the state of the machine, including installed hardware and software, might be crucial to reproducing the bug's behavior.

**Reduce Complexity to Increase Predictability**

Bugs are sometimes tough to nail down. They can be intermittent or disappear altogether as you attempt to create a specific series of steps that will always result in a manifestation of the problem. This can be explained in two ways: Either an important step or initial state has been left out, or the bug cannot be reproduced because the system being tested is too complex to be deterministic. Even if the bug can be reproduced exactly, it might be difficult to create an explanation of the problem. In both of these cases, you must find a way to reduce the complexity of the system; only then can the problem domain become small enough to understand.

## Eliminating Complexity

A bug can only manifest itself if the code that contains it is executed. Eliminate the buggy code, and the bug will disappear. By the process of elimination, you can narrow your search over a series of steps to the exact line of code that is causing the problem. You can disable subsystems in your game, one by one. One of the first things to try is to disable the entire main loop and have your game initialize and exit without doing anything else. This is a good trick if the bug you're hunting is a memory leak. If the bug goes away, you can be sure that it only exists in the main loop somewhere.

You should be able to creatively disable every major system at a time, such as animation, AI, and sound. Once these systems are stubbed out, your game will probably act pretty strangely, and you don't want this strangeness to be interpreted as the bug you are looking for. You should have a pretty complete understanding of your game before you embark on excising large pieces of it from execution.

If your game has an options menu for sound, animation, and other subsystems, you can use these as debugging tools without having to resort to changing code. Turn everything off via your game options and try to reproduce the bug. Whether the bug continues to exist or disappears, the information you'll gain from the experiment is always valuable. As always, keep good records of what you try and try to change only one option at a time.

You can take this tactic to extremes and perform a binary search of sorts to locate a bug. Stub out half of your subsystems and see if the bug manifests itself. If it does, stub out half of what remains and repeat the experiment. Even in a large code base, you'll quickly locate the bug.

If the bug eludes this process, it might depend on the memory map of your application. Change the memory contents of your game, and the bug will change, too. Because this might be true, it's a good idea to stub out subsystems via a simple Boolean value, but leave their code and global data in place as much as possible. This is another example of making small changes rather than large ones.

## Setting the Next Statement

Most debuggers give you the power to set the next statement to be executed, which is equivalent to setting the instruction pointer directly. This can be useful if you know what you are doing, but it can be a source of mayhem when applied indiscriminately. You might want to do this for a few reasons. You may want to skip some statements or rerun a section of code again with different parameters as a part of a debugging experiment. You might also be debugging through some assembler, and you want to avoid calling into other pieces of code.

You can set the next statement in Visual Studio by right-clicking on the target statement and selecting Set Next Statement from the pop-up menu. In other debuggers, you can bring up a register window and set the EIP register, also known as the *instruction pointer,* to the address of the target statement, which you can usually find by showing the disassembly window. You must be mindful of the code that you are skipping and the current state of your process. When you set the instruction pointer, it is equivalent to executing an assembly level JMP statement, which simply moves the execution path to a different statement.

In C++, objects can be declared inside local scopes such as `for` loops. In normal execution, these objects are destroyed when execution passes out of that scope. The C++ compiler inserts the appropriate code to do this, and you can't see it unless you look at a disassembly window. What do you suppose happens to C++ objects that go out of scope if you skip important lines of code? Let's look at an example:

```
class MyClass
{
public:
  int num;
  char* str;

  MyClass(int const n)
  {
    num = n;
    str = new char[128];
    sprintf(str, "%d ", n);

  }

  ~MyClass() { delete str; }
};

void SetTheIP()
{
  char buffer[2048];
  buffer[0] = 0;

  for (int a = 0; a < 128; ++a)
  {
    MyClass m(a);
    strcat(buffer, m.str);  // START HERE...

  }
}                           // JUMP TO HERE...
```

Normally, the `MyClass` object is created and destroyed once for each run of the `for` loop. If you jump out of the loop using Set Next Statement, the destructor for `MyClass` never runs, leaking memory. The same thing would happen if you jumped backward to the line that initializes the buffer variable. The `MyClass` object in scope won't be destroyed properly.

Luckily, you don't have to worry about the stack pointer as long as you do all your jumping around within one function. Local scopes are creations of the compiler; they don't actually have stack frames. That's a good thing, because setting the next statement to a completely different function is sure to cause havoc with the stack. If you want to skip the rest of the current function and keep it from executing, just right-click on the last closing brace of the function and set the next statement to that point. The stack frame will be kept intact.

## Assembly Level Debugging

Inevitably, you'll get to debug through some assembly code. You won't have source code or even symbols for every component of your application, so you should understand a little about the assembly window. Here's the assembly for the `SetTheIP()` function we just talked about. Let's look at the debug version of this code:

```
void SetTheIP()
{
00411A10 55                          push     ebp
00411A11 8B EC                       mov      ebp,esp
00411A13 81 EC E8 08 00 00           sub      esp,8E8h
00411A19 53                          push     ebx
00411A1A 56                          push     esi
00411A1B 57                          push     edi
00411A1C 8D BD 18 F7 FF FF           lea      edi,[ebp-8E8h]
00411A22 B9 3A 02 00 00              mov      ecx,23Ah
00411A27 B8 CC CC CC CC              mov      eax,0CCCCCCCCh
00411A2C F3 AB                       rep stos dword ptr [edi]
  char buffer[2048];
  buffer[0] = 0;
00411A2E C6 85 F8 F7 FF FF 00        mov      byte ptr [buffer],0

  for (int a=0; a<128; ++a)
00411A35 C7 85 EC F7 FF FF 00 00 00 00 mov        dword ptr [a],0
00411A3F EB 0F                       jmp      SetTheIP+40h (411A50h)
00411A41 8B 85 EC F7 FF FF           mov      eax,dword ptr [a]
00411A47 83 C0 01                    add      eax,1
00411A4A 89 85 EC F7 FF FF           mov      dword ptr [a],eax
00411A50 81 BD EC F7 FF FF 80 00 00 00 cmp        dword ptr [a],80h
00411A5A 7D 35                       jge      SetTheIP+81h (411A91h)
  {
    MyClass m(a);
00411A5C 8B 85 EC F7 FF FF           mov      eax,dword ptr [a]
00411A62 50                          push     eax
```

```
00411A63 8D 8D DC F7 FF FF        lea     ecx,[m]
00411A69 E8 9C FA FF FF           call    MyClass::MyClass (41150Ah)
    strcat(buffer, m.string);
00411A6E 8B 85 E0 F7 FF FF        mov     eax,dword ptr [ebp-820h]
00411A74 50                       push    eax
00411A75 8D 8D F8 F7 FF FF        lea     ecx,[buffer]
00411A7B 51                       push    ecx
00411A7C E8 46 F7 FF FF           call    @ILT+450(_strcat) (4111C7h)
00411A81 83 C4 08                 add     esp,8

  }
00411A84 8D 8D DC F7 FF FF        lea     ecx,[m]
00411A8A E8 76 FA FF FF           call    MyClass::~MyClass (411505h)
00411A8F EB B0                    jmp     SetTheIP+31h (411A41h)
}
00411A91 52                       push    edx
00411A92 8B CD                    mov     ecx,ebp
00411A94 50                       push    eax
00411A95 8D 15 B6 1A 41 00        lea     edx,[ (411AB6h)]
00411A9B E8 FA F6 FF FF           call    @ILT+405(@_RTC_CheckStackVars@8) (41119Ah)
00411AA0 58                       pop     eax
00411AA1 5A                       pop     edx
00411AA2 5F                       pop     edi
00411AA3 5E                       pop     esi
00411AA4 5B                       pop     ebx
00411AA5 81 C4 E8 08 00 00        add     esp,8E8h
00411AAB 3B EC                    cmp     ebp,esp
00411AAD E8 F0 F8 FF FF           call    @ILT+925(__RTC_CheckEsp) (4113A2h)
00411AB2 8B E5                    mov     esp,ebp
00411AB4 5D                       pop     ebp
00411AB5 C3                       ret
```

One thing you'll realize immediately is that the disassembly window can be a big help in beginning to understand what assembly language is all about. I wish I had more time to go over each statement, addressing modes, and whatnot, but there are better resources for that anyway.

Notice first the structure of the disassembly window. The column of numbers on the left-hand side of the window is the memory address of each instruction. The list of one to ten hexadecimal codes that follows each address represents the machine code bytes. Notice that the address of each line coincides with the number of machine code bytes. The more readable instruction on the far right is the assembler statement. Each group of assembler statements is preceded by the C++ statement that they compiled from, if the source is available. You can see that even a close brace can have assembly instructions, usually to return to the calling function or to destroy a C++ object.

The first lines of assembly, pushing various things onto the stack and messing with EBP and ESP, establish a local stack frame. The value 8E8h is the size of the stack frame, which is 2,280 bytes.

Check out the assembly code for the `for` loop. The beginning of the loop has seven lines of assembly code. The first two initialize the loop variable and jump over the lines that increment the loop variable. Skip over the guts of the loop for now and check out the last three assembly lines. Collectively, they call the destructor for the `MyClass` object and skip back to the beginning part of the loop that increments the loop variable and performs the exit comparison. If you've ever wondered why the debugger always skips back to the beginning of `for` loops when the exit condition is met, there's your answer. The exit comparison happens at the beginning.

The inside of the loop has two C++ statements: one to construct the `MyClass` object and another to call `strcat()`. Notice the assembly code that makes these calls work. In both cases, values are pushed onto the stack by the calling routine. The values are pushed from right to left, that is to say that the last variable in a function call is pushed first. What this means for you is that you should be mindful of setting the next statement. If you want to skip a call, make sure that you skip any assembly statements that push values onto the stack, or your program will lose its mind.

One last thing: Look at all the code that follows the closing brace of `SetTheIP()`. There are two calls here to `CheckStackVars()` and `CheckESP()`. What the heck are those things? These are two functions inserted into the exit code of every function in debug builds that perform sanity checks on the integrity of the stack. You can perform a little experiment to see how these things work. Put a breakpoint on the very first line of `SetTheIP()`, skip over all the stack frame homework, and set the next statement to the one where the buffer gets initialized. The program will run fine until the sanity check code runs. You'll get a dialog box telling you that your stack has been corrupted.

It's nice to know that this check will keep you from chasing ghosts. If you mistakenly screw up the stack frame by moving the instruction pointer around, these sanity checks will catch the problem.

## Peppering the Code

If you have an elusive bug that corrupts a data structure or even the memory system, you can hunt it down with a check routine. This assumes that the corruption is somewhat deterministic, and you can write a bit of code to see if it exists. Write this function and begin placing this code in strategic points throughout your game.

A good place to start this check is in your main loop and at the top and bottom of major components like your resource cache, draw code, AI, or sound manager. Place the check at the top and bottom to ensure that you can pinpoint a body of code that caused the corruption. If a check succeeds before a body of code and fails after it, you can begin to drill down into the system, placing more checks, until you nail the exact source of the problem. Here's an example:

```
void BigBuggySubsystem()
{
  BuggyObject crasher;
  CheckForTheBug("Enter BigBuggySubSystem.");
  DoSomething();
  CheckForTheBug("Calling DoSomethingElse");
  DoSomethingElse();
  CheckForTheBug("Calling CorruptEverything");
  CorruptEverything();
  CheckForTheBug("Leave BigBuggySubSystem");
}
```

In this example, `CheckForTheBug()` is a bit of code that will detect the corruption, and the other function calls are subsystems of the `BigBuggySubsystem`. It's a good idea to put a text string in your checking code so that it's quick and easy to identify the corruption location, even if the caller's stack is trashed.

Since there's plenty of C++ code that runs as a result of exiting a local scope, don't fret if your checking function finds a corruption on entry. You can target your search inside the destructors of any C++ objects used inside the previous scope. If the destructor for the `BuggyObject` code was wreaking some havoc, it won't be caught by your last call to your checking function. You wouldn't notice it until some other function called your checking code.

## Draw Debug Information

This might seem incredibly obvious, but since I forget it all the time myself, I figure it deserves mentioning. If you are having trouble with graphics- or physics-related bugs, it can be invaluable to draw additional information on your screen such as wireframes, direction vectors, or coordinate axes. This is especially true for 3D games, but any game can find visual debug helpers useful. Here are a few ideas:

- **Hot areas:** If you are having trouble with user interface code, you can draw rectangles around your controls and change their color when they go active. You'll be able to see why one control is being activated when you didn't expect it.

- **Memory/frame rate:** In debug versions of your game, it can be very useful to draw current memory and frame rate information every few seconds. Don't do it every frame because you can't really see things that fast, and it will affect your frame rate.
- **Coordinate axes:** A classic problem with 3D games is that the artist will create 3D models in the wrong coordinate system. Draw some additional debug geometry that shows the positive X-axis in red, the positive Y-axis in green, and the positive Z-axis in blue. You'll always know which way is up!
- **Wireframe:** You can apply wireframe drawing to collision geometry to see if they match up properly. A classic problem in 3D games is when these geometries are out of sync, and drawing the collision geometry in wireframe can help you figure out what's going on.
- **Targets:** If you have AI routines that select targets or destinations, it can be useful to draw them explicitly by using lines. Whether your game is 3D or 2D, line drawing can give you information about where the targets are. Use color information to convey additional information such as friend or foe.

**Every 3D Game Needs a Test Object**

In 3D games, it's a good idea to construct a special test object that is asymmetrical on all three coordinate axes. Your game renderer and physics system can easily display things like cubes in a completely wrong way, but they will look right because a cube looks the same from many different angles. A good example of an asymmetrical object is a shoe, since there's no way you can slice it and get a mirror image from one side to another. In your 3D game, build something with similar properties, but make sure the shape is so asymmetrical that it will be obvious if any errors pop up.

## Lint and Other Code Analyzers

These tools can be incredibly useful. Their best application is one where code is being checked often, perhaps each night. Dangerous bits of code are fixed as they are found, so they don't get the chance to exist in the system for any length of time. If you don't have Lint, make sure that you ramp up the warning level of the compiler as high as you can stand it. It will be able to make quite a few checks for you and catch problems as they happen.

A less useful approach involves using code analysis late in your project with the hope that it will pinpoint a bug. You'll probably be inundated with warnings and errors, any of which could be perfectly benign for your game. The reason this isn't as useful at the end of your project is that you may have to make sweeping changes to your code to address every issue. This is not wise. It is much more likely that sweeping changes will create a vast set of additional issues, the aggregate of which could be worse than the original problem. It's best to perform these checks often and throughout the life of your project.

## Nu-Mega's BoundsChecker and Runtime Analyzers

BoundsChecker is a great program, and every team should have at least one copy. In some configurations, it can run so slowly that your game will take three hours to display a single screen. Rather, use a targeted approach and filter out as many checks as you can and leave only the checks that will trap your problem.

## Disappearing Bugs

The really nasty bug seems to actually possess intelligence, as well as awareness of itself and your attempts to destroy it. Just as you get close, the bug changes, and it can't be reproduced using your previously observed steps. It's likely that recent changes such as adding checking code have altered the memory map of your process. The bug might be corrupting memory that is simply unused. This is where your notes will really come in handy. It's time to backtrack, remove your recent changes one at a time, and repeat until the bug reappears. Begin again, but try a different approach in the hopes you can get closer.

### Bugs Fixing Themselves?

Another version of the disappearing bug is one where a known failure simply disappears without any programmer actually addressing it. The bug might have been related to another issue that someone fixed—you hope. The safest thing to do is to analyze recent changes and attempt to perform an autopsy of sorts. Given the recent fixes, you might even be able to re-create the original conditions and code that made the bug happen, apply the fix again, and prove beyond a shadow of a doubt that a particular fix addressed more than one bug.

What's more likely is that the number of changes to the code will preclude the possibility of this examination, especially on a large team. Then you have a decision to make: Is the bug severe enough to justify a targeted search through all the changes to prove the bug is truly fixed? It depends on the seriousness of the bug.

## Tweaking Values

A classic problem in programming is getting a constant value "just right." This is usually the case for things such as the placement of a user interface object like a button or perhaps the velocity value of a particle stream. While you are experimenting with the value, put it in a static variable in your code:

```
void MyWeirdFountain::Update()
{
```

```
  static float dbgVelocity = 2.74f;
  SetParticleVelocity(dbgVelocity);
  // More code would follow....
}
```

It then becomes a trivial thing to set a breakpoint on the call to `SetParticleVelocity()` to let you play with the value of `dbgVelocity` in real time. This is much faster than recompiling and even faster than making the value data driven, since you won't even have to reload the game data.

Once you find the values you're looking for, you can take the time to put them in a data file.

## Caveman Debugging

If you can't use a debugger, you get to do something I call *caveman debugging*. You might be curious as to why you wouldn't be able to use a debugger, and it's not because you work for someone so cheap that they won't buy one. Sometimes you'll see problems only in the release build of the application. These problems usually result from uninitialized variables or unexpected or even incorrect code generation. The problem simply goes away in the debug version. You might also be debugging a server application that fails intermittently, perhaps after hours of running nominally. It's useless to attempt debugging in that case.

**Logging Is Your Friend**

Make good use of `stderr` if you program in UNIX or `OutputDebugString()` if you program under Windows. These are your first and best tools for caveman debugging. Most games have a relatively complex logging system that uses a number of different logging and caveman techniques for displaying debug information. You should do the same.

In both cases, you should resort to the caveman method. You'll write extra code to display variables or other important information on the screen, in the output window, or in a permanent log file. As the code runs, you'll watch the output for signs of misbehavior, or you'll pore over the log file to try to discern the nature of the bug. This is a slow process and takes a great deal of patience, but if you can't use a debugger, this method will work.

**Being Hypnotized by the *Ultima Online* Login Servers...**

When I was on *Ultima Online*, one of my tasks was to write the *UO* login servers. These servers were the main point of connection for the Linux game servers and the SQL server, so login was only a small portion of what the software actually did. An array of statistical information flowed from the game servers, was collated in the login server, and was written to a SQL database. The EA executives liked pretty charts and graphs, and we gave them what they wanted. Anyway, the login process was a Win32 console application, and to help me understand what was going on, I printed debug messages for logins, statistics data, and anything else that looked reasonable. When the login servers were running, these messages were scrolling by so fast that I certainly couldn't read them, but I could feel them. Imagine me sitting in the *UO* server room, staring blankly at three login server screens. I could tell just by the shape of the text flowing by whether or not a large number of logins were failing or a *UO* server was disconnected. It was like looking at the *Matrix* in its raw form.

**Debugging with Music**

The best caveman debugging solution I ever saw was one that used the PC speaker. Herman was a programmer who worked on *Ultima V* through *Ultima IX*, and one of his talents was perfect pitch. He could tell you the difference between a B and a B flat and get it right every time. He used this to his advantage when he was searching for the nastiest crasher bugs of them all—they didn't even allow the debugger window to pop up. He wrote a special checker program that output specific tones through the PC speaker and peppered the code with these checks. If you walked into his office while his spiced-up version of the game was running, it sounded a little like raw modem noise, until the game crashed. Because the PC speaker wasn't dependent on the CPU, it would remain emitting the tone of his last check. "Hmm…that's a D," he would say, and zero in on the line of code that caused the crash.

## When All Else Fails

So you tried everything and hours later you are no closer to solving the problem than when you started. Your boss is probably making excuses to pass by your office and ask you cheerily, "How's it going?" You suppress the urge to jump up and make an example of his annoying behavior, but you still have no idea what to do. Here are a few last resort ideas.

First, go find another programmer and explain your problem. It doesn't really matter if you can find John Carmack or the greenest guy in your group, just find someone. Walk them through each step, explaining the behavior of the bug and each hypothesis you had—even if it failed. Talk about your debugging experiments and step through the last one with him (or her) watching over your shoulder. For some odd reason, you sometimes find the solution to your problem without that person ever even speaking a single word. It will just come as if it were handed to you by the universe itself. I've never been able to explain that phenomenon, but it's real. This will solve half of the unsolvable bugs.

Another solution is static code analysis. You should have enough observations to guess at what is going on, but you just can't figure out how the pieces of the puzzle fit together. Print out a suspect section of code on paper—the flat stuff you find in copy machines—and take it away from your desk. Study it and ask yourself how the code could fail. Getting away from your computer and the debugger helps to open your mind a bit, and it removes your dependency on them.

If you get to this point and you still haven't solved the problem, you've probably been at it for a few solid hours, if not all night. It's time to walk away—not from the problem, but from your computer. Just leave. Do something else to get your mind off the problem. Drive home. Eat dinner. Introduce yourself to your family. Take a shower.

The last one is particularly useful for me, not that I need any of you to visualize me in the shower. The combination of me being away from the office and in a relaxing environment frees a portion of my mind to continue working on the problem without adding to my stress level. Sometimes a new approach to the problem or, even better, a solution will simply deposit itself in my consciousness. That odd event has never happened to me when I'm under pressure sitting at the computer. It's scary when you're at dinner, it dawns on you suddenly, and you've solved a bug just by getting away from it.

## Building an Error Logging System

Every game needs to have a robust logging system. You can only go so far with the `assert()` macro from the standard C libraries. With the sheer size of games, you need the ability to define different levels of errors. Some errors are more important than others, and you want the ability to define different severities for them. You also need a way to disable certain errors altogether. Finally, these errors should be ignored in the release version of the game.

Logging informational messages is another thing we'll need. This is how we'll pepper the code to find out what's happening inside a particular system. This logging will be based on tags; you can turn certain tags on or off, which enables or disables logs for that tag. For example, the event system may have its own tag. Enabling this tag will allow you to see what's happening inside the event system as it updates without having to step through breakpoints.

For this logging system, there will be three basic levels of logging. The first is *error*, the second is *warning*, and the third is *info*. Logs at the error level will display a dialog box showing the error string along with the function name, filename, and line

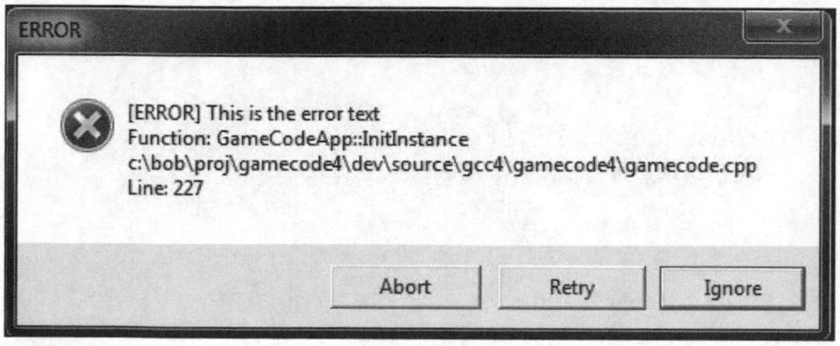


**Figure 23.3**
Debug error message.

number. There will be three buttons; Abort, Retry, and Ignore. Choosing Abort will cause the program to break into the debugger using the hard-coded breakpoint trick you saw previously in this chapter. Retry will cause the program to continue as if nothing happened. If this error is not recoverable, your game will probably crash. Choosing Ignore will cause the program to continue as well, but it will also flag that error as disabled. If that line is hit again, the error will not trigger. This is extremely useful for asserts and errors that are placed inside loops. Figure 23.3 shows what the error dialog looks like.

Warnings are less urgent errors. They shouldn't be ignored, but they aren't as dire as errors. A warning will log all the same information as an error, but it doesn't display a dialog box. Instead, it displays in the output window in Visual Studio.

Log messages at Info level are also displayed in the output window, but they don't include any of the extra debug information like function, filename, and line number. Info messages just show the message text.

Every log is tied to a tag that determines the behavior of any messages logged under that tag. There are a few hard-coded tags, but most are user defined. The hard-coded tags are "ERROR," "WARNING," and "INFO," which are used when throwing an error, a warning, or a generic info message. You can log to any other tag as well and set up flags for how those logs should be handled by the system. We'll see how that works later in this chapter.

With this design, we can now create a simple interface.

```
namespace Logger
{
  class ErrorMessenger
  {
```

```
    bool m_enabled;
  public:
    ErrorMessenger(void);
    void Show(const std::string& errorMessage, bool isFatal,
              const char* funcName, const char* sourceFile,
              unsigned int lineNum);
  };
  // construction; must be called at the beginning and end of the program
  void Init(const char* loggingConfigFilename);
  void Destroy(void);
  // logging functions
  void Log(const std::string& tag, const std::string& message,
           const char* funcName, const char* sourceFile,
           unsigned int lineNum);
  void SetDisplayFlags(const std::string& tag, unsigned char flags);
}
```

**Namespace > Class with Static Functions**

Notice the namespace above and how it's essentially acting like a class. In fact, this could have been written as a class with all static members, but using a namespace allows for several advantages. First, you have the ability to break up the namespace among multiple different files, similar to partial classes in C# and other languages. Second, since you can alias one namespace to another, you can set up conditionally compiled classes in a cleaner manner.

This namespace acts as the public interface for the logging system. Under the covers, there is another class called `LogMgr` that handles all the internals of actually logging. This class lives in *Dev\Source\GCC4\Debugging\Logger.cpp* and is not accessed outside this system. You can think of it as a private class. We'll examine this class a little later.

To start using this system, you must call the `Logger::Init()` function. This instantiates the internal `LogMgr` singleton class and initializes it. `Logger::Destroy()` must be called before the program exits to ensure this internal class is destroyed.

There are two basic ways to display a log with this system. The first is to instantiate a `Logger::ErrorMessenger` object and call the `Show()` function. This is used for error logs and will display the error message in the dialog box you saw in Figure 23.3. If the user presses the Ignore button, it will automatically set the `m_enabled` variable to `false`, and further calls to `Show()` will not do anything. Here's an example of how that might work:

```
if (somethingBadHappened)
{
```

```
    static Logger::ErrorMessenger* pErrorMessenger =
      GCC_NEW Logger::ErrorMessenger;
    pErrorMessenger->Show("Something bad happened", true,
      __FUNCTION__, __FILE__, __LINE__);
}
```

In practice, you don't ever type this out; rather, you put the whole thing in a macro. I'll show you how to do this later on.

The second way to log something is to call `Logger::Log()`. This will display the message according to the rules of that tag. The `SetDisplayFlags()` function is used to set those rules. Currently, the display flags are defined as follows:

```
const unsigned char LOGFLAG_WRITE_TO_LOG_FILE = 1 << 0;
const unsigned char LOGFLAG_WRITE_TO_DEBUGGER = 1 << 1;
```

If `LOGFLAG_WRITE_TO_LOG_FILE` is set for a given tag, the text is logged to a log file. If `LOGFILE_WRITE_TO_DEBUGGER` is set, the log is written to the output window in Visual Studio. These flags can be changed at any time by calling the `SetDisplayFlags()` function, but it's usually more convenient to set up a configuration file. That's what the parameter of `Logger::Init()` is for; you can pass it an XML file that defines the initial flags set for each tag. The default for most tags is 0, which means that tags will not display by default. The exception is for "ERROR," "WARNING," and "INFO," which are all set to display in the debugger by default.

Here's a sample logging configuration file:

```
<Logging>
  <Log tag="Script" debugger="1" file="0"/>
  <Log tag="Lua" debugger="1" file="0"/>
</Logging>
```

This configuration file will turn on debug logging for anything tagged with "Script" or "Lua." Such logs will be sent to the output window in Visual Studio.

Now that you have an understanding of the logging system interface, let's dig into the internals of it a bit. Here is the `LogMgr` class I promised to show you:

```
class LogMgr
{
public:
  enum ErrorDialogResult
  {
    LOGMGR_ERROR_ABORT,
    LOGMGR_ERROR_RETRY,
    LOGMGR_ERROR_IGNORE
  };
```

```
  typedef std::map<string, unsigned char> Tags;
  typedef std::list<Logger::ErrorMessenger*> ErrorMessengerList;

  Tags m_tags;
  ErrorMessengerList m_errorMessengers;

  // thread safety
  CriticalSection m_tagCriticalSection;
  CriticalSection m_messengerCriticalSection;

public:
  // construction
  LogMgr(void);
  ~LogMgr(void);
  void Init(const char* loggingConfigFilename);

  // logs
  void Log(const string& tag, const string& message, const char* funcName,
       const char* sourceFile, unsigned int lineNum);
  void SetDisplayFlags(const std::string& tag, unsigned char flags);

  // error messengers
  void AddErrorMessenger(Logger::ErrorMessenger* pMessenger);
  LogMgr::ErrorDialogResult Error(const std::string& errorMessage,
                                  bool isFatal, const char* funcName,
                                  const char* sourceFile,
                                  unsigned int lineNum);
private:
  // log helpers
  void OutputFinalBufferToLogs(const string& finalBuffer,
                               unsigned char flags);
  void WriteToLogFile(const string& data);
  void GetOutputBuffer(std::string& outOutputBuffer, const string& tag,
                       const string& message, const char* funcName,
                       const char* sourceFile, unsigned int lineNum);
};
```

At the top is the `ErrorDialogResult enum`, which defines the three possible results of an error dialog box. The `m_tags` variable is a map of tag strings to display flags. Whenever a log is triggered, this map is queried to find out the rules for displaying it. The `m_errorMessengers` variable is a list of all `Logger::ErrorMessenger` objects. Whenever an `ErrorMessenger` object is created, it's added to this list so that it can be destroyed when the program exits. The next two variables are critical sections needed to ensure that the logging system is thread safe.

`LogMgr::Log()` is called from `Logger::Log()`, which is just a wrapper function. It's responsible for building up the final output string, figuring out where it needs to go by querying the m_tags map, and sending it to those places. LogMgr::SetDisplay-Flags() finds the tag in the m_tags map and updates the display flags. If there is no tag in the map, it creates one. Logger::SetDisplayFlags() is just a wrapper for this function.

LogMgr::AddErrorMessenger() is called whenever a new ErrorMessenger object is created. It simply adds the ErrorMessenger object to the m_errorMessengers list. The LogMgr::Error() function is called from the ErrorMessenger::Show() function to display the appropriate dialog box. The return value of this function is used by ErrorMessenger::Show() to update the m_enabled flag, which determines whether or not the dialog is displayed next time.

The final three functions are private helpers.

This logging system is pretty neat, but it's missing two key things. First, it's not very easy to use. The code listing I showed you previously for using the ErrorMessenger class is a great example. Something like that really should be a single line of code. Second, and perhaps more importantly, there's no easy way to get rid of these errors and logs in release mode. Fortunately, there's a simple solution that will solve both of these issues. All you need to do is create a few macros to wrap the public interface of the logging system. These macros can encapsulate the coding overhead of using the logging system and can be completely compiled out in release mode.

Macros are a double-edged sword; they are typically harder to understand and debug since the compiler can't step into them. They can cause unforeseen problems as well. The compiler literally takes the macro call and replaces it with the macro text. For example, consider the following code:

```
#define MULT(x, y) x * y
int value = MULT(5 + 5, 10);
```

What would you expect value to be? It may not be what you think; in the code above, value will be 55, not 100. Since MULT() is a macro that replaces the call with the macro text, it ends up expanding to this:

```
int value = 5 + 5 * 10;
```

If MULT() were a function, it would behave as expected and return 100 because the parameters are evaluated before being pushed onto the stack. This is just one example of how a macro can bite you.

Here is the final version of the GCC_ERROR() macro:

```
#ifndef NDEBUG
#define GCC_ERROR(str) \
  do \
  { \
```

```
    static Logger::ErrorMessenger* pErrorMessenger = \
      GCC_NEW Logger::ErrorMessenger; \
    std::string s((str)); \
    pErrorMessenger->Show(s, false, __FUNCTION__, __FILE__, __LINE__); \
  } \
  while (0)\
#else // NDEBUG is defined
#define GCC_ERROR(str) do { (void)sizeof(str); } while(0)
#endif // !defined NDEBUG
```

The first line is a preprocessor check to see if `NDEBUG` is not defined. `NDEBUG` is only defined on release builds, so the full version of this macro is only defined on nonrelease versions of the game. The only parameter is `str`, which is the error string to send. First, the macro creates a new `Logger::ErrorMessenger` static instance. It's only created the first time this error is reached. The constructor of `ErrorMessenger` adds it to the list in `LogMgr` so that it gets cleaned up properly when `Logger::Destroy()` is called. This could just as easily be a static bool, but having a class gives you a lot more flexibility for the data you store at each `GCC_ERROR()` invocation. The next line wraps the `str` variable in an STL string. This is important because `str` can be an expression or even a naked `char*`. This forces `str` to be the format that you want. The last line inside the `do` statement calls the `Show()` function on the `ErrorMessenger` object to show the dialog box.

Notice how that whole block is wrapped in a `do...while(0)` block. The reason for this is to force the expanded macro (the code it becomes when the compile replaces the macro call) to be treated as a single statement. One thing people often try is to wrap it in curly braces, which will create a scope, but consider the following code:

```
if (fail)
  GCC_ERROR("Fail");
else
  DoSomethingGood();
```

If `GCC_ERROR()` used braces instead of a `do...while(0)` statement, attempting to compile this code, Visual Studio 2010 would give you the following error:

```
error C2181: illegal else without matching if
```

The reason is because of that semicolon on the end of the statement. The macro would expand as follows:

```
if (fail)
{
  static Logger::ErrorMessenger* pErrorMessenger =
    GCC_NEW Logger::ErrorMessenger;
```

```
  std::string s((str))
  pErrorMessenger->Show(s, false, __FUNCTION__, __FILE__, __LINE__);
}; // <-- NOTICE THE SEMICOLON HERE!!
else
  DoSomethingGood();
```

The semicolon after the `if` block closes that `if` statement, so the `else` is illegal. You could solve it by removing the semicolon from the call, like this:

```
if (fail)
  GCC_ERROR("Fail") // no semicolon
else
  DoSomethingGood();
```

This creates inconsistent code and calling conventions. Using the `do...while(0)` trick solves this problem completely since the semicolon is now just ending the `while` loop. The compiler is smart enough to know that `while(0)` will never loop, so it doesn't bother checking to see if it needs to go back. The performance is exactly the same. In fact, it generates the exact same assembly code.

The other debug and logging macros work in a similar fashion. They are all defined in *Dev\Source\GCC4\Debugging\Logger.h*. You can find the rest of the logging code in *Dev\Source\GCC4\Debugging\Logger.cpp*.

# Different Kinds of Bugs

Tactics and technique are great, but that only describes debugging in the most generic sense. You should build a taxonomy of bugs, a dictionary of bugs as it were, so that you can instantly recognize a type of bug and associate it with the beginning steps of a solution. One way to do this is to constantly trade "bug" stories with other programmers—a conversation that will bore nonprogrammers completely to death.

## Memory Leaks and Heap Corruption

A memory leak is caused when a dynamically allocated memory block is "lost." The pointer that holds the address of the block is reassigned without freeing the block, and it will remain allocated until the application exits. This kind of bug is especially problematic if this happens frequently. The program will chew up physical and virtual memory over time, and eventually it will fail. Here's a classic example of a memory leak. This class allocates a block of memory in a constructor but fails to declare a virtual destructor:

```
class LeakyMemory : public SomeBaseClass
{
```

```
protected:
  int *leaked;

  LeakyMemory() { leaked = new int[128]; }
  ~LeakyMemory() { delete [] leaked; }
};
```

This code might look fine, but there's a potential memory leak in there. If this class is instantiated and is referenced by a pointer to `SomeBaseClass`, the destructor will never get called.

```
void main()
{
  LeakyMemory *ok = new LeakyMemory;
  SomeBaseClass *bad = new LeakyMemory;

  delete ok;
  delete bad;         // MEMORY LEAK RIGHT HERE!
}
```

You fix this problem by declaring the destructor in `LeakyMemory` as virtual. Memory leaks are easy to fix if the leaky code is staring you in the face. This isn't always the case. A few bytes leaked here and there as game objects are created and destroyed can go unnoticed for a long time until it is obvious that your game is chewing up memory without any valid reason.

Memory bugs and leaks are amazingly easy to fix, but tricky to find, if you use a memory allocator that doesn't have special code to give you a hand. Under Windows, the C runtime library lends a hand under the debug builds with the debug heap. The debug heap sets the value of uninitialized memory and freed memory.

- Uninitialized memory allocated on the heap is set to 0xCDCDCDCD.
- Uninitialized memory allocated on the stack is set to 0xCCCCCCCC. This is dependent on the /GX compiler option in Microsoft Visual Studio.
- Freed heap memory is set to 0xFEEEFEEE, before it has been reallocated. Sometimes, this freed memory is set to 0xDDDDDDDD, depending on how the memory was freed.
- The lead byte and trailing byte to any memory allocated on the heap is set to 0xFDFDFDFD.

Windows programmers should commit these values to memory. They'll come in handy when you are viewing memory windows in the debugger.

The C-Runtime debug heap also provides many functions to help you examine the heap for problems. I'll tell you about three of them, and you can hunt for the rest in the Visual Studio help files or MSDN.

- `_CrtSetDbgFlag(int newFlag)`: Sets the behavior of the debug heap.
- `_CrtCheckMemory(void)`: Runs a check on the debug heap.
- `_CrtDumpMemoryLeaks(void)`: Reports any leaks to `stdout`.

Here's an example of how to put these functions into practice:

```
#include <crtdbg.h>
#if defined _DEBUG
  #define GCC_NEW new(_NORMAL_BLOCK,__FILE__, __LINE__)
#endif
int main()
{
  // get the current flags
  int tmpDbgFlag = _CrtSetDbgFlag(_CRTDBG_REPORT_FLAG);

  // don't actually free the blocks
  tmpDbgFlag |= _CRTDBG_DELAY_FREE_MEM_DF;

  // perform memory check for each alloc/dealloc
  tmpDbgFlag |= _CRTDBG_CHECK_ALWAYS_DF;
  _CrtSetDbgFlag(tmpDbgFlag);

  char *gonnaTrash = GCC_NEW char[15];
  _CrtCheckMemory();                            // everything is fine....
  strcpy(gonnaTrash, "Trash my memory!");  // overwrite the buffer
  _CrtCheckMemory();                      // everything is NOT fine!
  delete gonnaTrash;                      // This brings up a dialog box too...
  char *gonnaLeak = GCC_NEW char[100]; // Prepare to leak!
  _CrtDumpMemoryLeaks();                  // Reports leaks to stderr

  return 0;
}
```

Notice that the `new` operator is redefined. A debug version of `new` is included in the debug heap that records the file and line number of each allocation. This can go a long way toward detecting the cause of a leak.

The first few lines set the behavior of the debug heap. The first flag tells the debug heap to keep deallocated blocks around in a special list instead of recycling them back into the usable memory pool. You might use this flag to help you track a memory corruption or simply alter your processes' memory space in the hopes that a tricky bug will be easier to catch. The second flag tells the debug heap that you want to run a complete check on the debug heap's integrity each time memory is allocated or freed. This can be incredibly slow, so turn it on and off only when you are sure it will do you some good.

The output of the memory leak dump looks like this:

```
Detected memory leaks!
Dumping objects ->
c:\tricks\tricks.cpp(78) : {42} normal block at 0x00321100, 100 bytes long.
 Data: <                > CD CD CD CD CD CD CD CD CD CD CD CD CD CD CD CD
Object dump complete.
The program '[2940] Tricks.exe: Native' has exited with code 0 (0x0).
```

As you can see, the leak dump pinpoints the exact file and line of the leaked bits. What happens if you have a core system that allocates memory like crazy, such as a custom string class? Every leaked block of memory will look like it's coming from the same line of code, because it is. It doesn't tell you anything about who called it, which is the real perpetrator of the leak. If this is happening to you, tweak the redeclaration of `new` and store a self-incrementing counter instead of `__LINE__`:

```
#include <crtdbg.h>
#if defined _DEBUG
  static int counter = 0;
  #define GCC_NEW new(_NORMAL_BLOCK,__FILE__, counter++)
#endif
```

The memory dump report will tell you exactly when the leaky bits were allocated, and you can track the leak down easily. All you have to do is put a conditional breakpoint on `GCC_NEW` and break when the counter reaches the value that leaked.

**The Task Manger Lies About Memory**

You can't look at the Task Manager under Windows to determine if your game is leaking memory. The Task Manager is the process window you can show if you press Ctrl-Alt-Del and then click the Task Manager button. This window lies. For one thing, memory might be reported wrong if you have set the `_CRTDBG_DELAY_FREE_MEM_DF` flag. Even if you are running a release build, freed memory isn't reflected in the process window until the window is minimized and restored. Even the Microsoft test lab was stymied by this one. They wrote a bug telling us that our game was leaking memory like crazy, and we couldn't find it. It turned out that if you minimize the application window and restore it, the Task Manager will report the memory correctly, at least for a little while.

If you happen to write your own memory manager, make sure that you take the time to write some analogs to the C runtime debug heap functions. If you don't, you'll find chasing memory leaks and corruptions a full-time job.

**Don't Ignore Memory Leaks—Ever**

Make sure that your debug build detects and reports memory leaks, and convince all programmers that they should fix all memory leaks before they check in their code. It's a lot harder to fix someone else's memory leak than your own.

COM objects can leak memory, too, and those leaks are also painful to find. If you fail to call `Release()` on a COM object when you're done with it, the object will remain allocated because its reference count will never drop to zero.

Here's a neat trick. First, put the following function somewhere in your code:

```
int Refs (IUnknown* pUnk)
{
  pUnk->AddRef();
  return pUnk->Release();
}
```

You can then put `Refs(myLeakingResourcePtr)` in the watch window in your debugger. This will usually return the current reference count for a COM object. Be warned, however, that COM doesn't require that `Release()` return the current reference count, but it usually does.

## Game Data Corruption

Most memory corruptions are easy to diagnose. Your game crashes, and you find funky trash values where you were used to seeing valid data. The frustrating thing about memory corrupter bugs is that they can happen anywhere, anytime. Since the memory corruption is not trashing the heap, you can't use the debug heap functions, but you can use your own homegrown version of them. You need to write your own version of `_CrtCheckMemory()`, built especially for the data structures being vandalized. Hopefully, you'll have a reasonable set of steps you can use to reproduce the bug. Given those two things, the bug has only moments to live. If the trasher is intermittent, leave the data structure check code in the game. Perhaps someone will begin to notice a pattern of steps that cause the corruption to occur.

### The Best Hack I Ever Saw

I recall a truly excellent hack we encountered on *Savage Empire*, an *Ultima VI* spin-off that Origin shipped in late 1990. Origin was using Borland's 3.1 C Compiler, and the runtime module's exit code always checked memory location zero to see if a wayward piece of code accidentally overwrote that piece of memory, which was actually unused. If it detected that the memory location was altered, it would print out "Error: (null) pointer assignment" at the top of the screen. Null pointer assignments were tough to find in those days because the CPU just happily assumed you knew what you were doing. *Savage Empire* programmers tried in vain to hunt down the null pointer assignment until the very last day of development. Origin's QA had signed off on the build, and Origin execs wanted to ship the product, since Christmas was right around the corner. Steve, one of the programmers, "fixed" the problem with an amazing hack. He hex edited the executable, savage.exe, and changed the text string "Error: (null) pointer assignment." to another string exactly the same length: "Thanks for playing *Savage Empire*."

If the memory corruption seems random—writing to memory locations here and there without any pattern—here's a useful but brute force trick: Declare an enormous block of memory and initialize it with an unusual pattern of bytes. Write a check routine that runs through the memory block and finds any bytes that don't match the original pattern, and you've got something that can detect your bug.

### The Infamous Barge Bug

*Ultima* games classically stored their game data in large blocks of memory, and the data was organized as a linked list. If the object lists became corrupted, all manner of mayhem would result. A really bad one happened to me on my very first project, *Martian Dreams*. QA was observing a bug that made the Martian barges explode. The objects and their passengers would suddenly shatter into pieces, and if you attempted to move one step in any direction that game would crash. I tried again and again to fix this bug. Each time I was completely sure that the barge bug was dead. QA didn't share my optimism, and for four versions of the game I would see the bug report come back: "Not fixed."

The fourth time I saw the bug report, my exhausted mind simply snapped. I don't need to tell you what happened, because an artist friend of mine, Denis, drew this picture of me in Figure 23.4:

**Figure 23.4**
Artist's rendering of earwax blowing out of Mr. Mike's ears.

## Stack Corruption

Stack corruption is evil because it wipes evidence from the scene of the crime. Take a look at this lovely code:

```
void StackTrasher()
{
   char hello[10];
   memset(hello, 0, 1000);
}
```

The call to `memset()` never returns, since it wipes the stack clean, including the return address. The most likely thing your computer will do is break into some crazy, codeless area—the debugger equivalent of shrugging its shoulders and leaving you to figure it out for yourself. Stack corruptions almost always happen as a result of sending bad data into an otherwise trusted function, like `memset()`. Again, you must have a reasonable set of steps you can follow to reproduce the error.

Begin your search by eliminating subsections of code, if you can. Set a breakpoint at the highest level of code in your main loop and step over each function call. Eventually, you should be able to find a case where stepping over a function call will cause the crash. Begin your experiment again, only this time step into the function and narrow the list of perpetrators. Repeat these steps until you've found the call that causes the crash.

Notice carefully with each step the call stack window. The moment it is trashed, the debugger will be unable to display the call stack. It is unlikely that you'll be able to continue or even set the next statement to a previous line for retesting, so if you missed the cause of the problem, you'll have to begin again. If the call that causes that stack to go south is something trusted like `memset()`, study each input parameter carefully. Your answer is there: One of those parameters is bogus.

## Cut and Paste Bugs

This kind of bug doesn't have a specific morphology, an academic way of saying "pattern of behavior." It does have a common source, which is cutting and pasting code from one place to another. I know how it is; sometimes it's easier to cut and paste a little section of code rather than factor it out into a member of a class or utility function. I've done this myself many times to avoid a heinous recompile. I tell myself that I'll go back and factor the code later. Of course, I never get around to it. The danger of cutting and pasting code is pretty severe.

First, the original code segment could have a bug that doesn't show up until much later. The programmer who finds the bug will likely perform a debugging experiment where a tentative fix is applied to the first block of code, but he misses the second one. The bug may still occur exactly as it did before, convincing our hero that he has failed to find the problem, so he begins a completely different approach. Second, the cut-and-pasted code might be perfectly fine in its original location but cause a subtle bug in the destination. You might have local variables stomping on each other or some such thing.

If you're like me at all, you feel a pang of guilt every time you press Ctrl-V and you see more than two or three lines pop out of the clipboard. That guilt is there for a reason. Heed it and at least create a local free function while you get the logic straightened out. When you're done, you can refactor your work, make your change to *game.h*, and compile through the night.

## Running Out of Space

Everyone hates to run out of space. By space, I mean any consumable resource: memory, hard drive space, Windows handles, or memory blocks on a console's memory card. If you run out of space, your game is either leaking these resources or never had them to begin with.

We've already talked about the leaking problem, so let's talk about the other case. If your game needs certain resources to run properly, like a certain amount of hard drive space or memory blocks for save game files, then by all means check for the appropriate headroom when your game initializes. If any consumable is in short supply, you should bail right there or at least warn players that they won't be able to save games.

**Nine Disks Is Way Too Many**

In the final days of *Ultima VIII,* it took nine floppy disks to hold all of the install files. Origin execs had a hard limit on eight floppy disks, and we had to find some way of compressing what we had into one less disk. It made sense to concentrate on the largest file, SHAPES.FLX, which held all of the graphics for the game.

Zack, one of Origin's best programmers, came up with a great idea. The SHAPES.FLX file essentially held filmstrip animations for all the characters in *Ultima VIII,* and each frame was only slightly different from the previous frame. Before the install program compressed SHAPES.FLX, Zack wrote a program to delta-compress all of the animations. Each frame stored only the pixels that changed from the previous frame, and the blank space left over was run-length encoded. The whole shebang was compressed with a general compression algorithm for the install program.

It didn't make installation any faster, that's for sure, but Zack saved Origin a few tens of thousands of dollars with a little less than a week of hard-core programming.

## Release Mode-only Bugs

If you ever have a bug in the release build that doesn't happen in the debug build, most likely you have an uninitialized variable somewhere. The best way to find this type of bug is to use a runtime analyzer like BoundsChecker.

Another source of this problem can be a compiler problem, in that certain optimization settings or other project settings are causing bugs. If you suspect this, one possibility is to start changing the project settings one by one to look more like the debug build until the bug disappears. Once you have the exact setting that causes the bug, you may get some intuition about where to look next.

## Multithreading Gone Bad

Multithreaded bugs are really nasty because they can be nigh impossible to reproduce accurately. The first clue that you may have a multithreaded issue is by a bug's unpredictable behavior. If you think you have a multithreaded bug on your hands, the first thing you should do is disable multithreading and try to reproduce the bug.

A good example of a classic multithreaded bug is a sound system crash. The sound system in most games runs in a separate thread, grabbing sound bits from the game every now and then as it needs them. It's these communication points where two threads need to synch up and communicate that most multithreading bugs occur.

Sound systems like Miles from RAD Game Tools are extremely well tested. It's much more likely that a sound system crash is due to your game deallocating some sound memory before its time or perhaps simply trashing the sound buffer. In fact, this is so likely that my first course of action when I see a really strange, irreproducible bug is to turn off the sound system and see if I can get the problem to happen again.

The same is true for other multithreaded subsystems, such as AI or resource preloading. If your game uses multiple threads for these kinds of systems, make sure that you can turn them off easily for testing. Sure, the game will run in a jerky fashion, since all the processing has to be performed in a linear fashion, but the added benefit is that you can eliminate the logic of those systems and focus on the communication and thread synchronization for the source of the problem.

**The Pitch Debugger Comes to the Rescue**

*Ultima VIII* had an interrupt-driven multitasking system, which was something of a feat in DOS 5. A random crash was occurring in QA, and no one could figure out how to reproduce it, which meant there was little hope of it getting fixed. It was finally occurring once every 30 minutes or so—way too often to be ignored.

We set four or five programmers on the problem—each one attempting to reproduce the bug. Finally, the bug was reproduced by a convoluted path. We would walk the avatar character around the map in a specific sequence, teleporting to one side of the map, then the other, and the crash would happen. We were getting close.

Herman, the guy with perfect pitch, turned on his pitch debugger. We followed the steps exactly, and when the crash happened, Herman called it: A B-flat meant that the bug was somewhere in the memory manager.

We eventually tracked it down to a lack of protection in the memory system—two threads were accessing the memory management system at the same time, and the result was a trashed section of memory. Since the bug was related to multithreading, it never corrupted the same piece of memory twice in a row.

Had we turned multithreading off, the bug would have disappeared, causing us to focus our effort on any shared data structure that could be corrupted by multiple thread access. In other words, we were extremely lucky to find this bug, and the only thing that saved us was a set of steps we could follow that made the bug happen.

## Weird Ones

There are some bugs that are very strange, either by their behavior, intermittency, or the source of the problem. Driver-related issues are pretty common, not necessarily because there's a bug in the driver. It's more likely that you are assuming the hardware or driver can do something that it cannot. Your first clue that an issue is driver related is that it only occurs on specific hardware, such as a particular brand of video card. Video cards are sources of constant headaches in Windows games because each manufacturer wants to have some feature stand out from the pack and do so in a manner that keeps costs down. More often than not, this will result in some odd limitations and behavior.

Weird bugs can also crop up in specific operating system versions, for exactly the same reasons. Windows 9x–based operating systems are very different than Windows 2000 and Windows XP, which in turn are very different than Windows Vista and Windows 7. These different operating systems make different assumptions about parameters, return values, and even logic for the same API calls. If you don't believe me, just look at the bottom of the help files for any Windows API like `GetPrivateProfileSection()`. That one royally screwed me.

Again, you diagnose the problem by attempting to reproduce the bug on a different operating system. Save yourself some time and try a system that is vastly different. If the bug appears in Windows 7, try it again in Windows XP. If the bug appears in both operating systems, it's extremely unlikely that your bug is OS specific.

A much rarer form of the weird bug is a specific hardware bug, one that seems to manifest as a result of a combination of hardware and operating systems, or even a specific piece of defective or incompatible hardware. These problems can manifest themselves most often in portable computers, oddly enough. If you've isolated the bug to something this specific, the first thing you should try is to update all the relevant drivers. This is a good thing to do in any case, since most driver-related bugs will disappear when the fresh drivers are installed.

Finally, the duckbilled platypus of weird bugs is the ones generated by the compiler. It happens more often than anyone would care to admit. The bug will manifest itself most often in a release build with full optimizations. This is the most fragile section of the compiler. You'll be able to reproduce the bug on any platform, but it may disappear when release mode settings are tweaked. The only way to find this problem is to stare at the assembly code and discern that the compiler-generated code is not semantically equal to the original source code. This scenario occurs most often when you're doing something extremely tricky, which can expose an edge-case in the optimizer's logic. Finding this bug is not that easy, especially in fully optimized assembly.

By the way, if you are wondering what you do if you don't know assembly, here's a clue: Go find a programmer who knows assembly. Watch that person work and learn something. Then convince yourself that maybe learning a little assembly is a good idea.

**Report Every Compiler Bug You Find**

If you happen to be lucky (or unlucky) enough to find a weird compiler problem (especially one that could impact other game developers), do everyone a favor and write a tiny program that isolates the compiler bug and post it so that everyone can watch out for the problem. You'll be held in high regard if you find a workaround and post that, too. Be really sure that you are right about what you see. The Internet lasts forever, and it would be unfortunate if you blamed the compiler programmers for something they didn't do. In your posts, be gentle. Rather than say something like, "Those idiots who developed the xyz compiler really screwed up and put in this nasty bug ...," try, "I think I found a tricky bug in the xyz compiler ...."

# Profiling

Profiling is the act of improving the execution speed of your program and removing any bottlenecks from the code. This can be accomplished by measuring how long different parts of your code take to execute and rewriting the slow algorithms to be more efficient. Bottlenecks are particularly long frames that manifest as a momentary hitch in performance. They can occur if you have to wait for a piece of hardware, like waiting for the hard drive after suffering a cache miss, or if you're trying to do too much in a single frame.

## Measuring Performance

The first step in profiling is measuring the performance of your game. You can't fix what you can't see. There are a number of different programs available for measuring performance. Some are free, while others cost a lot of money. *VTune* by Intel is one of the better-known tools. It's extremely powerful but also very expensive. *Luke Stackwalker* is a program I use on my own projects that works pretty well. It's not as powerful as *VTune* or other commercial applications, but it has the huge advantage of being free.

Another method of measuring performance is to use a "poor man's profiler." This involves measuring the time between function calls with a high-resolution timer and logging the results. A function like `GetTickCount()` won't work since it's too low resolution, causing inaccurate results. One method I've used in the past is to take advantage of the ×86 Time Stamp Counter. The Time Stamp Counter is a high-resolution 64-bit counter that counts the number of CPU cycles since the computer was reset. You can read the value of this timer before a block of code and then read it again afterward to find out how many CPU cycles it took to execute. This isn't perfect because you'll get different results on different CPUs, but the results should be relatively accurate when run on the same CPU. All you're looking for is a delta so you can see if you were able to speed up some particularly complex algorithm.

## Optimizing Code

Once you've isolated the offending algorithm, it's time to fix the code. Optimizing code is very much an art form. You need to examine the code and try to understand why it's so slow. For example, consider the following code:

```
// assume this is defined
std::list<Actor*> actorList;

Actor* FindActor(ActorId id)
{
  for (auto it = actorList.begin(); it != actorList.end(); ++actorList)
  {
    Actor* pActor = (*it);
    if (pActor->GetId() == id)
      return pActor;
  }
  return NULL; // actor not found
}
```

This function loops through a list of actors to find the one that matches the ID. On the surface, it may appear okay, but this function is extremely inefficient. Once you have a few hundred or even a few dozen actors in the world, this function will cause some major performance issues in your game.

Computer scientists use a form of notation to estimate the performance cost of an algorithm with relation to the data that it operates on. This is called *Big-O* notation. The algorithm above is O(n), where n is the number of elements in the data structure. This means that as n goes up, so does the amount of time it takes to run this algorithm. In other words, the time it takes to run this algorithm scales linearly with the number of items in the list.

Let's say for the sake of argument that the evaluation of each iteration through the list costs 1ms. That means that if there are 100 elements in the list, it would cost 100ms to go through the entire list in the worst case.

The easiest fix for this problem is to create a map, which is typically implemented as a balanced binary tree (specifically a red-black tree for Visual Studio). Here is the revised code:

```
// assume this is defined
std::map<ActorId, Actor*> actorMap;
```

```
Actor* FindActor(ActorId id)
{
  auto it = actorMap.find(id);
  if (if != actorMap.end())
    return it->second;
  return NULL;
}
```

This function uses the map's `find()` function, which searches the tree for the key. A binary tree is a divide-and-conquer data structure, so as long as the tree remains balanced, you won't visit every node. This type of algorithm is O(log2n), which means that the time the algorithm takes to run is proportional to the base-2 log of the number of elements. If visiting each node takes 1ms and there are 100 nodes, the node has a worst-case time of about 6.64ms. That's *much* better than the 100ms that list was going to take! This is a huge improvement, assuming that the actor data structure is accessed often enough using the `ActorId` as the key.

The final optimization technique I want to talk about is with scripting languages like Lua. Scripting languages execute code slower than a compiled language like C++. One thing you can do is move some of the more expensive script functions into C++. This is commonly done for heavy math functions. For example, you probably don't want to do your pathing algorithm in Lua. This should be in C++ and called from Lua.

## Tradeoffs

Not every optimization is going to be as simple as swapping out an STL data structure. Most of the time, you'll have to make a trade. The classic trade is memory versus performance. In the actor example you saw in the previous section, you might do some tests and find that about 25 percent of the time, you're searching for the player's `Actor` object. One optimization would be to cache that actor directly so that retrieving the player is a simple getter function that doesn't have to go into the actor map at all. The cost of this is the memory required to store the extra pointer, which is probably worth it.

Caching values is a very common optimization. In general, you could precompute and cache everything you can, especially right before a big algorithm is about to run. On *The Sims Medieval*, we cached certain routing paths in the pathing system that were both extremely common and very expensive. This cost us a bit of memory because we had to store those paths, but many of our long-distance routes didn't have to run the expensive path-finding algorithm, it just had to verify that the path hadn't become invalid.

Another common optimization is to sacrifice reactivity for performance stability. A good example of this can be found in the event system in Chapter 11, "Game Event

Management." The `EventManager::VUpdate()` takes in a `maxMillis` parameter that only lets the Event Manager process for that amount of time. If it goes over that amount, the rest of the events are queued for the next frame, but it helps ensure that the Event Manager doesn't "spike" (for example, take a particularly long amount of time, causing a hitch in the frame rate). The cost is that events don't always get processed on the frame they are sent. Most of the time, this isn't a big deal, but it becomes possible to starve the Event Manager of CPU time. If you consistently push more events to the Event Manager than it can handle, the delay between events will grow until it's unmanageable and the poor Event Manager can't catch up!

**Sims Are a Bit More Thoughtful**

One of the big spikes in *The Sims Medieval* was the AI update tick. If you had a Sim in an area with a large amount of expensive objects, the AI tick could cause the game to visibly hitch. We fixed this issue by spreading the update across multiple frames, which got rid of the spikes but caused Sims to stand around and do nothing for a few frames. This was only noticeable on really low-end machines with a single-core processor and a lot of Sims in the world. The Sims appeared more "thoughtful," as if they were considering their actions.

### Over-Optimization

Optimization must be done in a triage fashion. Just because you can make an algorithm 10 times faster doesn't mean that you should, especially if this algorithm isn't showing up in your profiles. If the algorithm only takes 0.01ms, making it take 0.001ms won't do you much good. You should only concentrate on the top two or three issues at a time because those will give you the biggest overall performance gain.

Most of the time when you first run your game through the profiler, you'll be surprised at which algorithms show up the most. You might be calling an innocent getter function that's doing an inefficient search, or you might be calculating something in a large loop that you can easily cache. You can often make a big difference in performance with small changes.

The point is, you have to profile your game to see where the performance issues are and only concentrate on the biggest ones.

## Parting Thoughts

An important thing to keep in mind when debugging is that computers are at their core deterministic entities. They don't do things unless instructions are loaded into the CPU. This should give you hope, since the bug you seek is always findable.

You know that with enough time and effort, you'll squash that bug. That thought alone can be a powerful motivating force.

## Further Reading

*Reversing: Secrets of Reverse Engineering*, Eldad Eilam

# Chapter 24

*by Mike McShaffry*

# Driving to the Finish

At some point in your project, you begin to realize that you're a lot closer to the end than the beginning. While the calendar tells no lies about this, somehow your workload seems to increase exponentially. For every task that goes final, two or three seem to take its place. For a time, you and the team can take the added work with gusto—but after this drags on for a few weeks or months, everyone becomes exhausted. It's about that time the boss walks in and tells everyone another work weekend is ahead. Does this sound familiar?

This phenomenon is pretty common in many project-oriented businesses, but games are especially susceptible because there's something games are required to deliver that doesn't exist anywhere else. Games have to be fun.

I've said it a few times in this book already, but it deserves another mention. You can't schedule fun, and you can't predict fun. Fun is the direct result of a few things: a great vision, lots of iteration, a mountain of effort, lots of playtesting and redesign, and a flexible plan. I've also recently begun to believe there is a very healthy dose of luck involved, too. Any one of these things in abundance can make up for something lacking in the others. Most game companies simply rely on the effort component—a valiant but somewhat naive mistake.

If you've ever been in a sustained endurance sport like biking, you know that you start any event with lots of excitement and energy. Toward the end of the ride, you've probably suffered a few setbacks, like a flat tire or running out of water, making it hard to keep your rhythm. Your tired body begins to act robotically, almost as if your brain has checked out, and the highest thinking you are doing is working a few muscle groups. You refuse food and water, believing you don't need it. Then things really start to go wrong. You'll be lucky to cross the finish line.

The same thing happens to game development teams after a long stretch of overtime. Tired minds can't think, and not only do they make mistakes, but they don't even recognize them when they happen, and they attempt to solve the entire mess with even more mandatory overtime. This death march is not only damaging for the team and their families, but it is also a choice doomed to fail.

Getting a project over the finish line is tough, and you'll be called upon to solve some sticky problems along the way. Some of these problems will happen fast, too fast for you to have a solution in your back pocket. You'll have to think on your feet—not unlike someone who happens upon an emergency situation. When you learn first aid, you are taught that you must be able to recognize a problem when you see it, have the skills to do something about it, and most importantly, you must decide to act.

I can give you the first two. The final one is up to you.

## Finishing Issues

If your project is going well, you'll likely only need a few tweaks here and there to make sure you "stick the landing," so to speak. You can recognize this on your project by looking for a few telltale signs:

- **Your bug count is under control.** Your developers have fewer than four active bugs to fix per day until the "zero bugs" date.
- **Everyone is in good spirits.**
- **Bugs are easy to find and fix.** This is likely due to a lot of work on your game engine at the beginning of the project. Nice job!
- **The game is fun to play, performs well, and has only polishing issues remaining.**

If this describes your project, congratulations! But don't get too cocky, because there are some easy missteps you can make, even at this late stage.

### Quality

Perhaps the two biggest questions you and everyone else on the team asks at this point are likely to be: "Is the game good enough? Is it fun?" If a bug comes out of the testing group, it's because they want something changed to make the game better. Anyone on the development team can motivate a change as well, and they should do so if they think the game will become better because of it.

## Smoking the Build at Red Fly Studio

Red Fly Studio never had enough of anything we needed, especially testers. Our typical game took about five hours to play all the way through, which divided among three or four testers meant that each new build of our game took more than an hour for our testers to do a quick playthrough. Combine that with the problem of testing on multiple platforms or in multiple languages, and the testing time went up pretty fast. Because a build-breaking bug could happen at any time, we decided to have the entire team join in and help the testers play through the entire game, in every language. Split this job into as many as 20 or 30 developers and even our longer games got smoke tested in about 20 minutes.

## A Full-Time Job

At EA, we have a complicated build promotion process. Whenever you check something in, the build machine will sync up and build it. If the build passes, your change gets promotion to "latest," which means if anyone syncs to the "latest" data through the data tool, they will get your changes. Everyday, a few QA testers are assigned the task of promoting the last "latest" data to "LKG," or "Last Known Good." A complete smoke test is run with an established test plan. The whole process takes several hours. Once the testers sign off, the build is promoted. Anyone can grab the "LKG" data and have a decent, working copy of the game.

Later in the project, this turns into a full-time job. We had one or two testers on *The Sims Medieval* during the last six months or so who would do nothing but LKG testing. It took both of them the entire day to run through the whole game and write up bugs. When attempting to promote a major milestone like alpha, the entire test team was dedicated to running through the entire game, including each play path for the dozens of quests.

There are a lot of good ways to measure how important a particular bug is, one of which is user pain. Look for this blog article written in 2008 on it: http://www.lostgarden.com/search/label/User%20Pain. Basically, it measures a bug on many dimensions, such as what kind of bug it is, whether it blocks progress in the game, and how often it happens. This is boiled down to a number, the calculation of which is completely up to the team and what they feel is important.

I use a slightly different approach and measure bugs in four categories:

- Class AA: This is "drop everything you are doing and fix this bug," as it is significantly hampering the team from getting testing or work done.
- Class A: This bug must be fixed or the game can't ship. It might be a persistent crash during a level load, for example.

- Class B: This bug could ship, but players will definitely notice it; however, if the bug is rare, they will tolerate it. A good example of this might be a disappearing background object on the common play path.
- Class C: Fixing this bug won't effectively make any difference to the players—the team might know it is wrong, however. A good example of this might be the wrong music being played in a specific area or an incorrect texture on an object in a junk pile.

The closer the project gets to the scheduled zero bugs milestone, the less likely minor, C level bugs will actually get fixed. This rule of thumb is directly related to the fact that any change in content or code induces some risk. I've seen a single bug fix create multiple new bugs. This implies that any high-risk change should either happen much earlier in the schedule or there has to be some incredibly compelling reason, like there's no other choice, and the project is in jeopardy if the change isn't made. These problems are usually elevated to the highest level severity in the bug database, and your game shouldn't ship if it hasn't been fixed.

**Ghosts Are Supposed to Be Transparent, Aren't They?**

At some point in the final week of *Ghostbusters: The Video Game* for the Wii at Red Fly Studio, the producer noticed that none of the ghosts were transparent anymore. Evidently, a change had gone in weeks before, and everyone was so exhausted from crunch that no one noticed. The change to fix the problem was tricky, and it touched quite a few systems. As risky as the change was, it didn't take the team long to decide that it was worth fixing. After all, how can you really know you are seeing Slimer without seeing the hot dogs in his stomach?

Everyone on a project has his pet feature, something that person really wants to see in the game. The best time to install these features is before the code complete milestone (some people call this *alpha*). There are a few good reasons for this. First, it gives the team a huge burst of energy. Everyone is working on their top-tier wish lists, and tons of important features make it into the game at a time where the risk of these changes is pretty tolerable. Second, it gives the team a message: Either put your change in now or forever hold your peace. After code complete, nothing new code-wise should be installed into the game. For artists and other content folks, this rule is the same, but the milestone is different. They use the content complete milestone (or *beta*) as their drop-dead date for pet features. One more note about programmers and artists adding anything: If the game isn't reaching target performance goals, it's a bad idea to add anything. Adding things won't make your game any faster. Make sure the performance issues are completely taken care of before code complete and monitor those issues closely until the project ships.

### Lord British Must Die

It's a common practice to put inside jokes or "Easter Eggs" into a game. On *Ultima VII,* the team installed a special way to kill Lord British, especially since Richard Garriott wanted Lord British to be completely invincible. You need a little background first.

Origin was in an office building in the west Austin hill country, and the building had those glass front doors secured with powerful magnets at the top of the door. One day, Richard and some other folks were headed out to lunch, and when Richard opened the door, the large block of metal that formed a part of the magnetic lock somehow became detached from the glass and fell right on Richard's head. Lord British must truly be unkillable, because that metal block weighed something like 10 pounds and had sharp edges….

The team decided to use that event as an inside way to kill the monarch of Britannia. At noon, the Lord British character's schedule took him into the courtyard of the castle. He would pause briefly under the doorway, right under a brass plaque that read, "Lord British's Throne Room." If you double-clicked the sign, it would fall on his head and kill him straightaway.

Perhaps the weirdest thing about this story is that a few weeks later, the same metal block on the same door fell on Richard a second time, again with no permanent damage. The guy is truly protected by some supernatural force, but he did buy a hard-shell construction helmet, and he wasn't so speedy to be the first person to open the door anymore.

By the time the team is working solidly to zero bugs, all the code and content is installed, and there is nothing to do but fix bugs. It's a good idea to add a few steps to the bug-fixing protocol. Here's the usual way bugs get assigned and fixed:

1. A bug is written up in test and assigned to a team member to fix.
2. The bug is fixed and is sent back to test for verification.
3. The bug is closed when someone in test gets a new version and observes the game behaving properly.

Close to the zero bug date, a bit of sanity checking is in order. This sanity checking puts some safety valves on the scope of any changes. By this time in the project, it usually takes two overworked human brains to equal the thinking power of one normal brain.

1. A bug is written up in test and reviewed by the team lead.
2. If needed, it is saved for a triage team, usually the team leads, to discuss whether it should be fixed and who should fix it.

3. If the bug is serious enough, it is assigned to someone on the team to investigate a solution.
4. Someone investigates a potential solution. If a solution seems too risky, that person reports back to the triage team for a little advice.
5. The solution is coded and checked on the programmer's machine by a colleague. It doesn't have to be the lead programmer, just anyone with neurons and a reasonable familiarity with the subsystem being fixed.
6. The bug is sent back to test for verification.
7. The bug is closed when someone in test gets a new version and observes the game behaving properly.

If you think that the bureaucracy is a little out of control, I understand your concerns. It might be out of control, but it's out of control for a reason. Many bugs might never make it out of step #1. For those that do make it to a real fix, it is reviewed by a colleague who can really help ensure that the bug is fixed correctly, and it is never seen again by the testers or the team.

**Bug Meeting on *Martian Dreams***

My first experience with bugs in games was on *Martian Dreams* at Origin Systems. The whole team gathered in the conference room, and each new bug from testing was read aloud to the entire team. Sometimes the bugs were so funny the whole room was paralyzed with laughter, and while it wasn't the most efficient way to run a meeting, it sure took the edge off the day.

On *Ultima VII, Ultima VIII,* and *Ultima Online,* the teams were simply too big, and the bugs too numerous, to read aloud in a team meeting. Between the inevitable laughter and complaining about fixing the object lists again, we'd probably still be working on those games.

Even on smaller projects, like *Bicycle Casino* and *Magnadoodle,* we held bug meetings with the team leads. It turned out that the rest of the developers would rather spend their time making the game better and fixing as many bugs as they could than sitting in meetings. Outside of that, time away from the computer and sleep was a welcome diversion.

Of course, everything hinges on your active bug count. If you are two months away from your scheduled zero bug date, and you are already sitting at zero bugs (yeah, right!), then you have more options than a team skidding into their zero bug date with a high bug count. I hope you find yourself in the former situation someday. I've never seen it myself.

The only hard and fast rule is how many bugs your team can fix per day—this bug fix rate tends to be pretty predictable all through your testing period. It will be different for programmers than artists, because art bugs can be fixed faster and easier. Programmers tend to fix somewhere between three and ten bugs per day per person, but your mileage may vary. The point is, measure how fast your bugs are dropping to zero and draw the line out to see when you'll actually reach zero. If the date looks grim or doesn't even slope toward zero, you've got a serious problem on your hands. If things are looking good, loosen the screws a little and make your game better while you can.

**Getting to Zero Bugs on *Star Wars: The Force Unleashed II***

*Star Wars: The Force Unleashed II* should have been a nightmare project. It had an incredibly short production schedule and an aggressive scope, and we feared the worst. But in the same way that a downhill skier brings his "A" game to any double black diamond slope, everyone on the project did the same. By the time we hit Beta, the bug count was well under control, the team wasn't too exhausted, and the game was behaving well on all levels. This set us up to be super aggressive with our bug fixing. Nearly every bug that came in from QA was fixed, leaving only a few that had to be closed as "Won't Fix." On the day we were due to submit our final version to Nintendo, we all looked at each other and for once agreed that we were ready to let this game go with no regrets at all.

You could just decide to fix fewer bugs, closing them as "Won't Fix." While this will get your active bug count to zero, the live bugs in your game can create an overall game experience that seems sloppy. If you have no choice but to do this, make sure you focus on fixing bugs that materially affect the game experience. Minor graphical glitches you can ignore, but a repeatable crash on the common play path should get fixed no matter what.

## Code

At the end of every game project, the programmers, game designers, and audio engineers are the ones who are hammered the most. Artists and animators are hit especially hard during the content complete milestone, but after that their work levels off, mostly because it is usually more predictable. If you don't believe me, just ask an artist how long it will take him to tweak the lighting on a model. Or ask a level designer how long it will take to place a few more power-ups in a level, and she will not only give you a solid answer, but she will also be right about it. Audio engineers also have very predictable work, but they tend to get pushed about by way too many late changes by the rest of the team. Every time an animation gets tweaked, the audio will typically get tweaked to match.

Ask a programmer how long it will take to find the random memory trasher bug, and he will shrug and say something like, "I don't have any idea! A few hours maybe?" You may find that same programmer, 48 hours later, bashing his head against the same bug, no closer to fixing it than when he started.

These setbacks happen all the time, and there's not much that can be done except to get as much caffeine into the programmer's bloodstream as he can stand, get the other programmers to take up the slack in the bug debt, and maybe lend a few more neurons to the problem. Don't forget about the advice earlier in the book: Any two programmers looking at the same problem are at least three times as smart as a lone programmer.

When the bug is eventually found, there is often a decision that has to be made about the nature of the solution. A simple hack may suffice, but a "real" solution exists that will touch a lot of code and perhaps induce more risk. At the very late stages of a project, I suggest hacking. Wonton, unabashed hacking.

Some of you may be reeling at this sacrilege, but I'm sure just as many of you are cheering. The fact is that a well thought-out hack can be the best choice, especially if you can guarantee the safety and correctness of the change. "Hack" is probably a bad word to use to fully describe what I'm talking about, because it has somewhat negative connotations. Let me try to be specific in my definition:

**Hack – n.** *A piece of code written to solve a specific corner case of a specific problem, as opposed to code written to solve a problem in the general case.*

Let me put this in a different light. Everyone should be familiar with searching algorithms, where the choice of a particular search can achieve a "first solution" or a "best solution" criteria. At the beginning of a project, coding almost always follows the "best solution" path, because there is sufficient time to code a more complicated, albeit more general algorithm. At the end of the project, it is frequently the case that the best solution will lead a programmer down a complete reorganization of an entire subsystem, if not the entire code base.

Instead, games have a "get-out-of-jail-free" card, because the players don't generate the game data. Since the game inputs are fairly predictable, or even static, the problem domain is reduced to a manageable level. A programmer can be relatively sure that a specific bit of code can be written to solve a specific problem, on a specific map level, with specific character attributes. It seems ugly, and to be honest, it is ugly. As a friend of mine at Microsoft taught me, shipping your game is its most important feature.

The hack doesn't have to live in the code base forever, although it frequently does. If your game is even mildly successful, and you get the chance to do a sequel, you might have time to rip out the hacks and install an upgraded algorithm. You'll then be able to sleep at night.

### Hacks in *Ultima 7* and *Strike Commander*

At Origin it was common practice for programmers to add an appropriate comment if they had to install a hack to fix a bug. A couple of programmers were discussing which game had the most hacks—*Ultima VII* or *Strike Commander*. There was a certain pride in hacking in those days, since we were all young, somewhat arrogant, and enjoyed a good hack from time to time. The issue was settled with grep—a text file search utility. The *Strike Commander* team was the clear winner, with well over 500 hacks in their code.

*Ultima VII* wasn't without some great comments, though. My favorite one was something like, "This hack must be removed before the game ships." It never was. What's more, I think the same hack made it into *Ultima VIII*.

### Baby Maker

In *The Sims 3* code base, there's a file named BabyMakerSceneWindowGhetto UIDeleteMeSomedayPlease.cs. This was a last-minute hack that survived into the shipping version of the game and even found its way on *The Sims Medieval*! Old hacks are the hardest to kill.

Commenting your code changes is a fantastic idea, especially late in the project. This is especially true in any script languages, like Lua, that don't have the same analysis tools common in C++. After the code complete milestone, the changes come so fast and furious that it's easy to lose track of what code changed, who changed it, and why. It's not uncommon for two programmers to make mutually exclusive changes to a piece of code, each change causing a bug in the other's code. You'll recognize this pretty fast, usually because you'll go into a piece of code and fix a bug, only to have the same bug reappear a few versions later. When you pop back into the code you fixed, you'll see the code has mysteriously reverted to the buggy version. This might not be a case of source code control gone haywire, as you would first suspect. It could be another programmer reverting your change because it caused another bug.

That situation is not nearly as rare as you think, but there is a more common scenario. Every now and then, I'll attempt a bug fix, only to have the testers throw it back to me saying that the bug still lives. By the time it comes back, I may have forgotten why I chose the solution, or what the original code looked like. Even better, I may look at the same block of code months later and not have a clue what the fix was attempting to fix or what test case exposed the bug.

The solution to the problem of short-term programmer memories is comments, as always, but comments in the late stages of development need some extra information to be especially useful. Here's an example of a late-stage comment structure we used on the Microsoft projects:

```
if (CDisplay::m_iNumModals == 0)
{
   // ET - 04/10/02 - Begin
   // Jokerz #2107 - Close() here causes some errors,
   // instead use Quit() as it allows the app to shutdown
   // gracefully
   Quit(); // Close();
   // ET - 04/10/02 - End
}
```

The comment starts with the initials of the programmer and the date of the change. The entire change is bracketed with the same thing, the only difference between the two being a "begin" and "end" keyword. If the change is a trivial one-liner with an ultra-short explanation, the comment can sit on the previous line or out to the right.

The explanation of the change is preceded with the code name for the project and the bug number that motivated the change. Code names are important because the bug might exist in code shared between multiple projects, which might be in parallel development or as a sequel. The explanation of the change follows, and where it makes sense, the old code is left in but commented out.

**The Infamous [rez] Comments**

Whenever I write a comment in a system that isn't mine or make a change that isn't straightforward, I always precede my comment with "[rez]." I do the same thing for asserts and error messages that are on in the debug builds. That way, people don't have to hunt through the source control system to find out who made a particular change; they can just come to me and ask. This has worked really well for me, and if you're working on a project with multiple people, I suggest you do the same.

Most programmers will instantly observe that the source code repository should be the designated keeper of all this trivia, and the code should be left clean. I respectfully disagree. I think it belongs in both places. Code reads like a story, and if you are constantly flipping from one application to another to find out what is going on, it is quite likely you'll miss the meaning of the change.

### Each Change Gets a Bug Number

At the end of the project, it's a good idea, although somewhat draconian, to convince the team to attach an approved bug number with every change made to the code. This measure might seem extreme, but I've seen changes "snuck" into the code base at the last minute without any involvement from the rest of the team. The decision to do that shouldn't be made by a programmer at 3 a.m. on Sunday morning. Also, if you come across a change in code that has a bug number attached, it is a trivial matter to load up the bug to see what was going wrong and even how the bug can be reproduced if you have to try an alternate fix.

There are plenty of software companies that employ some form of code review in their process. The terms "code review" and "computer game development" don't seem to belong in the same universe, let alone the same book. This false impression comes from programmers who don't understand how a good code review process can turn a loose collection of individual programmers into a well-oiled team of coding machines.

When most programmers think of code reviews, they picture themselves standing in front of a bunch of people who laugh at every line of code they present. They think it will cramp their special programming style. Worst of all, they fear that a bad code review will kill their chances at a lead position or a raise.

I've been working with code reviews in a very informal sense for years, and while it probably won't stand up to NASA standards, I think it performs well in creative software, especially games. It turns out there are two primary points of process that make code reviews for games work well: who initiates the review and who performs the review.

The person who writes the code that needs reviewing should actually initiate the review. This has a few beneficial side effects. First, the code will definitely be ready to review, since the person needing it won't ask otherwise. Programmers hate surprises of the "someone just walked in my office and wants to see my code" kind. Because the code is ready, the programmer will be in a great state of mind to explain it. After all, they should take a little pride in their work, right? Even programmers are capable of craftsmanship, and there's not nearly enough opportunity to show it off. A code review should be one of those opportunities.

The person performing the review isn't the person you think it should be. Most of you reading this would probably say, "the lead programmer." This is especially true if you are the lead programmer. Well, you're wrong. Any programmer on the team should be able to perform a code review. Something that is a lot of fun is to have a junior programmer perform code reviews on the lead programmer's code. It's a great chance for everyone to share his tricks, experience, and double-check things that are critical to your project.

This implies that the programmers all trust each other, respect each other, and seek to learn more about their craft. I've had the privilege of working on a programming team that is exactly like that, and the hell of being on the other side as well. I'll choose the former, thank you very much. Find me a team that enjoys (or at least tolerates) code reviews and performs them often, and I'll show you a programming team that will ship their games on time.

When I worked on Microsoft's casual games, the programmers performed code reviews for serious issues throughout the project, but they were done constantly after content complete, for each change, no matter how minor. Most of the time, a programmer would work all day on five or six bugs and call someone who happened to be on his way back from the bathroom to do a quick code review before he checked everything in. This was pretty efficient, since the programmer doing the review was already away from his computer. Studies have shown that a programmer doesn't get back into the "zone" until 30 minutes after an interruption. I believe it, too.

Bottom line: The closer you get to zero bugs, the more checking and double-checking you do on every semicolon. You even double-check the need to type a semicolon. This checking installs a governor on the number and the scope of every code change, and the governor is slowly throttled down to zero until the last bug is fixed. This increases the quality of every change and the quality of the whole game as a result. After that, the game is ready to ship.

**Code Reviews on *The Sims***

Code reviews on *The Sims* are mandatory and somewhat automated. When a programmer is ready to check in, he right-clicks on the change list in Perforce and selects "Request code review." This launches a plug-in that posts the code review on an internal website and sends an email to the team. The website shows all the changes side-by-side and allows the reviewer to comment on any section of code. There's a check box that says "ship it!" that the reviewer must check before the code change is allowed to be checked in. This process must be done for every single change, no matter how small. It creates a bit of an overhead for each submission, but it ensures that at least one other person has seen the change and given it his blessing. When you're working on a team with over 200 people, this kind of thing is critical.

## Content

Programmers aren't immune to the inevitable discussions, usually late at night, about adding some extra content into the game at the eleventh hour. It could be something as innocuous as a few extra names in the credits, or it could be a completely new terrain system. You think I'm kidding, don't you?

Whether it is code, art, sounds, models, map levels, weapons, or whatever makes your game fun, you've got to be serious about finishing your game. You can't finish it if you keep screwing with it! If you are really lucky, you'll wind up at a company like Valve or Blizzard, who can pretty much release games when they're damn good and ready. The rest of us have to ship games when we get hungry, and the desire to make the best game can actually supersede basic survival. At some point, no matter how much you tweak it, your game is what it is, and even superhuman effort will only achieve a tiny amount of quality improvement. If you've ever heard of something called the "theory of diminishing returns," you know what I'm talking about. When this happens, you've already gone too far. Pack your game up, ship it, and hope it sells well enough for you to get a second try.

The problem most people have is recognizing when this happens—it's brutally difficult. If you're like me, you get pretty passionate about games, and sometimes you get so close to a project that you can't tell when it's time to call it done and schedule the Ship Party.

**Find Your Own Beta Testers**

Microsoft employs late stage beta testers. These people work in other parts of Microsoft but play their latest games. Beta testers are different from playtesters because they don't play the game every day. They are always just distant enough and dispassionate enough to make a good judgment about when the game is fun or when it's not. If you don't have Microsoft footing your development bills, find ad hoc testers from just about anywhere. Ask your friends or family. You don't need professional testing feedback. You just need to know if people would be willing to plunk down some money for your game and spread the word about how good it is.

**A Bug Becomes a Feature**

When I worked on the *Ultima* series, it wasn't uncommon for truly interesting things to be possible, code-wise, at a very late stage of development. On *Ultima VIII,* a particular magic spell had a bug that caused a huge wall of fire that destroyed everything in its path. It was so cool we decided to leave it in the game and replace one of the lamer spells. It wasn't exactly a low-risk move, completely replacing a known spell with a bug-turned-feature, but it was an awesome effect, and we all felt the game was better for it.

#### The Brave Executioner

The game world of *The Sims Medieval* has a big pit right in the middle of it where a horrible tentacled beast lives. If you've ever seen *Return of the Jedi*, you may remember the Sarlacc pit. The idea is basically the same. One of the things a hero Sim can do is jump in the pit and fight the beast. If he succeeds, he gets something special. If he fails, he dies.

There was a bug on *The Sims Medieval* that read something like this: "I was watching the executioner feed the pit beast when all of a sudden she just leapt into the pit! I couldn't reproduce it." There was a video attached that showed the executioner diving into the pit. The designers saw this video and loved it, so they asked us to figure out why the executioner was choosing to do this action and to turn it into a feature.

I'm trying my very best to give you some solid advice instead of some wishy-washy pabulum. The truth is there's no right answer regarding last-minute changes to your game. The only thing you can count on is 20-20 hindsight, and only the people that write the history books are the winners. In other words, when you are faced with a decision to make a big change late in the game, trust your experience, try to be at least a little bit conservative and responsible in your choices, and hope like hell that you are right.

#### Let the Team Vote on Bugs

On *Mushroom Men: The Spore Wars,* we did something unusual. We had already established a "Bug Triage" room where all the team leads could discuss each bug as it came in from the testing team and either kill it or assign it to someone. A few weeks before we went into total lockdown mode, we gathered a list of 100 bugs that the team really wanted to see fixed and let the entire team vote on them. This took a few rounds, but it was great to see things that were close to a developer's heart get fixed. We'll do this again.

## Dealing with Big Trouble

Murphy is alive and well in the computer game industry, and I'm sure he's been an invisible team member on most of my projects. At Origin Systems, I think Murphy had a corner office. I think his office was nicer than mine!

Big trouble on game projects comes in a few flavors: too much work and too little time, human beings under too much pressure, competing products in the target market, and dead-ends. There aren't necessarily standard solutions for these problems, but I can tell you what has been tried and how well it worked or didn't work, as the case may be.

## Projects Seriously Behind Schedule

Microsoft has a great way of describing a project behind schedule. They say it's "coming in hot and steep." I know because the first Microsoft *Casino* project was exactly like that. We had too much work to do, but too little time to do it. There are a few solutions to this problem, such as working more overtime or throwing bodies at the problem. Each solution can work, but it can also have a dark side.

### *The Dreaded Crunch Mode—Working More Hours*

It amazes me how many project managers choose to work their teams to death when the project falls behind schedule.

**84-Hour Workweeks at Origin**

On my very first day at Origin Systems, October 22, 1990, I walked by a whiteboard with an ominous message written in block letters: "84-Hour Workweeks—MANDATORY." With simple division, I realized that 84 divided by 7 is 12. Twelve hours per day, seven days per week was Origin's solution for shipping *Savage Empire* for the Christmas 1990 season. To the *Savage Empire* team's credit, they shipped the game a few tortured weeks later, and this "success" translated into more mandatory overtime to solve problems.

We were all young, mostly in our late 20s, and the amount of overtime that was worked was bragged about. There was a company award called the "100 Club," which was awarded to anyone who worked more than 100 hours in a single workweek. At Origin, this club wasn't very exclusive.

**Welcome to Planet Moon; We're in Crunch**

On my first day at Planet Moon, the project lead for *Brain Quest* said "Welcome to Planet Moon, we're in crunch." This was after the song and dance during the interview about how crunch is rare and a thing of the past.

All things considered, the crunch wasn't too bad until the very end of the project. We would do one week of 10–12 hour days followed by a week of 8-hour days, which was pretty manageable. Once alpha started to approach, all bets were off. By the end of the project, leaving the office at 2 a.m. was considered an early night, with 4 a.m. being much more common. That was the project that ushered me into the "100 Club."

Humans are resilient creatures, and under extraordinary circumstances they can go long stretches with very little sleep or a break from work. During World War II, Winston Churchill was famous for taking little catnaps in the Cabinet War Rooms lasting just a cumulative few hours per day, and he did this for years. Mr. Churchill had good reason to do this. He was trying to lead England in a war against Nazi

Germany, and the cost of failure would have been catastrophic for his country and the entire world.

Game companies consistently ask for a similar commitment on the part of their employees—to work long hours for months, even years on end. What a crime! It's one thing to save a nation from real tyranny, but it's quite another to make a computer game. This is especially true when the culprit is overscoping the project, blind to the reality of a situation, and has a lack of skill in project management.

It is a known fact that under a normal working environment, projects can be artificially time-compressed up to 20 percent by working more hours. This is the equivalent of asking the entire team to work eight extra hours on Saturday. I define a normal working environment as one where people don't have their lives, liberty, or family at stake. This schedule can be kept up for months if the team is well motivated.

### Take a Break—You'll Be Better for It

It was this schedule that compressed *Ultima VIII* after a last-minute feature addition: Origin asked the team to ship the game in two extra languages, German and French. The team bloated to nearly three times its original size, adding native German and French speakers to write the tens of thousands of lines of conversation and test the results. We worked overtime for five weeks—60 hours per week, and we took the sixth week and worked a normal workweek, which averaged 50 hours. This schedule went on from August to March, or eight months. Youth and energy went a long way, and in the end, we did ship the game when the team thought we were going to ship the game, but everyone was exhausted beyond their limits.

Weeks later, however, it was clear that the game wasn't all we wanted it to be. Our collective exhaustion at the end caused me and others to make some bad decisions about what we should fix. Reviews were coming in, and they weren't good. A few months down the road, the team got back together to fix many of the biggest problems, and we released a patch, which by all accounts was much better.

The moral of this story—it is possible to crunch like crazy, and it may seem like you are achieving your goals, but in the end, your game will suffer for it. Working overtime works only to solve short-term problems, not long-term disasters.

### Go Home

There's an odd competition among some game developers concerning how they deal with crunch. If you sleep in the office, you are somehow more dedicated than someone who goes home, even if you work the same hours. I have only slept in the office once in my career. I was 18 years old and working in QA at Maxis on *SimCity 3000*. It was late so I decided to get a few hours of sleep on a large stuffed alligator in the server room. I barely slept at all, I felt awful, and I probably didn't smell great since we didn't have a shower in that building. It's not worth it. I would rather sleep in my own bed for four hours than sleep on a stuffed alligator in the server room for six hours.

For short periods of time, perhaps a week or two weeks, truly extraordinary efforts are possible. Twelve-hour days for a short burst can make a huge difference in your game. Well managed and planned, it can even boost team morale. It feels a little like summer camp. A critical piece of this strategy is a well-formed goal such as the following:

- Fix 50 bugs per developer in one week.
- Finish integrating the major subsystems of the game.
- Achieve a playthrough of the entire game without cheating.

The goal should be something the team can see on the horizon, well within sprinting distance. They also have to be able to see their progress on a daily basis. It can be quite demoralizing to sprint to a goal you can't see, because you have no idea how to gauge your level of effort.

**Richard's Midnight BBQ**

On *Ultima VII,* Richard Garriott was always doing crazy things to support the development team. One night he brought in steaks to grill on Origin's BBQ pit. Another night, very late, he brought in his monster cappuccino machine from home and made everyone on the team some latte. One Saturday, he surprised the team and declared a day off, taking everyone sky diving. Richard was long past the time where he could jump into C++ and write some code, but his support of the team and simply being there during the wee hours made a huge difference.

There's a dark side to overtime in the extreme that many managers and producers can't see until it's too late. It happened at Origin, and it happens all the time in other companies. When people work enough hours to push their actual pay scale below minimum wage, they begin to expect something extraordinary in return, perhaps in the form of end-of-project bonuses, raises, promotions, and so on.

The evil truth is that the company usually cannot pay anything that will equal their level of effort. The crushing overtime is a result of a project in trouble, and that usually equates to a company in trouble. If it weren't so, company managers wouldn't push staggering overtime onto the shoulders of the team. At the end of the day, the project will ship, probably vastly over budget and most likely at a lower quality than was hoped. Unfortunately, these two things do *not* translate into huge amounts of money flowing into company coffers and subsequently into the pockets of the team.

A few months after these nightmare projects ship, the team begins to realize that all those hours amounted to nothing more than lost time away from home. Perhaps their firstborn took a few wobbling steps or spoke his first words, "Hey where in the hell is Mommy, anyway?" This frustration works into anger and finally into people leaving the company for what they think are greener pastures. High turnover right after a project ships is pretty common in companies that require tons of overtime.

Someone once told me that you'll never find a tombstone with the following epitaph: "I wish I worked more weekends." As a team member, you can translate that into a desire to predict your own schedule as best you can, try to scope your project within your means, and send up red flags when things begin to get off track. If you ever get to be a project lead, I hope you realize that there's a place for overtime, but it can't replace someone's life.

### *Pixel Fodder—Throw Warm Bodies at the Problem*

Perhaps the second most common solution to projects seriously behind schedule is to throw more developers on the project. Well managed, this can have a positive effect, but it's never very cost effective, and there's a higher risk of mistakes. It turns out there's a sweet spot in the number of people who can work on any single project.

#### More People Make Work Go Faster, Right?

*Ultima Online* was the poster child of a bloated team. In December of 1996, the entire *Ultima IX* team was moved to *Ultima Online* in the hopes that throwing bodies at the problem would speed the project to completion. This ended up being something of a disaster, for a few reasons. First, the *Ultima IX* team really wanted to work on *Ultima IX.* Their motivation to work on another project was pretty low. Second, the *Ultima Online* team had a completely different culture and experience level, and there were clashes of philosophy and control. Third, *Ultima Online* didn't have a detailed project plan, somewhat due to the fact that no one had ever made a massive multiplayer game before. This made it difficult to deploy everyone in his area of expertise. I happened to find myself working with SQL servers, and I didn't have a shred of experience!

Through a staggering amount of work—an Origin hallmark—on the part of the original *Ultima Online* team and the *Ultima IX* newcomers, the project went live less than nine months after the team was integrated. The cost was overwhelming, however, especially in terms of employee turnover in the old *Ultima IX* team. Virtually none of the programmers, managers, or designers of *Ultima IX* remained at Origin to see it completed.

One effect of overstaffing is an increased need to communicate and coordinate among the team members. It's a generally accepted fact that a manager's effectiveness falls sharply if he has any more than seven reports, and it is maximized at five reports. If you have a project team of 12 programmers, 14 artists, and 10 designers, you'll have two programming leads reporting to a technical director and a similar structure for artists and designers. You'll likely have a project director as well, creating a project management staff of 10 people.

If your management staff is anything less than that, you'll probably run into issues like two artists working on the same model, or perhaps a programming task that falls completely through the cracks. To be honest, even with an experienced management team, you'll never be completely free of these issues.

**Working in Parallel on *Bicycle Cards***

Occasionally, you get lucky, and you can add people to a project simply because a project is planned and organized in the right way. A good example of this was the *Bicycle Cards* project, basically a bunch of little games packaged up in one product. When some of the games began to run behind schedule, we hired two contractors to take on a few games apiece. The development went completely smoothly with seven programmers in parallel. Their work was compartmentalized, communication of their tasks was covered nearly 100 percent by the design document, and this helped ease any problems.

They say that nine women can't make a baby in one month. That's true. There is also a documented case of a huge group of people who built an entire house from the ground up in three days due to an intricately coordinated plan, extremely skilled people, and very specialized building techniques. Your project could exist on either side of these extremes.

### *Slipping the Schedule*

This solution seems de rigueur in the games industry, even with a coordinated application of crunch mode and bloating the team. There's a great poster of *Ultima VII* and *Strike Commander* that Origin published in 1992, in the style of movie posters that bragged "Coming this Christmas." It turns out that those posters got the season right, but they just had the wrong year.

There's a long list of games that shipped before their time, but perhaps the worst offender in my personal history was *Ultima Online*. There was even a lawsuit to that effect, where some subscribers filed a class action lawsuit against Electronic Arts for shipping a game that wasn't ready. Thankfully, it was thrown out of court. A case like that could have had drastic effects on the industry!

The pressure to ship on schedule is enormous. You might think that companies want to ship on time because of the additional costs of the development team, and while the weekly burn rate of a gigantic team can be many hundreds of thousands of dollars, it's not the main motivation. While I worked with Microsoft, I learned that the manufacturing schedule of our game was set in stone. We had to have master disks ready by such and such a date or we would lose our slot in the manufacturing facility. Considering that the other Microsoft project coming out that particular year was Windows XP, I realized that losing my place in line meant a huge delay in getting the game out. Console games can have the same problem. If you miss your submission date to Nintendo, Sony, or Microsoft, you get to go on "standby," waiting for another empty slot so they can test your game for technical standards compliance.

While things like manufacturing and submission can usually be worked out, there's another, even bigger motivation for shipping on time. Months before the game is done, most companies begin spending huge money on marketing. Ads are bought in magazines or television, costing hundreds of thousands or even millions of dollars. You might not know this, but those special kiosks at the end of the shelves in retail stores, called *endcaps,* are bought and paid for like prime rental real estate, usually on a month-by-month basis. If your game isn't ready for the moment those ads are published or those kiosks are ready to show off your game, you lose the money. No refunds here!

This is one of the reasons you see the executives poking around your project six to eight months before you are scheduled to ship. It's because they are about to start writing big checks to media companies and game retail chains in the hopes that all this cash will drive up the sales of your game. The irony is, if the execs didn't believe you could finish on time, they wouldn't spend the big bucks on marketing, and your game would be buried somewhere on a bottom shelf in a dark corner of the store. Oh, and no ads either. Your best advertising will be by personal email to all your friends, and that just won't cut it. In other words, your game won't sell.

The difference between getting your marketing pressure at maximum and nothing at all may only be a matter of slipping a few weeks, or even a few days. What's worse, this judgment call is made months before you are at code complete—a time when your game is crashing every three minutes. Crazy, huh?

Probably the best advice I can give you is to make sure you establish a track record of hitting each and every milestone on time throughout the life of your project. Keep your bug count under control, too. These two things will convince the suits that you'll ship on time with all the features you promised. Whatever you do, don't choose schedule slippage at the last minute. If you must slip, slip it once and make sure you give the suits enough time to react to all the promises they made on your behalf. This is probably at least six months prior to your release date, but it could be even more.

### *Cutting Features and Postponing Bugs*

Perhaps the most effective method of pulling a project out of the fire is reducing the scope of work. You can do it in two ways: nuke some features of the game or choose to leave some bugs in their natural habitat, perhaps to be fixed on the sequel. Unless you've been a bit arrogant in your project, the players and the media won't know about everything you wanted to install in the game. You might be able to shorten or remove a level from your game, reduce the number of characters or equipment, or live with a less accurate physics system.

Clearly, if you are going to cut something big, you have to do it as early in the project as you can. Game features tend to work themselves into every corner of the project, and removing them wholesale can be tricky at best, impossible at worst. Also, you can't have already represented to the outside world that your game has 10,000 hours of gameplay when you're only going to have time for a fraction of that. It makes your team look young and a little stupid.

**So, 70 Hours of Gameplay? Really?**

Always give yourself some elbow room when making promises to anyone, but especially the game industry media. They love catching project teams in arrogant promises. It's great to tell them things about your game, but try to give them specifics in those features you are 100 percent sure are going be finished.

After code complete, the programmers are fixing bugs like crazy. One way to reduce the workload is to spirit away some of the less important bugs. As the ship date approaches, management's desire to "fix" bugs in this manner becomes somewhat ravenous, even to the point of leaving truly embarrassing bugs in the game, such as misspelled names in the credits or nasty crashes.

Anything can be bad in great quantities, and reducing your game's scope or quality is no exception. One thing is certainly true—your players won't miss what they never knew about in the first place.

**This One Must Die so That Others May Live**

*Mushroom Men: The Spore Wars* on the Wii was in late development, and one of the levels was falling behind. Art was unfinished, scripted events were still undone, and many other things left the team with the distinct impression that getting the level done was going to take a lot of work. After some serious soul searching, the team decided to cut the entire level and spend time making the other levels in the game better. It was a very hard decision, because so much work and care had already been spent on it—and had it been completed, it would have been one of the cooler parts of the game. In the end, it was the right decision.

It is incredibly difficult to step away from the guts of your project and look at it objectively from the outside. I've tried to do this many times, and it is one of the most difficult things to do, especially in those final days. Anyone who cares about his game won't want to leave a bug unfixed or cut a feature.

Ask yourself three serious questions when faced with this kind of decision: Will my decision sell more copies? Will the players really notice this change? Will it keep someone from returning the game? If your answer is yes, do what it takes. Otherwise, move on and get your game shipped.

## Personnel-Related Problems

At the end of a project, everyone on the team is usually stretched to the limit. Good-natured and even-keeled people aren't immune to the stresses of overtime and the pressure of a mountain of tasks. Some game developers are far from good natured and even keeled! Remember always that whatever happens at the end of a project, it should be taken in the context of the stresses of the day, not necessarily as someone's habitual behavior. After all, if someone loses his cool at 3 a.m. after having worked 36 hours straight, I think a little slack is in order. If this same person loses his cool on a normal workday after a calm weekend, perhaps some professional adjustments are a good idea.

### *Exhaustion*

The first and most obvious problem faced by teams is simple exhaustion. Long hours and missed weekends create pressure at home and a robotic sense of purpose at work. The team begins to make mistakes, and for every hour they work, the project slips back three hours. The only solution for this is a few days away from the project. Hopefully, you and your team won't let the problem get this bad. Sometimes all it takes is for someone to stand up and point to the last three days of nonprogress and notice that the wheels are spinning, but the car isn't going anywhere. Everyone should go home for 48 hours, even if it's Tuesday. You'd be surprised how much energy people will bring back to the office.

One other thing: They may be away from their desks for 48 hours, but their minds will still have some background processes mulling over what they'll do when they get back to work. Oddly enough, these background thoughts can be amazingly productive, since they tend to concentrate on planning and the big picture rather than every curly brace. When they get back, the additional thought works to create an amazing burst of productivity.

#### 4 Hours > 15 Seconds

Late in the *Magnadoodle* project for Mattel Media, I was working hard on a graphics bug. I had been programming nearly 18 hours per day for the last week, and I was completely spent. At 3 a.m., I finally left the office, unsuccessful after four hours working on the same problem, and went to sleep. I specifically didn't set my alarm, and I unplugged all the telephones. I slept. The next morning, I awoke at a disgusting 11 a.m. and walked into the office with a fresh cup of Starbuck's in hand. I sat down in front of the code I was struggling with the night before and instantly solved the problem. The bug that had eluded me for four hours the day before was solved in less than 15 seconds. If that isn't a great advertisement for sleep gaining efficiency in a developer, I don't know what is.

### *Morale*

Team morale is directly proportional to their progress toward their goal, and it isn't related to their workload. This may seem somewhat counterintuitive, but it's true. One theory that has been proposed regarding the people who built the great pyramids of Egypt is that teams of movers actually competed with each other to see how many blocks they could move up the ramps in a single day. Their workload and effort were backbreaking, and their project schedule spanned decades. The constant competition, as the theory suggests, created high productivity and increased morale at the same time.

Morale can slide under a few circumstances, all of which are completely controllable. As the previous paragraph suggests, the team must be convinced they are on track to achieve their goal. This implies that the goal shouldn't be a constantly moving target. If a project continually changes underneath the developers, they'll lose faith that it will ever be completed. The opposite is also true—a well-designed project that is under control is a joy to work on, and developers will work amazingly hard to get to a finish line they can see.

There's also a lot to be said for installing a few creature comforts for the development team. If they are working long hours, you'll be surprised what a little effort toward team appreciation will accomplish.

#### Spend a Little Money—It's Your Team

Get out the company credit card and make sure that people on the project are well cared for. Stock the refrigerator with drinks and snacks, buy decent dinners every night, and bring in donuts in the morning. Bring in good coffee and get rid of the cheap stuff. Every now and then, make sure the evening meal is a nice one, and send them home afterward instead of burning the midnight oil for the tenth night in a row.

Something I've seen in the past that affects morale is the relationship between the development team and the testing team. I've seen the entire range, from teams that wanted to beat each other with pipes to others that didn't even communicate verbally—they simply read each other's minds and made the game better. Someone needs to take this pulse every now and then and apply a little rudder pressure when necessary to keep things nice and friendly. Some warning signs to watch for include unfriendly japes in the bug commentary, discussion about the usefulness of an individual on either team or their apparent lack of skill, or the beginnings of disrespect for anyone.

Perhaps the best insurance against this problem is forging personal relationships among the development leadership and testing leadership, and if possible, with individuals on the team. Make sure they get a chance to meet each other in person if at all possible, which can be difficult since most game developers are a few time zones away from their test team. Personal email, telephone conversations, conference calls, and face-to-face meetings can help forge these professional friendships and keep them going when discussions about bugs get heated.

This leads into something that may have the most serious affect on morale, both positive and negative. The developers need to feel like they are doing something worthwhile, and that they have the support of everyone. The moment they feel that their project isn't worth anything, due to something said in the media or perhaps an unfortunate comment by an executive, you can see the energy drain away to nothing. The opposite of this can be used to boost morale. Bring in a member of the press to see some kick-ass previews, or have a suit from the publisher shower the team with praise, and they'll redouble their effort. If you happen to work in a company with multiple projects, perhaps the best thing I've seen is one project team telling another that they have a great game. Praise from one's closest colleagues is far better than any other.

### *Other Stuff*

Perhaps the darkest side of trouble on teams is when one person crosses the line and begins to behave in an unprofessional manner. I've seen everything from career blackmail to arrogant insubordination, and the project team has to keep this butthead on the team or risk losing their "genius." My suggestion here is to remember that the team is more important than any single individual. If someone leaves the team, even figuratively, during the project you should invite him to please leave in a more concrete manner. No one is that important.

## Your Competition Beats You to the Punch

There's nothing that bursts your bubble quite as much as having someone walk into your office with a game in his hand, just released, that not only kicks butt but is exactly like your game in every way. You might think I'm crazy, but I'll tell you that you have nothing to worry about. The fact is that you can learn a lot from someone else's game simply by playing it, studying their graphics system, testing their user interface, and finding other chinks in their armor. After all, you can still compile your game, whereas they've shipped it and probably moved on to other things.

True, you won't be the first to market. Yes, you'd better be no later than second to market, and certainly you'd better make sure that you don't repeat their mistakes. At least you have the benefit of having a choice, and you also have the benefit of dissecting another competitor's product before you put your game on the shelf.

**Don't Give Away All Your Secrets**

They say that loose lips sink ships, right? This is certainly true in the game industry. *Strike Commander,* Origin's first 3D game, was due out in Christmas of 1992. In the summer of 1992, Origin took *Strike Commander* to the big industry trade show at the time, the Consumer Electronics Show, and made a big deal of *Strike Commander's* advanced 3D technology. They went so far as to give away technical details of the 3D engine, which the competition immediately researched and installed in their own games. Origin's competitive advantage was trumped by their own marketing department, and since the team had to slip the schedule past Christmas, the competition had more time to react. What a disaster!

The game industry tends to follow trends until they bleed out. That's because there's a surprisingly strong aversion to unique content on the part of game executives. If a particular game is doing well, every company in the industry puts out a clone until there are 50 games out there that all look alike. Only the top two or three will sell worth a damn, so make sure you are in that top two or three.

## There's No Way Out—or Is There?

Sometimes, you have to admit there's a grim reality—your game has coded itself into a corner. The testers say the game just isn't any fun. You might have gone down a dead-end technology track, such as coding your game for a dying platform.

What in the hell do you do now?

Mostly, you find a way to start over. If you're lucky, you might be able to recycle some code, art, map levels, or sounds. If you're really lucky, you might be able to replace a minor component and save the project. Either way, you have to find the courage to see the situation for what it is and act. Putting your head in the sand won't do any good.

**I Never Gave Up on *Ultima IX***

After *Ultima IX* was put on ice, and I was working hard on the *Ultima Online* project, I secretly continued work on *Ultima IX* at my house in the evenings and on weekends. My goal wasn't so much to resurrect *Ultima IX* or try to finish it single-handedly. I just wanted to learn more about 3D hardware-accelerated polygon rasterization, which was pretty new at the time. I was playing around with Glide, a 3D API from 3DFx that worked on the VooDoo series of video cards. In a surprisingly little amount of work, I installed a Glide-compliant rasterizer into *Ultima IX*, complete with a basic, ultra-stupid, texture cache.

What I saw was really amazing—*Ultima IX* running at over 40fps. The best frame rate I'd seen so far was barely 10fps using our best software rasterizer. I took my work into Origin to show it off a bit, and the old *Ultima IX* team just went wild. A few months later, the project was back in development with a new direction. *Ultima IX* would be the first Origin game that was solely written for hardware-accelerated video cards. A bold statement, but not out of character with the *Ultima* series. Each *Ultima* game pushed the limits of bleeding edge technology every time a new one was published, and *Ultima IX* was no exception.

## One Last Word—Don't Panic

There are other things that can go terribly wrong on projects, such as when someone deletes the entire project from the network or when the entire development team walks out the door to start their own company. Yes, I've seen both of these things happen, and no, the projects in question didn't instantly evaporate. Every problem can be fixed, but it does take something of a cool head. Panic and overreaction—some might say these are hallmarks of your humble author—rarely lead to good decisions.

Try to stay calm, and try to gather as much information about whatever tragedy is befalling you. Don't go on a witch hunt. You'll need every able-bodied programmer and artist to get you out of trouble. Whatever it is, your problem is only a finite string of 1s and 0s in the right order. Try to remember that, and you'll probably sleep better.

# The Light—It's Not a Train After All

It's a day you'll remember for every project. At some point, there will be a single approved bug in your bug database. It will be assigned to someone on the team, and likely it will be fixed in a crowded office with every team member watching. Someone will start the build machine, and after a short while, the new game will be sent to the testing folks. Then the wait begins for the final word the game has been signed off and sent to manufacturing. You may have to go through this process two or three times—something I find unnerving but inevitable. Eventually though, the phone will ring, and the lead tester will give you the good news. The final build has been accepted, and the game is going to be manufactured.

Your game is done. There will likely be a free flow of appropriate beverages. I keep a bottle of nice tequila or maybe a good single-malt scotch in my office for just such an occasion. You have a few weeks to wait for the channel to push your game into every store and online site, so what do you do in the meantime?

## Test the Archive

The first thing you do is take a snapshot of the build machine and the media files on your network. Your job is to rebuild the game from scratch, using all your build scripts, to make sure that if you ever need to, you can restore a backup of the game source and rebuild your game. Start with a completely clean machine and install the build machine backup. It should include all the build tools, such as your compiler and special tools that you used to create your game.

Restore a backup of the network files to a clean spot on your network. This may take some doing, since your network might be pretty full. It's a good idea to buy some extra hard drives to perform this task, since it is the only way you can be 100 percent sure your project backup will work.

After you have a duplicate of your build machine and a second copy of the network files, build your game again and compare it to the image that is signed off. If they compare bit for bit, make some copies of the backups and store them in a cool dark place, safe for all eternity. If you are working for a game publisher, they will want a copy of the backup, too, so don't forget to make enough for them. If the files don't match, do your best to figure out why. It wouldn't be completely unusual for a few bits to be mysteriously different on the first attempt. The existence of a completely automated build process usually makes the archive perfectly accurate, which is a great reason to have it in the first place.

As a last resort, if your files don't match, the best thing you can do is document the delta and have your testers run the rebuilt archive through the testing process once more. This will ensure that at least the game is still in a shippable state, even though some of the bits are different.

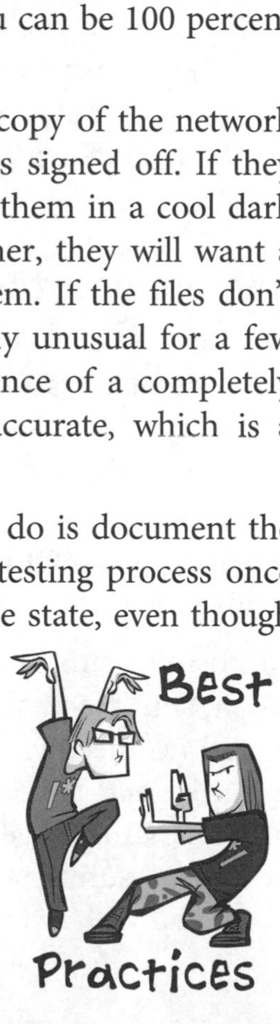


#### Archive the Bug Database

Don't forget to back up the bug database in some readable format, such as an Excel spreadsheet or even a CSV file. Store it along with your project archive, and if you ever want to start a sequel, the first thing you'll do is figure out which postponed bugs you'll fix.

## The Patch Build or the Product Demo

It's not crazy to start working on a patch build or downloadable demo immediately after the project signs off. The patch build is fairly common on almost every platform. If you know you need to build one, there's no reason to wait. A downloadable demo or trial version of your game is always a good idea.

I suggest you leave the patch build in your main line of development in your source code repository. The patch build should simply be the next minor version of your game and is exactly what you've been doing since your zero bug date. You can release the thumbscrews a little and consider some slightly more radical solutions to problems that you wouldn't have considered just a few days ago—it all depends on your schedule for the patch.

It wouldn't be uncommon to wait for initial customer feedback for finalizing the features and fixes that you'll include in your patch. Your customer base will likely find something your testers missed, or you may discover that a known problem is a much bigger deal than anyone expected.

The downloadable demo should exist in a separate branch in your source code repository. This is especially true if you code the demo with `#ifdef_DEMO` blocks or some such mechanism to cut your game down to a tiny version of itself. It wouldn't be crazy for some programmers to work on the demo and the patch simultaneously, and a separate code branch will help keep everything organized.

## The Postmortem

A good postmortem should be held a few weeks after you sign off your game. There are tons of ways to handle it, but there are a few common goals. Every project is a chance to learn about game development, and the postmortem is a mechanism that formalizes those lessons, which will ultimately change the way you work. It isn't a forum to complain about things that went wrong and leave it at that. Instead, your postmortem should identify opportunities to improve your craft. It is a forum to recognize a job well done, whether on the part of individuals or as a group.

In postmortems, it's really easy to get off track because everyone on the team wants to say his piece about nearly everything. That's good, but it can degenerate into a chaotic meeting. It's also not a crazy idea to split the team into their areas of expertise and have them conduct mini-postmortems in detail. For example, the programmers might get together to talk about aspects of the technology or their methodologies, surely stuff that will bore the artists to the point of chewing their own limbs off to escape the meeting. Each group—programmers, artists, designers, producers, and whoever—can submit their detailed report for any other similar group who wants to learn their lessons.

The team postmortem should focus on the game design, the project schedule, lines of communication, and team process. If someone believes he has a good idea of how to improve things, he should speak up, and if the group thinks the idea has merit, then they should act on the idea.

One thing that isn't immediately obvious is the fact that you won't learn everything in a public meeting. Some of the most important information might be better discussed in private, in the hopes that someone's feelings won't be bruised. If you get the chance to run a postmortem, don't forget to follow the public meeting with private interviews with the team. It will take a long time, but it's a good idea.

## What to Do with Your Time

When I reached the end of my longest project to date, *Ultima VIII,* my first act was to walk outside Origin's offices, sit down at a picnic table, and enjoy the light, smells, and sounds of a springtime Texas afternoon. I had been in a dark office working overtime for two years, and I'd forgotten what daytime was like. I went home and found a person there. After introductions and reviewing surprising evidence in the form of a photo album, I realized that the person in my apartment was actually my wife for over three years. I asked her out on a date, and she accepted. Then I asked her to accompany me on a diving trip to Cozumel. She accepted that, too.

I suggest you follow my lead. If you don't have a spouse, go somewhere fun with a friend. See the world. Get away from your computer at all costs. It will do you some good and may give you some fun ideas.

You won't be able to stay away from work forever. The desire to make another great game will soon overwhelm you. You may embark on a sequel to the game you just shipped, or you might get to do something entirely new. Either way, you'll be surprised at the energy level. People on the team who looked like the living dead just a few weeks ago will be ready to go around again.

There's nothing quite like starting a new project. You feel renewed and smarter, and if you're really lucky, you'll get to work with the same team. After what you've just been through, it's likely you'll have a good portion of mental telepathy worked out, and you won't need quite so many meetings.

One thing everyone will quietly do is make excuses to walk into computer game stores looking for the box. Eventually, you'll see it for the first time. There's nothing like it, holding a shrink-wrapped version of your game in your own hands. I sincerely hope you get the chance to do that someday. Everybody deserves that kind of reward for such a mammoth effort.

The game industry is a wacky place. The hours are long, and the money isn't that great. I know because I've been in it up to my neck since games ran on floppy disks. Somehow I find the energy to keep doing it. Am I just a glutton for punishment?

I guess there's a lot to be said for a profession that has one goal—fun. I learned in scouting that you should always leave a campsite better than you found it. I guess that working on computer games is a way to do that for much more than a campsite. My work in the computer game industry has hopefully had an effect on the people who enjoyed the games with my name somewhere in the credits. My work, and that of my co-author and friend Rez, on this book has hopefully made working on the games themselves more fun and more enjoyable for you.

Only time will tell, eh?

# INDEX

## G

## M

## P

## Q



## R

## S

## T

## U

## X-Z